CULTURE AND DEPRESSION

CULTURE AND DEPRESSION
Studies in the Anthropology and Cross-Cultural Psychiatry of Affect and Disorder

Edited by
Arthur Kleinman and Byron Good

UNIVERSITY OF CALIFORNIA PRESS

Berkeley   Los Angeles   London

University of California Press

Berkeley and Los Angeles, California

University of California Press, Ltd.

London, England

Copyright © 1985 by The Regents of the University of California

Library of Congress Cataloging in Publication Data
Main entry under title:

Culture and depression.

   (Comparative studies of health systems and
medical care)
   Includes bibliographies and index.
   1. Depression, Mental—Cross-cultural studies. 2. Psychiatry,
Transcultural. I. Kleinman, Arthur. II. Good, Byron.
III. Series. [DNLM: 1. Cross-Cultural Comparison.
2. Depressive Disorder—psychology.
WM 171 C968]
RC537.C85   1985   616.85'27   85-2535
ISBN 0-520-05493-8 (cloth)
ISBN 0-520-05883-6 (paperback)
Printed in the United States of America

2 3 4 5 6 7 8 9

Contents

Preface

The editors began planning this volume in 1975. But it was not until 1982 that they were able to bring the contributors together as participants of a double panel at the American Anthropological Association Annual Meeting in Washington, D.C. The panel on "Culture and Depression: Toward an Anthropology of Affect and Affective Disorder" was sponsored by the American Ethnological Society and included the senior authors of all the chapters in this volume, save two, along with several of the second authors. To provide a historical comparison from the Western tradition, the editors invited Stanley Jackson to modify a paper on acedia and melancholia that had been published in the *Bulletin of the History of Medicine*. They were also fortunate to enlist a contribution from Anthony Marsella and his collaborators in the Mental Health Unit of the WHO which both reviews that Unit's cross-cultural studies of depression and updates Marsella's overview of cross-cultural psychological and psychiatric contributions to this subject. With the exception of chapter 1, then, all of the papers in this volume are original writings.

A grant from the Rockefeller Foundation to start a Program in Cross-Cultural Psychiatry and Medicine at Harvard University provided partial support for the editing of the papers. The editors wish to acknowledge the very helpful contribution of Joan Kleinman to the editorial work. They thank Carol Casella-Jaillet for her fine secretarial services. An invitation from our colleague David Maybury-Lewis, when he was president of the American Ethnological Society, to organize a symposium gave us the chance to put planning into practice, for which we are grateful.

In 1980 we sent out letters of invitation. Along with them we included a specific charge to each contributor and a group of papers that we felt gave an overview of current studies of depression in psychiatry, psychology, and cross-cultural research. A year before the meeting, we sent each participant a second group of papers to update and extend the scope of the earlier batch. It was our interest that these papers along with participation in the panel would provide a common thread to the contributions and initiate interaction and feedback among the distinctive perspectives. After the meeting, we encouraged each of the authors to revise their contributions in light of the other presentations and the discussions. Finally, each paper has been extensively edited; most, including our own, have gone through several substantial revisions. For their serious commitment to this lengthy and burdensome process, their wit and grace in the face of deadlines, and best of all their willingness to engage in substantial rethinking and rewriting in response to critical dialogue, we offer our many thanks to the participants.

There is no more difficult (and less rewarded) act of scholarship than to step outside the accepted confines of one's discipline to argue with members of other disciplines about a cross-cutting subject that is constituted and expressed in greatly different ways when viewed here in an anthropological, there in a psychiatric and psychological problem framework. This book represents our attempt to bring such a cross-disciplinary colloquy to bear on depression, one of the more common emotions and disorders. The reader will find various traces of the colloquy: reworked disciplinary accounts that respond to paradigm conflicts as much as to questions of substance, debates between authors of the various chapters, actual attempts to construct interdisciplinary research frameworks, and the editors' overview of the exchange. Such an endeavor is likely to lead to (and in this instance has in fact produced) a large book and one that does not make for easy reading or simple conclusions. It is our hope that our readers will be rewarded in much the same way that we the editors have been: by coming away with a deeper sense of what distinguishes anthropological, psychological, and psychiatric approaches to depression in cross-cultural perspective, and by discovering those areas in which cross-disciplinary contributions are more availing and those in which they are less so.

In a field as broad as this one, even a large volume can accommodate only a few of the major perspectives. This is not an exhaustive compendium: that would exhaust the reader even more than this rich display of wares. We have concentrated most on anthropology, for it is our shared opinion that cross-cultural studies of emotions and illness can be faulted most frequently because of anthropological naiveté. We believe the resulting approach offers a more discriminating understanding—often of the problems in researching this subject as much as of the subject itself. We encourage our readers to enter and expand the colloquy. Enough hares have been started in these pages to keep us all busy for years to come.

Cambridge, Massachusetts   Arthur Kleinman
June 1984   Byron Good

Introduction:
Culture and Depression

Arthur Kleinman and Byron Good

CULTURE AND DEPRESSION:
INTRODUCTION TO THE PROBLEM

Why should a group of anthropologists, psychiatrists, and psychologists devote a volume to culture and depression? Historians tell us that the Greek and Roman medical writers described ''melancholic diseases'' among their populations which are quite similar to those seen by psychiatrists today, and that the terms ''melancholia,'' ''depression,'' and ''mania'' have a long and relatively stable history in European thought. Although writers such as Robert Burton, whose compendious *Anatomy of Melancholy* (1621) summarized clinical lore of his day, sought causes for the disorder in the black bile and described subtypes of melancholia that ring strange today, there seems little question that the ancients suffered depression as do people today. Furthermore, psychiatrists practicing in Third World clinics and mental hospitals see patients who are recognizably depressed and treat them with medical regimens current in Western clinics, including antidepressant medications and supportive therapy. This apparent universality arouses no surprise among contemporary biomedical researchers, who believe depression is a disease that is found in all human populations and that we are just beginning to understand. During the past decade, enormous strides have been taken in unraveling the complex set of interacting biochemical and psychological processes which produces depression. Although the picture is not as clear as many researchers thought five years ago, there is little question that neurotransmitters—bioamines involved in the transmission and regulation of neurological messages—and a set of hormones are implicated in depressive illness. So what is cultural about depression? What do anthropologists or cross-cultural psychiatrists have to offer to an understanding of such a disorder? Is there reason to believe that life in some societies is organized so as to protect their members from depressive illness? Is there evidence that the condition looks quite different in some cultures?

Growing evidence indicates the issues are not as clear as this picture of depression as a universal disease would suggest. First, the study of depression continues to be plagued by unresolved conceptual problems. Depression is a transitory mood or emotion experienced at various times by all individuals. It is also a symptom associated with a variety of psychiatric disorders, from severe and debilitating diseases such as schizophrenia to milder anxiety disorders. It is also a commonly diagnosed mental illness. Depression is thus considered mood, symptom, and illness, and the relationship among these three conceptualizations remains problematic. Is depressive illness a more severe and enduring form of depressed emotions, or is it an altogether different process? Are the boundaries between depressed mood and illness simply conventional, or are they related to more essential differences between them? Are depressive illnesses really discrete forms of pathology, separate from anxiety disorders, for example, or is depression a symptom—like fever—that may be associated with any number of disorders? These basic questions continue to bedevil researchers and preclude clear analysis of depressive illness.

Reading through the history of changes in conceptualization of the subtypes of depression does not give one confidence that such problems are about to be solved once and for all. The history of psychiatry is strewn with "nosologies," or systems of categorization of depression. Some are etiological categories, such as endogenous and reactive, reflecting interest in the underlying cause of a depression. Other distinctions, such as that between primary and secondary depressions, are relational, designating which is to be considered the illness, which the symptom. Other categories, such as neurotic and psychotic, are descriptive, indicating characteristics and severity of the disorder. The current wisdom, represented in the American Psychiatric Association's most recent Diagnostic and Statistical Manual (DSM-III), eschews cause altogether, treating psychiatric disorders as unitary diseases, precipitated by social precursors and superimposed on enduring personality characteristics. But is the depression of a basically healthy individual with unresolved grief over loss of a spouse or child the same disease as a depression of a more fundamentally troubled person? Anthropologists are not, of course, the first to raise questions such as these. They are debated regularly in the psychiatric literature. To the anthropologist, however, such disagreement over basic terms is a reminder that we are in the presence of culture. Psychiatric categories and theories are cultural, no less than other aspects of our world view. It seems reasonable, therefore, to ask to what extent depression itself is a cultural category, grounded both in a long Western intellectual tradition and a specific medical tradition.

Cross-cultural research offers evidence of cultural variations in depressive mood, symptoms, and illness which suggests the importance of pursuing this question. "Dysphoria"—sadness, hopelessness, unhappiness, lack of pleasure with the things of the world and with social relationships—has dramatically different meaning and form of expression in different societies. For Buddhists, taking pleasure from things of the world and social relationships is the basis of all suffering; a willful dysphoria is thus the first step on the road to salvation. For Shi'ite Muslims in Iran, grief is a religious experience, associated with recognition of the tragic consequences of living justly in an unjust world; the ability to experience dysphoria fully is thus a marker of depth of person and understanding. Some societies, such as the Kaluli of Papua New Guinea, value full and dramatic expression of sadness and grieving; Balinese and Thai-Lao, by contrast, "smooth out" emotional highs and lows to preserve a pure, refined, and smooth interior self. Members of such societies vary not only in how they express dysphoric emotion; they seem to experience forms of emotion that are not part of the repertoire of others. So dramatic are the differences in the cultural worlds in which people live that translation of emotional terms requires much more than finding semantic equivalents. Describing how it feels to be grieved or melancholy in another society leads straightway into analysis of different ways of being a person in radically different worlds.

What anthropological evidence we have indicates differences not only in depression as mood but also in symptoms of depressive illness. For members of many African societies, the first signs of illness are dreams that indicate a witch may be attacking one's vital essence. For members of many American Indian groups, hearing voices of relatives who have died is considered normal, not a sign of sickness. For members of other societies, hearing voices or dreaming of spirits may indicate a member of the spirit world is seeking a victim or demanding to establish a relationship with one who will become a follower and perhaps a healer. Dramatic differences are also found in expression of bodily complaints associated with depressive illness, indicating forms of experience not available to most members of our own society. Nigerians complain that ''ants keep creeping in parts of my brain,'' while Chinese complain of exhaustion of their nerves and of their hearts being squeezed and weighed down. In few societies of the world is depression associated with overwhelming guilt and feelings of sinfulness, as it often is in the Judeo-Christian West. Because such differences are found in the symptoms associated with depressive illness, determination of whether one is studying the same illness across societies is essentially problematic. There is no blood test for depression. If there were one, it would indicate some physiological disorder, but not the fundamentally social illness we call depression. Since symptoms serve as the criteria for depressive illness, and since symptoms vary significantly across cultures, the difficulty of establishing the cross-cultural validity of the category ''depression'' must be faced.

The world's cultures have offered researchers of various disciplines a natural laboratory for investigating the relation between depression and contrasting systems of social organization and cultural meanings. Questions asked reflect the theoretical orientation of the discipline and period. For years, psychoanalytically oriented researchers attempted to test theories of depression as aggression directed against the self, and to maintain the theory in the face of evidence that depression is often not associated with feelings of guilt and self-depreciation, and that the anger experienced by those who are depressed is commonly expressed toward others. Cross-cultural epidemiologists have sought variations in rates of depressive illness across societies, then looked for aspects of social life and culture that would explain the variance. Clinical researchers have looked at differences in levels of somatic and psychological symptoms across patient populations, some offering explanations of these differences in terms of the evolution of societies.

Although questions of the role of social and psychological factors in placing individuals at risk or protecting them from depressive symptoms and illness have great currency and are appropriate to put to the cross-cultural evidence, this book is organized around a prior question: Does the concept of depression have cross-cultural validity? Do members of other societies experience what we call depressive emotions and major depressive illness? Do differences in cultural meanings significantly alter the experience of depressed mood and the symptoms of depressive illness? If so, how are we to translate between our emotional world and those of other societies; how are we to establish criteria for depressive illness in other societies which will be comparable to those we use in our own?

In a sense, the great advances in biological psychiatry provoke these questions. Discovery of effective antidepressant medications in the 1960s initiated the most active period in the history of research on depression. Identification of effective psychopharmacology allows researchers to follow a strategy of comparing individuals for whom the drug is effective with a normal population and of investigating physiological changes in the individual which result from the medication. Both of these strategies are aimed at discovering biological mechanisms that correlate with depressive illness. In order to undertake such research, however, reliable diagnoses of depression must be made to serve as a basis for identifying samples to be studied. By the mid-1960s, it was clear that basing diagnoses on the "clinical judgment" of psychiatrists was unreliable. The same patient was likely to be diagnosed schizophrenic in the United States and manic-depressive in Great Britain, for instance.

To facilitate such research, the National Institute of Mental Health sponsored a major effort to establish clear diagnostic criteria for psychiatric disorders. These efforts resulted in a dramatically new diagnostic manual and innovative epidemiological instruments designed to assign psychiatric diagnoses to individuals (as contrasted with older instruments designed to determine level of psychiatric symptoms). Because these new diagnostic instruments are proving reliable, and because they are useful in identifying individuals with particular physiological as well as psychosocial characteristics, there is growing consensus in the psychiatric community that the current criteria of depression are valid and represent criteria of a universal, biologically grounded disease. It is just such certainty that our Western categories, in this case disease categories, are universal rather than culturally shaped which provokes anthropological response. When medical researchers act on an assumption of universality by directly translating our own diagnostic criteria into other languages to determine who is mentally ill in another society, anthropologists may be expected to challenge the validity of the entire enterprise.

This volume is designed to examine these issues. It represents the editors' conviction that cross-cultural research is of extraordinary importance in advancing our knowledge of human behavior, psychiatric illness, and, in particular, depression. It also represents our belief that disciplinary boundaries have greatly impeded examination of the questions raised here. Anthropologists often have little or no clinical experience and consequently criticize the psychiatric literature based solely on their research with normal populations. Psychiatrists seldom have extended experience with non-Western populations and consequently *underestimate* the great difficulty of translating between our Western analytic schemes, grounded as they are in our tacit cultural knowledge concerning emotion, interior experience, and psychological disorders, and the very alien psychological worlds of many of the societies studied by anthropologists. Epidemiologists so struggle to develop reliable approaches to measuring psychological disorders and social factors that they seldom seriously confront issues of validity. These great differences in perspectives have prevented the kind of serious scholarly exchange necessary to advance our understanding of depression in the context of cross-cultural studies.

This book is addressed to an interdisciplinary audience of researchers, scholars, and lay readers. We asked the authors—a distinguished group of anthropologists, psychiatrists, and psychologists—to present original data concerning depression in the societies they have studied, to address fundamental theoretical issues, to outline methodological issues raised by their work, and to engage members of other disciplines explicitly. Several common themes emerge from the contributions. The chapters submit the dominant psychiatric conceptualization of depression, in particular that represented by DSM-III, to sustained cultural analysis. Although there is no simple consensus about the cross-cultural validity of Western concepts of depression, the chapters document how differently dysphoric affect is interpreted and socially organized in many societies and suggest that depressive illness takes culturally distinct forms in several of the societies studied. The authors thus challenge current conceptualizations as parochial, as a form of "local" knowledge, and attempt to reinterpret "emotion," "symptom," and "illness" in thoroughgoing social and cultural terms. However, they do not stop at anthropological critique. A number of the contributors go on to outline research programs and to provide data, at times based on joint ethnographic, clinical, and epidemiological work, that significantly advance our understanding of the role of culture in shaping dysphoria and depression. We believe these contributions lay the ground for a new anthropology of depression.

ORIENTATIONS

Three distinctive disciplines dominate the cross-cultural study of depression: anthropology, psychiatry, and psychology. Though each has been interested in this subject for decades, they have gone about the descriptive and comparative tasks in separate ways, so that, as in the more general study of emotions and mental disorder cross-culturally, each discipline has constructed a more or less discrete literature. Theories have differed as much as methods, and within each discipline contributions have ranged along a spectrum of theory from materialist to idealist (Hahn and Kleinman 1983). So separate have these traditions become that one finds in each few references to recent work outside that tradition. If there ever was a situation accurately captured by the image of the blind men and the elephant, this would seem to be it.

This volume is an attempt to overcome the obvious and unavailing limitations that such splendid isolation creates. We have assembled papers from each tradition and asked contributors to deal with contributions from the other fields. Each contributor was also urged to set out fairly explicitly his or her theoretical paradigm and to illustrate it by working through empirical materials. The results vary, as they will in a large collection, but we the editors believe that taken together they portray (warts and all) both the present state of these distinctive disciplinary approaches to understanding culture and depression and the opportunities for and barriers to interdisciplinary colloquy and collaboration.

This volume is neither exhaustive nor truly representative. Rather, it reflects the chief preoccupations of the editors. We believe the biological component of clinical depression is important and cannot be disregarded, but we also share the view that biological studies divorced from clinical and ethnographic investigations have little to contribute to our understanding of the relation of culture and depression. Hence we have not sought to include a paper on this latter approach. During the preparation of the chapters, however, contributors were sent relevant reviews of the biology of depressive disorder, along with other papers on clinical, epidemiological, experimental, and ethnographic approaches, so that their discussions might include some attention to biology.

Similarly, because it is now so well known, we have not felt the need to include a strictly psychoanalytic account, though several of the contributions are informed by a psychoanalytic perspective. In place of a narrow experimentalist exposition, we have elected to have the relevant elements of this research tradition discussed in a more broadly based review of leading psychological research traditions. We have also eschewed sociological accounts that treat depression totally as an ideological or moral phenomenon, since with William James (1981:1068) we hold that "a purely disembodied human emotion is a nonentity."

What have we chosen to emphasize? Because it is our view that the single most troublesome problem plaguing the cross-cultural study of affect and affective disorder is the failure to take an anthropologically sophisticated view of culture, we have emphasized anthropological accounts, especially those that regard culture as the intersection of meaning and experience. We believe the cross-disciplinary study of culture and depression will be best advanced by coming to terms with the analytic questions raised by these accounts, and by critically examining the ethnocentric bias of psychiatric and psychological research categories. We also hope to stimulate further research in this tradition, especially studies that confront what we take to be a long-term weakness of anthropological accounts and the field's second most serious problem: a failure to grasp the clinical dimensions of depression. Hence we have included clinical and epidemiological studies that bridge anthropological and clinical frameworks. We have also sought out contributions that represent what we take to be some of the more innovative and productive approaches to the interdisciplinary study of emotion in society: sociolinguistic, cognitive behavioral, developmental, ethnoepidemiological, and sociosomatic analyses. Our bias is clearly integrative. Only accounts that relate meaning with experience, symbol with soma, culture with nature, and the three disciplines with each other, can overcome the sources of failure that have undermined most cross-cultural research on depression and mental disorder generally.

DEPRESSION: EMOTION OR DISORDER?

The contributors to this volume discuss two divergent forms of depression: depression as emotion and depression as disorder. It is important that the reader recognize which is the object of inquiry. For anthropologists, whose chief concern is the system of normative meanings and power relations which mediates the interconnections between person and society, emotions—here as personal feelings, there as expressions and constituents of social relationships—are commonly the focus of attention; not so for psychiatrists, whose interest centers on clinical disease.

Depression, then, simultaneously stands for two distinctive states of persons: one normal, the other pathological. But this distinction is usually not made in writings on depression in different societies and among ethnic groups in the same society. The result is a confusion so pervasive that researchers in this field often fail to agree or disagree with each other with adequate clarity to advance understanding. The contributors to this volume were asked to avoid this confusion, and we think for the most part they have. But if writings on depression as emotion and depression as disease are discourses about different subjects, how do these subjects relate? Here the reader will find the chapters reflect the chief ways of configuring this conundrum which dominate the literatures on depression. For some, there is a continuum between psychological state and clinical case, while for others the two are qualitatively different. For still others, each is a reification of Western categories which becomes problematic when viewed from the perspective of indigenous non-Western categories.

For the clinician, depression is a common, often severe, sometimes mortal disease with characteristic affective (sadness, irritability, joylessness), cognitive (difficulty concentrating, memory disturbance), and vegetative (sleep, appetite, energy disturbances) complaints which has a typical course and predictable response rates to treatment. Thousands of studies implicate neurotransmitter, neuroendocrine, and autonomic nervous system malfunctioning, and there is even early evidence, any biologically oriented psychiatrist will tell you, of genetic vulnerability. This is not the "depression" of the ethnographer, for whom the word denotes a feeling state of sadness, hopelessness, and demoralization that may be as fleeting as a momentary nostalgia or as lasting as prolonged grieving. For the clinician, grief is not clinical depression, though it may become so; for the ethnographer, depression is often conceived as a form of grief and grief as a type of depression. Psychologists oscillate between the two positions. For some behaviorally oriented psychologists, there is no "disease," though there most definitely is abnormal or maladaptive behavior; while for the psychoanalytically oriented, the two (emotion and disorder) partake of continuities and differences. In making headway through the chapters that follow it is essential that the reader know which one of these language games he or she has entered.

Other tensions characterize the field and are visible throughout the volume. Ethnography and epidemiological surveys sharply pose these differences. The former is qualitative and concerned principally with the problem of validity. The latter is quantitative and concerned primarily with the problems of reliability and replicability. The ethnographer masters the local language, spends many months, even years, in the field, and develops close working relationships with a relatively small number of key informants. He or she concentrates on translation and interpretation of meaning, often working with tacit and hidden dimensions of the social system. The epidemiologist spends weeks, at most a few months, in the field, usually does not know the indigenous language, and hence is forced to rely on questionnaires and measures of ''observable'' and ''quantifiable'' behavior. The epidemiologist views the ethnographer's task as ''impressionistic,'' ''anecdotal,'' ''uncontrolled,'' ''messy,'' ''soft,'' ''unrigorous,'' ''unscientific''; the ethnographer, in near perfect counterpoint, regards the epidemiologist's work as ''superficial,'' ''biased,'' ''pseudoscientific,'' ''invalid,'' ''unscholarly.'' Two unequal responses to this tension are apparent: the much more common—though to our minds less creative—is to put on blinders and disregard the work of the other; more rarely, researchers attempt to combine the two methods. Examples of both can be found in this volume.[1]

If anthropological ethnography and epidemiology differ fundamentally as methodologies, the clash between anthropology and psychology is one of conflicting paradigms governing what can be legitimately regarded as knowledge. Psychologists in the cross-cultural field do epidemiological, social survey, and clinical research. A few even make use of ethnographic methods, and many more utilize cross-cultural comparisons not all that different from those in which anthropologists engage. But it quickly becomes apparent their hearts are really in the experimental method. Underlying the method is an assumption that knowledge of human behavior, like that of the physical world, is generated by finding culture-specific instances of universal variables, then discovering laws that account for their covariation. Anthropologists generally scale another form of knowledge, based on interpretation of individual cases and careful translation across cases to make controlled comparisons. These approaches produce very different ideals of research, data analysis, and writing, and result in products as different as detailed ethnographies and short reports of statistical analyses. The epistemological paradigms of research practice in each field yield different kinds of knowledge, expressed in divergent styles and validated by distinctive tests of validity.

Although these differences prevail, anthropologists, psychologists, and psychiatrists increasingly combine methodologies. Psychological anthropologists have been strongly influenced by the core psychological methodology, and have imported it into field research. Psychiatrists have traditionally scorned all these approaches for clinical research methods of direct observation and counting of symptoms, charting of illness course, and evaluation of treatment outcomes. More recently, however, they too have employed epidemiological and social surveys, cross-cultural comparisons, and experimental research design. Only a few have felt comfortable with ethnographic methods, however, in spite of there being a long tradition of interpretive methodology in psychoanalytic, existential, and phenomenological clinical research. In each discipline, moreover, these tensions can be found among distinctive groups or schools of researchers. Increasingly these crosscutting research traditions have brought together scholars from the different disciplines.

We hold that these tensions in orientation—clinical/academic, quantitative/qualitative, meaning-centered/behavior-centered, cultural analysis/biological analysis, and so forth—represent a creative dialectic in cross-cultural studies, one that advances each discipline as much as it revivifies the subject. To exploit these scholarly tensions systematically, we have juxtaposed one kind of scholarship with another, mixed the traditions in which they are used to tackle the same set of problems, and in the final section of this book, presented three chapters that represent attempts to construct an interdisciplinary anthropological psychiatry (or epidemiology) and psychiatric (or epidemiological) anthropology. This strategy reflects a growing (though still minority) awareness that the old, established disciplinary approaches have led to dead ends. They increasingly appear conceptually and methodologically inadequate for their task, their products repetitious and off the mark. There is interest in new directions, new ways of configuring old problems as much as new methods for studying them. The field is starting to change, as scholars in each of the disciplines come to recognize the need for a new language to talk about sociosomatic and psychocultural interconnections, new paradigms of how to do research which integrate ethnographic and experimental methods and account for the *interaction* of nature and culture in the production and shaping of human distress.

We suggest that for each chapter the reader ask the following questions, which run like unifying threads through materials that are not nearly as disparate as they may at first glance seem, or as divergent as some of their authors would hold. Is depression configured as affect, affective disorder, or both? If as emotion, what view of emotion does the author hold—that emotion is a single state of arousal that is then shaped into anger, sadness, anxiety, or that particular emotions are from the start psychobiologically distinctive affective states? Is emotion configured as precognitive, cognitive, transactional, ideological, or various combinations of these?

For those papers dealing with affective disorders, the reader will want to ask: How do the authors define depressive disease (the end of a quantitative continuum or a qualitatively different clinical state)? Is a distinction drawn, and if so how is it handled, between depressive disease (expert's construction) and depressive illness (lay construction)? Where depression is configured as behavior, how is abnormal behavior distinguished from disease? How is normal depressive behavior thought to relate to the feeling state of being depressed? What are taken to be the sources of normal and abnormal depressive behavior, or depressive affect and depressive disorder?

How is culture configured, and what is the vision the writer holds of its interaction with depression? In what ways do the interpretations of how culture relates to depressive affect contrast with the interpretations of how culture relates to depressive disorder? What do these interpretations tell us about the particular societies under study, on the one hand, and about the study of normal and abnormal human experience, on the other? Do these distinctions, when applied to the practical reality of lived experience, matter clinically?

What are the universal and what the cultural varieties of depressive experience (be it emotion, disease, or behavior)? What are the sources of these continuities and divergences? Do cultural similarities and differences hold across gender, social class, and age? What opportunities do given chapters present for cross-disciplinary colloquy? What are the limitations authors foresee in the other perspectives, or in their own? What do each view as the salient questions in the cross-cultural study of depression?

While other questions also come to mind, these strike us as a grid that should help readers relate the chapters. Since many readers are likely to bring to the volume one of the disciplinary perspectives reviewed above and all will come to the chapters with particular theoretical assumptions, the reader may take this opportunity to search for relationships among chapters and thereby situate his or her particular perspective in relation to others. We see this conceptual tacking between divergent orientations as a means to liberate one's perspective from the tacit biases that confound all approaches to this subject. Those of us whose work is presented here have attempted to do this, albeit with mixed success. Anthropology suggests every cross-cultural encounter should make the challenge to particular perspectives unavoidable.

Our problem framework must be broadened to ask what the cross-cultural study of depression tells us not only about the social sources of depression but also about society. This anthropological orientation forces us to address both the impact of depression on society and the insight the social antecedents and consequences of depression provide into the nature and varieties of culture. Here then is yet another tension, this time between person and society, that can be avoided only at the expense of a more discriminating understanding. The creative dialectic between the two foci of interest centers our analysis on the symbolic bridge linking psychobiological and social realities.

OVERVIEW OF THE CHAPTERS AND THEIR ARGUMENTS

The following comments are our reflections on the important ideas raised in each of the papers and our interpretations of the relationships among them. They are the result of our having lived with these papers over the past two years and our attempt to come to terms with them based on a close reading. We share these fairly detailed comments with readers as reading notes that point up shared themes and special questions that will engage the reader's close reading.

Part I includes four anthropological pieces and a historical contribution. In chapter 1, Jackson describes the historical anthropology of two dominant Western idioms for configuring dysphoria: melancholia and acedia. He shows that their history is closely linked to changes in Christianity and medicine. Each took on different meanings at different times, and altered the meanings of the other. From the medieval period acedia in the religious texts became an interior quality like sorrow, while in the popular idiom it continued to radiate earlier meanings of a moral nature (sloth). At one time it conveyed an internal state, at another time an external behavior. Eventually it lost its coherence as a distinct condition in the West. Melancholia, in turn, came to mean both the disease and the affect. From the sixteenth century, with the transformation of Western society from a religious to a more secular state, acedia and the other cardinal sins gave way to the four temperaments and the humoral theory of behavior. Jackson shows that both acedia and melancholia mapped symptoms of great historical continuity across epochs as well as changing styles of symptom perception, expression, and labeling. Jackson demonstrates especially melancholia's changing association with distinctive explanatory idioms in Western history: somatic, psychological, religious, or moral. Hence the historical antecedents of "depression" disclose differing meanings, the remnants of which lend to "depression" today its ambiguous symbolic significance in lay and professional usage. The great virtue of this historical account is its demonstration of the anchoring of religious, illness, and behavioral categories in changing social structural arrangements. We may have moved from acedia and melancholia to depression, but we are warned of the same process that makes untenable the asocial, ahistorical professional tendency to reify names as things. Yet Jackson's diachronic analysis also indicates that beneath the flux and flow of social reality some continuing forms of human misery show a perduring, obdurate somatic grain. This grain clearly constrains experience as much as do the mutable categories that model it and the social arrangements that are the sources of such misery and shape the categories themselves.

Lutz (chap. 2), a psychological anthropologist, sketches a cultural critique of professional psychological categories—such as the emotion/cognition, subjective/objective, mind/body dichotomies—that she shows are tacit epistemological axes of the Western cultural tradition. Professional psychology and psychiatry draw on the West's ethnopsychological and ethnomedical systems. This creates an implicit ethnocentrism that only becomes apparent when our academic categories are contrasted with those of non-Western peoples. Translating the concept "depression" involves the translation of Western ethnopsychological and ethnomedical concepts of the nature, antecedents, and consequences of behavior which differ substantially from non-Western formulations of normal and abnormal behavior. Lutz's ethnography discloses that "thought" among the Ifaluk, a people living on a tiny South Pacific island, is not separated from "emotion," nor is depression seen as the opposite of the pursuit of happiness and equated with joylessness (anhedonia) as in the West. Depressive emotion as it is technically operationalized in psychology is a Western cultural category. Lutz suggests that emotion is best conceived not as psychobiological process but as cultural judgments that people use to understand the situations they find themselves in. These judgments are negotiated interpersonally and mediate events and relationships. Emotions, which are always embedded in ethnopsychological systems, support judgments concerning fact or value. They define situations, legitimate action in the real world. For this reason, Lutz argues cross-cultural psychological studies must break out of their ethnocentric cast by replacing the cross-cultural study of depressive affect with investigations of indigenous definitions of situations of loss and blocked goals and the socially organized response to them.

Lutz presents the strong argument in anthropology for the ethnocentric, egocentric and medicocentric biases of psychology, and offers a new problem framework for cross-cultural psychology. Her chapter is a vade mecum containing virtually all the major anthropological criticisms of psychological approaches applied to non-Western peoples. She shows why ethnography of others' emotional lives should lead to the discomfiting recognition that our very categories for doing the human sciences are culturally shaped. Her analysis is a challenge to cross-cultural research: translation—so often taken for granted in psychological and psychiatric studies—calls into question the very enterprise itself. Her refusal to privilege biological bases of emotion is likely to upset psychiatric readers as much as her cultural critique may provoke psychologists, and the colloquy that results will have to confront the limitations of relativism.

In the next chapter, Schieffelin extends the anthropological argument. Emotion is viewed as a system of social behavior, having a structural component external to personality and located in a social field of behavior, not just in the inner self. Schieffelin avers that affects are social inasmuch as they are experienced and provided with meaning in relationships with others, organized by cultural rules of expression and legitimacy, and communicate cultural messages. They are socially expected and even required as part of the appropriate participation in situations. Drawing on his extensive ethnographic experience with the Kaluli, a small-scale, preliterate society in the Highlands of Papua New Guinea, Schieffelin, following Bateson, uses the concept of ''ethos''—a culture's style of expressing emotion and model for emulating how to articulate emotion—to analyze how the Kaluli's egalitarian social structure of balanced reciprocity supports an ethos of male personal dynamism and assertiveness as well as dependency and appeal which gives a unique cultural form to anger and depression, respectively. The cultural value of balanced reciprocity is shown to be as relevant to Kaluli emotional behavior as it is to their economics. Schieffelin illustrates how this local system of the emotions operates by describing how the Kaluli handle grief reactions. He shows that their bereavement rituals constitute and express a movement from grief to anger and effective action. In these rituals the bereavement experience is resolved and the grieving person supported and compensated in keeping with the norm of reciprocity. The Kaluli, who do not recognize depression or have a label for it, appear to Schieffelin to suffer little of it (only one case in the villages he has worked in over the years). Schieffelin's analysis supports a psychoanalytic interpretation of how this cultural system protects the Kaluli against depressive disease, a not uncommon outcome of prolonged or abnormal grief in the West. Switching to a learned helplessness model of depressive disease, Schieffelin analyzes the single case of depressive disorder he encountered among the Kaluli as the result of that society's rather rare production of learned helplessness. This case of somatized depression is a harbinger of the discussions of somatization in chapters 9 through 13.

Schieffelin argues that if human affect is constituted in a social field, then affective disorders must also be essentially social phenomena. If this is so, then therapy must engage the sufferer in the social and cultural views in which the illness has its grounding. Schieffelin illustrates this by outlining a hypothetical therapy that would be specific to Kaluli society in the treatment of depression. This approach has the heuristic value of demonstrating how different a Kaluli treatment of depression would have to be from American treatment. It demonstrates the fundamentally cultural quality of depression and suggests we consider our therapies, including Beck's (1976) increasingly popular cognitive therapy, as a cultural response to a cultural disorder.

In chapter 4, Obeyesekere continues the anthropological line of analysis, but does so with a startling assertion. The generalized hopelessness that Brown and Harris (1978) and many others now take to be the basis of depressive disorder, Obeyesekere contends, is positively valued in Sri Lanka, as the foundational Buddhist insight about the nature of the everyday world. Pleasurable attachments to people and things in the world are the roots of all suffering, and recognition of the ultimate hopelessness of existence makes transcendence possible. Obeyesekere regards depressive affect in the contemporary Western world as "free-floating," not anchored in a shared societal ideology, and for that reason it conduces to medical labeling as illness. In Buddhist society private depressive affect is articulated in a publicly shared religious idiom, which echoes Jackson's discussion of acedia in medieval Europe. The "work of culture," Obeyesekere reasons, following the writings of the French philosopher, Ricoeur, involves the transformation of affects into meaning, providing unorganized and disorganizing private distress with a public form. For example, Freud argued that mourning is "work" that overcomes distressing affect engendered by loss. By means of the work of culture, feelings of loss become articulated as publicly sanctioned meanings and symbols, and in that movement from private world through social ideology to public symbol the feeling is mastered. Yet Obeyesekere openly admits some disquiet with this formulation, because, though it may explain what happens for the great majority, it does not explain those cases in which the work of culture fails to prevent the person from experiencing depression as disorder. Here he suggests that research is needed to determine the precise social structural, economic, and personal constraints that conduce to unsuccessful transformation of dysphoria.

Obeyesekere draws on Max Weber's concepts of rationalization and disenchantment to suggest why this process of cultural transformation, so widely present in the traditional non-Western world and in the West prior to the rise of modernism, is vitiated in the contemporary West and increasingly in the Westernizing sectors of the developing world. He illustrates successful cases of cultural transformation with ethnographic materials from his field research in Sri Lanka. There the striking Buddhist practice of *sil*, meditation on revulsion (death, feces), is shown to lead the meditator from private despair to generalization of negative affect from self to the world, and thereby to acceptance of its Buddhist meaning and significance. Again there are echoes of Jackson's treatment of the medieval Christian's positive evaluation of suffering as the starting point of religious transformation.

For the psychiatrist and psychologist reader in particular, Obeyesekere's critique of the methodology of psychiatric epidemiology and cross-cultural comparisons will be as unsettling as is his attempt to stand the Brown and Harris conceptualization of depressive disorder on its head. Provocatively, he asks us to suppose that a South Asian psychiatrist, drawing on the widely present culture-bound syndrome of semen loss, were to operationalize this indigenous Ayurvedic disease category by setting out clear-cut diagnostic criteria and incorporating them in a survey instrument whose findings could be quantified and assigned statistical probabilities. If this instrument were to be administered to Western populations to enumerate cases of semen loss and their epidemiological prevalence, the South Asian psychiatrist would be laughed at for being foolishly ethnocentric and tautological. Semen loss does not convey the same meaning in the West and hence we Westerners regard it as invalid as a measure of disease (but see Beiser's retort to this point in chap. 9). Obeyesekere uses this telling example of reverse ethnocentrism to attack the very idea of "operationalization" of criteria of depression and other disorders in the American Psychiatric Association's influential (even in Asia) Diagnostic and Statistical Manual. (In chapter 11, Manson and his collaborators review their efforts to construct a combined methodology that integrates anthropological and epidemiological techniques to study depression among American Indians which is aimed at resolving this question of cultural validity.)

Obeyesekere reasons that to give universal operational specificity to the vocabulary of emotions is to destroy its embeddedness in local forms of knowledge and to obscure what is integral to the rhetoric of emotion: its ambiguity, pluralism of meanings, and symbolic significance that "express emotional states that are not easily differentiated and indeed run counter to the very canons of operationalization." Having thrown down the gauntlet, or whatever its Sri Lankan equivalent would be, Obeyesekere goes on to criticize the methodology applied in a well-known psychiatric epidemiological survey conducted in India, that of Carstairs and Kapur (1976). For the anthropologist, the treatment of symptoms in isolation from their cultural context is problematic. Quantifying symptoms may help assess their intensity and quality, but for Obeyesekere and many other ethnographers no survey instrument can assess the personal meanings of symptoms, meanings that translate symptoms into motivations and human action. Moreover, reifying symptoms and stressors as individual things and failing to take into account their interrelationships in local cultural systems prevent epidemiological instruments from measuring the essential feature of sociocultural reality, namely, its meaningfully regularized interconnections that bring affect, symptom, stressor, and support together into a *system* (see chap. 13 where the Kleinmans extend this critique of studies in the stress-support-illness onset paradigm).

One objection to Obeyesekere's provocative paper is worthy of note here. The critique of the work of Carstairs and Kapur is directed against one of the most sensitive epidemiological studies in the cross-cultural literature. Finding that psychiatric instruments devised in the West are based on diagnoses that are not validated for the Indian context and that do not pay sufficient attention to "the psychiatric problems common in an Indian setting, such as the phenomenon of spirit-possession, preoccupation with symptoms of sexual inadequacy, and the frequency of vague somatic symptoms of psychological origin" (Carstairs and Kapur 1976:21), the research team developed an instrument specifically based on typical Indian complaints. Examining the relation between symptom level and care seeking, including resort to native healers, Carstairs and Kapur were able to test an important hypothesis about the mental health concomitants of legislated social change and to measure need for psychiatric services in a culturally sensitive manner. While such a study cannot investigate the personal meanings of public symbols and vocabularies of distress as can Obeyesekere's detailed life histories of individuals, we believe such survey work provides an important complement to the ethnographic method and enables the investigator to make generalizations about populations that cannot be made by the anthropologist.

The last chapter in this anthropological section is Keyes's review of the functions of cultural interpretation in the study of depression generally. Keyes shows that neither a materialist (only biological) nor a relativist (only cultural) account of depression provides an adequate understanding of the disorder. In their place, he sets out a dialectic approach that moves among and discloses the interactions between the concrete objective characteristics of human experience (both psychosocial and physiological) and their "practical interpretation in a particular cultural tradition." He begins, tracing some of the same pathways as Obeyesekere, with what he terms "moods"; while universal, both in the biological terms of the organism and the cultural terms of the person, these are not necessarily manifest as illness. Illness for Keyes, who draws on Schutz's phenomenological analysis of social problems, always involves a break from the commonsense (therefore cultural) stance a person normally adopts toward the world, and replaces it with a particular perspective based on awareness of painful distress. The work of culture may unite and dissipate the perception of painful distress that otherwise may conduce to labeling by self and other as illness. Even where distress is experienced, the religious or moral perspective on suffering may be regarded as more culturally appropriate; and if a medical perspective is applied, the particular cultural system of medicine will define how the illness experience is organized and treated.

Keyes also adopts Brown and Harris's (1978) model of the social origins of the disease depression to emphasize that though loss of important sources of value conduce to depression, if hope and awareness of new possibilities are present then loss will not lead to depressive disorder. Like Obeyesekere, Keyes sees the work of mourning as the work of culture. Crucial to the work of mourning in traditional societies is the idea of immortality. Keyes documents his argument with a case study from rural Thailand of prolonged grief which illustrates the interplay of risk factors and resources that either create or prevent depressive disorder. Keyes uses the case to show how suffering can be socially constructed either in religious or illness idioms, and how each brings in train distinctive pathways for seeking help, making sense of suffering, and mastering it. For example, the fact that grief following bereavement so uncommonly leads to lowered self-esteem, generalized hopelessness, and clinical depression is a consequence of mourning rituals that "serve to create for the living an image of the deceased as one transformed into an immortal and re-create the world of living such that all those who remain . . . are accorded social identities that no longer depend upon relationships with the deceased." Keyes regards biomedicine as unique, since it deals with illness by interpreting experience without reference to the problem of suffering, which is the point of departure not just for religious systems but for virtually all other healing systems. For this reason Keyes asks whether biomedicine's treatment of depressive disease (psychobiological dysfunction) is appropriate for dealing with depressive illness (the experience of suffering).

Part I ends, then, with an anthropological challenge to psychiatry and psychology which serves as starting point for the papers in each of the parts that follow. How do we take cultural meaning, historical change, social structure into account in studying the sources, experiences, and consequences of depressive disorder? What paradigms for psychocultural and biosocial interaction allow us to investigate depression as both disease and illness? What are alternative ways of configuring and researching depression as emotion which enable us to assess the interplay between personal and public domains so central to human experience?

Part II contains reviews of developmental, behavioral, and sociolinguistic answers to these questions. Shweder, a psychologist and anthropologist, makes explicit a series of distinctive substantive questions which orients and organizes research on the relation of culture and affect. These questions, which include taxonomic, ecological, semantic, communicative, social evaluation, and management queries, provide a clear set of issues that can be addressed by research to promote the growth of understanding. From a developmental perspective, Shweder shows that young children can express specific emotions even before they acquire language, but that these are not necessarily the same as what adults feel. Though there are both culture-specific and universal elicitors of emotion, there are fewer universal elicitors for adults than for children. Shweder argues that cross-culturally children experience loss as distress and frustration as anger, and that they perceive such universal ideas as "natural law" and sacred obligations, the transgression of which are universally felt on a continuum of shame-guilt-terror. The cross-cultural literature, he asserts, supports the view that though emotions have meanings that influence how we feel, affective meanings may be universal; for example, there is a seemingly universally understood emotional language of facial expression, voice register, and body posture which is understood even by three-year-olds. Shweder contends that the development of emotions and the development of cognition are not as many have held them to be—from undifferentiated states to differentiated ones—but are the other way around. "What the young child lacks are not complex differentiated mental structures but the knowledge and representational skills needed for talking about and making deliberate use of the complex structures available to him.'' For Shweder, culture, in providing these knowledge and representational skills, brings both universal and culture-specific meanings to bear on the constitution and expression of experience. For example, with Osgood, he regards emptiness as having universal implications and connotation (Osgood et al. 1975). This and other universal meanings of affects Shweder conceives to be articulated in all societies via a language of causal responsibility, a language of concomitant mood metaphor, and a language of physical consequences. For Shweder, the most common understanding of emptiness is ''soul loss,'' which has perceptual, legal, and moral significances that vary, but for which there is a universal substrate. Ordinary language utterances tell one how to feel soul loss; social role regulations and rules carry with them obligation to feel soul loss in certain situations and to manage the emotional experience of emptiness.

To illustrate the value of a semantic approach to emotion, Shweder presents a phenomenology of depression, in the tradition of Sartre's (1948) phenomenology of emotions, as soul loss. He suggests that where soul loss is still a leading component of the local cultural code (and it is in much of the non-Western world), this is how depressive affect is constituted and expressed. Even where this shared public idiom is unavailable, the actual experience of depressed emotion contains virtually all the phenomenological details of emptiness and the loss of soul. The basis for such universal signification is that differentiated ''emotional keyboard,'' possessed by four-year-olds worldwide, that can play out this common dirge. Because of the effect of culture-specific meanings and complex social relationships on the panhuman emotion keyboard, however, in adulthood the emotional scores that get played diverge considerably. Shweder reviews his field research with Oriya Brahman children in an ancient temple city in India to support this line of analysis. He shows that the universal affective meaning of touching is channeled in a culturally unique direction by local beliefs about menstrual pollution and its transmission via a mother's or a wife's touch. This is his model for what happens with depressive affect as it is transformed from universal psychobiological emotion to culturally shaped emotion.

Shweder's chapter alters both the traditional anthropological and psychological modes of analysis. First, he suggests that cultural meaning systems do not always particularize experience as most anthropologists hold. Some cultural meanings, Shweder contends, are anchored in a stubbornly panhuman grain of experience (e.g., the meaning of feelings of emptiness). Hence Shweder's model is based on *interaction* between psychological universals and the culturally particular and universal dimensions of social life that comprise the core dialectic of human experience. Shweder's second point challenges the traditional developmental model as much as his first contests the orthodox anthropological model. Development is not from less to more differentiated but the other way around. Biology (the genetic program) and universal aspects of early childhood development assure the potential for differentiation, but thereafter psychological development emerges from biocultural interactions, which increasingly upset our Western notions of developmental stages, and proceed in very culturally specific directions.

This chapter will stimulate enough questions for a generation of studies in the cross-cultural development of emotion. The phenomenology of the lost soul strikes us as a provocative tour de force that will upset the conventional wisdom of ethnographers and experimentalists alike, and that should offer clinicians wedded to "atheoretical" descriptive psychiatry a looking glass that challenges the fundamental assumptions of the phenomenology of depression as sadness. Here Shweder shows us that to be adequate, phenomenology must begin not with professional categories but with universal (read, cross-cultural) lay experience. When more than three-fourths of the world's population live in non-Western cultures, and greater than 90 percent are unfamiliar with psychoanalytic and other clinical constructs, symptom phenomenologies to be valid must begin with core meanings and experiences that may seem alien to educated, middle-class Americans and Europeans but that have been normative for most of human history, including our own.

In chapter 7, Beeman, a sociolinguist, examines depressive disorder as social communication. In linguistic perspective, the body is a prime source of metaphor, but that bodily metaphor is given distinctive social significance in different societies. Beeman criticizes simplistic psychiatric and psychological formulations of how emotional language differs across cultural and ethnic group, and notes that there is no scientific grounding for the ethnocentric claim that Western languages are more developed because they differentiate psychological states more explicitly and precisely.

Beeman outlines a sociolinguistic model for the study of depression. This model treats affect as a stylistic characteristic of speech, in which metacommunicative markers and change in grammar and lexicon signal emotion as a quality of a complex social interaction. He suggests that depression should be studied as discourse occurring in culturally marked communicative contexts, and uses the family therapy literature to argue that symptoms are products of microsocial systems, not reflections of psychobiology. From this perspective, he reinterprets Beck's (1976) cognitive theory of depression, presenting evidence and theory for a sociolinguistic process generating Beck's negative cognitive schemata and depressive illness. He also analyzes Beck's cognitive therapy for depressive disorder in the terms of rhetoric—as the adroit reconceptualization (and remoralization) of the depressed person's negative definitions of situations, self, and others, and hence as a type of rhetorical treatment.

The sociolinguistic perspective on the genesis and treatment of depression offers an impressive array of important research questions. Remarkably, the large number of studies on the linguistic aspects of schizophrenia are not matched by similar studies of major depressive disorder. Beeman lays out a model of how major depression may be created in vulnerable persons under the right stressful circumstances by sociolinguistic patterns that systematically undermine self-efficacy and enforce negative attributions of the self and the world. His analysis of cognitive therapy as a sociolinguistic process follows in a long tradition of studies of psychotherapy and healing which conceive the therapeutic process as a form of social persuasion (see Frank 1974; Pentony 1981), but he brings to this perspective a much more rigorous analytic tool than has heretofore been applied. The Kleinmans (chap. 13) draw on this model for their analysis of the generation of somatization and depression in modern China, but neither they nor the other participants in this volume develop Beeman's potentially powerful perspective on therapy. The virtue of the sociolinguistic model is that it analyzes symptoms as situated speech forms and psychocultural processes as socially patterned linguistic interactions that mediate cultural meaning, local power relations, and psychological experience.

Chapter 8 is written by two psychologists, Carr and Vitaliano, who initiate a substantial change in the direction the preceding chapters have taken. These authors challenge the view that depression is a universal psychobiological disorder (see also Obeyesekere's and Beeman's remarks on this topic). They overturn the widely accepted view that biology provides a "final common pathway" for diverse social and psychological conditions resulting in depressive illness (Akiskal and McKinney 1973), arguing instead that culture provides a final common *ethnobehavioral* pathway that channels diverse social and biological conditions into culturally specific behavioral repertoires. They base their challenge to the disease model on findings that individuals diagnosed as depressed demonstrate a wide range of behavioral symptoms that overlap with other psychiatric categories. These symptoms encourage a psychiatric fallacy based on the assumption that different affective behaviors imply different disease processes. They note that screening scales that assess symptoms in the population and psychiatric nosologies overlap very little (a point developed in a different direction by Beiser in chap. 9). Symptom checklists strike Carr and Vitaliano as measures of self-esteem, helplessness, hopelessness, dread, anxiety, sadness—a kind of nonspecific psychological distress analogous to fever in biomedicine.

The authors favor a distress approach over a disease model. They view distress as a complex biobehavioral response to antecedent stressors which is mediated by vulnerability and psychosocial resources (coping and support). They construe vulnerability as a combination of genetic and developmental variables in which the latter is the result of deprivations in sources of value and reward leading to low self-esteem, impaired self-mastery, and loss of self-confidence. Because loss is the universal antecedent of depression, Carr and Vitaliano hold that psychological universals are the chief determinants of depressive behavior. These universals are social learning processes (positive and negative reinforcement, stimulus and response generalization, discrimination, extinction, modeling, and imitation) that are fundamental to the human condition and that are an essential component of the causal web of depression, since they predispose individuals facing aversive events to develop learned helplessness. Past learning experiences, universal cognitive processes (differentiation, response flexibility, situational specificity), and cultural norms determine whether one's response to perceived aversive life event changes is violence, anxiety, or depression. This cognitive behavioral interpretation of depression complements and extends Beeman's analysis, but in a somewhat unexpected direction.

Carr and Vitaliano compare depressive disorder to *amok*, a culture-bound syndrome in Malayo-Indonesian culture. They analyze amok as a final common behavioral distress pathway along which is channeled, under the influence of cultural norms and meanings, various kinds of normal and abnormal behavior, including psychiatric disorder. Depression is also conceived as a culturally approved final common pathway of behavioral distress and a cultural alternative to amok and violence. The authors present an ethnobehavioral model to describe how universal

principles of social learning, psychobiological processes, and sociocultural structure interrelate to generate depressive behavior. They
conclude on a note that is the point of departure of the next chapter, that
psychiatric epidemiology should be based on a model of psychological
distress and not on one that reifies disease categories that cross-cultural
comparison reveals to be problematic.

Beiser, a psychiatric epidemiologist, begins Part III, on epidemiology
and clinical measurement, by discussing findings from comparable
studies in Senegal, among Southeast Asian refugees in Canada, and
people dwelling in midtown Manhattan. His research suggests that
depression and somatization, which have frequently been found to occur
together in clinical research in Western and non-Western societies, and
which many have asserted offer one of the most common examples of
cultural patterning of illness, are ''orthogonal'' or distinctive symptom
clusters that overlap only partially. He concludes that somatization and
depression are separate conditions and that both are valid cross-cultural
universals. He believes somatization to be associated more with anxiety
than depression. The fact that depression in non-Western populations is
much more commonly expressed by a somatic idiom of distress he
relates to differences in communicative contexts, legitimacy of symptom expression in those contexts, and help-seeking resources, rather
than to a real difference in experienced symptoms or underlying
pathophysiology.

Beiser reviews some of the important recent biological findings that
support his analysis, and also leads readers through an impressive set of
cross-cultural studies that he has conducted to determine population-
based rates of depression. He criticizes clinical studies because they
provide data on selective samples that are not generalizable to populations. Along the way, Beiser reviews many of the major concerns in the
epidemiology of depression and makes a powerful argument for using
statistically sophisticated quantitative studies to make cross-cultural
comparisons of mental health and illness. His review of the methodological issues will give readers a sense of much of the controversy that
surrounds the findings from cross-cultural research and that is provoked
by different disciplinary claims about what are the best ways to assure
valid and reliable knowledge.

Readers will note that it is not always clear when Beiser refers to
depression as affect and when as disease. An assumption of his methodology is that they fall along a continuum, but both earlier and later
chapters raise serious questions about such a continuum. Are symptom
statements in general populations where clinical depression occurs in

well under 10 percent of subjects comparable to symptom complaints in a clinical sample of patients disabled by a major depressive disorder? How are criteria established to determine who is a "case" in a population-based survey, and how can such criteria be used in populations in different societies? Is factor analysis in a general population measuring one thing (the global distress Carr and Vitaliano discuss) and clinical research another (psychiatric disorder)? Do somatization and depression relate in the same manner in a clinical sample of depressed patients as they do in a population sample where depressive affect may be present to a much greater extent than depressive disorder? These and other questions are provoked by a reading of Beiser's chapter in concert with chapters 12 and 13, where the Goods and the Kleinmans present different perspectives on this topic. The controversy is an accurate reflection of the current "state of the art" and the disputes within and outside of psychiatric epidemiology. Beiser's attempt to integrate cultural and biological bases of depression offers concrete opportunities for interdisciplinary collaboration.

In chapter 10, Marsella and his WHO collaborators (Sartorius, Jablensky, and Fenton) review the findings from the WHO multiculture study of depressive disorder. They discuss problems in conceptualizing depression as a disease category and in conducting cross-cultural epidemiological and clinical studies. They present some of the chief manifestations of depression in different cultures derived from clinical observational studies, matched diagnostic studies, matched samples, and international surveys. Marsella et al. show that the findings support the view of a core depressive disorder, but also of substantial cross-cultural differences in that disorder. They disclose why the way the WHO study was organized assures its contribution to the former will be greater than to the latter. In a scientifically commendable, open, and disarmingly self-critical manner, they review problems with sampling, data collection methodology, and data analysis in their own study, as well as in other studies, which limit its usefulness in detecting how culture affects depression. Marsella and his colleagues set out a number of hypotheses of how personality, family structure and dynamics, social organization, mourning rituals, and social stressors relate to depression so as to potentially yield both significant cultural differences and cross-cultural similarities. The conclusions they enumerate are a reasonable summary of the problems confronting epidemiological and clinical measurement of depressive illness cross-culturally, and point to what might be more useful directions for such studies in the future. The bibliography these authors cite is extensive and offers readers a valuable guide to the large body of studies in this field by psychologists and psychiatrists.

The fourth and final section of the volume provides three examples of integrations of anthropological, epidemiological, and clinical approaches. Though the types of integration differ, each chapter responds to questions raised in the earlier sections. Manson, Shore, and Bloom have built an anthropological epidemiology of depression among the Hopi and other American Indian groups. Their study commences with the recognition of differential cultural as well as lay and professional constructions of depressive disorder discussed in the contributions in Part I. Beginning with ethnoscientific techniques for eliciting indigenous illness categories, Manson and his collaborators developed an ethnomedical instrument to determine Hopi symptom domains that might plausibly be inferred to have some more or less close relationship to the American psychiatric category "major depressive disorder." They isolated five Hopi illness categories—each a cluster of cognitive, affective, and behavioral descriptors. These emic categories were associated with a range of psychosocial problems including personal loss, difficulties in subsistence, culture conflict, interpersonal strife, family problems, social/political tension, witchcraft, and supernatural sanction. Side by side with the systematic assessment of traditional Hopi illness categories, the authors modified a standard psychiatric evaluation questionnaire to make it appropriate for use with the Hopi. Not only did they use back translation and reliability techniques, they modified the questionnaire to address the problem of culturally divergent meanings. Hence guilt, shame, and sin, which are lumped together in the National Institute of Mental Health's Diagnostic Interview Schedule, had to be separated into discrete questions, since each conveys very different meaning in Hopi. Cultural sensitivities and restrictions on discussing sexual behavior required deletion of some questions and substitution with others more appropriate for Hopi informants. These instruments were then given to a clinical sample and a matched community sample.

Manson et al. present some of the more salient findings. One indigenous Hopi disorder correlated highly with the vegetative complaints of major depressive disorder but did not persist for the two weeks required by DSM-III to make the diagnostic criteria for major depressive disorder. The authors conclude that this criterion of duration may be inappropriate for the Hopi. Another Hopi disorder overlapped with the dysphoria but not the vegetative complaints, while several of the Hopi categories correlated not at all with clinical depression. Their sample consisted of a high proportion of cases who met the criteria for major depressive disorder (which has been shown to have very high rates among American Indians), a high proportion of females (a finding that holds for all Western societies and, importantly, most but not all non-Western societies), and high rates of bereavement. Major depressive disorder in men always began secondary to alcoholism. Women with major depressive disorder occasionally had culturally constituted auditory hallucinations that in another setting would lead to a diagnosis of psychosis. Manson and collaborators were able to relate depressive disorder to the high rates of loss in Hopi culture: death and acculturation that threatened self and group identity. These findings are employed by the authors to (1) sustain a critical review of cultural problems in DSM-III when applied to American Indian groups; (2) develop a more specific problem list of the chief behavioral and social problems afflicting this and other American Indian societies; and (3) explain why depression among American Indians is often misdiagnosed and inadequately treated. Hence this innovative methodological collaboration between anthropologist and psychiatrist makes significant practical as well as theoretical contributions based on concern to avoid both anthropological and epidemiological pitfalls. Problems may still be discerned, but this is a much more sophisticated integration of methodologies than has heretofore been applied in field research.

In chapter 12, Good, Good, and Moradi present another example of how clinical and survey techniques can be integrated with ethnography. The purpose of their triangulation of methods in the study of depression among Iranians is to connect clinical and behavioral measurements with the measurement of meaning. This is a central methodological problem in the social sciences and psychiatry. It has already been shown in the study of stressful life events that taking the meaning of stressful events into account can significantly improve the ability to predict individuals at high risk for illness onset. Good et al. apply their measures to a different question, namely, whether Iranians disclose culture-specific forms of depression. The combination of assessing symptoms and their meanings enables their ethnographically informed factor analytic study to describe a unique Iranian depressive syndrome associated with a distinctive cluster of symptoms and illness experience. The authors disclose, moreover, how this cluster can be interpreted within the historical and contemporary context of Iranian culture.

Like the preceding chapter, and the one that follows, chapter 12 illustrates ways of taking both indigenous meanings and those of the researchers into account in studying psychiatric disorder. Just as the author's ethnographic interpretation of the Iranian context of depression informs us about its social sources (including uprooting and refugee status) and psychocultural forms, so too their interpretive sociology of science approach—already applied to the study of the natural sciences—reveals how cultural orientations implicit in psychiatric models produce findings that are artifacts of those models and the methodologies they subsume at least as much as they are aspects of the illness phenomenon under study. Thus, in this chapter, the cross-cultural comparison of depressive disorders is shown to have the potential of freeing psychiatry from the tacit Western cultural categories that lurk behind its technical diagnostic criteria.

The final chapter in this section, by Kleinman and Kleinman, offers another example of combined anthropological and psychiatric research on depression. The authors review their studies of the relationship between depression and neurasthenia among patients in psychiatric and primary care clinics at the Hunan Medical College, in the People's Republic of China. They configure their research as an analysis of the social production (etiology) and cultural construction (conceptualization and experience) of depressive affect and disorder. Depression is examined as a social affect that emerges from the relation of individuals, the local systems of power relationships within which they live, and macrolevel societal and historical conditions. The unit of analysis becomes the organization of depressive experiences within particular local systems of family, work, and community relations which mediate the effect of macro-level conditions (e.g., the Cultural Revolution) on individuals. The authors show how stress and distress can be studied as transactional situations in these local systems; this enables researchers to operationalize cultural and personal meanings as research variables.

Individual clinical cases are described which express problematic aspects of Chinese society—for example, the humiliating and destructive experiences of the Cultural Revolution, structural tensions in the tightly controlled work system—so that the study of depression in China, when expanded to include its social and cultural constituents, opens a perspective on contemporary Chinese society not readily available through the study of "normal" social life. The Kleinmans' analysis oscillates between the distinctive inner world and subjective experience of individual Chinese and the embeddedness of the individual in local systems. Depressive discourse is seen to emerge from and express this dynamic dialectic of the human condition.

Kleinman and Kleinman study affect and affective illness through the investigation of the meanings and uses of physical complaints (somatization). The paradox that the most emotional of illnesses is expressed and experienced in primarily bodily terms poses important issues for research. How is the experience of troubling social conditions and conflicted interpersonal relations translated into somatic illness? Are symptoms provoked primarily by particular forms of distress or by communicative norms that legitimate specialized and context-dependent vocabularies? What is the relationship among somatization as a psychological coping style (for troubling affect), as an idiom of distress, as a style of care seeking, and as a situation-specific way of interpreting and talking about one's distress? What is the relationship between major affective disorder expressed in somatic terms and chronic somatization, a condition of chronic illness behavior and amplification of bodily distress often associated with unalterable social stress? The fact that somatization disorders are the most common illness forms in both Chinese and American medical care clinics and that chronic pain is among the most prevalent causes of disability in both societies suggests how critical the investigation of these questions can be.

Chapter 13 also assesses the relation of a Western psychiatric category, depression, to a medical category having great currency in both professional and lay medical culture in China, "neurasthenia." Epidemiological research indicates that most neurasthenic patients meet diagnostic criteria for major depressive disorder. However, results of both clinical and survey research indicate the poverty of an approach that would simply equate the two categories, interpreting the Chinese illness reality through the lens of Western biomedical categories. Neurasthenia as symbolic reality condenses a distinctly Chinese syndrome of experiences and social significance and thus maps a perduring illness form experienced by Chinese.

FUTURE DIRECTIONS

It is our hope that this collection will serve to stimulate a new beginning of research into the relation of culture and depression. The papers here are only forerunners of a fully developed cross-cultural enterprise. They represent a new beginning, however, in several ways. A number of questions that have produced great discussion but few significant advances over the years have simply been left aside. No paper poses as central the question of whether the depressed in various societies direct their aggression inward as guilt or project it outward onto the social or spiritual order. No paper focuses on the role of child rearing in configuring distinctive psychological conflicts, defensive styles, and character structures. None of the papers in this volume seek to determine differences in the prevalence of depression by society or social group and explain such differences with reference only to other social variables. Issues such as these have been replaced by several new concerns.

First, the papers in this volume reflect the "interpretive turn" in anthropology (Geertz 1983). Dysphoric affect and depressive illness are investigated through a sustained analysis of systems of meaning and discourse. Sociolinguistics, cognitive psychology, semantic analysis, and phenomenological methods are each employed in turn to study how dysphoria is "brought to meaning," how specialized idioms and explanatory frames are used to interpret, articulate, and respond to depressive illness. The interpretation model focuses not only on lay interpretations of distress but also on our own medical and social science discourse in terms of which we view and analyze the discourse of members of other societies. It is our belief that an interpretive analysis offers important directions for research in the field.

Second, these papers reflect the mutual challenge of the biological and cultural paradigms. Depression is neither a simple "reflection" in personal experience of psychophysiological processes nor a culturally constituted phenomenon free of physiological constraints. Depression is of such interest to anthropologists and psychiatrists alike because it provides a prime opportunity for exploration of the interaction of culture and biology. We believe this interaction will remain at the center of attention, and that future research will begin with the questions raised by its investigation. Indeed, we think a core contemporary concern of cross-cultural studies and behavioral science research generally is how to measure meaning in such a way as to be able to study its relationship to biological processes and social behavior.

Third, these papers reflect the growing awareness of the limitations inherent in any single methodological approach to studying depression. Anthropological, clinical, and epidemiological methods are inherently in tension with one another, but it is just such tension that is the strength of cross-cultural research. We believe interdisciplinary approaches are necessary to establish new standards for how research should be carried out and to move past reproduction of old knowledge to new insights.

Finally, we believe such studies will have a variety of direct applications. Enormous investments are being made in research based on DSM-III categories and associated epidemiological instruments. These approaches need to be critically examined in the light of cross-cultural research. Not only does the validity of diagnostic categories require critical attention but the axial structure of DSM-III also needs to be opened to cultural analysis. The various axes represent the predominant conceptual paradigms in the field—depression as disease, as personality, and as disruption of social functioning. However, "emic" assessments—the evaluation of the patients' disorder by members of the culture, their representation of the disorder using illness categories and explanatory forms, and thus the social and cultural configuration of depressive illness—are bypassed altogether. They are treated as irrelevant to the clinician's task. The chapters in this volume suggest this is hardly the case. Together they argue for a rethinking of the relation between culture and depression, of the models used to conceive and the methods used to study the relationship, of the way the three disciplines—anthropology, psychiatry, and psychology—go about cross-cultural research.

NOTES

1. See Rorty 1980 for many other examples of theoretical conflicts in the study of emotion as well as several attempts at integration, especially those of Averill and Ekman, and a commendable try at devising a new philosophical language to bridge old and no longer tenable theoretical differences.

REFERENCES

Akiskal, H. S., and W. T. McKinney
    1973   Depressive Disorders: Toward a Unified Hypothesis. Science
                182:20–29.
Beck, A. T.
    1976   Cognitive Therapy and the Emotional Disorders. New York:
                International Universities Press.
Brown, G. W., and T. Harris
    1978   Social Origins of Depression. New York: Free Press.
Burton, R.
    [1621]   The Anatomy of Melancholy. New York: Tudor Press.
    1955
Carstairs, G. M., and R. Kapur
    1976   The Great Universe of Kota: Stress, Change and Mental Disorder in an Indian Village. Berkeley: University of California
                Press.
Frank, J.
    1974   Persuasion and Healing. New York: Schocken.

Geertz, C.
1983   Local Knowledge. New York: Basic Books.
Hahn, R. A., and A. Kleinman
1983   Biomedical Practice and Anthropological Theory. Annual
            Review of Anthropology, 12:305−333.
James, W.
[1890]   The Principles of Psychology. Vol. 2. Cambridge: Harvard
1981   University Press.
Osgood, C. E., W. H. May, and M. S. Mirou
1975   Cross-Cultural Universals of Affective Meaning. Urbana: Uni-
            versity of Illinois Press.
Pentony, P.
1981   Models of Influence in Psychotherapy. New York: Free Press.
Rorty, A. O., ed.
1980   Explaining Emotions. Berkeley, Los Angeles, London: Uni-
            versity of California Press.
Sartre, J. P.
1948   The Emotions: Outline of a Theory. New York: Philosophical
            Library.

Meanings, Relationships, Social Affects: Historical and Anthropological Perspectives on Depression

INTRODUCTION TO PART I

The claim that cross-cultural studies of depression provide a significant challenge to contemporary theories and research methods rests first on the argument that dysphoria and depressive illness vary in important ways across cultures. If there are significant variations, the validity of the psychiatric conception of depression as a universal disorder is called into question, and social and cultural variables take on particular importance for understanding the sources of differences. Chapters in the first section of this book provide data—both historical and anthropological—for assessing the extent and nature of variation of depressive emotion and illness across cultures.

The assessment of cultural variability begins with empirical data, but immediately problems arise. What are to be considered data? What variation is to be considered significant? For example, anthropologists and psychologists often look at a phenomenon such as the expression of emotion by a member of a cultural group, but where one sees a universal facial expression, the other sees distinctive configurations of meaning and codes of communication. Similar differences exist in the recording of clinical data and the assessment of what constitutes variation. The chapters in this section frame their presentation of data with provocative arguments about how we should conceptualize culture and social organization and how data should be gathered, presented, and, not least of all, interpreted.

The five chapters in Part I, by a historian of psychiatry and four social anthropologists, ask how cultural meanings and social structures should be taken into account in studying the sources, experiences, and consequences of dysphoric affect and depressive disorder. Depression is shown to be grounded in diverse societal sources of human misery and integrated into quite different contexts of meaning (e.g., the Ifaluk have no concept of depression as joylessness; the Kaluli have no concept of depression at all; Thai peasants take a religious not an illness perspective on prolonged grief; in medieval Europe the sadness and sloth of acedia and the humors of melancholia merge). Each chapter responds somewhat differently to the questions posed by these findings, but all the authors would agree that cross-cultural studies of depression must respond in a substantial way or they are vitiated by ethnocentric and anachronizing bias and failure to configure illness as a social problem.

The authors of this section all argue that collection and analysis of cultural data is inherently problematic. There is no value-free language for recording cultural meanings. Cross-cultural work necessarily involves translation between distinctive systems of meaning, that is, between popular conceptualizations in non-Western societies, on the one hand, and both Western psychiatric theory and broader theories of self and society in American and European culture, on the other hand. These authors express discomfort with the vast corpus of clinical and epidemiological studies that regard translation as a minor and largely unproblematic task. For them, translation is *the* central concern if culture is taken seriously. Indeed, their presentations suggest that translation of disease categories and symptoms should be conceived as the final step in a lengthy process, beginning with intensive ethnographic accounts of illness meanings and experiences in the indigenous terms of the particular societies under study. Only after this difficult and time-consuming understanding is achieved can specific translations and comparisons be made.

The chapter by Lutz makes an even more radical departure from established methods in cross-cultural research, though one quite reasonable by anthropological standards, by demanding that researchers begin with an examination of their own professional psychiatric and psychological categories as Western "ethnotheories." Her provocative point, like the instance of reverse ethnocentrism in Obeyesekere's ironic account of a non-Western psychiatrist searching for cases of a South Asian culture-bound disorder in the West, is meant to force researchers to come to terms with translation not just as a process of making sense of different words in distinctive languages but as a more difficult and fundamental activity relating distinctive worlds (their own and their subjects') wherein depression is configured and experienced differently.

All of the anthropological accounts make a strong case for the role of culture in depression, and Jackson shows that historical changes have profoundly affected how we conceive of depression in the West and what it has come to signify and be for us. In addition to the focus on cultural meanings, however, the chapters by Schieffelin, Obeyesekere, and Keyes also emphasize the social origins and consequences of depression, which they view dialectically as oscillating between social structural constraints and personal agency. Obeyesekere, for example, registers his disquiet that only certain persons develop depressive disorder though many find themselves beset by similar sources of distress and all have available a shared cultural meaning system. One of the "works of culture" in Sri Lanka, he points out, is to transform dysphoria into Buddhist transcendence. Keyes depicts a case of mourning that seems for a time to be headed for melancholia, the disease, only to be transformed by the work of culture. Nonetheless, the sufferer could well have become a chronic patient. Schieffelin could locate only one case of depression among the Kaluli, but it fits precisely the model of learned helplessness that he feels explains how depression occurs in Highland New Guinea and worldwide. In each instance, the sensitivity of the ethnographer to specific conditions of the person, as well as to the context of social life, illuminates the particularity of vulnerability, precipitating, and mediating (buffering) factors in the genesis of distress and disease as much as in the shaping of illness as a cultural form of suffering. This has become the core orientation of the anthropology of medicine, and these contributions suggest that it is also the central thesis of the anthropology of mental illness and psychiatry.

In Obeyesekere's chapter a crucial anthropological critique of epidemiological studies is advanced which is echoed in the final section of this book. The anthropological understanding of local cultural systems places stressful life events, social supports, and coping processes in *systematic interrelationship* with each other. Assessing variables as autonomous, reified entities, as is routinely done in epidemiological studies that use separate instruments to assess each, is a spurious substitute for measuring the vital interaction among these variables, the sociosomatic reticulum that connects person to social world. More valid measurements of social sources of sickness would evaluate the local cultural system within which certain interactions among meanings, norms, and power relationships conduce to illness onset or amplification of existing disability in particular individuals, and protect others (see chap. 13). For Obeyesekere, epidemiology is not an atheoretical methodology, as it is frequently portrayed, but rather is laden with value orientations (e.g., positivist, empiricist, Cartesian, and asocial) that significantly impede its utility in studying illness as a social phenomenon. Obeyesekere challenges various efforts to "operationalize" cultural and social variables in cross-cultural research as discrete entities that undercut anthropological attention to the interactive context of lived experience (healthy and morbid).

To the nonanthropologist, it may be pointed out that several distinctive forms of anthropological theory and analysis are represented here. Schieffelin's analysis of depressive experience as a "cultural system" is grounded in contemporary symbolic anthropology, with its focus on ritual as an entrée to a society's organized understanding of self and the world. In previous work, Schieffelin has analyzed one of the most dramatic grief rituals recorded by anthropologists, the *gisaro* of the Kaluli people of Papua New Guinea. Here he uses this research for provoking questions about the "reciprocity" of grief and anger in social process. Keyes, similarly a symbolic anthropologist, explicitly undertakes a phenomenological analysis of grief and depression as distinctive "perspectives" or forms of "reality." He follows in the tradition of Hallowell, in this analysis, and more recently of Geertz and others who draw on phenomenological theorists (Schutz, Ricoeur, Gadamer) to advance a Weberian analysis of the human struggle for meaning. Obeyesekere's work links this tradition to the psychoanalytic. Here, as in previous work, he explores the relation of "public" and "private" meanings through which symbols articulate personal conflict and a society's response to ultimate limits. Finally, Lutz represents an alternative tradition, that of cognitive anthropology. This tradition advances a series of formal methodologies for representing cultural meanings and the relation of symbols to one another (through opposition, classificatory hierarchy, propositional forms, etc.), and holds important potential for linking anthropology, psychology, and psychiatry.

Even though they examine depression more as a feeling state than a disorder, all of the authors, save perhaps Lutz, who does not address the issue, would seem to acknowledge the stubbornly human biopsychological element in human nature that also constrains depressive experience. Keyes even outlines a seemingly panhuman paradigm of the phenomenology of distress. Each chapter suggests a somewhat different line of analysis for a cultural explication of depression. The editors think it essential that readers carry forward the questions generated in this section to those later chapters that present behavioral, epidemiological, and clinical accounts of depressive disorder. The power of the anthropological argument resides precisely in the tension between these divergent perspectives: interpretation and translation versus measurement. Heretofore that argument has either been disregarded or criticized as unfeasible. The gravamen of this book asserts that cross-cultural research can no longer avoid these questions, that there are ways in which they can (nay, must) become part of cross-cultural clinical and epidemiological studies.

There is no theoretical synthesis at present which marries relativism (depression is a socially organized cultural form) with interactionism (depression is the outcome of a dialectical relationship between the sociocultural world and psychophysiology). But these chapters along with those that follow show that for journeymen field researchers this cultural interactionism emerges repeatedly, if you will, from wrestling with the slippery theoretical problems provoked by the relationship of culture and depression. Perhaps there is as much for anthropology to gain from this interdisciplinary confrontation as there is for psychiatry and psychology.

1

Acedia the Sin and Its Relationship to Sorrow and Melancholia*

Stanley W. Jackson

To replace the complex acedy by sadness or sloth is to evade a difficulty.
—James Hastings, *Encyclopedia of Religion and Ethics*, Vol. I:66

Dejected states of one form or another seem to have been part of the world of Western man as far back as his literature allows one to look, and the terms for them have long been familiar ones. As with today's use of the term "depression," earlier eras have sometimes used these terms carefully and sometimes carelessly. At varying moments a particular term might indicate a passing frame of mind, a passion or emotion, a mood, a symptom, or a disease.

Within the larger context of the Western world's ways of thinking about and dealing with various dejected states, there are several patterns with significant histories of their own yet clearly with some connection with one another. The most prominent among these is melancholia—the disease that belongs to the history of medicine and that can be traced back at least to the Hippocratic writings of classical Greece. For the Hippocratics in the fifth and fourth century B.C., melancholia was associated with "aversion to food, despondency, sleeplessness, irritability, restlessness," and they stated that "fear or depression that is prolonged means melancholia" (Hippocrates [Jones and Withington, trans.] 1923–31: I, 263; IV, 185). For Galen in the second century A.D. and for

*This chapter is an adapted version of a paper originally published in *Bull. Hist. Med.* 55 (1981):172–185.

Western authorities during the next fifteen hundred years, melancholia was conceived of as a chronic, nonfebrile form of madness, in which the patients were commonly fearful, sad, misanthropic, and tired of life, usually accompanied by the symptoms noted by the Hippocratics, often accompanied by a particular, circumscribed delusion, and sometimes accompanied by various gastrointestinal symptoms (Jackson 1969). During the sixteenth and seventeenth centuries, a reference to guilt gradually became an element in many descriptions of melancholia. The state following on the loss of a loved one or of material possessions was sometimes conceived of as a separate sort of dejected state and sometimes as just another instance of melancholia. More and more the presence of a delusion was thought to be an essential feature. Increasingly it was argued that melancholia was a partial insanity with sound mental functioning outside the limits of a single, circumscribed delusion, but this view was eventually abandoned (Jackson 1983). Beginning in the late seventeenth century, the hypochondriacal form of melancholia was gradually isolated as a nonpsychotic dejected state referred to as "hypochondriasis," "the hyp," or "the spleen." Eventually the category of melancholia was streamlined further by pruning those few mania-like states that had often been included. The term "depression" gradually came into use.[1]

Acedia and its kindred sin tristitia emerged after Galen in the second century A.D. These dejected states belong to the history of religion, in particular to the religious scheme of the cardinal sins of Christianity. By the late fourth century A.D., the Christian church had come to use the term "acedia"[2] to designate a constellation of feelings and behaviors that were considered unusual, undesirable, and indicative of a need for remedial attention. In the words of John Cassian (ca. A.D. 360–435), it was a "weariness or distress of heart," "akin to dejection," and "especially trying to solitaries" (Cassian [Gibson, trans.] 1955: XI, 266–267).

The gradual development of acedia as a distinct condition and the beginnings of a systematic concern about it had their roots in the experiences of the Egyptian desert monks near Alexandria in the fourth century. The symptoms of this condition were intimately associated with the struggles of the anchorites against the hazards of isolation and the temptations of their own fleshly inclinations while they strove for spiritual perfection and oneness with God. Important among these early ascetics and of primary importance in the development of the notion of acedia was Evagrius Ponticus (A.D. 345–399). He was a direct influence on Cassian, whose description of acedia was diffused throughout the medieval Christian world and remained the main point of reference for many later considerations of the subject. Although somewhat transformed in its applications to the cenobitic life and eventually employed beyond the walls of the monasteries, acedia continued as a familiar notion throughout the medieval era.

Some modern authors have viewed acedia as little more than a medieval term for what we would call depressive states or as a synonym for melancholia in its own time. Others have thought of it as merely a term for sloth or laziness. These are clearly misleading simplifications. This troublesome state was not merely dejection or sorrow. Nevertheless, from its beginnings it was associated with tristitia (dejection, sadness, sorrow), and this connection continued; there were frequent references to *desperatio* (despair) in writings about acedia; and it was intermittently brought into association with melancholia in the late Middle Ages. Similarly, despite having come to be referred to as "the sin of sloth" in the later medieval period and subsequently, acedia was not merely sloth, although lassitude, weariness, inaction, carelessness, and neglect were all aspects of acedia to varying degrees in various instances.

Viewed another way, this unusual mental state and its associated behaviors were both troublesome and common enough to receive considerable attention in medieval times. As in other times and places, there were various ways to deal with unusual mental states and their associated behaviors.[3] In the case of acedia it was mainly religious beliefs and, to a lesser extent, medicine that were used in attempting to explain and ameliorate the condition. Thus the history of acedia was intimately connected with changes in Christianity and medicine.

The scattered uses of the term "acedia" in extant writings from before the time of Evagrius indicate the following meanings—carelessness, weariness, exhaustion, apathy, anguish, sadness, low spirits, sloth, or negligence from excessive attention to worldly matters (le Pontique [A. and C. Guillaumont, eds.] 1971:I, 84–86; Wenzel 1960:3–12). Evagrius used as his frame of reference the eight main temptations or evil thoughts against which the monk had to fight, this being akin to the sometimes eight, sometimes seven, cardinal sins of later Christendom. In this scheme his description of acedia was considerably more comprehensive and systematic than those of his predecessors. The condition was characterized by exhaustion, listlessness, sadness or dejection, restlessness, aversion to the cell and the ascetic life, and yearning for family and former life (le Pontique I, 84–90, II, 520–527, 562–571; Ponticus [Bamberger, trans.] 1970:18–19, 23–24).

With the work and writings of Cassian, the concept of acedia was effectively transmitted to the West in a context of the eight chief vices. In his *Institutes of the Coenobia*, Book X is devoted to "Of the Spirit of Accidie." There he describes the condition as follows:

> Our sixth combat is with . . . [acedia], which we may term weariness or distress of heart. This is akin to dejection, and is especially trying to solitaries, and a dangerous and frequent foe to dwellers in the desert; and especially disturbing to a monk about the sixth hour, like some fever which seizes him at stated times, bringing the burning heat of its attacks on the sick man at usual and regular hours. Lastly, there are some of the elders who declare that this is "the midday demon" spoken of in the ninetieth Psalm. . . . It produces dislike of the place, disgust with the cell, and disdain and contempt of the brethren. . . . It also makes the man lazy and sluggish about all manner of work which has to be done within the enclosure of his dormitory. (Cassian XI, 266–267)

The afflicted monk became restless; he complained that his situation was no longer spiritually fruitful and that he was useless in it; and he thought that he would never be well unless he left the place. In his continuing restlessness, time seemed to pass very slowly; he yearned for company and considered seeking solace in sleep. In short, he tended either to remain idle in his cell or to wander from it in restless pursuit of diversionary activities, in either case to no spiritual end (ibid., pp. 267–268).

In keeping with some previous references to "this disease" (ibid.), when he took up the question of a remedy Cassian approached it in terms of a sustained medical metaphor. He referred to Saint Paul as being "like a skillful and excellent physician," and to his advice as "the healing medicines of his directions" for the treatment of "this disease, which springs from the spirit of accidie" (ibid., p. 268). Cassian consistently urged manual labor as a remedial measure, again using Saint Paul as his authority. While at first describing a gentle, soothing approach, when he discussed afflicted persons who were unresponsive or rebellious, he urged a much sterner approach, including such measures as brethren of the afflicted withdrawing from them and avoiding them. Throughout these passages there are injunctions against idleness and an emphasis on work (ibid., pp. 268–275).

Another significant feature of early accounts of acedia is related to the use of demons in the Christian system of explanation. For the desert fathers, the struggle with their own inclinations had frequently come to be viewed as a struggle with demons which came from outside to tempt them. Following a tradition with Stoic origins, they strove for an inner peace against their own inclinations toward passions. With the stirring of the passions, disturbing thoughts might arise and interfere with this inner peace. So these ascetics frequently turned to the notion of demons playing on their passions to stir up evil or disturbing thoughts. These became the demons' tools or weapons for tempting the person to consent to sin. In the writings of Evagrius the language of demons and evil spirits came into more systematic use with regard to the various temptations to sin, among which he included acedia. Acedia was an evil spirit; the demon of acedia, or "noonday demon," attacked the ascetic or tempted him. Sometimes acedia meant the demon, and sometimes it meant the evil thought that the demon provoked the ascetic to entertain. In these terms, as demon *and* evil thought, acedia was one of the eight main temptations (le Pontique I, 57, 94–98; Wenzel 1960:12–14).

Cassian established acedia as a troublesome condition within the context of the Christian scheme of eight principal faults or chief vices. For many centuries thereafter, the chief vices or cardinal sins, either eight or seven in number, constituted the basic frame of reference for the continuing history of acedia. Cassian had recognized eight chief vices— gluttony, fornication, covetousness, anger, dejection, accidie, vainglory, and pride. Gregory the Great (ca. A.D. 540–604), however, altered the composition of the list of cardinal sins and reduced the number to seven—vainglory, anger, envy, dejection, covetousness, gluttony, and fornication. While he dropped pride from the list, in a sense he retained it by setting it apart as the root of all the other sins. He added envy and dropped acedia, although apparently for him dejection had come to subsume both conditions. Certainly his descriptions of the latter included several elements that were commonly associated with acedia, and these vices shared a good many symptoms with the Evagrian and Cassianic descriptions. "Such effects as dejection and sorrow, absence of the wonted elation in spiritual exercises, impatience in work and devotion, wrath against the brethren, and despair of ever reaching one's spiritual goals, are all common to both *tristitia* and *acedia*" (Wenzel 1960:25).

During the next several centuries, both the Gregorian list and the Cassianic list were in frequent use, but with the former tending to predominate. Whether a list included tristitia or acedia, the sin was often described in a way that could subsume both. Gradually Gregory's total of seven became the accepted number, and pride and vainglory were merged, with pride as the surviving term. By the twelfth century, Gregory's tristitia had been replaced by Cassian's acedia, at times cited as "acedia or tristitia."

Another important point to note in the relationship of acedia to tristitia stemmed from the distinction made by Saint Paul, and by various ascetic authors, between a positive and a negative kind of tristitia, the former leading to penance and salvation, the latter to death (Bloomfield 1952: 73, 84−86; Wenzel 1960:28−29). Cassian had characterized the ''wholesome sorrow'' as stemming from ''penitence for sin'' or ''desire for perfection,'' whereas the more objectionable sorrow resulted from worldly frustration and distress (Cassian XI, 264−266). Over the centuries, this positive sorrow appeared in the lists of cardinal sins within the notion of tristitia but gradually disappeared along with the term ''tristitia'' itself. However, the negative sorrow, the dejection about worldly matters, continued to be associated with the sin of acedia.

Through the eleventh century, writers on acedia tended to emphasize the physical phenomena of idleness and somnolence, while, in the twelfth century, they ''laid greater stress on its inner phenomena of . . . spiritual slackness, weariness and boredom with religious exercises, lack of fervor, and a state of depression in the ups and downs of spiritual life'' (Wenzel 1960:30−31). That is, there had been a shift in emphasis from mode of behavior to state of mind, a shift more in keeping with the original perspective of the desert monks and Cassian. Also of note is the more benevolent view of acedia manifested by some medieval writers who recognized how natural it was for someone's attention to slacken and for him to have difficulty in continuing at the same activity for a prolonged period of time (ibid., p. 32).

Although from the time of Cassian to the spiritual treatises of the twelfth century acedia was largely an affliction of monks and contemplatives, in conjunction with the whole system of cardinal sins the concept gradually became part of the moral life of all Christians. Various lists of sins, commonly the cardinal sins, were used by priests as guidelines for the ritual of confession. Such lists became the basis for numerous penitentials, or handbooks of penance, which served confessors as systematic keys to the questions to ask the penitent and to the various penances to impose. When confession was made obligatory by the Fourth Lateran Council (1215−16) and the requirement was instituted that clergy should preach regularly to their parishioners, there was an extensive production of penitential literature, manuals for preachers, and catechetical handbooks in the period from 1200 to 1450. This meant that knowledge of the cardinal sins—of which the notion of acedia was a crucial part—spread among the general population (Bloomfield 1952: 91−92, 97−99; Wenzel 1960:68−69).

Acedia's designation as a cardinal sin meant that there were moral injunctions against it. However, the penitentials clearly reveal an additional perspective on this sin of a more benevolent nature. While they often chastised different aspects of acedia, the handbooks frequently implied that confession was a form of healing and the sins of the penitent were afflictions for which he was to be treated and cured. This theme can be traced back through the various penitential writings, and it probably reflects some influence from the sustained use of a medical metaphor by Cassian, whose works were so influential in other ways (McNeill 1932). This literature frequently involved "the conception of penance as medicine for the soul," with the medical principle of contraries curing contraries as the most common governing notion (McNeill and Gamer 1938:44). The processes of penance were conceived of

> as constituting a treatment in itself effective toward the recovery of the health that has been lost through sin. . . . The authors of these handbooks . . . had a sympathetic knowledge of human nature and a desire to deliver men and women from the mental obsessions and social maladjustments caused by their misdeeds. . . . "Not all are to be weighed in the same balance, although they be associated in one fault" but there must be discrimination according to cases. The physician of souls must . . . identify himself as far as possible with the patient. . . . [Despite a severity of prescription at times] the penitentials often reveal the considerateness of the experienced adviser of souls, wise in the lore of human nature and desiring to "minister to the mind diseased." (McNeill and Gamer 1938:45−46)

The tradition of the pastor/confessor as "physician of souls" can be traced back further still (Clebsch and Jaekle 1975:102−112), probably having roots in the idea of Christ as healer and in the notion of philosophers as "physicians of the soul" (McNeill 1951). Perhaps too the medical knowledge of the early Church Fathers and their commitment to ministering to the sick might have been a factor (D'Isray 1927).

With the flowering of Scholasticism, the sustained efforts at a systematic analysis of matters of faith included a considerably greater attention to acedia in the strictly theological literature (Wenzel 1960: 47−67). In the process, acedia, while continuing to be thought of as a sin, became integrated into theories of the passions and emerged as a disorder in man's emotional life. At times, it came to be thought of in medical terms.

For Saint Thomas Aquinas (1225?−1274), the traditional seven vices derived from the interaction of the will with the world of its objects: "objects move the appetite, the appetite responds in a certain way, certain kinds of responses are capable of leading to moral evil, or sin, if consented to'' by the will (ibid., p. 45). In this framework, acedia arose out of the will shrinking from some good because the concupiscible desires were perverted, either by an inappetence for or an aversion to the spiritual good.

In a usage not to be confused with its place in any system of sins, the term ''tristitia'' also referred to one of a small number of basic passions within a system of passions that took shape as part of Scholastic psychology. Tristitia and gaudium (sorrow and joy; cf. pain and pleasure) were paired as opposites to which many other feelings could be reduced. Tristitia was the basic reaction of man's sensitive nature in withdrawing from an evil, whether present or anticipated, real or imagined. Within this generic use of tristitia, Saint Thomas's fundamental definition of acedia as species was ''*tristitia de spirituali bono*: the sorrow about, or the aversion one feels against, man's spiritual good. 'Sorrow' is here understood as the negative reaction of man's sensitive appetite to an object which is either truly evil, or evil only in appearance but good in reality. The latter reaction constitutes *acedia* properly speaking'' (ibid., p. 48). From the early twelfth century on, accounts of acedia increasingly emphasized some form of sadness or grief. Eventually the definition of acedia as a severe or ''depressing sorrow'' became a significant use of the term, and was shared by Saint Thomas. Finally, it came to be viewed as a species of tristitia the passion *and* as the sin, which subsumed dejection or sorrow in the scheme of cardinal sins.

In acquiring this connection with the passions, acedia began to be described occasionally in physiological terms. The passions were conceived of as varying in strength and in combination with the various temperaments or constitutions of individuals, so some persons were thought to be more disposed to acedia than others. Many Scholastic writers considered some instances of acedia to be derived from an imbalance of the humors, thus making it a disease or the outcome of a disease. At times, this involved the notion of a temperamental disposition to the condition. Scattered passages in their writings indicate that it was sometimes associated with ''the cold and moist disposition'' (i.e., the humor, phlegm, and the phlegmatic temperament) and sometimes with ''the melancholy humor'' (i.e., the black bile and the melancholic temperament) (ibid., pp. 59, 191–194). The presence of such a natural cause tended to lessen the sinfulness of the vice in the eyes of these authors; it resulted more from disease than moral failing. This view could lead to some modification of the usual rigorous remedial advice in favor of suggesting relaxation in the sufferer's way of life. Some suggested that the afflicted could be helped by listening to music, although this led to the qualification that such matters should be left to physicians.

The spiritual authors of the twelfth century and the Scholastics of the thirteenth century had tended to emphasize the state of mind in acedia (weariness, disgust, lack of fervor, sorrow), but, influenced by the increased activity of confessors and preachers, the common man's image of acedia came to center around spiritual idleness or neglect in the performance of spiritual duties. During this period the standard English term for the sin became *sloth* (or similar terms from the adjective *slow*), and similar changes occurred in other vernacular languages (ibid., p. 89). With this shift of emphasis to idleness and negligence, *busyness*, in addition to the traditional pair of fortitude and spiritual joy, emerged as a significant antidotal virtue. Also, by the late Middle Ages, this sin sometimes came to include many rather worldly faults of neglect or dereliction. There were indications that it sometimes meant "neglect of the obligations of one's *status* or profession" and it became intimately associated with the notion that the obligation to work was an essential element of man's nature, with the result for many that the sin included the simple failure to work which might lead to poverty (ibid., p. 91). Nevertheless, the predominant popular view of the sin of sloth still remained that of sloth in one's service to God.

In the numerous literary works that portrayed acedia in the late medieval period, the condition took one or another of the various forms already outlined. Chaucer's views in *The Parson's Tale* have often been noted: the condition was presented as stemming from bitterness, being associated with heaviness, moodiness, and anger, and involving neglect of spiritual and worldly duties, idleness, tardiness, sorrow, and despair (Chaucer [Hill, trans.] 1974:523–526). Petrarch's view of acedia, in which the emphasis was on grief, sorrow, and dejection, is also well known. While his account may be said to deal with a somewhat secularized version of the condition, it clearly represents one aspect of acedia's traditional meanings. He placed it in a historical tradition dating back to the *aegritudo* (grief, sorrow) of classical times (Petrarch [Draper, trans.] 1911:84–106; Wenzel 1961).

As we have seen, acedia clearly did not mean merely sloth or merely sorrow and dejection, although some have tried to portray it as such. Both sorrow-dejection-despair and neglect-idleness-indolence were important themes in the earliest accounts of this condition, and each recurred in varying combinations with the other in descriptions of acedia throughout the Middle Ages. The question is how these apparently disparate features might be integrated rather than which description was truly characteristic of acedia. One solution to this problem is to view them as different types of acedia, as David of Augsburg did in the thirteenth century:

> The vice of *accidia* has three kinds. The first is a certain bitterness of the mind which cannot be pleased by anything cheerful or wholesome. It feeds upon disgust and loathes human intercourse. This is what the Apostle calls the sorrow of the world that worketh death. It inclines to despair, diffidence, and suspicions, and sometimes drives its victim to suicide when he is oppressed by unreasonable grief. Such sorrow arises sometimes from previous impatience, sometimes from the fact that one's desire for some object has been delayed or frustrated, and sometimes from the abundance of melancholic humors, in which case it behooves the physician rather than the priest to prescribe a remedy.
>
> The second kind is a certain indolent torpor which loves sleep and all comforts of the body, abhors hardships, flees from whatever is hard, droops in the presence of work, and takes its delight in idleness. This is laziness (*pigritia*) proper.
>
> The third kind is a weariness in such things only as belong to God, while in other occupations its victim is active and in high spirits. The person who suffers from it prays without devotion. He shuns the praise of God whenever he can do so with caution and dares to; he hastens to rush through the prayers he is obliged to say and thinks of other things so that he may not be too much bored by prayer. (Wenzel 1960:160)

Another way of reconciling the two main themes would be to think them both present as potentially observable parts of a whole condition, but with different observers emphasizing one or the other part. Thus sorrow or dejection could be viewed as the state of mind, and slothful behavior as the external manifestation. While traditionally acedia had implied just such a combination of inner state and mode of behavior, through the eleventh century there had been a trend toward more emphasis on the physical phenomena of idleness and drowsiness. During the following century, though, spiritual authors laid more stress on the inner phenomena of spiritual slackness, weariness and boredom with religious exercises, and a dejected state of mind.[4] The Scholastic contributions of the thirteenth century tended to confirm this "interiorization," and acedia came to be viewed as a severe or depressing sorrow. In contrast, the popular views of the late Middle Ages often focused more on external behavior and cited the person's idleness or sloth. It has been suggested that this shift in emphasis toward external behavior was related to the "practical" concerns of both the clergy and their flocks, that is, their preoccupation with sinfulness in general, its assessment in confession, and penance. In short, acedia may well have been a single, although complex, condition that was vulnerable to a distorting emphasis on one or another of its facets, depending on the social context and the purposes of the observer.

At first acedia was one of several unusual mental states and associated behaviors that tended to occur in the lives of the early desert monks. Then, through the earlier medieval centuries, these conditions came to affect those in both the anchoritic and the cenobitic life. So, in these early phases, acedia was the term for a condition experienced by some members of a restricted group, the Christian ascetics. While today we might wonder about the impact of isolation on the anchorites, and about the effects of the loss of customary human relationships and usual social comforts on both anchorites and cenobites, at the time the affected persons were judged as suffering from a troublesome state of the soul as a result of sin or as committing a sin by allowing their souls to be in such a state. In those early centuries there seems to have been little or no tendency to approach the afflicted in any other terms than religious ones. In the later medieval period, the use of the notion of acedia was extended to Christians in general. It seems to have been only then that medical ideas came to be of some significance for this condition.

By the late Middle Ages, it was accepted that a broad range both of members of the clergy and of lay persons might experience dejected states, and be thought of, and dealt with, as suffering from acedia the sin. To say this, however, only begins to address the complexities of the relationship of acedia to states of sorrow and dejection. While dejection was an element of acedia from its beginnings, it was also the central feature of tristitia, another of the chief vices or, later, cardinal sins. Thus, for a religious in the earlier medieval period, a state of sadness might be thought of as a sin in either of two different forms—as tristitia or, if there were significant elements of neglect or physical inaction, as acedia. As already noted, these two notions were gradually merged, first under the rubric of tristitia and then of acedia. This development seems to have further accentuated the place of sorrow-dejection-despair in the complex condition referred to as acedia in the later medieval era.

Further, as tristitia faded from the list of sins, so too did the positive sorrow that arose from remorse for one's sins and that led to penance and salvation. But the negative sorrow, or dejection about worldly matters, continued to be viewed as a sin and to evolve within the notion of acedia. Tristitia, as this positive sorrow, became more identified with the Christian tradition of the sufferer as an object for care, concern, and cure; the negative sorrow was associated with the idea of the afflicted person as an object to be moralized against.

Another important issue to consider is the relationship of acedia to the medical explanation of the illness known as melancholia. Throughout the medieval era the term "melancholia" referred to the traditional Galenic picture of a condition in which the sufferer was fearful, sad, misanthropic, suspicious, tired of life, and often, but not always, afflicted with one of a number of circumscribed delusions. Thus the sorrow-dejection-despair aspect of acedia the sin shared some common ground with melancholia the disease. Cases of acedia, though, did not tend to include delusions, in contrast to what was often the case in conditions diagnosed as melancholia. It was therefore usually fairly clear whether a dejected state might be diagnosed as melancholia or considered to be acedia. Yet there was some tendency for the more seriously dejected, but not deranged, states of that period to be included under melancholia, while at the same time acedia clearly included instances of severe dejection to the point of despair, and even suicide, without reference being made to melancholia. Therefore, some dejected states may have posed a problem in "differential diagnosis" between the two explanatory systems.[5]

At least in later medieval times, some religious authors assessed some conditions as cases of acedia *and* brought them into frank connection with the system of mental disorders in a medical framework, so there was a tendency to consider their treatment as the province of physicians. In such contexts, the associations of acedia with being phlegmatic certainly suggest the condition's traditional state of idleness;[6] its associations with being melancholic similarly suggest its commonly noted inner state of dejection.

Also of interest are the indications that the medical frame of reference implied a lesser degree of sinfulness and reduced responsibility, thus at times allowing the person suffering from acedia to be judged less harshly. During the medieval period a dejected person dealt with in medical terms was likely to have met with concern for his distress and to have been ministered to in a relatively compassionate way, but, if such a person was dealt with in religious terms as being afflicted with acedia, the tendency was toward a harsher approach. One cannot attribute this solely to a religious approach, however, as it was religious authorities who, in the later medieval period, introduced the medical perspective for some instances of acedia and thereby found the afflicted less culpable.

Further, earlier Christian functionaries had sometimes approached the sinner in religious terms with an emphasis on concern for the person's distress and on the introduction of measures to make him feel better. McNeill has brought this out in his studies of the penitential literature, though the extent to which a medical metaphor was used for expressing this attitude and its accompanying "prescriptions" is significant (McNeill 1932; McNeill and Gamer 1938). Thus, while a more benevolent approach was by no means restricted to a particular set of social functionaries, it does seem that it was more readily integrated with a healing outlook. To place all this in perspective one needs to take note of the fact that, over the centuries, there have been many troublesome mental conditions for which the afflicted person might be moralized against with an outcome of judgment and punishment or might meet an empathic concern with an outcome of care or cure. Ultimately, a focus on outward manifestations was more likely to have been associated with moralizing against, while a focus on the unusual mental state of the distressed person was more likely to have been associated with empathic concern. So, rather than one's social role or one's frame of reference determining whether one approached the sufferer with judgmental harshness or healing concern, the aspect of the troubled person's condition to which one was most sensitive may have been more critical.

The fifteenth and sixteenth centuries saw a weakening of the powerful central position held by the Christian church and an associated loss of its integrative influence in the explanation of human behavior. The increased interest in classical authorities, the trends toward more secularized thought, and the splintering effects of emerging Protestantism were all factors in this gradual change. In the process, the cardinal sins became less significant and the notion of acedia gradually lost the important place it had held in the scheme of sins, the neglect-idleness-indolence aspect became more and more the focus, and the trend toward the use of sloth and related terms became more predominant. While the surviving notion of the sin of sloth never totally lost its association with some element of sadness, to a significant degree the sorrow-dejection-despair aspect became associated with other terms.

Gradually, this latter aspect of acedia seems to have become interwoven with trends in both terminology and meaning associated with melancholia. The Latin *melancholia* was often translated as melancholia in English, but increasingly it was also translated as melancholy or other, nearly identical terms in other vernacular languages. The Renaissance rehabilitation of Aristotelian melancholia as a character correlate of genius or giftedness rather than as essentially an illness brought melan-cholia/melancholy forward as popular terms. During the sixteenth cen-tury, melancholia/melancholy continued to refer to the mental disorder in a medical context but the terms were also used to mean the black bile or to denote the person of melancholic temperament, *and*, more loosely, they were often used to refer to almost any state of sorrow, sadness, grief, dejection, despair. To complicate matters further, tristitia in particular, but also other related Latin terms, came to be frequently translated as melancholia/melancholy.[7] Over time the tendency seems to have been for melancholia to come once again to be restricted to denoting the illness, while melancholy remained both a synonym for melancholia and a popular term used with a breadth and diffuseness not unlike our use of the term "depression" today. Many states of dejection which might have been conceived of as acedia during the medieval centuries came to be viewed as melancholy, occasionally in the sense of a medical condition but more frequently in the sense of an unhappy, sad, or grief-stricken condition without significant clinical implications.

A further indication of the continuity between the sorrow-dejection-despair aspect of acedia and the melancholy of the sixteenth century is to be found in the world of pictorial representation. In the shift from the religious to a more secular outlook, the conventional illustrations of the cardinal sins were gradually appropriated to depict the four tempera-ments or characters as derived from humoral theory. As a part of this process, in the sixteenth century images that had traditionally portrayed acedia came to be used to portray melancholy (Klibansky, et al. 1964: 300−304).

In subsequent centuries acedia received much less attention in the Western world as a distinct condition, and sloth became the usual denotation of the sin when it was mentioned.[8] Further, sloth acquired a certain life of its own in postmedieval religious and secular writings. The emerging Protestant concerns about the importance of work meant that idleness became a danger to be guarded against (Weber [Parsons, trans.] 1958:155−163). Also, the uneasy concerns of urban leaders when faced with the problem of growing masses of able-bodied poor led to strenuous efforts to contain such idle persons who were considered to be culpable because of their inactivity (Foucault 1965, chap. 2). Sloth came more and more to mean a reprehensible idleness that was preached against by lay and religious leaders alike, usually with no indication of attention to the presence or absence of dejection in the persons under criticism. The neglect-idleness-indolence aspect of acedia seemed to have acquired a history of its own.

Melancholy reached the height of its popularity around the end of the sixteenth century with manifestations such as its use as a common theme in Elizabethan drama. There was also the detailed attention of Burton and others. Medical as well as nonmedical writers dealt with a variety of melancholic states during the later seventeenth century and eighteenth century. And there was the Romantic melancholy, ennui, and Weltschmerz of the early nineteenth century. But these are not what acedia became—rather they are each a part of a long tradition of attention to sorrow, grief, sadness, and so forth, to which the aspects of dejection in acedia always seemed to have some relation and into which at times they tended to merge. Western man has always been concerned with states of sorrow, dejection, and grief, whether conceived as unhappy states that elicited compassion, sympathy, or consolation; as troubled conditions that stirred impatience and irritation in others; as "fear or depression that is prolonged" (Hippocrates IV, 185) and thus came to be diagnosed as melancholia; as a melancholic cast of mind which became the focus for romanticizing in whatever form; or as reprehensible evidences of sinfulness which were moralized against as acedia or as tristitia.

Further, however, we must recognize that much of this discussion reflects a historical perspective on depressive states and what Western man has done to understand them, explain them, and deal with them. From this point of view, the notion of acedia was merely one of the ways employed to cope with *some* depressive states. But this is only one perspective. As part of the scheme of cardinal sins, acedia also served to cope with certain behaviors that troubled the members of particular social groups when the persons so behaving were derelict in their adherence to group values or in their contribution to group ends. We might also use the history of acedia as an example in the study of the recurrent and complex question of which social institution, which system of belief, and which values should govern the manner of dealing with any particular disturbing mental state or troublesome behavior.

When considering such "across-time" (historical) matters in conjunction with cross-cultural matters, it soon becomes clear that these two perspectives have some important features in common and that each can make useful contributions to the other. In historical studies such as this, as in cross-cultural studies, we are faced with such questions as: How much has the unusual mental state under study, and its associated phenomena, shown a significant continuity from context to context? How much are any apparent differences accounted for by the nature of an era's or an institution's selection for emphasis from a complex of potential observables, or by its choice of favored metaphors and preferred explanatory schemes? How much has an era or a culture so shaped the behaviors and symptoms of its members that it is more a matter of discontinuity than continuity? To state matters more in the language of cross-cultural studies: To what extent has there been a basic condition that has transcended the various moldings and shapings given to it by different cultures and different eras, and to what extent has any particular dejected state been basically a culturally relative phenomenon?

In the case of melancholia the disease, there has been a clear tendency toward a collection of symptoms which has cohered around a basic dejected state. In spite of the variations in explanatory schemes over the centuries, and in spite of some significant variations in the content of the syndrome, the continuity is striking. It seems likely that we have here a condition that has transcended a wide variety of influences from different eras and different cultures, and its various versions appear to be related to modern depressive disorders.

In the case of acedia the sin, a dejected state of mind seems to have been a common feature, and yet not always one that was emphasized. Eventually, though, this condition lost its coherence. With the diminishing emphasis on the sinfulness of this unusual mental state and at least some of its associated behaviors, it lost much of its place as a distinct condition for Western man.

Finally, in considering cross-cultural studies of depressive states, there is a particular theme that this historian of melancholic and depressive conditions finds of special interest. This is the relative emphasis on psychological factors in Western perspectives on depressive disorders versus the relative emphasis on somatic factors in non-Western perspectives (Kleinman 1977:3 – 10, 1980: chap. 4; Marsella 1980). As a psychiatrist who has been struck by this dichotomy in certain subgroupings in our own culture, the study of this issue by cross-cultural authorities has been of special interest. As a historian of medicine, I have wondered whether their work might offer me a crucial explanation for the long-standing scheme of three types of melancholia, one of which (hypochondriacal melancholia) laid special emphasis on somatic factors in its clinical description.

NOTES

1. These various themes are dealt with in detail in the forthcoming book, Stanley W. Jackson, *A History of Melancholia and Depression*, to be published by Yale University Press.

2. The Latin *acedia* was the transliteration of the Greek meaning heedlessness, sluggishness, torpor, literally noncaring state. *Accidia* became the accepted term in the later Middle Ages. *Accedia* and *acidia* also occurred. In English, spelling has ranged from the *accidie* and *accydye* of Chaucer to the later *acedy*, still recognized but obsolete, and the *acedia* of modern historical writings on the subject.

3. Acedia is thought of here as an "unusual mental state," a generic term for a variety of conditions. In medieval times some of the more common unusual mental states were conceived of as syndromes of mental disorder within the medical system. Others were conceived of within the Christian framework as atypical "states of the soul." Of those conceived of in the Church's terms, some—e.g., ecstatic states, mystical states—were often thought to be blessings rather than afflictions and were often honored rather than treated; others—e.g., acedia, tristitia—were considered sinful afflictions and in need of corrective measures.

4. This might be an instance of the larger shifts in attitude outlined in Radding (1978:577−597).

5. A further separate, and yet difficult to distinguish, theme was that of despair (Snyder 1965). Deriving from *tristitia saeculi*, the negative sorrow of Saint Paul which works death, despair was often the translation of *tristitia*, but it was also often the translation of *desperatio*, found at times in accounts of tristitia and at other times in accounts of acedia.

6. In an interesting paper that appeared after this study was essentially completed, it is argued that acedia was strictly a phlegmatic condition (see Brann 1979). I find Brann's argument unconvincing. He seems to be speaking from the context of a sixteenth-century argument that had little application to the medieval period, a controversy from a period when some could argue that acedia was merely melancholia and others could argue that melancholia was too fine a thing to be equated with acedia the sin. To my already stated view that acedia was not merely melancholia, I would only add that acedia was not merely lethargy.

7. Twentieth-century translators have further complicated the modern perspective on relevant late medieval literature by their use of "melancholy" when it was frequently "tristitia" in the original, but rarely, if ever, "melancholia," for example, Caesarius of Heisterbach [Scott and Bland, trans.] (1929); Petrarch [Draper, trans.] (1911).

8. The condition was occasionally taken serious note of in more recent centuries under its original name, as Paget indicated in his interesting essay, "Concerning Accidie," in which he did the same (1902:1−50). Tuke gave it the status of a syndrome in psychological medicine as "acedia" (1892:I, 51). In the twentieth century Connell termed it "accidie" in his Ph.D. dissertation (1932). But "sloth" has been the common term in the goodly number of volumes entitled "The Seven Deadly Sins."

REFERENCES

Bloomfield, M. W.
  1952   The Seven Deadly Sins: An Introduction to the History of a
                Religious Concept with Special Reference to Medieval English
                Literature. East Lansing: Michigan State University Press.

Brann, M. L.
  1979   Is Acedia Melancholy? A Re-examination of this Question in
                the Light of Fra Battista da Crema's *Della Cognitione et Vittoria
                di se Stesso* (1531). Journal of the History of Medicine 34:
                180–199.

Caesarius of Heisterbach
  1929   The Dialogue on Miracles. 2 vols. H. Scott and C. C. Swinton
                Bland, trans. London: George Routledge and Sons.

Cassian, J.
  1955   The Twelve Books . . . on the Institutes of the Coenobia.
                E. C. S. Gibson, trans. and ed. *In* P. Schaff and H. Wace,
                eds., A Select Library of the Nicene and Post-Nicene Fathers of
                the Christian Church. Grand Rapids: William B. Eerdmans.

Chaucer, G.
  1974   The Canterbury Tales. F. E. Hill, trans. Avon, Conn.: Heritage
                Press.

Clebsch, W. A., and C. R. Jaekle
  1975   Pastoral Care in Historical Perspective. New York: Jason
                Aronson.

Connell, M. A.
  n.d.   A Study of Accidie and Some of Its Literary Phases. Ph.D. diss.
                Cornell University, 1932.

D'Isray, S.
  1927   Patristic Medicine. Annals of Medical History 9:364–378.

Foucault, M.
  1965   Madness and Civilization: A History of Insanity in the Age of
                Reason. R. Howard, trans. New York: Pantheon Books.

Hastings, J., ed.
  1908–   Encyclopedia of Religion and Ethics. 13 vols. New York:
  1927   Charles Scribner's Sons.

Hippocrates
  1923–   Works of Hippocrates. 4 vols. W. H. S. Jones and E. T.
  1931   Withington, trans. and ed. Cambridge: Harvard University
                Press.

Jackson, S. W.
  1969   Galen—On Mental Disorders. Journal of the History of Be-
                havioral Science 5:365–384.

1983   Melancholia and Partial Insanity. Journal of the History of Behavioral Science 19:173–184.

n.d.   A History of Melancholia and Depression. New Haven: Yale University Press.

Kleinman, A. M.

1977   Depression, Somatization and the "New Cross-Cultural Psychiatry." Social Science and Medicine 11:3–10.

1980   Patients and Healers in the Context of Culture: An Exploration of the Borderland between Anthropology, Medicine, and Psychiatry. Berkeley, Los Angeles, London: University of California Press.

Klibansky, R., E. Panofsky, and F. Saxl

1964   Saturn and Melancholy: Studies in the History of Natural Philosophy, Religion, and Art. New York: Basic Books.

McNeill, J. T.

1932   Medicine for Sin as Prescribed in the Penitentials. Church History 1:14–26.

1951   A History of the Cure of Souls. New York: Harper and Row.

McNeill, J. T., and H. M. Gamer

1938   Medieval Handbooks of Penance: A Translation of the Principal "Libri Poenitentiales" and Selections from Related Documents. New York: Columbia University Press.

Marsella, A. J.

1980   Depressive Experience and Disorder across Cultures. *In* Handbook of Cross-Cultural Psychology. H. C. Triandio and J. G. Draguns, eds. Boston: Allyn and Bacon.

Paget, F.

1902   The Spirit of Discipline. London: Longmans, Green.

Petrarch

1911   Petrarch's Secret or The Soul's Conflict with Passion. W. H. Draper, trans. London: Chatto and Windus.

Ponticus, E.

1970   The Praktikos and Chapters on Prayer. J. E. Bamberger, trans. Spencer, Mass.: Cistercian Publications.

le Pontique, E.

1971   Traite Pratique ou le Moine. 2 vols. A. Guillaumont and C. Guillaumont, eds. Paris: Les Editions du Cerf.

Radding, C. M.

1978   Evolution of Medieval Mentalities: A Cognitive Structural Approach. American History Review 83:577–597.

Snyder, S.

1965   The Left Hand of God: Despair in Medieval and Renaissance Tradition. Studies of the Renaissance 12:18–59.

Tuke, D. H.
  1892   A Dictionary of Psychological Medicine. 2 vols. Philadelphia:
                P. Blakiston.
Weber, M.
  1958   The Protestant Ethic and the Spirit of Capitalism. T. Parsons,
                trans. New York: Charles Scribner's Sons.
Wenzel, S.
  1960   The Sin of Sloth: Acedia in Medieval Thought and Literature.
                Chapel Hill: University of North Carolina Press.
  1961   Petrarch's Accidia. Studies of the Renaissance 8:36–48.

2

Depression and the Translation of Emotional Worlds

Catherine Lutz

INTRODUCTION

One of the fundamental goals of anthropological studies of depression has been to understand how the emotional lives of culturally diverse peoples resemble or differ from our own. A widespread and passionate thematic premise attached to this goal has been that it is at the level of emotions that the human race is most unalterably uniform. Symbolic systems, institutional arrangements, even the conceptual handling of the natural environment may vary widely, goes this line of thought, but underneath the magnificent array lies a numbered and invariant set of impulses, desires, or ways of feeling. Emotions, in this view, are natural, precultural facts. *What* we feel about may be variable (for some it is Jesus, for others the sight of an outrigger canoe headed for open ocean), but *how* we feel is universal. I will argue, however, that the distinction between the what and the how of depressive experience and the dichotomy of "emotion" and "cognition" make sense only in the context of the Euro-American cultural system within which they developed; they are also less than useful concepts for cross-cultural research if left in their current unexamined state.

I examine here the concept of depression as a specifically Western cultural category. It is argued that this concept is informed by other more general and implicit notions about the nature of the person and emotion held by laypersons, academics, and clinicians, and that it is these Western "ethnopsychological" ideas that have instigated and structured the search for evidence of depression in other cultures. I will be focusing on the emotion of depression rather than the syndrome of depression with its variety of other nonaffectively defined symptoms. As the emotional state of sadness or depression is seen as one of the defining characteristics of the pathological state, if not the most central, analysis of the ethnopsychological ideas embedded in the latter sense of the term will also be important.

The chapter proceeds by first outlining a framework for looking at emotions in relation to cultural knowledge systems. A range of cross-cultural variation in ethnopsychological propositions relevant to psychosocial distress is reviewed and compared with the ethnopsychological ideas implicit in the notion of depression. One particular aspect of Western ethnopsychological thought—the nature and dichotomization of the categories of "emotion" and "cognition"—is explored in some detail, and the contrasting understandings of the Ifaluk people of Micronesia are described. Finally, it is suggested that failure to recognize the cultural assumptions built into the concept of depression results in misleading and often pejorative characterizations of the emotional lives of cultural others.

CULTURAL KNOWLEDGE SYSTEMS AND EMOTIONS: A PRELIMINARY FRAMEWORK

The state and syndrome of depression are defined as fundamentally emotional in nature. Thus, academic theories about the nature of depression are also necessarily theories about the nature of emotion. Let me begin, then, by outlining an approach to the cross-cultural examination of emotions such as depression. The approach is twofold: a critique of the implicit cultural meaning system involved in the concepts of emotion and depression as currently used, and suggestions for an alternative sense of the term "emotion" for use in cross-cultural research.

The American English concepts of emotion and depression can be examined within the framework of what might be called an anthropology of knowledge. The framework attempts to explain variation in the experience of reality by different individuals by reference to the notion that psychosocial reality is "constructed" by our positions within it and our understandings of it. This idea has been advanced most systematically in the idiom of the cultural by Hallowell (1955), the idiom of the social by Berger and Luckmann (1967), and the idiom of the clinical by Freidson (1970) and Kleinman (1980). Analytic and phenomenological priority is given, in these views, to the terms in which people themselves construe their experience. Culturally provided knowledge systems constitute the structures of existence in a fundamental way; they determine how people experience themselves and each other. In this scheme, cultural knowledge is not merely a tool used by the thinking person, it is rather both the form and substance of consciousness. This characteristic of cultural knowledge makes it invisible, in large part, to its bearer.[1] It also causes this knowledge, "although it is relative to a particular socio-historical situation, [to appear] to the individual as the natural way of looking at the world" (Berger and Luckmann 1967:8).

This framework can illuminate the anthropological search for "depression" in other cultures as well as the use of the concept of emotion in interpersonal judgment. From the perspective of the anthropology of knowledge, our own Western, academically acquired knowledge cannot be separated from its cultural base, as we take our "natural way of looking at the world" to the academic enterprise. It is important, therefore, to examine our own unstated assumptions about the nature of emotion and person in order to understand what sort of judgment we make when we use the term "depression" in descriptions of others.

Most social scientific research on emotions has been concerned with discovering and describing the "essence" of emotion, which is assumed to be primarily internal and psychobiological, a species of "feeling." Emotion words like "depression" are treated as linguistic labels for those events. Although the concept of emotion has a wide range of such culturally specific meanings in the West, it is possible to "reconstruct" the concept in a way that makes it more useful for cross-cultural research.

In contrast to this prevailing view (which I will describe in greater detail in a moment), I here treat specific emotions (and the generic "emotion") as culturally constructed judgments,[2] that is, as aspects of cultural meaning systems people use in attempting to understand the situations in which they find themselves. These judgments are made within and across cultural contexts, and, in the former case, they are socially negotiated. Ethnopsychological knowledge, or the meaning system surrounding the concept of person, describes what criteria are important for justifying one's own judgment or deciding on the appropriateness of another's judgment. In talking about ongoing events in their own and other lives, the idiom of emotion words may be used by people to simultaneously make and negotiate judgments about the meaning of those events. The concept of emotion is here placed in a mediating position between events or relationships and individuals; culturally constructed and recognized emotions define events or relationships for people and they define people's roles and behavior within them. Whether that meaning is construed as primarily moral or psychobiological (or both), social or individual (or both), is culturally specific.

Cultural knowledge systems implicit in the notions of depression and other emotions are necessarily evaluative. They are used by people to define and understand events, particularly those seen as amoral, abnormal, and/or unpleasant, and, perhaps, to alleviate the condition. These judgments are conceptualized as simultaneously involving assessments of fact and value, and thus can be termed "emotional" only in a reconstructed sense of the term; to look at ethnotheories of emotional distress in the framework of what has traditionally been meant by "cognition" is to artificially extract the value orientation from those theories. To look at depression in the framework of what is usually meant by "emotion" is to extract the rationality and social judgments involved (see below).

With this brief outline of the framework to be used, it is possible to move on to a closer examination of some of the varieties of ethnopsychological knowledge relevant to an understanding of what we in the West mean by "depression."[3]

ETHNOPSYCHOLOGICAL KNOWLEDGE AND DEPRESSION

Depression, as any emotional judgment, depends on the more fundamental cultural knowledge system commonly termed "ethnopsychology." The study of ethnopsychologies, or the symbolic systems and conceptualizations surrounding the person, has had a long tradition (e.g., Geertz 1976; Hallowell 1955; Leenhardt [1947] 1979; Mauss [1938] 1979; Radin 1927; Read 1955; Rosaldo 1980; Valentine 1963). Those who have focused on ethnopsychology have almost always done so based on the conviction that such an approach allows for "seeing [others'] experiences within the framework of their own idea of what selfhood is" (Geertz 1976:225). Hallowell noted that it also permits us to question the "relation . . . between varying self concepts and differential behavior" (Hallowell 1955:81). The far-reaching implications of ethnopsychological knowledge for all aspects of social life mean that "the entire psychological field in which [others] live and act is . . . unified through their conception of the nature and role of 'persons' in their universe, [and] by the sanctioned moral values which guide the relations of 'persons' '' (Hallowell [1960] 1976:386). Thus, to understand both consciousness *and* behavior, we need to begin by looking at the ways in which people describe others as well as themselves to each other.

Variation exists in the approaches taken to ethnopsychology. Most common has been a focus on the symbols and signs of the self, and the articulation of those symbols with other aspects of culture (e.g., Fajans n.d.; Geertz [1966] 1973; Rosaldo 1980). Others have been concerned more directly with the phenomenological aspects of ethnopsychology and particularly with the encounter or dialogue between two psychologies (Briggs 1970; Crapanzano 1980; Riesman 1977; Singer 1980). The interpretation of ethnopsychologies in terms of Western psychoanalytic and other models has been attempted by yet others (Levy 1973, n.d.). "Cognitive" perspectives on the subject have involved the examination of classification, inference, and propositional representations in ethnopsychologies (Kirk and Burton 1977; White 1979; Lutz 1983).

Although all of these approaches are complementary and contribute to understanding, basic disagreement exists (although often not in articulated form) over two issues: the epistemological status to be granted ethnopsychologies (see Heelas and Lock 1981), and the relationship between ethnopsychologies and experience. In regard to the first of the issues, a distinction is often implicitly being made between ethnopsychology and a scientific psychology, between a "subjective" and an "objective" psychology. This raises the issue of the relation between scientific psychology and current Western academic psychology. Strong evidence has been collected which suggests that American ethnopsychological notions are fundamentally involved in the current concepts, theory, and practice of academic psychology (e.g., D'Andrade 1974; Gergen 1973; Goodnow 1976; Lutz and LeVine 1983) as well as in clinical psychiatrists' views and practices (Gaines 1979; Townsend 1978). I leave aside the issue of whether a scientific psychology is possible, and view all extant psychological theories as cultural products. In one sense, therefore, the "ethno" in ethnopsychology is superfluous.

The second important point of actual or potential disagreement arises over the issue of the relation between any particular psychology and experience. Variation in responses to this question depends partly on whether ethnopsychology is conceptualized as an ideological veneer obscuring a fundamentally real personal experience or as one of the most fundamental symbolic forms through which people perceive and experience themselves. The latter position is taken here. Thus, ethnopsychological knowledge about ''depression'' and emotions like it is conceived as a much more exhaustive set than simply explicit, verbalized, shared cultural belief. Ethnopsychological premises may be available for use at varying levels of awareness. They may be directly communicated to inquiring others as in the form, ''We think that anyone who is 'depressed' should be surrounded with people,'' or they may be evident in myths (e.g., ''Loss is a rejection'') but be unavailable for explicit discussion (Hutchins 1983).[4]

Four aspects of cultural knowledge systems relevant to distress can be distinguished. (1) We can expect to find knowledge in every society that attempts to explain what constitutes behavioral deviance, and the proper responses to it (i.e., therapies). As a corollary to this, normalcy is defined. (2) Stances are taken which define what is knowable, how ''it'' is known, and what is ultimately real. (3) ''Natural'' responses to various kinds of recurrent life events such as frustration, aloneness, human error, helplessness, and loss are enumerated or assumed in all cultures. (4) Ethnotheories speak to the characteristics and forms of consciousness, and their origins and purposes. An appreciation of each of these aspects of ethnopsychological systems is essential to understanding the role of culture in structuring distress such as ''depression.'' In examining each of these factors in turn, I will look particularly at the ideas that are evident in Ifaluk everyday behavior and discourse and at the ideas and emphases that are evident in European and American academic psychological discourse on depression and emotion.

Definitions of Abnormality, Therapy, and Personhood

Translating the concept of depression involves translating ethnotheoretical statements detailing the nature, causes, evaluations, and responsibilities associated with abnormal states. Investigations in the fields of ethnomedicine and ethnopsychiatry have long focused on the diverse ways in which cultural groups have classified abnormality. These studies have pointed out that conceptions of abnormality often provide what might be termed ''negative definitions'' of cultural values, norms, and expectations concerning the behavior and states of persons. To the extent that the deviant is defined as a person, however, cultural conceptions of the nature of the person and of the origins of behavior will fundamentally inform the view taken of those who are classed as abnormal.[5] These two aspects of the relation between culturally defined personhood and abnormal states will be examined in turn as they relate to the problem of "depression."

Ethnotheories of abnormality may or may not make use of the mind-body dichotomy that in Euro-American thought and practice leads to a great concern with differentiating mental illness from physical illness. Thus, discussions about the nature of depression have often been organized around the issue of whether or to what extent the illness may be seen as biologically based *or* mentally (i.e., culturally) based. The concept of psychosomatic illness, whereby mental deviance is transferred to and experienced in the physical domain, represents a relatively recent and poorly integrated attempt to bridge that gap. As White and Marsella (1982) point out, people in most cultures talk about the interactions between the body and consciousness; it is only when a very sharp boundary is set up between the two systems that a concept such as psychosomatic illness—or somatopsychic illness as in the Japanese case (Lock 1982)—becomes necessary. In general, then, the extent to which the person is seen as a body-with-a-mind or a mind-with-a-body, rather than as a unified system with mental and physical elements more freely intermingling, will play a fundamental role in structuring the way in which any illness is described.

It has often been noted that there is a concern with identifying and treating disturbances in interpersonal relationships (including relationships with other-than-human beings) in many societies. Among the Ifaluk of Micronesia, a person who experiences a longer than optimal period of mourning for a dead loved one is not seen to have a primarily intrapsychic problem; rather, the problem is defined as that of an inadequate replacement of the lost relationship with another. This contrasts with the Euro-American concern to conceptualize and treat depression and other mental illnesses on an intrapersonal level; overcoming depression therefore often involves psychotherapy aimed at developing personal coping skills and/or drug therapy aimed at altering the person's biopsychological organization.

Definitions of abnormality are predicated on definitions of normality. The latter are usually unstated, however, as Clement (1982) has noted. Fajans (n.d.) has shown that among the Baining of New Britain states of deviance are explicitly named and described, while conceptualizations of normal human functioning remain implicit but provide the meaningfulness, as contrast, to abnormal states. We may thus understand the normal state to which depression is contrasted by examining the dimensions implicated in the latter. What is most striking about the Western view of depression is its implicit insistence that the normal state is the opposed one of happy or at least positive affect. In their discussions of the nature of depression, many Western psychologists place primary emphasis on the depressed person's self-reproach and loss of interest in "pleasurable activity." What is particularly deviant about the depressive is his failure to engage in the "pursuit of happiness" or in the love of self that is considered to be the normal and basic goal of persons. This seemingly natural goal is in fact a culturally molded goal, one that contrasts with other possible definitions of normalcy in which, for example, primary emphasis might be put on taking care of children and other relatives, or on experiencing morally correct but perhaps unpleasant emotions such as shame or righteous indignation.[6]

Ethnopsychological notions are implied in the kinds of therapies adopted for depressive or related experiences. It has been widely demonstrated that theories of illness causation and therapy are related to each other. Where social conflict is seen as causative, therapies may involve group discussion or group treatment. Where intrapsychic "unconscious conflicts" are seen as the root of the problem, individual therapy is used to reach the source of the conflict. In the description of his interaction with Chinese patients complaining of distress, Kleinman (1980:71−145) evidences his frustration with the nonsharing of therapeutic goals between himself and his clients. In the Chinese view, "feelings" are private and embarrassing events that are best not explored. The goal of therapy, then, cannot be analysis of feelings; they are not implicated as the perceived root of distress, nor do they represent a moral concept. What Kleinman describes as "limited psychological insight" (ibid., p. 161) on the part of his patients represents a limit in terms of the goals of therapy within a psychodynamic framework. Within the Chinese framework, limited *social* insight would appear to be the more serious problem, as this might lead one to cause shame to one's family by allowing a stigmatized nonphysical diagnosis for one's symptoms. The American's "psychological insight" is the Chinese person's "self-absorption." The heavy value loading evident in each of the latter two phrases indicates the extent to which the theories underlying both therapies and definitions of depression are simultaneously descriptive and evaluative.[7]

In addressing how one should respond to the distress of others, ethnotheories may speak not only to the specialist but to the layperson. Individuals in every society have developed expectations about how one should respond to the behavior of others in distress. Interactional "scripts" exist which detail typical scenarios following a particular accepted definition of the situation. In the case of loss, for example, ethnotheory may state: "People want to forget; talk about the weather" or "Encourage people to cry about it, or they will get sick later." The victim may be expected to respond with declarations of pain, to "resist" with numbness, or to nod in agreement with the counselor. These expectations about how people should deal with loss are based on other important premises such as ideas about the nature of interpersonal influence. Can people affect each other and *should* they? The Ifaluk place high value on giving "emotional advice" to one experiencing loss. Fairly stereotyped counsel is given to such a person, including the admonition to "stay around other people" so as not to dwell on the loss. In cultures where it is *not* assumed that people are the ultimate arbiters and owners of their interpreted experience, that is, where a central and positive role is attributed to interpersonal counsel, we may expect to find more of this type of behavior. Whether or not such counseling is restricted to specialists may also depend on existing cultural notions about how change is effected in individuals.

Ethnoepistemology: Words, Knowledge, and Action in the Judgment of Distress

Ethnoepistemological premises, or indigenous ideas about the sources and reality status of knowledge about self and other, play a fundamental role in the experience of distress. Marsella (1978, cited in Marsella 1980:273) first raised the question of the relation between a culture's "epistemic orientation" and depression, suggesting that "the expression and experience of depression may vary as a function of a culture's position on a continuum of subjective versus objective epistemological orientations." His use of this particular continuum as a focus (rather than, for example, an emphasis on human versus superhuman knowledge) follows, however, from a particular epistemic orientation within Western cultures. With this orientation, the objective and the subjective meanings of "depression" are seen as two separate problems. This epistemological stance is also reflected in the meaning of the concepts of thought and emotion, which are associated, respectively, with objective and subjective viewpoints. (This point will be returned to below.) The existence of this particular dualism in Western thought may play an important role in giving depression and other affects the "detached" experiential nature and the "traditional psychiatric representations" that Marsella notes (ibid., p. 274).

Marsella suggests that an objective epistemic orientation, which is seen as the result of a combination of "individuated self-structures, abstract languages, and a lexical mode of experiencing reality" (ibid., p. 273), encourages the "labeling of psychological experience while other epistemological orientations do not" (ibid., p. 276). From an ethnoepistemological perspective, however, the more relevant point may not be the relation between linguistic "labels" and things, psychological or otherwise; the ethnotheory of language from which this empiricist view of language is derived (Good and Good 1982) may or may not be shared widely among cultures. Of first concern is the way the inner and outer are indigenously conceptualized and related to each other, and which (if any) among the many concepts used to talk about distress are considered ultimately real and which epiphenomenal and/or unknowable. Psychodynamic theories posit that the psychic depths hold causal priority, that they can be reached, and that they constitute the "really real." Other ethnotheories vary on this epistemological point; the Ifaluk, for example, are unsure about the accessibility of "the insides" of other people. On the one hand, "We cannot see our insides," they say, and that is reason enough not to worry about that aspect of the unknown. On the other hand, "our insides," in their view, are not private in the way that Taiwanese and Americans see them as private; the privacy of Taiwanese insides is a result of the polluting/shameful qualities they are seen to have (Kleinman 1980), while the privacy of American insides arises in part from the extent to which the contents of consciousness are seen as sacred, individualizing markers of the self.

Given these views, introspection takes a correspondingly different role and meaning in these three societies. As already noted, introspection focusing on "feelings" is antithetical to Chinese ethnopsychologically constructed goals. For Euro-Americans, it is the method par excellence for discovering the really real. This is true not only in psychoanalytic approaches but also in more recent "cognitive" theories of depression. Beck (1967, 1976), who views faulty internal cognitive representations as the ultimate cause of depression, advocates a therapy consistent with this theory. Introspection is seen as the key to uncovering the silent assumptions that direct the individual's pessimistic view of herself or himself and the world, and the therapist's job is to train the patient to retrieve the rapid and often unnoticed chain of ideas and images that occur between an event and an emotion. For the Ifaluk, introspection is not a goal except insofar as moral self-monitoring requires people "to sort the good from the bad" in their thoughts and feelings. People nonetheless speak freely about their mental/emotional perception of events, in part because that perception is seen as morally infused.

The question often passionately asked in cross-cultural studies of emotion and depression—"What are they *really* feeling?"—is based on the assumption that ultimate psychosocial reality is internal; what may be ignored in the process of focusing on that question are indigenous epistemological notions about what *can* be known, what is worth knowing, and where a problem "really" lies.

Ethnoepistemological premises also underlie the approach people in various cultures take to the interpretation of speech, and thus to the relation between language and distress. Ethnotheory is developed to answer some of the following sorts of questions: Where do words come from? Are they to be interpreted as acts expressive of internal events, as vehicles for the exercise of power, as disguises for actual intentions or meanings? Can intentions differ significantly from either acts or words? When distress is identified in others or reported for oneself, how are those words to be taken? There is a continuum of possibilities along at least one dimension which in the West is fairly rigidly dichotomized into the "true" and the "false." For middle-class Americans, a word is "true" if it is accurately matched with its referent thought or personal process. A person "lies" or malingers if the correct referent cannot be identified by an observer. The Anem of New Britain provide a contrast: it is expected that people speak in ways that are predictable from their situations. More important, the negative connotations of the English term "lie" are absent from the Anem term for a false statement.

> The Anem tell what Europeans call lies to selected groups for particular purposes; knowing not only that they are lying, but also that the people to whom they are lying know the fact of their lying and the underlying motives. To a European, a lie is a lie; to the Anem, statements are made in a context. (Thurston 1981:6)

Psychoanalytic theory contains an elaborate framework for interpreting the words of the depressed. In the clinical use of this framework, the goal is to go beyond the word, not primarily to the subject-formulated purposes of their statements, but to an inner world of unarticulated unconscious experience. Crapanzano (1981:126) traces this kind of concern to Freud's (and a general Euro-American) emphasis on the referential, to the neglect of the pragmatic, functions of languages. Abu-Lughod (n.d.) describes how Bedouin women's distress at such things as the loss of their husbands through divorce is articulated in two very different forms: in seemingly disinterested and casual terms in conversation, and in impassioned poetic protest. From a Western epistemological perspective, only one of these forms can ultimately be valid, the other being denial or disguise. Abu-Lughod shows, however, that one form need not be reduced to the other, as the Bedouin recognize the pragmatics and process involved in speaking about one's situation.

Situation Frames in the Ethnotheoretical Understanding of Distress

One of the primary goals of ethnopsychological discourse or reasoning is to understand actions. We can therefore expect to find elaborate models detailing the origins of particular kinds of actions and defining the situations that make such actions intelligible. Ethnotheories will explain what constitutes a remarkable situation such as one of loss or frustration and what actions can be expected to follow from a mature person. Is adoption, for example, defined as a situation of loss for any of those concerned, for only particular persons involved, or for no one? Or is it instead seen as primarily a situation of gain—of a second set of parents by the adoptees, and of a wider network of kin and resource access by the transacting parents? Understanding the ethnotheoretically aided interpretation of such situations is obviously crucial for translating emotional worlds.

I have discussed in more detail elsewhere the ways in which situations may serve as frames for emotional meaning (Lutz 1981). Cultural values and knowledge (which are here being termed ethnotheories) determine which events will be seen as meaningful units, that is, they determine what will count as an event. Emotion concepts appear to universally involve definitions of the situations that frame particular emotions. They also involve ethnotheoretical propositions about the kinds of behavior to be expected from those who find themselves in such situations.

The emotion concept of depression links together situations of various types. Beck (1967) and Seligman (1975) have primarily drawn on the ethnotheory of their American clinical populations in identifying situations of loss from the "personal domain" and of "hopelessness" as linked with the concept of depression. Seligman and his associates (Abramson et al. 1978) delineate two types of situations of helplessness which the clients he has encountered apparently distinguish. These include cases where the inefficaciousness of action obtains only for themselves and cases where the powerlessness is shared by all individuals in the person's environment. Seligman links the concept of depression only to the former situation. Ethnotheory is also the data base when Seligman goes on to describe the reasons given for the lack of relation between outcomes and actions. Thus, people distinguish between causes that are stable or unstable, global or specific, and internal or external. People are more likely to judge themselves or be judged as "depressed" when they theorize that their actions are ineffectual or futile for reasons that are enduring (e.g., "It's in my genes"), global in nature (e.g., "No one ever listens to anything I say") and internal (e.g., "I alienate people by always asking questions").

It may be that ethnotheories universally identify certain types of situations and see them as problematic. Loss and the blocking of personal goals are certainly likely to call for understanding and response everywhere. For cross-cultural investigators to approach the question of suffering or distress via the ethnotheories that make particular kinds of situations culturally meaningful and that link those situations to cultural values and institutions is to begin with a less culturally specific set of meanings and correlations than that contained in the concept of depression. With this goal in mind, I will describe in a moment some Ifaluk ethnotheoretical notions about the nature of situations of loss and frustration.

Ethnopsychology and Consciousness

One of the most important tasks involved in translating concepts such as depression is to identify the underlying model that describes and interrelates concepts of mental and behavioral processes. Variation in consciousness and behavior has been observed by all peoples, and they have developed theories to describe and account for it. A primary distinction in Western ethnopsychology is that made between "thought" and "emotion," or between cognitive and affective processes. The Ilongot of the Philippines, described by Rosaldo (1980), set *liget* 'passion/wild or chaotic energy' against *beya* 'knowledge/creative and focused energy', not as nature against culture but as two forms of motivation necessary for adult human functioning. The Ifaluk of Micronesia speak in terms of the overlapping phenomena of *nunuwan* 'thought/emotion' and *tip-* 'will/emotion', thereby stressing the practical inseparability of thoughts and feelings.

In describing personal processes, people across cultures seem to be more interested in explaining action than in explaining autonomous internal experience. Thus, the processes detailed by ethnotheories in this area are only inadequately described as mental. Marquesans are described by Kirkpatrick (n.d.) as more interested in the links between events, thoughts, abilities, and acts than in "a typology of subjective meaning." Thus, "when cognition and feeling are dissociated from action or from a complex social world, Marquesans see an incomplete process, not pure cognition or feeling. For example, Marquesans view opinions—'thinking' expressed but not acted upon—dubiously, treating them as 'worthless' or suspecting that they do not reflect an agent's convictions'' (ibid.). The Ilongot likewise describe consciousness in relation to action; in their discourse, "the heart does not desire, reflect, or otherwise oppose itself to events that stand outside it. Narrations comment, 'My heart said shoot it, and I shot it'; 'My heart said he is coming, and he came' '' (Rosaldo 1980:38). In contrast, the Balinese see actions and inner events as occupying separate domains that are not causally linked. This fact makes issues such as expression, suppression, privatization, or substitutions from one realm to the next irrelevant. The Balinese wish to be "pure/refined/polished/smooth" in both their inner and outer forms, but with their compartmentalized view of self (the inner being "ungestured feeling," the outer "unfelt gesture") they must attempt to attain that refinement by two separate means; meditation calms the inner, while etiquette "regularizes" the outer. Geertz has obviously reached this understanding of the Balinese only after the shock of encountering, with his own ethnopsychological interpretative framework, behavior such as that of

> a young man whose wife—a woman he had in fact raised from childhood and who had been the center of his life—has suddenly and inexplicably died, greeting everyone with a set smile and formal apologies for his wife's absence and trying, by mystical techniques, to flatten out, as he himself put it, the hills and valleys of his emotion into an even, level plain ("That is what you have to do, 'he said to me,' be smooth inside and out"). (Geertz 1976:227)

With the possibility of such different views of the "inner" in mind, I would like to explore in some detail the role of the concepts of emotion and thought in explaining depression in present-day Euro-American ethnopsychological thought. In particular, it will be suggested that views of depression are fundamentally informed by the nature of, and emphasis on, the distinction between "emotion" and "thought."

WHAT DOES IT MEAN TO SAY THAT DEPRESSION IS AN "AFFECTIVE DISORDER"?

Depression is considered to be an affective disorder and is so classified in the official diagnostic manual of the American Psychiatric Association (1980). This is in contrast to such "thought disorders" as schizophrenia. "Depression" has parallel but extended meaning in lay discourse where the term is used to speak about (a) a temporary emotional state (closely related to such terms as "sad," "blue," and "bummed out"), (b) a mood or long-term emotional state (as in the sense of "I'm really depressed about all the work I have to do this month"), or (c) a serious and treatable mental problem or nervous breakdown that includes the feeling of depression as perhaps its most central and distinguishing symptom. Thus, judgments that someone is depressed in any of these senses are made, by both laypersons and psychiatrists, primarily by use of signs of disturbed affect.

One primary way in which affect is defined is in contrast to thought. The distinction between thought and emotion is as central to Western psychosocial theory as those between mind and body, behavior and intention, the individual and the social, or the conscious and the unconscious. Before going on to discuss some of the features of the dichotomy, it is important to note that emotion shares a fundamental characteristic with thought in this ethnopsychological view—they are each an internal characteristic of persons. The "essence" of both emotion and thought is to be found within the boundaries of the person; they are features of individuals rather than of situations, relationships, or moral positions. Thus, they are construed as psychological phenomena. Although social, historical, and interpersonal processes are seen as *correlated* with these psychic events, thought and emotion are taken to be the property of individuals, that is, they are located in individual minds. In addition, as already noted, both processes are considered to constitute a more authentic reality in comparison to the relative inauthenticity of speaking and other forms of interaction. (See, e.g., the portrayal of persons in the popular theories of Goffman [1959].)

Thought and emotion and their associated concepts form large and important contrast sets. Emotion is to thought as energy is to information; as heart is to head and as physical is to mental; as subjective is to objective; as irrational is to rational; as impulse is to intention; as chaos is to order; as preference is to inference; as knowing something is good is to knowing something is true, that is, as value is to fact, belief, or knowledge; as the unconscious is to the conscious; and as the natural is to the cultural. Although people will of course vary in the extent to which they would emphasize any one of these paired associations, each appears as a cultural theme underlying much academic and everyday discussion of the nature of emotion and, hence, of depression. Several of these themes will be briefly examined, particularly as they relate to understandings of depression.

Emotion as a Physical Event

For many middle-class Americans, emotions are a subset of feelings; emotions may be seen by them as the visible, expressive aspect of feelings and/or as a particularly strong kind of feeling. In both lay and academic approaches, the *essence* of emotion is found in feelings. While lay opinion appears to place some emphasis on defining feelings as opinions, most people stress two other aspects of feelings, including their physical nature and their location at the innermost and individuated, and hence sacred, part of the person. The somewhat contradictory implications of these two views account for some of the ambivalence felt toward the concept of emotion, an ambivalence evident in some of its other connotations that will be explored below.

The physical aspects of emotion are an important concern of both lay and academic theorizing, although the emphasis is particularly strong in twentieth-century academic psychology. Thus, Tomkins, whose theory of emotion has been one of the most influential, gives the following definition: "affects are sets of muscular and glandular responses located in the face and also widely distributed throughout the body, which generate sensory feedback that is either inherently 'acceptable' or 'unacceptable' " (1980:142). Although "cognitive" theories of emotion have been developed more recently (e.g., Beck 1971; Lazarus 1977; Mandler 1975) in an attempt to balance the former view with a concern for the ways in which cognition regulates emotion, "feelings" or perceived physiological state changes remain central to the definition of emotion in these latter theories as well. For example, in his model of affect and affective disorders, Kleinman defines primary affects as "uncognized universal psychobiological experiences" (1980:173) that are transformed into secondary (and culturally specific) affects by cognitive processes of perception, labeling, and evaluation.

Consistent with this aspect of the ethnotheory of emotion in which it is embedded, depression tends to be viewed as a physical problem. The closer association of emotion with physical than with mental processes is amplified in the case of emotional disorder by the tendency, found particularly among clinicians, to view depression within a biomedical framework (Fábrega 1982). "Many psychiatrists think of the behavioral changes of depression (e.g., sadness-despondency, psychomotor retardation, sleep disturbance) . . . as sensorimotor in nature" (ibid., p. 52), that is, as stemming directly from changes within the brain. The causal priority given to biological processes among psychiatrists is reversed by Beck, who has developed the most comprehensive cognitive theory of depression (Beck 1967; Beck and Shaw 1978). The central distinction between emotion as feeling and cognition as a more purely mental process is evident in this theory as well, however, as is the more recent common notion that cognition can control emotion. The feelings of sadness and hopelessness, in his scheme, are caused by faulty thought patterns or cognitions, which he defines as "characteristic ideas, perceptions, evaluative processes, and beliefs," while affect is defined as "subjective feeling" (Kovacs and Beck 1979:424).

This view of emotion as a psychobiological fact has several implications. Emotion tends to be associated with some of the same qualities as does physicality; like the body, emotions are generally seen as either orthogonal or opposed to personal responsibility, rationality, and culture. Each of these will be examined briefly in turn.

Emotion as an Unintended Act

Emotion is seen as something requiring "control" and as resisting our attempts to exercise this control. In ordinary discourse, we advise each other to "get a grip on" ourselves; we speak of being "overcome" by emotion and of those whose emotions "get the best of them." Emotions come in "waves," although we can try to "steel" ourselves as protection against being overwhelmed. These metaphors are consistent with the view of emotions as biological imperatives, and several observers (Averill 1974; Kagan 1978; Sartre 1948; Soloman 1977) have noted that this tends to absolve the individual of responsibility for emotions.[8] Thus, depression, like all emotions, predominantly "happens" to one; this is evident in the description of depression contained in the letters of the seventeenth-century Dutch melancholic, Barlaeus. To his friend he wrote:

> I did not write back in answer to your first letter, but you must not think that
> I omitted to do so from negligence or because I had forgotten you, but
> attribute it to the turbid blood [melancholia] which, if we are to accept what
> the philosophers and doctors tell us, constitutes no part of our ego. After all,
> Hippocrates, as far as I remember, makes a distinction between that which
> is affected and that which affects. (C. Barlaeus, in Block 1976:46)

Behavior that is emotional is thus not fully intentional; the executive or cognitive self may be called upon to rein in emotional responses, but if it is overcome by the material conditions of the self, which include emotion, responsibility is diminished.

Emotion as Subjectivity

Emotions contrast with thoughts as irrationality does with rationality. While thoughts may be seen as irrational and emotions as making sense, Euro-American ethnotheory places much more stock in the ability of thought to reach the valued "objective" viewpoint. Emotions are by definition subjective, and therefore lead to erroneous (i.e., irrational) judgments. D'Andrade (1981:190) has identified the brilliant yet emotionless Mr. Spock of *Star Trek* as representing the contradiction Americans see between intelligence and emotion. Although "reasons for" the occurrence of depressive affect are often posited, there is a strong block against viewing it as reasonable, as problem solving, or as rational. Like all emotions, depressive feelings tend to be seen as disruptions, or barriers to understanding and rationality.

The essential subjectivity of emotions, however, gives them a sacred role in individuating the person. Given the importance, in the American value system, of the individual personality, this aspect of emotions elevates them to a special place. In this view, emotions are Me in a way that thoughts are not. As thoughts are objective, they will be the same in whatever mind in which they appear. Feelings, however, are subjective; they therefore are not completely communicable, and very possibly are uniquely my own. They are also often seen as the source of personal values. In this view, "emotions are the life force of the soul, the source of most of our values" (Solomon 1977:14). Romantic views of the depressive individual which have had some currency in recent periods in the West (Sontag 1977) partake of this more general tendency to see emotions as personal and moral positions.[9]

Emotion as a Precultural Fact

The nature-culture distinction that is of such interest in Western cultures (Wagner 1975) is implicitly aligned with the emotion-thought distinction. The emphasis on emotion as physical feeling means that the transformations wrought by culture on the affective base (as on the physical base) become "secondary" (e.g., Kleinman 1980; Levy n.d.). Where culture is predominantly seen as a conscious, cognitive process, emotion then takes its place as the natural complement to cultural processing—as material that culture may operate upon, but that is not culture. Where an interest in emotional aspects of culture has arisen, an attempt has often been made to introduce the idea of "sentiment," or culturalized emotion, as standing apart from private, natural feeling or emotion (e.g., Fajans n.d.).

The evaluation given to things natural and things cultural are both variable and changing. As Strathern notes,

> at one point culture is a creative, active force which produces form and structure out of a passive, given nature. At another, culture is the end product of a process, tamed and refined, and dependent for energy upon resources outside itself. Culture is both the creative subject and the finished object; nature both resource and limitation, amenable to alteration and operating under laws of its own. (1980:178)

Emotions are seen in fundamentally the same way; thus, emotions are alternately the pliant material upon which acculturative forces have their way, or the energy (quite literally in many theories of emotion, e.g., Zajonc 1980) that animates cultural forms. Although the ambivalent or multivalent stances taken toward emotions arise in part from these shifts in the way that the relation between emotion and thought (as well as nature and culture) is conceptualized and evaluated, emotions are commonly seen as "less good" or lower than thought in more global evaluations. This evaluative bias is evident in such things as common American English metaphors; for example, people are commonly said to "rise above" or "triumph over" their emotions. (See Lakoff and Johnson 1980 for a discussion of the relation between "more" and "up" and "good" in metaphorical constructions.)

Culture and thought can also be viewed, however, as artifice or disguise—as themselves the limitations that in more common parlance are seen as characteristic of nature and emotion. From this latter perspective, thought and its offshoot, social speech, are seen as less authentic and less "really real" than emotion. It is only uncognized, unexpressed emotion that is truly natural, then, as it has not been reached and disturbed by cultural conventions for the conscious experience or display of emotion. The psychologist Tomkins (1979:208), for example, defines as "pseudo-emotion" any emotion that is at all socially constrained or suppressed, that is not "unconditionally free[ly] vocalized."

The importance of these aspects of the concept of emotion for understanding depression is evident in the debates and shared assumptions found in academic discourse on the disorder. In the first instance, the psychological literature tends to be oriented toward explaining depression as a natural fact; biological and/or psychological forces, in this view, create depression. "Cognitive" theories of depression (e.g., Beck 1967; Seligman 1975) share this assumption with other psychological approaches. They do, however, reverse the dominant logic, in which psychodynamic (i.e., natural, emotional) forces produce observed depressive symptoms, and state that cognitive (and by inference cultural) processes are primary in producing the syndrome of depression; that is, depressive affect yields to, or follows from, the creative force of cognition. Thus, for example, in Beck's view, certain types of premises, representations, or silent assumptions held by individuals intervene between an event and depressive affect. Here, in Strathern's terms, cognition is the "creative subject" and affect the "resource." Elsewhere, in the theory of depression advanced by Freud ([1917] 1963), emotion plays the role of the natural counterpart to the civilization of thought; here, emotion is generated within its own domain, and thought (like culture) emerges as "finished object."

Anthropological theories of individuals in cultural context borrow heavily from academic psychological paradigms as well as from the ethnopsychological theory which is also the ultimate source of inspiration for such academic paradigms. Thus, the cross-cultural study of depression has been defined predominantly as a question of the relationship between a natural fact—the affective response—and a cultural fact—the relevant ethnomedical beliefs and social institutions.

LOSS AND DISTRESS AMONG THE IFALUK

Against the background of this survey of issues in ethnopsychological interpretation relevant to normal and abnormal distress, it is possible to turn to a detailed examination of Ifaluk ethnotheory as it is used to understand and respond to loss.

Seen from a steamship offshore, the atoll of Ifaluk seems a tightly bounded and somewhat precarious community, sitting as it does at most fifteen feet above sea level in an area of frequent typhoons and few neighboring islands. Four hundred thirty people share one-half square mile of land and survive through fishing, the gathering of fruits and coconut, and taro cultivation. The cooperative and nonaggressive patterns they have successfully developed, in part in response to these material conditions, have made for dense networks of connections between individuals. One of the important sources of connection is the widespread practice of adoption; with a rate of over 40 percent for children, it is not unthinkable for someone to be able to claim four parents and sixteen immediate grandparents. Thus, losses from the island community, whether permanent through death or temporary through travel, are felt widely through the social system. Such losses are also felt intensely for a variety of reasons. Primary among them is the belief that a fundamental need—perhaps *the* most fundamental need— of persons is to be with other people. To be alone is to be lonely and fearful, and myths play out that prospect and its terrible consequences over and over again. Average household size on the atoll is thirteen, and adoption requests are enthusiastically made with the explicit purpose of bringing in more people, of having a child to share one's mosquito net at night. Only one person out of the island's 430 lives alone, and this is a senile seventy-year-old man, who in fact eats with relatives although he sleeps in a separate hut. The incredulity that greeted my expressed desire to live in a separate hut and my initial amazement at the sight of twenty or more people in one household sleeping each with their three-by-six-foot mats overlapping their neighbor's, are the mirror image of each other, the evidence of an encounter between two images of what it is that people desire. Being alone for a middle-class American connotes a strongly valued independence and privacy as much as it does the negatively felt absence of other people. This ambivalence is minimal among the Ifaluk.

The Ifaluk have a rich body of ethnopsychological knowledge which is used to interpret behavioral variation and changes in consciousness (Lutz n.d.). In these matters their notions are fundamentally *moral*, as they simultaneously name and evaluate actions and feelings. They portray themselves as basically undivided internally, where we speak of warring elements of the self, of rationality battling unruly emotions, of the reining in of our impulses. Thoughts are not separate from emotions; *nunuwan* (thoughts/feelings) are experienced by all and are necessary for properly conceived action. The child has few thoughts/feelings, the mature adult many; thus, maturation consists of the differentiation of consciousness, rather than of the gradual ascendency of one form over another (as thought over emotion in the American case). The child may have a "thought/feeling inside" but be unable to express it; the adult freely speaks about most thoughts/feelings. The mentally ill (*bush*) are also characterized as having problems with the expression of their thoughts/feelings. The moral evaluative connotations of the term *nunuwan* are evident in the use of the phrase "to have many nunuwan" to describe the socially intelligent person who is compassionate, considers the social wake his or her behavior will create, and anticipates the needs of others. The experience of having many thoughts/feelings can also be seen as disturbing, however; the Ifaluk see a large number of thoughts or feelings as m ist likely a confused and/or conflicting set and as thereby detrimental to functioning.

Given this understanding of the nature of mental events and their links to action, it is not surprising to find that people speak on a daily basis about their thoughts and feelings. To verbalize them is not seen as an expression of inferiority or of individuality; to speak of them is most often to present one's moral stance toward a particular event.

The Ifaluk have a relatively large number of words that are used to talk about types of particularly salient events, events we would describe as emotions. Examination of the use of these terms in everyday discourse, of folk definitions, and of a cluster analysis of the results of a sorting task reveals several basic classes of emotion in Ifaluk ethnotheory (Lutz 1982). The individual words and the classes are defined by the situations in which the emotion occurs. Two of the clusters that are relevant to the issues of loss and helplessness are reproduced in figure 2.1.[10]

The first cluster contains four emotions that all occur in the context of separation or the threat of separation, including especially death and travel off the island. These are the emotions of loss and connection with others and they are exclusively felt for or because of *other people*. Although the focus in all four cases is on a loss, the most commonly heard term, *fago* 'compassion/love/sadness', is primarily used to talk about the loss or misfortune of others. Fago is felt in a diverse group of

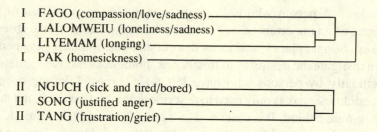

I FAGO (compassion/love/sadness)
I LALOMWEIU (loneliness/sadness)
I LIYEMAM (longing)
I PAK (homesickness)

II NGUCH (sick and tired/bored)
II SONG (justified anger)
II TANG (frustration/grief)

Fig. 2.1. Ifaluk Emotion Word Clusters.

situations; it is felt for those who are in need (of food, relatives, health, or humane treatment) as well as for the dead, the traveler, and the person who behaves in an exemplary way. The actions that follow fago in ethnotheory and in practice are often active, nurturant behaviors. This is not the hypo-emotion of "sadness," or the purely joyful "love" of peers. It is "sad love," "sadness-for-the-other," a sadness that activates. In keeping with this, the word *fago* takes an object more frequently than not. Consider the following dialogue:

Anthropologist: When was the time that your fago last appeared?

Young Woman: Every day I fago my relatives who are away. I fago them, that they might be sick, and because I don't see them. Or I fago you when you give me things, or [that old woman] because she might die.

Anthropologist: How can you tell if someone has fago?

Young Woman: If I take care of you, give you things and talk to you, I'll know you fago me. You talk calmly and politely to me and give me things and I'll know. If someone says "that sweetheart" about one of their relatives who has gone away, I'll know they fago.

Although considered a painful emotion, fago is positively evaluated. To assert one's fago is to implicitly claim to be a good person.

Three other concepts are used to talk about other aspects of loss. *Lalomweiu* 'loneliness/sadness' is felt when a particular person has died or left the island. The feeling is described as excessive thinking/feeling about the missed person, loss of the desire to eat or engage in conversation or other activities, and sleepiness. The emotion is defined in part by the disruption of other social ties; "people who are lalomweiu don't pay attention to others' talking, although they hear it—they stare off blankly.'' A person who is *liyemam* 'longing' focuses not just on the absence of an important other but on the desire and nostalgia the absence evokes. Songs, places, and faces that remind one of the missing person often instigate the desire. And finally *pak* 'homesickness' is experienced specifically by persons who have left their homes. Like the concept homesickness, pak is only used to describe those who have left, not those who remain behind. It is described as having "strong," "confused," or "many" thoughts/feelings about one's relatives and home. Weight loss is said to be a common accompaniment to homesickness.

These various interpretations for situations of loss all point to people as the primary object to which one can be attached and from which one can be separated. Unfocused or objectless loss responses are not spoken of, as far as I know.[11] All four emotions are considered normal states, although lalomweiu (loneliness/sadness) can lead to illness in children through its associated loss of appetite. Of the four, only fago (compassion/love/sadness) and pak (homesickness) are in common use.

Excessive focus on a loss is discouraged by advice to, for example, "cry big" during the twenty-four hours of a funeral, or risk later illness, and to forget about it as soon as possible thereafter by nurturing those who remain among the living. As one woman described her child's death, "They [my relatives] told me to think of my other children and to take care of the baby and I thought, maybe it's true [that I should stop thinking of him]."

Ifalukians distinguish between unavoidable losses, such as those caused by death and necessary travel, and losses that *might not* have occurred. In these latter cases, which might also be characterized as goal frustration, focus is placed on the human agency behind the loss, and another set of emotion concepts is used to talk about them. Relevant here are *nguch* 'sick and tired/bored', *song* 'justified anger', and *tang lanal* 'frustration/grief'. These three concepts are differentiated on two primary criteria, including the degree to which the frustration is socially legitimate or morally reprehensible and the degree to which the people involved in the situation feel able to change the situation for the better.

Nguch (sick and tired/bored) is used to talk about losses (from, in Seligman's terms, the "personal domain") that one must nonetheless accept because an important cultural value demands that one do so. Thus nguch is seen and used as a response to the thwarting of individual desires by social values. If a woman has been grating coconut in the midday heat for three hours, she will often declare herself nguch. If someone makes repeated requests for cigarettes or some other object, that request cannot be legitimately denied, but the severe drain on one's tobacco supply is nonetheless seen as a loss. To call oneself nguch in that situation is to call for some relief from a frustration while at the same time recognizing that the drains on one's time and resources are legitimate.

Song is best translated as "justified anger" because it represents a statement that one has observed a violation of cultural norms and values, and a demand that the transgression stop. Thus, to hear a woman say that she is song because she was not invited to the birthing of a relative is to know that the woman sees her claim as legitimate. It is also to know that the woman expects her erring relative to be "paid back" in some way (as it turned out in the above instance, by not being invited to the subsequent birth of her own child).

There are situations, however, in which can be discerned a combination of the factors that go into judgments of song and nguch. These are instances of injustice or wrong which one feels powerless to affect. Whereas the justifiably angry person expects community opinion and sanctions to follow her and the sick and tired/bored person does not, the person who experiences tang lanal (frustration/grief; literally, cry inside) focuses on wrongs that have been done to him personally and his lack of redress. Although some situations given by Ifalukians as examples of tang lanal are pure losses such as death or absence of a relative, the vast majority refer to being excluded or abused by others. In the following account given by a young man, and in others, the two other emotions most associated with tang lanal (as sequential or simultaneous judgments) are song and fago.

> "Tang lanal [occurs] if you have no money to buy things and no one to help you [or] if your only son died and you live alone with no one to take care of you and bonito come to the lagoon and no one sends you fish—you think of your son and tang lanal. If you live alone and people really treat you bad or ignore you, you fago [feel sorry for] yourself, you tang lanal. If you think of things that should be happening to you, you feel song [justified anger] and you tang lanal."

It is not judgments of self-blame but of self-pity and the accountability of others that constitute tang lanal. The expectation that one's state of emotional and physical well-being is dependent on others and the cultural legitimacy of that expectation mean that loss is interpreted by means of a set of concepts that focus on the morality of the loss (i.e., is it a frustration that is legitimate?) and the responsibility of others for rectifying the situation. In this egalitarian society, it is expected that *no one* will go without what others have, from land to food to children, and it is correct to ask for it rather than wait for it to be given. In the course of growing up, children are taught to express their thoughts/feelings and to ask for what is rightly theirs; for example, children who complain about the theft of something from them are told by their parents to go ask for it back. But losses that are inevitable or justified call either for stoicism or laughter.

These aspects of Ifaluk ethnopsychology have important implications for the ways in which stress, and particularly loss, will be experienced and handled. What comes to the forefront in making a judgment about the meaning of a loss for the self or for others is the morality of or justification for (in terms of cultural values) the frustrating loss. A universal aversion to loss no doubt exists; how that loss is experienced will, on Ifaluk, depend fundamentally on the central judgment of the validity of the loss. Responses to loss have the ring simultaneously of "inner experience" and moral legitimacy; they are statements of moral point of view, a point of view, moreover, that is presumed to be shared by all. Legitimate frustration and loss are to be accepted; illegitimate frustration should be acted on.

Compare this view of emotion and loss with the classic psychoanalytic conceptualization of depression. Two aspects of that theory stand out as implicating fundamental views of the person, which in turn call for particular kinds of therapies and for particular kinds of theories of emotion generally. In describing the self-abasement of the "melancholic" patient of his experience, Freud explained that "the self-reproaches are reproaches against a loved object which have been shifted on to the patient's own ego" (1963:169), that is, anger toward others shifts inward toward the self. In the internal arena, this process is identified as a "splitting" of the person (qua ego): "one part of the ego sets itself over against the other, judges it critically, and, as it were, looks upon it as an object" (ibid., p. 168). This critical faculty, the superego, bears a relation to the rest of the person as does "cognition" to "affect" in more recent psychological theories. What the melancholic does in more extreme form, all people do to some extent in Euro-American ethnopsychological formulations. The person is split between "emotional" responses to loss and "thoughtful," rational, and controlled reactions to it. Our "thoughts" critically judge our "emotions." This alienation of questions of value and feeling from questions of "literal" meaning implies that loss will tend to be experienced in the West as an inner struggle between these two ethnotheoretically postulated aspects of the self.

THE TRANSLATION OF EMOTIONAL WORLDS

How are the emotional works of diverse peoples to be translated faithfully to each other? In the cross-cultural investigation of depression, Euro-American ethnotheories concerning affect in general and the depression syndrome in particular have been taken as the reference point, whether or not the universality of depression is hypothesized. Kleinman (1977) has identified this procedure—of reifying a culturally constructed concept and using it in cross-cultural research procedures—as flawed by the "category fallacy." The use of this procedure has resulted in the "discovery" of depression cross-culturally (albeit sometimes unnamed indigenously and/or with frequent symptomatic variation), or in the declaration that depression does not exist because the conceptual equivalent to depression does not exist.

To phrase this another way, the use of Euro-American ethnotheories to guide research has meant that translation has proceeded predominantly in one direction, with American English being the source language and all others being target languages, that is, the languages into which translation is to be achieved. Werner and Campbell (1970) note that such an approach ignores Sapir's warning that the worlds of different language speakers are not simply the same worlds with different labels attached. They suggest that translation proceed not in this "one-to-many" way, which results in asymmetrical translation, but by providing a set of many equivalent or nearly equivalent statements in each language. This approach is, they note, a "method . . . for providing more context in both languages" (1970:407). Good's (1977) call for an analysis of "semantic networks" makes a similar plea for an increased concern with wider webs of meaning or conceptual relations and less of an exclusive emphasis on the relations between words and things. The latter approach leads to the "treating [of] disease terms as if they were names attached to their denotata like gummed labels" (White 1982:73), and to the search for biopsychological "entities" as a first step in translating emotion worlds.[12]

The set of statements which provides the context for translating emotion worlds includes the kinds of ethnopsychological premises about person, consciousness, and action which have been reviewed here.

Ignoring that context results not only in asymmetrical cultural translation but also in deficit models of psychological and social functioning. A striking example is provided by the work of Leff (1973, 1981), who looks cross-culturally for the "ability" to differentiate the affect of depression from anxiety and from irritability. Leff makes use of several Euro-American ethnopsychological notions including: emotions are in essence biological and intrapsychic phenomena, introspection is a necessary and sufficient condition for the discovery of a discrete emotional state in one's self, and "psychological" or individual-centered definitions of reality are more progressive and more evolutionarily advanced than somatic (and by omission, social) explanations for "mental" events. Based on this cultural knowledge, Leff gave the "Present State Exam" to patients in nine countries and correlated their scores on the three emotion state scales of depression, anxiety, and irritability. High correlation between any of these scales was taken as evidence that the patient was unable to differentiate the emotions so correlated. In general, the greater the geographical or sociohistorical distance from London, the more deficient people are in the ability to tell depression from anxiety. This is *not* taken by Leff as evidence that the emotion concepts as scaled and chosen are only meaningful within the cultural and ethnopsychological context of their origin. Conversely, he does not think to test the ability of Euro-American patients to distinguish, for example, the Ifaluk emotion state of fago (compassion/love/sadness) from that of lalomweiu (loneliness/sadness). Leff takes it as a given that the goal of all peoples should be to distinguish depression as conceptualized by the British psychiatric community. He identifies and positively evaluates the process by which "psychiatrists both overtly and covertly encourage patients to present their distress in psychological rather than somatic terms and thus constitute one of the forces behind the continuing process of emotional differentiation" (1981:69). It may be noted that Western psychiatrists act to amplify the existing lay cultural theory of emotions (including depression) as intrapsychic events.[13]

Leff also hypothesizes that "in traditional societies the group overshadows the individual in importance," and describes the traits of cultures lying at the poles of a "traditional-modern continuum" (ibid., p. 70). Stressed in that scheme is the distinction between the existence of choice and other individualistic values in modern societies and the obligatory and stereotyped nature of behavior in traditional societies. Leff concludes that relationships between individuals in traditional societies are "emotionally stereotyped" (i.e., rigid and proscribed) rather than "emotionally differentiated." Although it is possible to object to this kind of typology on many grounds, here it can only be pointed out that it is unadulterated Western ethnotheory parading as "objective" social science.

It is worth quoting Leff at length here:

> It is our contention that, in societies in which a person's behavior to kin is specified in considerable detail, there is little opportunity to explore the emotional aspects of relationships. Emotions are important in determining the choice of action towards another person. Where there is little or no choice of action in relationships, there is also a restriction on the possibilities of consciously experiencing a variety of emotions. In traditional societies, where relationships are more or less stereotyped, emotions remain unexplored and undifferentiated. As a society moves from the traditional to the modern roles on the features enumerated above, individuals become more important than the roles they perform, freedom of action in relationships increases, and a variety of emotions begins to be explored in the context of relationships with others. The unique qualities of the individual become prized and introspection consequently flourishes. The effect of these profound changes on emotional life is to shift the expression of emotion from the somatic towards the psychological mode, and to increase differentiation between emotions. (Ibid., p. 72)

What is painted by Leff is a picture of "traditional" people who, when suffering, express their pain in somatic terms for lack not just of the linguistic resources to express psychological states but of the mental resources to realize what they must eventually modernize and see, which is the primacy of the reality of their insides over any other reality.

The notion that non-Western peoples have basically undifferentiated emotional lives is a particularly invidious statement given the middle-class Euro-American stance toward the value of a "rich" (i.e., introspective) inner emotional life. The evidence from the many cultures for which detailed ethnopsychological descriptions are emerging suggests that emotions may be conceptualized in ways very different from this internalized view. Emotions may be grouped with moral values rather than (or as much as) with internal disruption, they may be linked with logical thoughts as much as or more than internal conflict, and they may be seen as characteristics of situations or relationships rather than as the property of individuals. Where this is the case, emotional differentiation may increase—not with introspection as Leff claims, but with heightened moral, situational, or social sensitivity.

False exoticism and pernicious "description" (e.g., the statement

"Their lives are undifferentiated masses") result from the asymmetrical translation of the concept of depression. This situation persists in cross-cultural psychiatry in part because our ordinary language understandings are not acknowledged to be cultural constructs, are often not explicitly examined, and therefore remain shallow. Our ethnographic understandings, which are created by use of these constructs, can only suffer as a result. I have tried to demonstrate that it is in fact the extensive Euro-American cultural knowledge system surrounding the concepts of depression and emotion that results in our concern with finding the phenomena elsewhere, favors the use of depth psychological methods, and structures the ways in which we find "them" surprising.

If we are to go beyond (or, more accurately, widen) the cultural foundations of our questions, the cross-cultural investigation of depression might be replaced by the examination of indigenous definitions of situations of loss and the blocking of goals, and the social organization of responses to them. Although the concepts of loss and goal blocking are not "acultural," they each entail a less elaborate and less concrete (and therefore less restricting) cultural meaning system with which to begin cross-cultural explorations than does the concept of depression. Loss may be defined formally simply as A − B or as the subtraction of something of value (B) from the domain (A) to which it once belonged, with what constitutes value, "belonging," or a "domain" being defined in indigenous terms rather than a priori. The domain, for example, may be defined primarily in terms of the individual as a psychological system (as in Euro-American psychology) or it may be defined in terms of the clan; cultural values determine what objects are desired and by whom they ought to be desired, that is, where they "belong."

The concept of emotion, defined here as culturally constructed and socially negotiated judgments about such situations, remains useful, therefore, given the assumption that human groups universally find certain types of events to be especially problematic and that they attempt to make sense of them variously as biological, social, moral, psychological, or otherworldly dilemmas. If these events, or "emotions," are conceptualized not simply as psychobiological facts but as that which is found intensely meaningful in any culture's terms, we will be less likely to do violence to the ways in which the emotional lives of others are experienced. The culturally narrow question of how loss "feels," then, becomes transposed into the question of what loss means for people in the much fuller sense of its moral, political, and social implications.

ACKNOWLEDGMENTS

I would like to thank Byron Good, Robert Hahn, Arthur Kleinman, and Susan Montague for their helpful comments on an earlier draft of this chapter. Some of the research reported here was conducted with the generous help of the people of Ifaluk in 1977 and 1978 and was supported by an NIMH grant.

NOTES

1. I prefer not to draw a sharp line between that knowledge which is "inside" of awareness and that which is "outside"; what I here term ethnotheory is both folk knowledge and ideology in Gaines's sense of the latter terms (1982:168−169). An emphasis on whether or not one is aware of the "contents" of the mind (or of one's behavior) can reinforce a decontextualized view of consciousness. It would seem more useful to examine the emergence and use of particular kinds of ethnotheoretical understandings in particular kinds of interactions with others.

2. Although Solomon (1977) explores the idea of emotions as judgments (primarily to emphasize what he sees as the element of choice they involve), I do not want to implicate his thesis in what I have to say here.

3. In this and further references to Western or Euro-American culture, I am referring to an amalgam of distinct cultural and subcultural traditions whose "unpacking" would allow for more detailed analysis of diversity in ethnopsychological traditions relating to emotions. Although this diversity cannot be explored here in any detail, the important possible sources of variation include (1) what Gaines (1982) has identified as Protestant European and Latin European traditions (with the former being the cultural background for most of American psychiatry); (2) more specific cultural traditions (such as the German and the American explored by Townsend [1978]); (3) the "theoretical" and the "clinical" approaches and beliefs that may be represented in the same practitioner (Kleinman 1980); (4) the variations in beliefs held by lay persons, academic psychologists, and clinical psychologists (e.g., Townsend 1978) which correspond to the diverse adult "socialization" experiences of the three groups; and (5) class, ethnic, and individual differences within particular societies (e.g., Benoist 1965). Thus, the concepts of depression and emotion are embedded in the similar but nonidentical knowledge systems of these various groups in the West, and the degree of similarity between any two or more such systems remains an interesting empirical question. Where I do not specify a more precise locus (e.g., lay, American academic, etc.), I am

hypothesizing a widely shared American ethnotheory, evident in social science theorizing, lay discourse, and clinical practice.

4. See Lutz (n.d.) for further discussion of methodological and epistemological issues in ethnopsychological study.

5. See the excellent recent review of this issue in White and Marsella (1982).

6. Although the conceptualization of manic states indicates that excessive happiness can be abnormal, it is the absence of happiness (i.e., depression) that is more resonant in the West as a violation of more fundamental culturally constituted goals.

7. This is not to say that the Chinese eschew introspection altogether. Declarations about one's bodily state and moral stance, which are common (Kleinman, personal communication), may be conceptualized as requiring another sort of introspection.

8. This frequent critique of conceptualizations of emotion is itself a reflection of the intense Western concern with personal (rather than social) responsibility for action as well as mental disorder (see White and Marsella 1982).

9. Although emotions are seen as subjective, the positivist tradition in social science (which is particularly strong in psychology) has led to the notion that emotions are objectively identifiable. This tradition has also intensified the existing cultural emphasis on the nature of emotions as body states that are amenable to measurement in the laboratory.

10. This figure represents a somewhat distorting extraction from a larger set of terms and clusters, and is presented here for heuristic purposes only. The clustering method used here is the single distance rather than the average distance method described in Lutz (1982).

11. I never observed anyone who appeared to experience or who spoke of experiencing "depression" (i.e., general hopelessness, self-blame, or physical symptoms associated with the syndrome in the West), nor is there a term to describe an abnormal state of that sort.

12. There are other pitfalls in translation beyond those dealt with here. To cite but one, a translator's assumptions about the inherent rationality (or irrationality) of the informant can bias translation in particular directions not demanded by the words themselves (Hahn 1973).

13. See Beeman (chap. 7) for a critique of Leff's assumptions about the nature of language.

REFERENCES

Abrahamson, L. Y., M. E. P. Seligman, and J. Teasdale
    1978   Learned Helplessness in Humans: Critique and Reformulation.
                Journal of Abnormal Psychology 87:49–74.

Abu-Lughod, R. L.
n.d.   Bedouin Poetry, Sentiment and Self-presentation: Discourses
                on Loss among the Awlad 'Ali. Manuscript.
American Psychiatric Association
1980   Diagnostic and Statistical Manual of Mental Disorders. 3d ed.
                Washington, D.C.: American Psychiatric Association.
Averill, J. R.
1974   An Analysis of Psychophysiological Symbolism and Its Influ-
                ence on Theories of Emotion. Journal for the Theory of Social
                Behavior 4:147–190.
Beck, A.
1967   Depression: Clinical, Experimental and Theoretical Aspects.
                New York: Harper and Row.
1971   Cognition, Affect and Psychopathology. Archives of General
                Psychiatry 24:495–500.
1976   Cognitive Theory and the Emotional Disorders. New York:
                International Universities Press.
Beck, A. T., and B. F. Shaw
1978   Cognitive Approaches to Depression. *In* Handbook of Rational
                Emotive Theory and Practice. A. Ellis and R. Grieger, eds.
                New York: Springer.
Benoist, A., M. Roussin, M. Fredette, and S. Rousseau
1965   Depression Among French Canadians in Montreal. Transcul-
                tural Psychiatric Research Review 2:52–54.
Berger, P. L., and T. Luckmann
[1966]   The Social Construction of Reality: A Treatise in the Sociology
1967   of Knowledge. New York: Anchor/Doubleday.
Block, F. F.
1976   Caspar Barlaeus: From the Correspondence of a Melancholic.
                Amsterdam: Van Gorcum, Assen.
Briggs, J.
1970   Never in Anger. Cambridge: Harvard University Press.
Clement, D. C.
1982   Samoan Folk Knowledge of Mental Disorders. *In* Cultural
                Conceptions of Mental Health and Therapy. A. Marsella and G.
                White, eds. Dordrecht: D. Reidel.
Crapanzano, V.
1980   Tuhami: Portrait of a Moroccan. Chicago: University of Chi-
                cago Press.
1981   Text, Transference, and Indexicality. Ethos 9:122–148.
D'Andrade, R. G.
1974   Memory and the Assessment of Behavior. *In* Measurement in
                the Social Sciences. H. Blalock, ed. Chicago: Aldine-Atherton.
1981   The Cultural Part of Cognition. Cognitive Science 5:179–195.

Fábrega, H.
1982   Culture and Psychiatric Illness: Biomedical and Ethnomedical
              Aspects. *In* Cultural Conceptions of Mental Health and Ther-
              apy. A. Marsella and G. White, eds. Dordrecht: D. Reidel.

Fajans, J.
n.d.   The Ups and Downs of Baining Personhood: Ethnopsychology
              Among the Baining. *In* Person, Self, and Experience: Exploring
              Pacific Ethnopsychologies. G. White and J. Kirkpatrick, eds.
              Berkeley, Los Angeles, London: University of California Press.
              Forthcoming.

Freidson, E.
1970   Profession in Medicine: A Study of the Sociology of Applied
              Knowledge. New York: Harper and Row.

Freud, S.
[1917]   General Psychological Theory. New York: Collier Books.
1963

Gaines, A. D.
1979   Definitions and Diagnoses. Culture, Medicine and Psychiatry
              3:381−418.
1982   Cultural Definitions, Behavior and the Person in American
              Psychiatry. *In* Cultural Conceptions of Mental Health and
              Therapy. A. Marsella and G. White, eds. Dordrecht: D. Reidel.

Geertz, C.
[1966]   Person, Time, and Conduct in Bali. *In* The Interpretation of
1973   Cultures. New York: Basic Books.
1976   "From the Native's Point of View": On the Nature of Anthro-
              pological Understanding. *In* Meaning in Anthropology.
              K. Basso and H. Selby, eds. Albuquerque: University of New
              Mexico Press.

Gergen, K.
1973   Social Psychology as History. Journal of Personality and Social
              Psychology 26:309−320.

Goffman, E.
1959   The Presentation of Self in Everyday Life. New York: Anchor/
              Doubleday.

Good, B. J.
1977   The Heart of What's the Matter: The Semantics of Illness in
              Iran. Culture, Medicine, and Psychiatry 1:25−58.

Good, B. J., and M. D. Good
1982   Toward a Meaning-Centered Analysis of Popular Illness
              Categories: 'Fright Illness' and 'Heart Distress' in Iran. *In*

Cultural Conceptions of Mental Health and Therapy. A. Marsella and G. White, eds. Dordrecht: D. Reidel.

Goodnow, J. J.
1976   Some Sources of Cultural Differences in Performance. *In* Aboriginal Cognition. G. Kearney and D. W. McElwain, eds. Psychology Series no. 1, Australian Institute of Aboriginal Studies, Canberra. Atlantic Highland, N.J.: Humanities Press.

Hahn, R.
1973   Understanding Beliefs: An Essay on the Methodology of the Statement and Analysis of Belief Systems. Current Anthropology 14:207−229.

Hallowell, A. I.
1955   Culture and Experience. Philadelphia: University of Pennsylvania Press.

[1960]   Ojibwa Ontology, Behavior, and World View. *In* Contributions
1976   to Anthropology: Selected Papers of A. Irving Hallowell. Chicago: University of Chicago Press.

Heelas, P., and A. Lock
1981   Indigenous Psychologies: The Anthropology of the Self. London: Academic Press.

Hutchins, E.
1983   Myth and Experience in the Trobriand Islands. The Quarterly Newsletter of the Laboratory of Comparative Human Cognition 5(1):18−25.

Kagan, J.
1978   On Emotion and Its Development: A Working Paper. *In* The Development of Affect. M. Lewis and L. Rosenblum, eds. New York: Plenum Press.

Kirk, L., and M. Burton
1977   Meaning and Context: A Study of Contextual Shifts in Meaning of Maasai Personality Descriptors. American Ethnologist 4: 734−761.

Kirkpatrick, J.
n.d.   Some Marquesan Understandings of Action and Identity. *In* Person, Self, and Experience: Exploring Pacific Ethnopsychologies. Berkeley, Los Angeles, London: University of California Press. Forthcoming.

Kleinman, A.
1977   Depression, Somatization, and the New Cross-Cultural Psychiatry. Social Science and Medicine 11:3−10.

1980   Patients and Healers in the Context of Culture: An Exploration of the Borderland between Anthropology, Medicine, and Psychiatry. Berkeley, Los Angeles, London: University of California Press.

Kovacs, M., and A. T. Beck
1979   Cognitive-Affective Processes in Depression. *In* Emotions in Personality and Psychopathology. C. Izard, ed. New York: Plenum Press.

Lakoff, G., and M. Johnson
1980   Metaphors We Live By. Chicago: University of Chicago Press.

Lazarus, R. S.
1977   Cognitive and Coping Processes in Emotion. *In* Stress and Coping. A. Monat and R. Lazarus, eds. New York: Columbia University Press.

Leenhardt, M.
[1947]   Do Kamo: Person and Myth in the Melanesian World. Chicago:
1979   University of Chicago Press.

Leff, J.
1973   Culture and the Differentiation of Emotional States. British Journal of Psychiatry 123:299–306.
1981   Psychiatry Around the Globe: A Transcultural View. New York: Marcel Dekker.

Levy, R. I.
1973   Tahitians: Mind and Experience in the Society Islands. Chicago: University of Chicago Press.
n.d.   Emotion, Knowing and Culture. Manuscript.

Lock, M.
1982   Popular Conceptions of Mental Health in Japan. *In* Cultural Conceptions of Mental Health and Therapy. A. Marsella and G. White, eds. Dordrecht: D. Reidel.

Lutz, C.
1981   Situation-Based Emotion Frames and the Cultural Construction of Emotions. Proceedings of the Third Annual Meeting of the Cognitive Science Society. Pp. 84–89. Berkeley.
1982   The Domain of Emotion Words on Ifaluk. American Ethnologist 9:113–128.
1983   Goals, Events and Understanding in Ifaluk Emotion Theory. Paper presented at the Folk Models Conference, Institute for Advanced Study, Princeton.
n.d.   Ethnopsychology Compared to What? Explaining Behavior and Consciousness among the Ifaluk. *In* Person, Self, and Experience: Exploring Pacific Ethnopsychologies. G. White and J. Kirkpatrick, eds. Berkeley, Los Angeles, London: University of California Press. Forthcoming.

Lutz, C., and R. A. LeVine
  1983   Culture and Intelligence in Infancy: An Ethnopsychological
                View. *In* Origins of Intelligence: Infancy and Early Childhood.
                2d ed. M. Lewis, ed. New York: Plenum Press.
Mandler, G.
  1975   Mind and Emotion. New York: John Wiley.
Marsella, A. J.
  1980   Depressive Experience and Disorder Across Cultures. *In* Hand-
                book of Cross-Cultural Psychology. Vol. 6, Psychopathology.
                H. Triandis and J. Draguns, eds. Boston: Allyn and Bacon.
Mauss, M.
  [1938]   Sociology and Psychology: Essays. London: Routledge and
  1979   Kegan Paul.
Radin, P.
  1927   Primitive Man as Philosopher. New York: D. Appleton.
Read, K. E.
  1954   Morality and the Concept of the Person among the Gahuku-
                Gama. Oceania 25:233–282.
Reisman, P.
  1977   Freedom in Fulani Social Life: An Introspective Ethnography.
                Chicago: University of Chicago Press.
Rosaldo, M. Z.
  1980   Knowledge and Passion: Ilongot Notions of Self and Social
                Life. Cambridge: Cambridge University Press.
Sartre, J.
  1948   The Emotions: Outline of a Theory. New York: Philosophical
                Library.
Seligman, M. E. P.
  1975   Depression and Learned Helplessness. *In* The Psychology of
                Depression: Contemporary Theory and Research. R. J. Fried-
                man and M. M. Katz, eds. New York: John Wiley.
Singer, M.
  1980   Signs of the Self: An Exploration in Semiotic Anthropology.
                American Anthropologist 82:485–507.
Soloman, R. C.
  [1976]   The Passions. New York: Anchor Press/Doubleday.
  1977
Sontag, S.
  1977   Illness as Metaphor. New York: Farrar, Strauss.
Strathern, M.
  1980   No Nature, No Culture: The Hagen Case. *In* Nature, Culture
                and Gender. C. MacCormack and M. Strathern, eds. Cam-
                bridge: Cambridge University Press.

Thurston, W.
1981   Some Initial Thoughts on Anem Reality. Paper presented at the
            annual meeting of the Association for Social Anthropology in
            Oceania, San Diego.
Tomkins, S. S.
1980   Affect as Amplification: Some Modifications in Theory. *In*
            Emotion: Theory, Research, and Experience. R. Plutchik and
            H. Kellerman, eds. New York: Academic Press.
Townsend, J. M.
1978   Cultural Conceptions and Mental Illness: A Comparison of
            Germany and America. Chicago: University of Chicago Press.
Valentine, C.
1963   Men of Anger and Men of Shame: Lakalai Ethnopsychology
            and Its Implications for Sociopsychological Theory. Ethnology
            2:441−477.
Wagner, R.
1975   The Invention of Culture. Englewood Cliffs, N.J.: Prentice-
            Hall.
Werner, O., and D. Campbell
1970   Translating, Working through Interpreters and the Problem of
            Decentering. *In* A Handbook of Method in Cultural Anthro-
            pology. R. Naroll and R. Cohen, eds. New York: Columbia
            University Press.
White, G.
1979   Some Social Uses of Emotion Language: A Melanesian Ex-
            ample. Paper presented at the annual meeting of the American
            Anthropological Association, Cincinnati.
1982   The Ethnographic Study of Cultural Knowledge of Mental
            Disorder. *In* Cultural Conceptions of Mental Health and Ther-
            apy. A. Marsella and G. White, eds. Dordrecht: D. Reidel.
White, G., and A. Marsella
1982   Introduction: Cultural Conceptions in Mental Health Research
            and Practice. *In* Cultural Conceptions of Mental Health and
            Therapy. A. Marsella and G. White, eds. Dordrecht:
            D. Reidel.
Zajonc, R. B.
1980   Feeling and Thinking: Preferences Need No Inferences. Amer-
            ican Psychologist 35:151−175.

3

The Cultural Analysis of Depressive Affect: An Example from New Guinea

Edward L. Schieffelin

INTRODUCTION

Anthropologists and psychiatrists have investigated cross-cultural differences in the symptomatology of mental disorders for a long time. Although such differences have been studied for schizophrenia and other psychoses (Breen 1967; Guthrie 1973; Sanua 1963; Schooler and Caudhill 1964), the most exciting advances in the last five or six years have been in the cross-cultural study of depression. The contrast between the depressive syndrome in Western patients with its emphasis on psychological factors (e.g., the feelings of sadness, hopelessness, worthlessness) and the primarily somatic symptomatology of non-Western patients (vague aches and pains, stomach malaise, insomnia, loss of vitality) has by now become classic. According to Marsella (1979:27), these differences in symptom patterns often appear so striking they could virtually represent different disorders. The matter is further complicated by the fact that many cultures like China (Kleinman 1980) classify symptoms of depression in a different way than we do in the West. Others do not recognize a depressive syndrome as an illness at all and have no conceptually equivalent word for it in their vocabularies (Marsella 1979:243). This does not mean that a Western physician could not find constellations of symptoms in those cultures which would be labeled depression in the West. The point is that these symptoms mean something different when they are embedded in an entirely different cultural context, and are experienced differently than they are in the West.

All this has raised challenging epistemological questions for Western psychiatry. Are we now to regard depression as one disorder with several guises? Or as several different disorders with a single name? Or (to take a radical stance) do we regard it as a culture-bound affective syndrome largely restricted to Western civilization? On what grounds are we to insist on the presence of depression in cultures that do not recognize or have a word for it?

On the basis of several factors, among them the apparent universality of some of the somatic symptoms of depression (principally anergia and insomnia with early morning awakening) in Western and non-Western patients and the fact that these patients may often be successfully treated with antidepressant drugs, the major investigators of this field have opted for the position that depression in whatever form has a common physiological underpinning, and to that extent represents a single disease. Unresolved, however, is whether depression really can be limited simply to its physiological underpinnings or whether its illness manifestation may also represent a fundamental, rather than epiphenomenal, dimension of the disorder. The fact that depression in the West has a much higher rate of suicidal tendencies (Marsella 1979:276) than it does elsewhere indicates that the cultural differences in its illness manifestations are not trivial. Similarly, Kleinman (1982:62ff) found that administering antidepressants to Chinese patients diagnosed as "neurasthenic" removed depressive symptoms but not other (mainly psychosocial) dimensions of their illness. How then are we to understand the significance of illness manifestations of depression cross-culturally, and does this have any significance for therapy? To deal with these questions we need to develop a model that accounts for the cultural construction of illness experience.

TOWARD A CULTURAL ANALYSIS

The cultural construction of depressive illness experience can best be understood if it is encompassed within a broader model of the cultural construction of everyday "feelings." Kleinman offers one such model in his discussion of Chinese depression, which is primarily experienced somatically.

> In [this] model affects are fundamental psychological phenomena engendered in an individual by external (e.g., inter-personal) and internal (e.g., intra-personal or somatic) stimuli. . . . Culture determines the evaluation of stimuli as stressors . . . what is perceived as a stressor in one culture may not be so perceived in another. . . .
>
> The affects engendered by these stimuli, such as anger, anxiety, depression, guilt, etc., are known to the person in whom they are invoked only via cognitive processes: perception, labeling, classifying, explaining, valuating. Thus affects exist as such for the individual only after they are cognized. Prior to cognition, affective states are an essential psychobiological phenomenon with physiological correlates, and as such are universal. Simply stated there is no difference in quality or intensity of the primary (uncognized) affects felt by Americans and similar affects felt by Chinese or individuals from any other culture. . . . There is a cultural difference in quality or intensity of secondary (cognized) affects, however, that is to say, once labeled, "anger," "sadness," or "huo-ch'i ta," affects differ. (1980:147)

For our purposes, the important feature of this model is the role that is assigned to cognition in the shaping of affect. Kleinman, like Soloman (1984), Rosaldo (1984), Levy (1984), and others, suggests, in effect, that affect comes into consciousness when a state of psychobiological arousal is given shape by a cultural judgment (the process of assigning an emotion label) made by the individual who suffers the arousal (or by others who observe his behavior). To suggest that affects are in this way in some sense cultural opens a radical and interesting new direction for investigation: cultural analysis.

Before pursuing cultural analysis, however, we should note that Kleinman himself takes another direction, one more in line with the conception of the relation between culture and affect traditionally held by culturally sensitive psychiatrists (cf. Devereux 1956). The question at issue here is: What does it mean to say that "feelings" or "emotions" are culturally organized or molded? The usually accepted model is grounded in the assumption of an underlying universal psychobiological nature of man. Culture then provides the cognitive and social environment to which the individual must learn to accommodate during his or her period of development. Particular contingencies of this cultural environment may subject the individual to culturally specific stresses during his lifetime, but at the same time it usually provides culturally

appropriate behavioral models and defense mechanisms for coping with
these stresses. The cultural shaping of affect is then largely a matter of
the development of culturally shared psychological mechanisms for
managing the entry of affects (derived from the underlying universal
human substratum) into awareness. Cognition plays the role of a
"secondary" process that acknowledges and labels affective experience, in order to deploy (or deny) it appropriately in accordance with
cultural values, sense of self, and social circumstances. Thus:

> Differences in the quality of secondary (cognized) affects result from their
> cognitive processing, not from their psychobiological substrate. For
> example, the somatic idiom for cognizing and expressing depressed feel-
> ings among the Chinese constitutes that affect as a vegetative experience
> profoundly different from its intensely personal, existential quality among
> middle-class Americans. . . . Chinese reduce the intensity of anxiety,
> depressive feelings, fears and the like by keeping them undifferentiated,
> which helps both to distance them, and to focus concern elsewhere. Other
> related coping strategies are (1) minimization or denial, (2) dissociation,
> and (3) somatization. (Ibid., p. 148)

What is important, for our purposes, is to point out here that although
this approach sees personality structure as developed through cultural
experience (albeit according to Western models of learning and development), as soon as it begins to describe and account for emotional
experience in terms of psychological mechanisms in the personality
structure (denial, displacement, dissociation, etc.) it loses contact with
the very cultural context that gives that emotional experience its significance. As a result, the model loses track of the way in which an
individual's feelings and behavior continue to be a part of the structures
of value, assumption, knowledge, and expression which are intrinsic to
the interactions in which he or she is continually engaged. When the
patient's feelings and reactions become viewed mainly in terms of
variables internal to personality, it becomes all too easy to overlook the
fact that the way he feels and what the situation means to him is largely
specified not by himself but by the cultural system of which he is a part.[1]
   Cultural analysis argues from the opposite direction. The basic conception is that while it is true that feelings are privately experienced, to
the extent that their content and expression are culturally organized, they
must be understood in terms of those culturally shared structures of
interaction extrinsic to the individual from which they derive their
meaning. Thus, to understand the role of culture in shaping affect, we

must look at emotions as a social and behavioral system with a structure in significant part external to the personality, located in the social field.

Cultural analysis takes the view that affects, though privately experienced, are fundamentally social in nature and therefore in significant part organized within the public domain. In taking this direction, it shifts focus from adaptive structures in the personality to patterned meanings of feelings within the cultural system and the relationship of affects and social action within the structure of the expressive order.

It is a matter of common experience that we understand what emotions are or mean for us not by first examining the structure of our own interiority but by attending to human interaction in the intersubjective world of common understandings. Affects are social in that they are experienced and given meaning in the presence of others, respond to cultural rules of expression and legitimacy, communicate cultural implications and messages, and are necessary and appropriate concomitants to any social situation. It is because they are situated in the cultural system that they have the significance they do for the personality. We may draw an analogy between affect and language. A language does not exist without speakers, but neither is it, as language, merely a product of their interiority, or of their biological capacity for speech. People may express themselves as individuals through speech, but they may only do so within a linguistic order and social context that are extrinsically given to them and determine the meaning of what they express. To understand what a speaker means, one must understand the structure of his language and perhaps of his society, not the anatomy of his larynx or the neurological structure of his brain. By the same token, to overstate the matter a bit, to understand what a person feels, and why he feels that way, one must attend to the cultural system in which his or her feelings are situated, and to the expressive system by which they are organized and given meaning.

It is to this aspect of meaning and expression in human feelings that Sapir referred when he remarked that before judging a person's feelings it was necessary to understand his culture's rules of expression (Sapir 1927, cited in Irvine n.d.). Thus, a Highlander from New Guinea who is jumping up and down and yelling with rage may merely be expressing anger in a conventional manner, while an upper-class Englishman engaging in the same behavior would, in the light of British expressive norms, be considered to be regressively acting out. The expressive order, however, is not merely a set of conventions for the appropriate expression of universal human emotions; it is an integral part of the social and personal meanings of those feelings, the way they are experienced, and the values and expectations they embody or entail. It is the means by which individuals create and maintain their social integrity in feeling the way they feel. Durkheim ([1911] 1961) pointed out long ago that what feelings are expressed, and how they are expressed, is closely linked to the social situation. Particular feelings are not only considered conventionally to be ''natural'' to a given set of circumstances (e.g., grief in situations of loss, anger in situations of frustration) but are also socially expected, or even required, as part of appropriate participation in the situation. In other words, particular feelings, or at least their expression, are normatively part of the constitution of, and the participation of, the self in a social situation.

Psychological commentators have criticized Durkheim for trying to factor the individual personality out of human interaction and have remarked that in any case one does not necessarily feel what he is required to express. Nevertheless, the point is that there is a culturally normative dimension to what a person must feel, no less than to how he must behave in social circumstances, which provide an opportunity, a compulsion, and a program for feeling that way (see also B. B. Schieffelin 1979); people normally do feel the way they are supposed to on a given occasion. Indeed, these norms of appropriate feeling represent the standard against which a person who feels something else may be judged deviant by himself and by others. Explanations or justifications may legitimately be required to account for his inappropriate sentiment or attitude.

The point is carried to the next level in the work of Goffman (1967), who sees the individual as continually creating and re-creating himself through others in the management of self-presentation in ongoing interaction. In this view, the boundaries and significance of the self are part of a continuous strategic negotiation with others. Here emotions are not merely normatively appropriate reactions to situations, but strategic postures within them through which an individual defines and legitimizes himself and his role in events vis-à-vis others, and projects his intentions. Who he is allowed to be, however, is therefore not entirely under his control but is critically dependent on his acceptance and validation by others in the interaction. In this context, feelings, both expressed and hidden, are themselves part of the social negotiation of the self.

The cultural analysis that follows will show how the system of cultural meanings, norms of expression, and concepts of the person—in terms of which this negotiation of self and feeling takes place—makes a significant difference for our understanding of the person's psychology and emotional economy and, ultimately, for the understanding of such disorders as depression. I wish to illustrate the procedure of cultural analysis by exploring the cultural structure of anger and grief as they are found among the Kaluli, a tropical forest people of the Southern Highlands Province of Papua New Guinea. Anger and grief do not, of course, exhaust the inventory of emotions among the Kaluli; it also includes, among others, joy, fear, desire, and compassion, which any fully complete cultural account would have to include. It is convenient for our purposes that anger and grief form an important nuclear group whose cultural significance is recognized by the Kaluli and presented prominently in their ceremonial performances (Schieffelin 1976). Anger and grief are also, of course, the primary affects considered in psychoanalytic theory to be involved in the psychodynamics of depression.

I will begin with a broad outline of the social context of Kaluli life and discuss the implications of their egalitarian social structure, dominant mode of interaction, and dual cultural ethos to show how these facilitate a particular emotional style. Kaluli social reciprocity will then be discussed to demonstrate the implications it has for the way Kaluli understand social events and, thus, the way it affects the shaping of emotional attitudes and expectations within the expressive order. I will then show how these factors are brought together in ceremonial performances to express their culturally conventional relationship. Finally, I will discuss the significance of Kaluli emotional expression for their experience of depression—a disorder that seems to be rare and is not culturally recognized. I will conclude with some remarks on the culturally specific treatment of depression both in our own culture and theirs.

ANGER AND GRIEF AS A CULTURAL SYSTEM

The Kaluli people (pop. about 1,200) live in twenty longhouse communities scattered approximately an hour's walk from each other in the tropical forest region north of Mount Bosavi. As with most Papuan societies, the social ties between Kaluli communities are based primarily on marriages between people in different longhouses. These ties are maintained, however, through the offering of support and hospitality, and the exchange of prestations of meat in a system of balanced reciprocity with delayed exchange.

Kaluli society is egalitarian. There are no big men or traditional positions of authority among the various longhouse communities. Each individual is customarily expected to take his own initiative in making his way in Kaluli society and gaining the support of others. A man achieves what influence he has through his ability to give vigorous support to his friends, play conspicuous roles in important events, initiate projects in which he can inspire the cooperation of others, and maneuver situations to his own advantage. This puts a premium on the individual's own initiative and force of character, and Kaluli men tend to adopt a posture of energetic assertiveness in any undertaking in which their interests are at stake.

Culturally, this posture of assertive energy is articulated in an ideology that emphasizes the productive vitality of male essence and supports the favored Kaluli ethos of exuberant vigor and personal dynamism (Schieffelin 1976, chaps. 6 and 7). This ethos infuses much Kaluli male public activity: the giving of an oration, the grabbing of weapons in response to a threat, the splendor of decorated bodies entering a compound on a ceremonial occasion to the accompaniment of drums. It expresses a man's energy, strength, health, pride, and personal force. It is meant to be provocative, intimidating, and beautiful and to arouse fear, excitement, admiration, and desire. Traditionally, a man who failed to show a certain amount of personal assertiveness was considered a weakling and person of no account, or was thought to be ill.

A few words must be said here about the meaning of ethos, a concept not much used in psychiatry. Bateson provided the original formulation for anthropology, characterizing ethos as "the expression of a culturally standardized system of organization of the instincts and emotions of individuals" (1958:118). Or, more briefly, it refers to the dominant emotional emphases of a culture. What does this mean for details of individual behavior and experience? It means, first, that individuals tend to adopt certain affective postures and styles of expression in relation to ordinary events and, second, that those modes of response are culturally normative. The individual is expected to assume certain appropriate emotional attitudes and postures as part of a normal human reaction, and is evaluated as a person according to the manner and degree that he does so. Ethos is thus not only a characterization of a culture's style of expressing emotions but represents a model for emulation as well.

In the Kaluli case, there are two dimensions to their dominant ethos: personal dynamism and assertiveness (especially emphasized in male behavior) and dependency and appeal. Within the assertive modality anger is an important emotion and expressive form. A man's temper, or "tendency to get angry" is an important feature by which Kaluli judge his character and assess the degree to which he is a force to be reckoned with.[2] It represents the rigor with which he will stand up for or pursue his interests vis-à-vis others and the likelihood that he will retaliate for wrong or injury. Anger is an affect that is both feared and admired.

The vigor or personal energy a person is expected to have is broadly exemplified in an emotional style that I have characterized elsewhere as volatile (Schieffelin 1976:119). It might be more accurately described as expressively passionate. When Kaluli feel strongly about something, they are not usually ones to hide their feelings. Rage, grief, dismay, embarrassment, fear, and compassion may be openly and often dramatically expressed. The expression of affect is in part aimed at influencing others, whether by intimidation (e.g., with anger) or by evoking their compassion and support (e.g., with grieving). A man whose expectations have been frustrated or who has suffered wrong or injury at the hands of another does not usually suppress his annoyance or try to "control" his anger. Rather, he is likely to orchestrate it into a splendid, frightening rage, projecting himself with threats and recriminations against his (often equally angry) opponent in a volatile exercise of social brinkmanship that occasionally leads to violence. Similarly, dismay or grief may be openly expressed in loud wails and sobbing speech, evoking others' sympathy and support. In the context of assertive individualism, these displays of affect have to be seen more as declarations of mind, motivation, and/or intention than as mere cathartic expressions of feeling.

This declarative dimension of Kaluli emotional expression is sometimes confusing to Western observers who see it either as an apparent "openness" of affect or as a childish lack of self-control. But it is neither of these. It also comes as some surprise to an outsider who asks an informant how another person feels about some set of events when he receives the common reply, "I don't know. How is one to know how another man feels?" Even if the informant observed the event in question, if the protagonists were less than completely explicit about their thoughts and feelings, he is likely to report that they acted as if they were angry (happy, dismayed, etc.). This does not mean, of course, that unless a person tells others explicitly what he or she feels or thinks, they really have no idea of it.

As Schieffelin and Ochs (1983) have pointed out, Kaluli, like most other people in the world, are able (most of the time) to shrewdly assess how others are likely to feel and respond to particular situations. But the point is they avoid making statements that attribute feelings, motivations, or intentions to others (even if they have a pretty good idea what they are) unless these feelings have been made explicit or publicly expressed in some way.

The reluctance to talk about the feelings and motivations of other people is bound up with a general reluctance to paraphrase or present interpretatively another's claims or statements of purpose when reporting them to others. Kaluli are careful when reporting a conversation or event to make clear whether they observed the situation themselves or only heard about it. They never paraphrase or summarize the substance of a conversation, but quote it verbatim so that they can not be accused of telling lies. To impute to a person any feelings, motivations, intentions or thoughts that he has not made publicly clear himself, is, in effect, putting words into his mouth and misrepresenting him. Insofar as expressed feelings are a public expression of thought and attitude, they can have significant (and troublesome) social implications, and the one who is said to have thought them may potentially be held responsible. Making speculative attributions about other people's feelings, like spreading misinformation, amounts to spreading mischievous and trouble-making gossip (*sadedab*), and may provoke suspicion and hostility.

Like everyone else, of course, Kaluli do not entirely refrain from gossip (indeed, much of the news passed from village to village is in the form of gossip). But it is significant that the feelings about which they most avoid making comments are those that are most likely to arouse socially problematic situations and conflict: desire for the opposite sex, anger, envy, and avarice. Messages about these things, when they are passed, are either based on statements the original speaker can be held accountable for or they are gossip.

While Kaluli ethos casts Kaluli expression of feeling in an explicit and declarative mode, it does not provide the measure and proportion for its expression; that is, though anger represents the extreme expression of the assertive ethos, it does not derive its justification from that ethos. The framework that gives anger its justification and social implications, that provides the sense of proportion that constrains it, and that outlines the order of events that it sets in motion is social reciprocity. I have already spoken of how social ties between different longhouse communities are maintained through exchange of prestations in a system of balanced reciprocity with delayed exchange. In this system, one person makes a gift or prestation to another with the understanding that the recipient will, at a later date, make an *exactly equivalent* return gift known as *wel*. What is important for our purposes is that this pattern of balanced reciprocity is not restricted to exchange of prestations, but also represents a fundamental pattern of behavior and a model for managing situations of many kinds beyond that of exchange in material objects or food. For example, just as in a prestation, where a gift of pork requires that an equivalent gift of pork be made in return (wel), so in the case of the theft of a pig, the enraged owner may appropriately resolve it by a countertheft of one of the thief's pigs (also called wel). (Alternately, he may settle for compensation, *su*, in objects of wealth.) And, if a man lost a relative to death by witchcraft, traditionally he might raid and attempt to kill the witch in return (once again, wel). There are similar reciprocal resolutions in fights, ceremonial performances, curing of illness, and relations with the spirit world (see Schieffelin 1976, chap. 5). What we would call exchange or reciprocity broadly represents for the Kaluli a system of social settlement (wrong and redress), a form of drama, and a general mode of action which returns situations to proper proportion by in some sense evening the score.

The reciprocity transaction provides the Kaluli with a model for dealing with many types of situations. If one can interpret a set of events as involving a loss and an opposition between protagonists, there is a shared understanding about the appropriate course of action to take. Implicit in this is a sense of proportion (reflected in the notion of wel) and a legitimate set of expectations and appropriate attitudes oriented toward the outcome of this well-understood type of resolution.

Returning to Kaluli anger, nearly every reason to be angry—any loss, wrong, injury, insult, or disappointment—is interpreted in terms of the scheme of reciprocity. The height of a man's rage is partly measured by the loss he has suffered, and redress is sought in proportion through the notion of wel (or su, equivalent compensation). There are two important implications of this for us. First, for the Kaluli anger almost always bears the implication that the angry person has suffered a loss of some kind, even if only in the form of a frustrated desire or disappointed hope. Second, because loss in a scheme of reciprocity implies one is entitled to return, the person who is angry is in some sense owed something: he has a legitimate (if often hopeless) expectation that he is due redress. In addition to being intimidating, therefore, an angry man is also a figure of pathos for the Kaluli; a display of anger is frequently meant to be a forceful plea for support. When a man has suffered wrong or loss (and the culprit has made himself scarce), he may stamp furiously up and down the hall of the longhouse, or the yard outside, yelling the particulars of his injury for everyone to hear in order to arouse their sympathetic attention and inspire their backing for redress. Anger thus obtains a particular rhetorical force, a certain kind of measure and legitimacy, and a set of implications from the way it is situated in the scenario of reciprocity.

Although the assertive posture, of which anger is a part, represents the dominant and favored cultural ethos for the Kaluli, it is not the only mode of pursuing one's ends and influencing others. Kaluli also tend to adopt the contrasting posture of appeal, which represents the ethos of intimate sentimentality and nostalgia which obtains between people who are close friends or relatives. If assertion exerts its influence by provoking, intimidating, exciting, and inspiring, and represents the stimulating application of productive energy, appeal exerts its force through the evocation of a sentimental intimacy, pathos, and compassion. An individual adopting this posture projects an attitude of need, vulnerability, and dependency, using a soft, intimate or even a begging, whining tone, inviting others to feel sorry for him or her and do something. In relation to the ethos of vigor and energy, it projects dependency and misfortune.

As anger is the extreme expression of the posture of assertion, grief is the extreme posture of appeal. Grief is given meaning, like anger, within the Kaluli sense of reciprocity. It represents a picture of a person reduced to powerlessness and vulnerability by devastating loss, of a figure of great pathos, of one entitled to redress. Powerful in rage, men are reduced to particular helplessness in grief, weeping in a hysterical and uncontrolled manner (*ganayelab*, see Feld 1982). Women, who are more subdued in anger, are not so devastated expressively by grief. They turn their weeping into a form of wept song (*sayelab*, ibid.).

Loss is the point of contact between anger and grief. It also forms the point at which, through the scenario of reciprocity, grief may be transmuted into anger and effective action. The raid to kill a witch responsible for a death is the satisfying result of the transformation of grief into anger. This movement from grief to anger is also the theme of most Kaluli ceremonial performances (Schieffelin 1976, chap. 11). It is important here to point out that though anger and grief show the greatest possible contrast in the projection of power versus the projection of vulnerability of self in a situation, they are alike in the context of reciprocity in that both are the result of loss and both contain the implication that one is entitled to redress. The angry claim redress through demand for compensation or a move toward vengeance, while the grief stricken wait upon the compassion of others to provide it (or transmute their grief into anger).

ANGER AND GRIEF IN CEREMONIAL PERFORMANCE

The culturally structured relationship between anger, grief, assertion, appeal, and social reciprocity forms a cultural configuration that is given aesthetic expression by Kaluli in their major ceremonies. Because these ceremonies in effect present and sum up the ordered relationship between cultural ethos, emotion, and reciprocity, a brief examination of them will be useful. Kaluli ceremonies are customarily held to celebrate some notable happy event such as a wedding, a formal presentation of pigs, or a bountiful harvest. The ceremonies, *gisaro*, *heyalo*, and *koluba*, differ in costuming, dancing, and the songs employed, but all share a similar dramatic structure and aesthetic intent. The dances take place at night in the central hall of the longhouse and are performed by the guests for the benefit of their hosts. In the performance, a group of elaborately costumed male dancers take turns dancing and singing in the light of torches held by the audience. The songs are newly composed for each performance and refer to places—streams, hills, gardens, and house sites on the audience's clan lands. These references to their lands remind the listeners of loved ones, now dead or far away, who once lived there. As they listen, the audience falls into a mood of profound nostalgia and pathos. The images of lost loved ones and times past which are evoked by the songs become so poignant that many of the listeners are deeply moved and burst into tears. Then, becoming angry at the anguish they have been made to feel, they leap up, grab a torch from a bystander, and stamp it out on the back of the dancer's bare shoulder. Others leap up supportively from the sidelines, brandishing weapons and yelling war cries, and making a terrific clamor. The dancer continues to sing relentlessly amid the pandemonium, without any sign of pain, until his turn comes to an end and he is replaced by another. Dancer follows dancer throughout the night. Each song moves more people to weeping and anger and burning the dancers. The performance finally breaks up at dawn. The dancers then perform an important act: they pay compensation to those in the audience whom they caused to weep, and everyone returns home in a mood of exuberance.[3]

To understand the significance of these ceremonies for our discussion, it is first important to note that the violence of the burning ordeal and its endurance by the dancer are not the important aspects of the ceremony for the Kaluli, though they are the most striking features to the Western eye. From the Kaluli point of view, the important thing is that the songs move the audience to tears. The violence is the release and retaliation for the emotion felt and reflects the excellence of the songs.

Second, the ceremonies do not seem to represent a safety valve for releasing repressed hostility between hosts and guests. Kaluli emphasized that groups feeling such hostility would not dance for, or allow themselves to be moved by, one another. The ceremony takes place in an atmosphere of relative openness and intimacy between friendly groups, an atmosphere in which the audience can allow itself to be vulnerable to the songs. The tension, weeping, anger, and violence are all generated within the "theater" of the performance which evokes deeply moving cultural situations having to do with the loss of loved ones and times past. That this is taken as a provocation by members of the audience who then retaliate reflects the fact that grief and anger are constituted and related to each other within the scenario of reciprocity: the grief and anguish are quite real even though they are generated within a theatrical context. They can only be resolved appropriately by retaliation and payment of compensation. Bad feeling arises only if the compensation is *not* paid. The payment of compensation not only signals good faith and sympathetic feeling between performers and audience, it also completes the experience of the latter and gives meaning and dignity to their feelings. Far from engendering or representing antagonism, it draws them closer together in shared sympathetic feeling.

For our purposes, the ceremonies can be seen to arrange all the elements of the expressive order of anger, grief, and reciprocity in the way that they are ideally ordered in life. The ceremonies further demonstrate that anger and grief (and, I would add, human emotions in general) must be seen not only as parts of the structure of personality but also as integral to the patterns of the culturally constituted expressive order. The relationship of emotions to events that arouse them is not merely a question of a personal psychological response to a stimulus. It is part and parcel of the more complex social construction of the situation in which certain emotional reactions are expected and are part of the meaning of the situation (indeed, they are part of the construction of the situation). The culturally constituted expressive order is thus deeply involved in the organization of psychological attitudes; emotions represent more than reactions to situations, they are interactional postures with rhetorical force which create situations and make claims on them. The ceremonies, with their real grief, real violence, and real compensation are themselves real emotional transactions as well as models of Kaluli emotional economy in regard to grief and loss, anger and retaliation.

IS THERE A KALULI FORM OF DEPRESSION?

What does all this reveal about a Kaluli tendency toward depression? I should remark at the outset that there is no epidemiological data on depression available for the Bosavi area (indeed, there is some question as to how one would look for it). Neither have I worked in a clinical setting serving the mental health needs of Kaluli people (no such facilities exist). Consequently, it is difficult to claim with certainty that cases of depression of the type marked by dysphoric mood do not exist. The organization of the Kaluli experience of grief and anger within the scenario of reciprocity would seem, however, to give powerful cultural protection against depression as it is understood by many Western theories.

It seems highly unlikely that Kaluli would develop depression along the lines of classic psychoanalytic theory (Freud 1956; Abraham 1948), which views depression as aggression-turned-inward over the loss of a love object. Kaluli do not blame themselves over their misfortunes in life; anger and blame over loss or disappointment is always turned outward according to the view of reciprocity as a sense of feeling wronged and owed rather than as a sense of inward blame, guilt, or self-hate. Similarly, for views such as the one that holds that depression results from an unresolved grief experience in childhood (e.g., Bowlby and his associates [1980]), Kaluli cultural modalities for dealing with grief and anger would seem to minimize the possibilities of this and related factors being the basis of Kaluli depression. Grief is publicly expressed (children grieving along with adults) and worked through in weeping and song, not just at funerals but on many occasions after them in ceremonial contexts where it has social support, is allowed retaliation, and receives compensation.

A similar conclusion can be drawn with regard to cognitive theories of depression. The kinds of self-defeating thought processes described by Beck (1972, 1976) and Burns (1980), which continually undermine self-esteem and feelings of self-worth and construct a situation of self-defeat among depressed middle-class Americans, are simply contrary to the predominant Kaluli style of allocating blame to others and feeling owed. Moreover, notions of personal success, competence, and adequacy as measured in a competitive postindustrial social environment are not important concerns for Kaluli self-esteem.

Are we to say, then, that Kaluli do not suffer depression? The Kaluli themselves do not culturally recognize such a disorder or have a word for it in their vocabulary. The question is: Do Kaluli people ever suffer from a constellation of symptoms which Western medicine would call depression and, if so, by what underlying system of causes or predisposing factors is it likely to have come about? Akiskal and McKinney (1973:21) have suggested an approach that views depressive phenomena as neither inherently psychosocial nor biological in origin, but rather as a final common pathway, the culmination of a number of possible causes, describable on several different levels. Although they view depressive symptomatology in the Western cognitive-affective form, their model will serve equally well for non-Western, primarily somatic depressions. For our purposes, the advantage of the model is that it allows for several different kinds of psychosocial conditions to culminate in depression. In terms of the processes underlying depression, Akiskal and McKinney support a "loss of reinforcement" theory of depressive etiology which, based on broad behavioral concepts,

> postulates that depression is the name given to behaviors that result from the loss of major sources of reinforcement, followed by operant conditioning in the form of attention and sympathy. Depression is equated with chronic frustration stemming from environmental stresses that are beyond the coping ability of the individual, who views himself as helpless and finds relief in the rewards of the "sick role." (Ibid.)

In other words, a person is likely to become depressed when placed in a situation in which his or her social moves are repeatedly frustrated and in which unhappiness and mental suffering are grounds for legitimately obtaining sympathy and support by entering the illness role. The rewards of entering this role in this situation are such that the individual develops a kind of "learned helplessness" in which motivational passivity and depression become a kind of self-perpetuating coping strategy.[4]

With regard to the Kaluli, this model suggests the most promising hypothesis for what kind of circumstance might be most likely to generate depression, who is likely to be at greatest risk, and how the disorder might be manifested. I would not expect depression to arise out of a situation in which the individual has sustained a definable concrete loss, since loss is vigorously managed in traditional Kaluli society. Rather, I would expect depression to arise in circumstances where an individual was placed unwillingly into a long-term life situation in which his or her assertive moves were regularly rebuffed or frustrated and in which there were no socially acceptable grounds for expressing anger or feeling owed. This, in the Kaluli case, would make for a somewhat different situation from that of the pure "reinforcement" model since if there are no grounds for feeling angry or owed, there are no grounds (among the Kaluli) for making an appeal for sympathy and support and hence no grounds for receiving reinforcement, at least in psychological ways, for learning helplessness. In such a situation where the modalities of both assertion and appeal were continually frustrated or cut off, a person might feel self-pity or resentment, but in the circumstances these feelings are denied socially supportable legitimacy. It is at this point that the posture of appeal might be taken up in the guise of somatic illness.

A person who is physically ill among the Kaluli, as among many other peoples, is a focus of sympathetic attention and is normally granted temporary release from mundane social responsibilities. Both men and women among the Kaluli can avoid garden labor or other activities by complaining of headaches, stomachaches, sore feet, fever, painful boils, and so on. People who are ill with minor ailments crouch in the sun in the house yard or huddle by a fire in the longhouse, rubbing their aching stomachs or sore limbs with stinging nettles to stimulate them back to health. Often they sit near others, remaining a little to one side, not participating fully in the ongoing social activities but obviously constituting a presence. The sick role, then, especially for mild illness, projects a posture of (passive) appeal on the basis of the suffering of bodily pain.

For the expression of depression among the Kaluli, then, I would expect the experience to take a somatic form analogous to that found in Asia. It would manifest itself as vague symptoms: headaches, stomach malaise, and low energy, plus a tendency to act subdued or abstracted in social interactions. Depressive symptoms would be essentially indistinguishable from the normal aches, pains, and minor illnesses of everyday life, except, perhaps, for their prolonged, chronic character. Here one can find social expression and receive sympathy for one's frustration and self-pity. (Indeed, complaints of headaches, sore feet, stomach distress, etc., are sometimes used by Kaluli to gain sympathetic attention when they are in disgrace for something or as an excuse for getting out of unwanted work obligations.)

The person most likely to inhabit such a situation, and hence be at greatest risk for depression in Kaluli society, is an unhappily married woman. Marital expectations in Kaluli society are different from those in the West, and happiness is not necessarily one of them. In theory, a woman is under the complete domination of her husband, although a clever and forceful woman may often have a great deal to say about household affairs and sometimes even about her husband's exchange plans. Kaluli do feel that husband and wife should feel affection for each other and hope that it develops, but a working relationship, not a romantic one, is the main expectation for the relation between husband and wife in marriage. More important are the social relationships that marriage establishes between the groom and his in-laws, and between the two communities linked by marriage. Marriage is a political and social alliance and its continued existence is often very much in the interest of not only the couple but also their relatives. If for some reason a woman is genuinely unhappy in her marital situation, she has little recourse. Divorce is almost impossible to obtain if her husband and her relatives have an interest in continuing the marriage. In such circumstances, she may be trapped in exactly the sort of situation of powerlessness without legitimate recourse which I have described.

Taking all these things into consideration, including the difficulty of distinguishing depression from normal aches and pains, I knew of only one person in Bosavi who, on just the basis of my impression, I would say might be suffering from major depression. This young woman was a bright, lively person before her marriage. She was married very much against her wishes as number three wife to a prominent man who was well known, even among the Kaluli, as a strong-willed character who occasionally beat his wives. To make things more complicated, the marriage was arranged by her brother as part of a traditional sister-exchange so that he could marry her new husband's sister. This meant that if she left her husband, her brother's marriage would have to break up also. After a little more than a year of marriage she had lost her sparkle. While she continued to perform wifely duties, she had become markedly subdued and seemed inattentive and distracted in social interactions. She complained of a constant headache, which she said she had had for over a year. Both she and others recognized that she was not herself. On two occasions she had consulted a mission doctor about her physical complaints, but he had not been able to determine what was wrong with her.

While the woman's most striking symptoms (dispirited self-presentation, low social energy, chronic headache) are manifestations frequently found in somatic forms of depression, given the limitations of the data the possibility of some other disorder cannot be ruled out. Nevertheless, it is consistent with my overall impression, based on four years of observation of the Kaluli, both the sick and the healthy, including those under considerable social pressure and emotional stress, that major depressive disorder is comparatively rare in Bosavi.[5]

CULTURAL ANALYSIS: IMPLICATIONS FOR TREATMENT

At the beginning of this chapter I suggested that even if we assume a common physiological underpinning for all forms of depression, major differences in the symptom pattern, as seen across cultures, represent important differences in the underlying structure of the disorder. This idea is based not so much on how the *experience* of depression per se differs across cultures as on what that experience implies for prognosis. Thus, when depression appears as a mood disorder (as it primarily does in the West), its prognosis is much more grave (because of the presence of suicidal tendencies) than what it manifests somatically (as in China). This would appear to be the case also among the Kaluli where my genealogies, encompassing information on several thousand people over a number of generations, including their manner of death, record not one single suicide since the end of the last century.

The cultural analysis of affect advocated here provides a way to get at the different underlying structures of culturally different forms of depressive disorder because it provides a way to link the meaning and expression of affect and the structure of social motivation as elements of the same cultural system. At the same time, it suggests that to the degree the structure and experience of depressive disorders differ cross-culturally, such different forms of depression may be amenable to different types of treatment. Moreover, knowledge of the cultural organization of emotions in a people's expressive system can be an important element in the construction of therapeutic strategies for culturally different forms of depression. It is appropriate, therefore, to show how such a therapy might be designed for Kaluli depression of the kind I have described before concluding with a discussion of the implications of cultural analysis for the treatment of depression in the West. Designing a culturally appropriate therapy for the Kaluli cannot avoid being a somewhat speculative exercise; the mode of therapy I am going to suggest has not been tested with an actual trial in the field. Nevertheless, the effort is

worthwhile because it demonstrates how a cultural analysis of the
emotions and the sense of self can be useful in designing a therapy and
how such a project might be undertaken. Finally, in so doing, it provides
a set of testable research hypotheses.

In our analysis of anger and grief in Kaluli culture, we showed that
neither of these emotions was likely to be implicated in the dynamics of
Kaluli depression in the ways commonly laid out in Western psychoanalytic theory. Depression among the Kaluli appears to be related
instead to the continual frustration of the cultural posture of personal
assertion and the social delegitimation of the posture of appeal (at least in
regard to the particular issues involved in the depression). This situation,
as noted above, was most in tune with theories deriving depression from
''loss of major sources of reinforcement'' in life together with personal
stress beyond the coping powers of the individual. What is important,
however, is that the Kaluli emotional system, as embodied in the
expressive order, is centrally pivoted around social reciprocity, which
provides the set of implications and expectations which for the Kaluli
supplies anger and grief with their legitimacy and a large part of their
meaning. It is through the major moves of reciprocity scenarios—loss,
followed by retaliation and/or compensation—that anger and grief are
aroused or evoked and then intelligibly resolved, whether in real life or
symbolically in ceremonial performance. These emotions, in turn,
imply moves of social reciprocity. It is easy for a Westerner to underestimate the psychological significance of reciprocity. For example, in
looking at the ceremonies, we tend to see the major emotional resolution
as being achieved in the catharsis of weeping and violence. But while
retaliation against the dancers does release the listeners' anguish of the
moment and allows them to assume a posture of strength, it does not
ultimately reconcile their feelings or give closure to the events. For
Kaluli, emotional closure and completion come with the receipt of
compensation (see Schieffelin 1976:206).

Social reciprocity clearly is deeply involved not only in articulating
Kaluli emotional experience but in resolving and healing it as well. This
leads me to suggest that any culturally appropriate therapy for depression
among Kaluli must involve a reciprocity scenario as an important therapeutic dimension. In point of fact, the therapeutic significance of reciprocity is already implicit in traditional Kaluli healing practices. Kaluli
treatment of physical illness is traditionally performed by a spirit-
medium. In the curing séance, the illness situation is symbolically
phrased as a reciprocity scenario played out between the living and

invisible spirits and witches in the attempt to return the patient to health (see Schieffelin 1976:107–115). Similarly, in our suggested therapy for depression, the elements of the depressive situation must be encompassed in a reciprocity scenario that allows them to be consciously reframed, acknowledged, transformed, and resolved.

Returning to our example of depression in an unhappily married woman, if I am right about the cultural meaning of the conditions that put such a person at risk, then depression is associated with a chronic (somatic) illness role because the appeal that the depression represents is socially illegitimate and unacceptable. The young woman had suffered no tangible (i.e., no material) loss in being married, and therefore (so long as her husband treated her in a reasonably conventional manner) had no grounds for seeking sympathy or support from her relatives. On the contrary, any resentment and resistance to the marriage would threaten to subvert the interests of her brother. Given the traditional brother-sister loyalties, a socially acceptable marriage, and the practical political interests of marriage alliance, she had no culturally recognizable grounds for appeal—hence her apparent move into the sick role. The desirable outcome from the Kaluli point of view has to include the preservation of the marriage; in fact, it is difficult to see how a therapy could be acceptable to the Kaluli if it did not. This means, essentially, that a way must be found for the young woman to abandon depression by becoming emotionally reconciled to her situation. At the same time, this must be done (in the example cited) without implying blame on her husband or brother (who by Western standards are responsible for her plight) or revealing the underlying socially illegitimate appeal her depression represents. One effective strategy to encompass this situation in a reciprocity scenario might be to induce the young woman to rephrase her marital situation as though it involved a "loss" (e.g., of the kind of life she had as single), enable her to grieve for it, be angry about it, and finally be compensated for it.[6]

The point is to provide a framework in which the young woman may acknowledge emotionally that things cannot be changed and stop trying to wish them otherwise, while at the same time she may receive sympathetic acknowledgment and compensatory support from others in the community. Kaluli traditional ceremonies provide the exemplary therapeutic model for this process, and, in fact, the therapeutic moves might be incorporated most effectively in an actual ceremony. The therapeutic action would involve the woman's husband, and/or her brother and other relatives, composing songs about places that have been meaningful and important to her before she was married, evoking the contexts and memories of the things she has "lost." These would be sung by the dancers as part of the ceremony. For her to be moved by the songs, weep for them, and attack the dancer, would mean that she acknowledges these former contexts of her premarital life as *past and lost*. But by reframing the situation as one of nostalgia for the past rather than conflict with brother and husband in the present, the ceremony socially *legitimizes* the woman's unhappiness and allows it to be played out in grieving and retaliation against the dancer without threatening the network of social arrangements her marriage represents. Finally, with her receipt of compensation she accepts public acknowledgment and redress for her unhappiness. The fact that her brothers and husband are among those who compensate her proclaims their support and formally expresses their concern and affection. The underlying situational conflicts, at least by Western standards, are never explicated. Instead the situation is reframed as something different, and all of its socially awkward dimensions are kept from exposure.[7]

Unfortunately, until recently, performance of traditional ceremonies has been suppressed by evangelical pastors associated with the Asia Pacific Christian Mission and hardly any have been performed between 1970 and 1982. Thus, it is difficult to know, in the absence of actual observations or controlled tests, how effective this therapeutic action would be, or how many ceremonies it might take to get good results. (With the waning of evangelical influence in the past few years, there is some indication that Kaluli ceremonies are on their way back.) Nevertheless, on the basis of our knowledge of Kaluli culture, the suggested therapy would appear to have a reasonable chance of success. It is consistent with (indeed built on) an analysis of how Kaluli emotions are organized as a meaningful cultural system, and how they are involved in the fundamental processes of social reciprocity. It utilizes a traditional ceremonial form as a means of evoking and reframing the meaning of the depressive situation, and resolves it through the special cultural implications of social reciprocity. The *reframing of the situation*, however, is only half of it. The subsequent *repositioning of the woman's attitude* as one of acceptance toward this loss (by publicly acknowledging her feelings and compensating her for them) is of critical importance, for that is what gives the emotional resolution its proper direction and meaning (as well as closure) for Kaluli. Without compensation, the individual is merely left grieving, angry, and helpless, without redress: one has succeeded in outlining the depressive situation without resolving it.

To follow a more Western course, which would attempt to uncover the underlying conflicts in the situation, that is, reveal the marriage as a conflict between the woman, her brother, and her husband, would be counterproductive. This would simply reveal the illegitimacy (from the Kaluli point of view) of her feelings, provoke angry remonstrance from both husband and brother, remove further social support, and invite further repression. This "getting to the real root of the matter" in Western terms entirely misses the point here—which is how to reframe the situation for the young woman so that she might abandon her illegitimate appeal, accept her marriage as a working relationship, and get on with the rest of her life.

CONCLUSION

The aim of this chapter has been to present a cultural perspective on the study of depression through an analysis of emotions as a cultural system. This kind of analysis focuses on the meanings and strategic implications of emotions, both as they are understood in cultural ideology and as they are socially organized within the expressive order. The aim has been to show further how a cultural analysis might be helpful in understanding the particular forms depression takes in non-Western cultures and how it can be useful for designing culturally sensitive therapeutic approaches.

A few concluding comments are in order. First, it should be clear that the agenda for the outcome of a successful treatment of depression may differ in another culture from what we in the West might take it to be. Thus, for Kaluli, who do not recognize depression, treatment would have to include the preservation of certain social relationships rather than focusing exclusively on alleviation of personal distress. Second, it seems evident that treatment of depression in other cultural settings need not conform to a Western style of therapy. It may include artistic or ritual elements that are appropriate to the culture in question but quite foreign to Western ways of doing things. One advantage of cultural analysis is that it can alert us to these cultural resources and suggest how they might be utilized.

A particular pitfall to note for therapies designed along particular cultural lines is their range of applicability. Kaluli depression is very likely to manifest itself in somatic form. But in the event that the therapy we have suggested is successful among the Kaluli, it is problematic whether it would be successful in the treatment of somatic-type depression in other cultures. While some version of this therapy might be useful among other peoples of Papua New Guinea, where reciprocity plays a similar part in the meaning of emotions, it seems unlikely that it would work in China, where, although depression is also of the somatic variety, the cultural organization of affect is apparently very different.

This raises the intriguing question of whether the underlying structure of depression may differ from culture to culture even when the presenting symptoms are similar. The answer to this awaits further research on the structure of affect and the efficacy of alternative therapies in different cultures, but can hardly be found without cultural analysis.

Another interesting question is whether the suggested "Kaluli therapy" might have any application for Western-style mood disorders or depressions whose underlying structure may relate to repression of anger or grief. Clearly, the cathartic aspect of the ceremony would point in this direction, as the work of Scheff (1979) suggests. The use of artistic or dramatistic means for evoking strong emotional responses for the purpose of allowing a patient to work through difficult unresolved experiences from his past is of course not new. But the kind of audience/ actor relationship that allows a Kaluli audience member to attack the dancer, and the significance of reciprocity that enables emotional closure and acceptance to be achieved through payment of compensation, is quite foreign to American culture. Thus, some of the therapeutic aspects that presumably operate most powerfully on Kaluli would be lost on us.

An important final point concerns the usefulness of a cultural perspective in understanding depression or designing therapy in our own Western society. Effective psychotherapists already know that they must understand the values and world view of each of their patients if they are to communicate and carry out their therapeutic interventions effectively. However, what is lost is the sense in which the patient's world view is embedded in, derives from, and indeed is part and version of a larger culturally constructed reality. Instead the patient's world view is usually seen as primarily internal to the patient. This is because, to the degree that therapist and patient are members of the same culture, sharing substantially the same basic values and frames of reference, they already assume Western cultural understandings of affect and behavior as the natural order of things. The patient's world view is seen as deviating from this order and hence is viewed as internal to the patient. It is only when therapists are faced with patients of different ethnic or cultural background that it becomes clear that the patient is operating out of a larger systematic context of values and assumptions that give significance to what he or she feels and means. It then becomes clear that knowledge of cultural background is important, but in the circumstances, it often can leave us with the curious (and erroneous) impression that "others" have culture whereas we do not.

In a discussion of an exotic culture from Papua New Guinea, it is easy to overlook the fact that culturally designed therapies aimed at culturally constructed forms of depressive experience are also what we have in the West. It is a truism to say that any therapeutic action reflects a given culture's values and theories of illness as they are articulated in its healing procedures. In this sense, no therapy or system of medicine is culture-free. What is important for our purposes, however, is whether we can gain insights into the efficacy or limitations of a given mode of therapy (or type of disorder) by examining its cultural dimensions. For this reason I wish, in closing, to look briefly at one particular brand of Western therapy from a cultural point of view, namely, the "cognitive" form of therapy developed by Aaron Beck and his associates (Beck 1972, 1976; Burns 1980).

Cognitive therapy is a particularly interesting example because it is designed specifically to treat depression and because it is restricted (though unwittingly) to dealing with the specifically Western form of that disorder. Middle-class Americans experience depression primarily as a mood disorder with its emphasis on psychological symptoms: sadness, feelings of worthlessness, hopelessness, and low self-esteem, and negative internal thought processing about the self. It is these negative internal thoughts and feelings that are the most painful and discouraging aspects of the disorder for patients, leading them all too frequently to attempt suicide.

At the risk of oversimplification, we can characterize cognitive therapy as an aggressive and systematic application of the rational attitude well-meaning people sometimes voice to the depressed: "Oh come now, things aren't *that* bad!" Cognitive therapy is based on the theory that depressive mood is the result of distorted thinking or wrong-headedness. It therefore focuses directly on depressive thought content rather than on emotional factors, or the vicissitudes of the patient's childhood years. The therapist encourages the patient to adopt an attitude of rational self-observation in order to expose the negative distortions, logical fallacies, unjustified assumptions, and leaps-to-conclusions hidden in depressive thinking ("I can't do anything right," "Nobody likes me," "I'm a failure"). In so doing, he or she attempts to invalidate and delegitimate the seemingly implacable "truthfulness" of depressive thoughts so that patients can recognize their falseness, cease taking them so seriously, and loosen themselves from their spell. The therapist trains the patient how to recognize and counter illegitimate negative thoughts with more realistic positive thinking. Trained to counter depressive thinking, the patient, it is claimed, ceases to be depressed. Although this therapy is unorthodox and still controversial, it has been tested against other modes of treatment and proven on balance to be effective (Blackburn et al. 1981; Rush et al. 1977; Shaw 1977).

What is interesting for our purposes is not only the explicit tailoring of a theory to a particular constellation of depressive symptoms characteristic of the West but also the way Western resources, embodied in the values of rationality and "science," are used to construct an effective therapy. Cognitive therapy does not merely claim a rational scientific basis to legitimate its own approach, it attempts to train the patient to apply the same "scientific" canons of logic and empirical observation to his own thinking and behavior. It thereby gets the patient to enlist the prestigious and legitimating image of Science to undermine the meaning of his symptoms on his own behalf and to substitute more appropriate (healthy) thinking in their place.

The same questions arise with regard to cognitive therapy as arose in our therapy for depression in a culture of Papua New Guinea. What is its range of efficacy? Focused strongly on the cognitive symptoms of depression characteristic of Western emphasis and experience, how effective can this therapeutic approach be against the primarily somatic forms of depression in which mood and internal cognitive processing play a much lesser part?

We would suspect that cognitive therapy would be most helpful to people from highly verbal backgrounds, with strong tendencies to introspection and a psychologically oriented outlook on life. This would suggest that the patients for whom it would be most useful would be those in the educated middle class, or in ethnic groups such as WASPs or Jews (I do not, at present, know of any studies that evaluate the effectiveness of cognitive therapy for different social classes or ethnic groups). The point is that those people for whom self-evaluating internal processing and psychologized interpretations of others are not the normal way of relating to life may be less accessible both to mood-oriented depression and to cognitive therapy.

The cultural analysis of depression and of emotions in general emphasizes the way in which emotions and feelings are ordered and given meaning in social interaction through the expressive system. I have argued that this extrinsic order is as important to understanding emotions as are internal personality variables and structures. Thus it is fundamentally implicated in the way people experience emotions, and in the symptomatology and structure of the types of depression they experience. I have argued (as have others) that particular syndromes and structures of depression are related to the particular cultural structure of the emotional system of the people in whom they appear and, consequently, that different forms of therapy may be more (culturally) appropriate in dealing with depression in different cultural contexts. The fact that a form of therapy is not universally effective (e.g., outside the given culture area, or for other forms of depression) is not a cause to reject it if it is significantly effective in the milieu for which it was designed (indeed, a culturally specific therapy may work better in some situations than standard therapies). Understanding depression as part of a cultural system of emotions or feelings can help design specific therapeutic approaches appropriate to people of particular cultural outlooks, and can suggest explanations for why some therapies work best with some people and not with others.

ACKNOWLEDGMENTS

I would like to thank Bambi Schieffelin, Judith Irvine, Byron Good, Arthur Kleinman, Steven Feld, Gillian Sankoff, Larry Merkle, and Arjun Appadurai for their many helpful comments and suggestions on earlier drafts of this chapter. They must, of course, share responsibility for those changes that they have persuaded me to make.

Funding for the field research on which this paper is based came from National Institute of Mental Health Project Grant R01 MH 26727 and National Science Foundation Supplementary Grant No. BNS76-04777. The assistance of the Research Institute for the Study of Man and the Institute for the Study of Human Issues is gratefully acknowledged here.

NOTES

1. There is also another issue that, while important, we cannot pursue in detail here, namely, the problem of the reification of essentially Western ethnopsychological categories that are then taken as the conceptual foundation of scientific inquiry. This is particularly a problem when it comes to assumptions about the nature of the underlying psychobiological substrate in the kind

of model Kleinman proposes. This model pictures the human psyche on two levels: the underlying universal psychobiological substrate and the culturally molded level of individual personality structure. The way that Kleinman uses this model, the psychobiological substrate is conceived as containing (or generating) specific (humanly universal) emotions (anger, depressive feelings, anxiety, etc.), which are then shaped, repressed, or defended against in culturally appropriate ways through psychological mechanisms developed in response to cultural practices. However, the model is open to the question of how one is to determine which are the basic underlying human emotions from which "culturally molded" forms of emotional experience are seen to be derived. There is, in fact, little consensus in the academic literature about how many "basic" emotions there are and which ones should be included in the list (Ekman 1974; Scheff 1979; Darwin 1872; Osgood et al. 1975; Leff 1973). Moreover, we are hampered by our tendency to take as universal the emotions recognized in the West, so that there is a real danger of academic ethnocentrism. Lutz (n.d.) has made the point forcefully: given a limited cultural base,

> it would be surprising if the emotions, exactly as distinguished, conceptualized, and experienced in American society, emerged as universals. Exactly this has been assumed, however, and then "proven" by Western researchers (Ekman 1974, Sorenson 1976). While it has been considered of great importance to ascertain whether some non-Western people "feel guilt," the question does not arise as to whether Americans experience the New Guinea Hagener's emotion of *popokl* "outrage over the failure of others to recognize one's claims" (Strathern 1968) or whether they are deficient in the ability to experience the Ifaluk emotion of *fago* "compassion/love/sadness."

There are many other examples of emotions considered basic or extremely important in other cultures but not recognized in the West. Whether Balinese feelings of *lek* or Japanese feelings of *amae* are to be interpreted as derived from more basic universal psychobiological forms of feeling or whether they are themselves basic and Westerners repress, deny, or dissociate them, is a matter for debate. This debate arises, however, because the Western model insists that the "universal psychobiological substrate" of human personality contains specific types of emotions. The problem is obviated, however, if, following Parsons (1961), we reconceptualize the "universal substrate" of personality to see it as essentially undifferentiated, containing non-goal-specific, or at least very generalized, emotional energies, rather than specific emotional systems. If this is the case, culture may play a more central role in shaping goals and directions in the personality on a more basic level than is usually supposed. With this, it becomes possible to give an account of the diverse human personality systems as parts of larger cultural systems, and patterns of feeling may be more easily understood in their social as well as psychological dimensions.

   2. Kaluli words for affects are not nouns describing types of feelings, but

verbs describing states of the individual. They correspond to English usages such as "to be angry," "to be desiring," or "to be grieving." Kaluli have at least seven expressions denoting states of anger and two for grief or sadness:

gadiab	to be moderately to strongly angry
kulufeyab	similar to or a bit more intense than *gadiab*
imolab	to fly into a sudden furious rage
kegab	to have a spat; talk angrily to spouse or children
kanolab	to be angry a long time
migi hedab	to glower with anger (lit., face hangs)
ilib nagalab	similar to *migi hedab*; perhaps more hidden (lit., chest hurts)
nofolab	to feel sad; feel compassion, sorry for someone
kuwayab	to grieve (implies wailing) for death or misfortune

The variation in the numbers of terms for death or misfortune suggests that anger is a particularly salient emotion among the Kaluli, while grief is less so. However, this can only be determined by examining their use in discourse. It appears that anger is, in fact, the more discussed term because it has severer immediate social consequences. Grief appears to be equally deeply moving, but it *evokes* responses from others instead of making assertions on them.

3. Dancers for the Kaluli ceremonies are all volunteers who perform for a variety of reasons, not the least of which is the appeal of the powerful and dramatic role itself. While the dancers are repeatedly and extensively burned throughout the night, the burns are rarely worse than second degree because of the comparatively low temperature of the flame of the resin torch, and usually heal in a few weeks' time.

For a more complete analysis of these ceremonies in the context of Kaluli culture, see Schieffelin 1976. For insight into the strategies of Kaluli poetics and music, see E. L. Schieffelin 1979 and Feld 1982.

4. See also Seligman 1975 for another version of this approach.

5. This impression needs to be improved on by a controlled epidemiological survey. Such a survey could in principle be done in Bosavi, though not without difficulty. In the first place, it is questionable that it could be successfully carried out using standard research instruments based on DSM-III if Kaluli depression has a different presentation from that for which they were designed. A new (or modified), more culturally sensitive instrument would have to be developed to ensure that the survey would produce valid findings.

6. This is not meant to imply that Kaluli women characteristically value the young single life. All that is meant here is that this young woman would prefer her previous unmarried state, living in the household of her mother and brother, to being married as the third of three wives to an overbearing man.

7. To many Western readers the therapy suggested here may seem wrong or misguided because it perpetuates a situation of injustice in which the patient (or victim) is a woman whose illness may be a result of being compelled to be an unwilling pawn in the marital politics of men. The question that has to be

addressed here, however, is what kind of solutions are actually *possible* in this particular cultural environment. Divorce is out of the question. Kaluli social organization is held together in large part through marriage alliances, so that the marriage bond plays a much more critical role for Kaluli people than it does for us. In this particular case, if the woman's marriage broke up, it would require breaking up her brother's marriage as well, plus the re-collection and return of a large amount of bridewealth distributed to relatives on both sides: in the end it would require undoing a formidable array of transactions and relationships of fairly long standing. If this woman's unhappiness is the outcome of the way marriages are arranged in this male-dominated society, the therapist has to decide whether in designing treatment it is practical to try to change the whole social system or simply to try to enable the woman to cope with it more effectively. Given the fact that Kaluli society is not at present anywhere near a state of awareness where women are beginning to seek greater social rights, the former course of action is not feasible. Kaluli women do not have the same expectations of "happiness" in marriage as exist among women in the West and they have developed many ways to cope with marital relations in workable and amicable ways. Thus it seems both more practical and more likely of success to design therapy to facilitate the patient's adoption of customary modes of coping by endeavoring to get her to accept what cannot, for now, be changed.

REFERENCES

Abraham, K.
   [1911]   Notes on the Psychoanalytical Investigation and Treatment of
   1949   Manic-Depressive Insanity and Allied Conditions. *In* Selected
               Works of Karl Abraham. London: Hogarth Press.
   [1924]   A Short Study of the Development of the Libido. *In* Selected
   1949   Works of Karl Abraham. London: Hogarth Press.
Akiskal, H. and W. McKinney
   1973   Depressive Disorders: Toward a Unified Hypothesis. Science
               182:20–29.
Bateson, G.
   1958   Naven. 2d ed. Stanford: Stanford University Press.
Beck, A.
   1972   Depression: Causes and Treatment. Philadelphia: University of
               Pennsylvania Press.
   1976   Cognitive Therapy and the Emotional Disorders. New York:
               International Universities Press.
Blackburn, I. M., S. Bishop, A. I. M. Glen, L. J. Whalley, and J. E. Christie
   1981   The Efficacy of Cognitive Therapy in Depression. A Treatment
               Trial Using Cognitive Therapy and Pharmacotherapy, Each
               Alone and in Combination. British Journal of Psychiatry 139:
               181–189.

Bowlby, J.
1980   Attachment and Loss. Vol. 3., Loss. New York: Basic Books.
Breen, M.
1967   Culture and Schizophrenia: A Study of Negro and Jewish
            Schizophrenics. International Journal of Social Psychiatry 14:
            282−289.
Burns, D.
1980   Feeling Good: The New Mood Therapy. New York: William
            Morrow.
Darwin, C.
1972   The Expression of the Emotions in Man and Animals. London:
            Murray.
Devereux, G.
1956   Normal and Abnormal: The Key Problem in Psychiatric
            Anthropology. *In* Some Uses of Anthropology: Theoretical and
            Applied. Washington, D.C.: The Anthropological Society of
            Washington.
Durkheim, E.
[1911]   The Elementary Forms of the Religious Life. J. W. Swain,
1961   trans. New York: Collier Books.
Ekman, P.
1974   Universal Facial Expressions of Emotion. *In* Culture and
            Personality: Contemporary Readings. R. LeVine, ed. Chicago:
            Aldine.
Feld, S.
1982   Sound and Sentiment: Birds, Weeping, Poetics and Song in
            Kaluli Expression. Philadelphia: University of Pennsylvania
            Press.
Freud, S.
[1917]   Mourning and Melancholia. *In* Collected Works of Sigmund
1956   Freud, J. Strachey, ed. Vol. 4. London: Hogarth Press.
Goffman, E.
1967   Interaction Ritual. Garden City: Anchor/Doubleday.
Guthrie, G. M.
1973   Culture and Mental Disorder. Module in Anthropology 39. New
            York: Addison-Wesley.
Irvine, J.
n.d.   Language and Affect: Some Cross-cultural Issues. Paper pre-
            sented at the 1982 Georgetown University Roundtable on Lan-
            guage and Linguistics, Contemporary Perceptions of Language:
            Interdisciplinary Dimensions.
Kleinman, A.
1980   Patients and Healers in the Context of Culture. Berkeley, Los
            Angeles, London: University of California Press.
1982   Neurasthenia and Depression: A Study of Somatization and

Culture in China. Culture, Medicine and Psychiatry 6: 117–190.

Leff, J.
1973   Culture and the Differentiation of Emotional States. British Journal of Psychiatry 123:299–306.

Levy, R.
1984   Emotion, Knowing, and Culture. *In* Culture Theory. R. A. Shweder and R. A. LeVine, eds. Pp. 214–237. Cambridge: Cambridge University Press.

Lutz, C.
1985   Ethnopsychology Compared to What? Explaining Behavior and Consciousness among the Ifaluk. *In* Person, Self, and Experience: Exploring Specific Ethnopsychologies. G. White and J. Kirkpatrick, eds. Berkeley, Los Angeles, London: University of California Press.

Manschreck, T., and M. Petrie
1978   The Atypical Psychoses. Culture, Medicine, and Psychiatry 2:233–268.

Marsella, A. J.
1979   Depressive Experience and Disorder across Cultures. *In* Handbook of Cross-cultural Psychology, Psychopathology. Vol. 6: Psychopathology. H. C. Triandis and J. G. Draguns, eds. Boston: Allyn and Bacon.

McGoldrick, M., J. K. Pierce, and J. Giordano
1982   Ethnicity and Family Therapy. New York: The Guilford Press.

Osgood, C., W. H. May, and M. S. Miron
1975   Cross-Cultural Universals of Affective Meaning. Urbana: University of Illinois Press.

Parsons, T.
1961   Social Structure and the Development of Personality. *In* Studying Personality Cross-Culturally. New York: Harper and Row.

Rosaldo, M.
1984   Towards an Anthropology of Self and Feeling. *In* Culture Theory. R. A. Shweder and R. A. LeVine, eds. Pp. 137–154. Cambridge: Cambridge University Press.

Rush, A. J., A. T. Beck, M. Kovacs, and S. Hollon
1977   Comparative Efficacy of Cognitive Therapy and Pharmacotherapy in the Treatment of Depressed Outpatients. Cognitive Therapy and Research 1:17–37.

Sanua, V. D.
1963   The Socio-cultural Aspects of Schizophrenia: A Comparison of Protestant and Jewish Schizophrenics. International Journal of Social Psychiatry 10:27–35.

Sapir, E.
  1927   Speech as a Personality Trait. American Journal of Sociology
              32:892–905.
Scheff, T. J.
  1979   Catharsis in Healing, Ritual and Drama. Berkeley, Los
              Angeles, London: University of California Press.
Schieffelin, B. B.
  1979   How Kaluli Children Learn What to Say, What to Do, and How
              to Feel: An Ethnographic Study of the Development of Com-
              municative Competence. Ph.D., Columbia University.
Schieffelin, B., and E. Ochs
  1983   A Cross-cultural Perspective on the Transition from Prelin-
              guistic to Linguistic Communication. *In* The Transition from
              Prelinguistic to Linguistic Communication. R. Golinkoff, ed.
              Hillsdale, N.J.: Lawrence Erlbaum Associates.
Schieffelin, E. L.
  1976   The Sorrow of the Lonely and the Burning of the Dancers. New
              York: St. Martin's Press.
  1979   Mediators as Metaphors: Moving a Man to Tears in Papua, New
              Guinea. *In* The Imagination of Reality: Essays in Southeast
              Asian Conference Systems. A. L. Becker and A. Yengoyan,
              eds. Norwood, N.J.: Ablex Publishing Co.
Schooler, C., and W. Caudhill
  1964   Symptomatology in Japanese and American Schizophrenics.
              Ethnology: 3:172–178.
Seligman, M.
  1975   Helplessness: On Depression, Development, and Death. San
              Francisco: W. H. Freeman.
Shaw, B. F.
  1977   Comparison of Cognitive Therapy and Behavior Therapy in the
              Treatment of Depression. Journal of Consulting Clinical Psy-
              chology 45:543–551.
Soloman, R. C.
  1984   Getting Angry: The Jamesian Theory of Emotion in Anthro-
              pology. *In* Culture Theory. R. A. Shweder and R. A. LeVine,
              eds. Pp. 238–256. Cambridge: Cambridge University Press.
Sorenson, E. R.
  1976   Social Organization and Facial Expression of Emotion. Wash-
              ington, D.C.: National Geographic Society Research Reports,
              1968 Project.
Strathern, M.
  1968   Popokl: The Question of Morality. Mankind 6:553–562.

4

Depression, Buddhism, and the Work of Culture in Sri Lanka

Gananath Obeyesekere

Brown and Harris in their exploration of depression as essentially caused by social and psychological conditions make the following statement:

> The immediate response to loss of an important source of positive value is likely to be a sense of hopelessness, accompanied by a gamut of feelings, ranging from distress, depression, and shame to anger. Feelings of hopelessness will not always be restricted to the provoking incident—large or small. It may lead to thoughts about the hopelessness of one's life in general. It is such *generalization* of hopelessness that we believe forms the central core of depressive disorder. (1978:235)

This statement sounds strange to me, a Buddhist, for if it was placed in the context of Sri Lanka, I would say that we are not dealing with a depressive but a good Buddhist. The Buddhist would take one further step in generalization: it is not simply the general hopelessness of one's own lot; that hopelessness lies in the nature of the world, and salvation lies in understanding and overcoming that hopelessness. Thus the problem raised here: How is the Western diagnostic term "depression" expressed in a society whose predominant ideology of Buddhism states that life is suffering and sorrow, that the cause of sorrow is attachment or desire or craving, that there is a way (generally through meditation) of understanding and overcoming suffering and achieving the final goal of cessation from suffering or *nirvāna*? My contention is that what is called depression in the West is a painful series of affects pertaining to sorrow and is caused by a variety of antecedent conditions—genetic, socio-cultural, and psychological. These affects exist in Western society in a relatively free-floating manner: they are not anchored to an ideology and are therefore identifiable and conducive to labeling as illness. But this need not be the case in other societies where these affects do not exist free-floating but instead are intrinsically locked into larger cultural and philosophical issues of existence and problems of meaning.

Kraus, in his review of Margaret Field's data on Ashanti, says:

> Her salient point seems to be that there is a high incidence of involutional psychotic reactions of the depressed type among Ashanti women. This type of depression seems, in fact, not to be thought of as an illness but accepted as the inevitable lot of most women. (1968:25)

This perverse refusal of the Ashanti to conform to Western psychiatric norms of depression is also found among the Yoruba. According to Murphy, the Yoruba really suffer from depression though they do not see it as such. "Depression presented a special problem in that while the symptoms were recognized as painful, unpleasant and disabling, they were seen as more or less 'natural' results of the vicissitudes of life" (ibid., p. 26). It is clear that for the Ashanti and Yoruba the constellation of symptoms operationalized as depression in Western society has become an existential issue, a natural product of the vicissitudes of life. The general psychiatric attitude is to view this as a "conceptual problem" (ibid.). Underlying the conceptual problem is the reality, this being a set of depressive affects and their causes. If the reality is the same everywhere, then culture is something extraneous or superadded, hence the well-known term "culture-bound syndrome."

In my view, the conceptual problem does not lie with the Yoruba or the Ashanti but with the Western psychiatrist. If the Ashanti, the Yoruba, or the Sinhala of Sri Lanka were to say that certain "affects" arising out of a life condition (bereavement, loss, menopause, old age, etc.) do not constitute an illness, and furthermore if these affects cannot be separated from their involvement in an existential issue (such as the nature of life), could we seriously say that the Ashanti, Yoruba, or Sinhala are deluding themselves and that they are in fact suffering from an illness called "depression"? We may be able to make this kind of statement in relation to a physical disease and thereby make the well-known distinction between illness and disease. For example, malaria is the *disease* since it has an operationally identifiable etiology whether it is found among Yoruba or Sinhala, while the *illness* is the cultural conception surrounding the disease. In physical medicine the disease can be extracted from the illness, and this makes a great difference for control and treatment. In the realms of the so-called mental diseases, however, a different situation prevails. I doubt that the illness-disease distinction is applicable since the cultural conception of the disease is intrinsic to its character: it is both illness and disease at the same time. A determinate biological/genetic mechanism is absent in mental illness or, if present, is accompanied and superlaid by social-psychological conditions that are products of human experience in different sociocultural settings. In this situation the manner in which the so-called symptoms are put together and given cultural meaning or symbolization is intrinsic to their nature as illness/disease. The *conception* of the disease (i.e., illness) *is* the disease. Or to put it differently, there are only illnesses and no diseases.[1]

On one level it is possible to prove that depression in its various forms is universal. Depression in this sense is defined from the modern psychiatric perspective in the Diagnostic and Statistical Manuals I, II, and III. These handbooks have operationalized depression into clear-cut, specific, and unambiguous symptoms and types. The intention is laudable since it is assumed that this will facilitate the identification of the disease—depression—wherever it is found, and also provide for cross-culturally valid statistical and epidemiological information. The results also seem incontrovertible: the depressive affects or symptoms seem to exist everywhere even if culture bound. Therefore it is concluded that depression in its Western sense is a disease universally present.

It is easy to show that this conclusion is not as logical as it may seem and may indeed be tautological. To illustrate my argument, let me practice a piece of reverse ethnocentrism. Take the case of a South Asian male (or female)[2] who has the following symptoms: drastic weight loss, sexual fantasies, and night emissions and urine discoloration. In South Asia the patient may be diagnosed as suffering from a disease, "semen loss." But on the operational level I can find this constellation of symptoms in every society, from China to Peru. If I were to say, however, that I know plenty of Americans suffering from the disease "semen loss," I would be laughed out of court even though I could "prove" that this disease is universal. The trouble with my formulation is that while the symptoms exist at random everywhere, they have not been "fused into a conception" (as semen loss) in American society.[3] Yet if I were to employ the methodological norms implicit in the several Diagnostic and Statistical manuals and apply them from a South Asian perspective to the rest of the world (as Western psychiatrists do for depression), then it is incontrovertible that "semen loss" *is* a disease and is universally found in human populations.

It is the methodology of psychiatric epidemiology that I criticize here. In psychiatric epidemiology, symptoms are treated in isolation from their cultural context. While it is true that the disarticulation of symptoms from context will facilitate measurement, it is also likely that the entities being measured are empty of meaning. Consider the recent work by Carstairs and Kapur (1976) which attempts to isolate psychiatric symptoms and relate them to psychiatric need. The intention is to produce a value-free and an operationally specific instrument for measuring psychiatric illness on an all-India basis. It is doubtful whether this goal is realizable. How does one label "tiredness" (symptom no. 2), "indigestion" (no. 4), "burning sensation" (no. 6), "dullness" (no. 16), "poor concentration" (no. 22) as psychiatric symptoms without justification from either a Western theoretical position or from the perspective of the indigenous value system (Carstairs and Kapur 1976: 75)? Moreover, can these terms from ordinary English-language use be transferred to designate entities expressed in another language? A reverse procedure may be more justifiable, that is, formulating a list of the psychiatric terminology employed in the native language and then seeking appropriate terms or phrases in English. Furthermore, though the authors claim to construct a value-free instrument, are not Western theoretical and commonsense notions implicit in psychiatric terminology such as "depression" (no. 15), "sweating" (no. 13), "phobia" (no. 14), "delusions" (no. 24), and especially "pathological worrying" (no. 20) (ibid.)?

In Carstairs and Kapur's study, symptoms are operationally isolated and quantified in relation to psychiatric "need." "Need" here is not the *felt* need of the respondents but an objective need score based on the number of symptoms. The authors present a need scale ranging from a 0−5 need score. Thus 75 respondents (6%) in a population of 1,233 have a 5 need score. The authors then ask: What proof is there that those with the highest scores have the greatest need for help (ibid., p. 127)? Note the evidence: 10 out of the 13 respondents with psychotic symptoms scored 5, while the other three had 4 on this scale. It is certainly plausible that psychotics should exhibit four to five symptoms, but what about the 175 respondents who had this number of symptoms but were *not* psychotic? How can we be at all sure that they are in need of psychiatric help? For example, a man may experience "wind," "weakness," "indigestion," "other odd sensations," and "burning," that is, five symptoms (ibid., pp. 158–159). Does this mean he needs psychiatric help? And what about a person who has sexual preoccupations, masturbation, night emissions, and "other sexual problems" (ibid., p. 163)?

The most serious criticism of quantitative measurement of symptoms is this: quantity of symptoms cannot measure need, but *quality and intensity* of symptoms are relevant. For example, a man may have one symptom—phobia or hysterical paralysis or impotence—and this may be qualitatively more significant as indicating psychiatric need than any list of three to five symptoms. In other words, a quantitative scale of psychiatric need is a totally valueless and misleading instrument. It is a pity that the authors, infatuated by a not very useful instrument, ignored some of the more fascinating problems of how Indian villagers, even those with "psychotic" symptoms, define their symptoms and learn to function effectively in their society. That most Indians do so is also clear from their study. A "measurement of social functioning" was used in the questions adopted in the pilot survey but dropped from the final design (IPSS).

> The idea of developing "objective" norms of functioning was dropped because of the complexity of the task. As it turned out, respondents with symptoms showed no difference in social functioning scores from those without symptoms: hence social functioning as measured by this questionnaire was not therefore included in our eventual measurement of need. (Ibid., p. 87; see also p. 125)

This is, I believe, a serious error. If people who have *symptoms* can function in society as well as those without, surely the solution is not to drop this issue (which is of enormous significance) but to make it a central question for research.

The pilot survey itself was carried out among men and women in the nonsample area to avoid contamination of the final results. But note that the nonsample area is in the same general area of the three villages studied. Anyone who knows of gossip and communication networks in Indian villages would expect contamination of the sample area. The authors reflect with unconscious irony: "The villagers (even those in the sample area) came to know about our investigation and were prepared for us when we went to them" (ibid., p. 90). They go on to state: "Often we had to see men while they were working in their vegetable gardens, or mending their fishing nets, and women while they were engaged in cooking or cleaning the house" (ibid., p. 91).

It seems to me that one must give up the empiricist ideal of constructing a value-free instrument for epidemiological measurement. Quite to the contrary, the values of the people must be included in its construction, and theoretical considerations (which are also never value-free) must also become central to the research. It is best that one recognizes the existence of these values in the society studied and in the investigator rather than attempt to dissociate values from psychiatric symptoms and from the methodology of the research. These considerations also apply to any discussion of depression whether it be among the Yoruba or Ashanti or Sinhala. If a cluster of symptoms operationalized by a foreign psychiatrist does not exist as a conception of a disease (i.e., illness), it is neither disease nor illness but it may be something else, for example, religion. It is this idea that I want to explore here.

Let me start with a personal anecdote. A colleague of mine, a clinical psychologist from the United States, visited me in Sri Lanka many years ago. I introduced him to a friend of mine and the two of them got to know each other well. Before my colleague left for the United States, he told me: "Gananath, your friend is a classic case of depression." I was somewhat startled, for though my friend had a sad expression and a pessimistic view of the world, I never thought of him in quite that way. Neither did my friend regard *himself* as a depressive, nor did his wife or his physicians consider him one. My friend was a manager of a government corporation, but often used to get away from it all—not by going on a conventional holiday but by going to meditate in isolated hermitages. I think he was someone who had articulated "the depressive affect" with a vision of the world and, having done this, he tried to understand the nature of the world as a sorrowful place through systematic meditation. His was neither a disease nor an illness; he had generalized his hopelessness into an ontological problem of existence, defined in its Buddhist sense as "suffering."

In considering the relationship between "depression" and Buddhism one must, I feel, rule out a specific depressive ethos in Buddhist society parallel to notions such as a "paranoid ethos" (Schwartz 1973). Quite the contrary is true: the Buddha himself enjoined that renunciation and the achievement of nirvāna are not for the ordinary layman who must live in the world and provide for his family and dependents. The ordinary person knows that the world perforce is one of suffering, but he must live in it, often enough with good cheer. The householder is enjoined to lead a happy and contented life in accordance with the five precepts of Buddhism. However, in a fundamental eschatological sense, even the happiness that we experience is an expression of suffering inasmuch as it is temporary and impermanent as is everything in the universe. The ordinary householder in a Buddhist society like Sri Lanka *is a Buddhist* in the sense that he knows that the world of sense pleasure and domesticity which he inhabits is illusory and that salvation must lie in the recognition of its illusory nature. Around him are models of those who have renounced the domestic life for the homeless—monks, both monastic monks and hermit monks living in the isolation of forests and caves. Furthermore, there are occasions when laymen are made aware of the nature of life as suffering and impermanent, for example, at death, where the standard phrase on everyone's tongue is "impermanent are all conditioned things." The funeral sermons uttered by monks reinforce these sentiments. Another specifically Buddhist institution for laymen is *sil* or the observance of the ten precepts on holy (*pōya*) days during the four phases of the moon, but especially on the full moon. During these days, the layman temporarily becomes a novice of sorts and engages in a variety of religious activities including meditation. Anyone can participate in sil activities, but traditionally sil was practiced by the old as a way of life intermediate between lay life and monkhood, and as a voluntary rite of passage from middle to old age.

I have shown that while Buddhist laymen are, like other human beings, caught up in the world, on occasion they are provoked to have a vision of the world which accords with their textual traditions. If they are afflicted by bereavement and loss (which in turn mobilizes other kinds of social and infantile conflicts and genetic predispositions), they can generalize their despair from the self to the world at large and give it Buddhist meaning and significance. This happens in other great religious traditions also, but the Buddhist provides special occasions for ontological reflection on despair. My friend was a successful executive who gave Buddhist meaning in his own way to what one, for purely heuristic reasons only, might call "depressive affects." I shall now focus on how this may occur in an ordinary village on more conventional lines.

One of the most popular activities during sil is meditation or *bhāvanā*. Ordinary laymen practiced various types of meditative practices on pōya days, but two were especially popular, meditation on universal kindness-compassion (*karanīya-metta sutta*) and meditation on mindfulness (*satipatthāna bhāvanā*), based on a text known as *satipatthāna sutta*. The latter is a very complex exercise and only part of it is generally practiced by those observing sil. This section is known as *pilikul bhāvanā* (meditation on revulsion), probably the most common form of meditation practiced in Sri Lanka. It is the significance of meditation on revulsion that I shall relate to the theme of this volume.

Meditation on revulsion is a long and ancient tradition in Buddhism and is known in the texts and commentaries as *asubha bhāvanā*, *asubha* meaning "foulness" or "impurity" (Vajirānāna 1975:166–182). In the monk tradition, meditation on foulness pertained to the actual contemplation of the corpse in ten separate stages of decay, each stage associated with special techniques of meditation and goals of realization of the nature of life. The general intent of asubha bhāvanā is to produce in the meditator a sense of disgust for sense pleasure, which will then lead him to realize the sense of the transitoriness of the body. In the lay tradition, this is not the case: one does not meditate on an actual decaying corpse but one conjures in one's own mind the putrescence of the body, which in turn will eventually lead to a knowledge of the transitoriness of the body and the world. An old lay virtuoso or *upāsaka* whom I interviewed many years ago put it thus: "The body is full of feces, it smells badly like a dead rat snake; the body is broken in one hundred and eight places; the body is like a forest of wild animals: it is like a lavatory pit used for six months, so cleanse it often and keep it clean." The layman, then, has an especially difficult task. He has no physical object before him in order to conjure up the body's putrescence; he has to evoke this putrescence through various metaphors of revulsion, the most conspicuous being that of feces. Feces is the one object par excellence that everyone in the society is familiar with as a revulsive object. It then becomes a metaphor for the revulsiveness of the body in the "meditation on revulsion."

The above response is typical. In 1970 I asked three students in the University of Sri Lanka (Peradeniya) to administer a questionnaire to thirteen upāsakas who came regularly to meditate in a temple on pōya days. The questionnaire was designed to investigate the typical activities of these virtuosos during sil. All these respondents were over the age of 50, except for one who was 44; the mean age was 67. These were old men who had practically retired from active life. Let me give some representative statements from their interviews.

Case 1 (age 61)

"I try to control my body. I think: my hair, teeth, nails, nerves, bones, and so forth are impermanent. Why? They are not mine. They are of no use. There is no point in all of this. Though one enjoys life and dresses well while living in the world it is of no use for the other world. . . . My body is revulsive like a corpse, like feces. [Again the generalization:] The bodies of others are also foul. So's the female body. I care not for women. I feel nauseous toward them.''

Case 2 (age 80)

''By meditation on revulsiveness I mean the thirty-two defilements of the body. . . . It is not my body alone that is foul: so are the bodies of others. Though you apply talcum powder and scent on the body it is like feces; it is like a clay pot full of feces.''

Case 3 (age 66, female)

[After describing the techniques of meditation this woman said:] ''One must separately control all parts of the body, from the hair to the teeth. I list the thirty-two parts of the body separately and say this part is impermanent, it has no soul. . . . [Then:] This body is like a lump of feces. I think then of urine and feces. When you remove the skin from that lovely body it is like a *domba* seed [veined and shriveled]. The whole body is a heap of dirt. It is like a bag of millet which, when you untie it, leaves you nothing. . . . when I think of my mother or my children they too are like this. I think: their bodies are dirt also.''

Case 4 (age 85)

''I reflect on the thirty-two parts of the body from my hair to my bones. . . . I think that my teeth and wrinkled skin are impermanent. So is my life. My body is revulsive. I think: when my bowels are stretched out, my, how long they are! I feel I want nothing of the human body. [Again:] Why think of one's wife and children? They too have bodies like mine. All persons are like this: no finality.''

Case 5 (age 86)

''I meditate on the body. The body is a heap of dirt. It contains thirty-two heaps of dirt. It is something covered by skin. . . . This is what I'll be when I die. I think it is transitory. The body is a hell. A heap of dirt.''

[Interviewer:] Why do you think the body is dirt?

"It breathes, it eliminates. It is filth, filth. You rub soap to get rid of its dirt. . . . This dirt does not belong to me. It is transitory. It dies. The body is a heap of feces. Impermanent. [Again:] A few years after I got married I did not care about women. After my two children were born, I felt that sexual intercourse was useless."

Case 6 (age unknown, female)

"When I meditate I feel no fondness for my body. With the feeling of uselessness of life [*kalakirīma*] I lose my liking for my body. . . . I feel the impurity of the body and hence no desire for it. I am aware of *dukkha*, suffering. I think: the bodies of others are like mine also. When I think of my body it is thus: I think it is a heap of dirt. It is surely like a heap of feces. I think the same of the inside of my body. It is as if a pot containing feces has been polished on the outside."

Only two of the respondents stated that their sil and meditation activities were precipitated by specific antecedent events. Case 6 stated that she was regularly beaten and abused by her husband, who subsequently abandoned her and her children. He used to have flagrant liaisons with other women. Then her father died: "The sorrow [*sōkaya*] of my father's death was such that I took the white cloth that he wore during sil and his rosary and his books and I started taking sil myself." She did not remarry for she thought, "If this man was bad, so must they all be. The married life is troublesome. Several proposed marriage to me but I refused. There is no freedom here." The other was a seventy-two-year-old man who used to observe occasional sil from childhood. However, sixteen years earlier, when the head monk of his village died, he began to regularly observe sil four times a month. He loved this monk, he said, and suffered great shock (*kampanaya*) at his death. In both cases, the pain of mind and sorrow was articulated in Buddhist terms and expressed in the activity of sil and meditation. The signs of sorrow (unlike the symptoms of depression) are not free-floating: they are expressed in Buddhist terms. In all the other cases there were no specific antecedents: rather sil was a response to old age. It is likely (though no direct evidence is available from the interviews) that old age did produce in some of these respondents a sense of hopelessness and loss ("depressive affects") but these feelings were generalized and given Buddhist meaning. The problems of personal sorrow resulting from the conditions of old age with its attendant ills became a problem of existence in its ontological sense.

One of the problems of contemporary psychiatric methodology is the assumption that the language that expresses "depressive affects" can also be operationalized. Yet the attempt to give operational specificity to the vocabulary of emotion is to destroy what is integral to that form of speech (*parole*), namely, its intrinsic diffusiveness, multiplicity of meanings, and capacity to assimilate and express emotional states that are not easily differentiated and indeed run counter to the very canons of operationalism (Ricoeur 1974:347–375). Furthermore, and I specifically refer here to the vocabulary of suffering and despair, that speech is linked to specific traditions, such as those of Buddhism or Christianity. It is almost impossible for a Sinhala person to use words expressing sorrow without articulating them to the Buddhist tradition. Even if all the words he uses do not come from that tradition directly, the larger context of usage will eventually embody it in the doctrinal tradition. Let me give some examples of Sinhala words employed to express sorrow with a rough approximation in English.

I have already mentioned sōkaya, sadness or sorrow, and kampanaya or *kampāva*, the shock of loss; another word is *sanvēgaya*, pain of mind. The Buddhist term dukkha also has a variety of meanings ranging from ordinary sorrow to suffering in its doctrinal sense. One of the most common terms in the lexicon of sorrow is *kalakirīma*, a sense of hopelessness, or despair with life. Etymologically kalakirīrma is derived from the words *kāla* and *kriyā*, "the termination of time," that is, death. When the word is used in its formal etymological sense as *kālakriyā*, it refers euphemistically to "death." However, in its popular form as kalakirīrma, it refers to a sense of hopelessness, but not a free-floating one: it is a reaction against life itself. Specific emotional words for sorrow and loss—such as sōkaya, kampāva, sanvēgaya—are easily assimilated into more general terms that express an attitude to life in general, such as dukkha and kalakirīma. This is reflective of the Buddhist orientation of this culture. The situation is such that any kind of affect or sorrow or despair can and must be expressed in ordinary language that is itself for the most part derived from Buddhism or can be articulated to Buddhism. Moreover, one is socialized into myths, parables, and legends that deal with the phenomenon of personal loss and sorrow as part of the nature of existence in general. One of the most famous is the parable of the mustard seed, familiar to most Buddhists. This text deals with the story of Kisā Gotamī whose first and only child died in infancy. Distraught with pain and grief, she went from place to place seeking some medicine to resurrect her child. She eventually came to the Buddha and asked the sage whether he could revive the dead child. The Buddha said that he could if only she would bring a mustard seed from a house in which death had not occurred. Elated, Kisā Gotamī went from one house to another seeking the impossible mustard seed. She soon came to the realization that her own personal grief is simply a part of a larger universal problem of suffering. In this recognition of the nature of life lay her redemption. The parable of the mustard seed could as easily serve us as a parable on the nature of depression (see Kaufmann 1961:396—405 for a good discussion of a related text).

The lay virtuosi or upāsakas discussed earlier have read texts such as that of Kisā Gotamī and they have resorted to sil, a temporary movement away from domestic living, and to meditation. The text of pilikul bhāvanā deliberately denigrates the body in order to deny the self as real. The metaphor used in the denigration of the body and the self is feces. In major depression also the self is denigrated: lowering of self-esteem and self-worth is conspicuous in this state. But in Buddhist virtuosos this is deliberately undertaken. I do not know whether a person who suffers a sense of worthlessness can overcome it by techniques such as that of "meditation on revulsiveness." Perhaps some do and others do not. In some situations it is likely that a person who has *not* been afflicted by negative sorrowful affects may be encouraged to deliberately cultivate or resurrect them through meditation—that is, meditation itself may create the "depressive affects" as a step in the larger quest for understanding the world.

One thing is clear enough: that which may be labeled as depression in the West is given a radically different form of cultural canalization and expression. Furthermore, this idiom of feces is specially effective in conveying the emotional feel of the horror of putrescence. The meditation is designed to make the meditator feel that his body is something that belongs to him yet is outside of him, so that he can view it (and its parts) in detachment; it also exists in others and in the world. It is likely that the ideal virtuoso, once he effects full detachment, can transcend both feces and body, so that they become neutral objects existing outside himself. True detachment must free a person from both disgust and attachment. However, I believe that for most persons meditation sends taproots into infancy and childhood: to the infant, feces are part of himself yet also something that is differentiated from him. In other words, the detachment of the self from the self—in order to deny its ontological reality—is facilitated by the metaphor of feces.

The metaphor of feces as putrescence is also implicated in the values of Sri Lankan society and the socialization of its children. In Sri Lankan society, as elsewhere, what is important is not the technology of child care—its time and place—but the maternal attitude that in turn expresses the values of the culture. Freud noted this in *Civilization and Its Discontents* (1930), in which the socialization of the anal system is linked with the values of Western civilization: order, cleanliness, routine, and through a long detour, to aestheticism. In Sri Lanka the formal techniques of toilet training are similar to those in many parts of the non-Western world. There is extreme permissiveness: time and place are not defined; the child gradually moves from the home to the backyard and, when he is old enough to look after himself, to the outhouse or bush. But this idyllic picture is soon dispelled when we focus on the maternal attitude toward feces: the mother's reaction is one of horror if the child attempts to play with it. *Chi* is the typical Sinhala expression of revulsion, which prototypically refers to feces. In socialization, the child is soon made to feel that all dirt is feces: thus when a child plays with mud, the exclamation "chi, feces" is used. In training, the mother may even rebuke a child by saying "Chi, feces baby," which is the earliest usage of the metaphor of feces to lower someone's self-esteem. The idiom of feces and foul smells are extended to other contexts also, for example, to "shame": a person who has lost face is someone who "stank"; dirt, mud, and bad smells all appear in the idiom of shame. All these feelings are activated or reactivated in "the meditation on revulsion" to convey the horror of putrescence, which is a preliminary step in the very transcendence of the body leading to a recognition of the impermanence or transitory nature of life itself.

The preceding discussion demonstrates that certain affects and the antecedent sociocultural-psychological conditions that produce these affects are crystallized into a "conception" in Buddhist Sri Lanka. This conception is not a conception of disease/illness. The term "depression" itself is, I believe, such a cultural conception, but a Western one, in which a constellation of symptoms is defined as illness. Once defined in ontic or existential terms, as in Sri Lanka, it ceases to be an illness and the unpleasant affects associated with this existential condition are expressed and perhaps even resolved in a variety of meanings and activities provided by the Buddhist orientation of the culture. In such a situation, it would be meaningless to consider the conception here as disease/illness. The question I now raise is this: Are there situations in which the constellation of symptoms associated with depression is in fact defined as illness in Sri Lanka? The answer is "yes," but even in this situation it would be wrong to define the set or constellation as "depression." A constellation of social conditions and affects are once again defined as illness, but illness here is also a cultural conception.

In *Medusa's Hair* (1981) I dealt with case studies of ecstatic priestesses. Prior to their taking the priestess role, they were almost invariably afflicted with an attack by a spirit of a dead ancestor. This affliction was defined as illness. During the spirit attack, the ideal-typical priestess experiences a sense of abandonment and despair, a form of the dark-night-of-the-soul experience. This period of despair has a phenomenological resemblance to the affects associated with depression—abandonment, hopelessness, sadness, and also certain antecedent conditions such as guilt toward a parent or significant other. But even here the illness is an experience that is given an entirely cultural meaning, and therefore to abstract the constellation of affects from the meanings associated with them is to do violence to the data. This leads to an intriguing problem: the same, or at least a similar, constellation of social conditions and affects can produce in Sri Lanka at least two (and perhaps more) cultural definitions, as an ontological problem (in Buddhism) and as an illness (in spirit attack).

The consideration of this problem leads me to the final point I want to make here which concerns the notion of *work*. In his *Freud and Philosophy* (1974), Ricoeur deals with the centrality of this notion in both psychoanalysis and in the study of art. Work in psychoanalytic theory parallels the Marxist notion of labor. Work is the process whereby affects are transformed into symbols and meanings. Thus the "dream work" is the transformation of unconscious affects and motives (the latent dream) into the dream itself, an entirely creative process (which Freud tended to undervalue). The notion of work is also found in Freud's paper, "Mourning and Melancholia" (1917). Here mourning is work that overcomes the negative affects engendered through loss and bereavement. So it is with melancholia, but work in melancholia does not result in a successful resolution. Ricoeur (1974) extends the notion of work to art; he shows that *Hamlet* is not just a simple Oedipal conflict but a transformation of childhood conflict into something totally different: the *work* of art. I would argue it is thus with the anthropological view of culture. The *work of culture* is the process whereby painful motives and affects such as those occurring in depression are transformed into publicly accepted sets of meanings and symbols.[4] Thus the constellation of affects that I talked of earlier can, through the work of culture, be transformed in a variety of directions—into Buddhism and into spirit attack and no doubt into other symbolic forms also. To study work, one needs a case history approach contextualized in a specific culture. This would enable us to identify the mechanisms involved in symbolic transformation, as Freud did in the dream work. Work also implies failure; if mourning is successful work, melancholia is failure. Success and failure in turn entail a critique of culture—a critique through which one might be able to connect anthropology with critical theory.

The idea of work could introduce a whole host of fruitful problems in the study of symbolic systems, and I can only hint at them here. What are the social, economic, and personal conditions and processes that result in the transformation of similar affects into differing symbolic systems? Why does the same symbolic system (be it meditation on revulsion or spirit possession) work for some and not for others? Then there is the problem that is central to this volume. Is it indeed possible that sorrowful affects may not be capable of transformation into public meanings under certain circumstances? What these circumstances are cannot be predetermined, though we can make some guesses. For example, it is likely that in Western culture the affects of depression are not given cultural meaning and significance because of what Weber (1958) called the process of rationalization in Western society and the demystification of the world. In this situation, affects exist more or less in a free-floating manner, awaiting a different symbolic formulation: their conceptualization as a disease, "depression." A similar process may occur in Sri Lanka. It may be possible that under certain conditions the affects may not receive cultural crystallization and may exist in a free-floating manner. What these conditions are must become the subject of investigation—an inquiry into the conditions wherein the work of culture does not succeed in the symbolic transformation of affects. It may be that if affects are specially strong, they may elude the work of culture, but this is a problem for research and further investigation.

CONCLUSION: DISQUIET

On rereading the last paragraph, I begin to experience some disquiet, if not depression. If affects under certain circumstances elude the work of culture, it may well be that the distinction between illness and disease is valid and that there are some affects, generated by eventually isolable and identifiable biogenetic or sociocultural conditions, that are cross-culturally uniform and constitute the operational core of what is called depression—or at least one of its many forms in Western psychiatric nomenclature. It may be that Western psychiatrists are right and naive anthropologists must not avoid the strong clinical evidence for major depression as an illness. Here again I must inject some skepticism. It is undoubtedly true that there are patients who are diagnosed as depressives in hospital wards in Sri Lanka and elsewhere, and some of these patients may even be persuaded that they are in fact suffering from an illness known as depression. But in my view this situation may also be a result of the work of culture—not the culture of Sri Lankan Buddhism but that of the culture of modern medicine.

Western medicine has enormous prestige and cultural significance in modern society. The definition of painful affects as a disease known as depression is itself a product of the culture of Western medicine, and given the power and prestige of the medical establishment, it is easy to see how this new definition of human suffering begins to be accepted by people as the right definition, especially by elites in non-Western societies. Moreover, parallel to the culture of Western medicine are the institutions that it creates, as, for example, wards for taking care of the mentally sick. One must not forget, however, that the existence of the institution may indeed create the very patients who are kept there and who are diagnosed with the label "major depression." If the institution did not exist, people might be compelled by their kinship obligations to accommodate these patients in their own homes and this in turn would inevitably lead to the conceptualization of the depressive affects in Buddhist existential terms. Unfortunately, the conditions in urban society in Sri Lanka and in other parts of the Third World will continue to stimulate the "institution effect" of modern medicine. If the institution is available, it provides an easy way to vest the responsibility of caring for those who suffer in technically qualified modern medical personnel. People who suffer painful emotional stress are difficult to handle and the culture of modern medicine provides a rationale for their kinsmen to reject familial and kinship responsibility. I am not advocating, of course, that we do away with hospital wards, since it is likely that these institutions, or similar ones, may be necessary in modern life. But one must not delude oneself with the false notion that the existence of patients labeled depressives proves in any way the existence of a disease known as "major depression."

The preceding argument does not *disprove* the existence of an operational core in depression, and thus my disquiet persists. In my view, any such identifiable operational core of the "disease" must be bioge-

netic—either as an antecedent cause of the affects or as a consequence or
both. The identification of such factors may have universal cross-cultural
validity, although of a limited sort, since what is called depression (in
whatever form) is *also* invariably associated with psychosocial and
cultural conditions. It is these conditions that defy *operational* specificity
and cross-cultural uniformity: they are locked into issues of existential
meaning and significance, such as those sketched in this chapter. I also
believe, though I cannot discuss this issue here, that the study of these
sociocultural issues has been impeded by experimental studies of depression,[5] by attempts to operationalize symptoms, and by the increasingly
bizarre and seemingly endless classifications of types of depressive
disorders being developed in the Diagnostic and Statistical Manuals.
Akiskal and McKinney (1973:27) state that one of the impediments to a
scientific understanding of depression is "the use of metapsychological
concepts that are difficult to test." I take the opposite view: it is only
through the use of metatheoretical concepts that we can hope to achieve
sufficient conceptual flexibility to study "depression" in its existential
dimensions in varying sociocultural settings.

ACKNOWLEDGMENTS

I am indebted to Ellen Feinberg who undertook a survey of some of the
cross-cultural studies of depression in summer 1982 under a Princeton
University work-study program grant. I am also grateful to Arthur
Kleinman and Amélie Rorty for perceptive comments on this chapter.

NOTES

1. I think even well-understood Western diseases like malaria are not
exempt from this process. In diseases like malaria also, symptoms are not
disarticulated entities that have a phenomenological reality independent of
culture, even though it is the culture of contemporary science. Here, too,
symptoms are "fused into a conception," which is the disease known as
"malaria." Sometimes one can *talk* of a symptom/syndrome in isolation from
the disease, as, for example, when the specialist (or even the patient) has doubts
whether the patient is suffering from X disease or Y disease. But even in such
situations, once a diagnostic decision has been made, symptoms once again are
integrated into the disease conception. Western medicine is no more exempt
from this process than any other system. The key difference between a determi-

nate physical "disease" like malaria and "illnesses" like depression is that the latter are often fused into larger cultural or ideological meanings and consequently become invested with existential significance. In this situation, the disease/illness distinction is hard to maintain.

2. South Asians generally believe that both men and women have "semen" and both can ejaculate and experience night emissions.

3. In any system one might have bodily signs that have no meaning. For example, a villager in Sri Lanka might experience "palpitations," but to him it need be no more significant than a mosquito bite or occasional sneezing. But when *I* have palpitations I feel anxious, since, for me, this is a symptom of my conception of "heart disease," and not a fortuitous bodily sign.

4. I have deliberately limited the notion of "work of culture" to the symbolic transformation of affects, but one might want to extend it to larger areas of species existence.

5. I specifically refer to the experimental studies that involve the infliction of trauma on animals. It is doubtful whether the results of these studies could be meaningfully compared with *human* problems. Even human problems show considerable variations. When I slice onions I shed tears, but is this the same as when I shed tears owing to the loss of a loved one? If you tickle the sole of my foot I will laugh, but is this the same as when I laugh at your joke?

REFERENCES

Akiskal, H. S., and W. T. McKinney
   1973   Depressive Disorders: Toward a Unified Hypothesis. Science 182:20−29.
Brown, G. S., T. Harris
   1978   The Social Origins of Depression: A Study of Psychiatric Disorder in Women. New York: The Free Press.
Carstairs, G. M., and R. L. Kapur
   1976   The Great Universe of Kota: Stress, Change and Mental Disorder in an Indian Village. Berkeley, Los Angeles, London: University of California Press.
Freud, S.
   [1930]   Civilization and Its Discontents. J. Riviere, trans. London:
   1946   Hogarth Press.
   [1917]   Mourning and Melancholia. *In* Collected Papers, Vol. IV.
   1956   J. Strachey, ed. London: Hogarth Press. Pp. 152−170.
Kaufmann, W.
   1961   A Critique of Religion and Philosophy. New York: Doubleday.
Kraus, R. F.
   1968   Cross-Cultural Validation of Psychoanalytic Theories of Depression. Pennsylvania Psychiatric Quarterly 3 (8):24−33.

Obeyesekere, G.
1981   Medusa's Hair: An Essay on Personal Symbols and Religious
              Experience. Chicago: University of Chicago Press.
Ricoeur, P.
1974   Freud and Philosophy: An Essay on Interpretation. D. Savage,
              trans. New York: Yale University Press.
Schwartz, T.
1973   Cult and Context: The Paranoid Ethos in Melanesia. Ethos 1
              (2):153−174.
Vajirānāna, P.
1975   Buddhist Meditation in Theory and Practice. Colombo: Guna-
              sena and Co.
Weber, M.
1958   Science as a Vocation. *In* From Max Weber. H. H. Gerth and
              C. Wright Mills, trans. and ed. New York: Oxford University
              Press.

5

The Interpretive Basis of Depression

Charles F. Keyes

Recently, while leafing through a popular magazine on science, I came across an article that reported that a distinguished psychiatric researcher at the University of Chicago had established definitively that depression is caused by a particular form of chemical imbalance in the brain. Although the magazine put the case in rather stronger terms than I suspect the researcher himself would have done in his technical papers, the conclusion asserted is one widely shared among many practitioners of biomedicine. In such a view of mental functioning as reducible to the physical functioning of the brain (see, e.g., Place 1956; Smart 1959; Borst 1970), depression, like other "mental illnesses," is taken as having nothing to do with that illusion, the "mind." Rather, depression is seen as constituting an impairment of the neurophysiology of the human organism. It follows from such a radical, "materialist" biomedical view of depression that cultural factors are relevant only insofar as they get in the way of an appropriate diagnosis, serving, it is assumed, to mask the true nature of the impairment.

A completely opposite view, adopted by some fellow anthropologists, holds that "depression" is itself a cultural construct, one developed within but one particular cultural tradition—that of the West. The relativist position, in its strongest form, proceeds from an assumption such as that enunciated recently by Schneider (1976): "Nature, as a wholly independent 'thing,' does not exist, except as man formulates it" (p. 203).

It is my contention that depression can neither be dissolved through an insistence on the culturally constructed nature of experience nor reduced to an isolable malfunction of some part of the human organism. For me, the model of depression employed in Western psychotherapies is the dialectical product of "objective" characteristics of human experience and the practical interpretation of those conditions as constituted within a particular cultural tradition (cf., Bourdieu 1977). In this approach, one should not attempt to discover the "real" roots of depression, as those who take a radical biomedical view are wont to do, but to identify the characteristic predispositions found among humans everywhere which conduce to what in certain therapeutic practices is construed as a distinctive mental illness, depression. I argue (in accord with those psychiatrists and psychologists who assume that humans possess a mind as well as a body) that, whatever the physiological correlates of these predispositions, they stem from moods that entail mental assessments of the relationship of the self to the world in which one is an actor. Such moods, while universal, do not necessarily manifest themselves as illness. Illness entails a break from the commonsense stance a person normally takes toward the world, and the adoption of a perspective that stems from a consciousness of pain. The sense of painful distress which might otherwise lead one to see oneself and to be seen by others as ill could be muted and dissipated through some "work of culture" that makes sense of the distress as other than illness. The work of culture—a production that provides a coherent statement of what some experience means—that is turned to when a person feels personal distress might well be a religious ritual. In such a case, the person experiencing pain could view the experience from a religious perspective instead of seeing it as illness. When an illness perspective is adopted, the treatment that will function to restore the ill person to quotidian existence will depend on the available "medical" works of culture. It follows, therefore, that although the Western model of "depression," like other disease models, does entail a representation of the experience of pain rooted in moods found among peoples everywhere, it has practical significance only as an element within a distinctive work of culture.

HUMAN NATURE AND PREDISPOSITIONS TOWARD DEPRESSION

Let me begin with a consideration of depression as it is construed in that authoritative source published by the American Psychiatric Association, the *Diagnostic and Statistical Manual of Mental Disorders, Third Edi-*

tion (1980) (hereafter DSM-III). In this work, "depression" is classed as a major affective disorder whose essential characteristic is "a disturbance of mood, accompanied by a fully or partial manic or depressive syndrome, that is not due to any other physical or mental disorder." The critical concept, "mood," is said to refer "to a prolonged emotion that colors the whole psychic life" (p. 205). The presupposition here is that "moods" are an inherent aspect of human nature. This presupposition is echoed by Geertz, one of the very few anthropologists to have utilized the concept of mood in his writing.[1] While for Geertz moods are shaped by the particular culturally differentiated situations in which an individual finds himself, they are, nonetheless, spoken of in universal terms. Moods are "scalar" qualities, unlike motivations, which are "vectoral"; moods "vary in intensity," but "go nowhere. They spring from certain circumstances but they are responsive to no ends. Like fogs, they just settle and lift; like scents, suffuse and evaporate. When present they are totalistic" (Geertz 1973:97). There is no human being, whether he or she be a stockbroker in New York, a Kirghiz pastoralist in the southern Soviet Union, an Inuit seal hunter in northern Canada, a member of the Politburo of the Vietnamese Workers' Party, or a rice-producing peasant in Java, who does not experience at varying times in his or her life the heaviness and lightening of feelings that we call moods.

Associated with shifts in moods are, without question, interferences with the workings of the human organism, especially the brain. These organic interferences are, as Wallace (1972:396) has suggested, probably limited in number. It is likely the organic interferences that lead so many people—including many in societies like the United States in which there is a significant popular culture of psychology—to present emotional disorders somatically. It is also these interferences that have made possible the development of effective treatments of emotional disorders with psychotropic drugs (which, it should be added, also constitute organic interferences). To accept that mood shifts are associated with organic processes does not imply, however, that the "psychic life"—to use the language of DSM-III—can be reconstrued in exclusively biological terms. While some moods can be traced to organic factors, most can not.

Moods do not simply impress themselves on biological organisms as, in a basic sense, it can be said that a viral or carcinogenic agent does. To make sense of moods requires that we view the human as having more than a biological character. To put this in another way, there is some "I" for whom moods "settle and lift," "suffuse and evaporate." Shweder (chap. 6) argues that this "I" can best be conceived if we accept that each human possesses a ''soul'' that is as ''real'' as is the material body. While I find Shweder's proposal intriguing, I do not think that his notion of ''soul'' is adequate for a theory of moods. The soul as he conceives it is too passive, too unchanging; it also presupposes a rather old-fashioned dualism.

Instead of associating the ''I'' with ''soul,'' I prefer to think of it in terms of ''mind.'' I take my lead here from the formulation of the notion of *citta*, usually translated as ''mind,'' in Theravāda Buddhist thought. According to Johansson (1970), citta is posited in Buddhist thought as being ''the core of personality, the center of purposiveness, activity, continuity, and emotionality. It is not a soul (*attā*), but it is the *empirical, functional self*. It is mainly conscious contents and processes. On the contrary, it includes all the layers of consciousness, even the unconscious; by it the continuity and identity are safeguarded'' (p. 23, emphasis in original).[2]

While mind depends on the functioning of the brain, it emerges only as the world of actual experience is engaged and made meaningful. As Geertz (1973:76), who takes his lead from Ryle (1949), has written: ''the human brain is thoroughly dependent upon cultural resources for its very operation; and those resources are, consequently, not adjuncts to, but constituents of mental activity.''[3] Unlike the notion of soul with its implication, at least given the Judeo-Christian connotations it typically carries, of an unchanging essence of self, mind is a self that is ever-changing as a consequence of the new meanings acquired from the social world and made the basis for acting in that world. While mind entails meaningful reflection on the social world (cf. Mead 1962:308), such reflection is not necessarily at the level of conscious awareness; mind subsumes not only consciousness but also the products of reflexivity that are embedded in the unconscious. True awareness—''mindfulness'' (*Pāli*, *sati*) in the Buddhist sense—emerges from a process such as Buddhist ''meditation'' or psychological ''analysis'' whereby one gains insight (to use the Buddhist notion) into one's unconscious.

As a generalized attribute of human nature, mind is that faculty which leads every person to confront experience as more than bodily sensation. Mind impels each human to impute, if not to find, meaning in experience, although it is important to stress that such meaning need not necessarily be consciously sought or consciously held. Moods, then, can be said to be not only a feeling in the sense of bodily sensation but also an apperception of the mind entailing meaning. Geertz has distinguished between the mode of meaningfulness associated with moods and the mode associated with motivation, another way in which the mind orients the person toward experience: "motivations are 'made meaningful' with reference to the ends toward which they are conceived to conduce, whereas moods are 'made meaningful' with reference to the conditions from which they are conceived to spring" (1973:97). While Geertz's formulation must be modified to eliminate the implication that such "making meaningful" involves a conscious process on the part of the actor who is in a particular mood, it does serve well to orient us to the problem of etiology of moods.

Moods—or, rather, those moods which do not have a clear organic source (i.e., what DSM-III classifies as "organic mental disorders")—are the product of a communicational process (cf. Ruesch and Bateson 1968) between the meaning-seeking self and significant others in the world—the domain of social relations—in which this self assumes a social persona. As Brown and Harris (1978:247) have written: "it is in the perception of oneself successfully performing a role that inner and outer worlds meet, and internal and external resources come together." Through experiences in the lived-in-world, the "world of daily life" (Schutz 1970, esp. chap. 2), the individual is enabled to bring "himself, as an objective whole, within his own experiential purview; and thus he can consciously integrate and unify the various aspects of his self, to form a single consistent and coherent and organized personality" (Mead 1934:309n). This coherence of personality, it should be noted, is never assured but is always contingent on the individual having a "stock of knowledge," to use Schutz's term, with which he can make sense of a world that is often changing. Coherence of personality is not dependent on an individual having imposed coherence on his or her stock of knowledge. Indeed, "the knowledge of the man who acts and thinks within the world of his daily life is not homogeneous; it is (1) incoherent, (2) only partially clear, and (3) not at all free from contradictions" (Schutz 1970:75). What people require of their stock of knowledge derived from diverse cultural sources is that it serves them in making *practical*, not theoretical, sense of the world. This point is worth stressing given some tendency among those who have employed Kleinman's notion of "explanatory models" of sickness (see Kleinman 1980:104ff.) to reify and overrationalize the practical meanings employed by those who are ill and those who treat the sick.

The experiences that give rise to moods are those from which the individual acquires, often unconsciously, significant (to the individual) practical meaning about the self as an actor within a world. Often moods are but a brief duration, lasting no longer than the length of an encounter. More rarely, a mood becomes prolonged and shapes the way in which the individual acts in many different types of relationships; a truly powerful mood becomes totalistic, coloring the way in which the self is presented to the world in general. Such prolonged moods invariably entail feelings that are as much physical as mental; as a consequence, individuals often display their moods with reference to somatic indexes. Prolonged moods point to experiences whose practical meanings have stimulated some radical rethinking about the self within the world. Depression, as we assumed at the outset of this discussion, is one such prolonged mood.

Brown and Harris, in their important study *The Social Origin of Depression*, have developed a theory of depression that seeks, following a line of thought parallel to the one I have pursued here, the sources of depression in the meaningful relationship between self and the world. "While we do not rule out that at times physical factors may be largely responsible for clinical depression," they write, "we believe that in most instances a cognitive appraisal of one's world is primary—and it is from this that the characteristic bodily and psychological symptoms of depression arise" (Brown and Harris 1978:235). Since Freud, many have considered the loss of a significant love-object to be the major factor in provoking depression. Brown and Harris agree that loss is relevant. They maintain, however, that it is not the loss of a love-object but the "loss of important sources of value" that conduces to depression (ibid., p. 244). Even such loss will not cause depression if there is "awareness of new possibilities and an underlying sense of hope" (ibid., p. 238). Rather, it is when a loss of value stimulates an appraisal of one's place in the world as being profoundly hopeless that prolonged and clinically recognizable depression is likely to ensue (cf. Becker 1973:210–217).

Given this stance, it would seem likely that the death of a significant other might well be a catalyst for the emergence of a depressive mood in a person. Freud, who took up this hypothesis in his paper "Mourning and Melancholia" ([1917] 1957:124–140), considered there to be a major difference between grief, the mood characteristic of one deeply affected by the death of another, and melancholia (i.e., depression): "the melancholic displays something else which is lacking in grief—an extraordinary fall in his self-esteem, an impoverishment of his ego on a grand scale" (ibid., p. 127). Why does not this fall in self-esteem, which I here equate with Brown and Harris's "loss of important sources of value," occur among the grieving? Freud maintains it is because the bereaved comes to accept, through the "work of mourning," that the love-object no longer exists. I suggest that this work of mourning is actually—to adopt a notion Obeyesekere (chap. 4) has formulated with reference to Ricoeur's reading of Freud—a "work of culture." Obeyesekere speaks of the work of culture as "the process whereby painful motives and affects such as those occurring in depression are transformed into publicly accepted sets of meanings and symbols." This process entails, as Ricoeur has said, the substitution of a text for inchoate inner feelings.

> This notion of text—thus freed from the notion of scripture or writing—is of considerable interest. Freud often makes use of it, particularly when he compares the work of analysis to translating from one language to another; the dream account is an unintelligible text for which the analyst substitutes a more intelligible text. To understand is to make this substitution. (Ricoeur 1970:25)

In traditional societies, the grief experienced at the death of a significant other is worked through by means of a cultural process whereby a standardized set of texts—funerary rituals and memorial rites—literally "make meaning" of the loss. It is important to note in this connection the difference between these traditional religious texts and the texts employed by psychoanalysts, a difference that provides the central tension in Ricoeur's work on Freud. The meaning generated in the substitution of the psychoanalytic text, and of most psychotherapeutic texts, is an "archaeology" of meaning, the "primordial" meaning of the unconscious made conscious. The meaning opened up by religious texts is a "spiritual" meaning, a "teleology," a "revelation of the sacred" (Ricoeur 1970, esp. pp. 459ff.). The most effective work of culture, Ricoeur goes on to argue, is one that moves dialectically between these two types of meaning. The Cuna shaman who is able to effect a cure by providing a "sick woman with a *language*" that oscillates "between mythical and physiological themes" (Lévi-Strauss 1967:188, 193) and the Ndembu healer who treats the afflicted by "making hidden and secret things visible and thereby accessible, if harmful, to regressive and remedial action" (Turner 1963:303) that entails drawing on religious ideas clearly act in ways understandable in terms of the argument made by Ricoeur. So, too, do the cultural processes that in most traditional societies provide the meanings whereby the bereaved can undertake the work of mourning with reference to ideas of immortality (see Keyes n.d. for further development of this idea).

The awareness of death, which is certainly one of the most distinctive aspects of being human, the grief that is experienced as a consequence of being aware of the loss of a significant other, and the work of culture that serves to move one away from this sense of loss and from the attendant grief toward a state in which the self acquires value in a world without the deceased serves, I believe, as a paradigm for recognizing depression and for the course of action that serves to dispel it. While grief usually does not lead to depression, there are occasions when "particularly intense mourning reactions . . . lead to a generalization of the hopelessness that follows the loss" (Brown and Harris 1978:245) and thus to clinically recognizable depression. It is in this connection that I will consider a case drawn from my ethnographic researches in northeastern Thailand.[4]

DEPRESSION IN A THAI-LAO VILLAGER

Among the Buddhist Thai-Lao[5] villagers of northeastern Thailand, displays of mood of any type typically are of short duration. As Buddhists, villagers consciously seek to eliminate the "impurities" of the mind, a value that is usually expressed in village terms with reference to the ideal of maintaining a "cool heart" (*cai yen*). During the period totaling nearly two years when I lived among the Thai-Lao, carrying out ethnographic research in the village of Ban Nǫng Tụn in Mahasarakham Province,[6] I was impressed by the degree to which there seemed to be far less public expression of moods than I was aware of among the Americans with whom I normally lived. In particular, I was struck by the subdued displays of grief. While relatives did grieve, especially following the death of an adult who died unexpectedly, I can recall only one case where observable grief was prolonged beyond a week or so. This was the case of Mrs. K. She was 27 years old in January 1973 when her mother, her younger brother, and three other villagers were killed in a truck accident. The tragedy was compounded by the fact that the truck was owned by her husband, although he was not the driver at the time of the accident. Even more tragic, the truck was carrying a large number of villagers to another community in a distant province where Mrs. K.'s younger brother was to get married. The news of this accident reached my wife and me in Chiang Mai in northern Thailand where we were then living. We were deeply upset. We had lived with the K.s in 1963−64 when we were carrying out anthropological research in Ban Nǫng Tụn. Mother S., Mrs. K.'s mother, had been very close to us, and had been our mentor in traditional village ways.

In May 1973 I was able to travel to Ban Nọng Tụn. Mrs. K. was still very distraught, although Mr. K. had begun to regain his usual cheerfulness (this despite agreeing to pay indemnity to the families of the three other villagers who had died). While prolonged grief is not usual among Thai-Lao villagers, no one was surprised that Mrs. K. was still deeply upset by the tragedy. Mr. K. thought, however, that her interest in their children (four girls and one boy, then between two and nine years old) as well as her involvement in their business (a shop and rice mill) and in village affairs would soon reclaim her attention and lead her to feel less pain at the loss.

In July 1973 my wife Jane, our two children, and I made an unexpected brief visit to Ban Nọng Tụn. We made our way to the K.s' house where we were to stay. Scarcely had we arrived when Mrs. K. broke into tears and withdrew. Mr. K. explained that, far from experiencing a lessening of grief, she seemed to be even more upset, showing little interest in anything. We could see that she had lost weight since our visit two months earlier. That evening Mrs. K. told Jane that the night before we had arrived she had had a dream in which her mother appeared and told her that the two Westerners, that is, ourselves, were coming (we had not announced our visit in advance). Mrs. K. said her mother seemed so real that she had reached out to touch her.

Mr. K. and other relatives of Mrs. K. did evince concern about the unusually prolonged grieving on the part of Mrs. K., although no one seemed to feel it would be a good thing to seek help for her. We were sorry we could spend only a day in the village, but Mr. K. later told us he thought our visit had cheered her some. We saw Mr. K. again in April 1974, by which time he said that Mrs. K. had almost recovered. It was not until August 1979 that I was to see Mrs. K. again. By that time she was able to talk about her mother without giving way to any grief and had quite obviously long since "recovered" from her grief depression.

At one level, it would not seem surprising that Mrs. K. should experience such a prolonged depression after the tragic truck accident. Yet, her depressed mood, especially in July 1973, was unlike any I had witnessed among other villagers, despite the fact that several also had to cope with the sudden death of someone very close to them. Thus, I believe other factors were also involved.

Mrs. K. was born in Ban Nọng Tụn in 1946, the second of six children and the oldest daughter. Like her fellow villagers, she had four years of primary education at the local village school. Until after her marriage she essentially knew no world other than the village; she had been to a town—one about 40 kilometers away—only once in her youth. When she was ten her father died, leaving her mother with six very young children. From that point on, she assumed considerable responsibility for helping her mother, not only in looking after the younger children but also in farming the small holding the family owned. When we later came to know both Mrs. K. and her mother, we recognized that a closer relationship obtained between them than between Mother S. and any of her other children.

This relationship persisted even after Mrs. K.'s marriage. Mr. K. came to Ban Nọng Tụn (he was from a nearby village) in 1962 to establish a diesel-run rice mill purchased with some money saved from six years of work in Bangkok. He bought a small plot of land from Mother S. to use for his mill and also set up a small shop on this land. He then employed Mother S.'s eldest daughter to help him. Within a few months the relationship had been transformed into a marriage without the benefit of a wedding, a not uncommon custom for less wealthy villagers. After the marriage, Mr. K. assumed the traditional responsibilities of a Thai-Lao son-in-law, helping his mother-in-law and her family in working their holding as well as running (with his wife's help) his own business.

While Mrs. K.'s world was changed by her marriage, her mother continued to be, I believe, the most significant other in her life. Early in their marriage (as my wife and I knew since we shared a house with them), there were a number of quarrels and disputes between Mr. and Mrs. K., but they soon developed a close working relationship (one that continues to the present). The difference in their ages—Mr. K. is nine years older than his wife—together with the fact that Mr. K. assumed some of the responsibilities that would have been filled by Mrs. K.'s father had he been alive (e.g., he took charge of the first plowing of the family's holding and arranged for the building of a new house for Mrs. S.) contributed to a degree of distance between the two. In many senses, Mrs. K.'s wifely duties continued to be an extension of the role she had carried out relative to her mother since her father's death.

At the time of the tragedy, Mrs. K.'s children were still too young to have led her to reorient her world to them as significant persons in their own right; indeed, her mother was helping her to raise these children so that she could also run the shop and assist her husband in the rice mill. The sudden death of Mother S. meant more to Mrs. K., I believe, than just the loss of one significant other among several in her world. For Mrs. K., her place in the world, her sense of self, was defined primarily with reference to her relationship to her mother. The death of her mother produced, I suggest, a marked loss in her self-esteem, contributing (as we would expect following Freud) to a depressed mood rather than normal grief worked through in mourning. If the death had been what villagers considered to be an "ordinary death," she probably could have anticipated this loss to some degree. Moreover, she would have had the normal funerary rites to perform, rites that would have helped through the "work of culture" to construct a place for herself in a world without her mother. But her mother—and her brother—suffered what in the village is called a *hūng* death (*tāi hūng*; in Thai, *tāi hōng*). A hūng death is a sudden, unexpected, and often violent death. Those who die hūng are not cremated as are those who die ordinary deaths; their corpses are buried, and left in graves for several months or years before being disinterred and given proper rites of cremation. Mother S.'s death, as well as the deaths of the other villagers in the truck accident, were discussed at length by villagers as being hūng deaths.

According to the cultural tradition of the Thai-Lao (as in the tradition of all Thai-speaking peoples), the spirit of one who dies a hūng death becomes a troubled ghost (*phī hūng*) that continues to intrude itself in the lives of the living because it is not yet ready for rebirth. Although I never heard Mrs. K. speak of her dead mother as a phī hūng, the dream related to my wife (I suspect that this dream was one of many similar dreams) provided evidence of the troubled state of her mother's spirit.

I had no opportunity to return to Ban Nọng Tụn until 1979, and so had no opportunity to follow the course of events that had finally led Mrs. K. to come to terms with her mother's death. I was, nonetheless, able to reconstruct something of that process. One of the first things that was pointed out to me on my return to the village was the large bell tower that had been erected in the grounds of the village Buddhist temple-monastery. The tower, which had cost the equivalent of at least $1,000 (a very large sum by village standards) and had been built by a highly skilled traditional craftsman brought to the village from another province, was dedicated to the memory of Mother S. The costs of the tower as well as of the rituals that had been sponsored in conjunction with it had been paid entirely by Mr. and Mrs. K. Some four years after the accident, I was told, the K.'s and others sponsored rites at which the disinterred remains of the victims were cremated. It was in conjunction with these rites that the tower was also dedicated. According to village belief, these rites were presumed to have ensured that the souls of the deceased could now progress to a new incarnation and would be troubled no longer. While I cannot say that the public meanings of the rites were reflected in

Mrs. K.'s own thought at the time when the rites were performed, they certainly were expressed by her when we next met in July 1979.

What was even more obvious to me in 1979, and again in 1980 when I spent six weeks in Ban Nọng Tụn living with the K.'s, was that Mrs. K. was literally a changed person. Rather than playing a support role within a world in which for her Mother S. was the most significant other, she had come to assume a much more autonomous and independent role. I was struck by the fact that she often went off to town by herself to purchase goods for the (now much larger) shop she and Mr. K. ran. She also had assumed considerable responsibility for the business affairs of the family enterprise (including a now quite large rice mill as well as other activities), especially since Mr. K. had developed heart problems. From her children's perspective, Mrs. K. would be viewed unquestionably as a strong person. Mrs. K. had replaced her own mother as the pivotal person within her world.

ILLNESS, SUFFERING, AND THEIR INTERPRETATIONS

If it is accepted, as I have argued earlier, that the predispositions that conduce to what would be diagnosed by Western psychiatrists as depression are inherent in the human condition, then it must follow that from time to time in every society there are those who experience the pain that comes from a "profound sense of hopelessness" stimulated typically by a significant "loss of important sources of value." This experience of pain may not, however, entail a person seeing himself and being seen by others as being ill. Illness is only one possible *perspective* that might be adopted by a person who has been jarred out of his or her normal stance toward the world by the marked shift in mood that is associated with an irrevocable loss.

As self-conscious beings, humans are "endowed with the capacity and the will to take a deliberate attitude towards the world and to lend it *significance*" (Weber 1949:81; emphasis in original). This attitude or stance, as in Schutz (1970), or perspective, as in Geertz (1973),[7] is ordinarily one of common sense, that is, it is adopted with reference to the "reality of our everyday life," the "paramount reality" (Schutz 1970:253, and pp. 72ff. and 320 under "life-world"; Geertz 1973:111, 119–120; Geertz 1975). One acts with a commonsense perspective unless one has been "shocked" (Schutz 1970:254–255) in some way that leads one to break with it. In making a break, there is a shift to a different mode of consciousness, of awareness of self, and an associated necessity to make sense of the world in a way other than simply taking it for granted as one does when adopting a commonsense perspective.

The experience of pain may lead one to make such a break with the commonsense perspective on the world. The symptoms of pain serve as the impetus for a discourse carried out with others—a discourse that may lead to the conclusion that the individual is in a state of "un-health," that is, a state in which one's well-being can no longer be taken for granted, as it would if one were acting in a commonsensical way. If such a conclusion is reached, the individual may then see himself or herself and be seen by others as being ill. An illness perspective has thus been adopted.

It is important to note, however, that much experienced pain never leads to the adoption of an illness perspective. The shock of pain may be interpreted as being of no real consequence even though one may be "out of sorts" for a brief period. In contemporary America, for example, it is thought that colds are not serious and can be controlled (i.e., relegated to the background within one's normal existence) by medication. Similarly, in many societies, pains associated with an injury to a limb do not lead to the adoption of an illness perspective; rather, one's normal routine, or activity within everyday life, is only partially disrupted.

Even when one "becomes ill" there is a great reluctance to abandon completely the commonsense perspective. Whether or not an illness is all-consuming, leading one to single-minded attention to one's state of illness,[8] is a function in some instances of the severity of the pain and the concomitant physical incapacitation that a person experiences. But more important is whether the pain is viewed as signifying a real threat to one's ability to return to a normal life either because one might die or be permanently incapacitated. A single-minded awareness of oneself as ill may be forced on one if others determine that he or she is too ill to perform normal functions no matter how mild the actual sensation of pain may be. Indeed, a person in American society experiencing only minor discomfort may literally be shocked into a totalizing illness perspective by being told that he or she has cancer. Cancer-as-illness, it should be noted, is not the same as cancer-as-disease, even for oncologists; cancer-as-illness evokes a set of powerful images about one's self and one's relationships to others which may have little to do with the physical experience that has been diagnosed as cancer-as-disease (cf. Sontag 1979).

When illness assumes dominance in one's orientation toward the world, one abandons normal activity and assumes a distinctive role, the "sick role." This role, while differently construed in different societies, always entails a distinctive way of regarding one's self and of relating to others, of acting in the world. Being ill, in this total sense, one also adopts a characteristic time-perspective: time comes to be measured by the duration of the illness, by episodes of severity of pain, and by changes in the course of the affliction. The sick role persists until the ill person is pronounced well or at least well enough to resume some normal activities or until he or she dies.

An illness perspective is associated with a distinctive epoché, as Schutz uses this phenomenological concept: with illness, the taken-for-grantedness of everyday experience—or, at least, that aspect of everyday experience that pertains to oneself as a social person—is questioned. It is this questioning that leads the ill person or those close to the ill person to seek out a practitioner who can *make* sense of the illness, such making sense requiring the work of culture. This work consists in the first instance of situating the problem posed by illness within a framework—the text—wherein an interpretation (although not necessarily a "logical" explanation) can be offered. Such interpretation leads to the reconstruing of the illness as a disease. Once "diagnosed" as disease, the practitioner then offers a vision (in biomedicine, a "prognosis") of the world in which the individual no longer occupies the sick role. Finally, the practitioner "prescribes" a course of action (a "treatment") that will effect the restoration of the ill person to the everyday world, that is, to a world understood in terms of a commonsense perspective. In societies where there are different types of practitioners, there may be several different consultations, each associated with drawing on distinctive texts in the construction of the illness as disease, with a distinctive vision of the world as it will be when the ill person is restored to health, and a distinctive treatment that will lead to the realization of the vision.

As the distinction between "illness" and "disease" has assumed a fundamental importance in the medical anthropological literature, it is necessary, I believe, to indicate how my construal of this distinction differs from that of conventional usage. Most in the field adopt some version of the distinction enunciated by Kleinman in his *Patients and Healers*:

> The key axiom in medical anthropology is the dichotomy between two aspects of sickness: disease and illness. *Disease* refers to a malfunctioning of biological and/or psychological processes, while the term *illness* refers

to the psychosocial experience and meaning of perceived disease. (Kleinman 1980:72; emphasis in original)

Such a definition implies that the patient's "illness" constitutes "false consciousness" that can be dispelled only through a scientific analysis that results in the discovery of "disease," the *true* "malfunctioning of biological and/or psychological processes." As Hahn (n.d.) has shown in a recent critical review and reformulation of the illness/disease dichotomy, there is an error involved in this definition of disease, one that results in a confusing of "an account of the phenomenon with the phenomenon accounted for."

Kleinman himself has reformulated the distinction in a way that avoids this confusion:

> When we become sick we first experience *illness*: i.e., we perceive, label, communicate, interpret, and cope with symptoms, and we usually do this not alone but together with family members, friends, workmates, and other members of our social network. . . . When we visit medical professionals . . . the practitioner begins to construe the patient's problem as *disease*: i.e., he perceives, labels, interprets and treats it as a specific abnormality in his profession's nosological system. (Kleinman 1982: 53–54)

In this new formulation, "disease" no longer refers in some indexical way to a real "malfunctioning" but instead constitutes an *interpretation* of a displayed set of signs. "Depression," "neurasthenia," "soul loss," "spirit attack," and so on, must be seen, thus, as labels for some of the possible *texts* that might be used to interpret such signs. Such texts presuppose distinctive explanatory models, in Kleinman's terms, for what constitutes a disease. Disease models become salient, however, only when there has been a prior determination that a person is ill.

An illness perspective constitutes, at best, only a partial way of viewing the experience of pain and affliction. Even when an illness has been interpreted as a particular disease, the prescribed treatment may prove to be ineffectual and the affliction thus persists or leads to death. Even if an effective treatment can be found, any powerfully painful experience may still lead the afflicted person, or those for whom the affliction is also of concern, to bring to consciousness the question of why it is that humans must suffer. The break one makes from the commonsensical world when one becomes aware, as every person does at different points in his or her life, that one is a being who cannot escape suffering through means at the disposal of mere mortals, typically leads one to turn toward a mode of practical understanding quite different from that which serves to restore him or her to health. Such a mode of understanding comes from adopting a religious perspective on the world. This perspective, drawn from distinctive texts and often communicated through rituals, serves to situate problems of suffering within a cosmic framework and to orient those who know suffering toward a course of action that conduces not to the control but to the transcendence of suffering.

In many societies illness and suffering are not clearly distinguished as perspectives and even where they are, illness is rarely posited as being "mental." Thus, in perhaps the prototypical experience that stimulates the predispositions to depression, grief following the death of the other, the pain is seen, either implicitly or explicitly, as suffering and is worked through in a process constituted by religious rites. As Freud recognized, the fact that grief rarely results in a radical devaluation of self-esteem is a consequence not of some mysterious innate ability to generate the work of mourning but because funerary and memorial rites serve to create for the living an image of the deceased as one transformed into an immortal and to re-create the world of living such that all those who remain, and especially the grief-stricken, are accorded social identities that no longer depend on relationships with the deceased. This is what happened, although the process took longer than usual, in the case of the grief-stricken Thai-Lao woman, Mrs. K., whose case I presented above.

Mrs. K.'s abnormal grief led her husband, others, and probably herself to see her as being "not well" (*bǫ sabai*), but her unwellness was not interpreted as being a disease (*lōk*; Thai: *rōk*) that required treatment by a "medical" specialist.[9] The appropriate texts for interpreting the pain of grief were ones that incorporated the Buddhist message that the underlying character of human experience is "suffering" (dukkha). In traditional communities in Thailand, such as the village in which Mrs. K. lives, funerary rites appear to suffice—at least eventually—to establish a cosmic reality, one based on *kamma* (Sanskrit: *karma*), in which existential suffering can be accepted (see Anusaranaśāsanākiarti and Keyes 1980). And even modern urbanites in Thailand often continue to "view their illness in a larger cosmological Buddhist context of previous lives and the possible moral *cum* physical consequences of past actions on the present lives (*kam/karma*)" (Tambiah 1977:102).[10]

Some societies have evolved highly distinctive cultural means for making sense of moods emerging from significant loss. Among the Ilongot of northern Luzon, as Rosaldo has shown in her superb study,

Knowledge and Passion, head-hunting has long served as one culturally
sanctioned means for confronting grief: "When asked why they go
killing, Ilongots occasionally mention grief and the 'bad feelings'
(*'uget*) which, born of the loss of kinsmen, are felt as weights and
burdens until one 'reaches' the dumb body of a victim, slashes it, and
tosses off its head" (M. Rosaldo 1980:138–139; see also R. Rosaldo
1984). In a somewhat similar fashion, the Kaluli of Papua New Guinea
organize attacks against witches (*sei*) who are believed to be the cause of
all deaths:

> For us, a person dies, and there is no way to resolve or make up his loss. For
> the Kaluli, there is the *sei*. So devastating an event as death cannot be
> fortuitous; it must have a cause or it is unintelligible because there is no way
> to react. One's grief is only helplessness; there is no object for one's anger,
> no source of resolution or compensation for one's feelings. . . . From this
> perspective, the *sei* is not so much a belief (for the Kaluli it is an experience)
> as a requirement for making cognitive and emotional sense out of a
> situation so that it can be brought to meaningful closure. (Schieffelin
> 1976:147)

The resolution sought is the life of the sei determined to be responsible
for the death of the person for whom one grieves. In a sense, head-
hunting and killing of witches represent the ultimate form of
transference.

Western medical practice is perhaps unique in its effort to interpret
illness without reference to the problem of suffering. "Depression" thus
is to be understood as a distinctive Western medical interpretation of
certain mood shifts; it is the product of a process whereby what is taken to
be a mental illness is reconstituted as a disease. While this process has
led to reasonably effective therapy, one is left with a question as to
whether medical treatment for depression has been turned to less because
of its proven efficacy than because of the disappearance of more traditional works of culture that have served at least as well as either
preventive or redressive treatments. One also wonders if modern medical treatments for depression, even those that emphasize logotherapy
rather than administration of medication, are unduly restrictive in considering only the problem of illness without also recognizing the underlying problem of suffering. The afflictions that in biomedical terms are
classed as "mental illness" are ones that among most peoples, including, I believe, most in Western societies, often lead to a search for
practical meaning that cannot be obtained from those steeped in medical
texts alone. At the very least, it would seem important for those who treat

''depression'' within a Western medical context to be aware of the value of religious works of culture for those who have experienced a radical drop in self-value following the irrevocable loss of a significant other.

NOTES

1. I searched through a number of texts and basic works in the field of psychological anthropology and the related field of culture and personality and did not find one that includes ''mood'' in the index. It would appear moods are considered unproblematic by anthropologists, or at least they have been until quite recently for a number of papers in this volume bespeak a change.

2. The classical formulation of the Therāvadin notion of ''mind'' is to be found in the *Vissudhimagga*, ''the path of purification,'' by the fifth-century theologian Buddhaghosa (1976:506ff.). See, for example, pp. xiv, 81ff. I draw here on Buddhist thought primarily because of my own research experience in a Buddhist society, namely, that of Thailand. I also believe that Buddhist thought can serve to deepen the understanding of some issues entailed in the discourse on the relationship between culture and mental health.

3. While I accept the Geertzian and thus Rylean position that mind is constituted through meaningful action, I am aware that the Rylean position is being rethought in philosophy in light of reflection on work that proceeds from a theory that sees mental states as functional states (see Dennet 1978).

4. While it should be obvious, it is worth emphasizing that the case I will present is an ethnographic, not a clinical, one. While my case report lacks the concrete detail on the ''psychic life'' of Mrs. K. that a clinical report would contain because of the elicitation process employed (I would, for example, have liked to have had far more information about Mrs. K.'s dreams), it draws on a much more detailed knowledge of her social world than would typically have been acquired by a clinician. Moreover, I have also had the opportunity to follow Mrs. K.'s life over a much, much longer period than would most clinicians follow the life of any one patient.

5. I use the term ''Thai-Lao'' as a label for the ethnic group to which most people in northeastern Thailand belong because they are culturally Lao (and recognize themselves as such), but who have long since adapted themselves to Thai national culture. They call themselves either Lao, Khon Isan (northeasterner), or Khon Phɥn Mɥang (local people).

6. I began my research in northesthern Thailand in December 1962 and completed my initial fieldwork in April 1964. I made return visits to the Northeast in 1967–1968, 1972–1974, 1979, and 1980, most of these visits being concentrated in Ban Nɔng Tɥn.

7. The term ''attitude'' is used by Schutz (1970; see p. 316 for a definition), but is rejected in favor of ''perspective'' by Geertz (1973:110n.), who avoids it

"because of its strong subjectivist connotations, its tendency to place the stress upon a supposed inner state of the actor rather than on a certain sort of relation—a symbolically oriented one—between an actor and a situation." While agreeing with Geertz that a perspective arises primarily as a consequence of "a certain sort of relation," I would also like to retain the Schutzian notion that an attitude is "characterized by a specific tension of consciousness" (Schutz 1970:253). Geertz goes too far, I believe, in his effort to root out subjectivism. Thus, while I employ the Geertzian term "perspective," it should be understood that it incorporates Schutz's formulation.

8. Sartre (1948:80) has captured this sense of totalizing when he writes: "There is, in effect, a world of emotion. . . . It is necessary to speak of a world of emotions as one speaks of a world of dreams or worlds of madness, that is, a world of individual syntheses maintaining connections among themselves and possessing qualities."

9. If she had sought out a specialist, it would not have been a psychiatrist (*nak cittawētwitthayā*). There are extremely few psychiatrists up-country in Thailand and this medical specialty was totally unknown to villagers. In 1976, according to Brummelhuis (1980:60), there was a total of 103 psychiatrists in Thailand, 81 of whom practiced in the greater Bangkok metropolitan area.

10. Irvine in his extremely detailed and insightful dissertation has argued that Western-trained psychiatrists continue to use " 'scientific language' to equate mental health with adherence to 'Buddhist' values, and to define monks as local promoters of the means of health" (Irvine n.d.:92; also see Brummelhuis 1980). Irvine is very critical of this continued legitimation of Buddhist values by modern psychiatry because he argues that it contributes to the imposition of a conservative system of political domination on the underclasses of Thai society. I believe that his argument, which seeks to reduce Buddhist ideology to false consciousness, misrepresents the role of Buddhist ideology in Thailand. Buddhist values have been linked to revolutionary as well as conservative political ends. More important for our concerns here, the continued salience of Buddhist ideas for the interpretation and treatment of mental illness serves to provide a means whereby modern Thai can confront not only problems of illness but also problems of suffering. Moreover, neither of these problems can be dissolved by invoking a false consciousness argument.

REFERENCES

American Psychiatric Association
  1980   Diagnostic and Statistical Manual of Mental Disorders. 3d ed.
                Washington, D.C.: American Psychiatric Association.
Anusaraṇaśāśanākiarti, P. K., and C. F. Keyes
  1980   Funerary Rites and the Buddhist Meaning of Death: An Inte-

pretative Text from Northern Thailand. Journal of the Siam
Society 69(1):1−28.

Becker, E.
1973   The Denial of Death. New York: The Free Press.

Borst, C. V., ed.
1970   The Mind/Brain Identity Theory. New York: St. Martin's
              Press.

Bourdieu, P.
1977   Outline of a Theory of Practice. Richard Nice, trans. Cam-
              bridge: Cambridge University Press.

Brown, G. W., and T. Harris
1978   The Social Origins of Depression: A Study of Psychiatric Dis-
              order in Women. New York: Free Press.

Brummelhuis, H.
1980   Psychiatry in Thailand: A Sociologist's View. Journal of the
              Siam Society 68(2):57−69.

Buddhaghosa, B.
1976   The Path of Purification. Bhikkhu Nyāṇamoli, trans. Berkeley:
              Shambhala.

Dennet, D. C.
1978   Current Issues in the Philosophy of Mind. American Philo-
              sophical Quarterly 15(4):240−261.

Freud, S.
[1917]   Mourning and Melancholia. *In* A General Selection from the
1957   Works of Sigmund Freud. John Rickman, ed. Garden City,
              N.Y.: Doubleday/Anchor. Pp. 124−140.

Geertz, C.
1973   The Interpretation of Cultures. New York: Basic Books.
1975   Common Sense as a Cultural System. The Antioch Review
              33(1):5−52.

Hahn, R. A.
n.d.   Rethinking 'Illness' and 'Disease'. *In* South Asian Systems of
              Healing. E. Valentine Daniel and Judy Pugh, eds. Contribu-
              tions to Asian Studies.

Irvine, W.
n.d.   The Thai-Yuan 'Madman', and the Modernising, Developing
              Thai Nation, as Bounded Entities under Threat: A Study in the
              Replication of a Single Image. Ph.D. diss. University of Lon-
              don, 1982.

Johansson, R. E. A.
1970   The Psychology of Nirvana. Garden City, N.Y.: Doubleday/
              Anchor.

Keyes, C. F.
  n.d.   From Death to Rebirth: Ritual Process and Buddhist Meanings in Northern Thailand. Ms.

Kleinman, A.
  1980   Patients and Healers in the Context of Culture: An Exploration of the Borderland between Anthropology, Medicine, and Psychiatry. Berkeley, Los Angeles, London: University of California Press.
  1982   Neurasthenia and Depression: A Study of Somatization and Culture in China. Culture, Medicine, and Psychiatry 6: 117−190.

Lévi-Strauss, C.
  [1949]   The Effectiveness of Symbols. *In* Structural Anthropology.
  1967   Garden City, N.Y.: Doubleday/Anchor. Pp. 181−201.

Mead, G. H.
  [1934]   Mind, Self and Society: From the Standpoint of a Social
  1962   Behaviorist. Charles W. Morris, ed. Chicago: University of Chicago Press.

Place, U. T.
  1956   Is Consciousness a Brain Process? British Journal of Psychology 42:44−50.

Ricoeur, P.
  1970   Freud and Philosophy: An Essay on Interpretation. Denis Savage, trans. New Haven: Yale University Press.

Rosaldo, M. Z.
  1980   Knowledge and Passion: Ilongot Notions of Self and Social Life. Cambridge: Cambridge University Press.

Rosaldo, R.
  1984   Grief and the Headhunter's Rage: On the Cultural Force of Emotions. *In* Play, Text and Story. E. Bruner, ed. Washington, D.C.: American Ethnological Society. Pp. 178−195.

Ruesch, J., and G. Bateson
  [1951]   Communication: The Social Matrix of Psychiatry. New York:
  1968   W. W. Norton.

Ryle, G.
  1949   The Concept of the Mind. New York.

Sartre, J.-P.
  1948   The Emotions: Outline of a Theory. New York: Philosophical Library.

Schieffelin, E. L.
  1976   The Sorrow of the Lonely and the Burning of the Dancers. New York: St. Martin's Press.

Schneider, D. M.
  1976   Notes Toward a Theory of Culture. *In* Meaning in Anthro-
                pology. Keith H. Basso and Henry A. Selby, eds. Albuquer-
                que: University of New Mexico Press for the School of Ameri-
                can Research. Pp. 197–220.
Schutz, A.
  1970   On Phenomenology and Social Relations. Helmut R. Wagner,
                ed. Chicago: University of Chicago Press.
Smart, J. J. C.
  1959   Sensations and Brain Processes. The Philosophical Review
                68:141–156.
Sontag, S.
  1979   Illness as Metaphor. New York: Vintage Books.
Tambiah, S. J.
  1977   The Cosmological and Performative Significance of a Thai Cult
                of Healing through Meditation. Culture, Medicine, and Psy-
                chiatry 1:97–132.
Turner, V.
  [1964]   Lunda Medicine and the Treatment of Disease. *In* The Forest of
  1967   Symbols. Ithaca, N.Y.: Cornell University Press. Pp. 299–
                358.
Wallace, Anthony F. C.
  1972   Mental Illness, Biology and Culture. *In* Psychological Anthro-
                pology. Francis L. K. Hsu, ed. Pp. 363–402. Cambridge,
                Mass: Schenkman.
Weber, M.
  1949   'Objectivity' in Social Science and Social Policy. *In* The
                Methodology of the Social Sciences. Edward A. Shils and
                Henry A. Finch, trans. and eds. New York: Free Press.
                Pp. 50–112.

Depressive Cognition, Communication, and Behavior

INTRODUCTION TO PART II

Part II takes up the challenge to psychiatry and psychology presented by the chapters in the first section. Those chapters asked: How do we take cultural meaning, historical change, and social structure into account as a serious, indeed central, concern in studying the sources, experiences, and consequences of depressive emotion and disorder? What paradigms for psychocultural and biosocial interaction allow us to investigate depression as both disease and illness? What are alternative ways of configuring and researching depression as emotion which promote analysis of the interplay between the personal and social domains so central to human experience?

The chapters in this section proffer developmental, behavioral, and sociolinguistic responses to these questions. Shweder's overview of relevant findings from cross-cultural child development leads him to turn several well-established positions upside down. First, he argues that the development of an elaborated emotional life is a process of emotional *dedifferentiation*, that is, that infants have highly differentiated affective states that become less differentiated, though culturally specified, through socialization. Moreover, Shweder suggests that culture does not simply particularize; it also brings universal affective meanings to the constitution and expression of emotional experience. He proposes a schema of universal affective meanings articulated in all societies in three distinctive idioms: a language of causal responsibility, a language of mood metaphor, a language of physical consequences. This analytic grid, Shweder avers, will bring some order to the evaluation of comparative cross-cultural research and will help researchers sidestep a few of the more disastrous methodological pitfalls enumerated in preceding chapters. Shweder also sets out a provocative heuristic for what a more adequate phenomenology of the feeling state of depression needs to model. In cross-cultural perspective, soul loss is a much more common way of experiencing loss than is existential despair. Hence Shweder begins with a phenomenology of soul loss, then asks what this tells us about the depressive experience cross-culturally. Shweder's point is that professional phenomenologies are as grounded in "commonsense" cultural views as are popular phenomenologies. A less biased and more discriminating professional phenomenological account of depressive experience cross-culturally cannot begin with what is held to be normative in the West, but must result from a comparison of distinctive phenomenologies of depression in different societies and subcultural groups (e.g., existential despair, soul loss, somatic distress, possession states, particular religious states of suffering and transcendence, etc.) that then determines shared and particularistic aspects of depressive experience. This important exercise has yet to be undertaken. Whether or not the sadness and emptiness Shweder identifies as central to soul loss are valid descriptors of that experience in different societies and, more problematically, are central to the depressive experience cross-culturally, are questions for empirical research.

Shweder's heuristic purpose in all of this is to recast psychological methods so that they can become more anthropologically informed, while pressing anthropological studies to make use of the data base and methods of cross-cultural psychology. Using the universal affective significance of touching and the unique cultural connotation it takes on as menstrual pollution from a mother's or wife's touch among Oriya Brahmans, Shweder offers a model of what happens as depressive affect is transformed, through the social application of meaning, from psychological universal to culture-dependent emotion. This model is grounded in the interaction between psychological universals and culturally particular aspects of social life which comprises the core dialectic of human experience. Not the least of Shweder's achievements is to hold a looking glass up to contemporary understandings of depression by psychologists and psychiatrists which challenges the tendency to see clinical description as "atheoretical." Phenomenology (and, thereby, clinical and epidemiological accounts) to be valid must begin not with the biased reproduction of professional categories but with the emergent and exigent understandings of lay experience.

Beeman, an anthropological linguist, writes from a sociolinguistic concern with social communication. While agreeing that the body is a chief source of metaphors of the self in health and illness, Beeman shows that bodily metaphor is given distinctive social significance in different societies. He debunks the mischievous cross-cultural myth that Western languages are more developed because they discriminate among psychological states more explicitly and precisely. In the sociolinguistic model of depression, affect is a stylistic characteristic of speech: a rhetoric. Metacommunicational markers and change in grammar and lexicon signal emotion as a quality of complex social interaction. Depression, then, must be analyzed as discourse occurring in culturally marked communicative contexts, while the symptoms of depressive disease (which Beeman is hesitant to accept as a universal biological process) must be viewed as products of microsocial systems like families and work relationships. This model allows Beeman to explain how Beck's negative cognitive schema of depression are generated and maintained. Rhetorical analysis is also employed as a model to examine therapy for depression, especially cognitive therapy. Beeman regards cognitive therapy as the adroit reconceptualization of the depressed person's negative definitions of situations, self, and others, so as to remoralize the afflicted individual. The sociolinguistic paradigm leads to many new questions for cross-cultural research on the origins, form, and alteration of depressive disorder, seen now as principally a social psychological, rather than a psychobiological, event. Beeman's contribution is to unveil a mediating process between social and psychological worlds. Several of the chapters in Part IV engage the insights of this model, though none use the field methods of sociolinguistics. The questions Beeman voices about a sociolinguistic understanding of how depressive disorder is caused and cured await future interdisciplinary research efforts aimed at more precise determination of the mediating system.

In the final chapter of this section, Carr and Vitaliano change the direction of inquiry in a fundamental way. They, like Beeman and Obeyesekere, begin by challenging the view of depression as a universal psychobiological disease. In place of the view that biology provides a "final common pathway" for diverse social and psychological conditions, resulting in depressive illness, an argument advanced by many psychiatrists studying depression as a biological disorder, they argue that culture organizes a *final common ethnobehavioral pathway* that channels diverse social and biological conditions into culturally specific behavioral repertoires. Again in this section, a major research orientation to depression, in this case the dominant approach in contemporary psychiatry, is turned on its head.

Carr and Vitaliano see depressive symptoms (e.g., low self-esteem, hopelessness, anxiety, sadness) as complaints about nonspecific psychological distress, analogous to fever in biomedicine. They offer a distress model in place of a disease model, and review alternative psychological and psychiatric literature to rebut the former and sustain the latter. Carr and Vitaliano regard distress as a complex *biobehavioral* response, a response to antecedent stressors mediated by vulnerability and psychosocial resources. Because loss is the universal antecedent of depression, however, these psychologists hold that psychological universals are the chief determinants of depressive behavior. The universals are social learning processes, specified in the chapter, which the authors take to be fundamental to the human condition. These processes are essential to the causal system of depression since they predispose individuals facing aversive events to develop learned helplessness. In this cognitive behavioral interpretation of depression, past learning experiences, universal cognitive processes, and cultural norms interact to determine whether one's response to perceived aversive life event changes is violence, anxiety, or depression. This analysis complements and extends Beeman's but in an unexpected direction. It is surprising that heretofore neither anthropologists nor cross-cultural psychiatrists have drawn on this line of analysis in empirical studies. Carr and Vitaliano work hard to attract scholars to their approach by demonstrating it can be used to interpret culture-bound syndromes, and to recast depression as a culture-bound syndrome. The first chapter in Part III picks up this argument as a point of departure to show how psychiatric epidemiology can be conducted not as a reification of Western disease categories but as a description of particular and shared forms of psychological distress.

Thus Part II introduces readers to three distinctive ways of relating culture to depression: developmental, sociolinguistic, ethnobehavioral. These approaches cover some common ground but end up following distinctive paths. Each suggests ways that ethnographic, clinical, and epidemiological studies might be organized to better understand the causes and consequences of depressive disorder. Each offers a methodology for conducting comparative cross-cultural work. These chapters present some of the most innovative and powerful perspectives in this volume on how the actual study of affect and affective disorder in society might proceed in empirical research. Shweder's orienting questions outline an approach to the ethnography of emotions; it is remarkable that for no non-Western society do we have *both* an ethnographic analysis of emotional life *and* a detailed analysis of depressive illness. Linked to studies of human development, such an approach provides a frontier for research. Beeman's work suggests two potential directions for innovative studies. First, he describes the shared ground between cognitive psychiatry and anthropology. This borderland illustrates the importance of cross-cultural investigations to determine which of the "logical mistakes" central to the discourse and cognition of the depressed (as identified by Beck and his colleagues) are universal, which are specific to American culture, and whether alternative "mistakes" (pathologies of interpretation) may be characteristic of the culture-specific discourse of the depressed of other societies. Second, Beeman criticizes the failure of cognitive therapists to recognize the *interactive* context of discourse, and proposes a challenging approach to empirical research via forms of interaction (in families, with significant others) that may promote or maintain the logic and cognition of the depressed. Carr and Vitaliano's chapter also outlines a research program. They suggest the specific hypothesis that culture-bound syndromes of particular societies may provide alternative responses to situations that typically produce depression in Western societies.

These chapters are more sophisticated accounts than are usually found in their fields, we think, precisely because they begin with cross-disciplinary materials and end with a framework for interdisciplinary research. In contrast to the caution, hesitancy, and criticism expressed in the anthropological accounts in the first part of the book, which we see as an appropriate function for anthropology in cross-cultural research, Part II, which is in no sense uncritical, sparks the controversy and passionate partisanship of new approaches to the cross-cultural study of emotion and disorder. In the third and fourth sections some of the bloom wears off the flowers of theory in the heat of fieldwork, but the excitement of new approaches to old controversy persists and, as the reader can judge, is productive.

6

Menstrual Pollution, Soul Loss, and the Comparative Study of Emotions

Richard A. Shweder

There are three general questions in the comparative study of emotions: (1) What is an emotional life? (2) With respect to which aspects of emotional functioning are people alike or different? and (3) How are these likenesses and differences to be explained? While this essay is concerned with all three of these general questions, it is the second question that receives the most attention.

It is argued that to ask whether people are alike or different in their emotional functioning is really to pose several more specific questions, that is, whether people are alike or different in the type of feelings they feel (the taxonomic question), the situations that elicit those feelings (the ecological question), the perceived implications of those feelings (the semantic question), the vehicles for expressing those feelings (the communication question), the appropriateness of certain feelings being felt or displayed (the social regulation question), and the techniques or strategies utilized to deal with feelings that cannot be directly expressed (the management question).

The semantic approach is illustrated, with special attention to feelings of "depression." The symptoms associated with feelings of "emptiness" are given meaning by reference to the idea of "soul loss." Finally, some speculations are offered about the way cultural practices convey meanings that influence the ontogenetic development of emotional functioning. The discussion focuses on the development of feelings about touching, "untouchability," and pollution among Oriya Brahman children and adults in the old temple town of Bhubaneswar, Orissa, India.

ASPECTS OF EMOTIONAL FUNCTIONING

To speak of the emotional life is to talk about *felt* experiences. Three-year-olds, Ifaluk islanders, and psychoanalysts (in other words, almost everyone, except perhaps the staunchest of positivists) recognize that emotions are *feelings* (Lewis and Brooks 1978; Lewis and Michalson 1982; Lutz 1982). To understand the emotional life of a person is to understand the types of feelings (anger, envy, fear, depersonalization, shame, joy, love, homesickness, etc.) felt by a person, the distribution and frequency of those feelings across time and context, the kinds of situations that elicit those feelings, the wishes and fantasies that co-occur with those feelings, and the consequential action tendencies set off by those feelings.

Now, it is true that feelings cannot be seen; the only feelings we have direct experience of are our own feelings. I do not feel your feelings as you feel them and indeed I have no way to know for certain that you have feelings at all. I know that you move your face in complex ways, and change your posture and utter words like "pain" and "anger," but faces, postures, and words are not feelings—and it is the feelings that interest us, though they cannot be seen. For some, that fact marks the end of the study of emotions. Positivists, for example, committed to the "godforsaken" view that only what is perceivable is real, have forsaken the study of felt experiences and confined themselves instead to reportage of that which can be observed, facial movements, heartbeats, and hormone levels. Most of us, however, are willing to live with assumption, inference, and conjecture, for the study of facial movements, heartbeats, and hormone levels takes on interest only if they can be used to draw inferences about things that cannot be observed—namely, how other people actually feel.

Conjecture plays a large part in our understanding. Some of our most fundamental ideas—the idea that contiguity in time and space implies causation, the idea that objects continue to exist in the absence of an observer, the idea that what you see is what I see—are conjectures. It is a conjecture that other people have an emotional life and it is a conjecture that trees and plants do not. Without conjecture there could be no understanding, and there would hardly be any point to studying emotions if we were unwilling to conjecture that other people's feelings, while unseen, are nevertheless there.

There are several aspects to emotional functioning and many distinct but compatible questions one can ask about the emotional functioning of a person or people. Six aspects or questions are listed below.

1. There is the *taxonomic* question: What types of feelings do these people experience? The first step in any study of emotions is to document the range and types of feelings felt. Lexical studies can be quite misleading in such a taxonomic investigation, for there are documented cases (e.g., Robert Levy's Tahitians) of people who talk a lot about an emotion (e.g., anger) yet rarely experience it, or experience an emotion (e.g., guilt) yet have no word for it and rarely speak of it (Levy 1973:273−288, 1984; also see Beeman, chap. 7). A people's lexicon for emotions is a rather poor index of their emotional functioning.

It is a challenging fact about emotional functioning, a fact about which I shall have more to say later, that very young children display *situation-appropriate* facial expressions for a diverse set of discrete emotions. If you take a six-month-old child and hold a cookie just out of his reach or confine his arms to his sides, he will show you the face of anger. Not the face of pain or the face of distress, but the face of anger. The inference is nearly irresistible that by eighteen months of age, that is, prior to language learning, children experience and know the difference between anger, surprise, distress, interest, fear, and disgust. By the age of thirty months they experience jealousy, and by the time they are four years old they are quite competent at expressing through face, language, voice register, and posture a wide range of such emotions (Charlesworth and Kreutzer 1973; Cohn and Tronick 1983; Emde et al. 1976; Hiatt et al. 1979; Izard et al. 1980; La Barbera et al. 1976; Ochs 1982; Paradise et al. 1974; Sroufe 1979; Stenberg et al. 1983; Van Lieshout and Cornelis 1975).

It is also a fact about emotional functioning, and I shall return to this fact as well, that the type and range of emotions within the experiential repertoire of the young child are not necessarily the same as the types of emotions actually experienced by adults. Eskimo and Tahitian six-month-olds are probably capable of the experience of anger and may well experience anger more frequently than Eskimo and Tahitian adults (Briggs 1970; Levy 1973).

2. There is the *ecological* question: What are the emotion-laden situations for these people, and which emotions are elicited by which situations? The focus here is on the way situations are interpreted and experienced with one's feelings.

Obviously there are many culture-specific or person-specific elicitors. Not everyone finds the same situations emotion laden or feels them in the same way. Being offered help, being told what to do, being "mothered" elicits anger in some people, yet deference, respect, dependency, and gratitude in others. Being the center of attention elicits embarrassment and fear in some, yet self-satisfaction and pride in others. In matters of love and loss, the Samoans experience what has been called a "generalized nonchalance" where Americans feel agitated and distressed (Geertz 1959).

One should not, however, rule out the possibility that there are some universal elicitors. The more one looks at the emotional life of young children around the world the more it would seem that certain situations are emotion laden in the same way, at least in the first few years of life. Loss (e.g., your mother or caretaker disappears, leaving you with a stranger) is experienced as distress. Frustration (a cookie is kept from you just out of reach) or confinement (someone forcibly keeps you from lifting your arms) is experienced as anger. Unexpected events (a sudden sound or "pop!" goes the jack-in-the-box) is experienced as surprise. The "visual cliff" elicits fear (Campos et al. 1975; Hiatt et al. 1979). In the first few years of life certain events seem to get interpreted in similar ways and experienced or felt in the same way by almost everyone. There are probably fewer "universal elicitors" for adults than for young children, yet even with adults one should not rule out the possibility that certain ideas are widely shared and certain emotions widely experienced. For example, the idea of "natural law" or sacred obligations may be a universal idea, and so may be the experience of shame-guilt-terror associated with the transgression of sacred obligations. And, while "irreversible loss" may imply or suggest different things to different peoples, certain of those implications or suggestions do have a worldwide distribution. There is a common thread of meaning to "bereavement"; as Rosenblatt et al. (1976) discovered in an examination of mortuary rites in seventy-three societies, in all but one society "crying" is a featured mode of emotional display and expression at funerals. Bali is the notable, and ambiguous, exception.

3. There is the *semantic* question: What do the feelings imply? To study the meaning of emotions is not the same as identifying the lexical labels (happy, sad, angry) that are used to refer to emotions and, as noted earlier, such lexical study per se is relatively uninteresting and probably unrevealing. To study what something means is to study what it implies or suggests to those who understand it (Hirsch 1967, 1976; Solomon 1976, 1984). To say that the bed is "soft and lumpy" is to suggest that backs may ache on it. To say that the ball is "hard" is to imply that heads may be cracked by it.

Sometimes the meaning of something seems to be *in* the thing itself.

It's "square" implies "it won't roll." "She's your mother" seems to imply "she ought to care about your health." Sometimes the meaning of something seems to be more in our head than in the thing itself. He's your "father" does not *imply* "secretly he wants to mutilate or castrate you or remove you from the scene," but that's what it means to some people. When the ideas suggested by something are widely shared, those suggestions become *implications*. When the suggestions are not widely shared, they remain suggestions or "free" associations. Nevertheless, whether we study (what has been called) "meaning-in" or "meaning-to," things often carry with them implications, suggestions, and associations, and that is what the study of meaning is about.

Emotions have meanings and those meanings play a part in how we feel. What it means to feel angry, indeed what it feels like to feel angry, is not quite the same for the Ilongot, who believe that anger is so dangerous it can destroy society; for the Eskimo, who view anger as something that only children experience; and for working class Americans, who believe that anger helps you overcome fear and attain independence (Rosaldo 1980, 1984; Briggs 1970; Miller 1982).

Some emotions imply action tendencies. Surprise implies focus. Fear implies flight. Other emotions suggest certain wishes or fantasies. Anger suggests explosion, destruction, and revenge. Shame suggests exposure and banishment. Guilt suggests reparation, absolution, reintegration, and forgiveness. Sadness suggests withdrawal, self-criticism, loss, and the idea of being helped. These implications may or may not be universal. As in any study of ethnosemantics, some implications will be widely shared and others will not. Jealousy takes on a special meaning when you believe that illness and death are the result of the envy of others and that to wish someone ill is to practice witchcraft against them. Loyalty, respect, deference, and dependency do not have the same associations for autonomous, egalitarian Americans as they do for interdependent, hierarchical Indians. Shame does not have the same meaning for Americans, who tend to think they have a right to be let alone to do their own business and who have nearly reduced shame to embarrassment and blushing before the public eye, as it has for more tradition-bound folks, who believe that most of what they do is governed by natural law and who view with shame any action that discredits their standing in the natural order of things. The life of the emotions itself takes on a special meaning if you believe that emotions, *if unexpressed*, are dangerous and do not go away, or alternatively, if you believe that emotions, *if expressed*, are dangerous and do not go away.

4. There is the *communication* question: How are feelings expressed and what are the vehicles for the communication of an emotion?

There are many vehicles of emotional expression and communication—the face, voice register, body posture, words and sentences, and so on. Some expressive symbols we know how to read or interpret without much training or instruction. There is a common language (an "Esperanto") of the face, voice register, and body posture which is understood by nearly everyone, young and old, and I for one have little difficulty with the idea that there is "prior" knowledge of the code for reading *some* emotional expressions. Most three-year-olds can tell from certain common features of the voice, face, and body when someone is happy, sad, mad, or surprised; and even some of the metaphors for emotional expression ("down," "empty," "blue") may have a universal reading. D'Andrade and Egan (1974), for example, found that the colors associated with different emotions are very similar for Tzeltal-speaking Mayan Indians and English-speaking Americans. The way the visual experience of color is mapped onto, or used to express concepts of emotion (happy, worried, sad, frightened, angry), may not be all that variable either historically or cross-culturally. And even some of the notable, and often noted, exceptions to the rule (e.g., widows in India wear white, not black) may disguise a deeper similarity (e.g., the absence of gay hues or attractive colors). The association, for example, of red with anger and black (or white) with bereavement is no historical accident; the color-affect code is a code that very different kinds of peoples know how to translate and they translate it in a similar way.

Obviously, not all aspects of the code for communicating emotions involve "prior" knowledge. The language of deference and respect, for example, is highly developed in some cultures and there is simply no way to know the correct terms of address or reference without training or instruction. And not everyone bangs his head against the wall to express grief or knows what it symbolizes when someone else does it. And certainly some facial expressions are culture-specific and difficult to read without acquired knowledge of the code. For example, among the Oriya women with whom I have worked in Bhubaneswar, India, there is a facial expression of the following type: the tongue extends out and downward and is bitten between the teeth, the eyebrows rise and the eyes widen, bulge, and cross. It is the face of surprise-embarrassment-shame, a combination of feelings that might be felt by an American graduate student if she were to shout vulgar abuse at a passing motorist only to discover that the driver was her thesis advisor. That face of surprise-embarrassment-shame appears on pictorial representations of the Hindu goddess Kali. Tongue out, eyes bulging, she is shown stepping on the chest of her consort Shiva. From the Oriya point of view, the representation is often "misinterpreted" by Western observers, who tend to see in Kali's face ferocity and demonic rage instead of the shock and shame she conveys to Oriya observers. It is noteworthy, nevertheless, that even many of the culture-specific aspects of emotional communication codes seem to get learned rapidly and early in life. Ochs (n.d.), for example, has examined the diverse ways affect is encoded in the Samoan language (via special affect particles, pronouns, etc.). Her important finding is that "with the exception of respect vocabulary, the entire set of affect features is acquired by Samoan children before the age of three years and 10 months."

Language is a very powerful means of emotional expression and communication. Most ordinary language utterances tell you how to feel about the things being discussed (Searle 1979; Labov and Fanshel 1977; D'Andrade 1981, 1984; Much n.d.). Among the less emotive aspects of ordinary language are the terms for emotions. There is nothing particularly "hot" about such words as happy, sad, angry, or surprised. They are far less evocative than saying of someone's wife that she is "past her prime" or talking about "little things that squirm in the night," or simply uttering, " 'Twas brillig and the slithy toves did gyre and gimbel in the wabe." Nevertheless, despite variations in emotional intensity, there are very few ordinary language phrases that are without feeling tone, and even the most innocent descriptions ("she's my friend," "she's my mother," "she's my lover") tell you how to feel.

5. There is the *social regulation* question: What feelings or emotions is it appropriate or inappropriate for a person of this or that status to feel and/or display?

The having of certain feelings and the display of certain feelings are both subject to social regulation (Hochschild 1979). Social roles and role relationships, for example, carry with them a certain obligation to feel and/or express certain feelings and not others. One is not supposed to have sexual feelings toward blood relatives or express hatred toward a friend, and the emotions that get displayed have many implications for relationships. Respect is what inferiors express to superiors, not vice versa. Gratitude binds equals. Empathy links you to members of your own kind.

In thinking about the social regulation of emotions, it is useful to employ the often used metaphor of the "drama." To view life as a stage.

To view society as an arrangement of roles. To view social interactions as the enactment of role-based scripts. To view the communication of this or that feeling as quite distinct from the actual having of that feeling. The performance or spectacle we call "society" requires of its actors only the skillful, or at least competent, public display of appropriate feelings (e.g., empathy, seriousness, respect, loyalty), not the private experience of them. Consider, for example, the private experience of feelings of intimacy or closeness among various family members in Oriya Brahman households in the old town of Bhubaneswar, India. Informants were asked to rank the eight nuclear family dyads in terms of closeness or intimacy. As reported by married women and men, the most intimate relationship is between husband and wife. Next on the scale of intimacy or closeness come the four parent-child dyads (mother-son, father-daughter, father-son, mother-daughter); the relative ordering of these dyads varies by informant. The least intimate relationships are the three sibling dyads (sister-sister, brother-brother, brother-sister); again, the relative ordering of these three dyads varies by informant.

It is tempting, even if hazardous, to speculate that there might be a universal patterning of subjective feelings of intimacy across the eight nuclear family dyads such that in all societies there is an ordering of private feelings of intimacy: spouse > child > sibling. The ordering of those dyads by Oriya Brahmans is, after all, quite similar to orderings given by Americans despite the obvious and substantial differences between kinship and family in Orissa and America. At some very general level there may well be something about the marital bond, the filial bond, and the sororal-fraternal bond that organizes feelings of intimacy into a common pattern.

What is more relevant for the present discussion, however, is that in Oriya Brahman families the public display of intimacy is not coincidental with the private experience of intimacy. Indeed, among Oriya Brahmans the husband-wife relationship is scripted for mild avoidance. Spouses may not eat together. They do not address each other by name. They never touch or display affection to each other in public. They move through social life separately; women stay at home and do not, for example, go to the marketplace or even attend the ear-piercing ceremony of their sons. Husband and wife rarely present themselves or appear in public as a "couple."

An important implication is that choreographed displays of avoidance or aloofness of the type standardly reported in ethnographies (see Whiting and Whiting 1975 for a cross-cultural analysis of husband-wife aloofness and intimacy) are not necessarily revealing of the underlying private feelings of the actors, and it seems hazardous to interpret ritualized avoidance in terms of the psychodynamics of the actors. Oriya Brahman couples are far more likely to spend the night together in the same bed than to eat together. Bedding down together goes on in a realm defined as private, a realm where feelings of intimacy can be expressed. Eating goes on in a realm defined as public. The avoidance script applies—and there may be witnesses and gossip.

On stage, social actors communicate role-appropriate feelings; they do not necessarily experience those feelings, and they certainly do not convey everything they do feel. One suspects that if social actors did convey everything they actually felt, and only what they actually felt, the performance called "society," or at least the spectacle called "civilization," would be very difficult to mount. On stage, how you actually feel is far less relevant than how you act, far less important than the role appropriateness of the feelings conveyed by your actions. An Oriya Brahman feels "close" to his or her spouse but, in public, he or she cannot show it.

The problem of "avoidance," and its presumed opposite, the "joking" relationship, is a classic one in anthropology (Tylor 1889; Radcliffe-Brown 1940). Although there have been several noteworthy attempts at explanation and interpretation (Stephens and D'Andrade 1962; Driver 1966; Sweetser 1966; Witkowski 1972; LeVine 1984) the problem remains unsolved (for a brief overview on the limitations of current theory, see Levinson and Malone 1980:117–127). The area is rich with challenges.

For the most part, anthropologists have examined "avoidance" and "joking" in the context of kinship relationships. The more provocative findings (see Murdock 1971; Goody and Buckley 1974) can be summarized as follows. In most societies of the world (80–90 percent), the mother-in-law/son-in-law and father-in-law/daughter-in-law relationships are marked by avoidance-respect-formality. In most societies of the world (roughly 80 percent) the relationship between a man and his wife's younger sisters or between a woman and her husband's younger brothers is marked by informality, joking, or sexual license. The affect display script for each of those relationships is pretty much the same kind of script across quite diverse societies, and the script for each of those relationships seems to transcend societal variations in descent system, residence pattern, religion, economy, political system, and so on.

In contrast, the brother-sister script is a bit more variable cross-culturally (although worldwide it tends in the direction of avoidance-formality-respect), while the scripts for a woman and her husband's elder brother and a man and his wife's elder sister are highly variable from society to society. Societies with a matrilineal or bilateral descent system seem to promote avoidance-respect-formality between a brother and a sister; you do not joke around with your brother in societies where your children are going to inherit his property. Societies with patrilineal descent systems seem to promote avoidance-respect-formality with the wife's elder sister and the husband's elder brother.

What to make of all this? Any unifying theory of kinship avoidance has a lot of explaining to do. Why, for example, within a single community (e.g., among Oriya Brahmans) must a man treat his sister with informality, joke around with his elder brother's wife and wife's younger sister, yet avoid his younger brother's wife and wife's elder sister? And why are the scripts for the display of emotions to a brother or husband's elder brother more *variable* from culture to culture than are the scripts for a father-in-law or a husband's younger brother? A unifying theory should help us understand in a consistent way the meaning or function of any particular mode of affect display (avoidance vs. deference vs. informality vs. joking vs. abuse) and should help us relate each mode of affect display (e.g., avoidance vs. joking) to the underlying dynamics of the role relationship. By the "underlying dynamics," I mean the mix of necessary cooperation and unavoidable competition in the relationship, the relative balance of power or status, and the potential consequences or costs of a struggle or conflict over desired but limited resources. At the moment there is no unifying theory. Displays of emotions are socially structured and socially regulated; we still have much to learn about the dynamics of the choreography.

6. There is the *management* of emotions question: How are those emotions that are not expressed handled? We know, for instance, that certain feelings like anger or emptiness or envy are not displayed or directly expressed in some cultures, and it appears that the techniques for handling such emotions vary widely from denial to displacement to projection to somatization (LeVine 1973, chap. 17; Kleinman 1982).

The management of emotions question is, of course, a central one for culture and personality theorists (see, e.g., Whiting and Child 1953; Whiting 1964, 1977; Roberts and Sutton-Smith 1962a,b; Spiro 1965, 1983; Shweder 1979). Whether right or wrong, it is the main tenet of many culture and personality theorists that myths, rituals, games and religious beliefs, practices and symbols are "projective systems," that is, indirect ways of vicariously satisfying repressed wishes, disguised means for reducing anxiety or expressing deeply felt but forbidden desires. If the culture and personality theorists are right, many cultural practices—from prayer to head-hunting, from monastic retreat to adolescent circumcision, from obedience to the Ten Commandments to professional football—exist, or at least persist, as cultural practices for the sake of managing emotions (dependency, hostility, latent homosexuality, anxiety over sexual identity, etc.) and providing them with a safe outlet.

The fate of felt-but-unexpressed emotions is still poorly understood. It is plausible to imagine that certain emotions are functionally interconnected: to imagine, for example, that sexual arousal lowers the threshold for anger or aggression; to imagine that certain emotions (e.g., anger) will not go away until they are expressed or "acted out"; or to imagine that if they cannot be acted out one way (e.g., killing your father) they will be acted out in a less dangerous way (directing the hostility against "outsiders") or transformed into something else (e.g., depression) (see, e.g., Silverman 1976, which presents evidence that the subliminal presentation of hostile or aggressive imagery magnifies feelings of depression in depressed patients). The problem is that it is just as plausible to imagine the opposite: to imagine, for example, that anger, if unexpressed, slowly dissipates and ultimately disappears. The stage of our knowledge in this area is so limited that in 1984 it is still possible for Rosaldo (1984) and Spiro (1984) to disagree about whether Freudian defense "mechanisms" are a generic property of the human mind.

Rosaldo (1984) examines emotional functioning among Ilongot headhunters in the Philippines. Adopting the position that culturally constituted ideas have a decisive influence on mental processing, she argues against the notion of a psychic unity to mankind, against the notion of a generic human mind. Presenting illustrative material she notes that the Ilongot "did not think of hidden or forgotten affects [i.e., anger] as disturbing energies repressed; nor did they see in violent actions the expression of a history of frustrations buried in a fertile but unconscious mind." Rosaldo holds out the possibility that the way feelings work among the Ilongot is different from the way they work in our own culture; that, for example, among the Ilongot anger is not repressed and displaced, that defensive processes are the product of a Western way of constructing a self. Spiro (1984) demurs, and argues for a generic human mind and an inherent mental machinery including repression, displacement, and projection. It is also imaginable of course that defensive processes are not automatic defense "mechanisms" (inherent in the machinery) but rather habitual defensive "strategies," and that the strategy of choice (e.g., denial or projection vs. sublimation or intellectualization) may vary with a culture's construction of a self. Blame-externalizing defenses such as projection may be disapproved of in some cultures but not in others.

In sum, to ask whether people are alike or different in their emotional functioning is to ask whether they are alike or different in the types of feelings they feel (the taxonomic question), the situations that elicit those feelings (the ecological question), the perceived implications of those feelings (the semantic question), the vehicles for expressing those feelings (the communication question), the appropriateness of certain feelings being felt or displayed vis-à-vis certain types of relationships (the social regulation question), and the techniques or strategies utilized to deal with emotions that cannot be directly expressed (the management question). Undoubtedly there are universals and cultural specifics with regard to each of these aspects of emotional functioning. It is ludicrous to imagine that the emotional functioning of people in different cultures is basically the same. It is just as ludicrous to imagine that each culture's emotional life is entirely unique.

THE LOST SOUL: A PHENOMENOLOGY OF DEPRESSION

In illustrating the semantic approach to emotions, I attempt here an explication of the meaning of depression and attempt to identify what depressed feelings are about. I suggest that the idea of "soul loss" helps us make sense of the subjective experience of depression and some of its associated symptomatology (see, e.g., Beck 1976; Gada 1982; Kleinman 1982; Marsella 1980; Mathew et al. 1981; Mezzich and Raab 1980; Orley and Wing 1979). I try to give some unity to reports about what it feels like to feel depressed (e.g., Jackson 1980; Leff 1980) and what these feelings imply about the self and the world.

When you feel depressed you feel as though your soul has left your body. What you feel is empty, and a body emptied of its soul loses interest in things, except perhaps its own physical malfunctioning as a thing. The phenomenon of soul wandering is widely acknowledged among the world's cultures, and the phenomenology of soul loss has, for millennia, been a topic of theoretical and practical concern. A sophisticated and nearly universal doctrine has emerged which has it that the body is routinely emptied of its soul at the time of death and while sleeping or dreaming. Despite all the historical and cross-cultural variations in theories of the soul, most religious and cultural traditions associate death and sleep with soul loss. Against this background of common understanding it is perhaps not too surprising that when a fully conscious, awake person loses his soul, he finds it difficult to (is afraid to?) sleep or dream, and he spends much of his now extended waking time fantasizing about death and wondering why his soul has been withdrawn at such an uncanny time—while awake and still alive.

Emptied of a soul, some people fear they are "under desertion by God." Others think they are bad or evil people and this is their just dessert. Some imagine that the world is a lousy place in which it is impossible to have or keep the things you want, a place booby-trapped with unlooked-for disappointments, a place where striving is fruitless. Still others think there is an amine or a gene that has done it to them and that there must be some "thing" wrong with any "body" that cannot hang onto its soul. Some find comfort in the thought that it's the body and not the self that is to be blamed for suffering. Others wonder why such an unfair thing, a genetic deficiency, should have happened to them, and despair over the thought that life is absurd.

When your soul leaves your body you feel empty. "Emptiness" is a dark concept with many implications or connotations. It has spatial dimensions: to be empty is to be down (vs. up), low (vs. high), cut off (vs. connected), hemmed in (vs. free). It has a tactile feel: to be empty is to be dry and cold, not moist and warm. It has a familiar visual aura: to be "blue" or black. The idea of emptiness is rich in associations. It is passive and weak, sluggish and cheap, fragile, inert and headless. There are all too many testimonies to the felt implications of emptiness: to be empty is to be down, low, blue, cold, dried out, weak, cut off and alone, isolated without energy and without hope. It is to feel "depressed," to feel the blood stagnate in your veins. It is to have "tired blood" (is Geritol a magical therapy for women with the "blues"?).

It remains to be seen whether these implications or suggestions are universal. I would not be surprised if they were. Osgood, May, and Miron's (1975) cross-cultural analyses of affective meaning in twenty-one societies is suggestive in that adjectives such as empty (vs. full), dark (vs. light), and low (vs. high) are widely experienced as bad or unpleasant, and it is not unlikely that there are synesthetic or associative connections among those and other concepts. There is also good reason to suspect that the metaphorical meanings of a basic orientational dimension like down (vs. up) (e.g., "I'm on top of the situation"; "Things are looking up") are not arbitrary, and that vertical (up/down) imagery is put to similar use in many societies. The human head is up. The gods are up. The heavens are up. The mighty are up. Control is up.

What's good is up (see Lakoff and Johnson 1980*a,b*; B. Schwartz 1981). I would not, of course, rule out the possibility that with deliberate effort (e.g., in folk therapy or by means of the meditative disciplines of various religious traditions) intuitive feelings about the meaning of low, dark, down, and empty might be reversed or denied. It is also possible that in certain contexts the connotations can shift, perhaps radically. The relevant context of use for the present discussion, however, is the feeling of emptiness associated with soul loss, and soul loss, as we know, is widely associated with death and vulnerability. Of course, even death and vulnerability can, with effort, be infused with positive connotations, although typically that does not occur. People cry at funerals.

When you lose your soul you lose interest in things—basic things like food, sex, other people, and life's projects. You stop eating and you stop sex. You lose weight and you lose sleep. During soul*ful* functioning there is a constant, even if barely noticed, perception of ourselves and others as "spirited," as a dynamic center of initiative and free will organized around an "I" (the observing ego). The "I" I refer to is that ghostly but familiar transcendental "I." It is transcendental because it is more than or other than a list of body parts or an assemblage of muscle and blood and skin and bones. It is the "I" that looks out at the world and out at the "me" in the mirror. It is that sense of pure yet distinctive subjectivity that makes it coherent, even if somewhat fantastic, to conjure up the image of retaining our identity while dwelling in someone else's body. During soulful functioning, that "I," that dynamic center of initiative and free will, works in concert with one's senses, reason, imagination, memory, and body. When the soul is lost that changes. "Dispirited," all that remains is the body and the mind, and a body and a mind do not function very well without will and initiative. You feel listless and tired. The brain goes. You have headaches. You can't think straight and you forget things. The senses go. Your vision blurs and you feel dizzy. The body goes. Your gut aches. Your back hurts. You feel weak, shaky, and short of breath. To function effectively, a mind and a body require a soul.

Emptiness gets expressed (or discussed) in different ways in different cultures, and there appear to be three ways to convey the feeling of soul loss. There is the language of *causal responsibility*, the language of *concomitant mood metaphor*, and the language of *physical consequences*. Emptied of your soul you can either dwell on the "why" of it all (Am I under desertion by God? Did I inherit this from my mother? Why can't I keep the things I love?), or generate concomitant mood metaphors (I feel like I'm in a cold, dark room on a winter's night, down, dried up, blue, cut off; "made of glass"), or focus on what is left, a dispirited body depleted of its normal appetites.

The cross-cultural literature on depression has a lot to say about the "somatization" of depression (Climent et al. 1980; Mezzich and Raab 1980; Kleinman 1982). To "somatize" depression is to talk about the perceived physical consequences of emptiness—sleep loss, weight loss, energy loss, loss of the appetites, headaches, back pain, dizziness, blurred vision, stagnating blood, and hunger for air. Some populations do it more than others.

One is more likely to focus on the perceived consequences of emptiness if you are nonwhite, non-Protestant and nonmale. Catholic women somatize more than Protestant women. Somatization occurs more in West Africa and Taiwan than in Minnesota. That there are individual and cultural differences in whether you dwell on the causes, dwell on the mood state, or dwell on the physical consequences is noteworthy; it may tell us something about individual and cultural differences in the perceived implications and consequences of *displaying* a feeling (social regulation) and in *managing* one's moods and emotions. For example, it is tempting to speculate that somatization is more likely when the direct expression of felt emotion is thought to be dangerous, threatening to one's social status and disruptive of social relationships with others. It is also tempting to speculate that the belief that felt emotions, if expressed, are dangerous is more common among those who believe that society is built up out of interdependent social roles and less common among those who believe that individuals in pursuit of their wants and desires are the fundamental units of society. The less "personal" the society the more dangerous it is to expose anything so subjective as one's emotions, and the more personal the society the more it will be viewed as healthy to emote. As Mr. Rogers has told many American preschool children: "Everyone has a history. Everyone has a name. Everyone has a story. No one's story is quite the same." Personal biography and affect display go together.

The idea of soul loss gives some unity to our understanding of what it is to feel depressed. It does not tell us why we have lost our soul or how to get it back, but it does tell us what depressed feelings are *about*. "Not so fast," the reader may object. "One cannot lose what one never had." To which the answer is: That's right. To feel depressed one must have had experience with the soul, and almost everyone has had that experience.

Believing in the existence of souls is not quite like believing in fairies. Of course both souls and fairies have fallen into official disrepute in secular science-bound cultures like our own. Fairies have become the things of pretend, enchantment, medieval paintings, and children's stories. And the idea of the soul has come to be associated with theological doctrine, which means it is viewed by those of us who are secular and science-bound as prescientific, fuzzy-headed, and mystical, and thus hardly worthy of serious consideration.

Fairies should probably be left where they are, in children's stories; we seem to be able to get along quite well without them, and nothing in reason, experience, or direct intuition requires that we grant them more than a tongue-in-cheek reality. It would be a shame, however, to leave the soul in the hands of the theologians.

The presence of our *own* soul is something we know by direct intuition. That intuition is so widely shared and so compelling that each of us tends to perceive the actions of others as spirited, in ways that the reactive movements of billiard balls, robots, and computers are not. And that direct intuition of our own soul is powerful enough that it has shaped many of our social institutions. Indeed, if by some strange alteration of consciousness we were to start perceiving each other as billiard balls, robots, or computers, we would have to abandon the concept of free will and personal responsibility and we would probably have to strip society of its entire legal-moral fabric; for the concept of "crime" and the institution of punishment are both testimonies to our direct knowledge of our own souls and our faith that others have souls as well.

To acknowledge the reality of the soul it is not necessary to endorse any of the theological doctrines, specific articles of faith, or speculative ontologies that have grown up around the idea of the soul. It is not necessary to believe in a divine maker who reigns over the universe, or that each individual soul is the splintered fragment of a once unshattered universal soul, or that there is a place called "heaven" where souls reside, or that souls get recycled or transmigrate, or that they move into the bodies they deserve, or that bodies can be snatched or possessed by invading spirits. It is not necessary to believe that souls materialize or that they reside in some special gland or organ.

What it is necessary to believe can be summarized in three propositions: (1) Not everything that is real is material (has weight and extension in space); (2) The really real test of reality is not that something be material per se but that it have an effect on the way we understand, treat, and react to things that are; and (3) The reality of the soul is something that can be no more in doubt than the reality of ideas, values, and personal identity, and all other such real things that lack weight and extension in space.

The young Leonardo da Vinci conducted several grotesque autopsies in the vain hope of finding some "thing" missing after the soul had left the body of the dead. He failed, and so has everyone since. If you try to find the soul with a scalpel, it will elude you. But, just as you can believe in the existence of "memories" without being able to say where they are when you are not having them, so too you can believe in "souls" without being able to say where they go when they wander or where they hide when they are home.

The idea of the soul is widely acknowledged even among those of us who are so secularized that we do not recognize the soul when we see it. It is what is involved when we see another person as a person and not merely as a highly intelligent robot. It is what we name when we give people a "proper" name instead of designating them with a serial number. For what is named is not merely an object, a thing in this world, but a subject as well; that subject (the so-called ghost in the machine), once properly named, continued to be honored and have influence (e.g., in "wills") long after the body or the machine is gone. It is the soul that is involved when we hold others responsible for their actions. It is what we honor when we respect another's privacy or freedom of movement. It is what we see in others when we look beyond their visible movements and see behind those movements a dynamic center of initiative and free choice. Call it the soul, the spirit, the transcendental ego, the subjectivity, the free will, or the "atman," it connects the person with things beyond and with others, and it is as real to each of us as it is immaterial. Lose it and you feel dead, cut off, alone, "dispirited"—depressed.

Imagine one's "self" entering another person's body. Imagine retaining a continuous sense of "I-ness" while replacing in succession each and every cell in one's body. It is not that difficult to imagine such things because one recognizes within one's self a sense of self deeper than one's possessions, one's physical appearance, one's body parts, one's tastes, one's values, or one's goals in life, and one can vary each and every one of those things, or even give them up, and still retain a sense that something has remained the same. That is your soul and it is not a concoction by theologians or something that disappeared with the enlightenment or with the invention of machines or computers. It is a deeply intuitive idea and, apparently, a universal idea. It is an idea that makes the experience of depression something that everyone can understand.

Up to this point I have tried to characterize the meaning and phenomenology of depression in terms of soul loss. Of course what I have done is not unproblematic. I begged many questions. I did not tell you what caused depression or how to get rid of it. I did not tell you whether children get depressed or whether childhood depression is related to adult depression. I did not comment on the apparent worldwide pre-dominance of depression among women, or explain why there is a sex difference in reported depression among adolescents and adults but not among children, or why reports of depression are more common among European women than among Chinese women. What I did do is tell you what the feeling of depression is about, and in doing so I implied that moods and emotions have meanings, that to understand a person's emotional life it is necessary to engage in conceptual analysis, and that it is possible to understand what it implies to feel depressed without knowing what "really" brought it on or how "really" to get rid of it.

I performed several sleights of hand. I accepted without comment the widespread practice of interpreting certain clusters of physical com-plaints (I'm tired, dizzy, and short of breath; I can't sleep; I'm losing weight; I don't care about sex) as the somatic expression of a depressed mood state. In other words, I took it for granted that there are alternative ways to express depression, for example, by focusing on causes, concomitants, or consequences, and that when a person tells you that he is under desertion by God he is expressing the "same thing" as someone who tells you he is cold, dark, and sad, who in turn is expressing the same thing as the person who tells you he can't sleep at night and has lost his appetite. Of course the three formulations are not even remotely synonymous: to lose your appetite is not quite the same thing as to feel sad or to believe that God has abandoned you. My warrant for linking these three types of formulations was that they expressed in three different idioms—causation, concomitance, and consequence—a con-cern for the same thing, the emptiness associated with soul loss. But notice that, while identifying a core meaning to depression, I ducked the question of whether depression means the same thing to two people who feel as though they have lost their soul, one of whom believes he is a bad person under desertion by God and the other of whom believes that soul loss is a fortuitous disease for which drugs are the only sensible response.

Notice too all the things I did not do. I did not try to link the three types of expressions of depression by referring to a common hormonal, chemical, or genetic condition; nor did I try to establish their equivalence by referring to a common eliciting condition (e.g., loss or learned helplessness); nor did I raise doubts about whether they really are expressions of the same thing or whether they should be linked at all.

Rather, having identified the semantic question as one among several that might be asked about emotional functioning, I tried to explicate the underlying meaning of a feeling and give some unity to our understanding of what it feels like to *feel* depressed.

SEMANTICS AND EMOTIONS: A DEVELOPMENTAL PUZZLE

To this point I have identified six ways in which people may be alike or different in their emotional functioning, and I have given an example of the semantic or phenomenological aspect of emotional functioning with special reference to feelings of depression. In this final section I speculate about the ontogenetic origins of cross-cultural differences in emotional functioning. I consider the question: What is the role of cultural meaning systems in the growth of an emotional life?

To pose this question in the right way I would like to start with the image of an emotional "keyboard." Each of the keys is a discrete emotion: disgust, interest, distress, anger, fear, contempt, shame, shyness, guilt. A key is struck when a situation or object is interpreted in a certain way—as loss or frustration or novelty or as "a little thing that squirms in the night." There is evidence to suggest that for any normal member of our species the keyboard is intact and available by the age of four years (Campos et al. 1975; Charlesworth and Kreutzer 1973; Emde et al. 1976; Hiatt et al. 1979; Izard 1978; Izard et al. 1980; Ochs n.d.; Van Lieshout and Cornelis 1975).

Notice that the emotional keyboard of the young child is quite differentiated. Perhaps only simple tunes are played, but the young child knows the difference between the emotions listed above, and by four years of age probably experiences all of them. The image of growth as a movement from an undifferentiated system to a differentiated system seems as inappropriate for the development of emotions as it is for the development of cognition.

In recent years it has been discovered that the mind of the young child is far more differentiated than previously supposed (for an overview, see Shweder 1982; Gelman and Baillargeon 1983). Two-year-olds can distinguish the perspective of self from the perspective of others (Lempers et al. 1977; also see Shatz and Gelman 1973, on perspective taking in four-year-olds). Three-year-olds are able to distinguish intentional from unintentional behavior (Shultz 1980). Preschool children know the difference between conventional rules and moral rules (Nucci and Turiel

1978; Shweder et al. 1981). In fact, so many cognitive distinctions and competencies previously thought to be absent from the mind of the young child have now been discovered that a new image has emerged of the child's mind. What the young child lacks are not complex differentiated mental structures but the knowledge and representational skills needed for talking about and making deliberate use of the complex structures available to him. Given this new appreciation of the differentiated structures of childhood thought, it is perhaps not too surprising that young children are able to discriminate among basic emotions (happy, sad, angry, surprised, afraid, etc.) almost as well as adults (R. Schwartz n.d.). Indeed, in some cultures the emotional experiences of the four-year-old may be more varied than the emotional experiences of adults. Javanese adults, for example, according to Geertz (1975), strive to smooth out their emotions to a steady affectless hum. The goal is "an inner world of stilled emotions" in which the "hills and valleys" of an emotional life are "flattened out . . . into an even level plain." Describing the way a young Javanese man reacted to the death of his wife, Geertz seems to imply, with his reference to meditative and mystical techniques for smoothing the emotions, that even in bereavement the Javanese succeed, at least in part, at stilling their inner life and flattening out the feeling of distress in the face of irreversible loss. Presumably if we looked at Javanese four-year-olds we would find "hills and valleys," anger and surprise, distress and disgust, and many other discrete, differentiated emotions.

What is fascinating about the ontogeny of emotions is that, while a differentiated emotional keyboard may be available to most four-year-olds around the world, the tunes that get played and the emotional scores that are available diverge considerably for adults. Some keys do not get struck at all; the emotional symphonies that do get played are about as similar or different as Haydn is to Schubert or Mozart is to John Cage. Eskimos do not experience anger in situations in which Europeans would explode (Briggs 1970). On occasions where the Chinese feel sick, Americans feel depressed (Kleinman 1982). Wide variations are found in the hang-ups and anxieties of different peoples. Men in some cultures are hung up over their masculinity; in other cultures they are hung up over their dependency (Whiting and Child 1953). Semen loss and vaginal emissions are worrisome things to people on the Indian subcontinent; lack of semen loss is what worries Americans. Some peoples value formality and calm and dislike any strong expression of emotions; Samoans are nonchalant where we lose our cool (Geertz 1959). For some people, guilt has been bleached of everything but a rational concern for doing what is right; other people experience transgression with shame-terror-guilt all bound together. Life is a stage in Bali, and stage fright is the big thing (Geertz 1973). Honor and revenge still exist in the Mediter-ranean and the Middle East; in other parts of the world the idea of honor has not been experienced in years.

How does the distressed Javanese four-year-old become the smoothed-out Javanese adult? How does the angry Eskimo four-year-old become the angerless Eskimo adult? Little is known about the process, but some speculations are possible. One major transformation of emo-tional functioning is related to our emerging capacity to "decouple" elicitors from reactions and reactions from expressive signals. Young children cannot do what adults can do. They cannot suppress the signal of an emotional state; they cannot feel but not express. Moreover, they do not easily express an emotion they do not feel, nor do they understand the social function of expressing but not feeling. They are not yet ready for the spectacle called society. They let situations get to them; they lack the concepts and detachment to redescribe events and alter their emo-tional reactions to them. They cry when it hurts.

There is a vivid example of "decoupling" in the writings of Whorf (1956:267). He points out that the sound pattern "QUEEP" elicits a universal set of associations: "QUEEP" is fast (vs. slow), sharp (vs. dull), narrow (vs. wide), light (vs. dark). Our associative response to "QUEEP" is automatic and that automatic response is probably pre-programmed and the same for the Bongo-Bongo and for us. Whorf then asks us to consider the sound pattern "DEEP." "DEEP" is phonetically similar to "QUEEP" and elicits the same set of associations (fast, sharp, narrow, light) for everyone except speakers of English. For English speakers, "DEEP" is not simply a thing in the world, a sound pattern; it is a sound pattern with meaning, a meaning that totally overrides and alters our reaction to its sound. For English speakers, and for English speakers only, "DEEP" is slow, dull, wide, and dark. I suspect that the development of the emotional life of a people is not unlike the shift from "QUEEP" to "DEEP."

Let us consider ontogenetic changes in emotional reactions to "touching" among Oriya Brahmans in the old temple town of Bhu-baneswar, India. Touching is a universal elicitor of positive affects among newborns in our species and in other species as well; touching is the "queep" of our emotional life (Bowlby 1969; Harlow 1973; Harlow and Mears 1979). Associated with touching is a cluster of positive feelings: comfort, security, stress reduction, attachment, nurturance.

That universal early elicitor of positive affect takes on, in many contexts, exactly the opposite meaning among Oriya Brahman adults.

I cannot enter into a full ethnographic account of ideas about touchability, untouchability, and pollution in Oriya culture. Suffice it to say that there are many things that pollute: feces, menstrual blood, "unclean" castes, "unclean" animals. Birth pollutes. Death pollutes. There are many ways Oriyas protect themselves against pollution. They avoid pollutants and keep them isolated or at a distance. They wash themselves after any contact with a pollutant. They eat, drink, or apply to their skin as a purifying agent the "five products of the cow": milk, curd, ghee, urine, and dung. They wear special clothes when they defecate and remove those clothes immediately after defecation. And during defecation men drape their sacred thread over their ears.

Each Brahman boy receives a sacred thread at the time of his sacred thread ceremony, ideally at age seven or nine. The sacred thread is a caste insignia; for a Brahman boy it signals the end of parental permissiveness toward nudity, dietary practices, and moral responsibility. The sacred thread is worn over the left shoulder and across the right side. It is believed that the sacred thread protects its wearer against evil spirits and spirit possession. It helps keep the wearer's soul where it ought to remain for a while, in his body. The sacred thread loses protective power if it becomes polluted, and thus when Brahmans defecate the sacred thread goes over the ear. For it is believed that in the ear of every Brahman is a token of the sacred river Ganges and that draped over the ear the sacred thread will remain sacred. Indeed, if a Brahman touches a pollutant and is unable to immediately wash, you may well see him purify himself by touching his hand to his ear.

There are many other ways Oriya Brahmans guard themselves against pollution. They are scrupulous about what they eat, whom they eat with, whom they accept food from, and who cooks the food they do eat. They classify cloth and utensils on the basis of their potential for pollution. Cotton is more easily polluted than silk; white cotton more easily polluted than colored cotton. Earthenware plates, jars, and pots are more easily polluted than metal utensils, and so on.

One of the most dangerous sources of pollution for Oriyas is the touch of a menstruating woman, including one's mother. Adult men believe that menstrual blood is poisonous, capable of killing trees and plants, shrinking testicles, and contaminating the environment. One male informant put it this way: "If the wife touches her husband on the first day of her period, it is an offense equal to that of killing a guru. If she touches him on the second day, it is an offense equal to killing a Brahman. On the third day to touch him is like cutting off his penis. If she touches him on the fourth day it is like killing a child. So it is a sin.''

Menstruating women have less exaggerated views but share with men the belief that during menstruation they are unclean and untouchable. Both men and women believe that the touch of a menstruating woman will shorten the life of the person she touches, and that anything she touches—her clothing, her bedding, her children's clothes—must be washed and purified. Consequently, a menstruating woman does not sleep in the same bed with her husband, does not cook food or leave food for returning ancestral spirits or even enter the kitchen, does not enter the family prayer room or approach the family deity, does not dress her children or wash clothing, and does not touch anyone (an exception is made for nursing infants, but all clothing is removed from the child before breast-feeding commences). It is thought by women and men to be a great sin to do so. For three days she does not groom herself or take a bath after dark or do anything that might tempt and attract her husband. After three days of relative isolation and seclusion she purifies herself with a special bath (preferably using turmeric paste and a bit of cow dung), and then on the fourth day she returns to her normal routine of bathing, cooking, feeding ancestral spirits and family members, worshiping deities, cleaning house, napping, massaging the legs of the husband's parents, and tending children. (For an informative account of menstrual practices and pollution concepts in Madras, India, see Ferro-Luzzi 1974; there are many points of similarity with Orissa.)

Pollution is not the same as germs, and informants clearly distinguish the two. They know about germs and do not consider them pollutants. Nor is the isolation and distancing of pollutants and agents of pollution a way of protecting people against dirt or disease. A sick woman is permitted to enter the kitchen. A menstruating woman is not.

Pollution is a less tangible thing than a microorganism, but it is just as real. Pollution has to do with sanctity, the sanctity of the temple. One must bathe before entering the temple. Menstruating women are not allowed in the temple. Unclean castes are not allowed in the temple. No one can enter the temple for twelve days after a birth or death in the joint family. If a person dies in the temple, the temple must be purified. The temple must be cleansed if a dog, an untouchable, or a foreigner enters.

Moreover, for Oriya Brahmans in Bhubaneswar, ''the temple'' refers not just to the eleventh-century structure and its resident God (Lingaraj or Shiva) but to each and every home and each and every body that lives in the shadow of Lingaraj. There is among Oriya Brahmans what might be called a "temple complex." They believe that one's paternal home is a temple to which ancestral spirits return to be fed (hence the special sanctity of the kitchen and that corner of the kitchen where food and water is daily left for returning ancestral spirits) presided over by a family deity (hence the special sanctity of the prayer room). And they believe that the human body is a temple in which there dwells a spirit or god, the atman, the self, the observing ego.

Each of these three temples must be kept pure out of respect for God, the ancestors, and the self. The distinction between Gods, ancestors, and self or between the temple as temple, the home as temple, and the body as temple is not hard and fast. Adult men think of themselves as "moving Gods" and they are treated that way by their wives, who are the first to point out that the husband is to be worshiped. And while the daily ritual of washing the feet of the husband and swallowing a few drops of the water is in decline in the old town, a wife does not typically eat with her husband and if she does, it is considered shameful, comparable to eating with God. Rather, she prepares the food that is to be "offered" to the ancestral spirits and to the husband's spirit. Later she will offer food to herself or perhaps even eat the leftovers or remnants off her husband's plate, just as he may, on special occasions, offer food to the God in the Lingaraj temple and them remove the leftovers (the so-called prasad) to his home to be eaten.

The God in the Lingaraj temple does not eat with his wife (the Goddess Parvati). Typically he eats alone, and it is not uncommon for adults in the old town to do the same. Indeed, as if to deliberately blur the distinction between self, ancestral spirits, and God, the God in the Lingaraj temple is treated as a person. The deity is awakened each morning, washed, and fed; he takes a nap; he gets sick; he visits his relatives; he goes on outings; he confesses his sin; and he chews betel (Mahapatra 1981). The distinction between the God in the Lingaraj temple, the deity and ancestral spirits in the house, and the spirit dwelling in the body is not terribly important to Oriyas. They visit the Lingaraj temple in the morning, and in the afternoon they tell you that all the Gods can be found inside one's body. One is never quite sure where God ends and where you begin, but one is quite certain that life is a series of attempts to preserve or restore the sanctity of deities, in the Lingaraj temple, in the paternal home, and in one's body. Daily bathing is an ablution; daily eating is an oblation, an offering to one's self. And it is in the context of these ablutions and oblations of daily life that feelings about pollution are best understood.

"Mara heici. Chhu na! Chhu na!" is what a menstruating Oriya mother exclaims when her child approaches her lap. It means, "I am polluted. Don't touch me! Don't touch me!" If the child continues to approach, the woman will stand up and walk away. Oriya children, of course, have no concept of menstruation or menstrual blood. There is a ceremony involving bathing and seclusion that marks the first menstruation, and the date, time, and place of the first menstruation is sometimes treated as a matter of significance. Astrologers and the Oriya almanac have much to say about what it all means: If it happens on a Sunday, before 6:40 P.M., in the house of someone other than her father, she will suffer seven months of calamity and become a widow. There is even an annual festival (Raja, the festival of the Earth) during which Mother Earth bleeds and .is given a menstrual bath. Despite this, the first menstruation arrives as a total shock to adolescent girls in Bhubaneswar; they are not prepared for it by anyone. Mothers explain their own monthly "pollution" to their children by telling them that they stepped in dog excrement or touched garbage, or they evade the issue. Nevertheless, Oriya children quickly learn that there is something called "mara" (the term "chhuan" is also used) and when "mara" is there their mother avoids them, stays out of her husband's bed, and out of the kitchen (indeed, "Handi bahari heichi" "I'm out of the kitchen" is the euphemism used by Oriya women to talk about menses). Most six-year-olds think it is wrong for a polluted woman to cook food or sleep in the same bed with her husband. Most nine-year-olds think that "mara" is an objective force and that all women in the world have an obligation not to touch other people or cook food while they are polluted.

As you can see, in Orissa touching is transformed from a species-wide elicitor of attachment, comfort, and security to a dreaded instrument of pollution. The transformation takes place by various means. "Don't touch me!" is heard on many occasions and in many contexts. There is not only the menstruating mother: there is the father who does not want his child to touch him in the interim between bathing (a purification ritual) and worshiping the family deity; there is the grandmother who does not want the child to touch her or climb into bed with her until the child has removed all his "outside" clothes for they have become polluted by mixing with lower castes at school; and there is even a children's game on the theme, pollution "tag." Several children stand apart from a lone isolated child and all together sing "Puchu, Puchu (teasing sound). Hadi ghare peja piichhu. Mote chhu na!" ("You drank rice water in the house of a Hadi [the lowest untouchable caste]. Don't touch me!''). The children scurry off pursued by the hand of the ''polluted'' child.

Of course, touching as an instrument of pollution is only one of its transformations in Orissa. Touching the feet of a superior is a sign of respect, deference, and apology. Young women routinely touch, indeed massage, the legs and body of their father-in-law and mother-in-law, and male friends, adults as well as children, affectionately hold hands and lounge about entwined in each other's arms. Notably, each of these touching practices has a positive valence for Oriyas yet strike many American observers as offensive, exploitative, effeminate, and slightly anxiety provoking. The point, I suppose, is that after early childhood the ''queep'' of touching is transformed through diverse cultural practices into the ''deep'' of touching. The emotional impact of the affective elicitors of early childhood is altered and what ends up being touching to one people is not so touching to another.[1]

CONCLUSION

In this chapter I have focused on the inherent complexity of the emotional functioning of young children and the reworking of this inherent complexity under the influence of cultural practices. I have argued that the emotional functioning of people in different cultures is not ''basically the same,'' nor is it entirely unique. There are universals and cultural specifics with regard to each of the six aspects of emotional functioning, which were identified earlier. As researchers in the comparative study of emotions, the most role-appropriate feeling is ''curiosity.'' There is no special virtue in identifying oneself as either a ''relativist'' (each culture unique) or a ''universalist'' (everyone basically the same).

ACKNOWLEDGMENTS

Research in the old town of Bhubaneswar, Orissa, India, was supported by a grant from the National Institute of Child Health and Human Development: No. 1 RO1 HD/MH 17067-01, ''The Development of Conscience, Guilt, and Morality.'' While in Bhubaneswar I was affiliated with the Department of Psychology at Utkal University. My thanks to its chairman, S. K. Misra, for his support and encouragement. I am especially indebted to Manamohan Mahapatra, Department of Anthropology, B. J. B. College, Bhubaneswar, for his counsel and advice at every stage of the research.

NOTES

1. The following objection might be raised to my semantic approach to the development of emotional functioning. It is the objection raised by Daniel G. Freedman in a personal communication that "there is no universal infancy any more than there is a universal adulthood." What Freedman has in mind is a line of research, much of it conducted by Freedman and his associates (Freedman 1974; also see Super 1981), indicating that there are racial and populational differences in neonatal temperament and responsiveness to certain stimulus events. For example, under conditions of partial air blockage (a cloth is placed over a newborn's mouth or nose), Oriental babies are, on average, more passive and less agitated than Caucasian babies. The implication of Freedman's objection is that emotional differences between populations of adults will be matched by parallel or analogous innate differences in the emotional functioning of babies in those populations.

It would be a forceful challenge to the semantic approach if different cultural practices were "reflections" or "crystallizations" of innate differences in responsiveness; for example, if Oriya Causasian newborns displayed significantly greater aversive responses than American Caucasian newborns to dirt or excretia or greater fussiness about being touched, or if Tahitian or Eskimo six-month-olds did not display the face of anger when their wrists were confined to their sides or a desired object held just out of reach. While a lot more evidence is needed before the issue can be settled with confidence, it is my bet that Tahitian and Eskimo six-month-olds will display situation-appropriate anger, that Javanese four-year-olds will clearly discriminate between a variety of basic emotions (e.g., surprise, anger, sadness, disgust, fear, etc.), and that Oriya babies are not born with feelings of untouchability.

REFERENCES

Beck, A. T.
   1976   Cognitive Therapy and the Emotional Disorders. New York: New American Library.
Bowlby, J.
   1969   Attachment and Loss. Vol. 1, Attachment. New York: Basic Books.

Briggs, J. L.
   1970   Never in Anger. Cambridge: Harvard University Press.
Campos, J. J., R. N. Emde, T. Gaensbauer, and C. Henderson
   1975   Cardiac and Behavioral Interrelationships in the Reactions of
               Infants to Strangers. Developmental Psychology 5:589–601.
Charlesworth, W. R., and M. A. Kreutzer
   1973   Facial Expressions of Infants and Children. *In* Darwin and
               Facial Expression. Paul Ekman, ed. New York: Academic
               Press.
Climent, C. E., B. S. M. Diop, T. W. Harding, H. H. A. Ibrahim,
L. Ladrido-Ignacio, and N. N. Wig
   1980   Mental Health in Primary Health Care. WHO Chronicle 34:
               231–236.
Cohn, J. F., and E. Z. Tronick
   1983   Three-Month-Old Infants' Reaction to Simulated Maternal
               Depression. Child Development 54:185–193.
D'Andrade, R. G.
   1981   The Cultural Part of Cognition. Cognitive Science 5:179–195.
   1984   Cultural Meaning Systems. *In* Culture Theory: Essays on Mind,
               Self and Emotion. R. A. Shweder and R. A. LeVine, eds. New
               York: Cambridge University Press.
D'Andrade, R. G., and F. Egan
   1974   The Colors of Emotion. American Ethnologist 1:49–64.
Driver, H. E.
   1966   Geographical-Historical versus Psycho-Functional Explana-
               tions of Kin Avoidances. Current Anthropology 7:131–145.
Emde, R. N., T. Gaensbauer, and R. J. Harman
   1976*a*   Emotional Expression in Infancy. New York: International
               Universities Press.
   1976*b*   Emotional Expression in Infancy: A Biobehavioral Study.
               Psychological Issues 10:37.
Ferro-Luzzi, G. E.
   1974   Women's Pollution Periods in Tamiland. Anthropos 69:
               113–161.
Freedman, D. G.
   1974   Human Infancy. Hillsdale, N.J.: L. Earlbaum Associates.
Gada, M. T.
   1982   A Cross-Cultural Study of Symptomatology of Depression. The
               International Journal of Social Psychiatry 28:195–202.
Geertz, C.
   1973   The Interpretation of Cultures. New York: Basic Books.
   1975   On the Nature of Anthropological Understanding. American
               Scientist 63:47–53.

Geertz, H.
1959   The Vocabulary of Emotion. Psychiatry 22:225–237.
Gelman, R., and R. Baillargeon
1983   A Review of Some Piagetian Concepts. *In* The Handbook of
            Child Psychology. P. Mussen, ed. New York: John Wiley and
            Sons. Pp. 167–230.
Goody, J., and J. Buckley
1974   Cross-sex Patterns of Kin Behavior: A Comment. Behavior
            Science Research 9:185–202.
Harlow, H. F.
1973   Learning to Love. New York: Ballantine Books.
Harlow, H. F., and C. Mears
1979   The Human Model. Washington, D.C.: U. H. Winston.
Hiatt, S., J. J. Campos, and R. N. Emde
1979   Facial Patterning and Infant Emotional Expression: Happiness,
            Surprise, and Fear. Child Development 50:1020–1035.
Hirsch, E. D.
1967   Validity in Interpretation. New Haven: Yale University Press.
1976   The Aims of Interpretation. Chicago: The University of Chi-
            cago Press.
Hochschild, A. R.
1979   Emotion Work, Feeling Rules, and Social Structure. American
            Journal of Sociology 85:551–575.
Izard, C. E.
1978   Emotions as Motivations: An Evolutionary-Developmental
            Perspective. *In* Nebraska Symposium on Motivation.
            R. Dienstbier, ed. Lincoln: University of Nebraska Press.
Izard, C. E., R. R. Huebner, D. Risser, G. C. McGinnes, and L. M.
Dougherty
1980   The Young Infant's Ability to Produce Discrete Emotion Ex-
            pressions. Developmental Psychology 16:132–140.
Jackson, S. W.
1980   Two Sufferers' Perspectives on Melancholia: 1690's to 1790's.
            In Essays in the History of Psychiatry. E. T. Wallace and L. C.
            Pressley, eds. Columbia, S.C.: Wm. S. Hall Psychiatric
            Institute.
Kleinman, A.
1982   Neurasthenia and Depression: A Study of Socialization and
            Culture in China. Culture, Medicine, and Psychiatry 6:
            117–190.
La Barbera, J. D., C. E. Izard, P. Vietze, and S. Parisi
1976   Four- and Six-Month-Old Infants' Visual Responses to Joy,
            Anger, and Neutral Expression. Child Development 47:
            535–538.

Labov, W., and D. Fanshel
1977   Therapeutic Discourse: Psychotherapy as Conversation. New
            York: Academic Press.

Lakoff, G., and M. Johnson
1980*a*   The Metaphorical Structure of the Human Conceptual System.
            Cognitive Science 4:195−208.
1980*b*   Metaphors We Live By. Chicago: University of Chicago Press.

Leff, J.
1980   Psychiatry Around the Globe: A Transcultural View. New
            York: Marcel Dekker.

Lempers, J. D., E. R. Flavell, and J. H. Flavell
1977   The Development in Very Young Children of Tacit Knowledge
            Concerning Visual Perception. Genetic Psychology Mono-
            graphs 95:3−54.

LeVine, R. A.
1973   Religious Symbols and Religious Experience. *In* Culture, Be-
            havior, and Personality. Chicago: Aldine Publishing Co.
1984   Properties of Culture: An Ethnographic Account. *In* Culture
            Theory: Essays on Mind, Self, and Emotion. R. A. Shweder
            and R. A. LeVine, eds. New York: Cambridge University
            Press. Pp. 67−87.

Levinson, D., and M. J. Malone
1980   Toward Explaining Human Culture: A Critical Review of the
            Findings of Worldwide Cross-Cultural Research. New Haven:
            HRAF Press.

Levy, R. I.
1973   Tahitians: Mind and Experience in the Society Islands. Chi-
            cago: The University of Chicago Press.
1984   Emotion, Knowing, and Culture. *In* Culture Theory: Essays on
            Mind, Self, and Emotion. R. A. Shweder and R. A. LeVine,
            eds. New York: Cambridge University Press.

Lewis, M., and J. Brooks
1978   Self-Knowledge and Emotional Development. *In* The Develop-
            ment of Affect. M. Lewis and L. A. Rosenblum, eds. New
            York: Plenum Press.

Lewis, M., and L. Michalson
1982   The Socialization of Emotions. *In* Emotion and Interaction:
            Normal and High-Risk Infants. T. Field and A. Fogel, eds.
            Hillsdale, N.J.: L. Erlbaum Associates.

Lutz, C.
1982   The Domain of Emotion Words on Ifaluk. American Ethnol-
            ogist 9:113−128.

Mahapatra, M.
1981   Traditional Structure and Change in an Orissa Temple. Calcutta: Punthi Pustak.
Marsella, A. J.
1980   Depressive Experience and Disorder Across Cultures. *In* Handbook of Cross-Cultural Psychology. H. C. Triandis and J. G. Draguns, eds. Boston: Allyn and Bacon. Pp. 237–290.
Mathew, R. J., M. L. Weinman, and M. Mirabi
1981   Physical Symptoms of Depression. British Journal of Psychiatry 139:293–296.
Mezzich, J. E., and E. S. Raab
1980   Depressive Symptomatology Across the Americas. Archives of General Psychiatry (3)7:818–823.
Miller, P.
1982   Teasing: A Case Study in Language Socialization and Verbal Play. Quarterly Newsletter of the Laboratory of Comparative Human Cognition 4:29–32.
Much, N. C.
n.d.   The Microanalysis of Cognitive Socialization, Ph.D. diss., University of Chicago, 1983.
Murdock, G. P.
1971   Cross-sex Patterns of Kin Behavior. Ethnology 10:359–368.
Nucci, L. P., and E. Turiel
1978   Social Interaction and the Development of Social Concepts in Pre-School Children. Child Development 49:400–407.
Ochs, E.
n.d.   Affect in Samoan Child Language. Paper presented at The Stanford Child Language Research Forum, Stanford, 1982. (Available from Elinor Ochs, Department of Linguistics, University of Southern California.)
Orley, J., and J. K. Wing
1979   Psychiatric Disorders in Two African Villages. Archives of General Psychiatry 36:513–520.
Osgood, C. E., W. H. May, and M. S. Miron
1975   Cross-Cultural Universals of Affective Meaning. Urbana: University of Illinois Press.
Paradise, E. B., and F. Curcio
1974   Relationship of Cognitive and Affective Behaviors to Fear of Strangers in Male Infants. Developmental Psychology 10:476–483.
Radcliffe-Brown, A. R.
1940   On Joking Relationships. Africa 13:195–210.
Roberts, J. M., and B. Sutton-Smith
1962   Child Training and Game Involvement. Ethnology 1:66–185.

Rosaldo, M.
1980   Knowledge and Passion. Cambridge: Cambridge University
            Press.
1984   Towards an Anthropology of Self and Feeling. *In* Culture
            Theory: Essays on Mind, Self, and Emotion. R. A. Shweder
            and R. A. LeVine, eds. New York: Cambridge University
            Press. Pp. 137–157.

Rosenblatt, P. C., R. P. Walsh, and D. R. Jackson
1976   Grief and Mourning in Cross-Cultural Perspective. New Haven:
            HRAF Press.

Schwartz, B.
1981   Vertical Classification. University of Chicago Press.

Schwartz, R.
n.d.   A Developmental Study of Children's Understanding of the
            Language of Emotion. Ph.D. diss., University of Chicago,
            1981.

Searle, J. R.
1979   A Taxonomy of Illocutionary Acts. *In* Expression and Meaning.
            Cambridge: Cambridge University Press.

Shatz, M., and R. Gelman
1973   The Development of Communication Skills: Modification in the
            Speech of Young Children as a Function of Listener. Mono-
            graph of the Society for Research on Child Development 38
            (5):1–38.

Shultz, T. R.
1980   The Development of the Concept of Intention. *In* The Min-
            nesota Symposia on Child Psychology. Vol. 13. W. Andrew
            Collins, ed. Hillsdale, N.J.: Lawrence Erlbaum Associates.

Shweder, R. A.
1979*a*   Rethinking Culture and Personality Theory. Pt. 1. Ethos 7:
            255–278.
1979*b*   Rethinking Culture and Personality Theory. Pt. 2. Ethos 7:
            279–311.
1982   On Savages and Other Children. American Anthropologist
            84:354–366.

Shweder, R. A., E. Turiel, and N. C. Much
1981   Moral Intuitions of the Child. *In* Social Cognitive Development:
            Frontiers and Possible Futures. J. H. Flavell and L. Ross, eds.
            Cambridge: Cambridge University Press.

Silverman, M.
1976   Psychoanalytic Theory: The Reports of My Death Have Been
            Greatly Exaggerated. American Psychologist 31:621–637.

Solomon, R.
1976   The Passions. Austin: University of Texas Press.
1984   Getting Angry: A Critique of the Jamesean Theory of Emotions
            in Anthropology. *In* Culture Theory: Essays on Mind, Self, and
            Emotion. R. A. Shweder and R. A. LeVine, eds. New York:
            Cambridge University Press. Pp. 238–254.

Spiro, M.
1965   Religious Systems as Culturally Constituted Defense Mecha-
            nisms. *In* Context and Meaning in Cultural Anthropology.
            Melford E. Spiro, ed. New York: Free Press. Pp. 100–113.
1983   Oedipus in the Trobriands. University of Chicago Press.
1984   Reflections on Cultural Relativism and Cultural Determinism
            with Special Reference to Reason and Emotion. *In* Culture
            Theory: Essays on Mind, Self, and Emotion. R. A. Shweder
            and R. A. LeVine, eds. New York: Cambridge University
            Press. Pp. 323–346.

Sroufe, L. A.
1979   Socioemotional Development. *In* Handbook of Infant Develop-
            ment. J. Osofsky, ed. New York: John Wiley and Sons.

Stenberg, C. R., J. J. Campos, and R. N. Emde
1983   The Facial Expression of Anger in Seven-Month-Old Infants.
            Child Development 54:178–184.

Stephens, W. N., and R. D'Andrade
1962   Kin-Avoidance. *In* The Oedipus Complex: Cross-Cultural Evi-
            dence. William N. Stephens, ed. New York: Free Press.
            Pp. 124–150.

Super, C.
1981   Behavioral Development in Infancy. *In* Handbook of Cross-
            Cultural Human Development. Ruth Munroe, Robert Munroe,
            and Beatrice Whiting, eds. New York: Garland. Pp. 181–270.

Sweetser, D. A.
1966   Avoidance, Social Affiliation, and the Incest Taboo. Ethnology
            5:304–316.

Tylor, E. B.
1889   On a Method of Investigating the Development of Institutions:
            Applied to Laws of Marriage and Descent. Journal of the Royal
            Anthropological Institute of Great Britain and Ireland 18:
            245–272.

Van Lieshout, C. F. M.
1975   Young Children's Reactions to Barriers Placed by Their
            Mothers. Child Development 46:879–886.

Whiting, J. W. M.
1964   Effects of Climate on Certain Cultural Practices. *In* Explorations in Cultural Anthropology: Essays in Honor of George Peter Murdock. Ward H. Goodenough, ed. New York: McGraw-Hill. Pp. 511–544.
1977   A Model for Psychocultural Research. *In* Culture and Infancy: Variations in Human Experience. P. Hebert Leiderman, Steven R. Tulkin, and Anne Rosenfeld, eds. New York: Academic Press. Pp. 29–48.
Whiting, J. W. M., and I. Child
1953   Child Training and Personality. New Haven: Yale University Press.
Whiting, J. W. M., and B. R. Whiting
1975   Aloofness and Intimacy of Husbands and Wives: A Cross-Cultural Study. Ethos 3:183–207.
Whorf, B. L.
1956   Language, Thought, and Reality. Cambridge: MIT Press.
Witkowski, S. R.
1972   A Cross-Cultural Test of the Proximity Hypothesis. Behavior Science Notes 7:243–263.

7

Dimensions of Dysphoria:
The View from
Linguistic Anthropology

William O. Beeman

If depression is a disease,[1] there seems to be very little indication among psychologists and psychiatrists as to what kind of disease it might be. To be sure, "depression" as a concept has been operationalized, measured according to standard testing devices, and treated. Still, vast areas of confusion remain. Is depression biological in origin, or is it a configuration of wrong "cognitions"? Is it brought about as a result of specific events, or are certain subjects "organically" more prone to suffer it, as a result of heredity? Is it primarily a state of mind, a state of the body, or a form of culture-specific response to human environmental conditions? This third possibility has rarely been considered as a regular factor in the diagnosis of depression. Although many cross-cultural studies of depression have been undertaken, most start with the assumption that depression is a universal human disorder, differing only in its manifestations.

Anthropologists, who might challenge the assumption of the universality of depression, have dealt with clinical emotional disorders only rarely. Such seemingly culture-specific disorders as Windigo psychosis, or *amok*, have been described in the anthropological literature, with some speculation as to origins and causes. Depression presents a far greater methodological problem for anthropologists, however, because of the enormous body of literature in psychiatry and clinical psychology which already exists, and which presumes universality. Anthropologists tend to look on most human phenomena as culture-specific until enough cross-cultural data is amassed to enable substantiation of a universal pattern. At worst this leads to particularist excesses, but in general it shows a well-founded bias toward inductive methodology in cross-cultural research.

From an anthropological standpoint, the assumption of universality of depression seems ill-founded. The experimental and clinical literatures show the symptomatology to be wildly variant when examined cross-culturally. The anthropologist here becomes skeptical, since it looks suspiciously that, having formed a clear idea of depression in Western culture, psychologists and psychiatrists then merely assert its universality. The deductive question for research then becomes: How do all these depressionlike disorders vary from the "classic" mold? Fábrega, himself an anthropologist, simply begs the question:

> One is left with the conclusion that the question of the possible universality of depression (or that of any Western defined psychiatric entity) as ordinarily stated is rather simplistic and not particularly productive. (1975a:78)

What does seem to be agreed upon by psychologists and psychiatrists is that there are two groups of symptoms: one "psychological" and the other physical in nature. Psychological symptoms are the most variant cross-culturally; however, this may be the result of testing biases. Marsella (1980:249−250) counsels in a major review that all reports of the manifestation of depression across cultures are "difficult to evaluate as a group because of the variability in the research strategies used to examine [the phenomena]."

Indeed, although most societies surveyed seem to exhibit the four "classic" signs of depression—depressed mood, diurnal mood variation, insomnia with early morning awakening, loss of interest in the environment (ibid., p. 258)—researchers in many societies report none of these signs or infrequent manifestations of them.

Rather more universal in distribution seem to be somatic components, such as stomach pains, weakness, or more general sleep difficulties. Nevertheless, even these symptoms turn out to manifest quite different patterns in different cultures. The wide variation in patterns of manifestation leads Marsella (ibid., p. 261) to conclude that "depression apparently assumes completely different meanings and consequences as a function of the culture in which it occurs."

Without additional study, particularly rigorous ethnographic study, the general issue of universality will not be completely resolved. The question may be approached from more than one direction, however.

Depression may be thought of as a disorder that requires close attention to communication and language in all of its aspects: symptomatology, diagnosis, and treatment. One anthropological subfield in particular, linguistic anthropology, may be able to provide insights into the communicative processes that underlie depression. Consequently, in the discussion that follows, I focus on three prime theoretical concerns in linguistic anthropology which have consequences for understanding depression.

The first concerns issues in language and cognition, exploring the question of how the linguistic expression used in native descriptions of emotional states reflects the reality of those emotional states. The second explores the role of language and communication in the therapeutic process, with particular attention to the work of Aaron Beck. The third deals with the creation of collective meaning in the overall framework of an individual's social network, with attention to the work of "family therapists" in dealing with depression.

NON-WESTERN EXPRESSIONS OF DEPRESSION

One of the most puzzling aspects of the cross-cultural evaluation and diagnosis of depression for psychologists and psychiatrists seems to be that the concept of depression is expressed linguistically in widely varying ways in different societies. The literature seems to show particular interest in the fact that there are many languages that have no word at all for depression, or in which the concept is expressed in very different ways than in Western society (Resner and Hartog 1970; Schmidt 1964; Prince 1964; Edgerton 1966; Orley 1970, 1979; Boyer 1964).

This leads to the first broad question a linguist may address to the study of depression. This can be crudely stated: If they don't have a word for it, does it exist?

At least one prominent researcher in the field, Julian Leff, has categorized the kinds of linguistic representations one finds concerning depression, and has come up with an evolutionary schema for dealing with the entire range. According to Leff (1981), the structure of vocabulary of any particular language is directly reflective of the history of the emotional expression of the population using that vocabulary. Thus he posits that the earliest forms of language had a single primitive gruntlike word "presumably something phonetically similar to the root *Angh* in the case of the Indo-European languages [to denote] the somatic accompaniments of unpleasant emotional arousal" (p. 45).

Proceeding up Leff's evolutionary ladder one finds: languages that reflect societies that do not differentiate between bodily and psychological experiences (thus expressing their psychological feelings in somatic terms); languages that serve societies that do not differentiate between psychological experiences; until we finally arrive at languages that express rich feelings of distinct psychological experience (like English).

For a linguist it is indeed wearying to see that theories such as this are alive and kicking after so many years of effort by the ancestors of the field in trying to throw cold water on such empty and groundless notions. I must confess that I feel somewhat foolish addressing Leff's schema, since it is ground that has already been worn bare by the tread of many others who have come before me. Nevertheless, this schema is equally foolish and must be dealt with by someone before a generation of psychiatrists adopt it as doctrine.

First, I admit that I have no patience with persons who characterize languages as "advanced" or "primitive" because they fail to meet their own extracontextual needs. Leff presumably feels that any language that cannot handle direct translation of the MMPI or Beck Depression Inventory word for word is somehow "less evolved." Consequently, he makes the mistake that since the language does not provide for expression of the emotional world with the same, or at least as many, slots as European languages, then the ability of the societies that use these languages to differentiate emotional feeling and separate it from somatic discomfort is less evolved as well.

A similar argument was advanced in anthropology during the early days of interest in color categories. Roughly, it was felt that because some languages had fewer names for colors, therefore the abilities of speakers of those languages to discern colors was different. This was quickly proven false. People using a four- or five-color-category system can of course differentiate colors as well as someone using an eight- or nine-color system. The difference is that the colors are grouped differently for communication. In some cases, as shown in Conklin's (1955) studies of Hanunoo color categories, dimensions other than tint and hue are coded with color terms (see also Berlin and Kay 1969).[2]

It is tedious to go through the litany of reasons that linguists and anthropologists have rejected evolutionary schemes for classifying languages over the decades. It may be more satisfying to attempt to show why linguists and anthropologists find indirect expression and metaphor, which Leff seems to believe indicates that some languages are "living fossils" (1981:45), are as acceptable as direct classificatory terms within human communication systems.

The first question one must address is a question of function in language. As Malinowski maintained nearly fifty years ago, the meaning of any particular term must be understood in conjunction with its natural context of occurrence, or else distortion results. Moreover, language is far more than a series of indexes. Speakers use their language pragmatically to accomplish concrete acts. As Malinowski admonished in speaking about his own ethnographic situation in *Coral Gardens and their Magic*:

> It is obvious that words do not live as labels attached to pieces of cultural reality. Our Trobriand garden is not a sort of botanical show with tags tied on to every bush, implement or activity. It will be our business to reconstruct what speech *achieves* in a primitive culture, or, for that matter, in a highly developed one. (1935:21−22; emphasis mine)

The question of the pragmatic use of language is in fact central to the study of the meaning of any linguistic complex, whether it be Malinowski's Trobriand gardening terms, or an inventory of words used for talking about emotional states. Nor are such notions confined to anthropological esoterica. As psychiatrists Watzlawick, Beavin, and Jackson (1967:20−21) observe,

> a phenomenon remains unexplainable as long as the range of observation is not wide enough to include the context in which the phenomenon occurs. Failure to realize the intricacies of the relationships between an event and the matrix in which it takes place, between an organism and its environment, either confronts the observer with something "mysterious" or induces him to attribute to his object of study certain properties the object may not possess.[3]

Leff makes a distinction between direct referential terms for depression and anxiety, and words for the bodily experiences of emotion which are relatively undifferentiated. This ignores some of the primary functions of metaphor in human language. Metaphor is indeed the primary method of expressing emotion in all but the most clinical settings. In normal discourse metaphor serves as one kind of metacommunicational signal that something relatively unpredictable or unexpected is part of the communication. In another paper (Beeman 1982) I have suggested that other linguistic devices such as the use of unexpected or seemingly inappropriate stylistic forms signal emotional content in face-to-face interaction in Persian. Friedrich (1966, 1972), who pioneered this line of research, shows many stylistic devices in pronoun usage in Russian which convey emotional content in the context of communication.

Thus, there seems to be a clinical bias in Leff's discussion of language and emotion. In normal human interaction, metaphor, stylistic shifts, and even suprasegmental features such as tone of voice are far more prevalent as devices for conveying information concerning the emotional state of individuals. Indeed, Leff as a practicing psychiatrist should be more keenly aware of this than most individuals. The crux of the bias, one suspects, lies in the desire of the medical practitioner to value positively the ability of a patient to clearly label and categorize his own symptoms. The fact that contexts of interaction such as those that pit physician against patient in Western fashion do not exist in many places in the world seems not to be a factor in his discussion. With this observation we return once again to Malinowski (1935:58) who makes it clear that the difference that exists between abstract terminology and "primitive" language usage is one of contextualization:

> even in the most abstract and theoretical aspects of human thought and verbal usage, the real understanding of words is always ultimately derived from active experience of those aspects of reality to which the words belong. The chemist or the physicist understands the meaning of his most abstract concepts ultimately on the basis of his acquaintance with chemical and physical processes in the laboratory. . . . In short, there is no science whose conceptual, hence verbal, outfit is not ultimately derived from the practical handling of matter. . . . In one of my previous writings, I opposed civilised and scientific to primitive speech, and argued as if the theoretical uses of words were completely detached from their pragmatic sources. This was an error and a serious one at that. Between the savage use of words and the most abstract and theoretical one there is only a difference of degree. Ultimately all the meaning of all words is derived from bodily experience.

We may go Malinowski one better and assert that the body is ultimately the prime referent for all metaphor. Moreover, most of the vocabulary thought of as abstract expressions for emotional states can be shown to derive from words that indicate physical functions of the body. The twentieth century is the first period in intellectual history in which the notion that psychological states could be considered separately from physical body states became well established. Thus, it is arguably the case that words for the psychological experience of emotion as used in contemporary contexts are themselves metaphorical extensions of what were originally thought of as somatic expressions.[4]

One final point needs to be mentioned with regard to this topic. The ability to speak about disorder is also a function of the curing process. Thus when individuals in any culture seek to be cured of distress, emotional or otherwise, their idiom for speaking about that distress is related to the context of curing. As Good (1977), Good and Good (1981), and Kleinman (1980) have shown, traditional practitioners are adept in using less than precise descriptions in their healing practice. They may in fact depend on the sustaining of a particular metaphor in order to explain to their patients the care that they need to bring about a cure.

Western-trained psychiatrists have been socialized into their own system of communication about disease. Thus they may indeed have difficulty communicating with patients who have learned how to speak to practitioners in a particular idiom. It is both ethnocentric and medico-centric to blame such communication difficulties on the patients, their language, or culture.

In concluding this section of the discussion, I feel I should make some alternative suggestions to those of Leff for understanding non-Western terminology for emotional disorders. First, one should refrain from taking the vocabulary of emotion out of context and at face value. To assess the actual meaning of non-Western terminology used to describe emotional disorder, it is necessary to perform as thorough an investigation as possible of the way that terms are actually used in natural interaction contexts for describing emotional distress, as has been the practice of Good (1977), Kleinman (1980, 1982), and Rosaldo (1980), among others.

AMERICAN DEPRESSION AND BECK'S COGNITIVE THERAPY

A second area where linguistic anthropology can shed some light on depression and its treatment is in exploring the relationship between patient and therapist. It is close to being an article of faith among writers on depression that patients do not cure themselves of depression. Thus the nature of interaction between patient and practitioner must be a crucial factor in effecting a cure. Like any human communication, this kind of interaction has a structure that can be studied. If a particular kind of therapy is especially effective in providing a cure, then, an examination of its structure should provide insights into the disorder it is effective in curing.

In the last twenty years the work of Aaron T. Beck and his associates has come to be the base for a staple methodology in the treatment of depression. Known as "cognitive therapy," Beck's methodology is extraordinarily interesting because it is a non-Freudian "talking therapy" that seems to produce extraordinary results in curing patients of dysphoria.

Beck (1972:129−130) describes the basic theory that underlies this treatment thus:

> In brief, the theory postulates that the depressed or depression-prone individual has certain idiosyncratic cognitive patterns (schemas) which may become activated whether by specific stresses impinging on specific vulnerabilities, or by overwhelming nonspecific stresses. When the cognitive patterns are activated, they tend to dominate the individual's thinking and to produce the affective and motivational phenomena associated with depression.

At base is the belief of Beck and his associates that depression is not simply an affective disturbance. He writes:

> In recent years . . . we have collected a considerable amount of evidence that indicates that there is a thinking disorder in depression and that this thinking disorder may be more central than was previously believed. . . . In contrast to the highly generalized and bizarre thinking of schizophrenics, the thought disorder in depression tends to be more focalized and discrete and less bizarre. . . . In addition . . . depressives tend to have a number of other distorted or maladaptive thinking patterns. Such individuals tend to think, for example in an all-or-nothing manner. Other thinking errors in depressives include overgeneralization and selective abstraction. For example, depressed patients typically focus on the negative in the environment and overlook or discount the positive. (Beck and Burns 1978: 201−202)

Beck's therapeutic techniques differ from traditional psychotherapy in that they focus on the "here and now" with no excursions into childhood memories. Moreover, the "work" of therapy does not involve the classic "transference" process, but rather "training the patient in a number of exercises which must be done on a daily basis as homework between the sessions" (ibid., p. 201). His methods also differ from behavior therapy, since they concentrate on inner experiences: thoughts, feelings, wishes, daydreams, and attitudes. In addition, his therapy concentrates on trying to "change maladaptive thinking patterns" rather than trying to modify overt behavior (ibid., p. 202).

The strategies Beck advocates for treatment of patients is reminiscent of Albert Ellis's "rational-emotive psychotherapy" (Ellis 1958, 1962, 1971; Ellis and Whiteley 1979)[5] in that the patient assumes a great deal of personal responsibility for his cure, and is presented with a number of techniques that he himself uses in daily living to counteract what Beck terms "maladaptive thinking."[6]

At base cognitive psychotherapy assumes the rationality of sufferers. The problems are seen to lie not in possessing abnormal thought patterns but only in the calibration of those thought patterns. As Beck (1976:246) observes, "the ideas are generally not irrational, but are too absolute, broad and extreme; too highly personalized; and are used too arbitrarily to help the patient to handle the exigencies of his life." The techniques of therapy thus involve methods which force the patient to test his cognitive patterns against reality, and adjust them to the point where they become more productive. He writes in an early formulation of his therapy:

> Through the procedure of focusing on his distortions of reality and his unrealistic attitudes, the patient can loosen the grip of his erroneous ideas and sharpen his perception of reality. In this way he can become less vulnerable to the intrusions of his repetitive depressive thoughts and can formulate his experiences in a more realistic way. Consequently, the unpleasant affective consequences, such as depression, anxiety or agitation, are reduced. (Beck 1964:568)

The therapist aids in this process through techniques of what can only be described as persuasion—in point of fact, the exercise of effective rhetoric—to accomplish two things: (1) to persuade the patient to engage in activities that lead to concrete success, and (2) to help the patient to confront his cognitive distortions and test them to see if they are valid.

In the first case, the therapist sets up a series of graded assignments that he persuades the patient to engage in. They are simple at first, but lead to more complex accomplishments. "For example, a depressed housewife initially might be encouraged simply to boil an egg. With each successive mastered experience, she can build up to preparing an entire meal" (Beck 1976:272).

From the standpoint of linguistic anthropology, the second set of goals is extremely interesting since it involves direct engagement with the patient in interaction and, according to the case examples provided by Beck, in considerable role-playing and enactment in order for the therapist to effectively expose the patient's distorted cognitions to him. Beck makes the confrontational nature of the interaction very clear:

> Challenging the basic assumptions is important in treating patients, such as depressives, whose cognitive organization is essentially a "closed system." . . . Through questioning, a particular assumption may be subjected to argument. The procedure consists of: (1) eliciting the patient's reasons for believing the depresso-genic assumption, (2) marshaling, *as in a*

debate, the evidence in favor of or contradictory to the assumption. The notion, as in the Socratic dialogues, is to find the "truth" through verbalizing the opposite position on a given issue [emphasis added]. (Ibid., p. 270)[7]

Cognitive Therapy and Pragmatic Philosophy

In an early formulation of his thinking of cognitive therapy, Beck describes the basic thesis which underlies his entire theory:

The affective response is determined by the way an individual structures his experience. Thus, if an individual's conceptualization of a situation has an unpleasant content, then he will experience a corresponding unpleasant affective response. (Beck 1964:657)

Beck's approach here, and in his other prescriptions for the treatment of depression,[8] bears a remarkable resemblance to semantic analysis. Moreover, his therapeutic methods seem to follow the outlines of pragmatic philosophy in determining the nature of meaning.

At base, Beck describes depression and other emotional disorders as arising from meaning systems of patients which are out of phase with the demands of society. If we take a maladaptive cognitive system to be a particular species of meaning system, then the classic tenet of pragmatic philosophy, issued by the philosopher Charles Peirce, can be set alongside Beck's "thesis" above as a corollary:

Consider what effects that might conceivably have practical bearings, we consider the object of our conception to have. Then, our conception of these effects is the whole of our conception of the object. (Peirce 1878:287)

Peirce's insights have been slowly percolating into standard anthropological theory. Bean (1979), Beeman (1971, n.d., 1976a, 1977, 1981, 1982) and Silverstein (1972, 1976), among others, have made major theoretical statements on the applications of pragmatic theory in anthropology and linguistics.

A pragmatic approach to depression parallels Beck's notions in that it recognizes that phenomena in the mundane world have very different symbolic meanings for different individuals. Phenomena can be said to have meaning only insofar as they can be seen to link ongoing events for individuals. When an individual is confronted with an isolable phenomenon in his immediate environment, whether it be a word, an object, or a piece of behavior, he imbues it with meaning by performing three separate actions: (1) by isolating the phenomenon from other phenomena, (2) by identifying the antecedents of the phenomenon, that is, the historical linkages that the phenomenon has with himself and with his present condition, and (3) by predicting the consequences of the phenomenon, that is, the possible future events that could proceed from the phenomenon. By this definition, meaningless phenomena are those with unclear or absent precedents and consequences.

In this schema all phenomena are potentially symbolic in their functioning in human affairs, once they become isolated for attention. As symbols, they are able to span temporal boundaries by encapsulating both antecedent and consequent behavioral events for the individual—in this sense they may be seen as truly timeless. It is common to speak of symbols and other sign phenomena as if they were detached from the context of everyday reality; in fact, they should be thought of as multi-contextual, since they always exist in a reconstructed historicity, and in multitudes of constructed potential futures.

It now becomes possible to deal with Beck's notion of the question of maladaptive cognitive strategies of the depressed individual in pragmatic terms. If the creation of meaning by the individual is seen as a cognitive act in which antecedent events are fused with possible consequent events, then the isolated symbolic phenomena that are the subject of immediate attention become the focus for that act. All past events are not relevant to the present, and neither are all future possibilities. Those which are relevant are selected in the interpretation of events by every individual. Symbolically constructed phenomena serve as the linkages that allow the individual to identify and select particular events for inclusion in the chain of antecedent-consequent linkage which constitutes pragmatic meaning.

Understanding what a phenomenon portends also involves knowing the rules for performance of subsequent actions. In this respect, the cultural boundedness of the understanding of phenomena is circumscribed by the range of possible imaginable actions and events subsequent to encountering and isolating a given phenomenon.

Among all of these imaginable outcomes, a particular range will be identified as *probable*, still another range as *desirable*, and yet another range as capable of being affected by personal action on the part of an individual, among others.[9] Beck describes maladaptive cognitive structures in ways that suggest that the normal process of selection and evaluation of antecedents and consequents in the attribution of meaning is skewed for depressed patients in directions that do not accord with the norms for their culture. Moreover, this skewing is, for depressives, of a particular sort—biased in the direction of overgeneralization, selective abstraction, and negativism.

Looking at depression in this way allows us to posit a relationship between normal cognitive functioning and the cognitive functioning of depressive individuals. In short, normal cognitive functions of isolating phenomena and linking them to relevant antecedents and probable consequents, and acting on the meanings thus generated, become skewed. Improbable or unrealistic consequent events are projected for isolated phenomena. Irrelevant or incomplete sets of antecedents are dredged up for linkage.[10]

Two advantages of this conceptualization seem striking. First, it is possible to deal with the mechanics of the cognitive dimensions of depression without reference to particular cultural contexts. A depressive patient in any cultural setting can mis-select antecedents and consequents for a particular phenomenon. It is up to the practitioner, or other observer (the anthropologist?), to determine what the normal parameters of linkage actually are for the social and cultural setting in which the depressive patient is functioning.

Second, this schema allows for a conceptualization of depression which also can be used to describe mania and paranoia, symptoms sometimes found in conjunction with depression. Mania and paranoia can here be thought of as disorders of the linkage function which involve a qualitatively different skewing from culturally determined normalcy than that exhibited in depression.

Finally, this conceptualization helps to explain why Beck's cognitive therapy works in effecting cures. This explanation has a great deal to do with the rhetorical functions of speech and what these do to affect the course of thought in interaction.

Psychiatrists as Adroit Communicators

Beck's cognitive theory of depression seems weak in two respects. First, it may be the case that the techniques of cognitive therapy "work" not because they draw on an underlying "correct" conceptualization of depression and its mechanisms, but rather because the therapist is an especially adroit communicator. This does of course imply something very interesting about depressive disorder, namely, that it may yield to rhetoric. But if this is the case, then Beck's conception of depression as a set of patterns "possessed" by the patient is clearly erroneous, since its treatment is both highly contextualized and involves processes of social interaction.

In all human society we must recognize that there are different levels of adroitness in communication. Some individuals are poor communicators, and others are extraordinarily skillful. Being an adroit operator in interpersonal communication involves not only the ability to produce and recognize appropriate signs but also to achieve the communication of meaning with others: to make oneself understood. In carrying out that accomplishment, one is constantly involved in constraining the conditions under which interpretation takes place. This includes both the definition of context, and the definition of items that are important within that context.

The process that adroit operators control to a higher degree than other individuals is the semantic process of *redefinition*, the ability to convince an individual through the application of linguistic devices that a particular interpretation of phenomena is to apply during the process of interaction. The truly adroit operator is also able to direct the attention of other participants in interaction to specific phenomena—to force them to single out those phenomena for isolation. As I have shown in other publications (n.d., 1976a, 1977, n.d.) this process often involves the use of stylistic devices in communication which lead and direct the attention of individuals in directions that are predetermined by the adroit operator. The adroit operator in communication is well known. He or she is the super-salesperson, the superb rhetorician, the magician, the fine actor, the politician, the preacher, the excellent teacher, the labor negotiator, the diplomat, and, finally, the therapist.

Cognitive therapists practicing as Beck and others describe in their writings are masters at making redefinition of specific phenomena, contexts, and linkage processes incumbent on their patients. This is done through classic techniques of argumentation and persuasion—introducing contradictions and refutations to the patients' meaning system, and helping them to recalibrate their processes of phenomena isolation and antecedent-consequent linkage. One is reminded here of the techniques of Zen masters, who introduce paradox to their pupils as a strategic device to force them to test the parameters of their own sense of reality.[11]

The remarkable aspect of this kind of therapy is that it works at all. One has to ask what kind of disorder is it that responds to normal techniques of communication when applied in a rigorous way? The only parallel that comes to mind is that of physical therapy, applied to limbs that have been immobilized or inactive for long periods of time. They must be "convinced" through therapy to function once again along normal lines.

This brings me to the second point of criticism. Beck contradicts himself in a sense. He espouses a highly interactive form of therapy that emphasizes self-examination on the part of an individual of his or her social and communicative patterns, but then sees the disorder arising from those patterns as if they were "objects" isolated from the reality of everyday life—cognitions and cognitive schemas somehow possessed by the individual like a tumor or cyst. This I believe is an erroneous conceptualization. It cannot be said of a person that he "has certain idiocentric cognitive patterns" (Beck 1972:129) like he might have a piece of bad art. It is more accurate to emphasize—as Beck himself paradoxically does—that the process of imputing meaning to anything in one's environment is a dynamic process that involves complex inter-action between the individual, his immediate context, and the wider cultural context. The process of creating meaning, whether erroneous or accurate, is a dialectic between macrostructures of ideology and social values, and microstructures of individual ongoing interactions; between pragmatic foresight and after-the-fact rationalization. Any individual, depressed or not, must render an account of himself *to himself* and to the world at large. The resolution of all of these processes is the actual, visible, situationally based act of the creation of meaning.[12]

The difficulties above may arise in part from the fact that Beck does not appear to deal with the question of the genesis of depression. I raise this question again as a linguist, for it seems that in questions of semantic meaning individuals are rarely operating in isolation from each other. Thus, the social context of depression seems to be an inordinately important factor in determining the basic nature of depression itself, and by extension, means for its permanent cure. My feelings on this point are echoed by yet another group of therapists and researchers whose work is discussed in the following section.

DEPRESSION AND SOCIAL INTERACTION

Bateson and His Legacy

As has been suggested throughout this discussion, although depression has usually been diagnosed as an individual disorder, there is a strong current of opinion that suggests that it arises and is exacerbated through social interaction processes. For this reason, careful study of human interaction, particularly linguistic communication in interaction, is potentially of great use in understanding the dynamics of depression.

Among anthropologists who have made significant contributions to the study of communication and affective disorders, Gregory Bateson stands out as a giant. Paradoxically, he seems never specifically to have addressed the question of depression. Nevertheless, his numerous writings on schizophrenia and neurosis have had enormous influence on many therapists and researchers working to understand dysphoric conditions. Bateson's legacy for the study of depression seems to have been to point out that mental disorders are often extrasomatic, in that they reside, both in their genesis and in their maintenance, in the social networks of individuals who suffer from the disorder. Thus, therapists seeking to help patients achieve permanent recovery from depression, if they follow Bateson's lead, need to look at far more than just the individual sufferer: they need to focus on their patients' entire social environment to discover "dysphorogenic" interactive mechanisms. Bateson would go farther than this, however, and would claim that such mechanisms are features of the social and cultural system within which the patient lives.

In recent years, a whole group of highly practical therapists, known generally as practitioners of "family therapy," have operated on the principle that whole social systems, not individuals, need to be the objects of treatment. One of the principal leaders of this group has been Virginia Satir (1967, 1972; Satir et al. 1976*a*, 1976*b*). This work has also been supported by psychiatrists practicing a more standard variety of therapy, notably Watzlawick (1977, 1978; Watzlawick et al. 1967), Haley (1963, 1964, 1976), and Jackson (1968*a*, 1968*b*), all of whom, not surprisingly, have been influenced to varying degrees by Bateson's work.

One of the premises governing this line of study is that communication and interaction are ultimately the devices that bind individuals to their immediate social networks. Another premise is the well-known assumption drawn from symbolic interactionist studies that "noncommunication is an impossibility in human society." Yet a third is that metacommunication (communication about the nature of a given communication) is even more important than communication for determining the ultimate "meaning" of a given situation.[13]

Metacommunicational messages are transmitted often by attitudes, tone of voice, nonverbal behavioral signals, and other extralinguistic means. They are also coded in stylistic variation in language, and in things as subtle as word choice and juxtaposition of sentences. Satir (1972:25) offers this commonsense example:

> A mother may accept the bouquet clutched in her three-year-old's hand and say, "Where did you pick these?"—her voice and smile implying "How sweet of you to bring me these! Where do such lovely flowers grow?" This message would strengthen the child's feeling of worth. Or she might say "How pretty!" but add, "did you pick these in Mrs. Randall's garden?"—implying that the child was bad to steal them. This message would make him feel wicked and worthless.

Sociolinguistics is full of examples of the ways in which stylistic variation conveys a wealth of meaning through the choice of one variant over another in a matrix of contrasts (see, among many others, Beeman 1976, 1977, 1983; Friedrich 1966, 1972; Irvine 1974, 1979).

Bateson's early contribution was to suggest that metacommunicative patterns of behavior—body movement, gesture, stylistic variation in speech, tone of voice, and so on—could provide messages for individuals, particularly children, which would affect their self-image, and thereby their mental well-being (Bateson 1935, 1955, 1960a, 1960b, 1961; Bateson et al. 1956; Bateson and Jackson 1964). Although this theory has primarily been applied to the study of schizophrenia and neurosis, it has been given broad application by family therapists, who have made it the base of a wide variety of intervention therapies designed to modify the overall communication patterns in family and other close-knit social units, such as work groups.

This approach offers a theory about both the genesis of depression and its maintenance as a chronic syndrome for individuals. In general, feelings of low self-worth and pessimism are seen as reinforced by the members of the sufferer's immediate social environment. The physical and emotional incapacity of the depressive patient is then seen as fulfilling a functional role within the social constellation of which he is a member. This contrasts sharply with even Beck's cognitive approach, in that it stresses the social dynamics that underlie the maintenance of emotional states rather than looking on emotional disorders as an exclusively individual pathology.

Watzlawick et al. (1967:228) make the point clearly:

> Spouses who live lives of quiet desperation, deriving minimum gratification from their joint experiences, have been known to psychiatrists for a

long time. Traditionally, however, the reason for their misery is sought in the assumed *individual* pathology of one or both of them. They may be diagnosed as depressive, passive-aggressive, self-punishing, sadomaso-chistic, and so on. But these diagnoses obviously fail to grasp the *inter-dependent* nature of their dilemma, which may exist quite apart from their personality structure and may reside exclusively in the nature of their relationship "game."

Indeed, the model assumed here is one of a game where individuals are bound by a cognitive "frame" that locks them into a pattern of behavior from which they cannot escape as long as the relationship is maintained in its unchanged state. The game model too is derived from Bateson (1956), who noted that even animals are able to distinguish the cognitive frame "play" as a state of behavior and mental functioning apart from mundane reality. It is for this reason that intervention is used to break the existing pattern of interaction and communication operating in the social environment of the patient diagnosed as suffering from dysphoria or other emotional disorder.[14]

Sociolinguistics and Social Pathology

Theories of emotional disorder based on examination of interaction patterns, assuming frame/game orientation, are similar to current models in linguistic anthropology for explanation of the creation of meaning. Although some semanticists still insist on theories of meaning for linguistics which isolate words and their usage from social reality, pragmatic theory insists that meaning in culture is a social process. Far from being a property of words, meaning is a concrete accomplishment of communicators who have learned how to manage the dynamics of their social interactions.

In this manner, the conceptions that individuals form of the meaning of individual phenomena in their immediate environment are shaped by those individuals with whom they habitually interact. Transferring this insight to cognitive and interaction theories of depression, we might hypothesize that, in analogy to the linguistic model, individual maladaptive cognitive processes of the kind specified by Beck and the maladaptive interaction patterns replete with their destructive meta-communicational messages, as identified and treated by "family thera-pists," exist in a symbiotic relationship. At least one recent study suggests that this is the case. Beier (1980) suggests that depressive individuals tend to reinforce their depressogenic cognitive processes through the use of nonverbal metacommunicational devices. A person who feels that he or she is not desirable to others continually provides nonverbal signals that drive others away, thus proving the hypothesis, and allowing the person to maintain his or her depression.

Another remarkable study by Brown and Harris, *The Social Origins of Depression*, considers the total social environment of a group of 114 female psychiatric outpatients, and two control groups totaling 458 in Camberwell, England. The study was carried out by survey. The women's social *environment* was well documented in the study, but unfortunately no attempt was made to assess the nature or quality of the face-to-face interaction processes that the women engaged in with their friends, families, and neighbors. This is a pity, since evidence from the study indicates that this data would likely have been highly significant. This is especially indicated in one area of interactional data which was recorded: so-called triggering events, that is, social interaction and other life events that seemed to result directly in the women entering into a depressive state.

Except for the family therapists mentioned above, it is remarkable how little research is currently being carried out on the role of interaction processes in establishing and maintaining depression in individuals. Extensive bibliographic research for this chapter revealed only a few recent studies that linked interaction and depression, and the bulk of these dealt with patient-therapist interaction. It seems, moreover, that aside from Bateson and his followers, the chief source for interaction study as an approach to research on depression is a chapter in Jones and Girard's 1967 college text, *Foundations of Social Psychology*. To be sure, a person such as myself, coming to this problem as a commentator rather than an active researcher, may be unaware of various resources on this topic. Nevertheless, I do not believe I am too far wrong in saying that much more work needs to be carried out which provides for systematic investigation of the interaction structures in the social environment of depressive individuals.

In particular, it would seem that more study of this kind would go a long way toward solving some of the discrepancies that seem to prevent a clear picture of the principles that unify depression as a syndrome across cultures. Although symptomology and conceptions of depression seem to vary widely, it may well be in the processes of generation and maintenance of depression within the social system rather than in the individual psyche that the panhuman similarities are to be found.

NOTES

1. The controversy between those who view depression as a disease and those who view it as some other form of disorder continues to rage, and may not be resolved very soon. Part of the problem seems to be one of definitions. What is a disease, after all? Beck's summary of 1973 still seems valid:

> There are still major unresolved issues regarding its nature, its classification, and its etiology. Among these are the following:
> 1. Is depression an exaggeration of a mood experienced by the normal, or is it qualitatively as well as quantitatively different from a normal mood?
> 2. Is depression a well-defined clinical entity with a specific etiology and a predictable onset, course, and outcome, or is it a "wastebasket" category of diverse disorders?
> 3. Is depression a type of reaction (Myerian concept) [see Myer 1908], or is it a disease (Kraepelinian concept) [see Kraepelin 1913]?
> 4. Is depression caused primarily by psychological stress and conflict, or is it related primarily to a biological derangement? (Beck 1973:3−4)

2. Color term research has generated considerable interest in anthropology. Much of direct cross-cultural field research has focused on the question of whether language affects color memory. Heider's assertion (1972) that memory for color is based on certain "focal" areas in the color space, and is independent of language and culture has been disputed by Lucy and Shweder (1979) who demonstrate that language is an important aid for color memory. Other references are included in Lucy and Shweder's work. None, significantly, claim that basic discriminatory processes are affected by linguistic categorization.

3. As an example, Watzlawick et al. (1967) cite the example of the ethologist Konrad Lorenz in one of his imprinting experiments with ducklings in his garden. As he dragged himself, crouching, around the garden in figure eight configurations, quacking, he didn't notice a horrified group of tourists, unable to see the ducklings in the tall grass, viewing what seemed to be the absolutely insane behavior of an old man (p. 20).

4. These words that describe emotional states in English are metaphors, deriving from descriptions of actions that can be observed to result from those states. Among these are *joy* (from Latin *guadia*=to rejoice), *sad* (from Old English *saed*=sated, Latin *satis*=enough), *happy* (from Middle English *hap*= fortune, luck), *glad* (Old High German *glat*=shining, smooth), and so forth. English speakers, by this criterion, might well fail Leff's test.

5. Indeed, Ellis compiled a bibliography with Robert Murphy which combines sources in rational-emotive psychotherapy and cognitive psychotherapy (Ellis and Murphy 1975). It should be noted that Beck does not cite the work of

Ellis in his writings before 1976, indicating that he may only have noticed the parallel structures in their work after his theories were already well formulated.

6. There is some internal argumentation in Beck's work about the nature of "maladaptive thinking." Indeed, it seems that many of the environmental conditions that set off depressive reactions in sufferers arise not from questionable perceptions of reality but rather from real life trauma. Nevertheless, Beck (1976:236) notes that inability to deal with danger or trauma may itself be maladaptive:

> It would seem difficult to justify applying the label "maladaptive" to an accurate appraisal of danger (and its associated anxiety) or to the recognition of a real loss and the resulting arousal of grief. Yet under some circumstances, even such reality-oriented ideation may be regarded as maladaptive because of its interference with functioning. For example, steeplejacks, bridgeworkers and mountain climbers may not only suffer serious discomfort, but may be subjected to greatly increased risk by a stream of thoughts or images about falling. . . . People engaged in hazardous activities generally acquire the ability to disregard or extinguish such thoughts. With experience, they seem to form a psychological buffer that diminishes the force and frequency of such thoughts.

7. Beck includes in his writings a number of dialogues that illustrate this technique. Although they are rather long, they capture the flavor of the confrontational nature of the therapy, and are thus somewhat important for understanding the reasons for the effectiveness of the technique.

8. And other disorders, particularly various forms of neurosis, phobias, and so forth (Beck 1976, chaps. 6, 7, 8).

9. Of course these ranges can be seen as overlapping. The material in the above section derives from Beeman (1976*a*:76−85), and was originally developed as a general discussion of the processes of creation of meaning in language.

10. I wish to explain that the schema presented here is not a diagnostic schema, or one based on any clinical study of depression. It is rather a way of conceptualizing depression which may help to bring it into focus against some models for cognitive functioning in language which have proved useful in discussions of cognitive dimensions of semantics. I would be delighted if the medical community found these proposals conceptually useful.

11. The techniques of argumentation cited by Beck are coupled with rather sophisticated linguistic analysis in the work of Bandler and Grinder (1975, 1979; Grinder and Bandler 1975). In their best-known book, *The Structure of Magic*, they specifically advocate transformational-generative analysis of patients' sentences as a technique for ferreting out unsaid or intended meanings, as well as for detecting the kind of "maladaptive cognitive structures" noted by Beck. As an example, they write:

> There is a special case which we like to emphasize of certain words which
> have no referential index. This, specifically, is the set of words which
> contains universal quantifiers such as *all*, *each*, *every*, *any*. The universal
> quantifier is a different form when combined with other linguistic elements
> such as the negative element—*never*, *nowhere*, *none*, *no one*, *nothing*,
> *nobody*. . . . We use a special form of challenge for the universal
> quantifier and words and phrases containing it, for example, . . .
>> *Nobody pays any attention to what I say.*
> may be challenged as:
>> *You mean to tell me that NOBODY EVER pays attention to you AT ALL?*
>> (Bandler and Grinder 1975:82−83)

This form of challenge asks clients if there are any exceptions to their
generalizations. A single exception to the generalization starts the client on the
process of assigning referential indices and ensures the detail and richness in the
client's model necessary to have a variety of options for coping.

12. See Beeman 1976c and 1982:17−18, for additional discussion of this
point.

13. Note the difference between "metalanguage," which is communication about the nature of the code, and "metacommunication," which is an
additional set of messages given over and above overt linguistic codes by
individuals in interaction situations. Thus a wink can inform participants in
interaction that what is being said is not to be taken seriously. A particular tone
of voice can clue a sensitive individual that though someone they are interacting
with makes an offer, that person will be very unhappy if the offer is accepted.
Silverstein (1976:16) points out another level of understanding: "Meta-
semantics," which describes "language [used] to describe the semantics of
language."

14. The late Erving Goffman, while not dealing with depression per se,
treated many social anomalies and pathologies using the frame/game mechanism. See particularly his *Frame Analysis* (1974).

REFERENCES

Akiskal, H. S., and W. T. McKinney, Jr.
    1973   Depressive Disorders: Toward a Unified Hypothesis. Science
                182:20−29.
Anthony, E. J., and Therese Benedek, eds.
    1975   Depression and Human Existence. Boston: Little, Brown.
Arieti, S., and J. Bemporad
    1978   Severe and Mild Depression. New York: Basic Books.
Bandler, R., and J. Grinder

1975   The Structure of Magic I. Palo Alto: Science and Behavior
            Books.
1979   Frogs into Princes: Neuro Linguistic Programming. John O.
            Stevens, ed. Moab, Utah: Real People Press.

Bateson, G.
1935   Culture Contact and Schizmogenesis. Man 35:178−183.
1942   Social Planning and the Concept of 'Deutero-Learning' in Rela-
            tion to the Democratic Way of Life. *In* Science, Philosophy and
            Religion, Second Symposium. New York: Harper. Pp. 81−97.
1955   A Theory of Play and Fantasy. Psychiatric Research Reports
            2:39−51.
1956   The Message 'This is Play.' *In* Transactions of the Second
            Conference on Group Processes. New York: Josiah Macy, Jr.,
            Foundation. Pp. 145−242.
1958   The New Conceptual Frames for Behavioral Research. Pro-
            ceedings of the Sixth Annual Psychiatric Institute. Princeton:
            The New Jersey Neuro-Psychiatric Institute. Pp. 54−71.
1960*a*   The Group Dynamics of Schizophrenia. *In* Chronic Schizo-
            phrenia. Exploration in Theory and Treatment. Lawrence
            Appleby, Jordan M. Scher, and John Cumming, eds. Glencoe,
            Ill.: Free Press. Pp. 90−105.
1960*b*   Minimal Requirements for a Theory of Schizophrenia. Archives
            of General Psychiatry 2:447−491.
1961   The Biosocial Integration of the Schizophrenic Family. *In* Ex-
            ploring the Base for Family Therapy. Nathan W. Ackerman,
            Frances L. Beatman, and Sanford N. Sherman, eds. New York:
            Family Service Association. Pp. 116−122.
1972   Steps to an Ecology of Mind. Scranton: Chandler.
1979   Mind and Nature: A Necessary Unity. New York: E. P. Dutton.

Bateson, G., and D. D. Jackson
1964   Some Varieties of Pathogenic Organization. *In* Disorders of
            Communication. Vol. 42. Research Publications. Association
            for Research in Nervous and Mental Disease. Pp. 270−283.

Bateson, G., D. D. Jackson, J. Haley, and J. Weakland
1956   Toward a Theory of Schizophrenia. Behavioral Science 1:
            251−264.

Bean, S.
1978   Symbolic and Pragmatic Semantics: A Kannada System of
            Address. Chicago: University of Chicago Press.

Beck, A. T.
1961   A Systematic Investigation of Depression. Comprehensive Psy-
            chiatry 2:162−170.

1963   Thinking and Depression. Vol. 1, Idiosyncratic Content and
                Cognitive Distortions. Archives of General Psychiatry 9:
                36−45.

1964   Thinking and Depression. Vol. 2, Theory and Therapy.
                Archives of General Psychiatry 10:561−571.

1973   The Diagnosis and Management of Depression. Philadelphia:
                University of Pennsylvania Press.

1976   Cognitive Therapy and the Emotional Disorders. New York:
                Meridian-New American Library.

Beck, A. T., C. H. Ward, M. Mendelson, J. Mock, and J. Erbaugh
1961   An Inventory for Measuring Depression. Archives of General
                Psychiatry 4:561−571.

Beck, A. T., and D. Burns
1978   Cognitive Therapy of Depressed Suicidal Outpatients. *In* De-
                pression: Biology, Psychodynamics and Treatment. Jona-
                than O. Cole, Alan F. Schatzberg, and Shervert H. Frazier,
                eds. New York: Plenum. Pp. 199−211.

Beeman, W. O.
n.d.   Interaction Semantics: Preliminary Foundations for the Obser-
                vational Study of Meaning. Master's thesis, University of Chi-
                cago, 1971.

n.d.   The Meaning of Stylistic Variation in Iranian Verbal Inter-
                action. Ph.D. diss., University of Chicago, 1976.

1976a   Status, Style and Strategy in Iranian Interaction. Anthropo-
                logical Linguistics 18(7):305−322.

1976b   What is (Iranian) National Character. Iranian Studies 9(1):
                29−43.

1977   The Hows and Whys of Persian Style: A Pragmatic Approach.
                In Studies in Language Variation. Ralph W. Fasold and
                Roger W. Shuy, eds. Washington, D.C.: Georgetown Univer-
                sity Press. Pp. 269−282.

1981   Why Do They Laugh? An Interactional Approach to Humor in
                Traditional Iranian Improvisatory Theater. Journal of American
                Folklore 94(4):506−526.

1982   Culture, Performance and Communication in Iran. Tokyo:
                Institute for the Study of Languages and Cultures of Asia and
                Africa (ILCAA).

n.d.   Affectivity in Persian Language Usage. MS. *In* Affective
                Dimensions of Middle Eastern Culture. Byron Good, Mary Jo
                Good, Michael M. J. Fischer, and Marvin Zonis, eds.

n.d.   Iranian Interaction Styles. Bloomington: Indiana University
                Press.

Beier, E. G.
1980   Towards a Theory of Nonverbal Behavior. Annals of the New
            York Academy of Sciences 340:9—15.
Berlin, B., and P. Kay
1969   Basic Color Terms: Their Universality and Evolution.
            Berkeley: University of California Press.
Boyer, L.
1964   Folk Psychiatry of the Apaches of the Mescalero Indian Reser-
            vation. *In* Magic, Faith and Healing. A. Kiev, ed. New York:
            Free Press.
Brink, A.
1979   Depression and Loss. A Theme in Robert Burton's "Anatomy
            of Melancholy" (1621). Canadian Journal of Psychiatry: 24(8):
            767—771.
Brown, G. W., and T. Harris
1978   Social Origins of Depression: A Study of Psychiatric Disorder
            in Women. New York: Free Press.
Conklin, H.
1955   Hanunoo Color Categories. Southwest Journal of Anthropology
            11:339—344.
Edgerton, R.
1966   Conceptions of Psychosis in Four East-African Societies.
            American Anthropologist 68:408—425.
Ellis, A.
1958   Rational Psychotherapy. Journal of General Psychology 59:
            35—49.
1962   Reason and Emotion in Psychotherapy. New York: Lyle Stuart.
1971   Growth through Reason: Verbatim Cases in Rational-Emotive
            Psychotherapy. Palo Alto: Science and Behavior Books.
Ellis, A., and R. Murphy
1975   A Bibliography of Articles and Books on Rational-Emotive
            Therapy and Cognitive-Behavior Therapy. New York: Institute
            for Rational Living.
Ellis, A., and J. M. Whiteley
1979   Theoretical and Empirical Foundations of Rational-Emotive
            Therapy. Belmont, Calif.: Brooks-Cole.
Fábrega, H.
1975*a*   Cultural Influences in Depression. *In* Depression and Human
            Existence. E. James Anthony and Therese Benedek, eds. Bos-
            ton: Little, Brown. Pp. 67—90.
1975*b*   Social Factors in Depression. *In* Depression and Human Exis-
            tence. E. James Anthony and Therese Benedek, eds. Boston:
            Little, Brown. Pp. 91—119.

Fann, W. E., I. Kapacan, A. D. Pokorny, and R. L. Williams, eds.
   1977   Phenomenology and Treatment of Depression. New York:
                Spectrum Publications.
Friedrich, P.
   1966   Structural Implication of Russian Pronominal Usage. *In* Socio-
                linguistics. William Bright, ed. The Hague: Mouton. Pp. 214–
                259.
   1972   Social Context and Semantic Feature: The Russian Pronominal
                Usage. *In* Directions in Sociolinguistics. John J. Gumperz and
                Dell Hymes, eds. New York: Holt, Rinehart and Winston.
                Pp. 270–300.
   1979*a*   The Symbol and Its Relative Non-Arbitrariness. *In* Language,
                Context and the Imagination. Stanford: Stanford University
                Press.
   1979*b*   Language, Context and the Imagination. Stanford: Stanford
                University Press.
Gada, M. T.
   1982   A Cross Cultural Study of Symptomatology of Depression. The
                International Journal of Social Psychiatry 28(3):195–202.
Gallant, D. M., and G. M. Simpson, eds.
   1976   Depression. New York: Spectrum Publications.
Gaw, A., ed.
   1982   Cross-Cultural Psychiatry. Boston: John Wright.
Goffman, E.
   1974   Frame Analysis. Cambridge: Harvard University Press.
Good, B. J.
   1977   The Heart of What's the Matter. The Semantics of Illness in
                Iran. Culture, Medicine, and Psychiatry 1:25–28.
Good, B. J., and M. J. DelVecchio Good
   1981   The Semantics of Medical Discourse. *In* Sciences and Cultures.
                Vol. 5, Sociology of the Sciences. Everett Mendelsohn and
                Yehuda Elkana, eds. Pp. 177–212. Boston: D. Reidel.
Grinder, J., and R. Bandler
   1976   The Structure of Magic II. Palo Alto: Science and Behavior
                Books.
Haley, J.
   1963   Strategies of Psychotherapy. New York: Grune and Stratton.
   1964   Research on Family Patterns: An Instrument Measurement.
                Family Process 3:41–65.
   1976   Problem-Solving Therapy: New Strategies for Effective Family
                Therapy. San Francisco: Jossey-Bass.
Heider, E. R.
   1972   Universals in Color Naming and Memory. Journal of Experi-
                mental Psychology 93:10–20.

Irvine, J.
1974   Strategies of Status Manipulation in the Wolof Greeting. *In*
              Explorations in the Ethnography of Speaking. Richard Bauman
              and Joel Sherzer, eds. London: Cambridge University Press.
              Pp. 167–191.
1979   Formality and Informality in Communicative Events. American
              Anthropologist 81(4):773–790.
Jablensky, A., N. Sartorius, W. Gulbinat, and G. Ernberg
1981   Characteristics of depressive patients contacting psychiatric ser-
              vices in four cultures. Acta Psychiatrica Scandinavica 63:
              367–383.
Jackson, D. D.
1968*a*   Communication, Family and Marriage. Palo Alto: Science and
              Behavior Books.
1968*b*   Therapy, Communication and Change. Palo Alto: Science and
              Behavior Books.
Jones, E. E., and H. B. Gerard
1967   Foundations of Social Psychology. New York: John Wiley and
              Sons.
Kleinman, A.
1980   Patients and Healers in the Context of Culture: An Exploration
              of the Borderland between Anthropology, Medicine, and Psy-
              chiatry. Berkeley, Los Angeles, London: University of Cali-
              fornia Press.
1982   Neurasthenia and Depression: A Study of Somatization and
              Culture in China. Culture, Medicine and Psychiatry 6(2):
              117–190.
Kraepelin, E.
1913   Manic-Depressive Insanity and Paranoia. *In* Textbook of Psy-
              chiatry. R. M. Barclay, trans. Edinburgh: Livingstone.
Leff, J.
1973   Culture and the Differentiation of Emotional States. British
              Journal of Psychiatry 123:299–306.
1977   The Cross-Cultural Study of Emotions. Culture, Medicine, and
              Psychiatry 1:317–350.
1981   Psychiatry Around the Globe: A Transcultural View. New
              York: Marcel Dekker.
Lesse, S.
1980   Masked Depression—The Ubiquitous But Unappreciated Syn-
              drome. The Psychiatric Journal of the University of Ottawa
              5(4):268–273.
Lucy, J. A., and R. A. Shweder
1979   Whorf and His Critics: Linguistic and Nonlinguistic Influences
              on Color Memory. American Anthropologist 81:581–607.

Malinowski, B.
1935   Coral Gardens and Their Magic. Vol. 2. New York: American Book Company.
Marsella, A. J.
1980   Depressive Experience and Disorder Across Cultures. *In* Handbook of Cross-Cultural Psychology. Harry C. Triandis and Juris G. Draguns, eds. Boston: Allyn and Bacon, Inc. Pp. 237–290.
Meyer, A.
1908   The Problems of Mental Reaction Types. *In* The Collected Papers of Adolf Meyer. Vol. 2. Baltimore: Johns Hopkins Press. Pp. 591–603.
Orley, J.
1970   Culture and Mental Illness: A Study from Uganda. Nairobi: East Africa Publishing House.
1979   Psychiatric Disorders in Two African Villages. Archives of General Psychiatry 36:513–520.
1964   Indigenous Yoruba Psychiatry. *In* Magic, Faith, and Healing. A. Kiev, ed. New York: Free Press.
Resner, G., and J. Hartog
1970   Concepts and Terminology of Mental Disorder among Malays. Journal of Cross-Cultural Psychology 1:369–381.
Rosaldo, M. Z.
1980   Knowledge and Passion: Ilongot Notions of Self and Social Life. Cambridge: Cambridge University Press.
Satir, V. M.
1967   Conjoint Family Therapy. Rev. ed. Palo Alto: Science and Behavior Books.
1972   Peoplemaking. Palo Alto: Science and Behavior Books.
Satir, V., J. Strachowiak, and H. A. Taschman
1976*a*   Changing with Families. Palo Alto: Science and Behavior Books.
1976*b*   Helping Families to Change. New York: Aronson, Jason, Inc.
Schmidt, K.
1964   Folk Psychiatry in Sarawak: A Tentative System of Psychiatry of the Iban. *In* Magic, Faith, and Healing. A. Kiev, ed. New York: Free Press.
Silverstein, M.
1972   Linguistic Theory: Syntax, Semantics, Pragmatics. *In* Annual Review of Anthropology. Bernard J. Siegel, ed. Palo Alto: Annual Reviews 1:349–382.
1973   Linguistics and Anthropology. *In* Linguistics and Neighboring Disciplines. Linguistic Series, no. 4. R. Bartsch and T. Vennemann, eds. Leiden: North Holland.

1976   Shifters, Linguistic Categories and Cultural Description. *In* Meaning in Anthropology. Keith H. Basso and Henry A. Kelby, eds. Albuquerque: University of New Mexico Press.

Takahashi, R.
1974   Treatment for Depression in Japan. *In* Depression in Everyday Practice. P. Kielholtz, ed. Bern: Hans Huber. Pp. 213–228.

Tellenbach, H.
1980   Melancholy. E. Eng, trans. Pittsburgh: Duquesne University Press.

Watzlawick, P.
1977   How Real Is Real? Confusion, Disinformation, Communication. New York: Random House.
1978   The Language of Change: Elements of Therapeutic Communication. New York: Basic Books.

Watzlawick, P., J. H. Beavin, and D. D. Jackson
1967   Pragmatics of Human Communication. New York: W. W. Norton.

Watzlawick, P., and J. H. Weakland, eds.
1977   The Interactional View: Studies at the Mental Research Institute, Palo Alto, 1965–1974. New York: W. W. Norton.

8

The Theoretical Implications of Converging Research on Depression and the Culture-Bound Syndromes

John E. Carr and Peter P. Vitaliano

Despite remarkable advances in the pharmacotherapy and psychotherapy of depression over the past two decades, the phenomenon remains an intriguing challenge to researchers. A definitive etiology is still unavailable, and diagnoses are frequently conflicting and inaccurate (Gershon 1980). This situation has prompted researchers to address the need to develop a more comprehensive and heuristic theoretical approach capable of integrating the complexity of available research findings and focusing future research endeavors (Kleinman 1982).

In searching for alternative models, consideration must be given to incorporating not only biological and behavioral literature but also the rapidly increasing body of literature accruing from international and cross-cultural investigations. A comprehensive model of psychopathology should be capable of systematically incorporating phenomena such as the so-called exotic or culture-bound syndromes. Are disorders such as the *amok* phenomenon unique to specific cultures or are they simply culturally determined variants of universal forms of psychopathology like depression (Yap 1969)?

There is a sufficient body of evidence to warrant consideration of the point of view that presumed universal forms of psychopathology (as defined by current psychiatric nomenclature) are themselves culture-bound syndromes; that depression, like amok, is a culturally determined variant, not of a universal form of psychopathology but of a range of alternative responses to universal antecedent life events. A brief overview of the relevant research literature regarding depression is instructive in this regard and illustrates some of the inherent methodological and conceptual difficulties of the Western nosological system with which the researcher must contend.

1. Individuals diagnosed as depressed do not manifest a common set of behavioral symptoms but instead display varying combinations of a wide range of symptomatology that overlaps with other diagnostic categories. While there is a small set of specific behavioral signs that appear to form the basis for the eventual diagnosis, empirical studies show that the correlation among these behaviors, while sometimes statistically significant, generally is not sufficient to predict the occurrence of one depressed behavior based on the observation of another (Carson and Adams 1981; Robbins 1982; Lonnavist 1980).

2. Manifest symptomatology is subject to divergent interpretations in varying cultural settings among clinically trained as well as lay individuals (Sandifer et al. 1969; Katz and Sandborn 1973; Sandborn and Katz 1980; Leff 1981; Teuting et al. 1981).

3. There is sufficient evidence to question the universality of the concept of depression as defined within the Western biomedical tradition. It has even been noted that the concept has no linguistic equivalence, let alone conceptual analog, in certain non-Western cultures (Marsella 1979; Leighton et al. 1963; Terminsen and Ryan 1970; Tseng and Hsu 1969; Resner and Hartog 1970; Schmidt 1964; Prince 1964; Edgerton 1966; Orley 1970; Boyer 1964). This does not mean that depression is nonexistent in these cultures, but rather that the identifying cues, meaning, and behavioral response may be assigned within cultures.

4. Given this relative lack of universality in either manifest behavior or conceptualization, it is not surprising that there is substantial disagreement among trained clinicians regarding diagnosis, and that researchers encounter serious methodological difficulties in attempting to investigate depression across cultures (Marsella 1979; Dohrenwend and Dohrenwend 1965, 1969, 1974). These difficulties have been attributed variously to definitions of disorder, degree of case contact, and training of interviewers, as well as lack of norms, the inappropriate application of norms, inappropriate scale formats, lack of conceptual equivalence, and failure to determine indigenous baselines for problem behavior.

5. Given the above difficulties, it would follow, and indeed it appears, that there are significant variations in the reported distribution rates of depression around the world (Marsella 1979; Dohrenwend and Dohrenwend 1965, 1969, 1974).

The apparent confusion and inconsistency of these findings have been of increasing concern to researchers and suggest a fundamental fallacy in the process by which we have arrived at a definition of the illness. Psychiatric nomenclature presumes that a universal biomedical disease concept can be defined in terms of manifest affective behaviors presumed to be symptomatic of the underlying disease process. The fallacy in this conceptualization is the inherent assumption that differential affective behaviors imply differential disease processes. The research literature would suggest this assumption is unwarranted.

In a recent methodological review, Dohrenwend and Dohrenwend (1982) have reported that commonly used psychiatric epidemiologic research screening scales, while intercorrelated, do not measure dimensions that coincide with the psychiatric nosological system. They appear instead to be measures of self-esteem, helplessness, hopelessness, dread, anxiety, sadness, confused thinking, or a "nonspecific psychological distress" analogous to fever—"When it is elevated, you know that something is wrong but you do not know what specific thing is wrong until you learn more about the context" (p. 1272).

This conclusion is consistent with converging research findings from psychiatric epidemiology and community mental health and suggests support for a comprehensive model of "distress" as opposed to the traditional psychiatric model of arbitrarily differentiated affective disease states (Albee 1977, 1980; Swift 1980). In this model distress is defined as a complex of biobehavioral responses to antecedent stressors (perceived as well as real) mediated by vulnerability to stress (demographic factors; genetic, physiologic, and psychologic predisposition), and psychological and social resources (coping strategies, social supports).

VULNERABILITY

In their social-psychological theory of depression, Brown and Harris (1978) identify three groups of determining factors in depression based on their review of the relevant research literature: (1) provoking agents,

(2) vulnerability factors, and (3) symptom formation factors. According to their review, certain individuals appear to be highly vulnerable to depression as a result of an early developmental learning history characterized by a high degree of deprivation in sources of value or reward. This deprivation in learning conditions leads to a low sense of self-esteem, an excessively critical view of self and others, and a low sense of self-worth, mastery, and self-confidence. Hopelessness is the term chosen by the authors to describe this state which, they say, leads to a ''gambit of feelings ranging from distress, depression, and shame, to anger.'' The critical factor in this process is the generalization of the sense of hopelessness to all experiences encountered by the individual. Low self-esteem is viewed as both predisposing a person to a depressive reaction and, when exaggerated, becoming a prominent feature of the depressive disorder itself. Thus, the cognitive organization and conceptual processes of the individual play a critical role in the etiology of depression.

ANTECEDENT LIFE EVENTS

Given this vulnerability, the individual is especially at risk in the presence of precipitating agents defined in terms of severe life events encountered by the patient. However, life change in and of itself is not the critical factor. Rather, it is the meaningfulness of these events to the individual, mediated by cognitive process, that is of significance to the individual. Events involving only short-term threat, although they may represent considerable emotional distress, do not contribute to the onset of depression. Instead, it is the event which involves a long-term threat, that is, a major loss or disappointment with long-term consequences, that has significance.

The cognitively mediated meaning assigned to antecedent events ranges between the idiosyncratic and the universal. The specificity and nature of the ''loss'' phenomenon suggests certain antecedent life conditions may have acquired universal significance as precipitants of the depressive response.

The concept of universal antecedents has been advanced by a number of researchers, among them Boucher and Brandt (1981), who have provided evidence suggesting that the underlying meanings of antecedent events are the stimuli for the experience of emotion and that these meanings can be inferred across cultures. For example, they argue that ''if the loss of 'positive significant other' is a universal stimulus for sadness, and 'mother' is universally evaluated positively, 'death of mother' may be a universal antecedent for sadness'' (p. 281).

Osgood et al. (1975) also have provided evidence of the existence of universals of affective meaning, while Aberle et al. (1950) and, more recently, Lonner (1980) have argued in favor of the concept of psychological universals as determinants of behavior. The apparent universality of values assigned to life stress events by subjects in differing cultures (Holmes and Rahe 1967) would appear to be consistent with this concept.

SYMPTOM FORMATION

The literature on symptom formation factors does not appear to be as well developed as that on provoking agents and vulnerability factors. However, evidence is cited by Brown and Harris that is consistent with the view that sociocultural factors define the eventual symptom formation outcome of the disorder. Social factors play a formative role in the onset of depression at all treatment levels and with diverse symptom pictures. They play a role in determining both vulnerability and loss events and appear to determine the severity of the condition once it occurs. Again, the process by which sociocultural factors exert an impact is a function of the person's appraisal of the meaning of life events, with the somatic symptoms of depression being the sequelae of this basic cognitive appraisal (Brown and Harris 1978).

THE ROLE OF LEARNING

A review of the social learning literature by Carson and Adams (1981) agrees with that of Brown and Harris and indicates a preliminary set of ''anomalous reinforcement conditions'' that appear to be involved in the predisposition to and precipitation of depressive episodes. The origins of these reinforcement conditions remain unclear, and likely involve a range of factors including physiological dysfunction, history of early deprivation of reward sources, life history of continuous aversive events, and so forth. However, the subsequent impact of these events on the individual's life can be clearly documented. Lewinsohn and his colleagues (1974) report depressed individuals are less active interpersonally, provide less reinforcement for others, miss opportunities to emit and elicit behavior, and have restricted interpersonal contacts. Similarly, Coyne (1976a, 1976b) has reported that depressives lack specific skills requisite to eliciting support from others when life becomes stressful. This finding is especially important since Paykel et al. (1969) have reported that depressed patients may have experienced three times the number of stressful life events during the six months prior to onset of depression as controls. Stressful events appear to evoke stronger needs for social support and nurturance, and individuals who become depressed in response to life stress events may not have the ability to elicit the support they need without also inducing negative affect in others (Coyne 1976a, 1976b). Subjects diagnosed as depressed evoke significantly more depression, anxiety, hostility, and rejection from normal subjects than do nondepressed patients or normal controls (Hammer and Peters 1977).

COGNITION

As noted earlier, the anomalous reinforcement condition appears to exert an effect on subsequent cognitive appraisal capabilities, which are viewed by an increasing number of researchers as playing a central role in depressive phenomena. There is considerable disagreement, however, as to the nature of this role (Lazarus et al. 1970; Beck 1974; Depue et al. 1979; Coyne et al. 1981). According to Beck (1967, 1976) stressful life events precipitate severe affective reactions only in individuals who have a specific type of cognitive organization that predisposes them to negative idiosyncratic perception and appraisal of these events. Beck observes that cognition in the depressive is dominated by negative views of the self, the world, and the future, low self-regard, ideas of deprivation, self-blame, self-criticism, overwhelming problems of responsibility, self-injunctions, and "escapist desires." In addition, the depressive appears to notice and recall only the negative features of information. There is a marked preoccupation with a sense of loss frequently resulting in the perception of hypothetical and pseudo-losses construed and experienced as if they were actual events.

Beck and Rush (n.d.) have reported a number of laboratory investigations demonstrating mood changes in response to cognitive manipulation. Earlier researchers have provided evidence to suggest that the labeling of affective states is a function of the interaction of physiological, cognitive, and contextual factors (Schachter and Singer 1962), but the mechanisms of this interaction remain unclear. Further, the specific type of cognitive organization to which Beck refers remains undefined, as he tends to focus on content and subjective meaning, while ignoring a body of research relating cognitive structure to coping style.

Within cultural groups, language and conceptual structure are correlated (Whorf 1956), and lexical properties of a language can provide clues to the cognitive processes of a cultural group (Osgood et al. 1975; Carr 1980). The research of Barry and Annis (1974), Dawson (1969), Witkin (1967), Carr (1980), and others has shown that the ability of individuals to cope adaptively to ecological, cultural, and interpersonal demands is a function of the relative degree of *differentiation* of their cognitive structure. Operationally defined as the degree to which an individual is able to make fine discriminations between stimulus events, conditions, or persons, differentiation is both a product and determinant of socialization processes.

Differences in the structure of cognition (e.g., high versus low differentiation) should not be confused with differences in content or "domain" (e.g., somatic versus psychological concepts). Both features are to be found not only within but also between various socioeconomic, ethnic, and cultural groups. Within any culture one might find individuals with highly differentiated psychological concepts for defining emotions, while for others there may be highly differentiated somatic concepts referring to the same states. Given sufficient time, these individuals should be capable of "communicating," once they have discovered the structural equivalencies that exist between their conceptual systems (Carr 1980). Thus the health care practitioner who fails to appreciate these potential differentials in structure runs the risk of misperceptions, mislabeling, and misdiagnosis, a phenomenon that Leff (1981) has already reported and that seems a possible contributing factor to the confusion in epidemiological studies across cultures.

Thus, we identify two specific variables within the category of cognitive factors which have been shown to play a role in the development of depression: content and differentiation of structure. The former is especially important in determining the meaning assigned to behaviors, symptoms, and self-concept. The latter appears to relate more to the ability to delineate within a content category a wide range of perceptual and behavioral coping options. The individual with a more highly differentiated system of coping options will have a greater probability of successfully adapting to environmental or sociocultural stressors than a less differentiated individual. Thus, individuals defined as behaviorally "deficient" or "psychopathologic" should manifest significantly less differentiated cognitive structure in those domains which are central to or consistent with accepted cultural norms, resulting in a far more limited range of response alternatives.

COGNITIVE FLEXIBILITY

The notion of alternative responsivity is especially noteworthy since the majority of research conducted on the role of cognitive factors in behavior has been based on the assumption that individual cognitive styles are constant, like personality traits (Gardner et al. 1959; Shapiro 1965; Horowitz 1976). Several researchers have more recently argued, however, that coping strategies vary among individuals and within the same individual in response to differing phases of a stressful event, or from one event to another (Cohen and Lazarus 1979; Folkman and Lazarus 1980; Carr 1980; Coyne et al. 1981). Thus, the flexibility with which individuals are able to apply their cognitive structure to situational demands will serve to further influence the success of the individual adaptive efforts. If structure is applied "rigidly" without regard to situational demands, then important information or options for response may be inadvertently excluded. Zajonc (1968) has referred to this process as "cognitive tuning" and illustrates it with an example of interpersonal communications. The "receivers" of a message will "open up" this conceptual system to provide the broadest net of categories in order to receive from the "sender" a fairly specific message. Once it is received, they then begin a process of progressively "focusing down upon" or articulating the message, in terms of more and more specific parameters until agreement is reached with the sender as to its precise meaning. The example illustrates the importance of flexibility in applying cognitive structure or shifting between greater and lesser degrees of differentiation to meet the structural demands of complex (or simple) situations, messages, and so on. Our discussion leads us to the conclusion that cognitive process should be viewed as an ongoing and variable response process and should be defined in terms of (1) the range of cognitive differentiation of the individual, (2) the response flexibility of the individual in applying this structure, and (3) the specifics of the situation at any given time. Since these processes are a function of the interaction of biological, sociocultural, and environmental factors, we may anticipate a wide range of individual differences across human populations, but with small but measurable difference among groups differing along socioeconomic, cultural, and geographic dimensions (Witkin 1967; Dawson 1969; Barry and Annis 1974; Carr 1980).

VIOLENCE AND DEPRESSION

Behavioral scientists have long postulated a relationship between depression and violence, although the nature of the relation has been the subject of continuing controversy. In recent years Bandura (1973) has proposed a modification in the classic frustration-aggression hypothesis (Dollard et al. 1939), replacing frustration with the concept "aversive events," defined as insults, painful stimuli, reductions in level of rewarding conditions, losses, and so forth, that are physically and psychologically aversive to the organism.

Based on a review of his own and others' research, Bandura (1973, 1977, 1979) has proposed that aversive events affect a range of diverse responses, including increased adaptive striving, aggression, avoidance, apathy, or depression. Frequent changes in life events (Holmes and Rahe 1967), especially those perceived as aversive in nature, have been shown to produce high levels of distress, "increasing the probability of depression or anxiety as a response in certain individuals" (Johnson and Sarason 1978).

We have already noted the overlap in manifest symptomatology reported among patients diagnosed as anxious, depressed, or aggressive (Dohrenwend and Dohrenwend 1982; Robbins 1982). Stefanis et al. (1980) have demonstrated empirically the existence of interactional patterns among aggression, anxiety, and depression as a function of varying personality characteristics. Specifically, they found depression to be negatively correlated with hostility but positively correlated with self-criticism, which in turn was positively related to both state and trait anxiety. The more self-critical persons are the more likely they are to be anxious in general, to respond to challenging situations with high anxiety, and to be depressed by perceived inadequacy of outcome.

We have also observed that cognitive process plays an important mediating role in determining the nature and direction of the range of coping and the attendant affective responses. According to Kelly (1955) and, more recently, Antonovsky (1980), human conceptualization emerges in response to the individual's attempts to predict and control events, to assign meaning and make manageable the experiences of life. The effectiveness of one's cognitive process, therefore, is inevitably reflected in the sense of self-esteem and personal competence derived from successful coping experience. Bandura (1977) has shown individuals with strong expectations of efficacy (confidence in one's own ability to control outcomes) are adept at coping with aversive events through the use of proven adaptive responses that are sanctioned by society, or through more blatant control-taking measures, such as aggression. Individuals with poor expectations of efficacy perceive aversive life events as uncontrollable and thus engage in "blunting" or distracting activities (e.g., eating, sports, TV, drugs, alcohol), withdrawal behavior, or learned helplessness (e.g., apathy, depression, resignation) or somatization.

Thus, through socialization practices that provide for both direct and indirect learning experiences, individuals learn to terminate or reduce the impact of aversive life events through a range of response strategies. Evidence consistent with this position has been provided by Suarez et al. (1978), who concluded that the behavioral suppression observed in depression appears to be a coping strategy or alternative response style developed to avoid noxious events and acquired by the depressed person through repeated learning experiences. This conclusion is supported by evidence of autonomic overresponsivity and a tendency for the depressed individual to utilize more passive-avoidant as opposed to active manipulation techniques than nondepressed controls in attempting to cope with aversive stimuli.

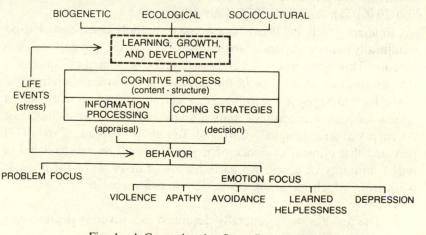

Fig. 1   A Comprehensive Stress-Response Model

Bandura's research on self-efficacy, when combined with Seligman's (1975) work on learned helplessness, provides added empirical support for the hypothetical link between stressful life events, coping style, and subsequent behavioral response. Violence, anxiety, and depression, this research suggests, are alternatives among a range of responses to common antecedent conditions, the choice of alternatives determined by past learning experience, cognitive process, sociocultural values and sanctions, and so on (see fig. 1).

A CROSS-CULTURAL TEST OF THE RESPONSE ALTERNATIVE HYPOTHESIS

If the response alternative hypothesis has merit, then we should observe that the "culture-bound syndrome" called amok occurs under circumstances in which depression might be an equally expected response. Specifically, we may pose the questions: Is there evidence that amok is (1) related to depression, (2) one of several response alternatives among a range of responses to common antecedent conditions, and (3) influenced by past learning experience, cognitive process, and sociocultural variables?

While generally regarded as a culture-bound syndrome, amok has been shown to be a common behavioral path way for multiple precipitants, an appropriate mode of response to certain situations, and a distinct form of violence, the conceptualization of which is traceable to social learning practices in the Malay culture of Southeast Asia (Carr and Tan 1976; Tan and Carr 1977; Carr 1978).

Clinicians practicing in Southeast Asia commonly assume amok to be a culturally defined variant of some form of psychosis, generally schizophrenia. This diagnosis is largely based on the presumed evidence of a thought disorder at the time of the act, that is, the assumption that one would have to be psychotic to engage in such an extreme act. However, a review of patient records of known amok cases in a large Southeast Asian psychiatric hospital (Carr and Tan 1976; Tan and Carr 1977) revealed that clinical evidence of psychosis could be substantiated in only a minority of cases. An earlier study (Tan 1974) of the forensic ward from which the amok cases were drawn revealed:

1. The inmates were generally described as "severely depressed or hostile."

2. Although 67 percent of the inmates were diagnosed as "schizo-phrenic," a surprisingly high percentage of these, 55 percent, were labeled as "depressed and/or suicidal" at the time of admission.
3. While all 67 percent were treated with phenothiazine (an anti-psychotic medication), in "about half the inmates" treated with phenothiazine (see 2 above), ECT was also given. This suggests that the phenothiazine was not effective and that ECT, effective with depressive disorders, was subsequently administered.

This therapeutic judgment that depressive illness is prevalent among amok patients is substantiated by data obtained from the adjacent women's forensic ward. Here the records showed that while *all* the patients were diagnosed as schizophrenic, 72 percent were treated with phenothiazines *and* ECT, but only 27 percent "responded to pheno-thiazine alone." Hence, there is evidence to suggest that a significant proportion of subjects, both in the sample of amoks and in the forensic ward from which they were drawn, showed evidence of a major de-pressive disorder.

In a definitive paper on the culture-bound syndromes, Yap (1969) described amok as an acute psychopathic reaction of a constitutionally predisposed or intellectually subnormal person who is subject to *stress*. He insisted that while similar it should not be confused with schizo-phrenia, nor was it due to brain dysfunction or other toxic, exhaustive, or infectious causes. Instead he attributed it to "a low frustration tolerance to interpersonal stress . . . attributable to . . . certain cultural forms . . . resulting in the individual . . . reacting to such stress with blind rage" (pp. 45–46).

Earlier descriptions of amok uniformly indicated a prodromal period of brooding or depression (Murphy 1972). For example, Clifford (1927:79) wrote that it

> results from a condition of mind which is described in the vernacular by the term *sakit hati*—sickness of liver. . . . The states of feeling which are described by this phrase are numerous, complex, and differ widely in degree, but they all imply some measure of anger, excitement, and mental irritation.
>
> A Malay loses something he values; he has a bad night in the gambling houses; some of his property is wantonly damaged; he has a quarrel with one whom he loves; his father dies; or his mistress proves unfaithful; any one of these things causes him "sickness of liver."

The cross-cultural distribution of the phenomenon and its antecedent conditions is indicated by Schmidt et al. (1975:9), who noted that in the Philippines, as well as Sarawak, ''the brooding-explosion-killing-amnesia sequence is the same. The causes frequently revolve about *offended sensitivity* and *intolerable loss of self-respect*'' [emphasis mine].

The critical antecedent conditions noted here are not dissimilar from those reported earlier in the reviews of depression research by Brown and Harris (1978) or Carson and Adams (1981), and support the concept of universality of antecedent events. The prodromal period of brooding and depression is preceded by a critical life event involving a significant loss either of property, support, or self-esteem. It has aready been noted in earlier work (Carr and Tan 1976; Tan and Carr 1977; Carr 1978) that has its origins in the socialization processes of the Malay, which affect idiosyncrasies in cognition and response-based reinforcement that in turn influences the definition of and response to antecedent stress conditions. We are now able to address the classic question: Given these preconditions of Malay culture, why don't all Malays run amok? The answer, of course, is that those who are not amok are either depressed, withdrawn, blunted or diverted, or coping effectively.

AMOK AS A DISTRESS RESPONSE

Our hypothesis is that depression and amok are related and among the several alternative *distress* responses individuals may make to aversive (stressful) conditions. The specific behavioral response represents a final common pathway of multiple etiological determinants, among them environmental, biological, psychological, cognitive, and sociocultural factors. Further, we would hypothesize that all so-called culture-bound syndromes are in fact by-products of this process; they are clinical manifestations of the ''final common pathway'' distress response in which sociocultural variables especially have played a prominent role in determining the idiosyncratic nature of the response. The proposition we are advancing is that both depression and amok are culturally determined variants, not of universal forms of psychopathology but of a response to universal antecedent life stress conditions or, as we have called them, aversive events. The critical question remains as to why some people respond with aggression, some with depression, and still others cope adaptively. The research literature indicates that idiosyncratic responses to stress are a function of a complex interaction of physiological responses, life experiences leading to the development of predisposing personality style, cognitive process, and learned problem-solving skills. These in turn determine perceptual style, self-concept, expectations of efficacy, and adaptive competence.

Our model maintains that as forms of human behavior, both amok and depression can be accounted for in terms of similar empirically derived principles of human behavior at biological, psychological, and sociocultural levels. Hence, empirically derived research findings relevant to these basic principles should have reasonable applicability cross-culturally and provide insight into these behaviors. The following examples appear to support this contention.

1. It has been noted that when it occurs, amok, like depression, is frequently in response to an actual or perceived grief loss. Research by Horowitz et al. (1980) indicates that different types of pathological grief reaction after the death of a loved one depend in part on preexisting self-concepts. Persons who experience themselves as incomplete have more difficulty with the frightening sadness of bereavement; persons whose self-concepts involve hatred of self or others have difficulty dealing with the normal frustration or rage reaction that follows bereavement and are at risk for out-of-control episodes.

2. Given the highly inhibited nature of traditional Malay culture, it is interesting to note that Horowitz et al. (1980) also found that individuals who habitually use extensive inhibition have a greater tendency to experience painful and overwhelmingly intrusive episodes of ideas and feelings following a stressful event than noninhibited individuals. "Disturbed thoughts" are a frequently reported feature of the prodromal amok state.

3. Horowitz et al. (1980) also reported that persons who tend to distort or avoid the painful meanings of a loss are likely to enter long periods of dulled, apathetic, and listless reactivity following serious life events, unless social relations help them counter these tendencies to avoid the implications of loss. The behavior described here is typical of the prodromal state of amok and often signals impending disaster. Malay tradition maintains that wise and sensitive community elders or family members can often identify such situations in which a person is at risk for running amok and, through judicious and subtle social intervention, the pressure can be relieved and a catastrophe averted.

THE ETHNOBEHAVIORAL MODEL

In an earlier paper Carr (1978) described an ethnobehavioral approach to the conceptualization of behavior disorders based on five general assumptions amplified below.

> *Learning*: There is a basic set of principles of human learning that is universal. We include here the empirically demonstrated behavioral principles of respondent and operant conditioning derived from the research of Pavlov (1927), Skinner (1953), Guthrie (1952), Hull (1943), Spence (1956), Miller (1969), and others. While theoretical interpretation of "how" and "why" may vary, the basic principles of positive and negative reinforcement, stimulus and response generalization, discrimination, extinction, modeling, and imitation are generally accepted. Biological mechanisms underlying the learning process provide a basis for the relative constancy of these principles across cultures. However, the outcome of the learning processes (and related biological functions) have been shown to be subject to influence by environmental or cultural factors.

> *Cognition*: Learning principles define the mechanisms by which cultural norms, beliefs, and expectations, as well as behavior, are acquired, providing the basis for assigning meaning to stimulus events and culture-specific behaviors. Thus, the learning process involves cognitive as well as behavioral dimensions. It does not necessarily follow that these principles are recognized or have conceptual equivalents in the indigenous belief system.

> *Antecedent Conditions—Stress*: All humans regardless of race or culture are faced by certain basic existential problems, such as survival, protection of young, social support and acceptance, the need for a sense of individual competence or worth. In each of these stated areas there are goals that are culturally specific. The challenge to the individual of each of these conditions represents a potential antecedent stressor.

> *Coping Response*: The basic principles of human learning define the mechanisms by which individuals of all races and cultures acquire (1) culturally specific goals and (2) culturally appropriate

coping responses to blocked goal attainment. This particular aspect of the model appears to be consistent with the more highly elaborate theory of social-behaviorism developed by Staats (1981). According to this theory, "intelligence consists of specific repertoires—systems of skills learned according to specific learning principles" (p. 241). The repertoires consist of language-cognitive, sensorimotor, and emotional-motivational skills or response patterns that determine learning and coping ability in various situations.

Pathology: These coping responses may be judged appropriate or inappropriate based on culturally relevant criteria. Those coping responses defined as "inappropriate" constitute the phenomena of pathology or illness within any given culture (Carr 1978: 270–271).

While this model was originally conceived to address the concept of culture-bound syndromes, Kleinman (1982) has pointed out that the approach has applicability to a broader range of behavioral phenomena and is consistent with a body of literature indicating that all psycho-pathologic behavior is in part culture bound. Thus, we find that significant commonalities exist between this model of psychopathology, derived from a comprehensive study of a "culture-bound syndrome," and a model based on a comprehensive review of the depression literature. The arrival at this common ground from different starting points attests to the view that depression, amok, and other forms of deviant behavior represent culturally determined variants in response to antecedent life stress conditions, some more adaptive, some less, and include among them active coping, withdrawal, avoidance, apathy, depression, and aggression. The basis for defining a response is not simply the subsequent behavior or the biologic state but also the context, the nature of the *perceived* stress event, the cognitively mediated coping style, and the supportive resources of the individual. In this respect, research in psychiatric epidemiology can profit greatly from the further development and advancement of a nosological system based on a heuristic distress model.

REFERENCES

Aberle, D., A. Cohen, A. Davis, M. Levy, and F. Sutton
  1950   The Functional Prerequisites of Society. Ethics 60:100—111.
Albee, G.
  1977   Strategies of Primary Prevention. Primary Prevention Working
              Conference, National Council of Community Mental Health
              Centers, Tucson, Arizona.
  1980   A Competency Model to Replace the Defect Model. *In* Com-
              munity Psychology: Theoretical and Empirical Approaches.
              M. Gibb, J. Lachenmayer, and J. Segal, eds. New York: John
              Wiley and Sons.
Antonovsky, A.
  1979   Health, Stress, and Coping. San Francisco: Jossey-Bass.
Bandura, A.
  1973   Social Learning Theory of Aggression. *In* The Control of
              Aggression. J. Knutson, ed. Chicago: Aldine.
  1977   Social Learning Theory. Englewood Cliffs, N.J.: Prentice-
              Hall.
  1979   The Social Learning Perspective: Mechanisms of Aggression.
              In Psychology of Crime and Criminal Justice. H. Toch, ed.
              New York: Holt, Rinehart and Winston.
Barry, J., and R. Annis
  1974   Acculturative Stress: The Role of Ecology, Culture and Dif-
              ferentiation. Journal of Cross-Cultural Psychology 5:382—405.
Beck, A.
  1967   Depression: Causes and Treatment. Philadelphia: University of
              Pennsylvania Press.
  1974   The Development of Depression: A Cognitive Model. *In* The
              Psychology of Depression: Contemporary Theory and Re-
              search. R. Friedman and M. Katz, eds. New York: Winston-
              Wiley.
  1976   Cognitive Therapy and the Emotional Disorder. New York:
              International University Press.
Beck, A., and A. Rush
  n.d.   Research on Suicide, Depression, and Anxiety. Paper presented
              at the annual meeting of the Association for Advancement of
              Behavioral Therapy. New York, December 1976.
Boucher, J., and M. Brandt
  1981   Judgment of Emotion: American and Malay Antecedents. Jour-
              nal of Cross-Cultural Psychology 12:272—283.
Boyer, L.
  1964   Folk Psychiatry of the Apaches of the Mescalero Indian Reser-

vation. *In* Magic, Faith, and Healing, A. Kiev, ed. New York: Free Press.

Brown, G., and T. Harris
1978   Social Origins of Depression. New York: Free Press.

Carr, J. E.
1978   Ethno-Behaviorism and the Culture-Bound Syndromes: The Case of Amok. Culture, Medicine, and Psychiatry 2:269–293.
1980   Personal Construct Theory and Psychotherapy Research. *In* Personal Construct Psychology: Psychotherapy and Personality. L. Landfield and L. Leitner, eds. New York: John Wiley and Sons.

Carr, J. E., and E. K. Tan
1976   In Search of the True Amok: Amok as Viewed within the Malay Culture. American Journal of Psychiatry 113:1295–1299.

Carson, T. P. and H. E. Adams
1981   Affective Disorders: Behavioral Perspectives. *In* Handbook of Clinical Behavioral Therapy. S. Turner, K. Calhoun, and H. Adams, eds. New York: John Wiley and Sons.

Clifford, H.
1927   In Court and Kampong. London: Richard Liesh.

Cohen, F., and R. Lazarus
1979   Coping with the Stresses of Illness. *In* Health Psychology: A Handbook. G. Stone, F. Cohen, and N. Adler, eds. San Francisco: Jossey-Bass.

Coyne, J.
1976*a*   Depression and the Response of Others. Journal of Abnormal Psychology 85:186–193.
1976*b*   Toward an Interactional Description of Depression. Psychiatry 39:28–40.

Coyne, J., C. Aldwin, and R. Lazarus
1981   Depression and Coping in Stressful Episodes. Journal of Abnormal Psychology 90:437–439.

Dawson, J.
1969   Theoretical and Research Bases of Bio-Social Psychology. University of Hong Kong Gazette 16:1–10.

Depue, R. (ed.)
1979   The Psychobiology of the Depressive Disorders. New York: Academic Press.

Dohrenwend, B., and B. Dohrenwend
1965   The Problem of Validity in Field Studies of Psychological Disorders. Journal of Abnormal Psychology 70:52–69.
1969   Social Status and Psychological Disorder. New York: John Wiley and Sons.

1974   Social and Cultural Influences on Psychopathology. Annual
              Review of Psychology 25:417−452.
1982   Perspectives on the Past and Future of Psychiatric Epidemi-
              ology. American Journal of Public Health 72:1271−1279.

Dollard, J., L. Doob, N. Miller, O. Mowrer, and R. Sears
1939   Frustration and Aggression. New Haven: Yale University
              Press.

Edgerton, R.
1966   Conceptions of Psychosis in Four East African Societies. Amer-
              ican Anthropologist 68:408−425.

Folkman, S., and R. Lazarus
1980   An Analysis of Coping in a Middle-Aged Community Sample.
              Journal of Health and Social Behavior 21:219−239.

Gardner, R., P. Holzman, G. Klein, H. Linton, and K. Spence
1959   Cognitive Control: A Study of Individual Consistencies in
              Cognitive Behavior. Psychological Issues 1:4.

Gershon, E.
1980   Progress in the Pharmacotherapy of Depression. Psychiatric
              Annals, vol. 10, no. 9, supplement.

Guthrie, E.
1952   The Psychology of Learning. Rev. ed. New York: Harper.

Hammer, C., and S. Peters
1977   Differential Responses to Male and Female Depressive Reac-
              tions. Journal of Consulting and Clinical Psychology
              45:994−1001.

Holmes, T., and R. Rahe
1967   The Social Adjustment Rating Scale. Journal of Psychosomatic
              Research 11:213−218.

Horowitz, M.
1976   Stress Response Syndromes. New York: Aronson.

Horowitz, M., N. Wilner, C. Marmar, and J. Krupnic
1980   Pathological Grief and the Activation of Latent Self-Images.
              American Journal of Psychiatry 137:1157−1162.

Hull, C.
1943   Principles of Behavior. New York: Appleton-Century Crofts.

Johnson, J., and I. Sarason
1978   Life Stress, Depression, and Anxiety: Internal-External Control
              as a Moderator. Journal of Psychosomatic Research
              22:205−208.

Katz, M., and K. Sandborn
1973   Multi-Ethnic Studies of Psychopathology and Normality in
              Hawaii. International Programs. NIMH.

Kelly, G.
1955   The Psychology of Personal Constructs. New York: W. W.
            Norton.
Kleinman, A.
1982   Neurasthenia and Depression: A Study of Somatization and
            Culture in China. Culture, Medicine, and Psychiatry 6:
            117—190.
Lazarus, R., J. Averill, and E. Opton
1970   Towards a Cognitive Theory of Emotion. *In* Feelings and Emo-
            tions. M. Arnold, ed. New York: Academic Press.
Leff, J.
1981   Psychiatry Around the Globe. New York: Marcel Dekker.
Leighton, A., T. Lambo, C. Hughes, D. Leighton, J. Murphy, and D. Mecklin
1963   Psychiatric Disorder Among the Yoruba. Ithaca: Cornell Uni-
            versity Press.
Lewinsohn, P.
1974   Clinical and Theoretical Aspects of Depression. *In* Innovative
            Treatment Methods in Psychopathology. K. Calhaun,
            H. Adams, and K. Mitchell, eds. New York: John Wiley and
            Sons.
Lonnavist, J.
1980   Affect, Symptoms, Syndrome or Illness. *In* Psychopathology of
            Depression. Proceedings of the Symposium by the Section of
            Clinical Psychopathology of the World. K. Achte, V. Aalberg,
            and J. Lonnavist, eds. Psychiatric Association, Psychiatria
            Fennica Supplementum 11—15.
Lonner, W.
1980   The Search for Psychological Universals. *In* Handbook of
            Cross-Cultural Psychology. Vol. 1. H. Triandis and W. Lam-
            bert, eds. Boston: Allyn and Bacon.
Marsella, A.
1979   Depressive Experience and Disorder Across Cultures. *In* Hand-
            book of Cross Cultural Psychology. Vol. 6. H. C. Triandis and
            J. Draguns, eds. Boston: Allyn and Bacon.
Miller, N.
1969   Learning of Visceral and Glandular Responses. Science
            163:434—445.
Murphy, H.
1972   History and the Evaluation of Syndromes: The Striking Case of
            Latah and Amok. *In* Psychopathology: Contributions from the
            Social, Behavioral and Biological Sciences. M. Hammer,
            K. Salzinger, and S. Sutton, eds. New York: John Wiley and
            Sons.

Orley, J.
  1970   Culture and Mental Illness: A Study from Uganda. Nairobi: East
                Africa Publishing House.
Osgood, C., W. May, and M. Miron
  1975   Cross-Cultural Universals of Affective Meaning. Urbana: Uni-
                versity of Illinois Press.
Pavlov, I.
  1927   Conditional Reflexes. G. Anrep, trans. London: Oxford Uni-
                versity Press.
Paykel, E., J. Meyers, M. Dienelt, G. Klerman, J. Lindenthal, and M. Pepper
  1969   Life Events and Depression: A Controlled Study. Archives of
                General Psychiatry 21:753–760.
Prince, R.
  1964   Indigenous Yoruba Psychiatry. *In* Magic, Faith, and Healing.
                A. Kiev, ed. New York: Free Press.
Resner, G., and J. Hartog
  1970   Concepts and Terminology of Mental Disorder among the
                Malays. Journal of Cross-Cultural Psychology 1:369–381.
Robbins, L.
  1982   Life Styles of Young Adults. Eleventh Herbert S. Ripley Lec-
                ture. University of Washington. October 6, 1982.
Sandborn, K., and M. Katz
  1980   Perception of Symptomatology in Ethnic Groups. *In* Psycho-
                pathology of Depression. Proceedings of the Symposium by the
                Section of Clinical Psychopathology of the World. K. Achte,
                V. Aalberg, and J. Lonnavist, eds. Psychiatric Association,
                Psychiatria Fennica Supplementum. Pp. 315–319.
Sandifer, M., A. Hordern, G. Turberg, and L. Green
  1969   Similarities and Differences in Patient Evaluation by U.S. and
                U.K. Psychiatrists. American Journal of Psychiatry 126:
                206–212.
Schachter, S., and J. Singer
  1962   Cognitive, Social, and Physiological Determinants and Emo-
                tional State. Psychological Review 69:379–399.
Schmidt, K.
  1964   Folk Psychiatry in Sarawak: A Tentative System of Psychiatry
                of the Iban. In Magic, Faith, and Healing. A. Kiev, ed. New
                York: Free Press.
Schmidt, K., L. Hill, and G. Guthrie
  1975   Running Amok. Unpub. ms.
Seligman, M.
  1975   Helplessness: On Depression, Development and Death. San
                Francisco: Freeman.

Shapiro, D.
1965   Neurotic Styles. New York: Basic Books.
Skinner, B. F.
1953   Science and Human Behavior. New York: Macmillan.
Spence, K.
1956   Behavior Theory and Conditioning. New Haven: Yale University Press.
Staats, A., and L. Burns
1981   Intelligence and Child Development: What Intelligence Is and How It Is Learned and Functions. Genetic Psychology Monographs 104:237−301.
Stefanis, C., A. Liakos, A. Kokkevi, and M. Markidis
1980   Interactional Pattern of Aggression, Anxiety, and Psychotic Depression. *In* Psychopathology of Depression. K. Achte, V. Aalberg and J. Lonnavist, eds. Helsinki: Psychiatria Fennica.
Suarez, Y., N. Crowe, and H. Adams
1978   Depression: Avoidance Learning and Physiological Correlates in Clinical and Analog Populations. Behavior Research and Therapy 16:21−31.
Swift, C.
1980   Task Force Report: National Council of Community Mental Health Centers Task Force on Environmental Assessment. Community Mental Health Journal 16(1):7−26.
Tan, E. K.
1974   Forensic Psychiatry in Hospital Bahagia, Ula Kinta. Unpub. Report. University of Malaysia.
Tan, E. K., and J. E. Carr
1977   Psychiatric Sequelae of Amok. Culture, Medicine, and Psychiatry 1:59−67.
Terminsen, J., and J. Ryan
1970   Health and Disease in a British Columbian Community. Canadian Psychiatric Association Journal 15:121−127.
Tseng, W., and J. Hsu
1969   Chinese Culture, Personality Formation, and Mental Illness. International Journal of Social Psychiatry 16:5−14.
Whorf, B.
1956   Language, Thought and Reality: Selected Writings of B. L. Whorf. J. Carroll, ed. New York: Wiley.
Witkin, H.
1967   A Cognitive Style Approach to Cross-Culture Research. International Journal of Psychology 2:233−250.

Yap, P. M.
   1969   The Culture-Bound Reactive Syndromes. *In* Mental Health
                  Research in Asia and the Pacific. W. Candell and Tsung-Yi
                  Lin, eds. Honolulu: East-West Center Press.
Zajonc, R.
   1968   Cognitive Theories in Social Psychology. *In* Handbook of
                  Social Psychology. Rev. ed. G. Lindzey and E. Aronson, eds.
                  Reading, Mass.: Addison-Wesley.

PART III
Epidemiological Measurement of Depressive Disorders Cross-Culturally

INTRODUCTION TO PART III

An abiding problem in the cross-cultural study of mental illness concerns the way cases of schizophrenia, depression, and other psychiatric disorders are to be identified and the severity of these disorders measured. The chapters in the first two parts of this volume raise serious and usually unanswered questions about cultural categories and norms that bias standard assessments of depressive disorder, and thereby render them questionable tools for valid cross-cultural evaluation. The clinical and population-based epidemiological surveys reviewed in this section provide major examples of comparative cross-cultural research projects that have attempted to confront these problems. While both chapters conclude that valid and reliable cross-cultural assessments can be (and have been) undertaken, the authors are honest and appropriately humble about the difficult problems that continue to plague leading research methodologies. The nonanthropological reader is likely to be chastened by these accounts, whereas anthropologists may well conclude that sensitive and sophisticated cross-cultural measurements, while difficult and uncertain, are nontheless still feasible.

In chapter 9, Beiser introduces readers to findings from the many sophisticated psychiatric epidemiological studies he has conducted among the Serer of Senegal, Southeast Asian refugees in Canada, and inhabitants of midtown Manhattan. Here he reanalyzes his data from previous studies to address directly a major hypothesis in cross-cultural studies of depression: that while depression is present in non-Western populations, it is highly "somatized," that is, experienced and expressed as bodily distress rather than primarily in psychological terms. Whereas other authors have viewed somatization as an impressive instance of the cultural patterning of depressive disorder, Beiser's factor analysis of expressed symptoms among populations in communities indicates that somatic and depressive complaints form distinctive, heterogeneous symptom clusters, though both may be found in the same individual. Beiser concludes that depression and somatization, in like

fashion, may be separate conditions both of which occur cross-culturally. His findings suggest a closer association of somatic complaints
to anxiety. That depression in non-Western populations may be much
more commonly expressed through a somatic idiom of distress, Beiser
argues, is due to differences in communicative contexts, legitimacy of
symptom expression in those contexts, and available help-seeking
resources, not to actual differences in perceived symptoms or existing
psychopathology. In support of this argument, he reviews some of the
more recent and interesting biological research findings as well as the
extensive series of international studies he has conducted to determine
population-based rates of depression and to assure valid cross-cultural
comparisons. Beiser criticizes clinic- and hospital-based studies because
they use highly selective samples, whose characteristics are not generalizable to entire populations. While describing the major epidemiological issues in the measurement of depression, Beiser explains why
statistically rigorous quantitative studies are essential to make cross-
cultural comparisons of mental health and illness. The review of the
methodological concerns should inform readers about the epidemiological perspective on the controversy that swirls around cross-cultural
data and that reflects discrepant epidemiological, clinical, and anthropological claims for the most appropriate methods to assure valid and
reliable knowledge.

In chapter 10, Marsella and his World Health Organization collaborators review WHO's multicenter study of depressive disorder. Since the
centers are in markedly dissimilar societies, the problems in conceptualizing depression as a disease category and in translating that conceptualization into cross-cultural (epidemiological and clinical) measurements, which Marsella et al. discuss, will be of particular interest to
readers of this volume. The authors review some of the chief manifestations of depression in different cultures derived from clinical observational studies, matched diagnostic studies, matched samples, and international surveys. The WHO researchers conclude that the findings
support both the view of a core depressive disorder and substantial
cross-cultural differences in that disorder. The WHO study was so
contrived as to assure that it would contribute more to our understanding
of the former than the latter. The authors are self-critical of the sampling,
data collection methodology, and data analysis in their own study and in
others because standard research approaches interfere with the detection
of cultural differences. In the past, for entirely understandable reasons
that reflect the practical requirement of projects in developing societies

to provide baseline data for the planning of clinical programs, the emphasis has been to search for cross-cultural universals; but now the cross-cultural research agenda has matured in an anthropological direction to encourage examination of cross-cultural differences.

Marsella et al. rethink their work to develop hypotheses concerning the influence on depressive disease of psychosocial and cultural factors, which might bring better balance to the emerging picture of cross-cultural differences and similarities. The authors thereby provide an insiders' view of which directions are likely to be more practicable for future cross-cultural comparisons. Few anthropologists have actually engaged in such clinical and epidemiological comparisons, but this chapter, like the preceding one, attests to the increased openness to anthropological concerns on the part of some of the leading researchers. At the same time, these chapters offer the great opportunity to anthropological theory to test leading propositions against the empirical data base by informing clinical and epidemiological studies.

9

A Study of Depression among Traditional Africans, Urban North Americans, and Southeast Asian Refugees

Morton Beiser

Clinicians are, or should be, interested in the influence of culture on depression for at least three reasons. First, it is important to understand how patients from different ethnic groups experience and express depression, one of the most ubiquitous of all disorders (Duncan-Jones and Henderson 1978; Goldberg et al. 1976; Weissman and Myers 1978; Weissman et al. 1978; Brown and Harris 1978) and one frequently misdiagnosed by primary care physicians (Goldberg et al. 1976, Johnstone and Goldberg 1976). If, as has been alleged, patients from certain subcultural groups express depression primarily through somatic symptoms (Kleinman 1977, 1980; Teja et al. 1971; Tseng 1975; Yap 1965; Marsella 1978; Binitie 1975; Abad and Boyce 1979; Engelsman 1982), it would be unfortunate indeed to miss the opportunity to help such persons with the right combination of antidepressant drugs and specific forms of psychotherapy, instead of referring them through an often needless, sometimes harmful, round of medical consultations. If the presentation of depression in different cultural groups is the same as it is in the dominant North American culture, and therefore, familiar to North American physicians and psychiatrists, the problem of ''missed'' cases may be equal across all cultural groups. This could be remedied by physician education about general psychiatric concepts. However, if depression in non-Western or non-Westernized groups is different from that in Euro-Americans, North American physicians may be missing even more cases in subcultural groups than in the general population.

Second, the effect of culture on the presentation of depressive illness is important for etiologic studies. Studies in the psychobiology and genetics of depression are opening up new therapeutic possibilities. One of the important ways of studying the contribution of genetics to depression is to study depressed people who can be identified as emanating from differing gene pools. However, people who can trace their genetic heritage to a specific gene pool often share a common culture as well and, thus, culture and genetics become intertwined. If we do not understand the way in which culture may obscure or affect the presentation of depression in different cultural groups, the study of the biology of depression will be vitiated.

Finally, the relationship of culture to depression plays an important role in the development of theory. Early reports that Africans did not suffer depression were interpreted by neo-Rousseauian adherents as due to Africans' "lack of responsibility" in a primitive paradise (Carrothers 1953). However, since the late 1950s an ever-increasing literature suggests that, although the form and content that clinical depression typically assumes in Africans differs somewhat from that of the average North American patient, the rates of this disorder are at least as high among Africans as they are in any other population (German 1972; Leighton et al. 1963; Prince 1968; Orley 1979).

My purpose here is to present population-based data that test the proposition that certain non-Western groups somatize depressive affect. I also suggest that the behavioral sciences remain bedeviled by a language problem. A single word—depression—refers to different phenomena, ranging from the upset of frustrated ambition, to the affective component of an illness for which many thousands of ambulatory patients are treated per year, to a condition requiring hospitalization.[1] Research in depression has suffered from confusion. Some investigators, for example, have (inappropriately) extrapolated from data derived from depressed patients to speculate about how people in general experience depression. Others have assumed that the illness, depression, is merely a severe form of a commonly shared experience also called depression. Such problems in studying depression are, in part, the products of language. In this chapter, although the term "depression" is retained, I attempt, despite a certain awkwardness of phrasing, to separate depression as experience from depression as illness.

BACKGROUND OF THE STUDY

A number of research scholars and clinicians, impressed by differences among patients from different cultures, have concluded that the experience of depression varies with culture. Comparing depression in Indonesian and German patients, Pfeiffer (1968) found that the former displayed a loss of vitality and somatic symptoms, and the latter, decreased efficiency, feelings of guilt, and suicidal tendencies. Binitie (1975) studied a consecutive sample of patients attending the Nervous Diseases Clinic in Uselu, Nigeria, for a period of eighteen months, comparing them with patients attending a London psychiatric clinic. He examined these patients, all of whom received a diagnosis of affective disorder, utilizing the Present State Examination (P.S.E.), a structured, systematic, psychiatric interview that yields a number of symptom ratings (Wing 1970). Binitie found that both groups reported depressed mood, but feelings of guilt, anxiety, and active contemplation of suicide were more characteristic of Londoners, somatization and motor retardation of Nigerians. In the most ambitious study of all, Leff (1973, 1981) reports results from interviewing patient samples, also using the P.S.E., in nine countries—Denmark, India, Colombia, Nigeria, England, the Soviet Union, Czechoslovakia, Taiwan, and the United States. The variables used for analysis were P.S.E.-derived scales measuring depression, anxiety, and irritability. In Nigeria and Taiwan—that is, in countries where the language is not Indo-European—the correlation coefficients among the three scales were higher than in the remaining countries. Leff suggests an evolutionary process in language to explain his findings: Chinese and African languages have not yet evolved to a point where they differentiate bodily and psychological experiences to the extent that Indo-European languages have, and, therefore, Chinese and Africans have more difficulty differentiating emotional states than do Indo-Europeans.

Leff's report exemplifies a common problem. While patients in treatment constitute the source of data, the argument about depression is loosely extrapolated from the clinical to the general situation. The author begins by studying illness but ends by talking about how people of different cultures experience the affect of depression.

Tanaka-Matsumi and Marsella's (1976) study of word associations to the term ''depression'' is one of the few to have utilized nonclinical samples. These investigators report that Japanese nationals' associations to the term were largely external referent words such as ''rain'' or "dark," while Japanese Americans and Caucasian Americans produced internal referents such as "sadness" and "loneliness." Arguing on the basis of such data, Marsella (1978) has suggested that Japanese and middle-class Americans suffer two different forms of disease. He calls for surveys of normal populations, preferably using multivariant techniques such as factor analysis to test out ideas.

This chapter, a report on mental health surveys conducted among three normal population groups, the Serer of Senegal, West Africa, residents of a borough of New York City, and Southeast Asian refugees in western Canada, explores the relationships between depressive affect and somatization. It also raises questions about the role of these two experiences in the occurrence of the illness, depression.

STUDY SAMPLES AND METHODS

The first group, the Serer, a nation of settled agriculturalists, have inhabited Senegal for at least seven hundred years. The respondents come from the region of Niakhar, the home of some 35,000 Serer who were, at the time of the survey (1970), one of the most traditional peoples in Senegal, if not in all of West Africa. The sample consists of Niakhar residents as well as Serer migrants living in the city of Dakar. A total of 456 adults make up the sample, which, with appropriate weighing, can be considered representative of all adult Serer born in Niakhar and living at the time of the survey. Details of the sample are more fully described elsewhere (Beiser et al. 1976). The subjects were interviewed using a Serer-language structured interview schedule containing questions about sociodemographic characteristics, acculturation experiences, health, and mental health. All subjects also received extensive physical and laboratory examinations. (More details about the examination and the construction of the questionnaire are supplied in Beiser et al. 1976.)

The New York survey area consisted of seven urban census tracts, six in Brooklyn and one in Queens. The 531 interviewees, a probability sample of adults living in the census tracts during the time of the survey, 1965 and 1966, are predominantly white, middle-class, and Catholic or Jewish. Most have at least some high school education. (Details of the sampling are more fully described in Benfari et al. 1972.) Interviews were conducted by trained, nonpsychiatric interviewers from the National Opinion Research Center.

One thousand seventy adult refugees from Vietnam, Laos, and Cambodia, resettled in Vancouver, British Columbia, during 1979 and 1980, were chosen using a multiwave probability technique (see Scheaffer et al. 1979) and constitute an urban Southeast Asian refugee sample.[2] All adult refugees who located in a rural area of the province make up a rural sample, adding 278 people to the total sample. Approximately one-half of this sample are ethnic Chinese, the rest Vietnamese and Laotian. They are predominantly young: 70 percent are between eighteen and thirty-four years old. While fewer than 15 percent have received secondary schooling or more, the educational spectrum is wide, ranging from some older persons who are functionally illiterate, to young adults whose experience interrupted their schooling, to a few highly trained professionals. Bilingual interviewers, most of them refugees themselves, surveyed the respondents using appropriate language questionnaires that contained many of the items appearing in the New York City and Senegal Mental Health Scales.

In all three instances, the survey, derived from the Stirling County interview schedule (Leighton et al. 1963), contained approximately one hundred items covering a variety of psychoneurotic and psychosomatic symptoms. Each of these studies was designed for a unique purpose. Although comparison across the three was considered a desirable goal, it did not constitute a first priority at the time each study took place. Thus, while many common items occur in all three interview schedules, the overlap is not perfect.

Used with Africans and Southeast Asians, the interview could be considered an etic instrument. However, prior to the surveys, the schedules were adapted for these two cultures. The process of adaptation, more fully described elsewhere (Beiser et al. 1972, 1973, 1974, 1976), began with a careful delineation of emic categories for describing psychological disturbance. This in turn generated a lexicon of culture-specific ways of expressing distress, some of which were added to the interview schedule. Thus, the African and Southeast Asian schedules each contain culture-specific items that do not appear on the New York questionnaire. "Decentering" procedures and back-translation were used with all etic items to ensure translatability of items and underlying concepts (Brislin 1970). Measures of psychopathology derived from the questionnaires were validated by comparing responses obtained from indigenously defined ill people with normal ones (see Beiser et al. 1976).

Before the items in the respective questionnaires were entered into the factor analysis, the distribution of responses to all items in each of the study samples was examined. Any item with less than 10 percent positive response was discarded. In each of the studies, between 90 and 100 items remained, on which we performed standard score transformations for each variable. The variables were then subjected to a factor analysis and rotation based on Hotelling's principle component solution and a Varimax rotation. We used the Scree test for determining the optimal number of factors for a solution in each of the three studies (Cattell 1966, 1977).

The Stirling County Questionnaire and other instruments similar to it (Brodman et al. 1949, 1951; MacMillan 1957; Langner 1962; Srole et al. 1962; Goldberg 1976; Goldberg and Blackwell 1970) have been used in one of two ways to identify psychiatrically ill people in the general population. In the first, quasi-clinical, method, psychiatrists examine data obtained from research subjects and arrive at a decision about whether or not a respondent can be considered clinically ill (Leighton et al. 1963; Srole et al. 1962). The second approach utilizes statistical techniques to arrive at cutoff scores on mental health scales derived from the questionnaires. People whose scores exceed the cutoff are considered to be psychiatric "cases" (Srole and Fisher 1980).

Questionnaire data are used differently in the present study. For our purposes, the 100-odd items may be considered a distillation of decades, if not centuries, of clinical lore about the ways people experience and/or report distress. Clinicians group these phenomena, to which they assign the term "symptoms," into conceptual categories called "diagnoses," which become hallowed by use and concretized by the assignment of statistical designations. That these are not immutable categorizations is attested by the frequency with which they are revised. The latest such North American revision, the American Psychiatric Association's (APA) DSM-III (1980), scores a great advance over previous diagnostic systems by clearly specifying which symptoms, in which combination, constitute a psychiatric diagnosis.[3] However, the clinical or consensus approach imposes on phenomena an order that may exist more in the minds of clinicians than in nature. In this study, we utilize, as an alternative, a statistical technique that searches for actual rather than imputed relationships among indicators of distress in designated populations. Factor analysis, the most frequently used tool for such purposes, may be viewed as an exercise in the validation of constructs such as depression and somatization (Harman 1970; Horst 1968; Brislin et al. 1973). Factor analyses do not produce diagnoses but, rather, continuous dimensions. Unlike diagnoses, which rest on a dichotomous model of illness (people either do or do not "have" a clinical "depression"), everyone in a designated population receives a score on a factorially derived dimension. While psychiatric patients typically score high on dimensions of distress (Eysenck 1982; Beiser et al. 1976), a high score on a factor is not the same as a diagnosis. Building bridges between factor scores and diagnosis, a high priority for research, will require refinements of scoring such as assigning appropriate weights to items and the utilization of other multivariate techniques such as discriminant function and cluster analysis. Comparing factor structures among population groups provides one approach to understanding whether distress is experienced differently or similarly in diverse cultures.

RESULTS

The New York City and Senegal samples yielded four factors and the Southeast Asian, five. In Senegal, the four factors accounted for 32 percent of total item variance; in New York City, four factors accounted for 60 percent; and among the Southeast Asian, five factors accounted for 39 percent of total variance. The factors derived from each of the three studies bear remarkable similarities to each other. Two factors—Depression and Somatization—are presented in tables 9.1 and 9.2, respectively.

TABLE 9.1

FACTOR LOADINGS ON "DEPRESSION" FACTOR IN THREE DIFFERENT CULTURES

	Item	Senegal	New York City	Southeast Asian
1.	Are there times when you feel low or hopeless?	.48	.42	.67
*2.	Do you have trouble making up your mind, even about minor decisions?	.33	.34	.59
3.	Do you wonder if anything is worthwhile anymore?	.36	.57	.66
4.	Do you worry about what people say about you?	.56	.46	.51
5.	Do you feel that for no apparent reason people criticize you or pick quarrels with you?	.41	.34	.35
6.	Have you had periods when you couldn't get going?	.50	.45	.30

TABLE 9.1 (Continued)

Item	Senegal	New York City	Southeast Asian
*7. Have there been times when you lost interest in everything?	.43	0	.60
8. Have you been feeling unhappy, in spirits?	0	.41	.66
9. Do you sometimes feel lonely or apart even when among friends?	–	.47	.56
*10. Do you have periods of great restlessness?	–	.36	.48
*11. Do you find it hard to concentrate?	.51	–	.46
12. Do you worry about money?	.46	.52	0
13. Do you worry about family problems?	.44	.52	0
14. Do you worry about getting ahead?	–	.54	0

"CULTURE-SPECIFIC" ITEMS

A. *SENEGAL*

1. Do you feel you are an unlucky person?	.43	0	0

B. *NEW YORK CITY*

1. Have you felt you were going to have a nervous breakdown?	0	.31	0

C. *SOUTHEAST ASIAN*

1. Have you been feeling troubled, in turmoil?	0	0	.67
2. Have you felt things were sad and boring?	0	0	.73
3. Have you felt worthless?	0	0	.49
4. Have you felt remorseful?	0	0	.64

NOTES:

0 Item not included in this particular questionnaire.

– Item was included in questionnaire but loading on factor is <.30.

* Item is part of DSM-III criteria ancillary to Dysphoric Mood for diagnosis of Major Depression.

TABLE 9.2

FACTOR LOADINGS ON "SOMATIZATION" IN THREE DIFFERENT CULTURES

	Item	Senegal	New York City	Southeast Asian
+ 1.	Does your heart beat hard?	.36	.57	.54
2.	Do you have a sense of pressure in your head?	.48	.50	–
3.	Do your hands tremble enough to bother you?	.45	.50	.31
4.	Are you ever troubled by a feeling that your hair is standing on end?	.36	.42	0
5.	Do you ever have creeping feelings in the skin?	.31	.41	0
+ 6.	Do you have spells of dizziness?	.44	.31	.62
+ 7.	Do you feel you are bothered by all sorts of ailments?	.34	.47	.62
+ 8.	How is your health? (Excellent, Good, Medium, Poor)	–	.34	.62
+ 9.	Have you been bothered by shortness of breath when not exerting yourself?	–	.66	.59
+ 10.	Does your food ever seem tasteless, hard to swallow?	.53	–	.47
+ 11.	Have you felt nauseated as if you were going to vomit?	.29	–	.49
12.	Have you been troubled with constipation?	.54	–	.34
*13.	Do you have loss of appetite?	.46	–	.46
+ 14.	Are you ever troubled by upset stomach?	.37	–	0
15.	Do you take medicines for constipation?	.37	–	0
16.	Are you bothered by nightmares?	.38	–	.32
17.	Does your head feel heavy?	.57	–	0
*18.	Do you feel tired all the time?	.39	.30	.60
*19.	Do you wake up earlier than you want to and then can't get back to sleep?	0	0	.49
+ 20.	Have you had back pain?	–	–	.51

NOTES:

0   Item not included in this particular questionnaire.

–   Item was included in questionnaire but loading on factor is   .30.

*   Item is part of list of DSM-III criteria ancillary to Dysphoric Mood for diagnosis of Major Depression or Melancholia.

+   Item is part of list of DSM-III criteria for Somatoform Disorders.

Factor I, Depression, accounted for 26 percent of the common factor variance in Senegal, 21 percent in New York, and 55 percent among the Indochinese. On the Depression Factor, six items display consistent loadings in all three cultures. These are all ways of describing unhappiness in psychic terms—hopelessness, indecisiveness, feelings of futility, hypersensitivity to the opinions of others, and anergia (lack of energy). Loneliness, which loads on the New York and Indochinese factors, does not load on Senegal. Other items that load in two of the samples but not in a third are restlessness (absent in Senegal) and inability to concentrate (absent in New York City).

"Culture-specific" items, derived from pretesting and from disease lexicons developed prior to the construction of our questionnaires, are also included. "Nervous breakdown," an item in the New York City questionnaire, could not be translated conceptually for the other two cultures. "Unlucky," a rough translation into English from the original Serer, cannot adequately convey the power attributed to luck or fate in an African universe where everything happens because of spirits. Some of the Southeast Asian culture-specific depression items (presented in only an approximate English translation) have been reported in other studies (see Kinzie et al. 1982). Some items were not included for all three studies. For example, the "worry" items found on both the New York City and Serer factors were not asked of the Asian refugees. "Worry about getting ahead" forms part of the Depression factor in New York City, but not in Senegal.

Items 1, 3, and 8 are ways of reporting Dysphoric Affect. Besides Dysphoric Affect, the DSM-III classification lists a number of criteria for the diagnosis of Major Depression: Items 2, 7, 10 and 11, if reported in addition to Dysphoric Affect, would qualify one for a diagnosis of Major Depression.

Factor II, Somatization, contains a number of items that contribute to a diagnosis of Somatoform Disorder in DSM-III. They include complaints about palpitations, dizziness, persistent poor health, and shortness of breath. While the former are fairly consistent across all three groups, the Senegalese and Southeast Asian factors contain complaints referable to the gastrointestinal tract which do not load on the New York City factor. One of these—loss of appetite—is a DSM-III item for a diagnosis of Melancholia. Feeling fatigued loads on all three factors and is one of the DSM-III criteria for Depression. Factor II accounts for 27 percent of the common factor variance in Senegal, 24 percent in New York City, and 12 percent among the Southeast Asians.

DISCUSSION

If it were true that Asians somatize distress while middle-class Euro-Americans psychologize, or that members of technologically less evolved societies such as the Serer lack the language or the ability to make conceptual distinctions between affective and somatic experience, different factors should have emerged from these analyses. In the cases of the Serer and the Southeast Asian refugees, one might have predicted a factor with loadings on one or two depressive items plus many somatic complaints. In contrast, one might have predicted the emergence of a pure psychic dysphoria item for New Yorkers. In all three cases, however, the affect of depression is expressed in psychic terms, illustrating that neither the Africans nor the Southeast Asian refugees lack a vocabulary for such expression and that the experience is not an unfamiliar one. Furthermore, among the two non-Western groups, the depression factor explains much of the variance among the mental health items included in the surveys' questionnaires, just as it does in New York City.

Interesting differences do exist. All three groups of respondents were asked about feeling lonely. New Yorkers and Southeast Asians who are depressed complain about feeling lonely, whereas depressed Serer do not. This may reflect the extreme sociocentrism of Serer village society. In Serer villages, one is literally never alone. To be alone, or to wish to be alone, is madness to the Serer. A Serer can usually count on the support and interest of his community even if he is ill or disabled. Depressed New Yorkers do suffer loneliness. In general, Vietnamese, Chinese, and Laotian cultures are more sociocentric than North American. However, the refugees, most of whom come from urban centers rather than rural areas where social cohesion might be expected to be strong, experience loneliness. Moreover, many of the refugees have left behind them families, kin, and communities. They therefore feel both lonely and depressed. Depressed New Yorkers differ from depressed Serer in worrying about getting ahead. This item is meaningless in Serer society where individual advancement is subordinated to the welfare of family and community.

In all three cultures, somatization, the expression of distress through bodily symptoms, emerges as a factor separate from depression. In Senegal, we were able to conduct physical examinations of all sample respondents. Analyses of these data indicate that the somatic preoccupation factor bears no relationship to measures of physical health. However, Senegalese respondents identified by their indigenous healers as having "illness of the spirit" and by Western psychiatrists as being psychiatrically disturbed have higher somatization scores than the general population (Beiser et al. 1976). Southeast Asian refugees receiving mental health care in Vancouver similarly have high somatization scores (Beiser, unpublished data). Differences in item loadings on the somatization factor recall suggestions that the form that hypochondriacal complaints assume varies across cultures (see, e.g., Kenyon 1976).

Factors are orthogonal structures. This means that one can be depressed without having any somatic complaints, can complain about bodily symptoms without being depressed, can be both depressed and somatically preoccupied, or can be happily free of both types of symptoms. Somatization does not appear to be an equivalent, or substitute way, of expressing the feeling of depression.

How can one reconcile these findings with the frequent reports that depression does not exist in the disease lexicon or as part of the illness repertoire of non-Westerners, and that patients who are not Indo-European language speakers do not complain about depression to their doctors. (See Schieffelin, chap. 3.; Leff 1981; Marsella 1980 and chap. 10.) The paradox becomes resolvable through an appreciation of the differences between concepts of illness based only on cases coming to treatment and those based on community surveys, and of the difference between depression defined as illness and as a behavior. Leff (1981) suggests that patients and healers in non-Western cultures are unfamiliar with the affect or behavior, depression. There are several possibilities. (1) The behavior does not occur at all in many non-Western cultures. (2) The behavior occurs, at least at a metapsychological level (as "disease" to use Kleinman's [1980] psychobiological framework, or "soul loss" in Shweder's formulation [chap. 6]), but assumes different forms cross-culturally. These forms are often so different that their manifestations can no longer be subsumed under the Western conceptual rubric "depression." Instead, they, and Western depression, must be considered culture-specific dimensions of experience. As a corollary to this proposition, some authorities have postulated that, whatever the upset is which occurs at a subcognitive level (whether disease or soul loss), the disequilibrium is subject to so much culture shaping that it constitutes a different experience from one culture to another (see, e.g., Marsella 1980). (3) Equivalent behaviors (which can be called depression) occur in all cultures, but are handled by different regulatory systems. (4) Equivalent behaviors occur, but culture determines that they will be singled out for regulation in some societies and disregarded in others.

Our data refute Proposition 1. They also suggest that some of the claims that have been made within the framework of Proposition 2 are overstatements. It appears that the perception of dis-ease among Africans, Southeast Asian refugees, and North Americans in our samples was more alike than dissimilar. In each culture, individuals expressed dysphoria in psychic terms that were clearly separable from another experience, the experience of somatized distress. It is interesting to compare the results of the present study with others conducted in general populations. Butcher and Pancheri (1976), in one of the largest of such studies, compared factors derived from administering the MMPI (Minnesota Multiphasic Personality Inventory) to normal populations in seven different cultures. These authors were more impressed with similarities than with differences in the factor structures. However, studies such as those of Leff (1973, 1981) and Binitie (1975) found differences among patient samples from different cultures. In general, research workers who have conducted general population surveys seem impressed with the stability of affective dimensions across cultures, while those who work with clinical populations are impressed by differences.[4]

Given these observations, Propositions 3 and 4 seem the most tenable. In other words, depression as an affect seems more alike than dissimilar across the cultures studied, but depression as illness—that which is recognized and handled by a societal regulatory system—may vary greatly across cultures.

Despite its drawbacks, one of the great achievements of DSM-III is its clear specification of what is to be considered psychiatric disorder. It is a codification of the symptom requirements for the role of psychiatric patient in North America.[5] In DSM-III, depressive illness is defined by the presence of depressed mood and a number of associated complaints. "Melancholia" is a variant of depression in which somatic symptoms are thought to suggest a more severe form of the illness, one that will probably require treatment with drugs or convulsant therapy. While many of the DSM-III Major Depression symptoms are found on our depression factor, some Depression and some Melancholia symptoms come from the somatization dimension. This would lead one to predict that a major difference between "normals" and psychiatrically depressed patients is that, while depressive affect and somatization occur independently of each other among the former, they will tend to co-occur among the latter. While our data did not permit a test of this hypothesis, it finds support in the work of Mathew et al. (1981), who report that Eysenck's neuroticism dimension predicts (weakly) the presence of somatic symptoms in a group of clinically depressed North American patients and that depressed patients achieve higher somatic symptoms scores than normals. The proposition also finds support in a review of numerous studies of the Zung Depression Scale in normal and in clinical populations. Factor analyses from these studies suggest different structures among the two groups, with more coalescence of psychic and somatic symptoms among patients than among normal populations (Hedlund and Vieweg 1979).

Not all North American depressive patients, however, have high scores on somatization. Mathew et al. (ibid.) found, after all, only weak correlations between depression and somatization among patient groups. Furthermore, according to DSM-III, one may receive a diagnosis of depression (Dysthymic Disorder) with purely psychic complaints. A high score on depression alone thus is a qualification for patienthood in North America. This leads one to speculate that at least two types of people come into psychiatric care in North America and receive clinical diagnoses of depression—those who would receive high scores on a depression factor like ours and those who receive high scores on both depression and somatization—and it may well prove that the psychophysiology of these conditions is very different. Other investigators using techniques like cluster analyses have also suggested that clinical depression constitutes a heterogeneous diagnostic category. Paykel (1971), for example, was able to classify nonpsychotic depressed patients into three subgroups, one of which, "anxious depression," was characterized by depressive affect, somatic anxiety, and hypochondriasis. Patients in another subcategory, "nonanxious depression," had experienced more recent life events prior to the onset of their illness than the anxious depressives had. This finding suggests that "pure" depression, that is, depressive complaints without an admixture of anxiety or somatoform symptoms, may be a more reactive phenomenon than other forms of depression. The research of Lechman et al. (1983) demonstrates that relatives of patients with depression and an associated anxiety disorder are at greater risk for major depression, and for anxiety disorder, than are relatives of individuals suffering a purer form of depression.

In non-Western cultures, it seems likely that it is mainly the person with both psychic dysphoria and somatic distress who becomes a patient. In Africa, for example, depression as illness seems to be made up of both psychic and somatic complaints, with the somatic symptoms dominating the clinical picture.[6] Kleinman (1980, 1982) points out that entry into and exit from the treatment system entails a set of negotiations with important individuals and groups in the patient's environment. Kleinman's important paper on neurasthenia (1982) demonstrates that somatic symptoms are part and parcel of this negotiation process. Neurasthenic patients in Hunan were found to suffer a high proportion of depressive symptoms. While antidepressant medication helped some of these symptoms, it in no way resolved any of the illnesses. Cure apparently required a set of negotiations that, using the somatic symptoms as rationale, could result in altering the socioenvironmental context.

German's (1972) and Kleinman's work demonstrates that non-Western patients do not lack a vocabulary for describing their illness in psychic terms. However, relatively few Hunan patients spontaneously complained of dysphoria. When interviewed with a schedule that contained detailed questions about psychic complaints, they answered in sufficient detail to convince Kleinman that many qualified for a DSM-III diagnosis of depression. In fact, all of them reported some form of dysphoria.

Complaints about feeling depressed do not regularly enter into physician-patient interactions among Chinese or Africans. One of the reasons for this difference between Western and some non-Western cultures is that different ideas prevail about what is legitimate to bring into a treatment encounter. While majority culture North Americans will complain of dysphoria with physicians, Vietnamese and Chinese feel that such things can be discussed with family and friends, perhaps with priests or fortune-tellers, but not with doctors (Tung 1980; Kleinman 1980). Another reason for not discussing psychic problems in psychic terms is fear of stigma. In Southeast Asian culture, mental illness is even more stigmatizing than it is in North America (Tung 1980; Kleinman 1980).

During patient-physician encounters, Non-Westerners and lower-class North Americans will tend to downplay dysphoric symptoms and to emphasize somatic ones (see also Kleinman 1980, 1977; Leighton et al. 1963; Cheung et al. 1980–81; Fernando 1975). One suspects that many non-Westerners who become patients suffer from something very much like DSM-III Depression with Melancholia but do not volunteer psychic symptoms unless systematically asked. However, a number of authors (Lin et al. 1979; Kleinman 1982; Kinzie 1983) report that Southeast Asians will, if specifically asked, report psychic depression.

The work of Perris et al. (1981) also highlights the fact that the person who asks questions about symptoms plays a significant role in what is reported. In a preliminary study, these authors investigated depressed psychiatric inpatients in Naples, Italy, and Umea, Sweden, using a psychopathology rating scale filled out by physicians and a self-report inventory filled out by patients. In line with expectations, the doctors' ratings on Italian patients yielded higher scores on hypochondriasis, whereas the Swedish patients were perceived as suffering more from agitation and inability to feel. In contrast with the authors' predictions and with the physicians' ratings, however, the depressed Swedish patients' self-ratings yielded higher scores in disturbances in bodily functioning than the Italians', whereas Italian patients expressed more intense feelings of hopelessness and loss of interest.

The findings from all these studies suggest that, although the core experience of depressive illness may be more similar than different across cultures, what is emphasized or reported in physician-patient interactions varies greatly. Each society creates its own threshold for the translation of troubling experience into illness. One likely determinant of the threshold beyond which depression becomes illness is the dimension of sociocentrism versus egocentrism. Shweder (chap. 6) and Kleinman (chap. 13) suggest that egocentric societies permit the expression of affect and legitimize such expression. According to Shweder, "Personal biography goes along with affect display." As societies become more egocentric, the expression of inner emotional life becomes part of the repertoire of behavior for more and more people. One can trace the development of this in Western society. Shakespearean drama, the artistic product of a Western society in a more sociocentric phase than it is now, reserves melancholy madness as the exclusive province of princes and kings. Commoners in Shakespeare's plays are one-dimensional; if they suffer inwardly, one never knows it because no public display of affect is permitted. Soap operas, the mass theater of a present-day egalitarian society, make it clear that anyone can be depressed and anyone can be ill with purely psychic symptoms.

SUGGESTIONS FOR FUTURE RESEARCH

Depression may be more ubiquitous than sometimes thought, and the way it is experienced more similar than different across cultures. We need no longer rely on speculation: survey tools exist to test this proposition in various societies. Findings to date support the proposition that depression as an experience has many core features, suggesting a common biological upset. This generalization requires the qualification that there are apparent subtle differences in the experience of depression in different cultures. Japanese nationals' more external associations to the experience compared with Japanese Americans' more internal referents and the differences in feelings of loneliness between depressed North Americans and depressed Africans may be pathoplastic differences determined by culture.

It is tempting to attribute variations in feeling states to culture, emphasizing that affect is interactive as much as it is interpersonal. However, future research must address both cultural and genetic explanations as alternate hypotheses. It has been pointed out, for example, that suicidal behavior is rare among depressed Africans compared with depressed North Americans and Europeans (Asuni 1961; Binitie 1975). Perhaps this is because African culture is different from Euro-American cultures, but recent work (Rydin et al. 1982) reveals that suicidal behavior may be linked to serotonin levels in the brain. The fact that serotonin levels are stable over time leads Rydin to suggest that the tendency toward impulsive behavior is partially attributable to genetically determined susceptibility. Persons with such a susceptibility, when depressed, may be particularly vulnerable to suicide. It is possible, of course, that brain serotonin levels vary across ethnic groups, accounting for differential propensities toward suicidal behavior. Testing a hypothesis relating behavior to culture will call for some ingenuity in accounting for strong competing hypotheses, such as genetic variation.

Depression as illness is not the same in all cultures. This raises certain questions for research. When, how, and under what conditions do experiences such as depression become defined as disorder and what is the role of somatic symptoms in this definition? Research by Westermeyer et al. (1983) suggests that among Laotians somatic symptoms play a powerful role in predicting entry into the mental patient role. Westermeyer interviewed a sample of Hmong refugees shortly after their arrival in Minnesota, using the Symptom Checklist-90 (SCL-90) (Derogatis et al. 1973). Scores obtained on the SCL-90 were then used as predictors in a study of who among the refugees became clients of the mental health care system. The identified patients had initially higher mean scores on depression and somatization than the rest of the Hmong. While both scores differentiated patients from normals on a statistical basis, it is striking to observe from Westermeyer's data that the mean somatization score for those who became patients is twice that for nonpatients, whereas the depression score differences are not as dramatic.

Does depression become illness in the presence of somatic symptoms because their co-occurrence raises discomfort above a threshold level of tolerance, or do somatic symptoms legitimize entry into the patient role? Under what conditions do the requirements for admission to the patient role change?

We now possess the conceptual and methodological tools to conduct research into the determinants of patient roles in different cultures, and measures derived from social psychiatry and social psychology can be used to test hypotheses. The search for equivalences in feeling states or levels of illness has been aided by the use of multivariate techniques such as factor analysis which can be applied to population data and by the evolution of systematic clinical examinations based on well-defined inclusion and exclusion symptom criteria. Psychophysiological measures such as sleep patterns in depressive patients (Kupfer et al. 1982; Passouant 1979) and various biochemical assays (Kasa et al. 1982; Limoila et al. 1982; Carroll et al. 1981; Rydin et al. 1982) hold forth the promise of further refinement of clinical taxonomies.

A note, however, about "sickness." Words used to denote illness categories acquire connotations that make scientific discourse difficult. Instead of being the conceptual conveniences they are meant to be, categories for classifying behaviors often become battlegrounds. For example, Obeyesekere (chap. 4) stands Western culture on its ear by stating that if he were to suggest that anorexia, sexual fantasies, and nocturnal emissions together constitute a category of disturbed behavior, he would be "laughed out of court." In fact, this constellation of behaviors makes a good deal of psychodynamic sense. The problem comes with the name he chooses for this syndrome—semen loss. The connotation that it is semen loss that causes this constellation of behaviors becomes ridiculous in Western society, which values the opposite. (One should not retain semen; the more one loses, the better.) At a purely descriptive level, however, the syndrome Obeyesekere describes possesses heuristic value. It is the connotation of the term which makes it ridiculous. This is also true, as Lutz (chap. 2) points out, for labels like "depression" and "neurasthenia." Their denotative value may be obscured because of connotations regarding etiology and "proper" courses of treatment which these labels have acquired. An Esperanto of denotative description of patterns of disorder across culture would be a boon to research.

In passing, one must note the real achievement of DSM-III in making diagnosis both more denotative and more operational. Evolving taxonomies for depression as experience and depression as disorder, relating these taxonomies to the dynamics of health-seeking behavior and to the cultural context in which they evolve, are important research goals.

Differentiating the affective from the somatic components of depression has implications for treatment as well as for research. Mathew et al. (1983), for example, treated a group of depressed patients with a particular antidepressant—Amitryptiline—and compared the results obtained with those of another group of depressed patients who received Desipramine, an antidepressant with chemical characteristics different from Amitryptiline. While both groups of patients improved in the affective sphere, only the Amitryptiline-treated group reported relief from their somatic symptoms. The authors felt this was because Amitryptiline possesses anxiolytic, in addition to antidepressant, properties. Kleinman (1977, 1982) has also suggested that the neurovegetative upset sometimes called anxiety may be a source of somatization and has illustrated how culture, operating through the work role, may create a process by which the disease of anxiety is transformed into a somatoform illness.

Another important area of depression research is the search for cause. It is clear from the work of Brown and Harris (1978), Beck (1974), and others (Abrahamson et al. 1978; Akiskal and McKinney 1973) that cause is complex, that it involves factors such as personal historical vulnerabilities, stress, and social context. At another level, it probably involves vulnerabilities based on neurophysiological predisposition (Akiskal 1973; Kasa et al. 1982; Kupfer et al. 1982; Rydin et al. 1982; Weissman et al. 1982, 1984). Carr and Vitaliano (chap. 8) suggest that, in depression research, we should develop taxonomies based on such factors as perceived stress, cognitively mediated coping styles, and the supportive resources available to an individual. The idea of such a taxonomy of antecedents is very appealing. It is clear that the day of simplistic notions of etiology, such as depression is anger turned inward, is over. Data about complex interactions relating to depression have begun to emerge: what is needed now are conceptually based taxonomies of antecedents which can take such data into account and which can be related to the occurrence of depression.

Such complex research questions cannot be addressed by the practitioners of any one discipline, be it psychiatry, psychology, or anthropology. Instead, such questions suggest exciting and potentially fruitful areas for interdisciplinary study. Such study will help to replace the rancor that has sometimes characterized the interaction of anthropology, psychology, and medicine with constructive collaborations devoted to understanding persistent and troubling phenomena like depression.

ACKNOWLEDGMENTS

The research on which this report is based was made possible in part by a research award from Canada Health and Welfare, National Health Research Directorate Program, and a National Health Research Scholar Award from the National Health Research Directorate Program; a research grant awarded by the Secretary of State, Multiculturalism Directorate; and an award from the P. A. Woodward Foundation, Vancouver.

NOTES

1. In the past, the term "melancholia" evolved into similarly confused usage (Jackson 1980).
2. Throughout this chapter, "Southeast Asian" is used to refer to these refugee groups from Vietnam, Laos, and Cambodia. The refugees have informed us that this is the term by which they prefer to be described rather than the Indo-Chinese, "Boat people," and the like.
3. Since the Stirling County Questionnaire derives from the same body of lore underpinning DSM-III, it incorporates many of the symptoms attributed to diagnoses such as depression in the latter system. However, since all three studies reported in this chapter antedated DSM-III, the overlap in items is not complete.
4. Clinically based research in illness is prey to an ascertainment bias that has been called "Berkson's fallacy." Berkson (1946, 1955) makes the point that persons who have disabilities not related to a condition being investigated are more likely to enter the formal treatment system. He offers as an example that people with diabetes and cholecystitis are more likely to be in hospital than those with cholecystitis alone. There may, as a result, be an apparent association between the two conditions when, in the general population, there is no such relationship (Berkson 1946, 1955; see also Cohen and Cohen, in press).
5. Of course, other considerations besides symptoms enter into the process of becoming a patient, for example, considerations such as family dynamics and social position. These factors are, however, beyond the scope of the present report.

6. The differences are relative, however, not absolute. German (1972), for example, working in Uganda, reports that while African patients complain of depression in somatic terms, the more acculturated they become, the more likely they are to describe it using complaints of psychic discomfort.

REFERENCES

Abad, V., and E. Boyce
  1979   Issues in Psychiatric Evaluations of Puerto Ricans: A Socio-
                Cultural Perspective. Journal of Operational Psychiatry 10(1):
                28–39.
Abrahamson, L. Y., M. E. P. Seligman, and J. D. Teasdale
  1978   Learned Helplessness in Humans: Critique and Reformulation.
                Journal of Abnormal Psychology 87(1):49–74.
Akiskal, H. S., and W. T. McKinney
  1973   Depressive Disorders: Towards a Unified Hypothesis. Science
                182:20–29.
American Psychiatric Association
  1980   Diagnostic and Statistical Manual of Mental Disorders. 3d ed.
                (DSM-III.) Washington, D.C.
Beck, A.
  1974   The Development of Depression: A Cognitive Model. *In* The
                Psychology of Depression: Contemporary Theory and
                Research. R. Friedman and M. M. Katz, eds. New York:
                Winston-Wiley.
Beiser, M., J. L. Ravel, H. Collomb et al.
  1972   Assessing Psychiatric Disorder Among the Serer of Senegal.
                Journal of Nervous and Mental Disease 154(2):141–151.
Beiser, M., W. Burr, J. L. Ravel et al.
  1973   Illnesses of the Spirit Among the Serer of Senegal. American
                Journal of Psychiatry 130(8):881–886.
Beiser, M., W. A. Burr, H. Collomb et al.
  1974   Pobough Lang in Senegal. Social Psychiatry 9:123–129.
Beiser, M., R. C. Benfari, H. Collomb and J. Ravel
  1976   Measuring Psychoneurotic Behaviors in Cross-Cultural
                Surveys. Journal of Nervous and Mental Disorders 163(1):
                10–23.
Benfari, R. C., A. H. Leighton et al.
  1972   Some Dimensions of Psychoneurotic Behavior in an Urban
                Sample. Journal of Nervous and Mental Disease 155(2):77–90.

Berkson, J.
1946   Limitations of the Applications of Fourfold Table Analysis to
              Hospital Data. Biometrics Bulletin 2:47−53.
1955   The Statistical Study of Association Between Working and
              Busy Cancer. Proceedings of Staff Meetings, Mayo Clinic
              319−348.
Binitie, A.
1975   A Factor Analytical Study of Depression Across Cultures—
              African and European. British Journal of Psychiatry 127:
              559−563.
Brislin, R. W.
1970   Back-Translation for Cross-Cultural Research. Journal of
              Cross-Cultural Psychology 1:195−216.
Brislin, R. W., W. J. Lonner, and R. M. Thorndike
1973   Cross-Cultural Research Methods. New York: John Wiley &
              Sons.
Brodman, K., A. J. Erdmann, I. Lorge et al.
1949   The Cornell Medical Index: An Adjunct to Medical Interview.
              Journal of the American Medical Association 140:530−534.
1951   The Cornell Medical Index—Health Questionnaire. Vol. II, as
              a Diagnostic Instrument. Journal of the American Medical
              Association 145:152−157.
Brown, G. W., and T. P. Harris
1978   Social Origins of Depression: A Study of Psychiatric Disorders
              in Women. London: Tavistock.
Butcher, J. N., and P. Pancheri
1976   A Handbook of Cross-National MMPI Research. Minneapolis:
              University of Minnesota Press.
Carrothers, J. C.
1953   The African Mind in Health and Disease: A Study of Ethno-
              psychiatry. Monograph Series, no. 17. Geneva: World Health
              Organization.
Cattell, R. B.
1966   The "Scree" Test for the Number of Factors. Multivariate
              Behavioral Research 1:245−276.
Cattell, R. B., and G. Vogelman
1977   A Comprehensive Trial of the Scree and KG Criteria for Deter-
              mining the Number of Factors. Multivariate Behavioral Re-
              search 12:289−325.
Cheung, F. M., B. W. K. Lau, and E. Waldmann
1980−81   Somatization among Chinese Depressives in General Practice.
              International Journal of Psychiatry in Medicine 10:361−373.

Cohen, P., and J. Cohen
  n.d.   The Clinician's Illusion. Archives of General Psychiatry. In
                    press.
Derogatis, L. R., R. S. Lipman, and L. Covi
  1973   SCL-90: An Outpatient Psychiatric Rating Scale: Preliminary
                    Report. Psychopharmacology Bulletin 9:13−28.
Duncan-Jones, P., and S. Henderson
  1978   The Successful Use of a Two-Phase Design in a Population
                    Survey. Social Psychiatry 13:231−237.

Engelsman, F.
  1982   Culture and Depression. *In* Culture and Psychopathology.
                    I. Al-Issa, ed. Baltimore: University Park Press.
Eysenck, H. S., and S. B. G. Eysenck
  1982   Culture and Personality Abnormalities. *In* Culture and Psycho-
                    pathology. I. Al-Issa, ed. Baltimore: University Park Press.
Fernando, S. J. M.
  1975   A Cross-Cultural Study of Some Familial and Social Factors in
                    Depressive Illness. British Journal of Psychiatry 127:46−53.

German, A.
  1972   Aspects of Clinical Psychiatry in Sub-Saharan Africa. British
                    Journal of Psychiatry 121:461−479.
Goldberg, D. P., and B. Blackwell
  1970   Psychiatric Illness in General Practice: A Detailed Study Using
                    a New Method of Case Identification. British Medical Journal
                    2:439−443.
Goldberg, D., C. Kay, and L. Thompson
  1976   Psychiatric Morbidity in General Practice and the Community.
                    Psychological Medicine 6:565−569.

Harman, H. H.
  1970   Modern Factor Analysis. Chicago: University of Chicago Press.
Hedlund, J. L., and B. W. Vieweg
  1979   The Zung Self-Rating Depression Scale: A Comprehensive
                    Review. Journal of Operational Psychiatry 10(1):51−66.
Horst, P.
  1968   Personality: Measurement of Dimensions. San Francisco:
                    Jossey-Bass.
Jablensky, A., N. Sartorius, W. Gulbinat, and G. Ernberg
  1981   Characteristics of Depressive Patients Contacting Psychiatric
                    Services in Four Cultures. Acta Psychiatrica Scandinavica 63:
                    367−383.
Jackson, S. W.
  1980   Two Sufferers' Perspectives on Melancholia: 1690's to 1790's.
                    In Essays in The History of Psychiatry. E. R. Wallace and

L. C. Pressley, eds. Columbia, S.C.: Wm. S. Hall Psychiatric Institute.

Johnstone, A., and D. Goldberg
1976   Psychiatric Screening in General Practice: A Controlled Trial. Lancet 1:605−608.

Kasa, K., S. Otsuki, M. Yamamoto et al.
1982   Cerebrospinal Fluid of Aminobutyric Acid and Homovarellic Acid in Depressive Disorders. Biological Psychiatry 17(8): 877−883.

Kenyon, F. E.
1976   Hypochondriacal States. British Journal of Psychiatry 129: 1−14.

Kinzie, D., and S. Manson
1983   Five Years' Experience with Indochinese Refugee Psychiatric Patients. Journal of Operational Psychiatry 14(2):105−111.

Kinzie, J. D., S. M. Manson, D. T. Vinh, N. T. Nolan, B. Anh, and T. N. Pho
1982   Development and Validation of a Vietnamese Language Depression Rating Scale. American Journal of Psychiatry 139: 1276−1281.

Kleinman, A.
1977   Depression, Somatization, and the New Cross-Cultural Psychiatry. Social Science Medicine 11:3−10.
1980   Patients and Healers in the Context of Culture. Berkeley, Los Angeles, London: University of California Press.
1982   Neurasthenia and Depression: A Study of Somatization and Culture in China. Culture, Medicine, and Psychiatry 6(2): 117−190.

Kupfer, D. J., E. Targ, and J. Stack
1982   Electroencephalographic Sleep in Unipolar Depressive Subtypes. Support for a Biological and Familial Classification. Journal of Nervous Mental Disorders 170(8):494−498.

Langner, T. S.
1962   A Twenty-Two Item Screening Score of Psychiatric Symptoms Indicating Impairment. Journal of Health and Human Behavior 3:269−276.

Leckman, J. F., K. R. Merikangas, D. L. Pauls, B. A. Prusoff, and M. M. Weissman
1983   Anxiety Disorders and Depression: Contradictions Between Family Study Data and DSM-III Conventions. American Journal of Psychiatry 140:880−882.

Leff, J.
1973   Culture and the Differentiation of Emotional States. British Journal of Psychiatry 123:299−306.

1981   Psychiatry Around the Globe: A Transcultural View. New York: Marcel Dekker.

Leighton, A., T. Lambo, C. Hughes et al.
1963   Psychiatric Disorder Among the Yoruba. New York: Cornell University Press.

Leighton, D. C., J. S. Harding, D. B. Macklin, A. M. MacMillan, and A. H. Leighton
1963   The Character of Danger. New York: Basic Books.

Limoila, M., F. Karoum, and W. Z. Potter
1982   High, Positive Correlation Between Urinary Free Tyramine Excretion Rate and "Whole Body" Norepinephrine Turnover in Depressed Patients. Biological Psychiatry 17(9): 1031−1036.

Lin, K., L. Tazuma, and M. Masuda
1979   Adaptational Problems of Vietnamese Refugees. Archives of General Psychiatry 36:955−961.

MacMillan, A. M.
1957   The Health Opinion Survey: Technique for Estimating Prevalency of Psychoneurotic and Related Types of Disorders in Communities. Psychological Reports Monograph, Supp. 7.

Marsella, A. J.
1978   Thoughts on Cross-cultural Studies on the Epidemiology of Depression. Culture, Medicine, and Psychiatry 2:343−357.
1980   Depressive Experience and Disorder Across Cultures. *In* Handbook of Cross-Cultural Psychology. Vol. 6. H. Triandis and J. Draguns, eds. Boston: Allyn and Bacon.

Mathew, R. J., M. L. Weinman, and M. Mirabi
1981   Physical Symptoms of Depression. British Journal of Psychiatry 139:293−296.

Orley, J., and J. K. Wing
1979   Psychiatric Disorders in Two African Villages. Archives of General Psychiatry 36:513−520.

Passouant, P.
1979   Depression et Sommeil. Encephale 5(5):533−545.

Paykel, E. S.
1971   Classification of Depressed Patients: A Cluster Analysis Derived Grouping. British Journal of Psychiatry 118:275−288.

Perris, C., M. Eisemann, H. Perris, D. Kemali, A. Amati, M. delVecchio, and L. Vacca
1981   Transactional Aspects of Depressive Symptomatology. Psychiatria Clinica 14:69−80.

Pfeiffer, W.
1968   The Symptomatology of Depression Viewed Trans-culturally. Transcultural Psychiatric Research Review 5:121−123.

Prince, R.
1968   The Changing Picture of Depression Syndromes in Africa: Is It
            Fact or Diagnostic Fashion? Canadian Journal of African
            Studies 1:177–192.
Rydin, E., D. Schalling, and M. Asberg
1982   Rorschach Ratings in Depressed and Suicidal Patients with Low
            Levels of 5-Hydroxyindolacetic Acid in Cerebrospinal Fluid.
            Psychiatric Research 7(2):229–243.
Scheaffer, R. L., W. Menderhall, and L. Ott
1979   Elementary Survey Sampling. North Scituate, Mass.: Duxbury
            Press.
Srole, L., T. S. Langner, S. T. Michael et al.
1962   Mental Health in the Metropolis: The Midtown Manhattan
            Study. New York: McGraw-Hill.
Srole, L., and A. K. Fisher
1980   The Midtown Manhattan Study vs. "The Mental Paradise
            Lost" Doctrine: A Controversy Joined. Archives of General
            Psychiatry 37:209–265.
Tanaka-Matsumi, J., and A. J. Marsella
1976   Cross-cultural Variations in the Phenomenological Expression
            of Depression: Word Association. Journal of Cross-Cultural
            Psychology 7:379–396.
Teja, J. A. S., R. I. Narong, and A. K. Aggarwal
1971   Depression Across Cultures. British Journal of Psychiatry 119:
            253–260.
Tseng, W. S.
1975   The Nature of Somatic Complaints Among Psychiatric Patients:
            The Chinese Case. Comparative Psychiatry 16(3):237–245.
Tung, T. M.
1980   Indochinese Patients: Cultural Aspects of the Medical and Psy-
            chiatric Care of Indochinese Refugees. Falls Church: Action for
            Southeast Asians.
Weissman, M. M., and J. K. Myers
1978   Affective Disorders in a United States Urban Community:
            The Use of Research Diagnostic Criteria in an Epidemio-
            logical Survey. Archives of General Psychiatry 35(11):
            1304–1311.
Weissman, M. M., J. K. Myers, and P. Harding
1978   Psychiatric Disorders in a United States Urban Community.
            American Journal of Psychiatry 135:549–562.
Weissman, M. M., K. K. Kidd, and B. A. Prusoff
1982   Variability in Rates of Affective Disorders in Relatives of De-
            pressed and Normal Probands. Archives of General Psychiatry
            39:1397–1403.

Weissman, M. M., E. S. Gershon, K. K. Kidd, B. A. Prusoff, J. F. Leckman et al.
    1984   Psychiatric Disorders in the Relatives of Probands With Affective Disorders. Archives of General Psychiatry 41:13−21.
Westermeyer, J., T. F. Vang, and J. Neider
    1983   A Comparison of Refugees Using and Not Using a Psychiatric Service: An Analysis of DSM-III Criteria and Self-Rating Scales in Cross-Cultural Context. Journal of Operational Psychiatry 14(1):36−41.
Wing, J. K.
    1970   A Standard Form of Present State Examination. *In* International Symposium on Psychiatric Epidemiology. E. H. Hare and J. K. Wing, eds. London: Oxford University Press.
Yap, P. M.
    1965   Phenomenology of Affective Disorders in Chinese and Other Cultures. *In* Transcultural Psychiatry. D. Reuck and K. Porter, eds. Boston: Little, Brown.

10

Cross-Cultural Studies of Depressive Disorders: An Overview

Anthony J. Marsella, Norman Sartorius, Assen Jablensky, and Fred R. Fenton

INTRODUCTION

Depression is one of the oldest known psychiatric disorders. References to depressive experience and disorder abound in the Old Testament and in many classical Hindu medical texts. Hippocrates (460−377 B.C.), the father of medicine, listed melancholia as one of the major forms of mental disease more than two thousand years ago. In 1621, Robert Burton (1577−1640) published *The Anatomy of Melancholia*, a text that has remained an important resource for understanding the nature and experience of depressive disorders. By the nineteenth century, depression had become a pervasive concern of Western psychiatry. Scores of practitioners and theorists, including Esquirol, Haslam, Falret, Baillarger, Kraepelin, and Freud, made contributions to our understanding of depression. Yet, in spite of the longevity of our concern, depressive disorders remain an elusive problem.

Today, the number of people suffering from depressive disorders is increasing. Sartorius (1974) estimated that there are more than 100 million people worldwide who suffer from depressive disorders. Depression has become such an extensive problem that Klerman (1979) suggested this period in our history may well come to be called the Age of Melancholy.

Among our current approaches to depression research, cross-cultural studies represent an important strategy for investigating universals and specifics in the etiology, expression, and experience of depressive disorder. The cross-cultural literature on depression has been reviewed by Pfeiffer (1968), Prince (1968), Milenkov (1969), Sartorius (1973), Fábrega (1974, 1975), Singer (1975), Marsella (1981), and Kleinman (1982). These reviews concluded that many of our conceptions regarding depression may be highly ethnocentric.

Our purpose in this chapter is to discuss the cross-cultural literature on depressive disorders and experience with special attention to the following topics: (1) cultural conceptions of depression, (2) epidemiological aspects of depression, (3) manifestations of depression, (4) the assessment of depression, (5) personality correlates of depression, and (6) cultural hypotheses of depression. In beginning this review, it is important to recognize that cultural factors have not been incorporated into our major theories of depression. One reason for this has been our confusion about the definition of culture. For many, culture is considered to be an "external" variable involving artifacts and practices of particular ethnic groups. But the fact that culture is also an "internal" variable as represented in knowledge, beliefs, attitudes, cognitive styles, self-referent systems, and other varieties of subjective experience relevant to depression is frequently ignored. We argue that cultural factors constitute an important context for all aspects of depressive experience and disorder and they must be considered if an accurate understanding of depression is to be achieved.

CULTURAL CONCEPTIONS OF DEPRESSIVE DISORDER

The current medical conception of depression asserts that it is a psychiatric syndrome characterized by specific affective, cognitive, behavioral, and somatic symptoms. Popular conceptions of depression are similar to the medical description. As a result, Indo-European languages have many words that refer to depressive experience. This view may, however, be unique to European and North American cultures since equivalent concepts of depression are not found among many non-European groups, including, for example, Nigerians (Leighton et al. 1963), Chinese (Tseng and Hsu 1969), Canadian Eskimos (Terminsen and Ryan 1970), Japanese (Tanaka-Matsumi and Marsella 1976), and Malaysians (Resner and Hartog 1970).

That no conceptually equivalent terms for depression exist in many non-European cultures does not mean depressive disorders do not exist. Rather, it is possible that the subjective experience of depression, its behavioral manifestations, and the social responses to it may vary across cultures. A definitive answer would require a careful appraisal of the "emic" conceptualization of depression. Moreover, even if some types of depression are shown to have primary biological causes (e.g., catecholamine deficits at the neural synapse), cultural factors could still exert powerful pathoplastic effects and modify the behavioral expression of the biological factors. Individuals experiencing a biochemical deficit must still *interpret* the abnormal experience, *translate* the experience into active behavior, and *respond* to the social reaction to that behavior. Thus, if a language conveys the abnormal subjective experience generated by a common biochemical disturbance differently in one culture than in another, the experience and manifestations of the disorder in the two cultures would likely be different. In addition, apparent similarities in the manifestations of depressive disorders across cultures must not be automatically interpreted to mean their causes are identical. The same behavior could have different causes and different consequences across cultures. To date, the relative contributions of "universal" biological causes (if these are shown to exist) and of culture-specific psychological and social influences to the etiology, experience, and expression of depression in different parts of the world remain, by and large, unknown.

THE EPIDEMIOLOGY OF DEPRESSION ACROSS CULTURES

Studies of the epidemiology of depression, although numerous, have yielded few firm conclusions about ethnocultural variations in the frequency and distribution of depressive disorders (see Sartorius 1973, 1975; Marsella 1978; Clayton 1981; Fenton 1981; Boyd and Weissman 1982). The major reasons for this are: (1) the point at which a mood change ceases to be "normal" and becomes pathological has not yet been defined with precision, (2) diagnostic criteria used in epidemiological studies vary, (3) case finding and sampling procedures differ, (4) "non-European" patterns of depressive experience are not often considered, and (5) issues of diagnostic reliability in different ethnocultural groups have received little or no attention. Furthermore, at present there are no reliable psychophysiological, biochemical, or other indicators measurable by routine laboratory methods which can be used to supplement clinical observation in the diagnosis of affective disorders.

Sartorius (1975) and Marsella (1978) identify four steps in the conduct of cross-cultural epidemiological studies: (1) considering relevant anthropological and ethnographic material when designing the studies, (2) developing glossaries and operational definitions for symptoms and diagnostic categories to be studied, (3) deriving symptom patterns using multivariate analytic techniques rather than relying exclusively on a priori diagnostic categories, and (4) using similar research methods in cross-cultural studies.

The third step is particularly important. Relying solely on diagnosis to interpret differences in rates of depression in different cultures is risky because similar diagnostic labels may mask wide differences in symptom patterns. Assuming that valid information is collected and recorded systematically, multivariate techniques such as factor analysis may be used to supplement clinical judgment as to how symptoms cluster irrespective of the final diagnostic labels applied. Marsella et al. (1972, 1973) and Binitie (1975) have used factor analysis to derive symptom profiles across cultures and have found that patterns thus generated indicate considerable cultural variation.

MANIFESTATION OF DEPRESSION ACROSS CULTURES

There have been numerous studies on cultural variations in the manifestation of depressive disorders. These studies have been reviewed by Prince (1968), Racy (1970), German (1972), Kleinman (1977, 1982) and Marsella (1980). One of the earliest observations on the manifestation of depression across cultures was made by Kraepelin ([1904] 1974) during his visit to Indonesia: "Depression, when it did occur, was usually mild and fleeting, and feelings of guilt were never experienced." Nevertheless, Kraepelin maintained that depression was a universal human phenomenon. Cross-cultural studies on the manifestation of depression have been conducted using a wide array of research strategies and methods including clinical observation, matched diagnostic groups, matched samples, and international surveys. They will be discussed in that order.

Clinical Observation

Clinical studies of depressive symptomatology in non-Western cultures have been reported from Afghanistan (Waziri 1973), Iraq (Bazzoui 1970), India (Rao 1973; Teja and Narang 1970; Sethi and Gupta 1970), Indonesia (Pfeiffer 1967), Japan (Shinfuku et al. 1973; Ohara 1973), Nigeria (Ebigbo 1982), the Philippines (Sechrest 1963, 1969), Taiwan (Kleinman 1979), and the People's Republic of China (Kleinman 1982). All of these studies allude to the reduced frequency or absence of psychological components of depression and the dominance of somatic aspects. This is true especially for guilt, existential despair, self-denigration, and suicidal ideation. A limitation of clinical observation is its a priori assumption about the presence of certain symptoms; it is also subject to numerous observer disagreements because of low reliability. These problems are compounded in cross-cultural studies because of ethnocentric perceptions.

Matched Diagnostic Groups

The matched diagnostic groups strategy compares symptoms of patients from different cultures who have received the same clinical diagnosis (e.g., paranoid schizophrenia, neurotic depression). The basic assumption is that, given a common diagnosis, a common disease process is likely to be present and that variations in specific symptoms could be attributed to cultural factors. This approach has been used to compare symptoms among endogenous depressives in 'Japan and Germany (Kimura 1965) and among neurotic and psychotic American blacks and Caucasians (e.g., Tonks et al. 1970; Simon et al. 1973). The basic assumption of this strategy is sound; however, it does not consider that diagnosis is often unreliable. Thus, when symptom differences emerge between two groups who share the same diagnosis, it is logical to ask why they received the same diagnosis in the first place.

Matched Samples

This approach compares patients from different cultures who are matched for such key variables as age, sex, social class, educational level, and so forth. It assumes these variables account for common variances in symptomatology, while differences in symptomatology may be attributed to ethnocultural factors. This approach has been used to compare symptomatology of Mexican-American and Anglo-American patients (Stoker et al. 1968), Filipinos and Americans (Sechrest 1969), Japanese and Americans (Draguns et al. 1971), and Argentinians and North Americans (e.g., Fundia et al. 1971). In all these instances, cultural variations in symptoms were reported. For example, Stoker et al. found that Mexican-American patients presented much higher frequencies of complaints and symptoms associated with agitated depression, including hostility, hyperactivity, crying, and sleeplessness. In contrast, Anglo patients reported more guilt feelings and more psychological and physical retardation.

If the matched samples method were used on a large-scale basis to compare the presenting symptomatologies of first admission patients prior to the influence of medications or hospital environments, it is conceivable that researchers would be able to identify the major types of symptoms that characterize given cultures. This approach requires standardized psychiatric interviews with high reliability across cultures. The same results could be achieved from community-based epidemiological surveys using quota sampling methods (e.g., samples of 5,000 people in each culture stratified for age, gender, and social class characteristics and examination of their symptom profiles).

International Surveys

The international survey was one of the first research strategies used to study cultural variations in depressive symptomatology. Murphy et al. (1964) surveyed depressive symptomatology in thirty countries. They found similarities in the expression of depression across four classic signs (i.e., depressed mood, diurnal variation, insomnia, and loss of interest in the environment) in twenty-one countries, but in nine other countries, largely "non-Western," these signs were not found with great frequency among depressed patients. Instead, the primary symptoms included somatic disturbances like fatigue, anorexia, weight loss, and loss of libido. Although this approach is valuable, it has many limitations. Clearly, without prior training, it is unlikely psychiatrists from different cultures would use similar interview methods and criteria for assessing symptomatology. If these could be controlled, however, it would offer a good opportunity to compare cultural variations in depressive symptomatology. Such an approach was used in the WHO Collaborative Study on Depression (Sartorius et al. 1980; Jablensky et al. 1981; WHO 1983).

The WHO study represents one of the most extensive cross-cultural comparisons of depressive symptomatology. Five hundred and seventy-three patients from five countries (Canada, India, Iran, Japan, and Switzerland) were interviewed by experienced clinicians using standardized interview schedules (The WHO Schedule for Standardized Assessment of Depressive Disorders [SADD]); all interviewers were to use specified diagnostic criteria for depression. The results revealed similar patterns of depressive disorder in all settings, but there were considerable cultural variations in the frequencies with which certain symptoms appeared across the samples. For example, guilt feelings were present in 68 percent of the Swiss sample, but in only 32 percent of the Iranian sample; suicidal ideas were present in 70 percent of the Canadian sample, but in only 40 percent of the Japanese sample. Somatization was present in 57 percent of the Iranian sample, but in only 27 percent of the Canadian sample. Thus, even when a priori concepts of depression guide the assessment of patients, ethnocultural variations in the manifestation of symptoms of depression are still evident. A major difference across the research sites was the level of severity in the patients. Patients in Basel and Montreal evidenced more "anergic-retarded" and "vital" depressions than patients in Tokyo and Teheran. The former patients also had more personality abnormalities and more nonaffective psychiatric disturbances in their predisorder history.

The WHO study provides a good foundation for future comparative studies of depressive disorders. For example, the SADD has high interviewer reliability coefficients, suggesting it can be used in a variety of cultural settings to appraise depressive symptomatology. In addition, the range of symptoms it addresses includes the full spectrum of problems associated with depression in the Western cultures. Indeed, the patients in all the sites were found to have high frequencies of sadness, joylessness, anxiety, tension, lack of energy, loss of interest, concentration difficulties, and feelings of inadequacy. But these similarities do not rule out the existence of "culture-specific" disorders.

Modifications in the original study would be useful in clarifying and extending the findings. First, it would be helpful to add emically generated depressive symptoms to the SADD; for example, Ebigbo (1982) reported a successful clinical research study using indigenously generated somatic complaints. Second, efforts should be made to develop ethnic identity scales that would assess the degree of Westernization of patients. In the existing WHO study, the patients were highly educated and Westernized. This was less true of the Iranians and Indian patients, and it was in these groups that the phenomenology varied. Third, it may be necessary to include a wider range of diagnostic groups. The WHO study screen required patients to have depressive symptoms prior to inclusion. This probably resulted in greater symptom homogeneity of the cultural samples. Fourth, future research would benefit from a greater focus on such clinical parameters as onset, course, and outcome. Cultural variations in these parameters were found in the well-known International Pilot Study of Schizophrenia (IPSS) and it is likely they would emerge in studies of depressive disorders. Fifth, greater detail is needed in examining various dimensions of symptoms. It would be useful, for example, to study the frequency, intensity, and duration of symptoms rather than their simple presence or absence. Sixth, more cross-cultural research is needed on personality differences and depression in different cultural settings. Last, we need to investigate the nature of the illness experience and role in different cultures to better understand the contextual forces that encourage and maintain certain disorders.

Despite these diverse strategies, results indicate the experience and expression of depression varies across ethnocultural boundaries. Reviewers concur that feelings of guilt, self-deprecation, suicidal ideas, and feelings of despair are often rare or absent among non-European populations, whereas somatic and quasi-somatic symptoms, including disturbances of sleep, appetite, energy, body sensation, and motor functioning, are more common. For example, Collomb and Zwingelstein (1961; cited in German 1972:461) claimed that Senegalese depressed patients

> do not appear to be deeply unhappy or miserable; ideas of self-accusation and guilt are absent, and suicide is rare; the disorder is characterized rather by ideas of persecution, anxiety, hypochondriasis, and somatic complaints.

Sechrest, in his extensive study of Filipino psychiatric patients (1963:199), wrote:

> No instances were found of patients complaining of feelings of worthlessness, of hopelessness, of impending doom, and only two instances were

found of complaints of being or feeling guilty. . . . The investigator would conclude, then, that depression is quite infrequent among Filipinos.

Based on a review of the literature, Marsella (1980) suggested that the experience and expression of depressive disorders are not identical in all cultures, but vary according to the degree a society is "Westernized." He also contended that the presence of a "psychological representation"—symptoms including depressed mood, feelings of guilt, and self-deprecation—may affect the response to treatment as well as the course and outcome of depressive disorders. When the psychological dimension is added to the somatic dimension, the experience of depression assumes new implications: it is now exacerbated.

In conclusion, cross-cultural research on the manifestations of depressive disorder indicates that although so-called core symptoms of the depressive syndrome can be found in many cultures, the full range of manifestations of the depressive syndrome is not universal. In non-European cultures, somatic symptoms are more frequent manifestations of depressive illness and the so-called diagnostic symptoms of depression—reported or observable depressed mood, feelings of guilt, and suicidal ideas—are not common.

THE ASSESSMENT OF DEPRESSION ACROSS CULTURES

Although self-report scales, observational scales, and interview schedules have been developed to assess depression in the "Western" world, few efforts have been made to develop "culturally relevant" instruments. This is not entirely surprising. As demonstrated by Murphy et al. (1967), psychiatrists in different parts of the world adhere to very similar diagnostic "stereotypes" of the depressive disorders because of common experiences in medical training, which ignores ethnocultural considerations.

Instruments such as the Zung Self-Rating Scale (Zung 1969), the Depression Adjective Checklist (Levitt and Lubin 1975), the Minnesota Multiphasic Personality Inventory (Butcher and Pancheri 1975), the Hamilton Depression Scale (Binitie 1975; Teja and Narang 1970), the Beck Depression Inventory (Marsella et al. 1975) and the WHO Schedule for Standardized Assessment of Depressive Disorders (WHO 1983) have all been used effectively in different cultures. Some of them, in different degrees, allow the investigator to record culture-specific events. For example, the WHO/SADD contains, in addition to a pre-coded checklist of depressive symptoms, a number of open-ended items designed for the narrative description and rating of "other symptoms," including specific culture-related experiences and behaviors.

Unfortunately, however, most of the existing scales and schedules measuring depression have limited cultural validity, and thus limited clinical utility in non-Westernized populations. The psychometric properties of an effective cross-cultural clinical instrument should include the following: (1) the range of symptoms and signs should be sufficiently broad, (2) the information should be collected from more than one source if possible, (3) the wording and scaling of the items should be culturally appropriate, (4) the reliability should be measured in different ways (e.g. alternative forms, test-retest), (5) the validity of the instrument should be tested against different criteria (e.g., concurrent validity, predictive validity), (6) culture-appropriate glossary definitions and rules of scoring the items or factors should be specified, and (7) training procedures for the use of the instrument should be specified.

It is also important for depression researchers to recognize that cultural variations in measurement may be evidenced across descriptors of a symptom rather than by its presence or absence. Marsella and Tanaka-Matsumi (1976) found that Japanese nationals, Japanese-Americans, and Caucasians reported differences in the frequency, duration, and severity of depressive symptoms rather than in their mere presence or absence. It is these parameters that capture the subtle influences of cultural experience.

When we construct measures of depression for use in different cultures, we should try to avoid ethnocentric biases that frequently constitute sources of error in cross-cultural psychiatric research generally. Brislin et al. (1973) and Lonner (1979) discuss the important properties of a culturally relevant measure. These include the use of behaviors that reflect experience in that culture (anthropological investigations can often provide clues as to what kinds of items might be appropriate); the use of back-translation to ensure equivalent linguistic meanings in different cultures; and the use of measurement formats that are culturally relevant.

Since some languages do not encourage the use of adjectives to describe human behavior, the use of adjectives either as items or as qualifying terms can be troublesome (Marsella et al. 1975). The same can be said of "true" and "false" items. How the items are scaled may also be important. In the Philippines, Marsella showed an uneducated, impoverished respondent a diagram of a flight of seven stairs; the top step was designated as "being very happy," the bottom step as "being very sad." The respondent was asked to rate how happy he was by placing himself on a particular step. The respondent chose the bottom step because he didn't "want to fall off the top step and hurt himself." The lesson of this anecdote is obvious: one should not assume equivalence in measurement formats. The respondent had perceived the steps in a concrete fashion, not as an abstract scale of satisfaction.

Before closing our discussion on measurement, some comments on biological measurement are warranted. Recent developments in the use of dexamethasone suppression (DMS) tests, hormonal assays, and even in vivo brain function suggest the biological measurement of depression may be feasible in the future (Bunney et al. 1983). These approaches may enable us to assess common biological responses in the face of culturally specific manifestations. It is possible to envision a study where similar scores on dexamethasone suppression tests among individuals from contrasting cultures can be used to separate patient groups. This could be followed by examinations of differences among symptomatology, social disabilities, and personality correlates.

In brief, the minimal requisites of a culturally relevant measure of depression include anthropological knowledge of a group's cognitive structure, including the experience and behavior of clinically depressed individuals in different cultures; accurate translation of both the connotative and the denotative meanings of the instrument's contents; and the use of measurement formats that involve culturally appropriate scales, questions, and parameters. Biological approaches to measurement may be useful in future cross-cultural research.

PERSONALITY CORRELATES OF DEPRESSION

Among Western conceptions of depression, it is assumed that personality variables covary with depressive experience. This variation may be a precursor (depression-prone personality) and/or a correlate of depression. Among the variables most associated with depression are hostility, guilt, low self-esteem, and body image dissatisfaction. These variables have been investigated cross-culturally. Fernando (1969) and Kendell (1970) examined the role of hostility and aggression in depression. They concluded that depression is more likely to occur among cultural groups that strongly inhibit aggressive impulses. This finding is consistent with psychodynamic notions that repressed hostility results in increased risks of depression.

The question of guilt has already been discussed; the results indicate that guilt does not assume the same proportions in depression among non-Western samples that it does in Western groups. Some researchers, such as El-Islam (1969), contend that guilt is present in non-Western cultures but is masked by tendencies to project blame to others. If this is the case, however, it is clear that guilt may not be the same experience for them. Guilt is a function of a particular self-structure (individuated), and to the extent self-structures vary across cultures, guilt must differ.

Low self-esteem is another personality variable influenced by culturally mediated self-structures. In some cultures, the presentation of a positive image of self is considered impolite and offensive because it elevates and celebrates the individual. Thus, in these instances, it is conceivable that individuals may present low levels of self-esteem without pernicious implications. In studies of self-esteem and depression among Japanese-American and Caucasian-American youth in Hawaii, Marsella et al. (1973) and Yanagida and Marsella (1978) found low correlations between depression and real ideal self-concept discrepancy for Japanese-Americans and high correlations for Caucasian Americans. For the former, being depressed did not imply low self-esteem because of the normal ritualistic tendencies to engage in self-debasement. In brief, Western assumptions about self-esteem and depression are not universal; they vary as a function of cultural differences in self-structure. Some cultures continually encourage self-debasement, deference, and personal denigration. Thus, these may not be indicative of depression.

Last, Western researchers have suggested that body image dissatisfaction often accompanies depressive experience. In a comparative study of Americans of Chinese, Caucasian, and Japanese ancestry residing in Hawaii (Marsella et al. 1981), this assumption was supported. However, the ethnocultural groups differed in the particular areas of the body with which they were dissatisfied—among Caucasians the principal dissatisfaction was the face; among Chinese, height, weight, and nose; among Japanese, weight, height, waist, hips, and posture. These variations in body image dissatisfaction stem from differences in how groups normally perceive themselves and how they believe other see them.

The relationship of personality to depression in Western psychiatric theory has been reviewed by Akiskal et al. (1983). They point out psychiatrists have long linked characterological constellations such as dependency, introversion, obsessionalism, and self-deprecation to depression without adequate evidence. Based on their analysis, they concluded that introversion may be a possible premorbid trait for non-bipolar depression, while extraversion, cyclothymia, and work-oriented achievement may be associated with bipolar disorders. The conclusions represent useful hypotheses for cross-cultural study because of ethno-cultural variations in personality structure and dynamics. For example, Japanese culture encourages dependency (*amae*) and does not consider it to be a negative personal quality (Doi 1979). In addition, locus of control is generally external among Japanese people, while achievement drives are very high. Given this constellation of personal qualities, it would be valuable to examine how depressive disorders are modified, shaped, or formed in Japanese culture.

In general, it seems logical that personality should influence the etiology, manifestation, course, and outcome of depressive disorders, since personality represents the sum total of unique inborn and acquired personal qualities that facilitate an individual's adjustment to the environment. Clearly, no form of psychopathology can be considered apart from this potent mediator of behavior. To the extent cultures vary in personality, it is to be expected that depressive disorders may vary. Part of the variation is a function of language. We perceive and experience a world that language describes. Each language represents an arbitrary and limited codification of the chaos of objects, events, and processes that surround us. In many respects, different languages create different universes. Within this context, our sense of self, consciousness, time, and space co-vary with language. Marsella (1981) argued that in cultures in which metaphorical languages and imagistic mediation of reality dominate, individuals may not psychologize experience and this may reduce the risk of the isolation, detachment, separation, and alienation we associate with depression in the West. Culture, personality, self-hood, and language are filters for human behavior, whether it is normal or abnormal.

CULTURAL HYPOTHESES OF DEPRESSIVE DISORDERS

There are many aspects of depressive disorders which are determined, to a greater or lesser extent, by cultural influences. For more than three decades researchers have offered a variety of cultural hypotheses to account for these influences. This section will summarize some of the major hypotheses, including those related to family structure and dynamics, social organization, psychological-defense operations, self-structure, and social rituals.

Family Structure and Dynamics

A number of researchers (e.g., Stainbrook 1954; Collomb 1967; Vitols 1967) concluded that extended family structures, child-centered family relationships, and strong family support processes may help reduce risks of depression by increasing psychosocial resources for coping with stress and by reducing childhood insecurities and losses. Thus, both formative vulnerabilities and precipitative risks are reduced.

Social Organization

Social organization refers to organizational dimensions that a society encourages, including particular roles, statuses, and acceptable behavior patterns. It also refers to the extent of shared values, goals, and beliefs. A review of the research (e.g., Weissman and Klerman 1977) on gender and depression indicated that women have higher rates of depression than men and that these rates cannot be attributed to biological differences between the sexes. It has been speculated that role stresses are the primary reason for the higher rates. A national survey of depressive symptomatology in the United States revealed that blacks had higher rates than whites. This could be a function of role and status deprivation; there are limits to the number and type of behavioral alternatives available to blacks and this may increase a felt sense of helplessness and inadequacy.

Psychological Defenses

Many investigators have suggested rates of depression may be lower among certain ethnocultural groups because of socially sanctioned and encouraged defense mechanisms that serve to protect individuals from certain stresses. Stainbrook (1954), for example, argued that certain societies may promote persecutory delusions to reduce self-blame and

Vitols (1967) contended that blacks living in the southern United States have low rates of depression because of limited self-expectations and relatively simple ways for maintaining self-esteem. Savage and Prince (1968) observed that certain Nigerian subcultures rely heavily on projection and denial, thus minimizing risks from unacceptable impulses.

Mourning Rituals

Death is one of the most potent sources of depression in all societies. To the extent societies foster mourning rituals that can reduce the stress of loss by death, depressive disorders can be minimized. Some Asian societies endorse the practice of ancestor worship in which love objects are not lost through death but instead become spiritual resources which are omnipresent as long as they are cared for through prayer and ritual (Yamamoto et al. 1969). Still other societies conceive of death as a relief from life's burdens or as an opportunity for new forms of consciousness. Within these contexts, grief may be minimized or effectively channeled into socially acceptable patterns of behavior (Prange and Vitols 1962).

Social Stresses

To the extent that stressful life events and experiences are capable of influencing the formation, precipitation, and exacerbation of depressive disorders, then cultures that minimize these changes can be expected to have fewer cases and/or different patterns of depression. The literature on crowding, poverty, racism, malnutrition, illiteracy, family disintegration, and social disintegration indicates all these factors have pernicious consequences for mental health; however, more research is needed to identify whether particular depressive disorders are specific to particular social stresses or whether they are a generalized response to any major stressor among vulnerable individuals.

The cultural hypotheses provide useful starting points for understanding the relationship between sociocultural factors and depressive disorders; however, they should not be mistaken for facts that have been empirically validated. What is needed are comparative studies designed to systematically test these hypotheses. Such a task is not easy, for there is still considerable debate about the nature and classification of the depressive disorders. Ideally, efforts should be made to differentiate subtypes of depression that can then be linked to specific cultural hypotheses. It is necessary also to specify the relationship between cultural variables and the different aspects of depressive disorders. For example, in some disorders cultural factors may serve as formative causes, while in others they may serve as precipitative, exacerbative, or maintenance causes. Further, cultural factors may influence the type of onset, the manifestation of symptomatology, the extent of disability, the course of disorder, and its outcome. We need specificity. The question is: What relationships exist among different clinical parameters of various depressive disorders in particular cultures?

FUTURE CONSIDERATIONS

Depression incorporates a broad spectrum of psychobiological disorders that vary considerably in severity and duration. To understand this spectrum of disorders, it is necessary to recognize the interdependency of culture, psychology, and biology. Scientists and professionals alike have too often chosen to focus on one of these levels to the exclusion of the others. As a result, we frequently think of depression as a psychological or biological disorder; it is not.

Depression involves the totality of human functioning—biological, psychological, and sociocultural. We need to understand the relationships across all these levels. Biological psychiatrists often scoff when scientists and/or professionals with nonbiological orientations seek explanations of depression at sociocultural or psychological levels. The idea that "Westernization" or "unemployment" or "cultural disintegration" may be associated with the development of depression often finds little support in the face of our reliance on neurotransmitters, adrenal output levels, and potassium-sodium balances. But it is time to put aside narrow theoretical interests in favor of conceptual frameworks that acknowledge the complexity of depression.

Here, in the closing section of our chapter, we would like to propose a research agenda for future studies of depression, an agenda that addresses four basic questions associated with depression research: (1) What is the relationship among different clinical parameters of depression, that is, onset, symptoms, course, outcome? (2) What is the relationship between different clinical parameters of depression and alternative levels of conceptualization, that is, macrosocial, microsocial, psychosocial, biopsychosocial? (3) What are the relationships among different levels of conceptualization for any given clinical parameter of depression? (4) Do these relationships hold true across cultural boundaries?

Figure 1 provides a foundation for our agenda. It demonstrates that variables used to explain depressive disorders exist in interdependent hierarchical levels. Macrosocial-level variables do not, in and of themselves, cause depression; they can, however, be considered part of a variable network that helps determine biochemical and/or physiological dimensions of the problem. The macrosocial and the biopsychosocial levels are simply different contexts in which various patterns of forces operate on one another. We need to understand relationships across these levels. There is a small but growing amount of research in psychosomatic medicine, stress, medical sociology, and other related cross-disciplinary topics which provides support for the assumption of interdependency (see Goldberger and Breznitz 1982 for detailed reviews). It is not unreasonable to assume that the sociocultural context of an individual's life could partially determine norepinephrine concentrations, adrenal output patterns, and dopamine receptor site densities via such mediating variables as child rearing, stressor exposure patterns, resource availability, breeding and nutritional patterns, and role conflict and role deprivation configurations. This is the basic premise of figure 1; variables such as acculturation are not only macrosocial in nature but also ultimately microsocial, psychosocial, and biopsychosocial.

Figure 2 builds on the premise of interdependent hierarchical levels by displaying a matrix of clinical parameters by variable-level categories, and represents a conceptual framework for research on depression. It suggests we examine onset, symptomatology, course, outcome, and diagnostic patterns in relation to one another, in relation to a given conceptual level, and in relation to many conceptual levels. For the most part, clinical research has focused on symptoms; attention needs to be given to onset, course, and outcome since these may be relatively independent of symptomatology.

The question of cultural differences among the variable relationships proposed in figure 2 is very important. Do cultures vary in the onset, course, and outcome of depressive disorders? Are there differences in the relationship between microsocial variables and depressive disorder parameters across cultures? How do macrosocial variables influence biological variables in different cultural settings? These questions are examples of the issues we feel need to be addressed in future cross-

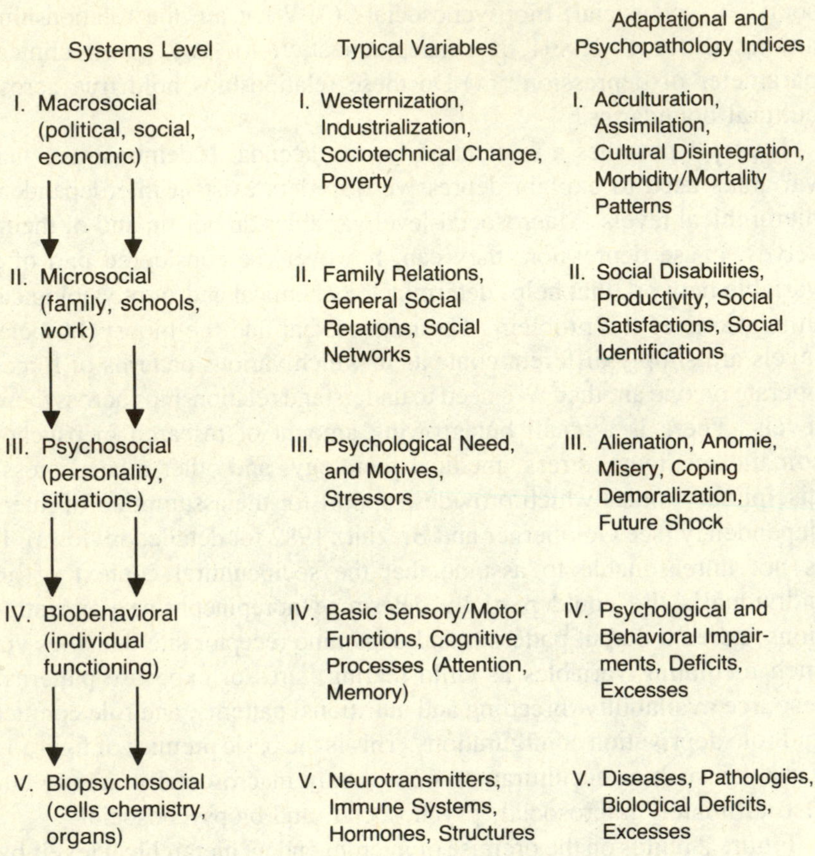

Systems Level	Typical Variables	Adaptational and Psychopathology Indices
I. Macrosocial (political, social, economic)	I. Westernization, Industrialization, Sociotechnical Change, Poverty	I. Acculturation, Assimilation, Cultural Disintegration, Morbidity/Mortality Patterns
II. Microsocial (family, schools, work)	II. Family Relations, General Social Relations, Social Networks	II. Social Disabilities, Productivity, Social Satisfactions, Social Identifications
III. Psychosocial (personality, situations)	III. Psychological Need, and Motives, Stressors	III. Alienation, Anomie, Misery, Coping Demoralization, Future Shock
IV. Biobehavioral (individual functioning)	IV. Basic Sensory/Motor Functions, Cognitive Processes (Attention, Memory)	IV. Psychological and Behavioral Impairments, Deficits, Excesses
V. Biopsychosocial (cells chemistry, organs)	V. Neurotransmitters, Immune Systems, Hormones, Structures	V. Diseases, Pathologies, Biological Deficits, Excesses

Fig. 10.1. Hierarchical Systems in Human Adaptation and Psychopathology.

cultural studies of depressive disorders. They must be asked if we are to gain new insights into old problems.

CONCLUSIONS

1. Depressive disorders constitute a major psychiatric disorder in European and American cultures and there is reason to believe the extent of the problem will increase in the future. However, efforts to understand and resolve the problem of depressive disorders are hampered by debate regarding the definition, classification, and conceptualization of depressive disorders.

		CLINICAL PARAMETERS			
		ONSET	SYMPTOMS	COURSE	OUTCOME	DIAGNOSIS
CONCEPTUAL LEVEL	MACROSOCIAL					
	MICROSOCIAL					
	PSYCHOSOCIAL					
	BIOPSYCHOSOCIAL					

Fig. 10.2. Conceptual Framework for Clinical Research.

2. Cross-cultural research offers a unique opportunity for addressing some of these problems by using a comparative analysis of similarities and differences in human behavior which can be attributed to shared acquired experiences transmitted from one generation to another for purposes of adjustment and adaptation.

3. Different cultures conceptualize the problem of depressive disorders in different ways. In certain non-Western cultures, there are no equivalent concepts for depression, but this does not mean depression is absent—it may be experienced, expressed, and responded to in different manners.

4. In spite of the numerous epidemiological studies that have been conducted, it is difficult to investigate differences in the rates of depression because of variations in conceptualization. If any progress is to be made in comparing differential rates of depression, it is necessary to implement a series of common methodological procedures which will permit equivalency in case definition and assessment.

5. A variety of research methods have been used to study the manifestation of depressive disorders across cultural boundaries. As a group, these methods are based on agreement that depressive disorders among non-Western people are characterized by strong somatic components. In contrast to Western cultures, feelings of guilt, self-deprecation, suicide, and depressed mood are frequently absent among non-Western cultures. This raises interesting questions about the universality of depressive disorders.

6. Within the context of cultural variations in the conceptualization, expression, and experience of depressive disorders, the problem of measurement assumes formidable proportions. If measurement is to be cross-culturally valid, a number of criteria must be met.

7. An ignored topic of research on depressive disorders which can be enhanced by cross-cultural studies is personality. Since cultures vary in personality structures and dynamics, it is logical that depressive disorders may also vary. Part of this variation may be due to personality needs, motives, and traits, while others may be a function of language differences that mediate different self-structures and constructions of reality.

8. Many cultural hypotheses of depressive disorders have been advanced. However, the majority of these hypotheses have not received empirical validation. It will be necessary in the future to examine specific linkages between cultural factors and distinct patterns and parameters of depressive disorders in different cultures.

9. A research agenda for the future is proposed which seeks to examine the relationship among different clinical parameters of depressive disorders both within and across different hierarchical levels of conceptualization (i.e., macrosocial, microsocial, etc.) for different cultures. This agenda provides for greater specificity in our efforts to understand the problem of depressive disorders.

REFERENCES

Akiskal, H., R. Hirschfeld, and B. Yerevanian
    1983   The Relationship of Personality to Affective Disorder. Archives
                of General Psychiatry 40:801−810.
Amsterdam, J., A. Winokur, I. Lucki, S. Caroff, P. Snyder, and K. Rickels
    1983   A Neuroendocrine Test Battery in Bipolar Patients and Healthy
                Subjects. Archives of General Psychiatry 40:515−524.

Bazzoui, W.
1970   Affective Disorders in Iraq. British Journal of Psychiatry 117: 195−203.

Binitie, A.
1975   A Factor-Analytical Study of Depression Across Cultures (African and European). British Journal of Psychiatry 127: 559−563.

Boyd, J., and M. Weissman
1982   Epidemiology. *In* Handbook of Affective Disorders. E. Paykel, ed. New York: Guilford Press.

Brislin, R., W. Lonner, and R. Thorndike
1973   Cross-Cultural Research Methods. New York: John Wiley.

Bunney, W., et al.
1983   Advances in Visual Imaging Techniques in Mental Disorders. Psychiatric Annals 13:420−426.

Butcher, J., and P. Pancheri
1975   A Handbook of Cross-National MMPI Research. Minneapolis: University of Minnesota Press.

Clayton, P.
1981   The Epidemiology of Bipolar Affective Disorder. Comprehensive Psychiatry 22:31−43.

Collomb, H.
1967   Methodological Problems in Cross-Cultural Research. International Journal of Psychiatry 3:17−19.

Collomb, H., and J. Zwingelstein
1961   Depressive States in an African Community (Dakar). *In* First Pan-African Psychiatry Conference Report. T. Lambo, ed. Abeokuta, Nigeria.

Doi, T.
1976   The Anatomy of Dependence. Tokyo: Kodansha Press.

Draguns, J. G., L. Phillips, I. K. Broverman, W. Caudill, and S. Nishimae
1971   Symptomatology of Hospitalized Psychiatric Patients in Japan and in the United States: A Study of Cultural Differences. Journal of Nervous and Mental Diseases 152:3−16.

Ebigbo, P.
1982   Development of a Cultural Specific (Nigeria) Screening Scale of Somatic Complaints Indicating Psychiatric Disturbance. Culture, Medicine, and Psychiatry 6:29−43.

El-Islam, F.
1969   Depression and Guilt: A Study at an Arab Psychiatric Center. Social Psychiatry 4:56−58.

Fábrega, H.
1974   Problems Implicit in the Cultural and Social Study of Depression. Psychosomatic Medicine 36:377−398.

1975   Cultural and Social Factors in Depression. *In* Depression and
                Human Existence. E. Anthony and T. Benedek, eds. Boston:
                Little, Brown.

Fenton, F.
1981   Occurrence and Manifestations of Affective Disorders in Dif-
                ferent Cultures: A Selective Review. Unpublished manuscript.

Fernando, S.
1969   Cultural Differences in the Hostility of Depressed Patients.
                British Journal of Medical Psychology 42:67−75.

Fundia, T., J. Draguns, and L. Phillips
1971   Culture and Psychiatric Symptomatology: A Comparison of
                Argentine and United States Patients. Social Psychiatry 6:
                11−20.

German, A.
1972   Aspects of Clinical Psychiatry in Sub-Saharan Africa. British
                Journal of Psychiatry 121:461−470.

Goldberger, L., and S. Breznitz, eds.
1982   Handbook of Stress: Theoretical and Clinical Aspects. New
                York: The Free Press.

Jablensky, A., N. Sartorius, W. Gulbinat, and G. Ernberg
1981   Characteristics of Depressive Patients Contacting Psychiatric
                Services in Four Cultures. ACTA Psychiatric Scandanavica
                63:367−383.

Kendell, R.
1970   Relationship Between Aggression and Depression: Epidemio-
                logical Implications of a Hypothesis. Archives of General
                Psychiatry 22:308−318.

Kimura, B.
1965   Vergleichende Untersuchungen uber Depressive Erkrankungen
                in Japan und in Deutschland. Forschritte der Neurologie und
                Psychiatrie 33:202−215.

Kleinman, A.
1977   Depression, Somatization, and the "New Transcultural Psy-
                chiatry." Social Science and Medicine 11:3−9.
1979   Patients and Healers in the Context of Culture. Berkeley, Los
                Angeles, London: University of California Press.
1982   Depression and Neurasthenia in the People's Republic of China.
                Culture, Medicine, and Psychiatry 6:1−80.

Klerman, G.
1979   Is This the Age of Melancholy? Psychology Today 12:36−42,
                88−89.

Kraepelin, E.
1974   Vergleichende Psychiatrie (1904). *In* Themes and Variations in

European Psychiatry. S. R. Hirsch and M. Shepherd, eds. H. Marshall, trans. Bristol: John Wright and Sons.

Leighton, A., T. Lambo, C. Hughes, D. Leighton, J. Murphy, and D. Macklin
1963 Psychiatric Disorder Among the Yoruba. Ithaca: Cornell University Press.

Levitt, E., and B. Lubin
1975 Depression: Concepts, Controversies and Some New Facts. New York: Springer.

Lonner, W.
1979 Cross-Cultural Research Issues. *In* Perspectives in Cross-Cultural Psychology. A. Marsella, R. Tharp, T. Ciborowski, eds. New York: Academic Press.

Marsella, A. J.
1978 Thoughts on Cross-Cultural Studies on the Epidemiology of Depression. Culture, Medicine, and Psychiatry 2:343−357.
1980 Depression Experience and Disorder Across Cultures. *In* Handbook of Cross-Cultural Psychology, Vol. 6, Psychopathology. H. Triandis and J. Draguns, eds. Rockleigh, N.J.: Allyn and Bacon.

Marsella, A. J., M. Escudero, and P. Gordon
1972 Stresses, Resources and Symptom Patterns in Urban Filipino Men. *In* Transcultural Research in Mental Health, Vol. II. W. Lebra, ed. Honolulu: University of Hawaii.

Marsella, A. J., V. Kameoka, L. Shizuru, and J. Brennan
1975 Cross-Validation of Self-Report Measures of Depression Among Normal Populations of Japanese, Chinese and Caucasian Ancestry. Journal of Clinical Psychology 31:281−287.

Marsella, A. J., D. Kinzie, and P. Gordon
1973 Ethnic Variations in the Expression of Depression. Journal of Cross-Cultural Psychology 4:435−456.

Marsella, A. J., L. Shizuru, J. Brennan, and V. Kameoka
1981 Depression and Body Image Satisfaction. Journal of Cross-Cultural Psychology 12:360−371.

Marsella, A. J., and J. Tanaka-Matsumi
Unpublished data. Baselines of Depressive Symptomatology Among Normal Samples from Different Cultures. Honolulu, Hawaii.

Marsella, A. J., E. Walker, and F. Johnson
1973 Personality Correlates of Depression in College Students from Different Ethnic Groups. International Journal of Social Psychiatry 19:77−81.

Milenkov, K.
1969 Cyclophrenia and Comparative Psychiatry. Neurol., Psihitr., i

Neurohirurg 8:321–330.

Murphy, H., E. Wittkower, and N. Chance
1964   Cross-Cultural Inquiry into the Symptomatology of Depression. Transcultural Psychiatric Research Review 1:5–21.

Odegaard, O.
1961   The Epidemiology of Depressive Psychoses. ACTA Psychiatrica Scandanavica 37:33–38.

Ohara, K.
1973   The Socio-Cultural Approach for the Manic Depressive Psychosis. Psychiatrica et Neurologica Japonica 75:263–273.

Pfeiffer, W.
1968   The Symptomatology of Depression Viewed Transculturally. Transcultural Psychiatric Research Review 5:121–123.

Prange, A. J. and M. M. Vitols
1962   Cultural Aspects of the Relatively Low Incidence of Depression in Southern Negroes. International Journal of Social Psychiatry 7(2):104–112.

Prince, R.
1968   The Changing Picture of Depressive Syndromes in Africa: Is It Fact or Diagnostic Fashion? Canadian Journal of African Studies 1:177–192.

Racy, J.
1970   Psychiatry in the Arab East. ACTA Psychiatrica Scandanavica Supplement 21:1–171.

Rao, A.
1973   Depression: A Psychiatric Analysis of Thirty Cases. Indian Journal of Psychiatry 15:231–236.

Resner, G., and J. Hartog
1970   Concepts and Terminology of Mental Disorder Among Malays. Journal of Cross-Cultural Psychology 1:369–381.

Sartorius, N.
1973   Culture and the Epidemiology of Depression. Psychiatria, Neurologia et Neurochirugia 76:479–487.
1974   Depressive Illness as a Worldwide Problem. *In* Depression in Everyday Practice. P. Keilholz, ed. Berne, Switzerland: Huber.
1975   Epidemiology of Depression. WHO Chronicle 29:423–427.

Sartorius, N., A. Jablensky, W. Gulbinat, and G. Ernberg
1980   WHO Collaborative Study: Assessment of Depressive Disorders. Psychological Medicine 10:743–749.

Scheaffer, R. L., W. Menderhall, and L. Ott
1979   Elementary Survey Sampling. North Scituate, Mass.: Duxbury Press.

Sechrest, L.
1963   Symptoms of Mental Disorder in the Philippines. Philippine Sociological Review 7:189–206.
Sethi, B., and S. Gupta
1970   An Epidemiological and Cultural Study of Depression. Indian Journal of Psychiatry 12:13–22.
Shinfuku, N., A. Karasawa, O. Yamada, S. Tuasaki, A. Kanai, and K. Kawashima
1973   Changing Clinical Pictures of Depression. Psychological Medicine 15:955–965.
Simon, R., J. Fleiss, B. Gurland, P. Stiller, and L. Sharpe
1973   Depression and Schizophrenia in Hospitalized Black and White Mental Patients. Archives of General Psychiatry 28:509–512.
Singer, K.
1975   Depressive Disorders from a Transcultural Perspective. Social Science and Medicine 9:289–301.
Stainbrook, E.
1954   A Cross-Cultural Evaluation of Depressive Reactions. *In* Depression. P. Hoch and J. Zubin, eds. New York: Grune & Stratton.
Stoker, D., L. Zurcher, and W. Fox
1968   Women in Psychotherapy: A Cross-Cultural Comparison. International Journal of Social Psychiatry 14:5–22.
Tanaka-Matsumi, J., and A. J. Marsella
1976   Cross-Cultural Variations in the Phenomenological Experience of Depression: Word Association. Journal of Cross-Cultural Psychology 7:379–396.
Teja, J., and R. Narang
1970   Pattern of Incidence of Depression in India. Indian Journal of Psychiatry 12:33–39.
Terminsen, J., and J. Ryan
1970   Health and Disease in a British Columbia Community. Canadian Psychiatric Association Journal 15:121–127.
Tonks, C., E. Paykel, and G. Klerman
1970   Clinical Depressions Among Negroes. American Journal of Psychiatry 127:329–335.
Tseng, W., and J. Hsu
1969   Chinese Culture, Personality Formation and Mental Illness. International Journal of Social Psychiatry 16:5–14.
Vitols, M.
1967   Patterns of Mental Disturbance in the Negro. Unpub. ms. Cherry Hospital, Goldsboro, N.C.

Waziri, R.
1973   Symptomatology of Depressive Illness in Afghanistan. Ameri-
            can Journal of Psychiatry 130:213—217.
World Health Organization
1983   Depressive Disorders in Different Cultures. Geneva, Switzer-
            land: World Health Organization.
Yamamoto, J., K. Okonogi, I. Iwasaki, and S. Yoshimura
1969   Mourning in Japan. American Journal of Psychiatry 125:
            1660—1665.
Yanagida, E., and A. J. Marsella
1978   The Relationship Between Self-Concept Discrepancy and De-
            pression Among Japanese-American Women. Journal of Clini-
            cal Psychology 34:654—659.
Zung, W.
1969   A Cross-Cultural Survey of Symptoms in Depressions. Ameri-
            can Journal of Psychiatry 126:116—121.

PART IV
Integrations: Anthropological Epidemiology and Psychiatric Anthropology of Depressive Disorders

INTRODUCTION TO PART IV

The three chapters in this section represent different attempts at integrating anthropological, epidemiological, and clinical approaches in the study of depression. The types of integration differ, but the authors of each chapter initiated their studies in response to many of the questions discussed in the preceding chapters. In each of the three studies described, researchers not only combined multidisciplinary methods but also sharply focused attention on the relation of depression as a clinical phenomenon to culture-specific forms of illness presentation and popular categories of distress.

Manson, an American Indian anthropologist, and Shore and Bloom, psychiatric epidemiologists and clinicians with extensive experience with various American Indian groups, have developed a two-sided anthropological epidemiology of depression among the Hopi and other American Indian groups aimed at assessing depression both from the standpoint of indigenous illness categories and from that of American psychiatry. Their study is based on the recognition that lay and professional categories of depressive disorder contribute to its cultural construction in keeping with the ideas expressed in Part I. Manson and his collaborators employed ethnosemantic techniques to elicit systematically and rigorously both indigenous Hopi illness categories and culture-specific symptoms. The authors then created an ethnomedical survey instrument based on these categories and forms of symptom expression to determine Hopi symptom domains that their ethnography suggested showed a family relationship to the American psychiatric category major depressive disorder. The emic or indigenous categories they isolated were associated with a range of psychosocial problems. Together with this epidemiology of traditional Hopi illness categories, the authors revised a standard psychiatric evaluation questionnaire to make it culturally appropriate for use with Hopi. Translation, back translation, and reliability techniques all were used, but the authors dealt further with the problem of meaning by modifying the questionnaire to take into account Hopi meanings divergent from those mainstream American ones underlying the questionnaire.

Manson et al. find evidence for the diagnosis of major depressive disorder among the Hopi as well as evidence that this professional disease category correlates highly with one indigenous diagnostic category, save for the two-week duration required by the third edition of the American Psychiatric Association's Diagnostic and Statistical Manual. This criterion of duration seems culturally inappropriate for the Hopi. Several of the Hopi categories correlated not at all with clinical depression. Like the disorder, social indexes of the sufferers disclosed both key similarities and differences with mainstream American norms. The authors correlate depressive disorder with the high rate of loss in Hopi culture: death and acculturation that threatened group and self-identity. These findings enable the authors to develop a critical review of cultural problems in DSM-III when applied to American Indian groups and to explain why clinical depression among American Indians is often misdiagnosed and inadequately treated. This interdisciplinary collaboration between anthropologist and psychiatrist makes several significant contributions, while avoiding serious anthropological and epidemiological errors. In contrast with many efforts currently under way which translate epidemiological instruments from English into non-Western languages, the research team reporting here shows that more sophisticated efforts to address questions of cultural patterning and validity are feasible and produce useful findings, even though they require a major investment of time and serious cross-disciplinary cooperation.

In chapter 12, Good, Good, and Moradi offer another example of how clinical and survey techniques can be integrated with ethnography. The purpose of their triangulation of methods in the study of depression among Iranians is to connect clinical description and population-based symptom measurements with the assessment and interpretation of meaning. Incorporating findings from meaning-centered accounts, whether ethnographic or clinical, into survey methods and relating findings of the two approaches is a central methodological problem in the social sciences and psychiatry. Research into the culture-specific meanings of sadness and grief for Iranians and into the semantic structure of the discourse of patients suffering from depressive illness led the researchers to hypotheses about the clustering of symptoms among depressed Iranians. These hypotheses were tested in a factor analytic study, and the findings are interpreted to describe a unique Iranian depressive syndrome associated with a distinctive cluster of symptoms and illness experience grounded in the historical and contemporary context of Iranian culture.

The authors of chapter 12 draw on recent literature in the sociology of the sciences to critically assess contemporary psychiatric epidemiology. They argue that failure to incorporate distinctive meaning frames within epidemiological instruments leads to research approaches that produce findings that are artifacts of those models and methodologies they subsume at least as much as they are aspects of the depressive illness phenomenon. Thus, chapter 12 returns the reader to the vexing issues discussed in the first section, but in so doing the cross-cultural comparison of depressive disorder is shown to have the potential of liberating psychiatry from the tacit Western cultural biases that lurk behind its technical, allegedly value-free diagnostic criteria.

The concluding chapter in this section, by Kleinman and Kleinman, presents yet another illustration of combined anthropological and psychiatric research on depression. The authors review their studies of the interconnections between depression and neurasthenia among patients in psychiatric and primary care clinics at the Hunan Medical College in the People's Republic of China. They analyze the social production (etiology) and cultural construction (conceptualization and experience) of both depressive affect and disorder as social processes that spring from the relation of individuals, through the local system of power within which they live, to macro-level societal and historical conditions. The unit of analysis becomes the organization of depressive experiences within particular local systems of family, work, and community relations which mediate the effect of macro-level forces on individuals. Stress and distress, then, are investigated as transactional situations in these local cultural systems, and thereby the investigators can operationalize cultural and personal meanings as research variables. The Kleinmans focus on the somatic articulation of personal and social distress—somatization—about which a number of the chapters in this volume have had something to say. That disorders of somatization are the most common illness forms in both Chinese and American primary care clinics means that the analysis of this pattern of symptom phenomenology and illness behavior holds practical as well as theoretical significance.

To what extent the contributions to this final section succeed in overcoming the obstacles identified throughout the volume is up to the reader to judge. Obviously, some large problems remain. These chapters are not presented as solutions, but as illustrations of differing interdisciplinary attempts to come to terms with a few of the major difficulties besetting cross-cultural studies of depression and mental illness generally. In linking anthropological, clinical, and epidemiological approaches, they alter each of these disciplinary frameworks and configure the problem itself through a rather different set of questions than has been the starting point of earlier studies. In the Epilogue, the first authors of chapters 12 and 13, who are also the editors of this volume, build on the ideas presented in these chapters to outline how they see the relationship between culture and depression. The point of the Epilogue is not to answer questions that have not been answered here and may well be unanswerable at this time. Rather, the editors formulate those questions they take to be most central for future theory building and empirical research in both psychiatric anthropology and anthropological psychiatry.

11

The Depressive Experience in American Indian Communities: A Challenge for Psychiatric Theory and Diagnosis

Spero M. Manson, James H. Shore, and Joseph D. Bloom

Anthropologists and psychiatrists have had a long-standing interest in the American Indian experience of psychopathology and beliefs about cause, treatment, and prognosis.[1] Such interest has, in turn, engendered valuable insight into the nature of depression within this special population. Some investigators have described the psychodynamics of dysphoria and related mood states in terms of tribal definitions of self (Devereux 1940; Hallowell 1963; Opler 1936; Parker 1962). Others have documented the effects of contemporary social pressures on native life, revealing the relationship between culture change and risk of depression (Leighton and Hughes 1961). Several scholars have shown that indigenous therapeutic forms serve to express repressed affect and to restructure cognitively mediated appraisal processes (Jilek 1974, 1982). Our own work is largely epidemiological in origin, and seeks to develop diagnostic instrumentation by which to reliably and validly identify depression in American Indian communities (Manson and Shore 1981). Each of these lines of inquiry—though different in emphasis—has eventually confronted the same questions: How is depression conceptualized and experienced by American Indians? To what extent is this view and experience similar to those of other cultural groups? For a variety of reasons, the answers, until now, have proven to be elusive.

It is well known that American Indians employ rich and varied lexicons for describing cognitive, affective, and spiritual states of being (Trimble et al. 1984). Moreover, the ethnographic record clearly indicates that Indians relate to one another and to the world in a way that is quite different from that of American society in general (Manson and Trimble 1982; Medicine 1982; Mohatt and Blue 1982). Thus, early in our epidemiologic research, it became evident that the development of reliable, culturally valid diagnostic instrumentation has to take into account the explanatory models to which American Indian people themselves subscribe in making sense of their illness (Kleinman 1980).

Depression in particular warrants systematic study for a number of clinical as well as theoretical reasons. It is the most frequently diagnosed problem among American Indians presenting for treatment at mental health facilities (Sue 1977; American Indian Health Care Association 1978; Rhoades et al. 1982), accounting for as much as 40 percent of the daily patient case loads in many of these clinics. This remarkably high rate of treated depression is in keeping with the available epidemiological data, which indicates that the prevalence of depression within select Indian communities may be four to six times higher than that observed in the U.S. population at large (Shore et al. 1973; Roy et al. 1970; Sampath 1974). Yet, despite its apparently high prevalence in this cultural group, depression is easily misdiagnosed and not well understood. Accurate diagnosis is complicated by its occurrence with alcoholism, antisocial behavior, physical illness, and prolonged grief, each of which is common among American Indians and typically masks their depressive experience (Shore and Manson 1981, 1983). Furthermore, various indigenous forms of illness have been naively equated with specific psychiatric disorders such as depression, thereby confusing the possible relationship among these phenomena (Marano 1982). Examples include recent discussions of *tawatl ye sni* (totally discouraged) (Johnson and Johnson 1965) and *wacinko* (to pout) (Lewis 1975) among the Lakota, and of *windigo* (Kiev 1972) among the Northern Ojibway and Cree.

This chapter reports our progress in describing certain illnesses among the Hopi of northeastern Arizona, in articulating their explanation of these illnesses, and in discovering points of interface with psychiatric diagnosis and theory. The discussion opens by briefly summarizing the salient aspects of the study's multistage design. We outline how the indigenous model for explaining illnesses of the mind or spirit was elicited, indicate the manner in which two different methodologies were blended to construct a special diagnostic interview schedule, and describe the process by which known psychiatric cases and noncases were identified and subsequently interviewed. Preliminary analyses of the results are then reviewed with special attention given to the relationship among Hopi categories of illness and the relationship of these categories to depression. These analyses are amplified by clinical impressions derived from interviews of known psychiatric cases. We conclude with a discussion of the issues that such findings pose for current diagnostic practice and future theory building.

THE STUDY

Field Site

The Hopi reservation is located in the northeastern corner of Arizona and encompasses approximately 650,000 acres of semiarid land, the elevation of which ranges from 3,500 to 6,000 feet or more above sea level (see fig. 11.1). Ten thousand individuals are registered members of the tribe. Recent estimates indicate that over 8,000 Hopi people currently reside on the reservation. Several hundred members live in the nearby towns of Flagstaff, Winslow, and Holbrook, Arizona. The population is distributed among twelve villages that, with one exception, are situated on or at the base of four mesas. These mesas constitute the southern escarpment of the coal-rich Black Mesa and fall along a line running roughly from east to west.

The Hopi are part of the Pueblo cultural complex but clearly differ from their Rio Grande counterparts in several ways, for example, language (Uto-Aztecan), certain ceremonial activities, and some aspects of kinship behavior. The Hopi universe is divided into two parts, the upper world of the living and the lower world of the dead (Titiev 1944:173). Space, time, color, and number combine to form a paradigm for ordering the symbolic relationships within this dual universe (Hieb 1979), relationships expressed through elaborate ceremonial activity (Frigout 1979). "The Hopi Way" represents a behavioral formulation of these relationships and is a guide for everyday action.

Hopi social structure consists of a number of interlocking groups, both named and unnamed. The former includes village sites, clans, and sodalities; the latter includes households, lineages, and phratries. Membership in one group can and often does cut across membership in other groups, leading to a fluid set of social and economic alignments and

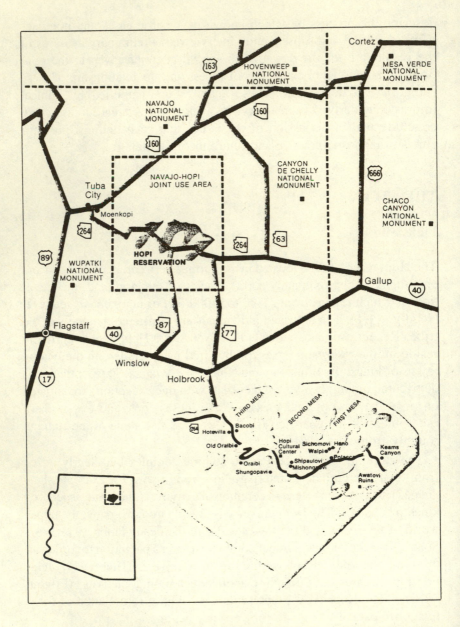

Fig. 11.1 Hopi Indian Reservation.

obligations that are context dependent. Personal identity is rooted in one's maternal group and is reinforced by close association with kin as a function of matrilocal residence. Connelley (1979) provides an excellent detailed overview of Hopi social organization.

Health and human services are rendered by the Indian Health Service (IHS), Hopi Tribal Health Department, and traditional healers. Though each operates independent of the others, there is considerable collaboration and cross-referral, much of which, for a variety of reasons (Dinges et al. 1981), is conducted on an informal basis. The IHS operates the Keams Canyon Hospital, a 60-bed facility that houses dental, social, and mental health programs as well as a variety of outpatient services. Two satellite clinics, one at Second Mesa and another at Low Mountain, provide limited medical and dental care. Third Mesa residents also frequent the IHS facilities at Tuba City. The Hopi Tribal Health Department administers an alcohol treatment/rehabilitation program and a center for mentally handicapped adults, conducts health education activities, and functions in related planning capacities. Traditional healers are active and constitute an important part of the health delivery structure (Levy 1983). Most often, they serve in their capacity as members of the ceremonial societies that are invested with ritual knowledge specific to the cure of given diseases or ailments. Some healers practice outside this role, yet inevitably cite aspects of their social genealogy as the source of individual efficacy.

Our work with the Hopi on this study began in spring 1980. Interest in them arose out of a serious concern for the increasingly negative impact of contemporary social pressures and of the recognition that Western diagnostic assumptions disregard Hopi views of themselves and their life experience, resulting in less effective mental health care. The study was initiated after presentation to each village and tribal council review. It proceeds in the consultative model previously discussed by Shore (1977) and Manson and Shore (1981).

Elicitation of Hopi Illness Categories

It is not a straightforward task to conceptualize psychiatric disorder, especially depression, cross-culturally, as several recent reviews indicate (Bebbington 1978; Kleinman 1977; Marsella 1978). In some groups, there appear to be no semantic equivalents for the word "depression" (Resner 1970; Tanaka-Matsumi and Marsella 1974; Tseng and

Hsu 1970; Terminsen and Ryan (1970). Moreover, when such equivalences have been demonstrated, the manner in which an individual may manifest depression has varied considerably by cultural background (Collomb and Zwingelstein 1961; German 1972; Kleinman 1977; Marsella et al. 1973; Prince 1968; Sechrest 1963). It is therefore critical that judgments about psychiatric disorder and presumed symptoms thereof be derived in part from the experience and perceptions of the subject population (Beiser et al. 1976; Leff 1981; Meile and Gregg 1973).

Ethnosemantic interview procedures have enabled investigators to elicit lexicon taxonomies of disease entities in other cultures (D'Andrade et al. 1972; Kay 1977; Werner 1965; Werner and Begishe 1966). We employed a similar, but less rigorous, technique to identify a broad range of Hopi categories of psychopathology, including etiology, context, and potential sources of assistance.

The interview began by asking an informant to name illness categories: "What are the sicknesses or things that can be wrong with people's minds or spirits?" Behavioral, affective, and cognitive dimensions were subsequently elicited through inquiries about how the informant can tell when a person becomes or feels such ways. A question concerning causation followed. Then, using paired comparisons, the interview contrasted each illness category with the others to ascertain differences among them. Probes were designed to indicate whether these differences are attributable to personal characteristics ("Do only certain kinds of people become/feel this [illness category]?") and/or specific events ("Do only people who experience certain kinds of situations become/feel this [illness category]?"). The remaining questions dealt with duration ("How long might a person be/feel this [illness category]?"), assistance ("Where do people find help for this [illness category]?"), and the basis of the ineffectiveness or inappropriateness of other forms of assistance ("What are the reasons for not needing/ wanting help from [source of assistance] for this [illness category]?").

The interviews were conducted by a bilingual member of the Hopi community. Informants were systematically recruited with special attention to sex, age, and place of residence. Thirty-six individuals were interviewed, 2 males and 2 females within each of three age groups (18−30, 31−50, and 51 and older) across First, Second, and Third mesas. Interviews lasted approximately one hour and were conducted over a three-month period.

In this fashion, five categories of illness were identified: *wu wan tu tu ya/wu ni wu* (worry sickness), *ka ha la yi* (unhappiness), *uu nung mo kiw ta* (heartbroken), *ho nak tu tu ya* (drunkenlike craziness with or without alcohol), and *qo vis ti* (disappointment; pouting).[2] Each of these categories of illness is associated with a cluster of cognitive, affective, and behavioral states (see fig. 11.2).

Wu wan tu tu ya is characterized by dysphoria with accompanying mood swings, low self-esteem, a lack of control over one's self and the surrounding environment, constant worry, and anger. There also may be partial loss of memory and visual or auditory hallucinations. Exhaustion, insomnia, poor appetite, dizziness, increased physical complaints, and argumentative behavior are reported to also be indicative of this illness. Of the various phenomena described by Hopi informants, wu wan tu tu ya most closely approximates the English equivalent of mental illness. Its particular meaning, however, is contingent on a number of factors and, in this sense, illustrates the fluid referential nature of each of these linguistic forms. For example, the significance attached to wu wan tu tu ya depends in part on the relationship between symptoms and subsequent help-seeking behavior, specifically, whether one solicits the advice of a lay person or a specialized healer such as a religious priest. Causal attributions as well can figure importantly in the assigned meaning. Wu wan tu tu ya takes on special significance if associated with witchcraft, personal sins, misconduct, spiritual imbalance, or certain supernatural experiences. Thus, it is important to recognize that these terms constitute glosses for varying states of being. For the sake of discussion, they are presented as distinct phenomenological categories. In point of fact, their meaning often is situation specific and ultimately must be considered in context.

Ka ha la yi is described in many of the same affective terms as wu wan tu tu ya. Literally translated, it means "unhappy." There is an element of cognitive disorientation, there can be thoughts of death, and in some cases one may experience limited memory loss. Individuals may be tearful, unable to sleep, suffer a loss of appetite, and voice increased problems with their physical health. Some informants associated ka ha la yi with loneliness and even with wanting to die. Other informants believed the latter interpretation mistakenly imputes intention and that it is best understood as one way of describing many problems of unhappiness. For example, ka ha la yi may be the term used initially to characterize the state of mind resulting from the death of a family member as well as a Hopi farmer's reaction to discovering that his cornfields have been devastated by wind.

Uu nung mo kiw ta, heartbroken, refers to the despair or acute sadness

	Wu wan tu tu ya/wu ni wu	Ka ha la yi	Uu nung mo kiw ta	Ho nak tu tu ya	Qo vis ti
Affective					
Worry	X	X		X	
Anger	X	X		X	X
Contempt for others		X			
Wanting to die		X			X
Not feeling in control	X	X			
Noneffective			X		
Sadness	X	X			
Low self-worth	X				
Wide mood swings	X	X		X	
Loneliness		X			X
Cognitive					
Confusion		X		X	
Thoughts of death		X			X
Suicidal ideation					X
Partial memory loss	X	X			
Visual/auditory hallucinations	X			X	
Behavioral					
Crying		X			
Exhaustion/tiredness	X		X		
Loss of appetite	X	X			X
Inability to sleep	X	X	X		
Constantly sleeping					X
Argumentative	X	X		X	
Self-critical	X				
Inability to move			X		
No facial expression			X		X
Dizziness	X				
Complaints of physical illness	X	X	X		

Fig. 11.2. Illness Categories and Associated Clusters of Affective,
Cognitive, and Behavioral States.

that derives from unrealized expectations or disrupted interpersonal relationships; literally, the ''heart is broken.'' The situations involved were described as perplexing, shocking, and sudden. Examples include being ignored by one's mother or the breakup of a teenage romance. Feelings of ineffectiveness, sleep loss, exhaustion, and physical complaints were frequently associated with uu nung mo kiw ta.

Ho nak tu tu ya is characterized by psychological agitation: worry, anger, wide mood swings, cognitive disorientation, visual and auditory hallucinations, and constant argumentation. Alcoholics or the severely mentally ill with psychotic symptoms were cited as examples of ho nak tu tu ya.

Qo vis ti or ''turning one's face to the wall'' refers to various stages of disappointment. It can entail social, psychological, and even physical withdrawal. In some instances, the associated symptoms include loneliness, despondency with thoughts of death, and suicidal ideation. Anger and argumentation may surface in response to attempts by family or friends to dissuade the individual from withdrawing.

Ho nak tu tu ya and qo vis ti appear to be independent constructs in terms of the thoughts, feelings, and actions said to be experienced by the individuals suffering from them. Various symptoms such as worry, anger, wide mood swings, appetite loss, insomnia, argumentativeness, and increased physical complaints are reported to be typical of a majority of these illness forms. However, no single set of symptoms is common to all conditions. The data suggest, then, that these categories can represent distinct entities. In some situations, however, these referents may be used interchangeably, which underlines the importance of social context in determining specificity of meaning.

No clear patterns emerge from the informants' descriptions of the lives of the people who typically experience these illnesses or of the circumstances that often surround the onset of a given illness. The kinds of problems and situations that were reported to be associated with each of the illnesses in question fall within seven general domains: personal loss (death of a spouse, relative, or close friend), subsistence difficulties (unemployment, failed crops), cultural conflict (disrespectful youth, disregard for ceremonial obligations), interpersonal strife (fights between neighbors and friends, jealousy), familial problems (divorce, ignoring household responsibilities), social/political tension (village politics, disputed tribal council decisions), witchcraft, and supernatural sanction (for having improperly performed a ceremony or ignoring necessary ritual observances). All these situations or problems were frequently mentioned in association with each of the five indigenous categories of illness. There was disagreement on whether wu wan tu tu ya is ever linked to witchcraft or to supernatural sanctions.

Apart from Titiev's (1972:14) earlier, brief discussion of qo vis ti and several case histories of auditory hallucination among older Hopi women (Matchett 1972), these observations appear to be new to the ethnographic record.

Modification of the Diagnostic Interview Schedule (DIS)

The DIS is a highly structured instrument designed to allow lay interviewers (with one week of training) to render psychiatric diagnoses according to DSM-III criteria, Feighner criteria, and Research Diagnostic Criteria (Robins et al. 1981). Robins and her associates demonstrated its reliability and validity in a test-retest design that compared lay interviewers and psychiatrists, both of whom administered the DIS in a randomized, alternating order to 216 subjects (inpatients, outpatients, former patients, and nonpatients). Reporting a number of measures of the lay interviewers' ability to provide correct psychiatric diagnosis, Robins et al. (ibid., p. 389) concluded that "at present it appears to be a reasonably satisfactory instrument for making psychiatric diagnosis whether in the hands of clinicians or in the hands of lay interviewers." The accuracy of the DIS can be attributed in large part to a descriptive, rather than etiologic, approach to diagnosis; clear standards of severity of symptoms, to the exclusion of physical illness, medical experiences, and drug or alcohol use as potential explanations of symptoms; and explicit interviewer probes that reduce information variance. The DIS generates diagnoses on a lifetime basis and indicates if the disorder is current or defined for four periods of time (which vary with the three major diagnostic systems): the last two weeks, the last month, the last six months, and the last year. It also determines age at the last symptom(s), age at which the first symptom(s) emerged, and whether medical care was ever sought for any of the symptoms of the disorders in question. Moreover, the DIS yields a total symptom count across diagnoses and a count of the number of criteria met for each diagnosis, whether positive or not. A computer program is available to process DIS data along these lines.

Given the special focus of this study, only certain portions of the DIS were selected for use, specifically, those questions that deal with depression, somatization disorder, and alcohol-related behavior. Observations by Kleinman (1977), Tseng (1975), Tseng and Hsu (1969), Rin et al. (1973), and others that psychopathology tends to be somatized among non-Western peoples fit closely with our clinical experience in treating American Indian patients. Marked alcohol consumption and alcoholism in Indian and Native communities are also frequently cited problems. Since both phenomena may co-occur with depression and are of intrinsic interest, we included the relevant DIS items.

The DIS is constructed for administration to native speakers of American English, as are all Western diagnostic instruments. English, though ubiquitous on the reservation, is a second language among the Hopi; their own language is the one most frequently spoken in the home and at social events. The DIS questions therefore required considerable modification to be understood. We initially attempted a back-translation procedure, employing tape-recorded Hopi translations and English back-translations, but found this approach to be untenable.[3] As a result, the changes assumed the form of developing a sociolinguistically appropriate version of the DIS that approximates local English use, which has been shown to vary from the standard in Indian communities (Leechman and Hall 1955; Leap 1979). The primary objective was to *retain* the intended meaning of the original question, regardless of ultimate relevance to the Hopi world view—a difficult task. One DIS item combined the concepts of guilt, shame, and sinfulness, whereas our informants—23 bilingual Hopi health care professionals and paraprofessionals—clearly distinguished each of these concepts from the others and indicated that three separate questions are required to avoid confounding, potentially different responses. Informants also noted cultural restrictions on the discussion of sexual behavior, the subject of a large number of questions in the DIS. Some questions of this nature were therefore deleted; the interviewer is now permitted to exercise personal discretion in deciding whether or not to ask questions about sexual behavior. It was in this manner, then, that the DIS sections specific to depression, somatization disorder, and alcohol-related behavior were modified for inclusion in an interview schedule designed for this particular field site.

American Indian Depression Schedule (AIDS)—Hopi Version

The overarching goal of the study is to construct a culturally appropriate diagnostic instrument of demonstrated reliability and validity. In this case, the criterion for validity may derive from indigenous categories of psychopathology, from Western psychiatric nosology, or from their intersection. AIDS is designed to permit examination according to all three points of reference. Its application across linguistically distinct tribal communities requires prior knowledge about the social ecology and indigenous concepts of illness, and pretesting of the modified DIS questions.

The AIDS consists of five sections, which contain an extensive set of biodemographic questions, a series of linked, recurring questions about one's knowledge and personal experience of indigenously defined psychopathology, and select portions of the DIS as described above. The biodemographic items include the usual questions with regard to age, sex, marital status, family size, recent deaths, residential pattern, religious affiliation, occupation, and brief medical history. Questions pertinent to Hopi address such matters as tribal and clan membership, blood quantum, languages spoken and fluency, and participation in ceremonial activities. The second section asks whether or not the respondent is familiar with any of the indigenous categories of illness, their meaning, if he or she has ever used any of the categories to describe someone else and the relevant circumstances, whether or not the respondent has ever felt these ways and, if so, why, if it was to be expected, and normal frequency of occurrence and duration. The remaining questions in this section focus on the nature of assistance sought and rendered, compliance, and effectiveness of treatment(s). The third section, the DIS items relevant to depression, covers symptoms of dysphoric mood, psychophysiological symptoms (e.g., poor appetite, difficulty sleeping, loss of energy, agitation or retardation, loss of interest in usual activities or decrease in sexual drive), certain cognitive features (feelings of self-reproach or guilt, diminished ability to think or concentrate, and recurrent thoughts of death or suicide), and specified duration in the absence of other psychiatric conditions. The fourth section is equivalent to the DIS questions concerning alcohol abuse and dependence, specifically, the extent to which there is an identifiable pattern of pathological alcohol use (defined in terms of level of social or occupational functioning, quantities consumed, frequency of consumption, amnesic periods, and inability to decrease or cease alcohol consumption). DIS questions with respect to somatization disorder constitute the fifth and last section. The diagnostic criteria include a history of physical symptoms lasting several years which began prior to thirty years of age, a predetermined number of physical complaints ranging from general sickliness to symptoms of gastrointestinal distress, psychosexual problems, and cardiopulmonary problems.

The interview procedure is patterned after the DIS, which elicits information on whether a given symptom was brought to the attention of a health care professional and whether it ever occurred in the absence of physical illness or injury or use of medication, alcohol, or nonprescribed drugs. If not, then the report of the symptom in question falls below diagnostic requirements. The AIDS extends this logic of inquiry to distinguish whether or not symptoms that meet these diagnostic criteria occurred in association with the experience of indigenously defined forms of psychopathology.

Reliability of Psychiatric Interview

The Schedule for Affective Disorders and Schizophrenia—Lifetime Version (SADS-L) was selected as the basis for establishing criterion validity in the ongoing study. The SADS-L is a structured diagnostic interview designed for administration by research psychiatrists, clinical psychologists, and psychiatric social workers (Endicott and Spitzer 1978). It provides a progression of questions, items, and criteria that systematically rule in and out specific diagnoses according to the Research Diagnostic Criteria. By more clearly articulating defined levels of severity, duration, and course of illness, the SADS-L significantly reduces the criterion and information variances that contribute to the unreliability of previously available evaluation procedures. There are three versions of the SADS: a regular version (SADS), which assumes a current episode of psychiatric illness and focuses on the individual's present (and prior two weeks') functioning; a lifetime version (SADS-L), which reviews one's entire life as well as current disturbance; and a version for measuring change (SADS-C). We chose the SADS-L because it offers the greatest flexibility for, and most information about, the mental health history of the respondent.

Since the study involves diagnostic assessments by multiple interviewers across different field sites, we conducted an inter-rater reliability test of the SADS-L as administered by the participating research psychiatrists—four (including Shore) members of the Department of Psychiatry, Oregon Health Sciences University, who are actively involved in service to and research among Indian and Native communities, and have had lengthy experience in this regard. For the purposes of the inter-rater reliability test, 20 subjects were drawn from the patient population of a local urban Indian mental health program.[4] Each psychiatrist interviewed 5 subjects who were randomly assigned to him. The three psychiatrists conducting the initial diagnostic assessments in the Hopi community demonstrated 74 percent agreement on occurrence of major diagnoses and 100 percent agreement on occurrence of major affective disorder as rated from videotapes of his colleagues' interviews.[5]

Clinic Index Group

The SADS-L is being employed to identify a clinically depressed index group (CIG) of Hopi people. Individuals who, in the opinion of local health care professionals, exhibit significant signs of depression are interviewed by the research psychiatrists. Respondents diagnosed as depressed constitute the index group, which serves as the criterion referent. Psychiatric interviews continue until fifty such CIG members are identified.

Administration of the AIDS

The Hopi version of the AIDS is being administered to the CIG and to a community sample of Hopis, a Matched Community Group (MCG), the members of which are matched with the former on a 2:1 basis according to age and sex. Previous clinical experience suggested that response patterns might vary along these dimensions and, for our purposes, had to be controlled. The MCG is being recruited through the general outpatient clinics of the IHS medical facilities at Second Mesa and Keams Canyon.[6] Potential subjects with past or present mental health problems (including alcoholism) are eliminated from further consideration. Members of the clinic index group are interviewed at a time and place convenient for them. The matched community group is interviewed at the medical facilities in an isolated room that can be accessed unobtrusively, without calling undue attention to the subject. Depending on level of distress, administration of the AIDS requires between 45 minutes and 1¼ hours. All interviews are conducted in English by a bilingual Hopi mental health paraprofessional who has received extensive training in the interview procedure and has participated in an inter-rater reliability test of like interviewers across the field sites.

PRELIMINARY RESULTS

Since the study is only partially completed, the reliability and validity of the instrumentation will determine the strength of conclusions drawn from the data at this time. However, the preliminary results provide some indication of (1) the study groups' general knowledge and previous experience of the indigenously defined illnesses, (2) relationships among these illnesses, (3) the kind and degree of correspondence between this set of illness categories and depressive symptoms, and (4) the pattern of symptoms that may characterize depression in this special population. Our discussion of the results in these terms proceeds as an attempt to answer a series of related questions that represent specific formulations of the overarching questions stated at the outset: How is depression conceptualized and experienced by American Indians? To what extent is this view and experience similar to those of other cultural groups?

Subject Characteristics

The results reported here are based on interviews with 54 Hopis. As noted above, there are two groups of subjects, a clinic index group (CIG) and a matched community group (MCG). Twenty-two of the 54 subjects belong to the clinic group; the other 32 constitute the matched group.[7] The matching of MCG members with CIG members on a 2:1 basis was not completed at the time of this report, hence the disproportionate sample sizes. Table 11.1 summarizes various characteristics of the two groups of subjects.

Each group is predominantly made up of females, though roughly in equal proportions. The average age is 34.8, with ages ranging from 17 to 54. Virtually all subjects are full-blood Hopi (96%). Hopi is the native (first and most frequently spoken) language of 82 percent of the CIG and 72 percent of the MCG. There are significant differences between the two groups of subjects in terms of marital status and amount of formal education. Many more CIG members (45%) than MCG members (6%) are separated, widowed, or divorced. Moreover, a markedly greater percentage of the MCG (38%) than of the CIG (9%) have received postsecondary education. All subjects completed a minimum of six years of formal education.

TABLE 11.1
SUBJECT CHARACTERISTICS

	Clinic Index Group n = 22		Matched Community Group n = 32	
Sex				
Male	4	(18%)	8	(25%)
Female	18	(82%)	24	(75%)
Age	34.6		35.0	
Blood quantum				
4/4−3/4	20	(91%)	32	(100%)
3/4−1/2	0		0	
1/2−1/4	2	(9%)	0	
< 1/4	0		0	
Marital status				
Married	9	(41%)	23	(72%)
Widowed	4	(18%)	0	
Separated	1	(5%)	1	(3%)
Divorced	5	(23%)	1	(3%)
Never married	3	(13%)	7	(22%)
Education				
College	2	(9%)	12	(38%)
Secondary	20	(91%)	20	(62%)
Primary	0		0	
None	0		0	
Native language				
Hopi	18	(82%)	23	(72%)
English	4	(18%	9	(28%)

Knowledge and Experience of Hopi Forms of Illness

To what extent are the subjects familiar with the indigenously defined illnesses that are the focus of this study? Have the subjects previously suffered from one or more of these illnesses? If so, are there any differences in this respect among the illness categories and between the two subject groups?

The subjects consistently reported they had heard of the illnesses in question and were familiar with the contexts in which they arise (see table 2). Ka ha layi (unhappiness) was known to the greatest percentage of subjects (93%). Uu nung mo kiw ta (heartbroken) was the relatively least well known illness (80%), but it too was quite familiar to the

TABLE 11.2
KNOWLEDGE AND EXPERIENCE OF HOPI ILLNESS FORMS

	Wu wan tu tu ya/ wi ni wu		Ka ha la yi		Uu nung mo kiw ta		Ho nak tu tu ya		Qo vis ti	
	CIG	MCG	CIG	MCG	CIG	MCG	CIG	MCG	CIG	MCG
Knowledge of Illness	22 (100%)	26 (81%)	21 (95%)	29 (91%)	17 (77%)	26 (81%)	20 (91%)	27 (84%)	19 (86%)	28 (88%)
Previously Suffered Illness	21 (95%)	26 (81%)	20 (91%)	26 (81%)	16* (73%)	14 (44%)	9 (41%)	7 (22%)	12 (55%)	15 (47%)

*p <.01, Chi square test, df = 1

subjects. No differences were evident between the two subject groups with respect to their knowledge about the indigenously defined illnesses.

There was considerable variation in the extent to which subjects reported having suffered from these illnesses, among illness categories as well as between the two groups of subjects. In decreasing order of frequency, the subjects had experienced wu wan tu tu ya/wu ni wu (worry sickness) (87%), ka ha la yi (unhappiness) (85%), uu nung mo kiw ta (56%), qo vis ti (disappointment) (50%), and ho nak tu tu ya (drunkenlike craziness with or without alcohol) (30%). Uu nung mo kiw ta is the only illness reported with significant greater frequency of occurrence among the CIG than the MCG (X^2 test, $p < .01$, df $= 1$).

Relationships among Hopi Forms of Illness

To what extent are these indigenously defined illnesses related to one another? In what terms? There are several interesting patterns of associ-ation among the above illnesses (see table 11.3). *Uu nung mo kiw ta* is strongly correlated with *wu wan tu tu ya/wu ni wu* ($r = .41$), *ka ha la yi* ($r = .43$), and *ho nak tu tu ya* ($r = .49$). It also is moderately correlated with *qo vis ti* ($r = .30$). *Wu wan tu tu ya/wu ni wu*, in turn, is strongly associated with *ho nak tu tu ya* ($r = .38$), but not with *ka ha la yi* ($r = .25$)

TABLE 11.3
CORRELATIONS AMONG HOPI ILLNESS FORMS

	Wu wan tu tu ya/wu ni wu	*Ka ha la yi*	*Uu nung mo kiw ta*	*Ho nak tu tu ya*
Wu wan tu tu ya/wu ni wu	—	—	—	—
Ka ha la yi	.25	—	—	—
Uu nung mo kiw ta	.41	.43	—	—
Ho nak tu tu ya	.38	.28	.49	—
Qo vis ti	.13	.31	.30	.28

or *qo vis ti* ($r = .13$). *Qo vis ti* exhibits weak to moderate associations with *ho nak tu tu ya* ($r = .28$) and *ka ha la yi* ($r = .31$). Likewise, *ka ha la yi* is weakly correlated with *ho nak tu tu ya* ($r = .28$).

The specific nature of these relationships is difficult to determine from our preliminary analyses. For example, the strong association of *uu nung mo kiw ta* with *wu wan tu tu ya/wu ni wu* and with *ka ha la yi* cannot be explained readily from the data at hand. As indicated in figure 11.2, limited overlap is reported between *uu nung mo kiw ta* and *wu wan tu tu ya/wu ni wu* in terms of the thoughts, feeling, and behavior informants believed to be characteristic of these forms of illness. Even fewer are said to be common to *uu nung mo kiw ta* and *ka ha la yi*. Similarly, inspection of table 11.4, which summarizes the correlations of depressive symptoms with each Hopi category of illness, reveals that there are few, if any, depressive symptoms strongly associated with *uu nung mo kiw ta* and *wu wan tu tu ya/wu ni wu* or with *uu nung mo kiw ta* and *ka ha la yi*. However, both *uu nung mo kiw ta* and *ho nak tu tu ya* have three depressive symptoms in common—trouble falling asleep, disinterest in sex, and feeling sinful—which may account in part for the extent of their relationship. Clearly, neither the idealized characteristics of these illnesses nor association with the depressive symptoms appears to be sufficient to account for the observed relationships among the categories in question. Other symptoms about which we did not inquire (or have not yet examined, given the preliminary status of this report) may represent their shared elements. Alternatively, as noted in the conclusion, quite different criteria—for example, healer sought or treatment provided—may underpin these associations.

Correspondence between Hopi Forms of Illness and Depressive Symptoms

To what extent do depressive symptoms as defined by DSM-III relate to these Hopi forms of illness? Are there differences among the latter in this regard? If so, what is the nature of such differences?

As we noted earlier, the section of the AIDS which focuses on indigenous categories of illness opens by asking the subject if he or she knows of any Hopi word or phrase that is equivalent to the term "depression." Fifty (93%) of the subjects indicated that none exists. Two individuals answered affirmatively, citing *wu wan tu tu ya/wu ni wu* as the closest approximation. The two subjects in question were not native Hopi speakers, described themselves as able to understand but not speak the Hopi language, knew virtually nothing about this form of illness beyond having heard the phrase, and, with one exception, exhibited no awareness of any of the other illnesses.

An examination of the correlation of depressive symptoms (ever experienced in the subjects' lifetime) with the indigenous forms of illness reveals some striking differences among the latter in terms of the kind and degree of associated symptoms (see table 11.4). These patterns could not have been predicated from the subjects' responses to the initial query about Hopi categories of illness.

A protracted period of dysphoria, lasting at least two weeks or longer, is one of the major DSM-III criteria of depression. If absent or reported to be below this threshold, an individual does not meet the requirements of a diagnosis of major depressive disorder. Only one of the five indigenously defined illnesses, ka ha la yi, was associated—and strongly so ($r = .48$)—with a positive response to having felt depressed, sad, or worried for two weeks or more. However, as one can see in table 11.4, ka ha la yi is moderately correlated with only two specific symptoms of depression, namely, significant weight gain ($r = .28$) and talking or moving more slowly than normal ($r = .30$). This pattern is in sharp contrast to the high degree of association between uu nung mo kiw ta and a number of different depressive symptoms; yet this particular form of illness exhibited little correlation with reports of a two-week period of dysphoria. In our closing remarks we discuss the symptom duration threshold and cross-cultural equivalence in the attribution (and reporting) of dysphoria as criterion issues of great importance to future work in this area.

The depressive symptoms fall into eight different categories of problems having to do with (1) appetite change, (2) abnormal sleeping patterns, (3) fatigue, (4) psychomotor retardation or agitation, (5) marked disinterest in sex, (6) a low sense of self-worth, (7) disoriented thought processes, and (8) suicidal ideation. Uu nung mo kiw ta includes seven of these eight categories and is more strongly associated with a significantly greater number of depressive symptoms than any of the other indigenous forms of illness. Uu nung mo kiw ta is characterized by weight loss, disrupted sleep, fatigue, and psychomotor retardation as well as agitation, loss of libido, a sense of sinfulness, shame, and not being likable, and trouble thinking clearly. The strength of its association with these symptoms ranges from moderate to strong. The diagnosis of major depressive disorder is contingent in part on the presence of one

TABLE 11.4
CORRELATION OF DEPRESSIVE SYMPTOMS WITH HOPI ILLNESS FORMS*

	Wu wan tu tu ya/wu ni wu	*Ka ha la yi*	*Uu nung mo kiw ta*	*Ho nak tu tu ya*	*Qo vis ti*
Felt depressed, sad, or worried	.11	.48	.18	.02	.00
2 years or more felt depressed, sad, or worried almost all of the time	.06	.12	.18	.02	.22
Lost appetite	.23	.09	.24	.09	−.12
Lost weight without trying	.21	.18	.29	.03	.16
Eating increased so much gained 10 lbs or more	.09	.28	.08	−.07	.11
Trouble falling asleep or staying asleep, waking too early	.20	.09	.34	.30	.15
Slept too much	.14	.25	.15	.15	.09
Felt tired out all the time	.15	.22	.33	.25	.15
Talked or moved more slowly than normal	.12	.30	.37	.20	.31
Moved all the time, couldn't sit still	.24	.02	.33	.10	.22
Lost interest in sex	.02	.09	.34	.30	.00
Felt not good at anything, not likable	.22	.21	.30	.20	.19
Felt sinful	.14	.25	.40	.33	.09
Felt guilty	.07	.25	.27	.20	.15
Felt shameful	.05	.25	.31	.06	.04
Trouble thinking as clearly as usual	.04	.10	.30	.12	.11
Thoughts came much slower than usual	−.02	−.43	.20	.14	.08
Thinking was all mixed up	−.04	.04	.08	.14	.26
Thought a lot about dying	−.06	−.08	.12	.09	.00
Thought you wanted to die	.09	.01	.24	.20	.04
Thought of killing self	−.06	−.04	.05	.03	.00
Tried to kill self	.20	.10	.16	.21	.18

*Unless otherwise specified, symptom duration is two weeks or more.

or more symptoms in five of the eight categories of depressive symptoms. Uu nung mo kiw ta is the only Hopi form of illness that exhibits such comprehensiveness in the kind and degree of depressive symptoms associated with it.

Neither wu wan tu tu ya/wu ni wu nor qo vis ti—both of which are fairly strongly associated with uu nung mo kiw ta, yet not with one another—appear to bear much, if any, relationship to symptoms of depression. Ho nak tu tu ya is correlated with sleeping difficulties, disinterest in sex, and feeling sinful.

Before considering the pattern of depressive symptoms which distinguishes known cases from the matched community group, it is interesting to note the subjects' responses to two questions that were reformulated in our modification of the depression section of the DIS. The nature of and reasons for these modifications are discussed earlier in this chapter. The changes involved expanding single questions that contained references to multiple, possibly different, affective states in one case and cognitive processes in the other case. The preliminary results indicate that this modification was well advised. For example, major differences are evident in the correlations of feeling sinful and feeling guilty with uu nung mo kiw ta ($r = .40$ and $.27$, respectively) and in the correlations of feeling sinful and feeling shameful with ho nak tu tu ya ($r = .33$ and $.06$, respectively). These differences suggest that the question, which in its original form asks whether the subject has ever experienced a two-week period during which he felt worthless, sinful, or guilty, wrongly assumes that these states of being are equivalent; they do not appear to be for the Hopi. Likewise, the strengths of association of slowness of thoughts and of mixed-up thinking with uu nung mo kiw ta ($r = .20$ and $.08$, respectively) indicate that these aspects of cognition also may be perceived differently by the Hopi, and should not be treated as simply linguistic variants on the same state of mind.

Pattern of Depressive Symptoms and Clinical Presentation among the Hopi

Are there any differences between the known cases of depression and the matched community group in terms of their reported experience of depressive symptoms? If so, what are these differences, and what do they suggest with respect to the clinical pattern of depression that one might expect among the Hopi? Does this pattern differ in any way from that which is characteristic of the general population?

A number of significant differences between the CIG and MCG are apparent in terms of the depressive symptoms that were reported as having been experienced (see table 11.5). With respect to dysphoric mood, 82 percent of the CIG indicated they had felt depressed, sad, or worried for two weeks or more, whereas this applied to 50 percent of the MCG. These feelings were also much more chronic among the CIG (73%) than among the MCG (38%) (X^2, p < .05, df = 1). CIG members reported significantly more frequent experience of a variety of other depressive symptoms than did MCG members. These symptoms include diminished appetite, weight loss, disrupted sleep, both psychomotor retardation and agitation, a sense of not being likable, and trouble thinking clearly. Though no significant differences between the two groups of subjects are evident in regard to kind or frequency of suicidal ideation, a markedly greater number of CIG members had attempted to kill themselves.

As noted previously, CIG members were interviewed using the SADS-L. Forty-four of these subjects—35 females and 9 males—were diagnosed as currently suffering from an affective disorder that involved depression: major depression (n = 32, 74%), minor depression (n = 5, 11%), intermittent depression (n = 4, 9%), cyclothymic personality (n = 1, 2%), or schizoaffective disorder, depressed type (n = 2, 4%).

The 32 cases of major depression included 25 females and 7 males. Sustained dysphoric mood was reported by them to have a duration of from one week to eighty-four weeks. Twenty-five (78%) of these cases had experienced dysphoria for a period of two weeks or greater. Seven (22%) cases indicated having experienced dysphoria for one week or more, but less than two weeks. Chronic depression was found to coexist in 16 (50%) of these 32 cases of major depression. These instances of "double depression" included 11 (44%) of the 25 females and 5 (71%) of the 7 males. A chronic depressive disorder was considered present if the individual was diagnosed as having either labile personality, intermittent depressive disorder, or chronic minor depressive disorder.

Twelve of the 44 subjects suffering from an affective disorder that involved depression also were diagnosed as being concurrently alcoholic or drug abusing. This group included all seven of the males with major depression, each of whom was found to have a coexisting alcoholic condition. Without exception, their depressive experience proved to be

TABLE 11.5
DEPRESSIVE SYMPTOMS ACROSS SUBJECT GROUPS[a]

	Clinic Index Group (N=22)	Matched Community Group (N=32)
Felt depressed, sad, or worried	18 (82%)[b]	16 (50%)
2 years or more felt depressed, sad, or worried almost all the time	16 (73%)[b]	12 (38%)
Lost appetite	12 (55%)[b]	7 (22%)
Lost weight without trying	14 (64%)[d]	4 (13%)
Eating increased so much gained 10 lbs or more	13 (59%)	12 (38%)
Trouble falling asleep or staying asleep, waking too early	17 (77%)[d]	9 (28%)
Slept too much	7 (32%)	7 (22%)
Felt tired out all the time	14 (64%)	14 (44%)
Talked or moved more slowly than normal	12 (55%)[c]	6 (19%)
Moved all the time, couldn't sit still	17 (77%)[c]	11 (34%)
Lost interest in sex	13 (59%)	13 (41%)
Felt not good at anything, not likable	16 (73%)[c]	11 (34%)
Felt sinful	7 (32%)	7 (22%)
Felt guilty	11 (50%)	13 (41%)
Felt shameful	12 (55%)	11 (34%)
Trouble thinking as clearly as usual	15 (68%)[b]	12 (38%)
Thoughts came much slower than usual	11 (50%)	9 (28%)
Thinking was all mixed up	11 (50%)	12 (38%)
Thought a lot about dying	11 (50%)	11 (34%)
Thought you wanted to die	11 (50%)	10 (31%)
Thought of killing self	9 (41%)	9 (28%)
Tried to kill self	9 (41%)[c]	3 (9%)

[a]Unless otherwise specified, symptom duration is 2 weeks or more.
[b]$p < .05$
[c]$p < .01$
[d]$p < .001$

secondary to their alcoholism. In no case did the history of significant depression precede the onset of alcoholism or occur independent of it.

Nine of the 44 subjects reported experiencing auditory hallucinations. Two women met the criteria for schizoaffective disorder, depressed type, although a careful review of their histories indicated they had experienced both major and chronic depression in association with occasional auditory hallucinations in the absence of other symptoms of thought disorder. Two other women met the diagnostic criteria for schizophrenic disorder with a coexisting history of major depression.

This picture of depressive symptoms among the Hopi and of their clinical presentation may be colored by several factors. First, we have not yet completed SADS interviews of a probability sampling of the matched community group to determine the extent to which cases of major depressive disorder might comprise its membership. Indeed, we suspect that the MCG includes cases of this type despite our initial screening effort. If so, the present differences between the two groups in their reports of these symptoms are likely to remain in future comparisons of known cases to known noncases; these differences may even be heightened. Other symptoms, however, may also assume greater importance. Thus, the pattern that has emerged from this data represents a minimal set of depressive symptoms.

Second, one cannot help but be struck by the high frequency with which the MCG reports the experience of many of these depressive symptoms. Recent deaths of family members and/or loved ones were frequent occurrences: 34 subjects, 64 percent of the entire sample, indicated that a spouse, relative, or close friend had died within the last two years. There are no differences between the two subject groups in this regard. According to DSM-III criteria, depressive symptoms reported in close association with such an event do not apply toward a diagnosis of major depressive disorder. Only two members of the MCG indicated that the symptoms they experienced were related to the death of a family member or loved one.

Last, the MCG members were recruited from a medical clinic. Their health status undoubtedly influenced the kind and frequency of symptoms they reported. We do not know the extent to which the health status of this particular sample approximates that of the Hopi community at large, though there is reason to suspect that the latter is not as good as the health status of the general U.S. population (Sievers and Fisher 1982). We will examine the possible effects of such differences on reported symptoms at the other field sites.

CONCLUSION

Anthropological interest in questions abut indigenous forms of illness—
and the nature of mental disorder cross-culturally—gained considerable
momentum in the early 1960s from the struggle to develop more explicit,
replicable ethnographic procedures. Formal linguistic models dominated the methodological approaches that were generated and seemed to
be most easily applied to illness concepts, resulting in the elicitation of
terminological systems and the classification of associated phenomena
(see Frake 1962; Conklin 1972). Anthropologists and their counterparts
in psychiatry eventually realized the limits of this perspective and concluded that little insight is offered into the contexts that underpin the uses
of such knowledge. Hence, the past decade has been characterized by the
search for a general conceptual framework to account for the cognitive,
affective, and behavioral dimensions of illness as experienced in different social and cultural settings (Fábrega 1974; Good and Good 1982;
Kleinman 1977; Kleinman et al. 1978). The most comprehensive of
these proposals integrates the notions of explanatory models and semantic networks with health-care-seeking strategies (Kleinman 1980).

Psychiatry wrestled with its own methodological problems during the
same period. Nosology and diagnostic criteria underwent major revisions that culminated in the DSM-III. Additional development of these
criteria stimulated the construction of interview procedures that are
capable of generating highly reliable diagnostic judgments by mental
health professionals as well as by trained lay people. This instrumentation includes the DIS.

Our work builds on these methods and theoretical advances. It represents an attempt to link developments in both fields to design and validate
a diagnostic tool that permits a culturally sensitive assessment of the
depressive experience in certain American Indian communities.

This chapter describes some of the specific findings of this effort to
date. The findings are preliminary and have been discussed without
reference to their full context: there is much more to the Hopi illness
experience than categories and related symptoms alone suggest. In
succeeding reports we will illustrate how these illness categories and
symptoms interact with presumed etiologies, various social situations,
and an array of health-care-seeking strategies. Yet, despite this partial
treatment, the above findings are instructive in several ways.

First, anthropological elicitation procedures can be employed on a
large scale to generate information abut indigenously defined illnesses in

a systematic fashion. A frequent criticism of past applications of these techniques is that the informants are usually few in number and consequently are often unrepresentative of the communities to which they belong. Our experience indicates that this need not be the case. Native members were trained fairly easily in such elicitation procedures, which, in turn, permitted a much broader sampling of the community's views on the phenomena in question. Moreover, we observed an unanticipated diffusion of the application of these techniques to the local mental health services. Staff use them to elicit the explanatory models that patients and families hold with respect to their illnesses, to identify attendant expectations, and to establish relevant therapeutic goals (Kleinman et al. 1978).

Second, elicitation procedures of this nature can be combined with highly structured diagnostic protocols to enable one to examine simultaneously indigenous forms of illness and psychiatric disorders. Extensive ethnographic observation and culturally informed clinical practice are valuable, in fact essential, sources of information about both domains. However, comparative reliability and the generalization of apparent patterns to the larger community are problematic in the absence of well-specified criteria and explicit, replicable methods of collecting data on a large scale. The approach being tested in the ongoing study has considerable promise in this regard. It offers a means of addressing these latter concerns, but may also allow the discovery of the context of illness and personally as well as culturally meaningful explanations.

Third, with respect to the substantive aspects of the reported findings, a number of indigenously defined categories of illness are widely known to and commonly experienced by the Hopi. The data suggest that some of these illnesses are related, albeit differentially, and that others are not. No conceptual equivalent of depression was immediately obvious to the subjects or was thought to exist in the Hopi language. Yet one form of illness, uu nung mo kiw ta, is strongly associated with many of the most salient symptoms of depression and occurs with significantly greater frequency among known cases of major depressive disorder than among a matched community group. There appear to be important Hopi distinctions between certain affective states, for example, contrasting sinfulness with shame and guilt. Presumably, similar cognitive processes—namely, slowing of thought and mixed-up thinking—also appear to be unrelated from the Hopi perspective.

Fourth, a series of recent publications has distinguished between "descriptive" and "etiological" categories of illness in folk nosological systems (Guimera 1978; Good and Good 1982). The former refer to illnesses that are classified solely in descriptive terms; the latter encompass illnesses that are classified purely on the basis of religious, magical, and/or social cause. Though many illness categories include both descriptive and etiologic elements, such a distinction has been useful in interpreting phenomena of this nature and in relating it to clinically meaningful entities. Good and Good (1982), for example, employed this distinction in a productive way to discuss the derivations and different functions of ''heart distress'' and ''fright'' among Iranians. Our data indicate that the five Hopi illness categories discussed here are essentially descriptive in nature. A wide range of situations and circumstances are thought to be associated with the occurrence of these illnesses, yet no special relationships seem to obtain among these situations or circumstances and the illness categories in question. This observation differs sharply from the current, predominantly etiologically based schemes for classifying illness among American Indians in general (Murdock 1980; Rogers 1944). It does not, however, preclude the possibility that these illness categories may be defined in part by the kinds of healers or treatments believed to be appropriate for an individual's care. If subsequent analyses support our initial findings, then we should be able to more fully specify the empirical bases for the five Hopi categories of illness and, in turn, can proceed with their comparison to clinically meaningful entities. Having systematically mapped one onto the other, even if only partial correspondence obtains between them, we will be in a position to conduct the cross-cultural psychiatric epidemiologic research that has been called for by Marsella (1978, 1979, 1980) and others (Good and Good 1982; Kleinman 1977).

The findings from the SADS-L interviews of the clinic index group reveal a number of important clinical aspects of the pattern of depression among the Hopi. First, 22 percent—almost 1 of 4—of the CIG members with major depression were definite in their statement of having experienced pervasive dysphoric mood for one but not two weeks. This pattern coincides with that previously noted in regard to the relationship between several of the indigenous forms of illness and depressive symptomatology. Ka ha la yi, for example, was frequently associated with dysphoric moods lasting two weeks or longer, yet was linked consistently to only two symptoms of depression. However, uu nung mo kiw ta, which was reported to occur regularly in association with at least nine depressive symptoms, was seldom associated with sustained dysphoric mood.

Hence, instruments such as the Diagnostic Interview Schedule or a strict interpretation of DSM-III criteria—both of which employ a two-week duration of dysphoric mood as the diagnostic threshold—would lead one to miss a significant number of the depressed conditions observed in this study. The importance of the duration of sustained dysphoria may vary from one cultural setting to another, and clearly warrants closer examination. Indeed, this issue remains unsettled even in the application of DSM-III criteria to the general U.S. population.

Second, 50 percent of the CIG members experienced the coexistence of chronic and major depression. Keller and Shapiro (1982), in a recent report of their findings from the NIMH Collaborative Study on Depression, described a similar diagnostic pattern in 26 percent of their sample, which was drawn from the general population. A later report further corroborated their findings (Keller et al. 1983), a phenomenon they termed "double depression." Double depression has both clinical and theoretical relevance for understanding the experience as well as extent of depression among American Indians. To begin with, the pattern of double depression that we found in this sample of Hopi subjects confirms the clinical reports (albeit anecdotal) of numerous Indian Health Service psychiatrists who have worked with other tribal groups. It provides some indication of why the course of depression within this population tends to be especially pernicious and debilitating. Moreover, if a condition of double depression does in fact place one at greater risk for the onset of a subsequent major depressive disorder, as Keller and Shapiro (1982) and others have proposed, then this phenomenon may help to explain the basis for the service utilization data which suggests the extremely high prevalence of depression among American Indians. Indeed, a high incidence of chronic depression in this population may be attributed to the significantly greater number of personal losses that American Indians suffer, in terms of either the death of relatives and friends or the acculturative pressures which threaten personal identity. Consider the high frequency with which the subjects in this study reported the recent death of a family member.

Third, the coexistence of alcoholism and depression among American Indian men also deserves closer examination. In this study, major depression was secondary to an alcoholic condition in every male subject, without exception. The onset of major depression never occurred independent of their alcoholism. Therefore, the relationship between alcoholism and depression—specifically, the extent to which the former may mask or perhaps precipitate the latter—and how diagnosis as well as treatment should proceed constitutes a key issue for future clinical inquiry.

The two female subjects with schizoaffective disorder, depressed type, introduce yet another clinical issue. Though they met the criteria for schizoaffective disorder, these women appeared to be experiencing major depressions with intermittent or auditory hallucinations which were culturally determined. By SADS-L criteria, they met the diagnostic standard for schizoaffective disorder. However, according to DSM-III criteria neither subject manifested sufficient deterioration from her previous level of functioning (except for increased depressive symptomatology) to warrant this diagnosis. The voices they heard did not seem to interfere with their adjustment and would not be described as abnormal in this particular cultural context (e.g., being visited by "people of the past"). In point of fact, 20 percent of the clinic index group experienced occasional or intermittent auditory hallucinations. Two of these subjects heard the voices of deceased relatives while grieving or suffering a major depression, similar to the experiences previously reported by Matchett (1974). Most of the individuals who reported auditory hallucinations typically heard a single voice. One subject indicated that the voice was the murmuring of a witch.

These observations suggest a number of areas in which DSM-III and the diagnostic instrumentation based on it may require modification for application among the Hopi and perhaps other American Indians. One should seriously consider shortening the diagnostic threshold for sustained dysphoric mood from two weeks to one week. The interview procedure must facilitate the description of the possible coexistence of chronic depression and major depression. Moreover, the underlying classificatory assumptions should allow for a diagnostic construct akin to the double depression described by Keller and Shapiro (1982). The interaction of alcoholism and depression, especially among males, requires careful scrutiny to ascertain the primacy of one over the other. Other sex-specific patterns also should be anticipated, notably the more frequent occurrence of depression among women. This greater frequency of depression may be related to the role of women in the families' attempt to cope with the psychosocial stressors intrinsic to rapid cultural change. Finally, given the common occurrence of and special meanings that may be attributed to auditory hallucinations in this population, one must pay close attention to the context as well as to the nature of the effects of such experience upon the individuals in question.

The answers beginning to emerge to the questions stated at the outset of this chapter have implications that reach far beyond the practical concerns of nosological validity, appropriate instrumentation, and epidemiology, and beyond the ethnography of illness among American Indians. These answers are requisite to the effective planning and delivery of cross-cultural mental health services, in a very immediate sense for this special population and, more generally, for other cultural groups in the United States and elsewhere. The degree of this effectiveness is tied directly to the ability to work with and across differently conceived illness forms. However, in its rush to generate highly specified criteria by which to reliably diagnose disorder, psychiatry has failed to consider the cultural dimension of illness: how it is conceptualized, experienced, manifested, explained, and treated. Anthropology, in turn, particularly to the extent that it has remained clinically and epidemiologically uninformed, suffers from a similar kind of ignorance, in this case a narrowness of view spawned by the wholesale and often poorly considered rejection of the biomedical model that guides psychiatric theory. In our opinion, future efforts should aspire to correct these shortcomings and should seek ways of bridging paradigmatic differences. A point has been reached in the knowledge-building process at which major new insights into these phenomena can be attained by combining the strengths of both disciplines. We see the ongoing study as a modest step in this direction. It is hoped the results will enable us to ask other, related questions in a productive fashion.

ACKNOWLEDGMENTS

The research described herein and authorship of this paper were supported by the Center for Epidemiologic Studies, NIMH, Grant No. 1-R01-MH33280. We wish to thank the staff of the National Center for American Indian and Alaska Native Mental Health Research, Ms. Rhonda Chamema, the Keams Canyon medical staff, the Hopi Tribal Health Department, the Hopi Tribal Health Committee, and Dr. George Keepers for their assistance and support in various aspects of the research on which this chapter is based.

NOTES

1. Pursuant to a 1978 resolution by the National Congress of American Indians, people indigenous to North America are referred to as American Indians and Alaska Natives except when specific tribal designations are appro-

priate. For the sake of discussion, we employ the term Indian in referring to this special population.

2. Hopi orthographic convention follows Kalectaca (1978).

3. Hopi is an unwritten language and has engendered at least five different orthographic systems.

4. Our thanks to Dr. Loye Ryan, Director, Mental Health Program, Urban Indian Health Program, Portland, Oregon, and to Ms. Ellie Tatum, Department of Psychiatry, Oregon Health Sciences University, for their assistance in this phase of the study.

5. The fourth research psychiatrist has just completed his ratings; the combined results will be reported when available. Agreement on occurrence is a conservative measure of reliability. Other relevant statistical measures of reliability will soon be available.

6. Various circumstances on the reservation currently prevent a communitywide search for potential subjects, which is the strategy employed at the other field sites. However, since the objective of this study is to develop a diagnostic instrument with demonstrated reliability and validity, such limitations do not bear importantly on the discussion at hand.

7. At the time of this report, the clinic index group numbered 44 subjects, all of whom had been interviewed with the SADS-L. Only 22 of these subjects had also completed the AIDS. Thus, comparisons of AIDS response patterns across the clinic index group and the matched community samples refer to the 22 members of the CIG who completed the AIDS. Elsewhere in the discussion, the reader will see references to all 44 members of the CIG when the SADS-L results are considered.

REFERENCES

American Indian Health Care Association
    1978   Six Studies Concerning Assessing Mental Health Needs in the
                Minneapolis-St. Paul Area: A Summary. Minneapolis: Ameri-
                can Indian Health Care Association.
Bebbington, P. E.
    1978   The Epidemiology of Depressive Disorder. Culture, Medicine,
                and Psychiatry 2(4):297−341.
Beiser, M., R. C. Benfari, H. Collomb, and J. Ravel
    1976   Measuring Psychoneurotic Behaviors in Cross-Cultural Sur-
                veys. The Journal of Nervous and Mental Disorders 163(1):
                10−23.
Collomb, H., and J. Zwingelstein
    1961   Depressive States in an African Community (Dakar). *In* First
                Pan African Psychiatric Conference Report. T. Lambdo, ed.
                Abeo Kunta, Nigeria.

Connelley, J. C.
   1979   Hopi Social Organization. *In* Handbook of North American
              Indians. Vol. 9, Southwest. W. C. Sturtevant, ed. Washing-
              ton, D.C.: Smithsonian Institution.
D'Andrade, R., N. Quinn, S. B. Nerlou, and A. K. Romney
   1972   Categories of Disease in American English and Mexican Span-
              ish. *In* Multidimensional Scaling: Theory and Applications in
              the Behavioral Sciences. Vol. 2, Applications. A. K. Romney,
              ed. New York: Seminar Press.
Devereux, G.
   1940   Primitive Psychiatry. Bulletin of the History of Medicine 8:
              1194−1213.
   1961   Mohave Ethnopsychiatry. Washington, D.C.: Smithsonian
              Institution Press.
Dinges, N., J. Trimble, S. Manson, and F. Pasquale
   1980   The Social Ecology of Counseling and Psychotherapy with
              American Indians and Alaskan Natives. *In* Cross-Cultural
              Counseling and Psychotherapy. A. Marsella and P. Pedersen,
              eds. New York: Pergamon Press.
Endicott, J., and R. L. Spitzer
   1978   A Diagnostic Interview: The Schedule for Affective Disorders
              and Schizophrenia. Archives of General Psychiatry 35:
              837−844.
Fábrega, H.
   1974   Disease and Social Behavior. Cambridge: M.I.T. Press.
Frigout, A.
   1979   Hopi Ceremonial Organization. *In* Handbook of North Ameri-
              can Indians. Vol. 9, Southwest. W. C. Sturtevant, ed. Wash-
              ington, D.C.: Smithsonian Institution.
German, A.
   1972   Aspects of Clinical Psychiatry in Subsaharan Africa. British
              Journal of Psychiatry 121:461−479.
Good, B., and M. DelVecchio Good
   1982   Toward a Meaning-Centered Analysis of Popular Illness
              Categories: 'Fright Illness' and 'Heart Distress' in Iran. *In*
              Cultural Conceptions of Mental Health and Therapy. A. Mar-
              sella and G. White, eds. Dordrecht: D. Reidel.
Guimera, L. M.
   1978   Witchcraft Illness in the Evuzok Nosological System. Culture,
              Medicine, and Psychiatry 2(4):373−396.
Hallowell, A. I.
   1963   Ojibwa World View and Disease. *In* Man's Image in Medicine
              and Anthropology. I. Galdston, ed. New York: International
              Universities Press.

Hieb, L. A.
  1979   Hopi World View. *In* Handbook of North American Indians.
                Vol. 9, Southwest. W. C. Sturtevant, ed. Washington, D.C.:
                Smithsonian Institution.

Jilek, W.
  1974   Indian Healing Power: Indigenous Therapeutic Practices in the
                Pacific Northwest. Psychiatric Annals 4(9):13−21.

Johnson, D. L., and C. A. Johnson
  1965   Totally Discouraged: A Depressive Syndrome of the Dakota
                Sioux. Transcultural Psychiatric Research Review 2(1):
                141−143.

Kalectaca, M.
  1978   Lessons in Hopi. Tucson: The University of Arizona Press.

Kay, M.
  1977   Health and Illness in a Mexican-American Barrio. *In* Ethnic
                Medicine in the Southwest. E. H. Spicer, ed. Tucson: Uni-
                versity of Arizona Press.

Keller, M. B., and R. W. Shapiro
  1982   Double Depression: Superimposition of Acute Depression Epi-
                sodes on Chronic Depressive Disorders. American Journal of
                Psychiatry 139(4):438−442.

Keller, M. B., P. W. Labori, J. Endicott, W. Coryell, and G. L. Klerman
  1983   "Double Depression": Two-Year Follow-up. American Jour-
                nal of Psychiatry 140(6):689−694.

Kiev, A.
  1972   Transcultural Psychiatry. New York: The Free Press.

Kleinman, A.
  1977   Depression, Somatization and the "New Cross-Cultural Psy-
                chiatry." Social Science and Medicine 11:3−10.
  1980   Patients and Healers in the Context of Culture. Berkeley, Los
                Angeles, London: University of California Press.

Kleinman, A., L. Eisenberg, and B. Good
  1978   Culture, Illness and Care. Annals of Internal Medicine 88:
                251−258.

Leap, W. L.
  1979   Studies in Southwestern Indian English. San Antonio: Trinity
                University.

Leechman, D., and R. A. Hall
  1955   American Indian Pidgin English: Attestations and Grammatical
                Peculiarities. American Speech 30:163−171.

Leff, J.
  1981   Psychiatry Around the Globe. New York: Marcel Dekker, Inc.

Levy, J. E.
In press   Hopi Shamanism. A Reappraisal. *In* Essays in Honor of Fred
Eggan. A. Ortiz and R. de Mallie, eds. Albuquerque: Univer-
sity of New Mexico Press.

Lewis, T. H.
1975   A Syndrome of Depression and Mutism in the Oglala Sioux.
American Journal of Psychiatry 1342(7):753−755.

Manson, S. M., and J. H. Shore
1981   Psychiatric Epidemological Research among American Indians
and Alaska Natives: Some Methodological Issues. White Cloud
JOurnal 2(2):48−56.

Manson, S. M., and J. E. Trimble
1982   Mental Health Services to American Indian and Alaska Natives
Communities: Past Research, Future Inquiries. *In* Reaching the
Underserved: Mental Health Needs of Neglected Populations.
L. Snowden, ed. Beverly Hills: Sage Publications.

Marano, L.
1982   Windigo Psychosis: The Anatomy of an Emic/Etic Confusion.
Current Anthropology 23(4):385−412.

Marsella, A.
1978   Thoughts on Cross-Cultural Studies on the Epidemiology of
Depression. Culture, Medicine, and Psychiatry 2(4):343−357.
1979   Cross-Cultural Studies of Mental Disorders. *In* Perspectives in
Cross-Cultural Psychology. R. Tharp and T. Cibowrowski,
eds. New York: Academic Press.
1980   Depressive Experience and Disorder across Cultures. *In* Handbook of Cross-cultural Psychology. Vol. 5, Culture and Psychopathology. H. Triandis and J. Draguns, eds. Boston: Allyn
and Bacon.

Marsella, A., J. D. Kinzie, and P. Gordon
1973   Ethnic Variations in the Expression of Depression. Journal of
Cross-Cultural Psychology 4:435−458.

Matchett, W. F.
1972   Repeated Hallucinatory Experiences as a Part of the Mourning
Process among Hopi Women. Psychiatry 35:185−194.

Medicine, B.
1982   New Roads to Coping: Siouxan Sobriety. *In* New Directions in
Prevention Among American Indian and Alaska Native Communities. S. M. Manson, ed. Portland: Oregon Health Sciences
University.

Meile, P., and W. E. Gregg
1973   Dimensionality of the Index of Psychophysiological Stress.
Social Science and Medicine 7:643−648.

Mohatt, G., and A. Blue
1982   Relationships between an Empirical Measure of Traditionality
              and Social Deviance. *In* New Directions in Prevention Among
              American Indian and Alaska Native Communities. S. M.
              Manson, ed. Portland: Oregon Health Sciences University.

Murdock, G. P.
1980   Theories of Illness: A World Survey. Pittsburgh: University of
              Pittsburgh Press.

Opler, M. E.
1936   Some Points of Comparison and Contrast between the Treat-
              ment of Functional Disorders by Apache Shamans and Modern
              Psychiatric Practice. American Journal of Psychiatry 92:
              1371–1387.

Parker, S.
1962   Eskimo Psychopathology in the Context of Eskimo Personality
              and Culture. American Anthropologist 64:76–96.

Prince, R.
1968   The Changing Picture of Depressive Syndrome in Africa: Is It
              Fact or Diagnostic Fashion? Canadian Journal of African
              Studies 1:177–192.

Resner, G., and J. Hartog
1970   Concepts and Terminology of Mental Disorder among Malays.
              Journal of Cross-Cultural Psychology 1:369–381.

Rhoades, E. R., M. Marshgall, C. Attneave, M. Echohawk, J. Bjork, and
M. Beiser
1980   Mental Health Problems of American Indians Seen in Out-
              patient Facilities of the Indian Health Service, 1975. Public
              Health Reports 96(4):329–335.

Rin, H., C. Schooler, and W. Caudill
1973   Symptomatology and Hospitalization: Culture, Social Structure
              and Psychopathology in Taiwan and Japan. Journal of Nervous
              and Mental Disorders 157:296–313.

Robins, L. N., J. E. Holzer, J. Croughan, and K. S. Ratcliff
1981   National Institute of Mental Health Diagnostic Interview
              Schedule. Archives of General Psychiatry 38:381–389.

Rogers, S. L.
1944   Disease Concepts in North America. American Anthropologist
              46(4):559–564.

Roy, C., A. Chaudhuri, and D. Irvine
1970   The Prevalence of Mental Disorders among Saskachewan
              Indians. Journal of Cross-Cultural Psychology 1(4):383–392.

Sampath, B. M.
1974   Prevalence of Psychiatric Disorders in a Southern Baffin Island

Eskimo Settlement. Canadian Psychiatric Association Journal 19:363–367.

Savage, C., A. H. Leighton, and D. C. Leighton
1965   The Problem of Cross-Cultural Identification of Psychiatric Disorders. *In* Approaches to Cross-Cultural Psychiatry. J. M. Murphy and A. H. Leighton, eds. Ithaca: Cornell University Press.

Sechrest, L.
1963   Symptoms of Mental Disorder in the Philippines. Philippine Sociological Review 7:189–206.

Shore, J. H.
1977   Psychiatric Research Issues with American Indians. *In* Current Perspectives in Cultural Psychiatry. E. F. Foulks, R. M. Wintrob, J. Westermeyer, and A. R. Favazza, eds. New York: Spectrum Publications.

Shore, J. H., J. D. Kinzie, and J. Hampson
1973   Psychiatric Epidemiology of an Indian Village. Psychiatry 36:70–81.

Shore, J. H., and S. M. Manson
1981   Cross-Cultural Studies of Depression among American Indians and Alaska Natives. White Cloud Journal 2(2):5–12.
1983   American Indian Psychiatric and Social Problems. Transcultural Psychiatric Research Review 20(3):152–168.

Sievers, M. L., and J. R. Fisher
1981   Diseases of North American Indians. *In* Biocultural Aspects of Disease. I. Rothschild, ed. New York: Academic Press.

Sue, S.
1977   Community Mental Health Services to Minority Groups: Some Optimism, Some Pessimism. American Psychologist 32:616–624.

Tanaka-Matsumi, J., and A. Marsella
1974   Ethnocultural Variations in the Subjective Experience of Depression: Word Association. Journal of Cross-Cultural Psychology 7:379–397.

Teftt, S. K.
1967   Anomie, Values, and Culture Change among Teen-Age Indians: An Exploration. Sociology of Education (Spring):145–157.

Terminsen, J., and J. Ryan
1970   Health and Disease in a British Columbian Community. Canadian Psychiatric Association Journal 15:121–127.

Titiev, M.
1972   The Hopi Indians of Old Oraibi. Ann Arbor: The University of Michigan Press.

Trimble, J. E., S. M. Manson, N. G. Dinges, and B. Medicine
    1984   American Indian Concepts of Mental Health: Reflections and
                  Directions. *In* Mental Health Services: The Cross-Cultural
                  Context. P. B. Pedersen, N. Sartorius, and A. J. Marsella, eds.
                  Beverly Hills: Sage Publications.

Tseng, W. S.
    1975   The Nature of Somatic Complaints among Psychiatric Patients:
                  The Chinese Case. Comparative Psychiatry 16:237–245.

Tseng, W. S., and J. Hsu
    1970   Chinese Culture, Personality Formation, and Mental Illness.
                  International Journal of Social Psychiatry 16:5–14.

Werner, O.
    1965   Semantics of Navajo Medical Terms (I). International Journal
                  of American Linguistics 31:1–17.

Werner, O., and K. Begishe
    1966   Anatomical Atlas of the Navajo. Unpublished manuscript.

12

The Interpretation of Iranian Depressive Illness and Dysphoric Affect

*Byron J. Good, Mary-Jo DelVecchio Good,
and Robert Moradi*

INTRODUCTION

Recent anthropological critics have charged that cross-cultural psychiatrists and other social scientists reify Western cultural categories, elevate them to the status of analytic categories, assume they reflect aspects of the natural order, and then use them uncritically in cross-cultural research. Along with distinctions between magic and religion or the natural and supernatural, the Cartesian categories mind and body often serve as prime examples of cultural categories treated as natural. It is surprising, then, to find that many anthropologists implicitly assume the distinction between diseases of the body and diseases of the mind to be universal. Most will be quick to deny such obvious heresy. A moment's reflection, however, will indicate how common this assumption is.

Anthropologists seldom challenge the naturalness of categories of diseases of the body. When Topley (1970) wrote that Cantonese in Hong Kong interpret measles as caused by "womb poisoning" and respond with elaborate ritual avoidances for one hundred days, or when Bowen wrote in her classic *Return to Laughter* (1953) of a smallpox epidemic experienced as a pestilence of witchcraft by the Tiv, none objected to their use of the disease categories measles and smallpox without placing them in quotes. Medical anthropologists pay great attention to how members of other societies *interpret* disease, how folk healers or lay people categorize disease or symptoms, explain their immediate and underlying causes, and respond with culturally appropriate treatments or rituals. But the correspondence of the disease category to a natural phenomenon is seldom challenged.

Diseases of the mind have quite a different history in anthropological theory. Such disorders have been viewed as forms of behavioral abnormality or deviance, and the focus of analytic attention has been on the cultural production and societal response to such behavior, rather than on the cultural interpretation of an underlying disorder.[1] The very notion that extreme emotional distress or problems in the perception of reality should be considered disease rather than, for example, matters of morality or possession is explained as resulting from the growing dominance of medicine in matters of the mind. Changes in conceptualization and categorization of psychiatric disorders over the past century are viewed not as the result of the growth of knowledge of the natural world but as evidence for the social construction of psychiatric knowledge. Differences in the form of psychopathology in various cultures are taken as evidence that psychiatric disorders are constituted in a manner unique to a society's culture, patterns of child rearing, or social organization of coping resources. In the 1930s, this anthropological view of psychopathology fit relatively easily with the psychoanalytic view that mental illness is a result of unique constellations of individual conflicts and defensive maneuvers. In the 1980s, with the development of biological psychiatry and growing agreement that at least the major psychiatric disorders are universal and heterogenous diseases, the inherited anthropological tradition is increasingly at odds with contemporary psychiatric "knowledge."

The challenge to anthropological understanding is especially true for the study of depression. In the past decade, there has been an unprecedented growth of research into the biological, pharmacological, and social aspects of depressive disorders. Stimulated by the discovery of effective antidepressant medication, extensive investigations into the role of specific neurotransmitters and neuroendocrine abnormalities in the major affective disorders are under way (e.g., Goodwin and Potter 1978; Sachar 1982). Such basic neurophysiological research is often linked with studies of sleep abnormalities, with efforts to discover laboratory diagnostic tests (e.g., Carroll et al. 1981) and with pharmacological studies. Drug research has been directed not only at basic physiological mechanisms but also at the relationship between clinical presentation and the effectiveness of particular combinations of medications, often studied through controlled clinical trials. Such investigations have depended on the establishment of research diagnostic criteria that reliably distinguish depressive disorders from others and identify specific subtypes of depression.

Since the mid-1970s, research diagnostic criteria, specific epidemiological instruments, and the new diagnostic and statistical manual (DSM-III) of the American Psychiatric Association (1980) have developed hand in hand. While previous epidemiological instruments had focused on the level of psychological symptoms, new ones were designed to assign individuals to diagnostic categories. This approach reflected a new research interest in the biological characteristics of particular diseases and a growing consensus that psychiatric disorders can be understood as a set of discrete and heterogenous diseases (Weissman and Klerman 1978). In addition, increasingly sophisticated social psychological studies investigated factors that protect individuals, provoke onset of depression, and increase vulnerability (Brown and Harris 1978). Taken together, these investigations have produced an impressive new understanding based on the assumption that depression is a disease. This scientific understanding is commonly reproduced in American popular culture, where depression has been domesticated as the ''common cold of the psychiatric disorders'' and a simple chemical imbalance.

While advances in the study of depression provide a major challenge to the traditional anthropological paradigm for studying disorders of the mind, efforts to apply the contemporary understanding of depression in cross-cultural research reveal fundamental difficulties and call for anthropological reflection and research. Something seems askew. A disorder long understood to be profoundly social in character is increasingly viewed as a psychophysiological phenomenon. Reading through the scores of research reports on depression that appear monthly in medical journals, one has little sense that losses of the most cherished human relationships, crises of personal meaning, and oppressive power relationships are involved as the very essence of depression. Current theory recognizes that onset of the disease may be triggered by social events in particularly vulnerable individuals. However, the social characteristics of depression are treated as secondary or epiphenomenal features, and the cultural meanings associated with the experience are treated as systematic bias or distortion, to be sorted out in an effort to study the underlying, essential condition. Cross-cultural research within this paradigm is explicitly ethnocentric. Diagnostic research instruments, such as the Present State Examination and the Diagnostic Interview Schedule, are currently being translated into a variety of languages, without any effort to first establish the local forms of the disorder or local idioms for articulating symptoms. The universality of the category is *assumed*, eliminating the need to establish validity, and the tautological circle is completed when the symptoms that serve as criteria of diagnosis, because they are believed to reflect specific psychophysiological and hormonal states, are assumed to be universal. The traditional anthropological critique of the reification of Western or American forms of experience as universal analytic categories again has special relevance.

What do these developments in psychiatry imply for the anthropological tradition? What does anthropology have to contribute to an understanding of depression? Several suggestions for needed research and theoretical development follow and provide a frame for the reflections in this chapter.

First, it is essential that anthropologists critically examine their assumptions concerning the differences between disorders of the body and those of the mind. The view that physical diseases are culturally interpreted while mental disorders are culturally produced is no longer viable. Similarly, the view that physical diseases are biologically constrained and follow a course independent of culture (the "natural history" of the disease) while mental disorders are matters of the mind and society is neither good anthropology nor biomedically acceptable. Although disease theories of psychiatric disorders should be submitted to a critical sociology of knowledge, the intellectual tradition that blinds cultural anthropologists to the usefulness of studying the relation of culture and disease in cases of psychiatric disorders should be abandoned.

Second, current developments in psychiatry provide the opportunity for renewed interest in the cross-cultural validity of diagnostic categories. While anthropologists should not ignore the potential power of conceptualizing depression as disease, they should also critically assess the extent to which reliable diagnostic methods, whether clinical or epidemiological, may produce universality as an artifact of the methods employed. It is far from clear whether depression and its subcategories as conceived in American psychiatry are universal, or whether they are culture-specific forms of an underlying depressive disorder. Anthropological investigation of these issues will require both creative theoretical work and innovative empirical studies, carried out in clinical settings or in conjunction with case-finding and epidemiological methods. Occasional reports of cases happened upon in ethnographic research cannot serve as a basis for an anthropology of depression.

Third, the relationship of depression and other psychiatric disorders to culture, conceived as systems of meaning and discourse, should become a renewed focus of research. Given the extent of research on depression in the past decade, it is extraordinary how little we know about the cultural meanings associated with dysphoric affect and depressive illness. The narrow focus on symptoms as diagnostic criteria has precluded attention in contemporary cross-cultural psychiatry to the shaping of depressive illness by the radically different systems of meaning provided by the world's cultures. It is in this domain we believe anthropology has the potential to develop an autonomous theoretical perspective, neither derivative of biomedicine nor ignorant of current psychiatric knowledge.

In this chapter, we explore the implications of an interpretive or meaning-centered anthropology for the study of depression. In the words of its leading practitioner, Clifford Geertz (1983:19), an interpretive anthropology has as its primary focus the study of the relation of human action to its sense rather than behavior to its determinants: "many social scientists have turned away from a laws and instances ideal of explanation toward a cases and interpretations one, looking less for the sort of thing that connects planets and pendulums and more for the sort that connects chrysanthemums and swords." Psychiatric anthropology, from this perspective, is an interpretive endeavor, an effort to understand how members of a society bring to meaning those disorders and emotions that appear as fundamental and unwelcome realities, how they construe the relationship of those realities to previous and concurrent difficulties in their lives, and how illness idioms are used both to articulate the experience of disorder and to construct it as a social reality.

Cross-cultural analysis in psychiatry necessarily involves translating across alternative discourses or ways of talking about emotion and illness. When one conducts research on a disorder such as depression in one's own society, the theoretical and popular discourses concerning the disorder are both local. It is easy to forget how much they share, to become blind to the cultural assumptions built into the analytic terms. In cross-cultural research, translating between psychiatric theory and local cultural forms becomes much more problematic. An interpretive analysis thus requires explicit attention to our theoretical discourse and its cultural content as well as to the popular discourse in the society studied.

The "interpretive turn" taken by recent anthropology is distinctly out of fashion in psychiatry, where it connotes a return to stultifying psychoanalytic discussions, more metaphysical than scientific. Biological paradigms produce new knowledge where others have failed. How then can an interpretive anthropology enter into dialogue with contemporary psychiatry? What can be learned from such an approach? Is there method to a disciplined craft of interpretation that can be replicated and yield assurance that we are not writing fiction? Can it yield insight that will complement the work of the epidemiologist or clinician, that will provoke development of new methods and less ethnocentric theoretical models?

In the following pages, we discuss several issues central to an anthropological account of depression. First, we critically examine aspects of the current psychiatric discourse on depression. Second, we outline an analytic approach focusing on aspects of meaning and interpretation which are often systematically excluded from current psychiatric research. Third, we illustrate this approach with an analysis of dysphoric affect and depression in Iranian culture.

DEPRESSION: EMPIRICIST AND CONTINGENT ACCOUNTS

Other authors in this volume have demonstrated some ways in which the contemporary psychiatric discourse on depression reproduces conventional knowledge in American society (see Young 1980 for an analysis of stress discourse in these terms). This discourse implicitly postulates an abstract, desocialized individual, whose symptoms are seen to reflect an inner psychophysiological state rather than aspects of social interaction (Beeman, chap. 7) or local power relations (Kleinman and Kleinman, chap. 13). Distinctions between affective disorders and thought disorders, and a focus on dysphoria and loss of pleasure are grounded in our tacit knowledge and often treated as facts of nature rather than social constructs (Lutz, chap. 2).

The discourse on depression is thus represented by anthropological critics as positivist, grounded in a particular disease paradigm, and ethnocentric. This is a fair account of how depression is constructed in much psychiatric writing and research. By contrast, however, recent ethnographic studies of the actual practice of psychiatrists give quite a different picture of the nature of psychiatric knowledge, particularly as employed in clinical settings (e.g., Gaines 1979, 1982; Good et al. 1982). These two forms of anthropological analysis provide competing accounts of psychiatric discourse and knowledge.

Similar contradictions in the accounts by sociologists and anthropologists of the work of scientists have recently provoked a sharp debate among sociologists of the natural sciences.[2] In a stimulating set of essays, Mulkay and Gilbert argue that sociologists of science use scientists' symbolic products—journal articles, public testimony in policy debates, personal comments during scientific controversies—to assemble an account of "how that science really is." However, "given the diversity of scientists' discourse it is possible . . . to produce radically different, yet quite plausible, stories by selecting from and reassembling that discourse in different ways" (Mulkay et al. 1983:196). They argue for the methodological priority of analyzing scientists' "discourse" (i.e., "all kinds of talk and all kinds of written documents" [Mulkay 1981:170]: "We have suggested that, at least initially, we should concentrate on understanding how scientists' discourse is organized to convey varying conceptions of scientific action and belief on different occasions and in different contexts" (Mulkay and Gilbert 1982*b*:588−589).

Mulkay and Gilbert (1982*b*, 1982*c*) argue that natural scientists use two primary "repertoires of discourse": an empiricist and a contingent discourse. Empiricist discourse is employed by natural scientists when they contribute to the formal research literature or give general accounts to laymen about their work. In these contexts they maintain the assumption that genuine scientific knowledge is determined by controlled, experimental revelation or logical discovery of "the facts" of the natural world. However, scientists also have a contingent interpretive repertoire, which treats action in science as much less uniform and places more importance on practical methodological skills, personal and social factors, and intuition. Scientists generally describe their own work to the public in empiricist terms; however, when called on to account for errors of others in scientific disputes, they often blame those errors on contingent factors (Mulkay and Gilbert 1982*c*).

Although psychiatry and the natural sciences differ in important respects, a parallel is clear. The psychiatric discourse on depression includes both empiricist and contingent accounts, and the two are significantly different. Social and symbolic variables are incorporated into the two accounts differently, and the empiricist accounts systematically exclude much of the knowledge embodied in contingent accounts. For these reasons, the two provide quite different bases for making systematic interpretations across cultures.

Empiricist Accounts of Depression

During the past decade, the predominant thrust of psychiatric research and professional publication has been aimed at accounting for depression as a discrete, naturally occurring disease (or a related group of diseases), distinct from other psychiatric disorders. Reports of research activities and the accounts of the depression are clearly empiricist, in Mulkay's terms. Research has focused on discovering physiological conditions that correlate with distinctive clinical syndromes, identified primarily as a set of specific symptoms of certain duration and level of severity. The clinical characteristics have been operationalized as "research diagnostic criteria," which served as the basis for research whose findings are embodied in the revision of the diagnostic and statistical manual (DSM-III). Because of discovery of links between neuroendocrine disruption and the "vegetative signs and symptoms," these symptoms have come to play an increasingly important role in the formal definition of the disorder, as well as in clinical practice. Physicians commonly refer to those depressions in which disruptions of appetite, sleep, energy, and sexual activity are prominant as "biological depressions," and treat them with "antidepressant" medication. Along with sustained dysphoria, these serve as the core criteria for major affective disorders. Thus, the empiricist account represents depression as a disease, whose symptoms reflect underlying psychophysiological processes. This discourse is most closely associated with epidemiologic, pharmacologic, and biological research, and clinical diagnosis.

It is important for anthropologists to appreciate the historical context of the empiricist discourse. Between World War II and 1970, a series of psychiatric epidemiological studies were undertaken in the United States and in several cross-cultural settings which focused on the relation of level of mental health to such social variables as poverty, urban anomie, rapid social change, and social stratification (see Weissman and Klerman 1978 and Murphy 1982 for excellent reviews). Because of serious difficulties of identifying psychopathology in a reliable and valid manner, these studies measured *level* of psychiatric symptoms and social impairment, rather than prevalence of cases diagnosed according to the then current nosology.

By the mid-1960s, psychotropic medications were in use which had differential effects on various psychiatric conditions. This provided great impetus to develop diagnostic criteria that could be used reliably in research, with the goal of identifying genetic, neurobiological, pharmacological and psychosocial features that distinguish populations meeting criteria for different disorders. The Research Diagnostic Criteria (RDC) evolved from a decade of research, particularly by a group at Washington University, St. Louis (see Feighner et al. 1972; Spitzer et al. 1975). The RDC, as well as the psychometric instruments designed to make RDC (or DSM-III) diagnoses, state explicitly the symptoms, duration, and level of impairment required for an individual to be given a particular diagnosis. These instruments are currently in wide use in epidemiological studies of the genetic and psychosocial concomitants of diagnostic groups as well as in clinical studies seeking biological concomitants. Thus a series of converging forms of research have led to a working assumption that there exist multiple, discrete psychiatric disorders and that epidemiology should proceed "on the heuristic assumption that there are discrete disorders" (Weissman and Klerman 1978:709).

The new approaches to diagnosis and epidemiological measurement—what we may call the empiricist paradigm[3]—have important advantages over previous forms. They are explicit, do not depend on confusing and overlapping etiological concepts, and may facilitate identification of biological concomitants or causes. However, application of these approaches in cross-cultural research reveals important limitations when viewed from an interpretive perspective.

The empiricist paradigm suggests a clear strategy for investigating depression in other societies. Since it is assumed that depression is a discrete and universal disorder and that the symptoms that serve as diagnostic criteria map onto underlying biological processes, it is also assumed that once semantic equivalents for these symptoms are found, the translated criteria can be used to identify the same disorder in another society. Research is thus directed at careful translation of those symptoms that serve as diagnostic criteria, identification of a cohort of individuals who meet criteria for depression, and examination of various characteristics (genetic, psychosocial, physiological) of that population in contrast with others. This approach is illustrated by the World Health Organization's studies of schizophrenia and depression and by a recent study by Orley and Wing (1979).

There are several fundamental difficulties with this approach (see Good and Kleinman 1984 for an elaboration of this critique in relation to anxiety disorders). First, it essentially begs the question of the cross-cultural validity of the concept depression. Do individuals who meet the translated criteria suffer from a single clinical syndrome, equivalent to that suffered in the society in which the criteria were developed, or is the disease that is constructed in this manner an artifact of the method used? (See Obeyesekere, chap. 4, for an argument that a culture-specific disorder such as "semen loss" could be shown to be universal using this methodology.) Although the RDC evolved from years of careful clinical description in the United States (see Robins and Guze 1972), for studies undertaken in the non-Western world, similar research does not precede the development of criteria for depression, which are merely transposed from Western publications.

Second, the "centri-cultural" strategy, that is, the translation of instruments or criteria developed exclusively in one culture into other languages (Wober 1969), often treats symptoms as decontextualized reflections of physiological states rather than as aspects of local idioms of distress. Diverse anthropological studies, including many in this volume, have shown that distress is articulated in a wide variety of culture-specific idioms. An approach that begins with symptoms significant to Americans and seeks semantic equivalents in another culture, rather than identifying local idioms of distress and relating them to clinical syndromes, is certain to produce knowledge that is artifactual.

In the best studies employing the empiricist paradigm, much of the negotiation across meaning systems is undertaken under the rubric "translation." For example, Orley and Wing (1979:517) adapted the Present State Exam by "translating the concept behind each item rather than simply translating the questions in the English version." They provide an admirable description of a long process of anthropological and clinical studies on which the translation was based. Even then, they used the question, "Do you sometimes blame yourself for something that was a mistake?" as the criterion for "pathological guilt"—a surprisingly innocuous experience to serve as a criterion for pathology—and expressed surprise that depressed Ugandan villagers exhibit higher rates of pathological guilt than depressed Londoners. It also appears from their report that culture-specific symptoms, such as concern with issues of fertility, dreams of being bewitched, and richly metaphoric somatic complaints, which one would expect to be prevalent (Turner 1967; Janzen 1978; Lambo 1962; Field 1958; Collis 1966; Ebigbo 1983), were not tapped by the interview because they are not present in European populations.

Third, in more general terms, the empiricist paradigm systematically excludes attention to the culture-specific contexts of meaning used for the interpretation and articulation of dysphoria and depressive illness.

Symptoms are abstracted from their symbolic and meaningful contexts, and social factors, such as local power relations associated with kin networks or employment, are conceptualized as vulnerability factors or provoking agents, not as essential characteristics of the disorder.

Because of these problems, cross-cultural research on depression based in the empiricist paradigm faces serious limitations. It is important for anthropologists to note, however, that these limitations are characteristic not of all psychiatric knowledge but of research and publications framed by empiricist discourse. Empiricist accounts are part of a situated discourse and contrast with contingent accounts of depression among psychiatrists.

Contingent Accounts

Two forms of contingent accounts of depression are found among psychiatric researchers: clinical accounts and informal discussions of research methods. We will note these briefly. When describing clinical work with depressed patients, psychiatrists typically discuss the disorder in terms quite different from those described above. The personal and social complexity of individual patients comes to the fore, and clinicians describe extended exploration of the relation between symptoms and relevant contexts of social conflict, loss, and characterologic issues.[4] While their analysis is not self-consciously cultural, their accounts of depression are not far from what anthropologists describe as "hermeneutic" analysis, circling from symptom to context to symptom to develop deepened understanding (cf. Good et al. 1983).

Psychiatric researchers also provide, in private discussions, contingent accounts of the research process, making it appear far less like the process of orderly discovery described in professional journals. For example, they describe the role of particular clinical experiences with individual patients as sources of ideas explored in further research and reported in empiricist terms. They describe serious difficulties with using standard psychometric instruments with some ethnic groups, particularly Puerto Ricans. They show an awareness of differences in the way primary care and psychiatric patients describe their symptoms, that is, in their idioms of distress.[5] Cross-cultural researchers often discuss major differences in clinical phenomena, which do not become part of the research reports. For example, very little of the contingent discourse of the researchers involved in the WHO international epidemiological projects are hinted at in the formal reports. Thus, not only is the object of research, depression, represented in far more sociocultural terms—as a response of particular individuals, who have unique life histories and psychological characteristics, to difficult life circumstances, producing culturally influenced expressions of distress and care-seeking responses—but the research process itself is interpreted in contingent terms.

We argued in the introduction that a significant task for anthropology is to reincorporate analysis of cultural meanings and interpretation into the study of depression. We might argue in a similar vein that an important conceptual task is to develop a theoretical framework that explicitly integrates psychiatry's contingent discourse into psychiatric research accounts.

DEPRESSION: INTERPRETED DISORDER OR DISORDERED INTERPRETATION?

We began with the contention that many anthropological accounts fail to recognize the disease-like characteristics of disorders such as depression, focusing on the cultural construction of the behavioral disturbance and ignoring the role of biological phenomena in constraining and patterning the disorder. We suggested, however, that empiricist accounts of contemporary psychiatry systematically exclude from attention the meaning of symptoms and the culture-specific symbolic domains in terms of which the illness is constituted. Thus, for example, dramatic cultural differences—psychosis experienced as possession in Sri Lanka (Waxler 1977), anxiety experienced as morbid fear of bewitchment in Africa (Lambo 1962), depression and anxiety experienced as heart distress in Iran (Good n.d., 1977), and exhaustion of the nervous system in China (Kleinman 1982)—are omitted from analysis of psychiatric disorders, giving the appearance of uniformity to psychiatric disorders when clinical and ethnographic phenomena have marked differences.

An interpretive account of depression mediates the epistemological and empirical contradictions of the cultural relativist and empiricist positions and points the way to new research strategies. An interpretive account of depression begins with the recognition that culture provides the means for responding to and interpreting "reality" ("a quality appertaining to phenomena that we recognize as being independent of our own volition [we cannot 'wish them away']" [Berger and Luckmann

1966:1]). Such reality may be external to the self—the natural world, social formations—or may be internal, subjective reality. Physical sensations (pain, heart palpitations), drives (hunger, sexual desire), and emotions (sadness, anger) are all experienced as realities—as *das Es*, an "it," as Freud said—requiring the "work of culture" to bring them to meaning. Depression is experienced by the sufferer as a reality, a set of symptoms or a condition expressed and interpreted in local idioms and using local explanatory frames. Depression as a condition of the sufferer is interpreted secondarily by family members, care givers, and others in the society. Depression is thus like any other disease: an *interpreted disorder*.

Depression as a social or clinical reality, however, is not merely produced as a result of culturally influenced interpretations of an underlying disease; depression is also *a disorder of the interpretive process*. Individuals suffering anxiety disorders interpret as threatening or fearful aspects of the environment others in the society interpet as nonthreatening (see Good and Kleinman 1984). Persons suffering from depression interpret the environment as overwhelmingly negative and hopeless and themselves as bad, as Beck (1976) and his colleagues have shown. Disordered interpretation is not unique to psychiatric disorders. Individuals suffering from such chronic medical disorders as heart disease dramatically alter their interpretation of themselves and the world around them. However, psychiatric disorders such as depression are fundamentally disorders of perception and interpretation. Because culture plays so critical a role in shaping perception and interpretation, in defining what kinds of interpretations are normal and valued and what kind are disordered, serious research is required to determine the extent to which disordered interpretation is universal or culturally particular.

The interpretive approach to the study of depression in the cross-cultural context provides important issues for research, which may be summarized in four questions: What are the local forms of discourse for interpreting depression in the society being studied? What are they used to interpret? What forms do disorders of interpretation take? How do we translate between our clinical or research discourse on depression and the local discourse?

1. *What are the local interpretive forms?* Anthropological analysis suggests we first identify the idioms of distress specific to a society, and determine which are commonly used to articulate depression (see, e.g., Nichter 1981; Kleinman 1982). Second, we should investigate the explanatory forms—popular illness categories (Good and Good 1983) and

explanatory models (Kleinman 1982)—that are used to make sense of depressive symptoms or the depressive syndrome and to relate them to past or concurrent social conditions and life events. Third, we should investigate the semantic networks (Good 1977), that is, the networks of symbols and meaningfully related experiences, associated with depression. This approach suggests the importance of replacing narrow focus on decontextualized symptoms of depression with attention to contextualized depressive discourse and its symbolic and rhetorical structure.

2. *What are they used to interpret?* The cross-cultural literature suggests systematic variation in the personal realities (somatic sensations, emotions and emotional conflict, visual or tactile experience, fears concerning fertility or personal status, and so on) and social conditions (family conflict, loss, witchcraft threats, incorrigible social conditions) that are associated with depression and made the focus of interpretation. Particular idioms or explanatory forms in a society may have specific interpretive foci, some characteristics of the sufferer, some of the social context. For instance, popular ''stress'' discourse in American society is an etiological discourse, explaining current distress (symptoms) in terms of specific social conditions, past or present (e.g., unemployment, a divorce). Fright discourse, such as *susto* in Mexican culture, focuses interpretation not on symptoms of the sufferer but on the past life events per se (O'Nell and Rubel 1976). Cross-cultural differences in the symptoms associated with depression may be due to differences in the focus of attention and perception as well as to differences in forms of interpretation, explanation, and communication.

3. *What forms do disorders of interpretation take?* Aaron Beck and his colleagues have outlined a theory of depression and developed a form of psychotherapy based on research into characteristic cognitive patterns of depressed patients. The depressed, they found, tend to think ''in an all-or-nothing manner''; they tend toward ''overgeneralization and selective abstraction''; they ''typically focus on the negative in the environment and overlook or discount the positive'' (Beck and Burns 1978:202). It is surprising that a generation of cognitive anthropologists (see Lutz, chap. 2) have failed to investigate whether these cognitive characteristics are specific to Americans or are more general. Given the extent of cultural patterning of cognition, we would expect significant differences in the alterations in interpretation among the depressed in other societies.

4. *What is the relationship between the psychiatric discourse on depression and the local discourse in the society being studied?* The interpretive approach assumes there is no value-free or acultural perspective from which to study depression in another society. Since there is no "gold standard" for identifying depression, no pathognomonic biological marker that distinguishes the disorder, the question of validity of the concept is inevitable. This does not leave us in a condition of hopeless relativity. It suggests, rather, that we should systematically compare discourses, identifying characteristics of the discourse on depression in our own society and investigating comparable forms of discourse in the society being studied. To paraphrase Wittgenstein, we cannot simply look for different labels attached to the same item in the hypothetical museum; we must rather look for "language games" that bear "family resemblances" to each other (see Bloor 1983:22−49 for a discussion), specify the resemblances and differences, and investigate their relation to alternative ways of life. Translation is a final step undertaken only after assessment of popular and professional interpretations.

We believe this approach has the potential for systematically reincorporating social meanings in the analysis of depression and for making the knowledge present in the contingent discourse of psychiatry relevant to the empiricist discourse. In the following pages, we illustrate this approach by analyzing some aspects of depression in Iranian culture.

THE INTERPRETATION OF DYSPHORIA AND DEPRESSIVE ILLNESS IN IRANIAN CULTURE

Research Setting

Our analysis of depression among Iranians is based on more than a decade of research in Iranian culture. Good and Good conducted field research in Maragheh, a Turkish-speaking town in Iran, from 1972 to 1974, participated in rural health delivery research in 1975 and 1976 with the Tehran School of Public Health and World Health Organization, and consulted on cases of Iranian psychiatric patients in California between 1976 and 1982 (Good and Good 1982). Moradi has treated a large number of Iranian patients (Muslim and Jewish) in his psychiatric practice and recruited patients to participate in interviews for the current study. The three authors collaborated in a study of emotional expression among Iranian students (Good et al. 1981), and cooperated in clinical research and a brief survey of psychiatric symptoms among Iranian immigrants. Although we have not carried out focused research projects on depression among Iranians, we base our analysis on a variety of ethnographic, clinical, and epidemiological studies of emotion and illness in Iranian culture.

Dysphoria—sadness, grief, despair—is central to the Iranian ethos, an emotion charged with symbolic meaning. Pious Shi'ite Muslims gather weekly to hear the cruel martyrdom of Hossein, the grandson of the Prophet, commemorated in poetry and preaching and to respond with open weeping. The secular literature, both classical poetry and modern novels, is filled with melancholy and despair. Tragedy, injustice, and martyrdom are central to Iranian political philosophy and historical experience. "Dysphoric affect" is thus not equated with simple unhappiness in Iranian culture; it has profound religious and personal significance.

Given a cultural context in which dysphoria may have positive valuation, special issues are posed for the study of depression. Is dysphoric affect experienced as illness? What are the boundaries between nonpathological dysphoria and pathological depression? What are the primary meaning contexts within which the experience of dysphoria is grounded, and how are pathological states shaped by these and by structural and historical conditions? Can we identify a culture-specific form of depression? Investigation of these issues is necessary for an understanding of how depression is manifested and experienced by Iranians.

In the following pages, we first describe the central cultural frames within which dysphoria is experienced and interpreted, focusing on sadness as a normal, even valued, affect. Second, we analyze data from clinical experience, identifying specific syndromes of symptoms and experiences associated with depression in the discourse of Iranian patients. Third, we report on a factor analysis of a symptom checklist administered to a group of immigrant Iranian women and discuss whether there are culture-specific syndromes of symptoms in a nonclinical population, how they relate to the cultural patterning of symptoms identified in the clinical research, and how symptoms vary across cohorts residing for different members of years in the United States.

Dysphoria and the Tragic in Iranian Culture

The experience of sadness, loss, melancholy, and depression is rooted in two primary meaning contexts in Iranian culture: one associated with an understanding of the person or self, the other with a deep Iranian vision of the tragic, expressed in religion, romance and passion, and in interpretations of history and social reality. This vision is articulated through the Islamic tradition of popular mourning rituals, through the classical traditions of Persian poetry and the popular literary traditions, including Azeri Turkish oral epics, and through contemporary secular artistic productions of films, novels, and modern poetry.

The Concept of the Self

Sadness for Iranians is associated with personal depth (*'omq*). A quiet, serious, gentle person is contrasted with one who is noisy and talks too much, who jokes inappropriately and is unmannerly. A sad person is considered a thoughtful person (*motafakker*), who has childishness and playfulness under control. A sense of the tragic in life is associated with depth of the inner self, as opposed to shallowness of the outer self. One who expresses happiness too readily is often considered to be a simple (*sâdeh*) or socially incompetent person. Indeed, the ability to express sadness appropriately and in a culturally proscribed manner is a mark of social competence as well as personal depth.

In Iranian culture, the self is frequently conceptualized as consisting of an inner core and a public self.[6] The core self houses a person's true feelings and constitutes an individual's true personality. In public inter-actions, the core self must be protected from disruption and emotional trauma if a person is to remain healthy, both mentally and physically. Yet it is a cultural ideal to establish intimate relationships through which the core self may be expressed and nurtured.

Some individuals are believed to be particularly "sensitive" (*hassâs*) and therefore vulnerable to disruption of the inner self (Good and Good 1982; Good et al. 1981). The core self may be weighed down by life's unresolvable burdens (poverty, political repression), disturbed by conflicted social relations, shamed by loss of face or honor, or disrupted by shocks or "frights" associated with sudden revelations of losses or threats to the person (Good and Good 1981, 1982). Social relations should be carefully managed to protect the inner self.

Although the core emotions should be guarded, the occasional un-restrained expression of emotion is "profoundly admired" as a complete and direct expression of the self. In bereavement, for example, aban-donment of the self to overwhelming grief expresses an inner passion seldom displayed in social interaction (Bateson et al. 1977:270–271). Thus, although pathological depression is not an ideal, there is no stigma associated with expression of deep sadness; indeed, the ability to express sadness is highly valued.

Iranians recognize that outer expression does not always match inner self. At times one is called upon to simulate sadness and melancholy, particularly in situations in which the quality of one's emotional reaction will be monitored and evaluated by others. One is expected, for example, to express deep mourning at funerals of family members, to indulge in ritual crying at religious ceremonies (referred to as "mourning parties" by cynics), and to exude modulated passion and sadness on socially designated occasions. One young Iranian scholar, commenting on the discrepancy between the private and the public self in the expres-sion of sadness, noted, "If someone in your family dies, you have to really act like you are sorry, to wail and kick, otherwise you'll be accused of having ill feelings toward that person, regardless of what your inner feelings are, especially if you stand to inherit something."

The requirement to express grief as a public emotion may itself become a burden, especially by those who are upwardly mobile and moving into social status groups having different codes for communi-cation of affect and participation in ritual. A twenty-two-year-old preg-nant teacher in Azerbaijan, daughter of a traditional shopkeeper, com-mented on the long mourning period and weekly wakelike rituals asso-ciated with the death of her grandmother and followed by the mourning month of Moharram:

> Why are the children of the rich so beautiful, especially when their parents are not so beautiful? Why do their children have white skin and red cheeks, while our children come out black like us? . . . We are just steeped in blackness, mourning, sadness, but not the rich. . . . The teachers at my school say my child will take on a black spirit if I always wear black.

Thus Iranians recognize discrepancies between personal feeling and public emotion and may chafe at the norms governing ritual expression. Nevertheless, the ideal of the self as possessing a depthful vision of the tragic and the capacity to experience grief is highly valued and is grounded in the most basic and pervasive religious traditions, in classical Persian poetry, and in Iranian interpretations of history.

Grief and the Tragic in Iranian Shi'ism

The core of Iranian Shi'ism embodies a vision of the tragic and of grief as a religiously motivated emotion. Ritual performances held throughout the year recollect the struggles and martyrdom of the Shi'a imams and recount the failures of the Shi'a to dominate the early Islamic movement. Those historical events are interpreted as evidence that the just and the righteous in the world will be cruelly suppressed by worldy and irreligious authorities. Religious grieving represents a recognition of the sacrifice of the community's martyrs and a commitment to strive toward righteousness, whatever the consequences.

The central ritual performances are held during the month of Moharram and commemorate the tragedy at Kerbala, where the grandson of the Prophet, Imam Hossein, and his band of followers were slain by the Ummayid Caliphate.[7] During the first two weeks of Moharram, the entire Iranian Shi'a community is caught up in elaborate rituals of grief. In the small town we studied in Turkish-speaking Azerbaijan from 1972 through 1974, eight religious performing groups staged over three hundred operatic dramas during a twelve-day period. These dramas, known as *ta'zieh* (or as *shabih* in Turkish), reenacted the events of the martyrdom; in each performance, one of the beloved of the Imam was portrayed as begging permission to go to the field of battle, bidding tearful farewells to mother, wife, betrothed, or kin, and requesting unpaid social debts be forgiven. As each player went to his death, the audience (which numbered in the hundreds for each drama) wept openly, beat their chests, and grieved. Separate performances were held for men and women, and many women were unable or forbidden to attend these public ta'zieh. However, the dramas were complemented by *marsieh* or *rawzeh*, held in homes and hosted by women, which were less elaborate musical ceremonies recounting the deaths of the martyrs and the tragic plight of their female kin left behind as prisoners.

The commemorations of this central religious event are associated not only with grief and modulated sadness but also with a paradigmatic cluster of emotions: guilt and repentance, righteous anger, and these fused in identification with the martyred. Participants are reminded that the ritual has its origins in the gathering at Kerbala of the ''Penitents,'' the Muslims of Kufa who had invited Imam Hossein to join them but abandoned him when the armies of the Caliph squashed a potential insurrection. Male participants in the ritual athletically pound their chests and strike their backs with chains, enacting not only their grief but their sharing of the community's guilt for its failure to be faithful. They also express their outrage at the perpetrators of ''the awful deed,'' a rage that historically spilled over into religious riots directed against Sunni Muslim, Christian, and Jewish minorities during Moharram. This passion was channeled into antigovernment demonstrations during the early phases of the Islamic revolution in 1978, and into anti-American demonstrations during the hostage crisis in 1979–80. In the provincial town we studied, some of the most ardent participants in the rituals—the ''madmen of Hossein''—directly expressed their identification with the martyrdom of the Imam by donning a white shroud, slashing their heads, and spilling their blood over their shrouds. This was the highest expression of grief interpreted as identification with the suffering and the cause of the martyred.

Many Iranian Muslims of all social classes explicitly and positively interpret their experiences of loss, grieving, and sadness in relation to the suffering of the community of martyrs. Most children first learn to grieve as a religious activity. The bereaved are comforted by reminders that their losses are like those of the kin of the martyrs, and they are encouraged to transform their personal grief into religious sentiment.

Since the Iranian revolution, the meanings of this tradition have been transformed. For participants in the revolution, political action and martyrdom replaced symbolic action and remembrance. Khomeini's call to act on religious sentiments continues to motivate a large segment of Iranian society. For many Iranians, however, including those in exile, the tradition of Moharram has been hideously distorted. The clergy, by taking on the mantle of authority, no longer represents the ideal of justice over repressive secular regimes. The traditional Shi'ite interpretation of grief as a religious emotion and of society and history as the stage for forces of justice and unrighteousness is thus challenged to the core, leaving the exiles ambivalent about their religious heritage and cynical.

Iranians, of course, have never all shared positive regard for the religious tradition. Status groups differed in their interpretation of Islam, and for non-Muslim groups such as Jewish Iranians, the tradition is anathema. Nearly all Iranians, however, share an underlying appreciation for the tragic, which is represented in secular literature, poetry, and the arts, and carried to the interpretation of history.

Despair and the Tragic in the Modern Secular Tradition

Secular Iranian literary works, including classical poetry and modern writings and film, provide an alternative discourse on dysphoria and its relation to society and history. They focus, however, on the same fundamental issue as the religious tradition—the struggle of the individual to maintain inner purity in the face of repressive social conditions and the meaning of melancholy and despair in this social context. In addition, they explicitly explore the boundary between pathology and a valued sense of the tragic, exploring the meaning of despair, pathological grief, and suicide. We will briefly illustrate with twentieth-century literary examples.

Two classic modern novels—*The Blind Owl* by Sadeq Hedayat (1937) and *The School Principal* by Jalal Al-e Ahmad (1958)—focus on the individual in despair. In Hedayat's surrealistic novel, sorrow and despair are not only the obsession of the author but have been perceived as pathological by Iranian commentators. The novel had a powerful influence on contemporary Iranian writers and intellectuals, who found in the book "the heroic black pessimism of a pure spirit refusing to be tainted with contemporary Iranian social and moral degeneration" (Hillman 1978:2). Al-e Ahmad, a contemporary writer, found in *The Blind Owl* "a new language, unnerving and full of melancholia . . . a surrealistic and strange anecdote full of sorrow and nostalgia" (1978:29). Hedayat's earlier short stories (1930, 1932) dwell on suicide and death of the self, and in 1951 Hedayat became a literary cause by committing suicide in Paris. Following his suicide, he was variously extolled as a fugitive from the triviality of his own society and criticized for "resorting to such a romantic antic" (Al-e Ahmad 1974:25).

Al-e Ahmad's *The School Principal* presents despair phenomenologically as tedious frustration and examines it in the context of the author's social critique of the Iranian educational system. Al-e Ahmad went on to focus social criticism on the enchantment of the Iranian bourgeoisie with the West, coining the term *Gharbzadegi*, "West-struckness," for the condition (1962), and notes with irony the uselessness of Western educated Iranians within Iranian culture and society (1974:13−18).

These and other modern Iranian writers provided a discourse that became central to Iranian students, intellectuals, and immigrants as they struggled to criticize the repression of their society and to express the conflicts between their cultural identity and their attraction to the West. These same issues are prominent in the discourse of Iranian patients.

One further example illustrates artistic exploration of an idiom commonly used by depressed Iranian patients. The film *Gav, The Cow*, based on a short story by writer and psychiatrist Gholam Hossein Sa'edi and produced by Daryoush Mehrjui, was one of the most popular Iranian films among the educated and intellectual middle classes of the late Pahlavi era. As noted by Fischer (1984:15), such films became "an important arena of discussion and self-reflection for the modern, new classes about themselves, about their relation to other classes, and about their cultural roots." The film features a villager who adores his cow and adorns it with beads and caresses. While he is briefly absent from the village, his neighbors discover the cow has died; they hide the body and debate how to break the devastating news to its owner. When he returns, his neighbors deny the cow's death, telling him it has wandered away, and attempt to soften the shock of the news. The man increasingly suspects his neighbors' denials, becomes withdrawn in quiet grief, and in scenes presented with tragic hilarity, eventually becomes mad with sorrow, finally settling in the stable and becoming the cow he has lost. The film is a remarkable commentary on the line between appropriate sorrow and pathological grief that leads to depression and madness. It is also art in an ironic voice, choosing pathos and comic style to enhance self-recognition and to criticize the Iranian mode of dealing with the news of death and with bereavement.

These secular literary works treat cultural themes prominent in the discourse of Iranian patients—pathological grief, feelings of entrapment in repressive social relations, the desire to maintain self-integrity unsullied by demeaning social conditions, and despair at the awareness of the disjunction of the idealized inner self and outward social actions. These issues have special poignance for Iranian immigrants.

The Immigrant Experience

The most salient structural and historical situation that framed the discourse on depression for those Iranians who participated in our clinical and survey research was the immigrant or refugee experience. Iranian immigrants' sense of being cut off from their cultural roots, their "up-rootedness" (see Coehlo and Ahmad 1980), and their loss of family, friends, homeland, and way of life is compounded by serious pressures from the American immigration service and by the increasingly repressive situation in Iran. Iranians who previously could maintain contact with home and yet live in the United States are more and more giving up hope of ever returning to Iran. Nearly all immigrants not only struggle with grief over their lost home and culture but are faced with adjusting and adapting to new cultural expectations and behavioral norms. For many, the grief is unresolvable, at least for a period, and results in depression. The themes of loneliness, sensitivity to being different and incompetent in American ways, fears of the fracturing of traditional family patterns of relating and communicating, and heightened mistrust and anger are particularly prominent for Iranian immigrant patients. There is special irony to being American immigrants for many Iranians. Having struggled to develop and maintain an Iranian identity in the face of growing intellectual influence from the West, they now must come to terms with the West as refugees seeking asylum. Thus the issue of how to maintain inner purity and still relate to the social order without loss of self or resort to despair is an important cultural theme in this new context and shapes the discourse of the clinically depressed.

Depressive Illness in Iranian Culture

Whereas in some societies, the expression of anger is central to the assertion of selfhood and self-worth (Schieffelin 1976; Rosaldo 1980; Chagnon 1977), in Iranian society the experience and competent communication of sadness and grief is essential to establish personal depth. Viewed from a cultural deviance model of psychiatric disorder, one might therefore hypothesize that dysphoria, labeled illness in American society, would be valued and sanctioned as normal rather than be considered sickness in Iranian culture. Our ethnographic and clinical experience indicates this is not true. Iranians value sadness, but they experience depression as *nârâhati*, distress, and seek care. Clinical depression is seen in psychiatric settings in a very recognizable form. However, it is articulated by patients in distinctive Iranian idioms and is interpreted by sufferers and their families using distinctive explanatory frames. Depressive symptoms are associated with verbal and behavioral syndromes that often leave American therapists puzzled. We will briefly indicate the meaning of the domain nârâhati, then outline several distinctive symptom complexes typically associated with depressive illness by Iranian patients.

The Domain of Nârâhati[8]

Iranians commonly complain of being nârâhat—"not comfortable," upset, or in distress. This general state of the person encompasses a wide range of conditions, from that of being upset by a conflicted social relationship, to that of experiencing a wide range of general anxiety and depressive symptoms, to more severe conditions of psychological breakdown or illness. A person who is severely troubled may be labeled as having a sickness of the nerves (*maraz-e a'sâb*) or a psychological illness (*maraz-e ravâni*) or, when most severely disturbed, as being crazy or mad (*divâneh*), all of which are stigmatizing (Good n.d.). The state of nârâhati provides the boundary between one who is melancholy in a valued sense and one who is troubled or ill.

The complaint of being nârâhat is very diffuse; it includes a range of mixed and undifferentiated anxiety and depressive phenomena in a manner similar to Leff's (1981) description of societies that do not distinguish the two forms of experience. However, there are a rich set of descriptors in Iranian languages (Persian, Turkish, etc.) used to label and express particular symptoms, indicate general syndromes, and describe etiology or associated social conditions. While there is a formal Persian term for depression—*afsordegi*—it is not commonly used in popular discourse. Symptoms of nârâhati typically include feelings of sadness and grief (*gham o gosseh*), which may be in reaction to loss or death, to ritual mourning or bereavement. They also include rumination or excessive worry (*ziâdi fekr kardan*) associated with various problems of living, poverty, or the difficulties of uprootedness, and include anxiety (*negarâni*) arising from interpersonal conflict, problems with the American bureaucracy, and fears of being deported, or general insecurity (for immigrants). In addition, symptoms of nârâhati include feelings of weakness and a variety of somatic complaints.

Labeled popular illness categories do not map directly onto specific depressive or anxiety disorders, as defined by psychiatric nosology; they describe typical syndromes of distress. *Nârâhati-e qalb* (distress of the heart) labels a condition associated with physical sensations of heart palpitations, pressure on the chest, and a sensation of the heart being squeezed. The heart is popularly conceived as both a central physiological organ and the center of emotion (following the Galenic tradition), and complaints of heart distress are often associated with feelings of sadness or dysphoria as well as anxiety. Heart distress is associated causally and semantically with problems of female sexuality and disorders of womanhood (with pregnancy, childbirth, "lack of blood" and weakness, concerns about fertility, use of the contraceptive pill, and aging) and with interpersonal problems and poverty (see Good 1977; Good and Good 1982; and Good 1980). It is most prevalent among middle-aged women, and rates are higher in the lower social classes (see Good and Good 1982 for prevalence rates).

Distress of the nerves (*nârâhati-e a' sâb*) describes a condition of irritability, weakness and tiredness, lack of patience in interpersonal relations, and "nervousness." A more acute manifestation, which may also be associated with heart distress, occurs when an individual is "angry" (*'asabâni*, from *a' sâb* or nerves) or irritable (*'asabi*), quick to take offense, and inappropriate in social interaction.

Distress is explained by several common etiological idioms. It is more likely to arise in an individual who is "sensitive" (*hassâs*), a personality characteristic explained in terms of one's childhood, or in one whose physiological temperament is imbalanced (e.g., by having too little blood). It may be caused by conflicted social relationships, embarrassment or shame, or by "fright." The etiological idiom "fright" is invoked to explain distress or illness in terms of sudden stress or shock, in particular the sudden breaking of bad news to an individual, especially if the person is not surrounded by a supportive kin network (Good and Good 1982).

Research is not currently available to determine the relationship between specific psychiatric diseases and these symptoms or idioms of distress, labeled syndromes, and etiologic discourses, although we believe such research is feasible and would clarify the relationship between Iranian culture and psychiatric disease. Our clinical research, however, suggests that several of these are typical in the discourse and experience of Iranians suffering from depressive illness. In American clinical settings, they are often communicated as symptoms or complaints; because clinicians are unaware of the syndromes of meaning associated with each of these complaints, they often interpret them narrowly as isolated psychiatric symptoms ("heart palpitations," "anxiety") and fail to pursue their cultural significance.

The following analysis of the discourse of depressed Iranian patients is based on clinical work with students and immigrants seen in several different psychiatric settings. We refer specifically to interviews with the following four patients.

A Refugee. Mr. Tehrani, a single, thirty-five-year-old university graduate, left Iran three months prior to the interview analyzed here, and had been in the United States only two weeks at first contact for psychiatric care. He met DSM-III criteria for major depressive disorder; he characterized himself as "depressed" and attributed his depression to sadness and loss, to his experiences in Iran, and to his sensitive personality and personal and family history. He had one previous episode of depression as a young university student in England, which led him to return to Iran. He later spent five years in an American university, where he received a bachelor's degree. Upon his return to Iran, he held a high level management position in a technical bureaucracy within the government. He left Iran surreptitiously when conditions became intolerable

A Student Immigrant. Mrs. Zohreh, a married twenty-nine-year-old university student, had been living in the United States for nine years at the time of the interview. She first presented to a university medical clinic in 1979 with weight loss and epigastric pain (tentatively diagnosed as due to reflex esophagitis) two months after marriage. She soon became pregnant, and her chart notes that she had fainting spells, was nervous and depressed, was fatigued and often spent much of the day in bed, had poor appetite, and reported marital difficulties. She was referred for psychiatric treatment in 1981 when she became more severely anorexic, three months after suddenly learning that her father had died almost a year before. She was seen in brief psychotherapy for several months, missing nearly half of her scheduled appointments; therapy ended when she tried to arrange marital counseling with her husband. Her discharge diagnosis was dysthymic disorder and marital problems. She identified her depression as resulting from isolation, an unhappy marriage, and the "shock" of the news of her father's death.

An Iranian Jewish Businessman. Mr. Davoudi, a thirty-five-year-old former retail merchant, immigrated to the United States shortly after Khomeini came to power. His sense of frustration in trying to re-estabish himself in a meaningful business and his anxiety about the future led him, in his view, to become "really nervous," irritable, easily angered, and mistrustful of his wife and family. He experienced psychological crises as a late adolescent, but these had largely resolved after he established his own retail business and independence from his father. He became troubled and was diagnosed as depressed before leaving Iran.[9] He was treated with antidepressants and began weekly psychotherapy sessions shortly after arriving in the United States.

A Socially Incompetent Young Mother. Mrs. Homa, a twenty-seven-year-old Iranian woman, first emigrated from Iran to Israel with her parents when she was a teenager. There she married an Iranian, and both she and her husband emigrated to the United States one year prior to the interview. Mrs. Homa sought treatment because she constantly fought with her family and her husband, was nervous and unhappy, and was without energy and anorexic; she had recently been given antidepressant medication. She related her sense of extreme unhappiness to her being angry ('asabâni) and lonely, and to her lack of maturity, excessive sensitivity, and feelings of worthlessness, for which she blamed her parents and her immigrant status.

These four patients described their problems using key symbolic elements in the Iranian lexicon of distress. When explored, each of these core symbols condense a complex of personal meanings, broader cultural themes, and experiences associated both with traditional Iranian marital conflicts and the special social and historical situation of Iranian immigrants. Four key symbolic domains are represented in the discourse of depressed Iranian patients.

1. Sadness and Grief (*Gham o Gosseh*)—Dysphoric Mood and Depressive Illness

> Everything has two sides—a bad and a good. Depressive character is the bad side of sadness, of the tragic sense.
>   —Mr. Tehrani, a depressed Iranian patient

Whether they express their distress in specifically emotional terms—as sadness, loss, loneliness, and feelings of worthlessness—or in more

somatic idioms of nerves or pain, these patients all seemed quite prepared to reflect on their personal feelings and its grounding in their social
conditions. Mr. Tehrani was most explicit. When asked what brought
him to visit the psychiatrist, he responded without hesitation, "I'm
depressed." He immediately went on to ground his depression in the
experience of being a refugee, and in the conditions in Iran from which
he fled.

> "I left Iran three months ago and left my mother and younger brother
> behind. You know that people are very close there and love each other. But
> no one is free, everyone is under pressure because of Khomeini. I was
> depressed in Iran for the past year, but now it is at its peak. Right now, I
> have no country, no family, no house. In Iran I had everything. I had a
> ten-year job with a ministry and was head of a department. For some time
> [after the revolution], I thought I could live in Iran. But then I couldn't any
> longer. All these people arbitrarily killed right on the street, being shot
> outside the window . . . friends too. [He suddenly burst into tears
> intensely and with deep feeling.] For a year, I was confused. What is the
> right way for my life? I suddenly decided to leave."

Mr. Tehrani expressed an enormous sense of loss, sorrow, and guilt at
having left his kin behind. He described experiencing classic symptoms
of major depression.

> "I have sadness, depression, that says it. I can't concentrate, especially in
> the morning. I smoke, chain smoke. I am restless in the morning. In
> Europe, I'd wake up at 2 a.m. and smoke cigarettes. I have no appetite. I
> eat only after 5 p.m. I'm restless. I don't want to eat."

He reflected in an obsessive and agitated manner on the course his life
had taken since he left Iran.

> "I am depressed. Everyone in Iran is depressed. I left three old women in
> Iran, my ninety-two-year-old grandmother, my mother, and my *naneh*
> [nursemaid]. I didn't support the system. Everyone was depressed. But
> when I got to Paris, I realized I was alone. The situation is worse than it was
> in Iran. I'm very alone. People in this country don't talk, don't touch, don't
> care about each other. I think now, what is my future? What will happen to
> my family in Iran? I've thought of going all the way back, but they will kill
> me. I don't care about my life, but someone likes me. My mother, my
> brother. . . . I'm thinking about my past life. Why did I sell my car? Why
> did I sell my house? Why did I leave my family alone? Why did I forget my
> responsibilities? Why? Why? Why? It's hopeless thinking about this kind
> of thing. . . . I have no energy. It's very difficult to do anything. It's a
> major effort to go out. I don't want to think about doing anything."

Mr. Tehrani explored the relationship between depression and his culture's sense of the tragic with us.

> "People in Iran are *ghamgin* [sad] because of the system, history, dictatorship. They cry easier than they laugh. It is because of the culture; it is deep. When you understand sadness, you can understand people better. Right now, Iranian people understand happiness is very good, because they are sad. Now that I'm sad, I understand what happiness is. [We asked about people who laugh or joke easily.] We say if people have an easy laugh, it is because they don't understand this life doesn't have a point to it. We understand tragedy better. Our history is tragedy—tragedy after tragedy. Dr. Mossadeq[10] for instance. Right now Khomeini's system is based on tragedy: Cry and be sad! The entire sense of the tragic and of tragic character is Iranian. You have to understand tragedy if you want to socialize with people."

Mr. Tehrani described how his family had given meals for the poor during Moharram when he was a child. He went on to express his anger at Khomeini's distortion of the Shi'a tradition and his ambivalence about the traditional frame for interpreting grief.

> "If religion gives power to someone like Khomeini, who is able to kill everybody, I don't like this religion. Imam Hossein is a good subject on which to cry [said with anger and irony]. Right now I feel depressed. When I cry I feel better. Crying is good for you. A kind of catharsis. Religious crying makes one feel better. No one thought of Imam Hossein. It got to be all politics. Now they kill in the name of God. They don't understand God."

Mr. Tehrani's discourse on depression represents his efforts to interpret the current situation in Iran and his own depression in terms of the cultural symbols of Shi'ite Iran. The Islamic view of the tragic and of sadness have special irony for him in the context of the Iranian revolution. The redeeming characteristics of grief as a response to an unjust society's cruel treatment of the just have been distorted and exploited by the current regime. This distortion challenged his ability to endow the troubled social order with meaning, transforming his experience of sadness and his vision of life's tragic trajectory into a frustrated depression.

The case of Mrs. Zohreh, outlined above, illustrates the integration of dysphoria into two other typical social contexts. Although her primary symptoms were somatic—epigastric pain and anorexia—Mrs. Zohreh was quick to reflect on her feelings and the social stresses she saw as causal. First, she described a very conflicted marriage to a man who is more traditional, less educated, and of lower social class than she. She said she made the mistake of marrying a man because she thought she could help him. However, he is jealous, accuses her of not having been a virgin at marriage (though she was), refuses to allow her to go out alone with her friends, throws tantrums at home, and is abusive to her in front of her friends. She is extraordinarily isolated. If she were in such a traditional marriage in Iran, she would have family members to associate with regularly who would provide her support. Here she is alone.

Mrs. Zohreh also described an experience that occurs fairly commonly in the Iranian immigrant community but is puzzling to American clinicians. Early in our conversation, she mentioned that her father had died in Iran more than a year ago, but that she had only learned of it three months ago. Later she described how she has become easily startled or frightened, describing how frightened she had been when she suddenly heard of the radio of an earthquake in her family's region of Iran and how she had telephoned to find out if everyone was all right. Her family assured her everyone was well, she told us, her voice trailing off. Knowing what was implied, we asked if she believed them. She said she did not know, then told us how she had learned of her father's death. Her family had hidden the death from her, fearing that she would be "frightened" or "shocked" if she learned the news while she was away from her family and friends. However, a cousin living in another state was accidentally told the news and immediately called the patient (at 2:00 in the morning) to tell her of the death of her father. She went into a state of shocked grief. She was particularly angry at her husband for his response at that time.

> "My husband got upset. He is very upset, but he didn't help me. He thought too much about himself. . . . I wanted a rawzeh [a religious gathering in which the ritual grief poetry is sung], but he said no, it isn't necessary. Your father died a year ago. We needed it to help our feelings, especially my brother [who lives in a town in the same state]. My husband didn't help, he didn't like the idea. So we finally had a mullah come over and say prayers at our home. We had to do it ourselves."

Given the extensive ritualization of grief in Iranian culture, one might expect that Iranians would deal openly and intimately with death. Instead, there is a great deal of institutionalized denial associated with death of a close relative. It is widely agreed, among all social classes in Iran, that to receive tragic news while one is alone or away from one's family can lead to a "fright" illness (Good and Good 1981, 1982). As a result, Iranians in the United States are often not told of the death of a relative until they return to Iran months or even years later. As a result, when Iranians hear the denial of bad news, they are always suspicious. This clinical case is a counterpart to the situation portrayed in the movie *Gav* (discussed above).

The expression of sadness and grief is thus associated with culturally distinctive complexes of experience—those associated with having to flee Iran in the face of personal threat and accept life in a very different society, living in repressive marital relationships, and the traumatic and "fright-producing" discovery that a family member has died sometime in the past. These experiences are commonly associated with complaints of dysphoric affect for Iranian patients.

2. *'Asabâni*—Anger

Uncontrollable anger is commonly expressed as a symptom by Iranians suffering depression. The word *'asabâni* or anger has its root in the word *a' sâb* or nerves. It refers to a state in which a person is irritable, agitated, easily angered, nervous, and loses self-control in social interactions. If a person becomes angry in public or has inappropriate fights within the household, that person will be described as being *'asabâni* and in need of treatment. It is an important Iranian ideal to maintain self-control and to be competent in highly stylized forms of polite communication (*adab*) in public interactions. Expressing anger to a person in front of others leads to acute shame and often a breach in a relationship that can only be repaired if the person who caused the embarrassment humbles himself and begs to be excused. In general, being angry is not experienced as a cathartic release or as an acceptable element of one's social repertoire. Thus, unlike sadness, anger associated with depression is particularly stigmatized and experienced as a symptom of disorder.

Several of the patients interviewed sought care specifically because they began to become angry and have fights in their homes. Mr. Davoudi sought care from a psychiatrist after he had had a fight and hit his wife. He said the condition began when he was in Iran during the revolution, particularly after he was picked up by the Revolutionary Guard for questioning.

> "I was very nervous. I used to shout and be angry at the children. At the time, I thought everybody was lying to me. I talked to my wife and said, there is something wrong with me, something is going on."

He began to experience "heart distress" and went to a doctor, thinking
he might have cardiac problems.

> "I went to the doctor for that. I had some pain in my chest. I thought there
> was something wrong with my heart. He said it was just the nerve, the pain
> and everything. There is nothing wrong with the heart or blood pressure.
> He told me, you know when you blame yourself, you have all those pains
> inside. I just think that I was making myself . . . I was real nervous, I just
> got angry, when I started shaking.
>
> [Would you call yourself 'asabâni since you have been here?] Very
> much. Some of the time I'm very cool [*khunsard*, 'cool blooded'], I try to
> be cool. When I get angry, I can't stop myself. As a child I would get out of
> control. But I had never been out of control that bad. Even when I am real
> angry, I can stand back and behave myself. . . . the reason I came to the
> doctor was that I got angry, not just slap my wife's face and then afterward
> become calm, but you know I . . . it's the second time in the last ten years.
> I said there must be something wrong with me. I should . . . I never . . . I
> tried to . . . not get really angry, not do that anymore."

Anger was thus experienced by Mr. Davoudi as loss of self-control and
as shameful and guilt provoking.

Mrs. Homa also sought psychiatric treatment, presenting primarily
with "anger."

> "I am not happy with my life. I have many problems with my husband and
> with my child. I am always sad, and I do not enjoy life. I have many pains in
> my back and neck, and I went to a doctor and he said it comes because 'you
> are angry, very angry.' And that's the reason I came to the psychia-
> trist. . . . I think my life will stop because I am very angry and I can't be a
> friend or find friends. I can't play with my child, I can't speak with my
> husband. If there is something I don't like, I go crazy and become angry. I
> can't stop myself."

She described herself as having become a very angry child when her
family emigrated to Israel when she was thirteen. She said she and her
mother would often fight, then become *qahr* with each other, that is
formally stop speaking. When her family moved from Iran to a "freer"
society, her parents put very strict controls on her. Now she had moved
again with her husband. She described herself poignantly—as not having an identity, as never having grown up, as not being a real woman.
Thus her depression and her anger were grounded in more basic problems of selfhood.

In both of these cases, the "anger" associated with depression, rather
than the sadness, triggered care seeking. Angry behavior in Iranian

culture is associated with insult and loss of control; such behavior is stigmatizing and a threat to essential, supportive relationships. This labeled behavioral syndrome is thus a primary marker of pathology for those experiencing dysphoria.

3. Insecurity and Mistrust

Issues of trust and mistrust are widespread themes in the talk of Iranians about each other and in social scientists' interpretations of Iranian culture (Zonis 1971; Banuazizi 1977; Beeman 1976). The discourse of mistrust is especially prominent for Iranians experiencing depression. For the depressed, mistrust is often exaggerated and focused on fears or delusions of infidelity on the part of a marriage partner, thus linking depression to a major aspect of Iranian kin and gender relations. Fear of a wife's infidelity is a basic psychocultural issue for Iranians; personal and family honor and religious purity are bound together in a woman's virginity until marriage, and her modesty and fidelity thereafter. A man's jealous attention to his wife is both a romantic ideal and a recognized pathology. For the depressed, this jealousy may reach delusional proportions.

Mistrust and paranoia are often focused both on Iranians of opposing political affiliations (explored dramatically in the recent Iranian film *The Mission*) and by immigrants, on the American government and American people. It is difficult to sort out paranoia from reality, given the historical experience of Iranian immigrants. Although such mistrust is part of the common discourse within Iranian culture, it becomes exacerbated and a major theme in the discourse of Iranians suffering depression.

Jealousy and delusions of marital infidelity were important themes for the patients interviewed. We described how Mrs. Zohreh's husband insinuated that she was not a virgin at marriage. She said that because his previous wife cheated on him, "deep inside he cannot believe that I won't leave him." He therefore prevents her from going out of the house to be with friends.

Mr. Davoudi also described having an irrational mistrust of his wife.

"I was very upset. I thought my wife was lying to me, that I couldn't trust her. I knew all the time it was wrong, but I couldn't help it. So I decided to see the doctor. [He went on to say he had experienced the same feelings about a girlfriend he had when he was a student in London. We asked if his feelings of mistrust had changed with therapy.] Very little . . . but other

problems, feeling sad most of the time, that's better. Wanting to be alone.
[Is that bad?] Yes. I just felt I wanted to be alone. We used to sit and listen to
music, being happy. I can't do that now. Maybe the reason is mistrust.
Someone who tries to be friendly may be just trying to rob my pocket, to get
close to the family or something. That was my feeling."

Our clinical experience indicates that while nearly all Iranian immigrants have experienced loss of important sources of self-esteem—their
work, their businesses, their kin, as well as more routine abilities to
function as competent linguistic and social actors—such experiences
take on new meaning for the depressed. They develop increasing feelings of worthlessness, are self-conscious about their relation to American society, feel unworthy of love, and as a result begin to feel that those
around them may not love them. This then stimulates a culturally
prevalent jealousy and mistrust of spouse, especially by men of their
wives. It also increases their experience of other Iranians as untrust-
worthy and of Americans as threatening. Thus mistrust and paranoia
become prominent in the complaints of the depressed.

4. *Hassâsiyat*—Sensitivity

"They think I am very, very angry. I don't know if I'm sensitive or angry, I
don't know. [What is the difference?] Angry is to be like sick, to be sick,
but sensitive is what you are, what you're born."

—Mrs. Homa

When trying to interpret the cause of an experience of emotional
distress or depression, Iranian patients often describe themselves as
being "sensitive" (hassâs). They describe themselves as being more
sensitive to difficulties in their social environment and thus more
bothered by such problems than other persons. When asked about the
roots of sensitivity, they often tell about difficult experiences in their
childhood. The core self or inner feelings of a sensitive person are
especially vulnerable to disruption and distress; they are less shielded by
formal public interactions, more exposed to disruption by conflict or
"fright" than are the feelings of others. The sensitivity idiom thus links
stressors in the environment with childhood experiences and personal
character and is used to interpret dysphoria and depression etiologically.

All four of the patients discussed here described themselves as unusually sensitive. Mr. Tehrani described his response to events in Iran
and his depression as rooted in his childhood experiences.

> "I was twelve when my parents divorced. My brother was nine. My mother and father didn't care for children. I was very, very sensitive. . . . Every day, my parents fought. It was hard for us. There was fighting and anger."

He went on to give examples.

> "When studying, I couldn't tolerate noise. I'd get angry ['asabâni] easily; I fought with my family. This was as a child. The reason I am sensitive is because of my background. My mother was so young, sixteen years old. She didn't understand what a child is. She was a child herself. . . . Being sensitive was a very bad problem. I cried a lot when I was young, I was so sensitive."

Mr. Tehrani contrasted his response to the current events in Iran with that of his brother.

> "My brother—he is working for a company, has two kids and his wife. He wasn't sensitive about these problems. He doesn't read the newspaper, listen to TV or the radio. He ignores the killings. My brother understood from the first day that Khomeini is not good for Iran, and he started to work for himself and his family."

Mr. Davoudi also described his sensitivity to events in Iran, which ultimately led him to give up his country, as being rooted in his childhood. He described how sensitive he was to social interactions as a child, how he would be hurt if he tried to help someone and it was not reciprocated, and blamed his parents.

> "To tell the truth, the problem with people my parents' age is that they think you can solve all problems with money. . . . They didn't train us how to act, how to have relationships with other people. That's the way they are, they've been trained in this way. I've never had a one-hour conversation with my father . . . which is very important. Talking about ourselves, being friends together. It doesn't mean that I don't care about him or he doesn't care about me."

He concluded our conversation by interpreting his sensitivity and fear that others will take advantage of him in the context of his idealized image of himself as "kind" (*mehrabân*), a quality of personhood highly valued in Iranian culture.

> [How would you characterize yourself right now? What kind of person are you?] "To my brother, I try to be a father, to do what they haven't done for him. To my child, I try to be a good father. . . . And if you asked my wife, she would probably say he is a good husband, he is kind [mehrabân]. I am. I

> accept that. The time I blame myself is when I do something for someone
> else, and then need something in return and they don't reciprocate. I blame
> myself for being a fool. Even if the same person comes asking for some-
> thing, I don't say no. . . . I have had very bad times the last several
> months, and I tell myself not to be kind anymore. I want to change my
> character . . . but I can't. You can't change your personality that has been
> with you for years.''

Thus, the sensitivity idiom provides a discourse for interpreting one's depression as being caused by a special vulnerability to hurtful aspects of social relations or public events, a vulnerability rooted in enduring characteristics of the person developed in childhood. It is a quality that leads to distress (nârâhati) and to anger and conflict. Feeling pain, however, is inevitable for one who is sensitive to conflict and injustice in the world and is kind and generous and strives to live justly.

Conclusion of Clinical Study

It has been our goal to identify several aspects of discourse prominent in our interviews with depressed Iranian patients and to describe the network of meanings and associated experiences to which they refer. First, we found that Iranians have a well-developed affective discourse related to sadness, loss, and grieving. This discourse is grounded in a culturally shaped conception of selfhood, in a highly ritualized tradition of religious grieving, and in a tragic view of history and society shared by religious and secular thinkers in Iranian culture. Second, the immigrant experience frames all other aspects of experience for Iranians in the United States; it necessitates grief work and results in depression. The reality of the losses and life changes are interpreted in terms of traditional Iranian discourse. Third, we found in our interviews with clinically depressed patients four specific forms of discourse to be common, focused around ''sadness and grief,'' ''anger,'' ''mistrust,'' and ''sensitivity.'' Each relates to a symbolic domain or cluster of meanings and to experiences associated with those meanings for members of Iranian society.

Finally, while some of the patients we interviewed complained of pain and somatic symptoms, ''somatization'' did not seem prominent among these patients. While a few described experiencing heart distress and had previously sought medical help for it, this was not as prominent a theme as we believed it might be. Discussion of symptoms in terms of the heart and nerves does not seem to be an undifferentiated somatic discourse for Iranians, as Leff (1981) claims it often is for patients in the developing world, but a sophisticated and subtle discourse on affect rooted in traditional understandings and metaphors of the body.

We believe these are common discursive forms used by Iranians for interpreting their experience of depression. In turn, the association of these cultural forms with depression leads to a shaping of the Iranian depressive experience, making relevant contexts of meaning and networks of experience that lend a distinctive character to depression in Iranian society.

SYMPTOM COMPLEXES AMONG IRANIAN IMMIGRANTS: A FACTOR ANALYTIC STUDY

In Spring 1981, we had the opportunity to participate in a brief quantitative survey of psychiatric symptoms among Jewish Iranian women, most of whom had recently immigrated to California. Moradi was invited to speak to a Jewish Iranian cultural organization in California about psychological difficulties associated with immigration. We decided to use the opportunity to develop and administer a brief questionnaire to test hypotheses based on our ethnographic and clinical experience. In particular, we were interested in identifying the range of losses experienced by Iranian immigrants and investigating the relationship between the experience of loss and psychological symptoms. Second, we were interested in investigating whether psychological symptoms cluster together in a culture-specific fashion, revealing the cultural patterning of psychological distress, or whether analysis would reveal more universal factors similar to those derived from analysis of psychological symptoms among Americans.

We developed a short, Persian-language instrument designed to elicit losses and measure level of psychological symptoms. First, we recorded basic demographic data, including number of years in the United States. Second, we asked respondents to list the five most important things they had lost by leaving Iran. We asked for losses in this open-ended way because we had no data on which to construct a scale. We also asked respondents to indicate where family members and close friends reside, in order to measure loss of close relationships and level of support. Third, the authors prepared a Persian translation of the Brief Symptom Index (BSI), a short form of the Hopkins Symptom Checklist 90

(HSCL-90) (Derogatis 1977). The BSI consists of fifty-three psychological symptoms; respondents are asked to rate, on a scale of 0 (= not at
all) to 4 (= extremely), how much they have been bothered by each
symptom during the past two weeks. Based on studies of various American populations, the BSI has been factor analyzed into nine subscales:
depression, anxiety, somatization, interpersonal sensitivity, hostility,
obsessive-compulsiveness, phobic anxiety, paranoid ideation, and psychoticism. The items and subscales of the SCL-90 were developed
through extensive research with populations of psychiatric patients in the
United States, and the SCL-90 and the BSI have been widely used
among psychiatric patients, primary care patients, and nonpatient populations in this country (see Murphy 1982 for a review).

As discussed earlier in this chapter, we have reservations about
translating a symptom checklist derived from work with an American
population for use in another culture. In spite of our hesitancy, we chose
to do so for this study because the opportunity for the research arose
suddenly and we had a very short time to develop an instrument. In
addition, our goal was to compare symptom factors for American and
Iranian populations, and this instrument served our purposes well. It is
also our feeling that the most important symptom domains of Iranian
depressed patients are included in the BSI as translated, although were
we to use the instrument in the future we would add several items derived
from our clinical work.

We proposed three hypotheses. First, we hypothesized that psychological symptoms in general, and depressive symptoms in particular,
would decrease with number of years in the United States (i.e., would be
less among cohorts residing longer in this country). Our clinical and
ethnographic experience suggested that Iranian immigrants grieve their
loss of family, home, work, country, and culture, especially since travel
between the United States and Iran has been severely restricted. We
believed these losses would be worked through as grief work, leading to
a decline of depressive symptoms, especially after one to two years.[11]

Second, we predicted that psychological symptoms would cluster in
culturally meaningful patterns. We hypothesized factors would not
merely reflect universal psychophysiological patterns, but would also
represent semantic domains, including items that "go together" in the
Iranian immigrant experience and represent primary meaning contexts in
Iranian culture. It should be noted that the questionnaire was administered to a nonclinical population, and that even the empiricist paradigm
would not predict symptoms to cluster in DSM-III categories. However,

factor analyses of symptom checklists administered in African and other cultural groups have suggested that several factors—"physiological anxiety, topical depression, health preoccupation, episodic anxiety"— may be quite similar across cultures (Beiser et al. 1976; Beiser, chap. 9).

Third, we predicted that items measuring anger, mistrust or paranoia, and sensitivity would be related to symptoms of dysphoric mood. We could not predict whether these would be part of a single factor or would form separate but associated factors.

Findings

Respondents constituted an opportunity sample of 126 Jewish Iranian women. Because not all questionnaires were fully completed, factor analysis was conducted for 100 of the respondents. The sample consisted of women aged 16−29 (14%), 30−39 (28%), 40−49 (36%), and 50 or over (24%).

We first tested our hypothesis concerning relation of level of symptoms and years in the United States. In our initial analysis, using mean symptom level and the subscales derived by Derogatis, it was clear that the more recent immigrants experience a higher level of psychiatric distress. Symptom scores were analyzed by years of residence in the United States. The sample was divided into those respondents who had been in residence less than one year and who left after the revolution in 1980−81; those in residence between one and two years, who left Iran during the early stages of the new Islamic Republic in 1979; those in residence between two and three years, who left Iran during the initial protests and turmoil in 1978; and those who were in residence three or more years and left Iran freely. Analysis of variance and analysis of group means utilizing F-tests were performed. Distress appeared to peak for those in the second year of residence in the United States, perhaps because the initial euphoria of leaving Iran had subsided. Global Symptom Index scores (the mean of all 53 items) and scale scores for depression were highest for this group of immigrants; differences in group scores for these two subscales were significant to $< .01$. Although differences in scores on the other subscales were not significant to $< .05$, the two groups of newest immigrants, resident for two years or less, scored consistently highest on all subscales except paranoid ideation.

No significant relationship between age and psychological symptom scale scores emerged, although women aged 16−29 consistently had the lowest scores on all the subscales, and middle-aged women between 30−49 tended to have the highest scores. Married women whose spouses were still in Iran or Europe tended to exhibit more distress than women whose spouses had accompanied them. Significant differences were found on scores for phobic anxiety (p < .01) and somatization (p < .05).

Although we were unable to analyze the relation between level of losses experienced and psychological symptoms, we examined the relationship between specific losses and symptoms. Expression of loss is often conveyed to others and in self-reflection in terms of objects and relationships left behind in Iran. When these Iranian women were asked what were the most important losses experienced by leaving Iran, many mentioned family members and close friends. Political refugees, because they cannot return, must contend with severed relationships. This group of women also experienced sadness over having lost their country, their homeland, and the cultural traditions, music, art, and artifacts that they associated with home. Many also faced material losses—of wealth, social position, their jobs and those of their husbands, their homes. The greatest distress was expressed by the one quarter of the respondents who responded that they had lost their "very life" (*zendegi*). These immigrants scored significantly higher on the BSI Global Symptom Index on depression, somatization, phobic anxiety, and anxiety subscales.

We first examined our hypothesis about the relationship between dysphoria and the symptom complexes identified in the clinical research—anger, mistrust, and sensitivity—by developing a correlation matrix of the Derogatis subscales of the BSI (see table 12.1). If we equate "anger" (ᶜasabâni) with the Hostility subscale, "mistrust" with the Paranoid Ideation subscale, and "sensitivity" with the Interpersonal Sensitivity subscale, our hypothesis is not confirmed. Depression correlates most highly with Anxiety and Psychoticism (which includes several depressionlike items, including "feeling lonely, even when with people"); moderately with Interpersonal Sensitivity; and least with Paranoid Ideation and Hostility.

To test our hypothesis that symptoms would cluster in culturally meaningful patterns, variables were subjected to a factor analysis with varimax rotation, creating an eight-factor solution. Relationships between these factors, and years in the United States and identified losses, were then analyzed using analysis of variance.

TABLE 12.1

CORRELATION MATRIX FOR BSI SUBSCALES, IRANIAN JEWISH WOMEN STUDY

	GSI	DEP	ANX	SOM	PAR	IP	OB/C	HOST	PHOB	PSYCHOT
GSI	—									
DEP	.82									
ANX	.84	.74								
SOMAT	.82	.59	.68							
PAR ID	.69	.52	.52	.47						
INTPERS	.76	.65	.56	.51	.58					
OB/COMP	.85	.67	.71	.71	.53	.58				
HOSTIL	.76	.57	.62	.55	.49	.58	.57			
PHOB ANX	.74	.54	.65	.60	.42	.53	.53	.57		
PSYCHOT	.78	.71	.61	.52	.58	.65	.66	.54	.47	

The Eight-Factor Solution

Our hypothesis that the BSI items would cluster in culturally meaningful constellations that reflect the experience of immigrant Iranians was realized in our eight-factor solution. Although the stability of factors may be limited, given our sample size, each factor clustered items that make sense in light of our clinical and ethnographic data. The first two factors most clearly represent culturally constructed syndromes of distress of Iranian immigrants. Factor I, which we have labeled NÂRÂHATI, includes several of the central elements in the general discourse of "discomfort" described above (pp. 391–393)—obsessive rumination, irritability, and anxiety symptoms. Factor II is a depression factor; it brings together sadness, sensitivity, and mistrust. The remaining six factors represent smaller, less culturally patterned categories, although the meaning of each of these factors needs to be interpreted within the context of the Iranian immigrant experience. A few further comments may indicate how these differ from factors found in other cultures and how scores related to losses and duration of residence in the United States.

Factor I. Nârâhati: "Discomfort," Rumination, and Irritability

This factor includes the primary elements described above as the general domain of nârâhati and nârâhati-e a'sâb or distress of the nerves. It includes rumination or excessive worry (the obsessive-compulsive items), irritability (restlessness), weakness, "anger" (the hostility items), and several somatic complaints ("somatization" items). While the factor includes several items that might be expected on a somatic anxiety scale, most such items load on the phobic anxiety factor (Factor III) and the somatic distress factor (Factor IV).

In the survey sample, new immigrants experience the highest level of symptoms of nârâhati; the longer one has been in the United States, the less one experiences this syndrome (see table 12.2 for details). The frustration of establishing oneself and one's family in a new country, the anxiety of trying to find employment or start a new business in an economically depressed market, and of attempting to live frugally when one has been able to run a profitable business in Iran in the past becomes expressed in this cluster of symptoms. Sadness is not an element in this factor, which primarily captures the sense of frustration and distress of being uprooted rather than the sense of the tragic. In our analysis of immigrant responses, we found that higher factor scores are primarily associated with material losses—of home, wealth, and occupational position of self or spouse—although immigrants who characterized their loss as "their very life" (zendegi) exhibited the highest factor scores for nârâhati. The factor scores of the thirteen women who were separated from their spouses were higher than those of other women; however, there was no statistically significant difference.

FACTOR I. NÂRÂHATI: "DISCOMFORT," RUMINATION, AND IRRITABILITY

Item Content	Factor Loading	BSI Subscale
Mind going blank	.80	OBCOMP
Trouble remembering things	.72	OBCOMP
Trouble concentrating	.69	OBCOMP
Feeling weak in body	.60	SOMAT
Numbness and tingling	.58	SOMAT
Have to check and double-check things	.54	OBCOMP
Something is wrong with my mind	.53	PSYCHOT
Feeling restless	.52	ANX
Trouble getting breath	.51	SOMAT
Feeling easily annoyed, irritated	.50	HOSTIL
Temper outbursts can't control	.47	HOSTIL
Feeling tense and keyed up	.47	ANX
Suddenly scared for no reason	.44	ANX
Nausea and upset stomach	.44	SOMAT

Eigenvalue = 17.5   Percent of variance = 33.1%

TABLE 12.2
ANALYSIS OF VARIANCE OF SCORES ON INDIVIDUAL ITEMS BY YEARS IN U.S.

Item	Level of Significance	High Scoring Groups
Feeling no interest in things	.003	1 and 2
Feeling inferior	.004	1 and 2
Feeling easily annoyed and irritated	.006	2
Feeling lonely	.017	2 and 1
Feeling hopeless about future	.022	2 and 1
Feelings of worthlessness	.025	2

Factor I Scores by Years in U.S.

Less than one year	(1980−81)	.23	(n=18)
One to two years	(1979−80)	.16	(n=20)
Two to three years	(1978−79)	.05	(n=39)
Three or more years	(before 1978)	−.16	(n=23)

F Ratio = .589 n.s.

Factor I Scores by Losses

Loss	Yes	No	T-Test Probability (Separate Variance Est.)
Friends	−.25	.09	.09
"Life"	.27	−.15	.11
Wealth	.15	−.21	.08
Home	.22	−.15	.09

Factor II. Iranian Immigrant Depressive Disorder: Dysphoria and Sensitivity

Factor II brings together dysphoria—sadness, loneliness, feelings of worthlessness, hopelessness about the future—with two of the three symptom syndromes we hypothesized would be associated with depressive affect. Mistrust and paranoia are represented by a number of items, indicating that others are unfriendly or cannot be trusted. Sensitivity (hassâsiyat) is represented by several interpersonal sensitivity items. "Anger," which we found associated with clinical depression, forms a separate factor (Factor VI), although several of the anger symptoms are also part of Factor I. Factor II thus appears as a distinctively Iranian depressive syndrome.

The vegetative symptoms are not part of this factor. That is not surprising, both because this is not a study of depressed patients, who would be most likely to suffer such symptoms, and because such symptoms might be expected to form separate factors (see Uhlenhuth et al.

1983). Indeed Factor IV includes several of the vegetative symptoms that are included in the BSI, where they are associated with "heart distress." It is not clear if this factor marks more severe depressive illness or if it is a general somatic symptom factor.

Scores on Factor II are significantly associated with years spent in the United States; highest scores were found among immigrants resident two years or less, lowest scores among Iranians who immigrated prior to 1978. High scores were associated with expression of losses of "my life" (zendegi), with separation from one's spouse and family members, and with loss of feelings of hope and happiness. The sense of despair, of the tragic, and of sadness is conveyed in this symptom cluster, as are feelings of insecurity due to disrupted relationships and uncertainty about one's worth, position, and future.

A curious relationship between stated losses and symptom scores emerged in the analysis of the survey data. Respondents who stated that one of their most important losses on leaving Iran was close friends (40 percent of the sample) consistently scored lower on all eight factors. This consistent trend suggests that the ability to have and to mourn the loss of close friendships is a mark of a healthier immigrant. Establishing new friendships, adjusting to a new society, and seeking new support groups from within the immigrant community may be an easier task for these people than for those who rely mostly on family members for intimacy and sociability.

FACTOR II. IRANIAN IMMIGRANT DEPRESSIVE DISORDER

Item Content	Factor Loading	BSI Subscale
Feeling people are unfriendly, dislike you	.77	INTPERS
Feeling lonely, even when with people	.62	PSYCHOT
Feeling no interest in things	.62	DEP
Feeling inferior to others	.62	INTPERS
Feeling watched or talked about	.61	PARANOIA
Feeling lonely	.59	DEP
Never feeling close to another person	.54	PSYCHOT
Difficulty in making decisions	.53	OBCOMP
Feeling sad (blue)	.50	DEP
Feeling most people can't be trusted	.50	PARANOIA
Feeling uneasy in crowds	.50	PHOB ANX

Feelings are easily hurt	.50	INTPERS
Feelings of worthlessness	.50	DEP
Feeling self-conscious	.48	INTPERS
Hopeless about the future	.47	DEP
Idea someone can control your thoughts	.45	PSYCHOT

Eigenvalue   2.7   Percent of Variance 5.1%

Factor II Scores by Years in U.S.

Less than one year	(1980−81)	.39
One to two years	(1979−80)	.42
Two to three years	(1978−79)	.03
Three or more years	(prior to 1978)	−.35

F Ratio = 3.09   F Probability = .03

Factor II Scores by Losses

Loss	Yes	No	T-Test Probability
Family	.25	−.12	.07
Friends	−.02	.16	n. s.
"Life"	.52	−.04	.05
Spouse Absent	.51	−.08	.14

Other Factors

The remaining six factors are less distinctively Iranian. Factor III is a fairly clear phobic anxiety factor. Factor IV, associating heart distress with sleep, appetite, and two anxiety symptoms, is not clear; it may be a general somatization syndrome, or may be associated more specifically with anxiety disorders or depressive illness. Factor V condenses obsessions about one's guilt; Factor VI includes the more severe "anger" or hostility items; Factor VII is the suicide item; and Factor VIII includes several specific paranoid complaints.

FACTOR III. FEARFULNESS AND ANXIETY

Item Content	Factor Loading	BSI Subscale
Avoid things because they frighten you	.65	PHOBANX
Afraid to travel in buses, trains	.62	PHOBANX
Feeling fearful	.54	ANX
Afraid in open spaces	.53	PHOBANX
Spells of terror or panic	.49	ANX
Nervous when left alone	.44	PHOBANX
Hot or cold spells	.42	SOMAT

Eigenvalue = 2.2   Percent of variance = 4.1%

Factor III Scores by Years in U.S.

Less than one year	(1980−81)	.05	
One to two years	(1979−80)		.09
Two to three years	(1978−79)	.12	
Three or more years	(before 1978)		−.18

n.s.

FACTOR IV. SOMATIC DISTRESS

Item Content	Factor Loading	BSI Subscale
Pains in heart or chest	.62	SOMAT
Nervousness or shakiness inside	.61	ANX
Faintness or dizziness	.61	SOMAT
Trouble falling asleep	.50	GLOBAL
Poor appetite	.36	GLOBAL

Eigenvalue = 2.05   Percent of variance = 3.9%

Factor IV Scores by Years in U.S.

Less than one year	(1980−81)	.02
One to two years	(1979−80)	.08
Two to three years	(1978−79)	−.22
Three or more years	(before 1978)	.13

n.s.

Factor IV Scores by Losses

Losses	Yes	No	T-Test Probability
Friends	−.37	.15	.01
'Life''	.25	−.15	.06
Home	−.33	.04	.04
Spouse Absent	.28	−.12	.10

FACTOR V. GUILT

Item Content	Factor Loading	BSI Subscale
Idea should be punished for sins	.74	PSYCHOT
Feelings of guilt	.72	GLOBAL
Feeling blocked	.47	OBCOMP

Eigenvalue = 1.8   Percent of variance = 3.5%

Factor V by Years in U.S.

Less than one year	(1980−81)	−.12
One to two years	(1979−80)	.15
Two to three years	(1978−79)	−.15
Three or more years	(before 1978)	−.32

n.s.

FACTOR VI. ANGER AND HOSTILITY: 'ASABÂNI

Item Content	Factor Loading	BSI Subscale
Urges to beat or harm someone	.83	HOSTILITY
Urges to break or smash things	.80	HOSTILITY
Having frequent arguments	.47	HOSTILITY

Eigenvalue = 1.64   Percent of variance = 3.1%

Factor VI by Years in U.S.

Less than one year	(1980−81)	−.17
One to two years	(1979−80)	.16
Two to three years	(1978−79)	−.04
Three or more years	(before 1978)	.27

n.s.

[No significant associations between Factor VI scores and reported losses.]

FACTOR VII. SUICIDAL THOUGHTS

Item Content	Factor Loading	BSI Subscale
Thoughts of ending your life	.70	DEP

Eigen value = 1.6   Percent of variance = 3.0%

Factor VII. Score by Years in U.S.

Less than one year	(1980−81)	−.18
One to two years	(1979−80)	.56
Two to three years	(1978−79)	−.25
Three or more years	(before 1978)	.19

F Ratio = 3.97   F Probability = .01

[No significant associatins between Factor VIII scores and reported losses.]

FACTOR VIII. PARANOIA

Feeling others to blame for trouble	.67	PARA
Feel others do not give you credit	.55	PARA
Feeling people will take advantage	.46	PARA

Eigenvalue = 1.5   Percent of variance = 2.7%

Factor VIII Scores by Years in U.S.

Less than one year   (1980−81)   −.13
One to two years   (1979−80)   −.22
Two to three years   (1978−779)   .00
Three or more years   (before 1978)   .15

                                n.s.

[No significant associations between Factor VIII scores and reported losses.]

Conclusion of Factor Study

First, our hypothesis that psychological distress would decline with years in the United States was confirmed. Symptoms seem to increase slightly or remain about the same for those in their second year of residence, then decline fairly sharply for groups who immigrated earlier. The Iranian Immigrant Depression Factor is most significantly related to years in the United States, suggesting that the grief model may be appropriate for understanding the process of dealing with the losses associated with immigration.

Second, two factors emerged which clearly represent the distinctive syndromes we described, based on our analysis of clinical data. The item content of these two factors (I and II) is significantly different from factors derived from analysis of comparable American data. One factor (Factor II) appears to represent a distinctively Iranian depressive syndrome.

Third, two of the three symptom complexes that our clinical research led us to hypothesize would be associated with dysphoria (mistrust and sensitivity) were joined with symptoms of dysphoric affect in a single depression factor. The third symptom complex (anger) formed a separate factor.

Finally, the individual psychiatric symptoms whose decline correlates most significantly with the respondent's number of years in the United States all load on Factors I and II (see table 2). This further corroborates our suggestion that these two factors represent syndromes of distress specific to Iranian immigrants. Additional research is necessary to clarify the relationship between these factors and psychopathology, including major affective disorder and the anxiety disorders.

Findings of the factor analysis support findings of the clinical research. In the previous section, we argued that symptoms "go to-gether" not simply as reflections of psychophysiological processes or discrete psychiatric diseases but also as syndromes of meaning and experience that are socially and culturally constructed. We identified several syndromes in the discourse of patients. In the factor analysis, we were able to test the hypothesis that symptoms cluster in the fashion we predicted from the clinical research. Findings support our hypotheses and thus our contention that dysphoria and depressive illness is culturally patterned among Iranian immigrants.

CULTURE AND DEPRESSION—REFLECTIVE, CONSTITUTIVE, OR INTERPRETIVE?

In the introduction to this chapter, we argued that anthropologists often write about psychiatric disorders such as depression as though they were *constituted* by culture. Those who hold this position fail to acknowledge the clinical evidence that depressive illness is recognizable across cultures, and the growing psychophysiological and genetic evidence that depression is significantly shaped by biology. However, we argued that the empiricist discourse in psychiatry increasingly represents depression as a *reflection* of an underlying disorder of neurotransmitters and the neuroendocrine system. Such an approach narrows attention to a small set of decontextualized symptoms, viewed as markers of underlying biological processes. Social and cultural factors are reinserted into the analysis as risk factors or triggering agents. However, the great cultural variation in the meaning of dysphoria, the great differences in cultural idioms for articulating distress, and the networks of meanings and experience that ground psychiatric complaints are systematically excluded from attention.

We proposed an *interpretive* or meaning-centered perspective as an epistemological and methodological alternative to the reflective and constitutive positions. This approach focuses attention on the discourse on depression for members of a culture—the structure of that discourse, its interpretive value in making sense of experienced symptoms and troubled social relations, its characteristics as rhetoric and form of communication, and its role in constructing depression as an illness reality for members of a society. An interpretive analysis as an episte-mological position offers a critique of both biological and cultural reductionism, and views social reality and illness as constructed through culture-specific interpretations of biologically constrained experience and local social formations. As a methodological approach, a disciplined craft of interpretation, used in conjunction with clinical and epidemiological methods, focuses analytic attention on the relation between cultural meanings and psychiatric disease. From an interpretive perspective, important cultural differences in the phenomenology of depression are suddenly cast in relief.

Our analysis of dysphoria and depression in Iranian culture indicates the potential value of this approach. We combined ethnographic, clinical, and epidemiological methods to investigate the question of what is culture specific about the experience and communication of dysphoria and depressive illness. Our findings from these approaches were convergent. An important part of the "work of culture" (see Obeyesekere, chap. 4, and Keyes, chap. 5) in Iranian society is the transformation of dysphoria into religiously motivated grief, an experience of personal depth, and a positively valued perspective on the tragic character of the social order. Depressive illness is experienced, in part, as distress (nârâhati) that results from an inability to find positive meaning in losses, conflicted social relations, and repressive conditions of the social order.

Our clinical research indicated several culture-specific symptom groups common in the discourse of depressed patients—"sadness," "anger," "sensitivity," and "mistrust." These represent semantic domains, which are linked to typical life experiences that are interpreted and articulated in these idioms. We hypothesized that a factor analysis of a symptom checklist administered to a nonpatient population would associate these four domains. We found that three of the domains load on a single factor, which appears to represent a distinctively Iranian depressive syndrome, and the fourth ("anger") loads on a separate factor.

Although our factor analytic study is preliminary, it suggests an important methodological issue for cross-cultural epidemiological research. Great care has been taken to ensure that domains of psychophysiological importance—in particular the vegetative signs and symptoms—have been represented and sampled in instruments designed to study depression, and this is as it should be. In cross-cultural research, however, no comparable effort has been made to identify the full range of *semantic domains* that constitute the discourse on depression in a culture and systematically sample from these. Such an approach requires far more ethnographic and clinical research than the simple translation of an American instrument, and raises the question of cross-cultural validity and reliability. However, inasmuch as depression is fundamentally a social and meaningful reality, such questions are inevitable.

An interpretive approach to the study of depression forces the reader to attend to the complex interactions of biology, social relations, and cultural meanings. It requires that we approach cross-cultural research with a willingness to submit to a real encounter with alternative constructions of reality and ways of configuring experience, and with an awareness that the foundations of our own interpretive system may be shaken by this encounter. Only with such an attitude can a truly cross-cultural understanding of depression be developed.

ACKNOWLEDGMENTS

We would like to thank Karen Trocki for managing the computer work for the data analysis, Gilbert Moradi and Gail Devlan Moradi for their help in administering the questionnaires, Roustam Pourzal and Kaveh Safa-Isfahani for discussing with us several of the issues addressed by this paper, and Wheeler Thackston for assistance with transcription. Partial support for our writing of this chapter was provided by a grant on cross-cultural issues in psychiatry from the Rockefeller Foundation. Morton Beiser and Edward Schieffelin offered helpful suggestions on the chapter.

NOTES

1. The view of psychiatric disorders as abnormality or deviance is represented in such classical articles as Benedict (1934) and Devereaux (1980). It continues to be represented both in explicit social response theorists (Waxler 1977), in much of the work on the culture-bound disorders, and even in studies of specific psychiatric disorders such as schizophrenia (Scheper-Hughes 1979).

2. Stimulated by ethnographic research of bench scientists, sociologists of science have recently addressed the issue of the "social construction of scientific knowledge" (Mendelsohn 1977) with renewed interest. Ethnographic reports (e.g., Latour and Woolgar 1979) have led to debates among "empirical relativists" (Collins 1981, 1983), "constructivists" (Knorr-Cetina 1981), and "discourse analysts" (Mulkay et al. 1983), each interested in both epistemological and methodological issues concerning the influence of social factors on scientific knowledge. All agree that scientific knowledge is "under-determined" by empirical findings, that it is socially "constructed" or "constituted" rather than a "reflection" of empirical reality (Woolgar 1983).

3. Reference to this paradigm as "empiricist" follows Mulkay (1981: "empiricist discourse"), Harrison (1972: the "empiricist theory of language"), and others, who refer to a positivist position on the relationship between empirical reality and the symbolic order (cf. Good and Good 1981). Criticism of this position does not imply criticism of empirical research.

4. These observations follow from the seven years Good and Good worked as social scientists in a department of psychiatry. For a single extended case analysis, see Good et al. 1982.

5. These observations follow conversations B. Good had with nationally renowned clinical and epidemiological researchers in the field of depression, including Hagop Akiskal and Myrna Weissman, during an NIMH-sponsored conference on "Anxiety and the Anxiety Disorders" at Tuxedo, New York, September 1983.

6. The study of concepts of the self in Iranian culture began to flower in the 1970s, when American and Iranian social scientists entered into an intellectual dialogue. Zonis (1971) sparked the debate with his analysis of psychological traits of the Iranian political elite; Banuazizi (1977) and Bateson et al. (1977) responded with work on concepts of Iranian personhood based on monthly discussions of a "culture and personality" group of Iranian and American social scientists; additional work was carried on by Beeman (1976, 1982), Fischer (1984), and Good and Good (1981, 1982).

7. Studies of Iranian ta'zieh and religious rituals include a collection edited by Chelkowski (1979), Beeman (1982), Thaiss (1972), and M. Good (n.d.).

8. Recent anthropological research on the Iranian concept of nârâhati originated with the dissertation work of B. Good (n.d.). Pliskin has conducted an intriguing study of the concept of nârâhati among Iranian immigrants to Israel and the interactions of Iranian immigrants with Israeli medical professionals (Pliskin 1981).

9. It is our impression that neither Mr. Davoudi nor Mr. Tehrani met criteria for posttraumatic stress disorder. Though their experiences in Iran after the revolution and during their travel from the country were stressful, neither complained of recurrent experiencing of these trauma or of constricted affect or detachment from others.

10. Dr. Mossadeq was a progressive nationalist Prime Minister from 1951 to 1953. His attempt to overthrow Mohammed Reza Shah, and to establish a democratic republic, was thwarted by the Shah and military with the assistance of the CIA.

11. An alternative hypothesis might be that immigrants would experience a moratorium of up to several years before a sudden onset of psychological symptoms. This was once clinical wisdom (Beiser, personal communication). Some research indicates such moratoria seldom last more than several months (Murphy 1982:126). There has been, of course, a long-standing controversy over levels of psychological problems among immigrants and whether increased symptom levels result from self-selection for migration of more symp-

tomatic individuals or from the stresses associated with immigration. Current findings indicate the stress of immigration produces increased levels of depression and other psychological and medical illnesses.

REFERENCES

Al-e Ahmad, J.
1974   The School Principal. Translated from the Persian by John K. Newton. Chicago: Bibliotecha Islamica.
1978   The Hedayat of The Blind Owl. *In* Hedayat's "The Blind Owl" Forty Years After. M. Hillman, ed. Austin: University of Texas Press, Middle East Monographs, no. 4.
American Psychiatric Association
1980   Diagnostic and Statistical Manual of Mental Disorders. 3d ed. Washington, D.C.: APA.
Banuazizi, A.
1977   Iranian "National Character": A Critique of Some Western Perspectives. *In* Psychological Dimensions of Near Eastern Studies. L. Carl Brown and N. Itzkowitz, eds. Princeton: The Darwin Press.
Bateson, M. C., J. W. Clinton, J. B. M. Kassarjian, H. Safavi, and M. Soraya
1977   Safa-yi Batin. A Study of the Interrelations of a Set of Iranian Ideal Character Types. *In* Psychological Dimensions of Near Eastern Studies. L. Carl Brown and N. Itzkowitz, eds. Princeton: The Darwin Press.
Beck, A.
1976   Cognitive Therapy and the Emotional Disorders. New York: Meridian-New American Library.
Beck, A., and D. Burns
1978   Cognitive Therapy of Depressed Suicidal Outpatients. *In* Depression: Biology, Psychodynamics and Treatment. J. Cole, A. Schatzberg, and S. Frazier, eds. New York: Plenum. Pp. 199–211.
Beeman, W.
1976   What Is (Iranian) National Character: A Sociolinguistic Approach. Iranian Studies 9(1):22–48.
1982   Culture, Performance, and Communication in Iran. Tokyo: Institute for the Study of Languages and Cultures of Asia and Africa, Tokyo University.
Beiser, M., R. C. Benfari, H. Collomb, and J. Ravel
1976   Measuring Psychoneurotic Behavior in Cross-Cultural Surveys. Journal of Nervous and Mental Disease 163:10–23.

Benedict, R.
1934   Anthropology and the Abnormal. Journal of General Psychology 10:59–82.

Berger, P., and T. Luckmann
1967   The Social Construction of Reality. Garden City, N.Y.: Doubleday.

Bloor, D.
1983   Wittgenstein: A Social Theory of Knowledge. New York: Columbia University Press.

Bowen, E. (L. Bohannan)
1964   Return to Laughter. Garden City, N.Y.: Doubleday.

Brown, G. W., and T. Harris
1978   Social Origins of Depression. New York: The Free Press.

Carroll, B. J., M. Feinberg, J. F. Greden, J. Tarika, A. A. Albala, R. F. Haskett, N. M. James, Z. Kronfol, N. Lohr, M. Steier, J. P. deVigne, and E. Young
1981   A Specific Laboratory Test for the Diagnosis of Melancholia. Archives of General Psychiatry 38:15–22.

Chagnon, N.
1977   Yanomamo: The Fierce People. Hnet, Rinehart & Winston.

Chelkowski, P. J., ed.
1979   Taziyeh: Ritual and Drama in Iran. New York: New York University Press.

Coehlo, G., and P. Ahmed, eds.
1980   Uprooting and Development: Dilemmas of Coping with Modernization. New York: Plenum Press.

Collins, H. M.
1981   Stages in the Empirical Programme of Relativism. Social Studies of Science 11:3–10.

1983   An Empirical Relativist Programme in the Sociology of Scientific Knowledge. *In* Science Observed. K. Knorr-Cetina and M. Mulkay, eds. Beverly Hills: Sage Publishers. Pp. 85–113.

Collis, R. J. M.
1966   Physical Health and Psychiatric Disorder in Nigeria. Transactions of the American Philosophical Society 56(4):1–45.

Derogatis, L.
1977   SCL-90: Administration, Scoring and Procedures Manual I for the Revised Version and Other Instruments of Psychopathology Rating Scales Series. Baltimore: Johns Hopkins School of Medicine.

Devereux, G.
1980   Normal and Abnormal. *In* Basic Problems of Ethnopsychiatry. G. Devereux, ed. Chicago: University of Chicago Press.

Ebigbo, P. O.
1982   Somatization among Nigerian Normals and Mentally Ill. Cul-
            ture, Medicine, and Psychiatry 6:29–43.
Feighner, J. P., E. Robins, S. B. Guze et al.
1972   Diagnostic Criteria for Use in Psychiatric Research. Archives of
            General Psychiatry 26:57–63.
Field, M. J.
1958   Mental Disorder in Rural Ghana. Journal of Mental Science
            104:1043–1051.
Fischer, M.
1984   Towards a Third World Poetics: Seeing through Short Stories
            and Films in the Iranian Culture Area. Knowledge and
            Society 5.
Gaines, A.
1979   Definitions and Diagnoses. Culture, Medicine, and Psychiatry
            3:381–418.
1982   Cultural Definitions, Behavior and Person in American Psy-
            chiatry. *In* Cultural Conceptions of Mental Health and Therapy.
            A. Marsella and G. White, eds. Boston: D. Reidel.
Geertz, C.
1983   Local Knowledge: Further Essays in Interpretive Anthro-
            pology. New York: Basic Books.
Good, B.
n.d.   The Heart of What's the Matter: The Structure of Medical
            Discourse in a Provincial Iranian Town. Ph.D. diss. University
            of Chicago, 1977.
1977   The Heart of What's the Matter. The Semantics of Illness in
            Iran. Culture, Medicine, and Psychiatry 1:25–58.
Good, G., and M. Good
1981   The Semantics of Medical Discourse. *In* Sciences and Cultures.
            Anthropological and Historical Studies of the Sciences.
            E. Mendelsohn and Y. Elkana, eds. Boston: D. Reidel.
1982   Toward a Meaning-Centered Analysis of Popular Illness Cate-
            gories: "Fright Illness" and "Heart Distress" in Iran. *In* Cul-
            tural Conceptions of Mental Health and Therapy. A. J.
            Marsella and G. White, eds. Boston: D. Reidel.
Good, B., H. Herrera, M. Good, and J. Cooper
1982   Reflexivity and Countertransference in a Psychiatric Cultural
            Consultation Clinic. Culture, Medicine, and Psychiatry
            6:281–303.
Good, B., and A. Kleinman
1985   Culture and Anxiety: Cross-cultural Evidence for The Pattern-
            ing of Anxiety Disorders. *In* Anxiety and the Anxiety Dis-

orders. A. H. Tuma and J. D. Maser, eds. Hillsdale, N.J.: Lawrence Earlbaum Associates.

Good, M.
n.d.   Social Hierarchy and Social Change in an Iranian Provincial Town. Ph.D. diss. Harvard University, 1977.
1980   Of Blood and Babies: The Relationship of Popular Islamic Physiology to Fertility. Social Science and Medicine 14B: 147—156.

Good, M., B. Good, and R. Moradi
1981   Illness Constructs and Emotional Experiences Among Iranian Students in the United States. Report to Workshop on Cultural Adaption of Foreign Students, East-West Center, Honolulu, Hawaii. September 16—22, 1981.

Goodwin, F., and W. Potter
1978   The Biology of Affective Illness. *In* Depression: Biology, Psychodynamics, and Treatment. J. Cole et al., eds. New York: Plenum Press.

Hillman, M., ed.
1978   Hedayat's "The Blind Owl" Forty Years After. Austin: University of Texas, Middle East Monographs, no. 4.

Janzen, J.
1978   The Quest for Therapy in Lower Zaire. Berkeley, Los Angeles, London: University of California Press.

Kleinman, A.
1982   Neurasthenia and Depression. Culture, Medicine, and Psychiatry 6:117—190.

Knorr-Cetina, K.
1981   The Manufacture of Knowledge. Oxford: Pergamon Press.

Lambo, T. A.
1962   Malignant Anxiety: A Syndrome Associated with Criminal Conduct in Africans. Journal of Mental Science 108:256—264.

Latour, B., and S. Woolgar
1979   Laboratory Life: The Social Construction of Scientific Facts. Beverly Hills: Sage Publications.

Leff, J.
1981   Psychiatry Around the Globe: A Transcultural View. New York: Marcel Dekker, Inc.

Mendelsohn, E.
1977   The Social Construction of Scientific Knowledge. *In* The Social Production of Scientific Knowledge. Pp. 3—26. E. Mendelsohn, P. Weingart, and R. Whitley, eds. Dordrecht: D. Reidel.

Mulkay, M.
1981   Action and Belief or Scientific Discourse? Philosophy of the Social Sciences 11:163—171.

Mulkay, M., and G. N. Gilbert
1982*a*   What Is the Ultimate Question? Some Remarks in Defense of
            the Analysis of Scientific Discourse. Social Studies of Science
            12:309−319.
1982*b*   Joking Apart: Some Recommendations Concerning the Analy-
            sis of Scientific Culture. Social Studies of Science 12:585−613.
1982*c*   Warranting Scientific Belief. Social Studies of Science
            12:383−408.
Mulkay, M., J. Potter, and S. Yearly
1983   Why an Analysis of Scientific Discourse Is Needed. *In* Science
            Observed. Perspectives on the Social Study of Science.
            K. Knorr-Cettina and M. Mulkay, eds. Beverly Hills: Sage
            Publications.
Murphy, H. B. M.
1982   Comparative Psychiatry: The International and Intercultural
            Distribution of Mental Illness. New York: Springer-Verlag.
Murphy, J.
1982   Psychiatric Instrument Development for Primary Care
            Research: Patient Self-Report Questionnaires. Contract Report
            to the Division of Biometry and Epidemiology. NIMH (report
            no. 80M014280101D).
Nichter, M.
1981   Idioms of Distress. Culture, Medicine, and Psychiatry
            5:379−408.
O'Nell, C. W., and A. Rubel
1976   The Meaning of Susto (Magical Fright). Actas del XLI Con-
            gresso Internacional de Americanistas 3:342−349.
Orley, J., and J. Wing
1979   Psychiatric Disorders in Two African Villages. Archives of
            General Psychiatry 36:513−520.
Robins, E., and S. B. Guze
1972   Classification of Affective Disorders: The Primary-Secondary,
            the Endogenous-Reactive, and the Neurotic-Psychotic Con-
            cepts. *In* Recent Advances in the Psychobiology of the Depres-
            sive Illness. T. Williams, M. Katz, J. Schied, eds. Washing-
            ton, D.C.: U.S. Government Printing Office. Pp. 283−293.
Rosaldo, M.
1980   Knowledge and Passion. Cambridge: Cambridge University
            Press.
Sachar, E. J.
1982   Endocrine Abnormalities in Depression. *In* Handbook of
            Affective Disorders. E. S. Paykel, ed. New York: Guilford
            Press. Pp. 191−201.

Scheper-Hughes, N.
1979   Saints, Scholars, and Schizophrenics: Mental Illness in Rural
             Ireland. Berkeley, Los Angeles, London: University of Cali-
             fornia Press.
Schieffelin, E.
1975   The Sorrow of the Lonely and the Burning of the Dancers. New
             York: St. Martin's Press.
Spitzer, R., J. Endicott, and E. Robins
1975   Clinical Criteria for Psychiatric Diagnosis and the DSM-II.
             American Journal of Psychiatry 132:1187−1192.

Thaiss, G.
1972   Religious Symbolism and Social Change: The Drama of
             Husain. *In* Scholars, Saints, and Sufis. N. Keddie, ed.
             Berkeley, Los Angeles, London: University of California Press.

Topley, M.
1970   Chinese Traditional Ideas and the Treatment of Disease: Two
             Examples from Hong Kong. Man 5:421−437.
Turner, V.
1967   The Forest of Symbols. Ithaca: Cornell University Press.
Uhlenhuth, E. H., M. B. Balter, G. D. Mellinger, I. H. Gisin, and
J. Clinthorne
1983   Symptom Checklist Syndromes in the General Population.
             Archives of General Psychiatry 40:1167−1173.

Waxler, N.
1977   Is Mental Illness Cured in Traditional Societies? A Theoretical
             Analysis. Culture, Medicine, and Psychiatry 3:233−254.

Weissman, M., and G. Klerman
1978   Epidemiology of Mental Disorders. Archives of General Psy-
             chiatry 35:705−712.
Wober, M.
1969   Distinguishing Centriculture from Cross-Cultural Tests and
             Research. Perceptual and Motor Skills 28:488.
Woolgar, S.
1983   Irony in the Social Study of Science. *In* Science Observed.
             K. Knorr-Cetina and M. Mulkay, eds. Beverly Hills: Sage
             Publications. Pp. 239−266.

Young, A.
1980   The Discourse on Stress and the Reproduction of Conventional
             Knowledge. Social Science and Medicine 14B:133−146.
Zonis, M.
1971   The Political Elite of Iran. Princeton: Princeton University
             Press.

13

Somatization: The Interconnections in Chinese Society among Culture, Depressive Experiences, and the Meanings of Pain

Arthur Kleinman and Joan Kleinman

THEORETICAL ORIENTATIONS

The theme we will develop is that the disorder depression, though diagnosable worldwide with standard criteria based on psychobiological dysfunction that appears to be universal, can be looked at in another way, as fundamentally a relationship between an individual and society. Depressive illness discloses how an individual relates to society, but it also suggests how society affects individuals: their interaction, behavior, and even their cognitive, affective, and physiological processes. Indeed, the study of depression in society shows us the sociosomatic reticulum (the symbolic bridge) that connects individuals to each other and to their life world. Depression is a profoundly social affect and disorder, certain of whose sources and consequences are structures and relations in the social world. Social structures and relations are deeply affective, thus embodied in the individual and his disorders.

This dialectical relationship between depression (or for that matter any disorder) and society is mediated by the meanings and legitimacies that symptoms take on in local systems of power. We will interpret chronic pain in the lives of patients we studied in the People's Republic of China through the meanings and legitimacies this "disvalued experience" holds for them, their families, their work relationships, and their physicians. Inasmuch as these individuals construed the experience as neurasthenia, we will briefly return to the controversy regarding neurasthenia and depression in China and the West. We will reexamine this controversy, which we dealt with at great length in an earlier publication (Kleinman 1982), to analyze the cultural construction of the depression-neurasthenia-chronic pain connection as a complement to our interpretation of its social production. That will also illumine the process "whereby any culture externalizes its social categories onto nature, and then turns to nature in order to validate its social norms as natural" (Taussig 1980). Hence depression, neurasthenia, and chronic pain open a window on Chinese psychiatry and society; they do the same for Western psychiatry and the culture from which it takes its origin.

To this connection, and the dialectic between symptom and society it expresses, we will apply the somewhat less unwieldy, yet admittedly still inelegant term, *somatization*. We define somatization as the expression of personal and social distress in an idiom of bodily complaints and medical help seeking. Somatization is, we believe, the appropriate focus for interdisciplinary collaboration between anthropology and psychiatry. If the psychiatric investigation of depression cross-culturally is to become more discriminating in its analysis of depression's social sources and cultural variation, it must draw on interpretive theory and methodology from anthropology. Similarly, if anthropological analyses are to account for the psychobiological processes in depression (and other disorders), and not to do so is to distort the nature of their cross-cultural subject matter, then anthropology too must proceed with an integrative (culture ↔ nature) framework for analysis and comparison, albeit one with different emphases than psychiatry. This chapter reviews our attempt to forge such an anthropological psychiatry and psychiatric anthropology.

PERSONAL ORIENTATIONS

We have developed this interdisciplinary approach in Chinese society over the past ten years, first in Taiwan and among Chinese-Americans, and since 1980 in the People's Republic. The studies that we discuss now were all conducted at the Hunan Medical College, one of China's leading centers of psychiatry. In 1980 we spent five months in the Department of Psychiatry at the Hunan Medical College interviewing

100 patients who carried the diagnosis of neurasthenia as outpatients there. We were intrigued by the fact that neurasthenia—a diagnosis invented in North America and popular in the first third of this century throughout the West but now no longer officially sanctioned or used in the United States and also much less frequently encountered in Western Europe—was the most common psychiatric outpatient diagnosis for neurotic disorders in China, whereas depressive disorder—the most frequent psychiatric outpatient diagnosis in the West and indeed one of the leading diagnoses in primary care in the United States—was, at the time of our study, hardly diagnosed at all in China. We wondered if our Chinese psychiatric colleagues labeled neurasthenia what American and Western European psychiatrists labeled depression. Our earlier research in Taiwan (Kleinman 1980) and interviews in various outpatient clinics throughout China in 1978 (Kleinman and Mechanic 1979; Mechanic and Kleinman 1979) suggested that this might well be the case. We also wished to determine if the prevalence (at least the treated prevalence since we were not authorized to conduct population-based research in China), symptomatology, and sources and consequences of depression in China and the United States were significantly different. If so, what could such findings inform us about the universal and culture-particular aspects of depression?

But we were also interested in two other questions: What could we learn from differences in the diagnostic approaches of psychiatrists in China and North America about the different varieties of clinical constructions of social reality in the two societies? What would a comparison of the antecedents and consequents of depression in each society, furthermore, tell us about those societies? We were interested, for example, in peering through the window of depression and neurasthenia at everyday life in China and observing its problems and the indigenous approaches that deal with them.

Different patterns of historical development of medical categories in China and the West lent additional interest to our investigation. As Jackson shows (chap. 1), depression (in the guise of melancholia) was labeled in ancient Greece and has a long pedigree in the West. Although classical Chinese medicine virtually from the beginning labeled major psychotic disorders and hysteria, and took an interactionist psychosomatic perspective on disease and emotion generally, it was not until fairly late in its historical transformation in the Ming Dynasty that anything approaching the Western concept of depression was elaborated (Tseng 1974). In modern times these indigenous Chinese categories of what in the West is called depressive disorder have not been widely used, and as already noted, even the Western category has been infrequently applied by psychiatrists in China, who employ a largely biological approach to mental disorder. Moreover, the actual practice of contemporary Chinese medicine has emphasized organically oriented somato-psychic models much more than the earlier psychosomatic ones. Thus the psychological and social aspects of disease (including depression) are not emphasized in China's medical system.

We will review the chief results of our 1980 study. In 1983 we returned to the Hunan Medical College to initiate two additional studies, conducted between April and August. In the first, we followed up a subsample of our 1980 subjects who had been diagnosed as suffering from both Major Depressive Disorder and Chronic Pain Syndrome. This three-year follow-up assessment examined the relationship of course of illness and treatment outcome to social problems in the workplace, family, and community which we had identified as sources of patient distress in 1980. The second study investigated the same issues in a sample of chronic pain patients drawn from the medical outpatient clinic, the hospital's primary care facility. We sought to determine what number of these patients were depressed, what relation depression had to pain, and what relation both had to patients' life circumstances and the broader social system. Pertinent findings from each of these studies will be described, and their significance for the theoretical questions we have raised will be reviewed.

Not surprisingly, our studies have attracted attention from our colleagues in China. They have debated our interpretations, initiated their own projects, and begun to rethink the place of neurasthenia and depression in their own society. Much of their interest and criticism has centered on our handling of the concept of somatization, for which we were invited by the editors of China's *Referential Journal of Psychiatry* to contribute a review article (Kleinman 1984). The questions of the social causes and consequences of depression and somatization which we have raised, however, have not been the subject of close analysis—at least not thus far—principally because psychiatrists in China for various reasons, including some shared by colleagues in the West, have found it more prudent to follow clinical and biological research paths rather than social ones, which in the People's Republic are particularly sensitive. Nonetheless, China's psychiatrists are now initiating studies of stress and social support (see Zheng and Yang 1983; Xu 1983) which should indicate how generalizable are the data from our small samples and in so doing tell us more, though perhaps not as much as we want to know, about the place of depression and somatization in Chinese society. We do not view our contribution as an answer to this question, rather we have brought the question more urgently to the attention of our Chinese colleagues and argued that it be addressed in a broader problem framework.

Our Chinese studies can be compared with studies on somatization and depression conducted in North America and the United Kingdom (e.g., Brown and Harris 1978; Katon et al. 1982, 1984), including our current clinical research on patients with chronic pain syndrome in Boston. The literature for North America not only suggests questions for research in China; clinical experience and research with more than two thousand chronic pain patients in Seattle and Boston, many of whom were also suffering depressive disorders, convince us that the general points from our cross-cultural studies are as relevant for the West as they are for China, that we are confronting a salient cross-cultural phenomenon, an obdurate aspect of the human predicament.

Of course, one should be cautious in generalizing from patient samples to a society as a whole. These are after all studies of pathology, not normality. But we Westerners know so little about everyday experience and especially life problems in China, in part because the Chinese let us see so little of the structural tensions that their society, like all societies, must face, that this perspective is a particularly revealing one, precisely because it discloses problems created by the major transformations in China, with whose often beneficial effects we are much more familiar. We believe that any serious examination of the evidence concerning changes in the living standards and health conditions of the great mass of Chinese people since 1949 must, on balance, come down on the side of progress, sometimes enormous progress. But there have also been great problems. They too need to be understood.

SOMATIZATION IN NORTH AMERICA, THE UNITED KINGDOM, AND THE NON-WESTERN WORLD

In many societies in the non-Western world somatization has been shown to be the predominant expression of mental illness. For example, high rates of somatization in depressive disorder have been found in clinic-based studies in Saudi Arabia (Racy 1980), Iraq (Bazzoui 1970), West Africa (Binitie 1975), India (Teja et al. 1971; Sethi et al. 1973), the

Sudan and the Philippines (Climent et al. 1980), Taiwan (Kleinman 1977, 1980), Hong Kong (Cheung et al. 1981), and in matched comparisons more for Peruvian than for North American depressed patients (Mezzich and Raab 1980) and for East Africans more than Londoners (Orley and Wing 1979). Marsella (1979), in a major review of the cross-cultural literature, finds the somatic expression of depression to have higher prevalence generally in non-Western societies. Ebigbo (1982) shows that Nigerians demonstrate styles of somatic complaints that are unique to their culture, and Good (1977) reveals the same for the Turkish population in Iran.[1]

What tends to get lost in such studies, however, is, first, that somatization is also very common in the West and, second, that somatization is not limited to depression and other psychiatric disorders. Indeed, it may not always represent pathology or even maladaptation. While we lack population-based studies to support the last point, there are a great number of studies substantiating the other two. These studies show that somatization cases account for between one-third and three-fourths of patient visits to primary care physicians in the United States and the United Kingdom (Collyer 1979; Regier et al. 1978; Hankin and Oktay 1979; Goldberg 1979; Hoeper et al. 1979; Widmer et al. 1980; Katon et al. 1982, 1984). Somatization in the West has been associated with lower socioeconomic and educational levels, rural origins, active and traditional religious affiliation, and behavioral ethnicity (Katon et al. 1982; Harwood 1981). Somatization appears to have had an even higher prevalence rate in the West prior to the emergence of an increasingly psychological idiom of distress in the Victorian middle class. This psychologizing process has been related to the cultural transformation shaped by modernism, in which a deeper interiorization of the self has been culturally constituted as the now dominant Western ethnopsychology (see Romanyshyn 1982; Lasch 1979; McIntyre 1981). It may be that this psychological idiom, one of Western culture's most powerful self-images, is the personal concomitant of the societal process of *rationalization* that Max Weber saw as modernism's leading edge, "the process by which explicit, abstract, intellectually calculable rules and procedures are increasingly substituted for sentiment, tradition and rule of thumb in all spheres of human activity" (Wrong 1976:247). That is to say, "affect" as currently conceived and even experienced among the middle class in the West is shaped as "deep" psychological experience and rationalized into discretely labeled emotions (depression, anxiety, anger) that previously were regarded and felt as principally bodily experiences. As bodily experience "feeling" was expressed and interpreted more subtly, indirectly, globally, and above all somatically. Both psychologization and somatization, then, are cultural constructions of psychobiological processes: the former the creation of the Western mode of modernization that now influences the elites of non-Western societies; the latter the creation of more traditional cultural orientations worldwide, including that of the more rural, the poorer and the less educated in the West. From the cross-cultural perspective, it is not somatization in China and the West but psychologization in the West that appears unusual and requires explanation.

In recent years political scientists, economists, and other social scientists studying the work disability system in North America have noted that the phenomenon we call somatization of personal and social distress constitutes a large component of disability payments and missed workdays, and is also frequently an emblem of worker dissatisfaction, demoralization, and alienation (Stone 1979*a*, 1979*b*; Yelin et al. 1980; Figlio 1982; Alexander 1982). Similar studies have disclosed how family processes and aspects of the medical care system itself can help maintain and amplify chronic illness behavior in medical as well as psychiatric disorders (Alexander 1982; Helman 1985; Lock 1983; Plough 1981; Stewart and Sullivan 1982). This line of research is particularly impressive for chronic pain syndrome. Here marital, family, work and medical relationships have been shown to act as environmental operants that condition, and thereby maintain, chronic pain behavior (Turner and Chapman 1982; Sternbach 1974; Fordyce 1976; Keefe 1982; Keefe et al. 1982; Roberts and Reinhardt 1980). Stone (1979*a*, 1979*b*) has shown that chronic illness behavior has become an important entry point in the American system of distributive politics, where the illness test has replaced the means test to control access to social welfare resources; while Yelin and coworkers (1980) reveal that local conditions in the workplace are a statistically significantly better predictor of return to work in patients with chronic disability than are biomedical tests and measurements. Indeed, the biomedical health care system is often shown to be dangerous for chronic pain and other somatization patients, because it produces addiction to prescription narcotic analgesic drugs, polypharmacy with drugs that cause potentially serious and frequent side effects, iatrogenesis from expensive and risky tests, unnecessary surgery, and anger and frustration for patients, families, and physicians (Katon et. al. 1982; Rosen et al. 1982; Turner and Chapman 1982). To reduce the prevalence of somatization that has negative consequences for person and health care system, these studies demonstrate its psychological and social sources must be addressed along with its biological bases.

Somatization, we may conclude, is a significant problem cross-culturally in Western as well as non-Western societies.

CHINA RESEARCH: 1980

Using the Schedule of Affective Disorders and Schizophrenia (SADS) and the diagnostic criteria of the American Psychiatric Association's Diagnostic and Statistical Manual, Third Edition (DSM-III 1980), which were modified for use with patients in China, we were able to diagnose most of the 100 neurasthenia patients we interviewed in the Department of Psychiatry at the Hunan Medical College as suffering from various forms of clinical depression (93 percent). Fully 87 percent demonstrated the symptoms of Major Depressive Disorder: though they suppressed most of the affective symptoms (irritability and depression) they were experiencing and complained principally of the so-called vegetative (i.e., autonomic nervous system and neuroendocrine) ones (sleep, appetite, energy, cognitive and sexual disturbances, and psychomotor retardation or agitation). Many of these patients also suffered from anxiety disorders (71 percent).[2]

We were thus able to confirm our hypothesis that neurasthenia patients in China can be diagnosed as suffering depression (and other psychiatric disorders) when using standard North American assessment techniques and diagnostic criteria. Does this mean that neurasthenia is depression (or anxiety)? The picture is much more complicated when the standard clinical evaluation is supplemented with an anthropological analysis. Neurasthenia looked at from a cultural perspective is an example of the social construction of clinical reality, a point clarified by our other findings and discussed later below.

Of the 100 neurasthenia patients, 90 percent suffered headaches as one of their chief complaints, 78 percent insomnia, 73 percent dizziness, 48 percent various pains other than headaches, while only nine percent of patients articulated depression as one of their chief complaints. These symptoms are found in Beard's 1880 list of the core neurasthenic complaints in the United States, though they are more peripheral to the American syndrome. There is then some common psychobiological thread in neurasthenia. But culture also looms large. Headaches, dizziness, and insomnia were described as early as the Han Dynasty in China as leading symptoms of mental disorder (Ch'eng and Chang 1962) and are especially salient complaints in contemporary Chinese culture. Weakness and loss of energy (or exhaustion), which were usually thought of as the essence of neurasthenia in the West and which Chinese psychiatrists still define as resulting from the hypothesized abnormality in cortical activity of the brain alleged by them (though with hardly any biological evidence) to underlie neurasthenia, were present in only 35 percent and 30 percent of patients in our sample, respectively. This surprised us since weakness and exhaustion are central problems in traditional Chinese medicine where they are related to lack of *qi* (vital energy) and imbalance between *yin/yang*. For this reason we assumed they would be a ready-made traditional Chinese cultural form for integration into the diagnosis of neurasthenia.

It remains unclear why they are present in only a minority of cases, unless it is because *shen kui* syndrome and other indigenous Chinese medicine diagnoses are still coherent categories in the popular culture to label such complaints. The symptoms of the two types of neurasthenia in China, moreover, overlap with those of depression and anxiety disorders, particularly when the chief somatic complaints are supplemented with the elicitation of suppressed psychological symptoms. Thus there appear to be several types of neurasthenia in China: one associated with weakness and exhaustion which is virtually identical with neurasthenia as defined in the West a hundred years ago, and another, more common kind that has as its central complaints some of the more peripheral symptoms of the classical Western diagnosis, but only those that are significant in Chinese society, albeit not all of the symptoms that are salient for Chinese are included. Thus both culture and biology interact in this disorder. That interaction gives rise to a picture that is not simply a sum of their separate effects, but involves both a continuation and transformation of the syndrome in two different cultures.

Ninety of the one hundred neurasthenia patients studied had pain of one sort or another, and forty-four had persistent pain in one or more sites lasting for at least two years and perceived as causing significant disability in family or work functioning that in the United States is diagnosed as Chronic Pain Syndrome. Both pain complaints and Chronic Pain Syndrome have been described in North America in high frequency among depressed patients (Sternbach 1974; Ward et al. 1979; Lindsay and Wykoff 1981; Blumer et al. 1980). The diagnosis of Chronic Pain Syndrome is not used in China, and pain was not singled out by our

Chinese medical and psychiatric colleagues as the chief problem although patients frequently regarded it as such.

In the 1980 report of these findings we suggested that neurasthenia and depression could be understood as distinctive cultural construals of the same psychobiological state in which Chinese and American cultural values influenced both lay and professional constructions of distress (see Townsend 1978). Our anthropological readers generally took this to be our interpretation, but our psychiatric readers in the United States or China did not. American psychiatrists interpreted our findings as showing that depression is underdiagnosed in China. While this empiricist interpretation fits with the North American nosology, it fails to take into account the clash of distinctive diagnostic categories and their grounding in cultural beliefs and values. The anthropological perspective that the controversy is solely one of opposing cultural construals is also inadequate. After all, there is some psychobiological reality, some perduring perturbation of human nature, associated with substantial distress that is being labeled differently in the two societies. The labels are not creating out of nothing the difficult social reality patients face, though they are organizing that exigent reality in different (sometimes greatly different) ways.

Our other findings point this out. Though their chief complaints were somatic, all of the neurasthenia patients experienced dysphoria (depression, sadness, irritability), even though they suppressed these complaints. Dysphoric emotion traditionally in Chinese culture has been regarded as shameful to self and family; for that reason it was not to be revealed outside the family and was seen to dangerously overlap with highly stigmatized mental illness. Psychological complaints did not have the same social efficacy that physical complaints had in generating support and care (Kleinman 1980:119−178). Moreover, in traditional Chinese medicine, the expression of disturbed emotions was viewed as a potential cause of illness (Tseng 1974). For all these reasons, as we have argued elsewhere following many others, Chinese tend to suppress depressive affect (Kleinman 1980, 1982; Tseng and Hsu 1969; Tseng 1975). Cheung and her colleagues (1981, 1982, 1983, 1984) have shown that this is in part a situational phenomenon: Chinese depressives (at least Westernized university students in Hong Kong) will complain of psychological problems to very close friends and key family members in the home situation, but in the medical situation will complain of physical problems. Anthropological studies have shown that bodily complaints may metaphorically express personal and interpersonal distress (Rosaldo

1980; Lutz, chap. 2), and this also appears to be the case in Chinese culture (Kleinman 1977, 1980:133–145). *Huo qi da* (a burning sensation in the upper abdomen, chest, and mouth, understood as excessive hot energy rising up in the body in traditional Chinese medical theory) denotes dyspepsia to physicians, but it also connotes anger and irascibility to friends and relatives.

In keeping with the somatic idiom of distress, all the neurasthenia patients believed that though they were attending a psychiatric clinic their problems were primarily physical. None held psychological or psychosomatic models of their problems. Nor did any of the patients label their problems as depression. Accordingly, they were high utilizers of medical services (averaging two visits per month, a high rate even for patients with chronic disorders in China), and had received many treatments (they were taking an average of five drugs per patient at the time of the interviews). These behaviors and explanatory models matched those of their physicians and psychiatrists who viewed these patients' problems as principally biological and treated them in those terms. Here we see the transactional nature of somatization: practitioners sanction the patient's bodily idiom of distress; both contribute to somatization.

In the six months prior to the onset of their symptoms, virtually all the neurasthenia patients had experienced stressful life event changes in work, family, school, or economic and political matters. Many patients had significant family experiences with chronic illness, neurasthenia, and mental illness (mainly depression), and most had had long-standing work (90 percent) and family (80 percent) problems. Hence they had the classical constellation of vulnerability (biological and psychosocial) factors, precipitating or provoking factors (stress), and inadequate social resources (coping, support network, financial) that Brown and Harris (1978) associate with the genesis of demoralization and the generalization of hopelessness into depression.

At the time of our interviews, 74 percent of these patients were engaged in negotiations to change jobs, return from distant separations from family owing to different work sites, or go on sick leave to reduce work and receive compensation. In more than 90 percent of cases, the chronic symptoms seemed to us to communicate otherwise unsanctioned personal or social distress in a legitimated bodily idiom, while in 74 cases the symptoms appeared to function to increase control over tension-ridden interpersonal relations. In one out of five patients, physical symptoms sanctioned failure (primarily in examinations and school). From an anthropological perspective the symptoms were multivocal symbols expressing different social meanings and exerting effects in local relationships of power, a theme developed in the Discussion section. From a psychiatric perspective, these cases of somatization resembled those in the West described above, and called to mind the important uses of neurasthenia in the Soviet Union to gain leverage over a highly controlled work and political system (Gluzman 1982).

The only available specific treatment for depression in the Psychiatry Outpatient Clinic, an antidepressant drug, was given to each of the eighty-four patients with Major Depressive Disorder. While 87 percent experienced some improvement in symptoms and 70 percent very substantial improvement, fewer decreased their help seeking. In spite of receiving care in the Psychiatry Clinic, most did not improve their perceived disability, and few experienced substantial improvement in family, school, or work problems. Thus, antidepressants removed many but not all the symptoms, yet had limited effect on the illness behavior and social problems associated with the illness. At the time they received antidepressants, each of the patients with depression was told the diagnosis and a medical explanation was offered of depression. Yet, even though 87 percent experienced some improvement in symptoms, only 11 percent of depressed patients at time of follow-up called their disorder depression.

Thus, patients actively rejected the psychiatric label "depression" and reaffirmed the organic medical label "neurasthenia." Not only did the traditional Chinese cultural factors already noted seem to foster this behavior, so did newer political considerations. During the Great Proletarian Cultural Revolution, all mental illness, including, most notably, depression, had been called into question by the Maoists as wrong political thinking. This penumbra of meaning still affects the term depression, which also connotes withdrawal and passivity, behaviors that in China's often passionate context of aroused political energy seem suspiciously like disaffiliation and alienation. Such connotations spelled disaster during the Cultural Revolution and even in the pragmatic political atmosphere of present-day, post-Maoist China these are not public attributions with which patients and families wish to be associated. Indeed, neurasthenia is a much safer, and more readily accessible and widely shared, public idiom of frustration and demoralization, to which Chinese continue to resort in great numbers. Though most demoralization relates to local issues in work and family, for some this is a dual discourse (overt physical complaints, covert political ones) to express dissatisfaction with the broader political situation. Because these insights are not unknown to Chinese psychiatrists, it is even more difficult for them to transform neurasthenia into depression and examine certain of the wider social structural sources of this form of human misery. Our analysis suggests that in spite of the undoubtedly great international professional pressures on Chinese psychiatry to recast neurasthenia as depression, neurasthenia and depression have a much more complex relationship, and the former, not the latter, is (at least at present) a more socially suitable and culturally approved diagnostic category in Chinese society.

Follow-Up Study of Chronic Pain Patients at the Hunan Medical College: 1983

In April 1983, we followed up 21 of 30 cases from the 1980 sample who at the time of their initial interview were suffering from both Chronic Pain Syndrome and Major Depressive Disorder and who lived near enough to the Hunan Medical College to return for interviews.[3] (Nine patients who declined to participate lived outside the city and wrote that they were too busy with agricultural or other work activities to be interviewed.) Our aim was to determine to what extent somatic complaints among these patients were amplified or dampened in response to work, family, and other social problems, and to what extent both chronic pain and depression responded to medical treatments. Based on the 1980 findings, we hypothesized that the social context of illness would be the major determinant of persistent somatization. We wanted to learn more about that context to obtain a deeper understanding of the life experiences of our patients. We wished to assess the influence on their illness experiences of important political, economic, and other large-scale social change in China.

Two-thirds of the patients were women; most were middle-aged workers and teachers (see table 13.1). Using the same diagnostic interview schedule as three years before, we determined that only one-third of the patients made the DSM-III diagnostic criteria for Major Depressive Disorder. A quarter of the sample made the criteria for Dysthymic Disorder (chronic neurotic depression, a less severe form of clinical disorder). Hence 57 percent were diagnosed as suffering some form of clinical depression, far fewer than in 1980. For many of the patients depression had become a less severe but very chronic problem; for others it had remitted but often without return to normal health. The same percentage, but not always the same patients, were suffering from anxiety disorders. Nineteen percent had no mental illness at all. Thus, almost one out of five psychiatric disorders remitted over the three years, while others displayed a more chronic low-grade character (see table 13.2).

TABLE 13.1
1983 FOLLOW-UP STUDY

Demographics: N = 21		
Age: mean − 39, range 25−29		
mean for men − 34		
mean for women − 42		
Sex: men − 7 (33%)		
women − 14 (67%)		
Occupations: Workers	=	10 (48%)
Teachers	=	9 (43%)
Cadre	=	1 (5%)
Technician	=	1 (5%)

TABLE 13.2
1983 FOLLOW-UP STUDY

		*Psychiatric Diagnoses**	N = 21
57%	Depressive disorders	Major Depressive Disorder	= 7 (33%)
		Dysthymic Disorder	= 5 (24%)
		Panic Disorder	= 6 (29%)
		Phobic Disorder	= 5 (24%)
57%	Anxiety disorders	(Simple 4, Agoraphobia 1)	
		Generalized Anxiety Disorder	= 0 (0%)
		Obsessive-Compulsive Disorder	= 1 (5%)
14%	Somatoform disorders	Conversion Disorder	= 2 (10%)
		Somatization Disorder	= 1 (5%)
		Personality Disorder	= 5 (24%)
		Hypochondriasis	= 6 (29%)
		Suicidal Ideation	= 1 (5%)
		No mental illness	= 4 (19%)

*Percentages add to more than 100 percent as there was more than one diagnosis made per case.

Over the course of the three years, one-third of the patients experienced no change in their chronic pain and other symptoms, just under half were somewhat improved but still experienced pain as well as other symptoms, and only 14 percent were greatly improved. Just one patient had experienced a complete cure (table 13.3). Most patients thus still complained of pain and other symptoms. Eight patients (38 percent) had changed work since 1980, and altogether ten (48 percent) had changed work at some point in the preceding five years (see table 13.4). In comparison, there was no reported history of changing work over the past three years among twenty-five patients with various nonneur-

TABLE 13.3

1983 FOLLOW-UP STUDY

Pain Complaints		
Completely improved (cured)	=	1 (5%)
Greatly improved (75% improved)	=	3 (14%)
Somewhat improved (50% improved)	=	10 (48%)
No change (pain same as before)	=	7 (33%)

TABLE 13.4

1983 FOLLOW-UP STUDY

Social Change		
Married	=	2 (10%)
Mother left home	=	1 (5%)
Obtained degree	=	1 (5%)
Wants divorce	=	1 (5%)
Wants to retire	=	1 (5%)
Daughter left home	=	1 (5%)
Work Related		
Illness affects work	=	12 (57%)
Dislikes work	=	9 (43%)
Wants to change work	=	7 (33%)
Retired	=	3 (14%)
Reunited from work separation	=	4 (19%)
Changed work since 1980	=	8 (38%)
Total changed work	=	10 (48%)

25 Matched Neurotic Nonneurasthenia Psychiatry OPD Patients,
0: Number changed work in past three years.

asthenic neurotic disorders in the psychiatric clinic at the Hunan Medical College who were matched with the patients in our sample for age, sex, and occupation. Three other chronic pain patients (14 percent) had retired from work during these three years.

All the patients whose chronic pain complaints improved either had changed work or retired or had undergone some other significant change in their social situation which in 1980 had been identified as a source of significant stress. For example, four (19 percent) were reunited with family after separation owing to different and distant work sites, two (10 percent), who had desired to do so for some time but had previously met with substantial bureaucratic and family obstacles, had married, one (5 percent) had earned a much desired college degree, and in one case a conflict-ridden home situation was resolved when a contentious mother-in-law moved out. All the retired patients had experienced symptom improvement, whereas 20 percent of the patients who changed jobs experienced no symptom improvement, and another 20 percent had experienced a worsening of complaints (see table 13.5). Each of the last, however, described current work problems as more severe than in the previous job. Among those whose change in work was an improvement over their prior work, four experienced symptom improvement, one had no change in symptoms, and none had a worsening of complaints. Of the three patients whose change in work was neither more nor less stressful, the symptoms of two improved, one stayed the same, and none were worse (see table 13.6). Thus, symptom amplification reflected worsening of work problems, symptom dampening improvement.

TABLE 13.5
1983 FOLLOW-UP STUDY

Change in Symptoms among Those Who Changed Work

Better = 6 (60%) N = 10
Worse = 2* (20%)
Same = 2 (20%)

*Both involved change to more stressful job.

Change in Symptoms among Those Who Retired

Better = 3	N = 3
Worse = 0	
Same = 0	

Much the same picture emerged when family problems were evaluated (see table 13.7). In one instance where a daughter, who was the major support of the family, had left home, her mother's chronic pain persisted, as it did in a woman whose marriage had deteriorated so badly that she was actively contemplating divorce—a stigmatized and infrequent act in the People's Republic. Of the six cases who resolved major family problems, two-thirds had experienced symptom improvement. Our data, therefore, demonstrate a close relationship between persistence of complaints and persistence of social sources of distress, and diminished disability and perceived improvement in social life, including most notably retirement, reunion after separation due to different work sites, work change associated with improved work situation (usually described as less stressful), and improvement in family situations.

Ninety percent of cases in 1983 still experienced headaches, by far the most common complaint, though frequently these were less disabling than in the past. Other symptoms of neurasthenia (both in Beard's classical account and in the Chinese diagnostic system) also persisted (see table 13.8).

TABLE 13.6
1983 FOLLOW-UP STUDY

Change in Symptoms among Those with Positive Work Change

N = 5

Better = 4 (80%)
Worse = 0 (0)
Same = 1 (20%)

Change in Symptoms among Those with Negative Work Change

N = 2

Better = 0 (0)
Worse = 2 (100%)
Same = 0 (0)

Change in Symptom among Those with Neutral[a] Work Change

N = 3

Better = 2 (67%)
Worse = 0 (0)
Same = 1 (33%)

[a] New job perceived as neither better nor worse than previous job.

TABLE 13.7
1983 FOLLOW-UP STUDY

*Change in Symptoms among Those Who Resolved Problems
in Family Situations*

N = 6	
Better = 4	(67%)
Worse = 0	(0)
Same = 2	(33%)

TABLE 13.8
1983 FOLLOW-UP STUDY

Sources of Pain			N = 21
Headache	19	(90%)	
Backache	1	(5%)	
Other pain	8	(38%)	
Other Symptoms			(95%)
Weakness, tiredness	20	(86%)	
Insomnia	18	(86%)	
Dizziness	15	(71%)	
Bad memory	13	(62%)	
Poor appetite	7	(33%)	

Patients' accounts of work continued to disclose a strong association of symptoms with work problems. Nine (43 percent) stated openly their dislike for their work, and of these 7 (33 percent) expressed a strong desire to change work. Altogether 12 patients (57 percent) believed that illness affected their work, while the 9 already mentioned viewed their illnesses as worsened by work. Most of these patients were either actually engaged in efforts to change work or were considering doing so. It is notable as well that almost one in five patients stated they had significant economic problems greater than those of coworkers, a quarter perceived themselves as having significant marital problems, and more than half described a serious family problem that was still incompletely resolved.

Over the three years, only two patients (10 percent) had come to regard their sickness as depression, while nine (43 percent), the same number as in 1980, still thought of it as neurasthenia. This lends further weight to the argument we are advancing that neurasthenia is a more acceptable diagnosis than depression in China. But our understanding of why this is so was altered a bit by the finding that a very significant change occurred in whether patients viewed their problem as organic or psychological, in a direction we would not have predicted. In 1980 all the patients regarded their pain as either entirely or primarily organic in etiology, but by 1983, 52 percent regarded their pain as chiefly or entirely psychological. This change in viewpoint reflected the researchers' communication of a psychosomatic stress model of patients' illnesses, which also had become a more widely used explanatory model in the psychiatric clinic. Surprisingly, then, in spite of cultural sanctioning for organic explanations the patients came to accept professionally proffered psychological ones. This switch in explanatory models was associated with a change in help seeking. Of those whose views of their illnesses became more psychological or psychosomatic, 70 percent decreased medical help seeking, whereas of those few whose views of their illness became more organic, only a third decreased contact with the medical care system. Thus, change to more psychological explanations had the important effect of reducing the overutilization of medical services.

Again we were surprised that 38 percent of the follow-up patients expressed a wish to be treated with psychotherapy, a treatment intervention that is neither well developed nor prevalent in psychiatric care in China, and one that goes against the grain of the group orientation and somatic idiom of both traditional Chinese culture and the People's Republic. Perhaps this finding suggests that psychiatry is contributing to the advance of modernism in the clinic, a kind of Westernization of Chinese culture by "rationalizing" psychological idioms and self-images and thereby transforming neurasthenia into a disorder of "affect." This sea change in cultural code of communicating distress has not yet overtaken the popular culture in the People's Republic, but on the basis of similar change noted for Chinese in the United States, Hong Kong (Cheung et al. 1983), Taiwan (Rin 1982), and other overseas communities, it is apparent that it is happening in other Chinese populations as they undergo modernization and can be expected to emerge—our data suggest it is perhaps already beginning to do so—at least among the more educated class of teachers, professionals, and other "intelligentsia" in China.

Not a single patient in our sample had experienced a cure due to medical treatment, nor had a new medical diagnosis (e.g., endocrinological disease, cardiovascular disease, neurological disease) been established over the three years for any patient which had explained his or her pathology and changes in the level of disability. None of the psychiatric diagnoses (depression, anxiety, no mental illness) predicted positive treatment response, though clearly diagnoses of both ''neurasthenia'' and ''chronic pain'' were associated with relatively poor treatment outcomes. The only robust predictors of course were the social indicators of work, family, and other social problems. This is an impressive confirmation of our hypothesis, though the small size of our sample means that caution must be applied when generalizing from the findings. These findings are similar enough to those from the West (e.g., Yelin et al. 1980; Stone 1979*a*, *b*), however, that further research with larger samples in different clinical sites in China seems warranted.

Our pain patients were ''problem patients'' for their medical system, inasmuch as almost one-third had experienced some important difficulty in their relationships with practitioners, a complaint rarely mentioned among patients in China. They were viewed by their physicians as ''problem patients'' for much the same reason we suspect that chronic pain patients are so viewed in health care settings in the United States and the United Kingdom: because they fail to get better, perdure in seeking medical attention, and make treatment demands on their health care system which cannot be fulfilled. Again, as in the West, the psychosomatic label enables practitioners to shift responsibility for the poor therapeutic outcome from themselves to their patients.

For each case we attempted to work out an understanding of the meaning of the illness experience which extended beyond work and family problems to the broader sociocultural context (see table 13.9). For four patients (19 percent) chronic pain and other somatic complaints appeared to provide a cultural sanction for *failure* (in college entrance examinations, in achieving career goals, in returning from the countryside to their urban homes, and in other aspects of social life). For five patients (24 percent) the pain was a palpable symbol, a physiological emblem, of their own terrible personal tragedies during the Cultural Revolution, though, as in the general population, many more had experienced some problems (usually less serious ones) in that dangerous and chaotic period without it taking on such significance. Both sets of meanings of illness are vividly illustrated in the case vignettes described below. In our assessment, almost half the sample appeared to regularly and fairly successfully use their chronic pain to control spouse, children, or parents. Among four patients (19 percent) pain effectively sanctioned

TABLE 13.9
1983 FOLLOW-UP STUDY

Significance of Symptoms		
Sanction failure	=	4 (19%)
Symbolize distress due to Cultural Revolution	=	5 (24%)
Desire to change work	=	6 (28%)
Wish to reunite from separation	=	2 (10%)
Control family members	=	2 (10%)
Sanction expression of anger	=	10 (48%)
Express frustration over unresolved family, work, or political problems	=	6 (28%)
Time off and away from stressful life situation	=	4 (19%)
Bereavement response	=	4 (19%)
Other loss	=	2 (10%)

the expression of anger, which otherwise could not be expressed openly, including anger at the political system. For six others (28 percent) pain seemed to less availingly legitimize expression of chronic frustration and demoralization over unresolved community problems, including political ones. Two patients' pain appeared to successfully sanction time off and away from what they perceived as overwhelming responsibilities in the community, and gave them otherwise unavailable time to rest. (Indeed, two other patients who had serious work stress were able to persuade our research team to provide certificates to take time off work in order to "rest.") For 19 percent of the sample physical pain complaints occurred in the context of bereavement over the loss of a close family member, and in several other patients pain complaints seemed to express a more complicated set of losses (i.e., health, youth, confidence, education, Communist Party affiliation). Two patients justified isolation and nearly total withdrawal from sources of life stress via their pain complaints. Thus, for the patients we studied, pain complaints, as in the original 1980 study, held substantial social cachet and symbolized more than one personally or socially significant meaning, a point we shall return to in the Discussion, where we review the social sources of depression and somatization.

Chronic Pain in Primary Care in China at the Hunan Medical College

Since the chronic pain patients in our 1980 and 1983 studies were attending a psychiatry clinic, we wished to determine if our results pertained to the much larger number of patients attending the General Medical Clinic of the Second Affiliated Hospital at the Hunan Medical College and as a result could be compared with the data on somatization in primary care in the West. Therefore, in July 1983, that clinic was first surveyed to determine what percentage of patients complained of the two most common chronic somatization complaints in China: headaches and insomnia, in the absence of a medical diagnosis.[4] The former accounted for 11 percent of all patients surveyed over a two-day period, while the latter made up 10 percent of the 658 patients attending the clinic during those two days. These symptoms, which frequently occur together, were single *diagnoses* written on patients' records and by and large these diagnoses did not overlap. Thus, this very conservative estimate of somatization cases suggests that about one out of five outpatients in this primary care clinic may have been somatizing. Of the 658 patients, 7.4 percent carried the diagnosis of neurosis or neurasthenia, and were composed almost entirely of those from the headaches or insomnia groups.

Besides the survey, twenty-six patients, who were diagnosed to be suffering from chronic pain, defined as more than six months of pain that patients themselves perceived as disabling, were selected roughly consecutively, and interviewed in the same manner as in the earlier studies. Two-thirds were middle-aged women, almost half workers, the rest mainly teachers, cadres, and professionals (see table 13.10).[5] All suffered headaches as their site of pain, though half had other pain sites as well. Fifty-four percent made the DSM-III criteria for Major Depressive Disorder when interviewed with a modified version of the SADS diagnostic interview translated into Chinese, though none was so diagnosed by the Clinic's internists or consulting psychiatrists. Almost a quarter (23 percent) were determined to make the criteria for Dysthymic Disorder (chronic neurotic depression), which also was not diagnosed in the clinic. A third of patients, mostly those who were depressed, also made the criteria for various Anxiety Disorders. Seven patients (27 percent) were assessed to have no mental illness (see table 13.11).

These findings are in keeping with those from the chronic pain study in the psychiatry clinic. Women predominated in both groups. In our 1980

TABLE 13.10
CHRONIC PAIN IN PRIMARY CARE STUDY

Demographics:		N = 26	
Age :	mean—36, range 20–59		
	men, mean—39		
	women, mean—34		
Sex :	men—9 (35%)		
	women—17 (65%)		
Married :	22 (85%)		
Single :	3 (12%)		
Divorced :	1 (4%)		
Occupation :	Workers	=	12 (46%)
	Peasants	=	1 (4%)
	Cadres	=	6 (23%)
	Teachers	=	3 (12%)
	Professionals	=	4 (15%)

TABLE 13.11
CHRONIC PAIN IN PRIMARY CARE STUDY

		Psychiatric Diagnoses	N = 26
18 (69%)	Depressive disorders	Major Depressive Disorder =	14 (54%)
		Dysthymic Disorder =	6 (23%)
		Double Depression =	2 (8%)
		Generalized Anxiety Disorder =	1 (4%)
9 (35%)	Anxiety disorders	Panic Disorder =	3 (12%)
		Phobia Disorder =	5 (19%)
		(Simple 2, Agoraphobia 3)	
		Personality Disorder =	2 (8%)
		Hypochondria =	5 (19%)
		No mental disorder =	7 (27%)

survey of the 100 neurasthenia patients, men had a very slight predominance, as they did in the psychiatry clinic generally. But women predominated in the chronic pain-depression subsample. Teachers and others who belong to the intelligentsia were overrepresented, but workers (especially skilled workers) were present in large numbers. The elderly were not overrepresented. Somatization, then, may affect a wide segment of the Chinese population. In the absence of population-based figures, it would seem that women, especially middle-aged women, teachers, other members of the intelligentsia, and skilled workers may be at greater risk for somatization in China.

Again depression and anxiety disorders were found to be common concomitants of chronic pain, even in a general medical clinic, although more than one out of four patients had no mental illness. That both the follow-up study and this study contained a significant minority of patients who exhibited no evidence of mental illness on a fairly rigorous assessment schedule, we take to indicate that somatization is not always mediated by psychiatric disorder, though it does seem almost always to be associated with social problems.

These chronic pain patients had visited medical services on the average fifteen times over the preceding twelve months, a very high utilization rate for this clinic and for China generally. Besides headaches and other pain, more than half of the patients complained of dizziness, more than three-quarters insomnia, one-third weakness, more than one-quarter blurring of vision and one-quarter tiredness—what we can now see is the "classical" symptom constellation of neurasthenia in China. Not surprisingly, then, 73 percent had been diagnosed as suffering from neurasthenia by the doctors they had visited or had labeled themselves with the term. No patients called their sickness chronic pain, and only two (8%) called it depression. More than a quarter of patients had family members with a history of chronic pain or neurasthenia, which was true of the psychiatry clinic sample too. Whether this is a genetic or socially learned vulnerability factor will have to be assessed in future research.

Serious work problems were experienced by more than half the sample, 15 percent had significant marital problems, and almost one-third severe family distress. Thirty-eight percent of patients described themselves as being in serious economic difficulties, and nine patients (35 percent) had experienced difficult political problems in the past or were experiencing them at present, most usually related to the Cultural Revolution. Five patients (19 percent) were separated from their families owing to distant work sites. Thus, again serious social problems of the same type as described in the follow-up study were intimately connected to illness experience (see table 13.12).

In working out the meanings of the often not-so-covert chronic illness behavior, ten patients (38 percent) wanted to change work and their illness legitimized their efforts to do so; four (15 percent) were actively negotiating time off and away from work and from what were perceived as overwhelming family responsibilities, from which they sought "rest." For two, their spouses and family members treated them better when they were ill. For two other patients the pain complaints appeared to express frustration over a strong desire to obtain divorce in untenable marriage situations, but one deemed by unit (*danwei*) leaders and family members as unsuitable for divorce. For two patients the language of pain sanctioned personal failure and gave voice to a cry for help in an impossible-to-alter social situation, respectively (see table 13.13). Thus, the picture of social genesis and cultural construal of somatization in this primary care clinic seems to be quite similar to what we described for the psychiatry clinic.

The following case vignettes (in which names and identifying details have been changed to protect anonymity) illustrate certain of these findings. We have selected cases that are not meant to be representative, but for which sufficient information is available to illumine the web of

TABLE 13.12
CHRONIC PAIN IN CARE STUDY

Social Problems
Work = 14 (54%)
Separation = 5 (19%)
Family = 8 (31%)
Economic = 10 (38%)
Political = 9 (35%)
School = 1 (4%)
Loss = 1 (4%)

TABLE 13.13
CHRONIC PAIN IN PRIMARY CARE STUDY

Significance of Illness
Affects work = 6 (23%)
Can't work = 6 (23%)
Can't do housework = 4 (15%)
Wants to change work = 10 (38%)
Time off and out = 4 (15%)
Better support at work = 3 (12%)
Spouse better to patient = 2 (8%)
Wants divorce = 2 (8%)
Cry for help = 1 (4%)
Sanction failure = 1 (4%)

richly complex interrelationships between social reality, affect, and somatization which are only partially evoked by numerical description and inadequately explained by the statistical correlations.

CASE ILLUSTRATIONS

1. Lin Hung is a twenty-four-year-old worker in a machine factory who complains of headaches, dizziness, weakness, lack of energy, insomnia, bad dreams, poor memory, and a stiff neck. Pain, weakness, and dizziness are his chief symptoms, along with bouts of palpitations. His symptoms began six months ago, and they are gradually worsening. His mother, who has had similar complaints for many years, has been diagnosed as suffering from "neurasthenia," and he fears he has the same problem. His factory doctors believe he has a heart problem, but repeated electrocardiograms at the Hunan Medical College have been normal. He states he has a serious bodily disorder that is worsened by his work and that interferes with his ability to carry out his job responsibilities.

   Lin Hung has all the symptoms of Major Depressive Disorder as well as classical attacks of Panic Disorder (a type of anxiety disorder associated with waves of panic, hyperventilation, and rapid heart rate). He feels suicidal.

   Until his father retired from the job Lin now occupies, he was a soldier living not far from home. He didn't want to leave the army, but his father was anxious to retire so that he could move to a new apartment owned by his factory in another city. Fearing that his son would not be able to stay in the army and thereafter would not find work, Lin's father pressured him to take over his job, a job the younger Lin never liked or wanted for himself.[6] Lin Hung reluctantly agreed but now finds that he cannot adjust to the work. He did not want to be a machinist, and cries when he recounts that this is what he must be for the rest of his life. Moreover, he is despondent and lonely living so far away from his parents. He worries that he is not around to look after them in their old age, and that an older sister, who was sent to the countryside in the early 1970s, cannot get permission to move to the city to be with them. He has no friends at work and feels lonely living in the dormitory. He has a girl friend, but he cannot see her regularly any more, owing to the change in work sites. They wish to marry, but his parents, who have a serious financial problem because of a very low pension, cannot provide the expected furniture, room, or any financial help. The leaders of his work unit are against the marriage because he is too young. They also criticize him for his poor work performance and frequent days missed from work owing to sickness. He, in turn, does not believe he has the skill to work as a machinist and fears further ridicule for his shoddy work.

Lin Hung thinks that his health problem would resolve if he could leave his job, join his parents, and marry. But he regards each as impossible. Lin tells us he is hopeless and helpless, but he attributes these feelings to his physical symptoms not his social situation. He plans to seek sick leave so that he can rest and recover. His parents and he fear that he has a serious heart disorder, even though the Internal Medicine Clinic at the Hunan Medical College has reassured him that his heart is normal and that his palpitations result from his anxiety attacks. Lin Hung rejects the diagnosis of a psychosomatic problem, "I am sad and agitated because of my physical illness! That is the real problem, my heart disease." Out of desperation he pleads that we give him a letter for his factory clinic indicating that he must rest and recuperate, preferably at his parents' apartment.

2. Huang Zhenyi is a worker from a rural county town in his late twenties who has Dysthymic Disorder (chronic neurotic depression). He attributes his chronic headaches and dizziness to a traumatic childhood experience during the Cultural Revolution, about which he can talk only to his wife. During winter vacation from school, Huang Zhenyi returned to the school yard to play. While there, the then twelve-year-old noticed that on the rear door of the school building someone had tacked up a piece of paper. "Throw down Chairman Mao," was written in bold characters across the paper. Not knowing what to do about this anti-Mao slogan, he ran to see his close friend, who told him to quickly inform their Commune leaders. This he did, and these cadres responded by calling in the Public Security (police) agents. Three of them interviewed Huang Zhenyi at his school. They asked him who wrote the poster, and when he could not respond, they accused him. These policeman threatened that if he didn't confess they would not let him return home. Frightened after being interrogated for several hours in a small room at the school, from which he was not allowed to go to the toilet in spite of a painful urge to urinate, he told the police that he had found the slogan but was not the one who wrote it. He was angry at his friend for not supporting his story by

telling what had actually happened. Eventually, late at night, his interrogators allowed Huang to return home. There he found his mother distraught over his absence. He told her what happened, and assured her he was not at fault.

The next morning the three agents came to Huang Zhenyi's home and took him to the Public Security building. Brutally, they assured Huang Zhenyi that this time he would never leave the small interrogation room until he confessed. Terrified that he would not be allowed to eat, relieve himself, or see his mother again, Huang Zhenyi signed the confession, accepting sole responsibility for writing the poster.

When he returned home, he told his mother that he had written the poster, fearing that if he told her the truth it would only create greater trouble for her and for him. Huang Zhenyi still recalls with obvious pain his mother crying and cursing him, "If I knew before you'd end up like this, I wouldn't have wanted you." He remembers breaking down in tears, but he found himself unable to tell his mother the truth. "I felt like a coward. I couldn't tell her."

This experience recalled for him an earlier one. At age 8, he had gone with several classmates to fish in a nearby pond, instead of walking to school. They were very late getting to school. The teacher punished them by locking the boys in a small mud-walled room. They escaped by knocking a hole in the wall, and hid in a nearby cotton field. Their strict teacher ran after them and caught Huang Zhenyi's two friends, but not him. "I was so frightened I froze in my place. I could not move." Later in the evening he returned home, and the next day went back to school. The teacher, greatly angered by Huang's behavior, ordered him to do menial work around the school rather than study. Huang Zhenyi refused to do the hard labor, which led his teacher to criticize him severely in front of other teachers. After this experience, Huang Zhenyi reported "my liver became small, and I became frightened, cowardly." From this time onward he felt "paralyzed" whenever he had to "stand up" for himself before adults.

Because of his confession, the twelve-year-old Huang Zhenyi—who again felt "paralyzed," unable to break his silence before his adult accusers—was marched through the local county town wearing a dunce cap, carrying a sign around his neck in which he had written a self-criticism for the "terrible act," surrounded by thousands of local peasants and cadres, who cursed him, spat at him, and threw dirt and pebbles at him. The next day he was sent to work as a peasant at a local commune. He was expected to do the work of an adult. No one would talk with him at first. The labor was so very difficult that Huang Zhenyi thought he would not survive. Each day he had to undergo self-criticism, while local groups of children jeered him. In a big criticism session, he felt himself go numb all over, as if paralyzed. He wanted to yell out the truth but couldn't get himself to do it, to break his silence. No one would believe him, Huang Zhenyi reasoned. He had been patient so far; he would endure the unendurable, since there was no way out. Finally after a year of hard labor, a year during which he several times thought he could no longer stand the work and the isolation, his fellow peasants praised him for doing the work of an adult and enduring his punishment in silence. They pleaded on his behalf with the local authorities that he be allowed to return to school, which he did.

Eventually, Huang left this commune and moved to a county town in another province, where he finished high school and where his past was unknown. He became a key worker and joined the Communist Party. He was able to do the latter because the local Party officials, owing to the chaos of the time, knew nothing about his past and because of his highly regarded poor peasant background. He never told his mother the truth. When she was dying he thought of confessing to her the full story but decided against it. "I was too frightened to speak out and didn't think it would do any good." Huang's mother died not knowing the truth of her son's innocence, a point he returns to again and again as a palpable reason for his current feelings of desperate shame and self-hatred.

Now looking backward, he feels depressed, hopeless, demoralized. He retains great anger at the three policemen and at his classmate, who would not admit to the interrogators that Huang Zhenyi had told him he had found, not written, the anti-Mao poster. He feels a searing sense of injustice, a feeling that he associates with a burning sensation in the head, dizziness, and exhaustion. He is fearful that someone in the Party will learn of his past and expel him on account of it.

Huang believes he will never recover from this event. "It has affected my character. I am withdrawn; I don't like to be too friendly with others. I am a coward. I cannot trust others." He sees his only hope as writing a novel about his experience which fictionalizes it to protect his anonymity and which generalizes it so that it comes to represent the "losses and defeat" his generation has experienced. "Like me we are a lost generation that has suffered so much." But Huang Zhenyi doubts he will accomplish this goal. He has no formal training or natural skill to write fiction. He actively fears the consequences of others learning about his past. Each time he takes up a pen to write the story, he is overcome by a self-defeating lassitude, dizziness, and sense of his inefficacy. Hence Huang's physical complaints are amplified (perhaps created) by the literal embodiment of chronic frustration, inability to act—if we use his word, "paralysis," but of will not muscle—and the unbearable inner hurt of shameful "injustice" that he can neither publicly articulate (save through the personally unavailing neurasthenic pain) nor privately resolve.

3. Hu Chengyeh is a thirty-seven-year-old cashier in a rice shop in a rural town who suffers from periodic bouts of headache, dizziness, and a burning sensation in the upper abdomen and chest. We diagnosed Dysthymic Disorder and a chronic personality problem in this sensitive but sullen, even haughty worker. He arrived at our three-year follow-up interview much like he entered the initial interview: alternating between acting irritable, complaining (this time about the side effects and lack of therapeutic effect of our treatment), and being silent and aloof, rarely smiling and with a defiant edge to his bearing and movements.

We asked him about himself, but he had come to tell us about something else, something he withheld at our first meeting. "My family is complicated. I was taken in by my stepfather when my mother remarried after my real father died when I was very young. My stepfather who came from a landlord background was sent to the countryside in the Anti-Rightist Campaign where he eventually died of TB. I hate him. His bad class background deeply affected my life. Because he was my source of support I was labeled as having a landlord background.[7] My older sister who stayed with my real father's relatives, who supported her, was assigned a very good class background, since they were poor workers and peasants. She benefited, went to senior middle school, joined the Party. I was discriminated against. I couldn't go to senior middle school, was not given good work to do, couldn't join the Party. My life was ruined. So I hate him."

Hu also spoke of his problem as a great and irremediable "injustice." In spite of his stigmatized background, he asserts, he naively believed in his stepfather, until he learned from other family members that his stepfather resented having him in the family and spoke ill of Hu Chengyeh behind his back. Hearing these words, Hu felt great shame. His ambivalence was driven away; from then on, he reports, he felt only bitterness: a growing, unappeasable hatred that affected every part of his life. So all-pervasive and terrible did this hatred become that in recent years Hu Chengyeh visited rebuilt Buddhist temples to find peace of mind. He copied down Buddhist epigrams and wrote them out on scrolls that he hung in his room. But the admonitions to empty the mind of rancor, unhappiness, and vengeful desire, and to forgive didn't work for him. Bitterness and anger spilled over into all his relationships: with his wife and child, his coworkers, his neighbors, his physicians, even with us. Over the years he saw himself become sullen, withdrawn, alienated, implacably vengeful.

> "I quarrel all the time with my wife: over what she wears, over being late for dinner, which happens often since she works late. Always over trivial things. I am irritable to my little daughter. I fear anger will seriously affect her, hurt her, drive her away from me."
>
> "Once when she was 5, she locked herself in my neighbor's room. She was too little to understand how to unlock the door. I became furious, shouting at her. It frightened her more. She was too terrified and could not do what I yelled at her to do. My neighbor calmed her down and coached her through the steps of unlocking the door. Everyone present was greatly relieved. Not me. I felt such rage, I wanted to hit her. I still feel the rage surge through me when I think back to that event. It rises upward in my stomach and chest. I feel *huo qi da*."

The greater the bitterness the worse his physical pain becomes. He believes the injustice he has experienced has ruined his emotions and health.

Recently his physical symptoms have improved somewhat, following a work transfer from a distant rice shop, which necessitated that he live away from home for seven years, to one situated near enough to home so that he now lives again with wife and daughter. This transfer took him away from a tension-ridden work situation, one in which he daily squabbled with coworkers over work assignments and practices. But now he has begun quarreling more with his wife and especially with the neighborhood committee that oversees assignment of apartments. Hu Chengyeh regards his present room as unacceptable and has pressed the neighborhood committee to find him a larger and healthier accommodation, but without success. Hu, his wife, and daughter live in a very small single room that contains only one narrow window. In the furnacelike heat of the redoubtable Hunan summer, Hu complains, it is too hot to sleep. The more he feels the situation is intolerable but unalterable, the more he finds himself quarreling with the neighborhood committee.

Anger and bad relationships also characterize his experiences with the personnel at the local county hospital. "The medicine is useless. They cannot find out what is wrong. They do no good. There is no sense in going back to them."

When his anger becomes unbearable, as Hu himself recognizes, his "neurasthenic headaches" and abdominal and chest complaints become much worse. Then he must lie down; he cannot help with housework or go to work. Sometimes his wife too must stay home to comfort and care for him. She treats him with great concern when his sickness worsens, fearful that he will suffer a stroke (like his biological father) because of his rage and pain. Both she and his friends attribute his anger to his neurasthenia. Since changing work sites these events are less frequent. When they lived far apart for most of each month, Hu would return home to his wife and child for days at a time when he was too ill to work. At such times he would read reprints of ancient Chinese medicine texts that extol diet, tonics, and herbal medicine to maintain health and thereby improve emotions.

But whenever he thinks of his stepfather the burning bitterness returns:

> "He ruined all my chances. I couldn't continue on in school, get a good job. I wanted to join the Party, but how could I with the taint of a landlord label. It is a tragedy: my sister benefited from my real father's good class background; I have been ruined by my stepfather's. There is no remedy. Sometimes I feel it would be better to be dead than to carry this curse any further."

4. Comrade Yen is a forty-year-old teacher in a rural town, intelligent, articulate, and deeply depressed. She sits immobile on the wooden stool opposite us, looking fixedly at the floor. Her black hair tied tightly in a bun behind her head is streaked with white; her handsome, high-cheekboned face is deeply lined with crow's feet radiating outward from each eye. She recounts for us the story of her chronic headaches.

"There are several sources. Before the Cultural Revolution I was outgoing, active, had high self-regard. As a teenager I had been secretary of the local Communist Youth League. I dreamed of a career with the Party and advanced education. My family and friends all expected great achievements. I had ambition and high goals. Then during the Cultural Revolution I was severely criticized. I had to leave my position in the Youth League. I went to the distant countryside to a very poor place.[8] I couldn't adjust to the conditions. The work was too hard; too little to eat. Bad smells were everywhere, and nothing was clean. Terrible living conditions."

All of this was made worse by the realization that her career aspirations were no longer tenable, and that even return to an urban environment was unlikely. The daughter of intellectuals, with several generations of professionals in the family, Comrade Yen felt deeply the lost opportunity for a university education and career in the Communist Party. Cut off from family and friends, and books and newspapers, yet not well accepted, at least initially, by the peasants among whom she lived, she grew aloof and solitary. As the Cultural Revolution accelerated, she occasionally bore the brunt of self-criticism sessions. On one occasion she was denied an injection by a nurse at a rural county hospital who accused her of being a "stinking intellectual." She began to experience a change in personality. Comrade Yen felt constantly demoralized, and in place of her former optimism she was generally hopeless and expected only the worst to happen. She became introverted, sensitive to what she perceived as the rejecting and criticizing eyes of peasants and cadres. She first began to depreciate her goals, then herself. Hesitant where she once had been assertive, lacking confidence where she once had radiated it, Comrade Yen felt increasingly inadequate and coped by narrowing even more her behavioral field and already limited options. She stayed to herself. Eventually she obtained a post as a primary school teacher in a rural town. When her native abilities became apparent to her fellow teachers, they wished to elect her the principal. But Comrade Yen declined because she feared the responsibility and did not want to expose herself again in a situation where she might well fail and suffer further losses.

She married a native of the region who is presently a peasant but previously was a cadre in a mine. They live apart, and it is clear she prefers it this way: he is in a distant production team, while she lives in the small commune town. They have three children, two adolescent sons who live with their father and one daughter who still lives at home with her mother. Comrade Yen is angry that her husband has not been rehabilitated and given back his post as a cadre. It is aggravating to her but her husband has given up, declaring that he will never regain his former status. This is a chronic source of frustration, another difficulty about which she feels nothing can be done. Her third source of anguish is her daughter.

> "I really did not want to have her. I wanted to be alone. We already had enough children. When I was very pregnant I hit myself several times quite hard against the wall, hoping I might abort. But my husband wanted a child and I could not decide on an abortion at the hospital. Thus I blamed myself when I gave birth to a baby girl with a withered arm. I felt I caused it."[9]

The daughter grew up to be beautiful and very bright, an outstanding student. But her mother grieved for her because of her deformity. "In China, normal people don't marry cripples. Even though she could do everything—cook, clean, play sports—I knew she would have trouble marrying." At this point in our interview, the patient silently cried, her gaze fixed on the cement floor beneath the table separating us. Her husband, who had accompanied her, looked much older than Comrade Yen and was wide-eyed in a provincial capital he had visited only several times before. His coarse peasant features may have contrasted with his wife's more refined face, but he joined her in weeping openly when she continued to talk about their daughter:

> "There is no hope for her. Even though she is one of the best students in the senior middle school, she cannot take the examination to go to the university. Her school principal and the secretary of the local branch of the Party decided that only completely healthy, normal children can take the examination. We appealed to the county authorities, but they upheld the decision. There is nothing that can be done. Our daughter will live at home and do what work she can."

There followed several minutes when the patient could not go on, but sobbed and wept. Finally she told us how she and her husband had arranged for their daughter to meet another "cripple" in a nearby town. But her daughter decided she would not marry someone else who was deformed; rather she would remain single.

Comrade Yen shared her full hopelessness with us. Often she thinks it would be preferable to be dead. Her headaches keep her to herself. She cannot face any more "stress," it is too upsetting.

''My health is too uncertain. I cannot do too much. I think only of my headaches, not of the future or the past.'' Comrade Yen severely restricts her world. She withdraws from all but essential responsibilities. She cannot plan any outing ''because of bad influences on my health: the weather, the noise, the crowds.''

Because of her feelings of inadequacy, failure, hopelessness, despair, she circumscribes her life to school and dormitory room. Only on occasional weekends does she visit her husband. Her daughter stays with her. They appear to be like two recluses, each grieving somewhat different losses. Comrade Yen's world is now that of pain: experiencing her hurt, waiting for it, fearing it, talking about it, and blaming her problems on it. It is the pain (and related complaints) that legitimizes her withdrawal at work and in the family life, sanctions her isolation, demoralization, and depression. Her chronic pain is an unavailing expression of her multiple losses. Before we departed she sent us a letter:

''I feel always sad about being ill for such a long time. I feel headache, dizziness, don't like to talk, take no pleasure in things. My head and eyes feel swollen. My hair is falling out. My thinking has slowed down. Symptoms are worse when I am with others, better when I am alone. Whenever I do anything I have no confidence. I think because of the disease I have lost my youth and much time and everything. I grieve for my lost health. I must work a lot every day just like the others, but I have no hope in what lies ahead. I think there is nothing you can do.''

5. Zheng Gueili is a thirty-five-year-old mother of two and head of a child care center. A plump, attractive, initially demure woman with a low voice, she becomes animated and insistent as she recounts her physical complaints. Zheng Gueili complains of a long list of bodily symptoms, but pays special attention to her chronic headaches, insomnia, and poor memory. She also mentions that she has fears of making a mistake at work and being blamed for it. Although volunteering no complaints of dysphoria while recounting her story, when specifically asked, she admits feeling depressed and answers affirmatively to the vegetative complaints of depression, with the exception of guilt and suicidal ideas. Though persistent since 1980, she hastens to add, her symptoms are now somewhat less severe. But periodically they become substantially worse.

The daughter of a retired head of a local factory and a head nurse in a nearby hospital, Zheng Gueili was sent to the countryside during senior middle school, as were many of her classmates. In the com-

mune, she met another student from her native city. They first
became close friends, and then years later married. They married at a
time when it appeared both would remain living their entire lives in
their rice farming commune. "We gave up hope of returning to the
city. We were very lonely. No family nearby, few friends. We were
happier together." Zheng Gueili and her husband arranged the marriage through the local authorities.

One year after marrying, Zheng's husband was given official
permission to return to their home city (owing to political changes).
He lived with his parents, and rarely visited his in-laws, since they
clearly disapproved of the marriage. They viewed the husband's
work as a nonskilled laborer and his family's similar background as
unsuitable. "They expected me to marry someone of higher status,"
she told us.

From 1975 to 1979, Zheng Gueili did all she could to seek official
permission to return home and join her husband. Finally, unable to
succeed in her quest and despondent that she would live "forever" in
the rural area she had come to abhor, Zheng Gueili illegally left her
commune and joined her husband. Because his parents had no room
in their small apartment for the married couple, they went to live with
Zheng's parents, who made apparent their dislike for the husband and
the living arrangement. From the first, daily life was filled with
quarrels between Zheng's parents and her husband. She feared inter-
vening because without an official residence permit she was totally
dependent on her parents for food and lodging. But after a year, she
received official sanctioning to live in the city, and thereafter was
able to find employment. In fact, her father arranged his retirement
earlier than required so that she could obtain a job in his factory.

During this year, Zheng felt herself becoming progressively more
depressed and anxious. She began to doubt her competence in her job
as a day-care center worker in the factory, fearing that she would
make an error that would in some way result in injury to the small
children she minded. She could no longer tolerate the squabbling at
home, yet felt unable to change the situation. It was in this context
that her headache, which she had begun to suffer from in the countryside, greatly worsened. Insidiously, the other symptoms slowly
developed and also worsened.

"This is a bad time. I could not adjust to work; and home life was tense and
difficult. I had to do everything. I worked, cared for others' children, came
home, took care of my own children, cooked, washed dishes, cleaned the

house. Some mornings I began at 5:00 a.m. to go to the market for food. No one helped me. My husband was so angry at my parents and me he refused to help. My mother and father demanded that I be responsible for my family. They showed their unhappiness with my decision to marry by paying little attention to me and giving very little help. I cried to myself. I felt exhausted. But what could I do?''

As her symptoms worsened, Zheng Gueili initiated a frequently repeated cycle of visiting different clinics (usually accompanied by her husband or her parents), trying many different medicines, altering her diet, drinking tonics, eating special foods, and avoiding ''cold'' foods because traditional Chinese-style practitioners diagnosed her as constitutionally overly ''cold.'' For short periods her symptoms became so severe that she stayed in bed. During these times her parents did the housework, child care, and also solicitously attended to their sick daughter.

''My parents and my husband treated me very well. They were as frightened as I was that something was seriously wrong. When we learned the problem was neurasthenia then we realized my health was bad and easily upset. I would need help for a long time. The doctors told us this, as did our neighbors. I felt bad to be a burden, but there was nothing I could do. The headaches and insomnia were so bad. Nothing did any good.''

At the end of 1980, Zheng Gueili was promoted to teaching in the factory's primary school. She felt unprepared for her new responsibilities; she feared making a mistake and thereby misinforming her students. She also had a bad relationship with her supervisor, whom she felt was insensitive to her health problem and expected too much from her. In this context her symptoms substantially worsened and she had to obtain sick leave to recuperate at home. After a few months, she received permission to return to her former position in the factory's child care center. Over the past year, and against her wishes, she was promoted to head her child care unit. She fears this will present too much stress and will make her health worse. She already has noticed more frequent and severe headaches and insomnia.

But the home situation has greatly improved. Her husband and parents regard Zheng Gueili's health as fragile and easily undermined. For this reason they have taken over many of the child care, cooking, and housecleaning activities. They fear exhausting her and making her bodily complaints worse. Her husband confided to us that he even feared expressing anger at his wife because "her health cannot endure it."

Zheng Gueili's relationship to her factory physicians has not been good. She told us that they seem to discount the seriousness of her problem. She does not accept their diagnosis of psychosomatic disorder and referrals for psychiatric treatment. Zheng Gueili was indignant when she reported to us her disgust with the factory doctors. "My problem is not a psychological one. I have headaches, other pain, can't sleep well, and have trouble with my memory. Perhaps my neurasthenia has affected my brain. I am tired all the time. This is a serious sickness and perhaps there is no treatment for it."

There was no evidence to us at the time of mental illness. Even Zheng Gueili was aware that her symptoms greatly worsened owing to work or family tension. But she adamantly rejected any connection between the two that suggested psychological problems contributed to her illness.

By the time our interview ended, Zheng Gueili became increasingly demanding and complaining. She manipulated her husband before our eyes. When he complained to us of the difficulty he had getting angry with his wife for fear he would worsen her symptoms, she grumbled about a headache, and he responded caringly and stopped talking about his discontent. We had the intuitive feeling that she was successful at controlling her husband and parents, and also probably would succeed in returning to a less stressful job in the day care facility. We found ourselves growing impatient, however, with her whining tone of voice and querulous insistence that we provide her with a medical excuse from work so she could rest for several days. We also were impressed by the tolerance and concern her husband (and by report her parents too) continued to show for her physical condition.

Discussion: Depression

The depressed patients we studied in the People's Republic unquestionably had experienced substantial political, financial, and social (i.e., work and family) distress. We have enumerated the nature and magnitude of distress, the prevalence of depressive and anxiety disorders, and the uses (and abuses) of a somatic idiom for expressing that distress. The case vignettes, however, amply indicate that the epidemiological and clinical statistics fail to explain the problems our patients suffered in sufficient ethnographic depth to enable the reader to "interpret" their significance in the Chinese context of particular meanings, norms, and power. The quantitative data, important in other respects, offer a thin, medicocentric, in places almost lifeless, reduction of richly emotion-laden, socially complex findings. The case descriptions and interpretations, however, make it hard to see the forest for the trees: how does one generalize and reliably assign weights to the different components of cases. Here quantification is essential.[10] If we use one source of data as a foil against which to rework the other, we obtain a clearer image of the structural yet dynamic dialectic linking culture to depression and pain in our patient sample.

First, we can speak of the social production of depression. Our findings would fit well into the causal model of depression sketched by Brown and Harris (1978) in their masterly monograph *The Social Origins of Depression*. Why the particular patients we studied developed clinical depression, whereas others who went through the same experiences did not, may reflect in part underlying genetic and psychological vulnerability, and in part the meaning of the stressors for them and the social resources available to them to buffer the effects of severely stressful life events. But there can be little question that other, and perhaps larger, determinants of depressive disease are the social sources of human misery, aspects perhaps of the human predicament, that generated hopelessness, demoralization, and self-defeating conceptions of self and situation (Moore 1970:40–77, 1978:49–109). These social sources of affliction give rise to situations that undermine self-esteem, block alternative behavioral options, further limit access to already limited resources, create untenable interpersonal tensions, delegitimate established roles, and in many instances are simply intolerable. One need look no further for the microdepressogenic system, and its macro origins. The social sources of human distress are local human contexts of power that distribute resources unequally, and that transmit the effects of large-scale sociopolitical, economic, and ecological forces unjustly. The microcontext may be a terrible marital relationship in which a wife's self-esteem is systematically undermined by the communication system established by cultural rules as much as by idiosyncratic discord, or it may be an oppressive relationship with a supervisor or boss which plays out as much a structural dialectic of authority and subordination as an individual evil. Sometimes macro-origins exert a small effect on local context, other times as in the Cultural Revolution they may be determinative. The local context itself can be thought of as a nested hierarchy of family, network, work, and community settings. This local cultural system systematically relates person to social structure, bridging physiological processes and social relations. The symbolic medium mediating sociophysiological processes is cultural meanings that connect affect and cognition and self-concept as a person-centered and small group system to ethnoepistemological and moral and political components of the macrosystem. The systematic relationships within this local system might be thought of as generating pathological processes as well as therapeutic ones (Hahn and Kleinman 1983).

It seems most plausible, then, to regard the core psychobiology of depression as the outcome of the interaction between personal vulnerability, major stressful life events, coping processes, social support *within* these local contexts of power which influence how risk, stress, and resources are configured and systematically interrelate. These local contexts, left out of most epidemiological studies but central to anthropological analysis, give stress and support vector and cachet. Serious stressors and inadequate support are not reified entities but systematic relationships among meanings, legitimacies, and structural arrangements of power in local cultural systems that conduce to distress (Young 1980). How these systems contribute to the social production of disease should be a central focus of what might be called anthropological epidemiology (or in the case of the social production of depression, anthropological psychiatry).

But this is not the way our patients regarded depression, which few acknowledged as suffering. Even for the few who admitted its presence, depression, in their somatopsychic cultural view of self and body, was the result, not the cause, of pain, a medical not a social psychological problem. This somatizing view was shared by many of their practitioners (somatization after all is a transactional process), and, as we have demonstrated elsewhere (Kleinman 1980, 1982), it is supported by the universe of symbolic meanings that comprises the Chinese cultural tradition. The core principles of this cultural world view center on the harmonizing of interpersonal relations, the sociocentric orientation of the self, and for these reasons the constitution of affect as moral position in a social field of reciprocal behavior. Denial of dysphoria is also of course a neutral and safe position to hold in an ideological context in which depression signifies potentially dangerous political implications: disaffiliation, alienation, potential opposition. Here, as a complementary process to disease causation, we have the cultural construction of illness.

It is worth analyzing the social production and cultural construction of depression in our Hunanese sample in somewhat more detail. We can posit that genetic vulnerability and childhood and adolescent experiences with depressed mothers and difficult family situations may contribute to the development of a self-concept in which self-esteem is fragile or already in doubt and in which Beck's (1979) negative cognitive schemata are reinforced. But our patients appear to have been at higher risk as well because of their place in local Chinese contexts of power and the sociopolitical and historical changes those contexts had undergone. A number of our patients came from highly stigmatized families that carried the "black" labels of rightist or landlord background. Growing up in that setting, our future patients had faced great discrimination and blocked access to resources (senior middle school, university, desirable jobs). Many had internalized a spoiled identity, one that was dramatically reaffirmed in large national campaigns (Anti-rightist, Cultural Revolution) in which techniques for enhancing feelings of shame and guilt (self-criticism sessions, criticism of and by family members and family friends) were regularly employed, and in which their traditional Chinese moral universe was quite literally stood on its head. The children of "stinking intellectuals" learned to criticize themselves and their families, for example, for the very intellectual values so central to China's millennial culture and most probably an active socializing force in their very families. More practically, they were sent to the "distant" (most impoverished) countryside to live with peasants, where they often were greeted with hostility and suspicion in the peasant world of limited goods: where the open mouths and empty stomachs of rusticated youth were seen as more of a threat than their usually unimpressive muscles were seen as a gain to the local economy. There they literally "wasted their years" without completing schooling, separated from other family members, often by great distances that blocked communication, without access to resources to sustain their intellectual development and urban interests, frequently without achieving full acceptance either in their impoverished rural communities; and they became increasingly cynical about the ideological shifts from the radical, rural-oriented rhetoric of their youth to the pragmatic, urban-centered policies of their majority. When they finally returned (those who could leave the countryside—many still cannot), they found themselves literally "lost." No jobs, no chance to successfully compete in university entrance exams, in which only 4 percent pass, against a new generation of well-prepared students whose scientific and technological education was up-to-date, not woefully behind the times. Often they lacked even the official residence permit required to live in the city, and thus were totally dependent on family and the "hidden economy." This was the trajectory of vulnerability among one group of our patients. Others had various but often equally disconfirming experiences in which severe threats to the self and serious multiple losses were normative.

But other things happened to those who developed depression besides these societywide threats to the integrity of the self. Some experienced such overwhelmingly destructive personal tragedies that they developed major personality changes: a few became so deeply embittered that every aspect of their lives radiated anger and hatred and alienation, others withdrew with fear and hurt into the inner privacy of the isolated self, diminishing performance to match greatly reduced expectations, to protect against further losses. Yet others organized their lives around their repeated and multiple losses as prolonged or even continuous grief reactions.[11]

The inadequate or ineffective social supports and personal coping responses to meet these assaults on self-esteem and uncontrollable losses that characterize the local contexts within which our research subjects live disclose a few social and psychological sources of distress that are perhaps unique to China along with others that are widely present in the West. The latter include severe marital disharmony that in several cases established sociolinguistic dialogues with spouse or in-laws which further undermined confidence and reinforced the negative cognitive schemata of self-inefficacy and a demoralized view of the world as basically frustrating. Others participated in tension-ridden, disconfirming relations with work supervisors or unit leaders in which their aspirations were blocked and they saw themselves as sentenced to a lifetime of numbing drudgery and bitter chronic stress. Each of these situations of high social risk and personal vulnerability in an intimate behavioral field comprised of inadequate coping and social support resources and desperate local power relationships seems to have followed the same final common pathway charted by Brown and Harris (1978) as the social production of clinical depression. Greatly diminished self-esteem and hopelessness "specific" to particular losses and other stressful life events, in vulnerable individuals, became generalized into a pervasive hopelessness attributed to most aspects of their lives; finally, there developed the psychophysiological symptoms of depression and illness careers. Depressive disorder, thereafter, seems to have conduced to the development of chronic somatization in most of our cases, though anxiety disorders contributed to many of these cases as well.[12] The primary point is that the origin, organization, and consequences of this pathophysiology are social.

Chinese culture affected this social psychological and sociosomatic process of disease production in the creation of particular kinds of stressors (self-criticism sessions, being "sent" to the countryside, etc.), the valuation of certain types of stressors as most stressful (those that broke up family system or undermined the sociocentric moral underpinnings of the Chinese self), and the labeling of the psychophysiological reactions these stressors produced as "neurasthenia," to which the tendency to amplify the somatic component and dampen the psychological component of the stress response contributed. Chinese culture also affected the pattern of excessive medical help seeking, the use of particular styles of illness behavior to communicate social and personal distress, and the special ways by which these idioms opened up behavioral options in tightly organized family and work systems.

Chinese cultural norms come into play in the very perception of a life event as a loss or threat (real or symbolic) so that the percept is as much cultural construct as neurological sensory input (see Pennebacker and Skelton 1982). Further scanning and monitoring of the psychophysiological state of arousal (reaction to the loss or threat) incorporate structuring principles based on cultural norms and meanings that together with personal significance organize that arousal into a particular pattern of dysphoria, which can now be more accurately regarded as a psychocultural process. The symbolic significance of the loss (both for the individual and as part of the collective representations of the group) will contribute to organize its psychobiology and social construction as "stress," "grief," "depressive affect," and so forth. In this structurally dynamic dialectic between meaning and biology, social relations also are tied to psychophysiology (e.g., who was lost, what was the nature, quality, and intensity of the loss, what are the setting and relationships within which the loss is experienced and communicated, what support is available and how is it regarded and mobilized) as are norms (e.g., the cultural rules governing how loss should be responded to). Hence the cultural construction of depressive disorder contributes to its social production, while the latter initiates the former. The upshot is a sociosomatic system in which neuroendocrine dysregulation might be thought of as a component of disrupted social relations, and disconfirming personal meanings might be regarded as both contributing to and expressing the malfunctioning of neurotransmitters (Hofer 1984).

Pain and Somatization

In our view, chronic pain is a form of somatization, an illness behavior (see Carr and Vitaliano, chap. 8) associated with depression, anxiety, and other psychiatric diseases. But it also occurs in the absence of mental illness, as a coping style, a form of social communication, a cultural symbol and its interpretation.

One way of categorizing somatization is by its course: acute, subacute, chronic (Rosen et al. 1982). *Acute* somatization, lasting days or weeks, is frequently caused by acute stress syndrome in which general arousal of autonomic nervous system (including activation of the neuroendocrine system) gives rise to combined psychophysiological symptoms. Somatization occurs when the patient (abetted by the family and health professionals) systematically focuses on and thereby amplifies the physiological symptoms (i.e., pain, weakness, rapid heart rate, hyperventilation, gastrointestinal complaints, etc.), while at the same time he minimizes and thereby dampens their affective and cognitive concomitants. As a result, a psychophysiological reaction becomes defined and is experienced chiefly as a physical problem and help is sought for treatment of what patient, family, and health professionals consider to be a medical sickness. *Subacute* somatization, lasting several months, is caused by either a more prolonged stress response or an actual psychiatric disorder, most usually depression and/or anxiety disorders.

Chronic somatization results from physical complaints accompanying chronic psychiatric disorder (e.g., chronic depression or anxiety, hysteria, personality disorder, schizophrenia, chronic factitious illness, etc.), or from amplification of symptoms and disability in the course of chronic medical disorder (e.g., asthma, arthritis, diabetes, epilepsy). In the former instance, the bodily symptoms of psychiatric disease (insomnia, appetite and weight loss, energy disturbance, pain, weakness, dizziness) are emphasized, expressed, and dealt with while their psychological concomitants are deemphasized, regarded as secondary, and therefore untreated. In the case of chronic medical disorder, psychosocial stress in local contexts of power (i.e., family conflict over differential access to insufficient resources, work problems stemming from abuses of employer power or quests for empowerment by workers, school and examination failure, or community problems) is often the chief source of symptom amplification and the exacerbation of disability, though depression and anxiety secondary to physical illness may also contribute.

But chronic somatization also has two other sources. *Illness behavior* in acute or subacute somatization may become prolonged and eventually frozen into a long-term sick role in which complaining about bodily symptoms and preoccupation with illness form a central part of one's everyday behavior and a means of dealing with other people, as in chronic pain syndrome. Here psychological and social factors behaviorally condition physical symptoms, for example, in the operant conditioning paradigm, and bring these bodily complaints under the control of concrete environmental forces in the local cultural systems we have described. These forces maintain the illness behavior in spite of medical treatment, which may remove the underlying disease process (e.g., stress response, depression, anxiety, acute biomechanical low back strain). The illness behavior becomes a crucial relationship in the ecology of the local system. Indeed, at times medical treatment itself may become one of those concrete environmental forces conditioning chronic illness behavior. In such a circumstance, the underlying disease may remit in response to pharmacological treatment while the illness behavior continues in response to the therapeutic relationship.

Alternatively, chronic somatization sometimes occurs in the absence of any medical or psychiatric disorder as a habitual *coping style* or *idiom of distress* that is learned via childhood socialization in family, in school, and in the other sectors of the local system under the aegis of societywide paradigmatic cultural norms. A somatic style of coping with stress and of articulating distress is widely shared in many societies where it is indirectly and often inadvertently supported by family, school, work/disability, health care, and other social institutions. Physical complaints, based on actual psychobiological processes, may be encouraged by a culture's behavioral norms, rules of social etiquette, and even by language usage. Disability, as has been well documented and is apparent from the findings from our Hunan studies, can be (and often is) supported or even worsened by financial reward and advantages resulting from enhanced personal efficacy and desired change in interpersonal relations with spouse, children, parents, in-laws, friends, work supervisors, co-workers, teachers, health professionals, and others. These altered social relationships and economic benefits are the "social gains" that reinforce psychobiological processes and maintain illness behavior in the ways we have described (see Barsky and Klerman 1983; Cacioppo et al. 1983; Cheung and Lau 1982; Katon et al. 1982; Kleinman 1983; Mechanic 1972, 1980; Pennebacker and Skelton 1978; Tessler and Mechanic 1978).

In anthropological perspective, somatization includes interpretive schema for making sense of life problems (Nichter 1981), rhetorical devices for controlling local relationships by persuading others to provide greater access to scarce resources and empower the somatizer (Csordas 1983; McGuire 1983), and symbolic forms that constitute and express salient modes of life in particular cultures (Good 1977). The ethnography of chronic somatization seeks to explore the way somatization is organized in local cultural systems through these and related communicative processes acting on the psychobiological and sociosomatic reticulum we have described.

As a result, disability may be amplified or dampened, though in complex and varied ways. Where desired change occurs in local relationships of power, psychophysiological amplification may be reversed if it is no longer needed to maintain change, or it may persist where it is needed. Damping as a sociosomatic and psychosomatic process may occur where the personal despair and demoralization associated with powerlessness and its mediating affect, depression, are altered so that there is an enhanced sense of self-efficacy even if there is little or no change in the local situation. Damping may also occur if other means are employed to alter local power relations, and the language of bodily distress no longer has major strategic significance in these relationships. Amplification may persist even where desired change has been achieved if it has become a fixed coping style, or if the somatizer is no longer able to effectively communicate through other channels. Therapy, then, can be seen as achieving damping through its influence on local power negotiations or through remoralizing the demoralized powerless (Frank 1974), or as a form of cultural rhetoric in which the therapist's adroit reconceptualization of the situation alters the channel of communicating distress and persuasively enhances self-esteem and thereby removes depressive dysphoria (see Beeman, chap. 7; Csordas 1984). Maladaptive somatization may be said to be present either when persistent amplification fails to achieve personally desired change, or when change has been achieved at too great a cost to the person, the family, or the medical care and work/disability systems.

Psychiatrists and psychologists emphasize the study of somatization as maladaptive coping style or expression of depression and other forms of psychopathology. They view somatization as a means of coping with emotional problems (discharging anger in a sanctioned way, fulfilling dependency needs, sanctioning perceived failure). Most have not considered its normative and adaptive aspects, nor have they detailed its function as discourse strategies to open up behavioral options (e.g., time off work, change of jobs, marital separation), to control interpersonal transactions (except where family therapists have focused on its pathological role within the family), to gain greater access over scarce resources (e.g., disability payments), to empower the relatively powerless (in gender-related work and political settings). These are precisely the problems that require an interpretive approach, be it ethnographic, historical, or integrated with quantitative analysis (see Figlio 1982; Good and Good 1981; Yelin et al. 1980; Rosen et al. 1982; Nichter 1981; Good 1977; Stein 1982; Lewis 1971; Pickering 1974).

From the perspective advanced in this chapter, we hypothesize that persons who are at greatest risk for powerlessness and blocked access to local resources are most likely to somatize (Katon et al. 1982; Nathanson 1977). There is already some evidence to support this hypothesis, since in North American society working-class patients comprise a disproportionately high percentage of patients attending pain clinics for chronic low back pain (though this also has something to do with biomechanical stress in certain types of physical labor), while women appear to be overrepresented among chronic pain patients in the middle class. Ethnic and refugee populations also have been reported to somatize extensively (Katon et al. 1982). But local relationships of power, as our case vignettes attest, are complex and vary so greatly even within class and gender and ethnic categories that the focus of analysis must be more precise. In distinctive sociopolitical settings, the effects of somatization on distributive politics may well influence its utilization (Stone 1979). When powerlessness produces demoralization and despair, as has been shown to occur in lower-class women in Great Britain who become depressed (Brown and Harris 1978), it is more likely that somatization may be socially ineffective and personally maladaptive.

One point repeatedly made by researchers of this subject is worth remembering. Somatization is only rarely due to "malingering." It is often out of the patient's awareness, which among our Chinese subjects was almost always the case. This does not mean, however, that it is always or even routinely "unconscious," in the strict sense. Patients, families, and practitioners differ substantially in their skill not only in articulating and negotiating distress discourses (Plough 1981; Stewart and Sullivan 1982), where those who are depressed may be least successful, but also with respect to their insight into the sociodynamics and psychodynamics of these processes, where depression may also block insight. Even where there is insight, it cannot readily be expressed in an open fashion since this removes the social sanctioning of the illness discourse and labels the patient a malingerer (Figlio 1982). But clearly there is at least partial personal recognition of the significance of the somatization discourse and the fact that it is multilevel—overt response to symptoms, covert negotiation of relationships and resources—although this recognition cannot, for the above reason, be publicly expressed.

When medical or psychiatric disease or stress do not provide the biological substrate of somatic amplification, normal physiological processes seem to be the source. For example, Demers et al. (1980) showed that normal American adults experience what they label as "symptoms" roughly once per week. The great majority of these complaints are minor and either quickly disappear, are regarded as insignificant and forgotten, or are monitored internally until they can be normalized. A very few complaints may be amplified. Research shows that under psychosocial stress, or owing to a habit of somatic introspection, or where such complaints fit into a culturally shaped and socially legitimated coping style and idiom of distress in a particular local context of power, such physiologically based headaches, dizziness, fatigue, and so forth are a ready source of somatization.

Coda: Depressive Affect

Affect (feeling) is integral to human nature. But even though we may all "feel" the same psychobiologically produced patterns of autonomic arousal and neuroendocrine dysregulation, our unique biography and interpersonal context and the particular collective representations of our culture lead to divergent social productions and cultural constructions of specific affects. Even when each of us feels depressed, the perception, interpretation, and labeling (the construction) of the experience are distinctive, and in that sense what we actually "feel" is different. There may well be an obdurately human core to the psychobiological and social experience of loss and of lowered self-esteem that is terribly similar; nonetheless, to experience depression principally as headaches or as existential despair is not to experience the same feeling, even if "headaches'' radiate symbolic meanings of frustration and unhappiness, and if despair causes headaches.

Depression and other affects can also be viewed as particular moral stances in an ideologically constructed behavioral field (Myers 1979). There is a long Chinese tradition of paradigmatic exemplars of moral behavior whose ethical stances are simultaneously conveyed as emotion and as political statement (see Metzger 1981). Perhaps it is this tradition that makes depression so potentially dangerous an affect in China: it points to the social sources of human misery that have not been altered by Communist revolution and the building of a new socialist state. Much the same can be said of our own society, though we are socialized to view affect as a natural (''gut'') component of the self, not an interpersonal response or manipulation or a moral act with political connotation. In our society, however, the commercialization of human feeling (''the managed heart'' of television and the movies and sports and politics) is a visible sign of the capitalist construction of affect (see Lasch 1979; Hochschild 1983), which has its surface (and probably equally superficial) counterparts in the socialist construction of enthusiasm, selflessness, and the other ''red'' emotions. Intriguingly, during the Gilded Age of late nineteenth-century America, when Beard was popularizing the term, neurasthenia sounded a note of moral criticism of an age of ''wear and tear'' in which the body's supplies could not keep up with society's demands, and when to be neurasthenic was to withdraw from the frenetic race for material success that characterized this great age of business and replace competition with rest, contemplation, and the sensitivities of an earlier age (Sicherman 1977). The cross-cultural parallels are striking.

But affect as moral position in a social field of behavior is not affect as private experience. To make either pole of this dialectic, as relativists and materialists do, stand for affect en tout is to mistake its thoroughly interactionist nature (Averill 1980; Eckman 1980). The outward movement from private feeling to public meaning that transforms affect in one direction has as its reciprocal the opposite inward cultural transformation that organizes meaning into feeling as personal experience.

We can regard universal psychobiological and social (loss, powerlessness, failure) processes as providing the substrate with which cultural norms react to create affect as a public and private form of experience. This cultural reaction is constrained both by the universal substrate and the culturally and personally particular reagent. The product, meaningful affective experience, is constituted out of both, but each has been changed. It is as unavailing to interpret only collective representation and personal significance in depression or headache as it is to explain them away either by neurophysiological processes or by social universals of the human condition. A disembodied affect is equally artifactual as an affectless body. Clearly, if psychiatry, anthropology, and anthropological psychiatry are to advance the cultural study of depression and other emotions, they must study both sides of the reaction.

Depression as an affect in China, the United States, and other societies for which we possess adequate clinical ethnographies appears to have something to do with loss of crucial social relationships, withdrawal from established social structural positions, and undermining of the cultural norms guiding the self. It is an emotion that poses a threat to social arrangements and symbolic meanings, and not just via suicide. Demoralization, despondency, hopelessness, withdrawal, loss of interest in the social environment are asocial. They call basic norms and relations and institutions into question, undoing the ties of the symbolic reticulum that connect person to society; thus these asocial emotions underline with poignancy and pathos the problems of bafflement and suffering and social order that Weber (1978) saw as so fundamental to the social enterprise. In egocentric societies such as our own, perhaps this affect is not nearly as threatening as it would be in sociocentric societies such as China. Indeed, perhaps the expression of personal alienation and existential despair is intrinsic to the egocentric community as a liminal state that discloses the limits of the possible and establishes the border for solipsism and narcissism. But in sociocentric China, it would be both more threatening to cultural norms and less useful for social control to sanction egocentric depression as a liminal state. Rather somatized affect—feeling as pain and bodily, not psychic, suffering— may be the appropriate liminal state.

Here pain is an opportunity to reintegrate the sick person into the social support group and to reaffirm (in the Durkheimian sense) the norms of solidarity and social control (see Turner 1967). Depressive affect is socially and culturally unsanctioned and therefore suppressed. Somatization is sanctioned and expressed, and carries both cultural cachet and social efficacy. Depressive affect is unacceptable in China because it *means* stigmatized mental illness, breakdown of social harmony—in modern terms political alienation;[13] in traditional terms display of excessively negative feeling harmful to health. It does not signify what it *means* in middle-class white American society—the heroic romance of the lonely individual testing his existential condition by being obdurately solitary, the equity of each independent person naked before his just god (see Burton's *Anatomy of Melancholy*), the immortality of the personal soul, the narcissistic conception of man's ultimate, egocentric rights, the bitter disillusionment with sentimentality at not "making it" in the marketplace.

How we see culture entering into this picture is as the *systematized relations* between feeling, self-concept, interpersonal communication, practical action, ideology, and relationships of power. These systematized relations are distinctive in different societies. This makes for a difference in more than content. There are differences in the very structure of the links between affect, self, and social reality which are produced and reproduced distinctively in different social worlds. Culture always particularizes. The cross-cultural continuities, and there are many, in emotion come from the constraining influences of the separate elements in the cultural system: shared psychobiological processes, universal aspects of social relations, the limited variations in the politics of power.

We will not continue in this line of analysis; our point is only that the social production of depression tells us something about universal *and* particular features of social structure, while its cultural construction tells us about meaning systems and norms. If we had traced biological and psychological themes, we would have arrived at the same place for those academic discourses. How we choose to interpret depression—clinically, poetically, in the societywide terms of social science—is inseparable from its construction. The vexing problem this poses for interdisciplinary work on emotions is to emphasize our divergent disciplinary "interests," to show how those help shape our subject, and to query how they can be integrated. We take this to be a simply immense barrier to the study of emotions. One of the central concerns of the academic colloquy on affect must be, therefore, the question of how we go about building an interdisciplinary discourse to talk together about a unified subject that always seems to hold a mirror up to each of our disciplines and becomes as fragmented as they are. Our Chinese findings hold up such a mirror, for both psychiatry and anthropology.

NOTES

1. Culturally specific forms of somatization have also been described for semen loss syndromes in South and Southeast Asia (Obeyesekere 1976; Wen and Wang 1981), and frigophobia among Chinese (Lin et al. 1981). But it is

unclear to what extent these and related syndromes are associated with depression or other affective disorders.

2. In an earlier study conducted in several primary care settings in Taiwan, we found a statistically significantly smaller proportion of somatization patients suffering from depressive (49%) and anxiety disorders (43%). We interpreted this discrepancy, since depression appears to have roughly the same prevalence in the two societies, by hypothesizing that somatization in primary care has a much broader array of sources than depression and anxiety disorders, which we would expect to be especially prevalent among patients in a psychiatric out-patient clinic. This hypothesis led to the primary care study in Hunan described in another section of the chapter.

3. This research was conducted with the support of a grant from the Social Science Research Council. The authors wish to acknowledge the help of their colleagues in the Department of Psychiatry, Hunan Medical College, especially the research assistance of Dr. Huang Nang-da, and the advice and administrative support of Professors Yang Derson and Shen Qijie. We ourselves are solely responsible for the interpretation of the data, which may well differ significantly from the views of our Chinese colleagues.

4. The authors wish to acknowledge the help of Drs. Shi Zuorong, Huang Nang-da, Chen Xieqing.

5. This study was carried out by Jennifer Haas, a Harvard medical student working in Chinese, and Dr. Huang Nang-da, to both of whom we express our thanks and appreciation. Support for the clinic survey and field research was made possible by a grant from the Rockefeller Foundation to the senior author for a Program in Cross-Cultural Psychiatry and Medicine, of which this was the first study. Again, the views presented in this chapter are solely our own and doubtless differ significantly from those of our colleagues in China.

6. Because of the difficulties youth experience finding employment in China, as a result of an extremely tight job market and the large number of those finishing school each year, units allow workers to take early retirement and transfer their jobs to thei̇. children. The employment situation is such that few have an opportunity to change type of work or even take up different work in the same work setting. The job you start off with is likely to be the one from which you will retire.

7. Class background in the People's Republic, which in the past strongly influenced one's life chances, is inherited from a child's father, while rural or urban residence is inherited from the mother. When the father is dead, the class background of the person providing financial support for the child determines the class of the child (Potter 1983).

8. During the Cultural Revolution, millions of Chinese adolescents left their urban middle schools and were rusticated in rural communes, often remote and poor ones, where they were expected to engage in agricultural labor and learn from the peasants.

9. From a biomedical perspective it is hardly likely that the congenital abnormality resulted from Comrade Yen's actions during the pregnancy. But she held fast to her guilt-laden explanatory model in spite of receiving contrary opinions from the clinic's physicians.

10. The small sample size, for example, makes us cautious in generalizing to the situation in China as a whole, though prior research by us and by others (Kleinman 1982), along with our reading of the literature and discussions with Chinese medical colleagues (Kleinman and Mechanic 1981; Lin et al. 1981), lends support to the limited quantitative findings from the study reported here. The fact that the control group of 25 nonneurasthenic neurotic patients in the psychiatry clinic experienced few job changes in a three-year period, however, makes us hesitant to extend all of our conclusions to nonneurasthenic somatization patients in China, though we think some are probably valid.

11. The China scholar Anne Thurston (n.d.), following the psychiatrist Robert Lifton, regards some of the experiences of those most psychically hurt in the Cultural Revolution as instances of Post-Traumatic Stress Syndrome. Although we did not employ this diagnosis during our field study, several of our patients showed the classic symptoms: recurrent and intrusive recollections of the traumatic event, recurrent dreams about it, feeling as if it were reoccurring, numbing of responsiveness to the external world, estrangement, constricted affect, avoidance, and survivor's guilt. But most did not.

Other sources paint in less technical and more personal terms the same portrait of traumatic human suffering during the Cultural Revolution: see Heng and Shapiro (1983), who provide a moving Hunanese case, and Frolic (1980) and Mosher (1983) for examples from Guangdong.

David Mechanic (personal communication) suggests that the Cultural Revolution may not have actually created an increased prevalence of depression. He argues rather it may have become a salient explanation available and acceptable in the 1980s in China as a prototypical cause that is drawn on as a publicly acceptable explanation in place of other sources of depression that are less socially acceptable. In the absence of pre- and post-Cultural Revolution incidence data on depression, we cannot answer this question. Our hunch is that the Cultural Revolution may have increased the incidence of Major Depression, Post-Traumatic Stress Disorder, and other mental disorders with a strong reactive causal component. But we concur with Mechanic that use of the Cultural Revolution as a causal attribution also has occurred for the reason he mentions. Brown and Harris (1978:78) make the same point under the rubric of reworking the past. This process of retrospective rationalization has also been discussed by Amarasingham (1980) for a non-Western society under the rubric of narratization of illness events.

12. It was not feasible to determine whether Major Depressive Disorder or anxiety disorders were a more important source of somatization in particular cases (Good and Kleinman n.d.). It is plausible to assume that their relative

contribution as the template for somatic amplification varied for different types of somatization. This is a topic that deserves careful assessment in future field research. Since our samples are treated samples and do not come from a population survey, it is reasonable to suspect that depression and anxiety are less important in the generation of somatic amplification syndromes in the general population, where these disorders are less prevalent. An indication that this hypothesis seems reasonable is our finding that on follow-up for a significant minority of cases no mental illness could be detected even though somatization persisted.

13. China's recently aborted Anti-Spiritual Pollution Campaign began with criticism of a leading cadre's assertion that alienation was legitimate in the Communist state. This enlightened viewpoint was swiftly criticized and recanted. Obviously, the idea is still regarded as too threatening by China's leaders. But it is a sign of changing times that articles have appeared in the Chinese journal *Medical Philosophy* which discuss social pathology, and research is being published in the PRC on social stressors.

REFERENCES

Alexander, L.
    1982   Illness Maintenance and the New American Sick Role. *In* Clini-
                    cally Applied Anthropology. N. Chrisman and T. Maretzki,
                    eds. Dordrecht: D. Reidel. Pp. 351–368.
Amarasingham, L. R.
    1980   Movement among Healers in Sri Lanka: A Case Study of a
                    Sinhalese Patient. Culture, Medicine, and Psychiatry 4:71–82.
Averill, J. R.
    1980   Emotion and Anxiety: Sociocultural, Biological, and Psycho-
                    logical Determinants. *In* Explaining Emotions. A. O. Rorty,
                    ed. Berkeley, Los Angeles, London: University of California
                    Press. Pp. 37–72.
Barsky, A., and G. Klerman
    1983   Overview: Hypochondriasis, Bodily Complaints and Somatic
                    Styles. American Journal of Psychiatry 140:273–283.
Bazzoui, W.
    1970   Affective Disorders in Iraq. British Journal of Psychiatry 117:
                    195–203.
Beck, A. T.
    1976   Cognitive Therapy and the Emotional Disorders. New York:
                    International Universities Press.
Berton, R.
    1621   The Anatomy of Melancholy. Oxford: Lichfield and Short.
Binitie, A.
    1975   A Factor-Analytical Study of Depression across African and

European Cultures. British Journal of Psychiatry 127: 559−563.

Blumer, D., N. Heilbronn, E. Pedraza, and G. Pope
1980   Systematic Treatment of Chronic Pain with Antidepressants. Henry Ford Hospital Medical Journal 28:15−21.

Brown, G., and T. Harris
1978   The Social Origins of Depression. New York: The Free Press.

Cacioppo, J. T., and R. E. Petty, eds.
1983   Social Psychophysiology. New York: Guilford Press.

Ch'eng, C. F., and C. S. Chang
1962   Some Early Records of Nervous and Mental Diseases in Traditional Chinese Medicine. Chinese Medical Journal 81:55−59.

Cheung, F.
1984   Preferences in Help Seeking among Chinese Students. Culture, Medicine, and Psychiatry 8:371−380.

Cheung, F., B. Lau, and E. Waldmann
1981   Somatization among Chinese Depressives in General Practice. International Journal of Psychiatry in Medicine 10:361−362.

Cheung, F., and B. Lau
1982   Situational Variations of Help-seeking Behavior among Chinese Patients. Comprehensive Psychiatry 23:252−262.

Cheung, F., S.-Y. Lee, and Y.-Y. Chan
1983   Variations in Problem Conceptualization and Intended Solutions among Hong Kong Students. Culture, Medicine, and Psychiatry 7:263−278.

Clayton, P., and J. Darrish
1979   Course of depressive symptoms following the stress of bereavement. *In* Stress and Mental Disorder. J. Barrett et al., eds. New York: Raven Press.

Climent, C. E., B. S. M. Diop, T. Harding, H. H. A. Ibrahim, L. Ladrido-Ignacio, and N. N. Wig
1980   Mental Health in Primary Health Care. W.H.O. Chronicle 34:230−231.

Collyer, J.
1979   Psychosomatic Illness in a Solo Family Practice. Psychosomatics 20:762−767.

Csordas, T.
1984   The Rhetoric of Transformation in Ritual Healing. Culture, Medicine, and Psychiatry 7:333−376.

Cummings, N. A., and W. Follette
1976   Brief Psychotherapy and Medical Utilization. *In* The Professional Psychologist Today. H. Dorken et al., eds. San Francisco: Jossey-Bass.

Cummings, N. A., and G. R. Vanden Bos
1981   The Twenty Year Kaiser-Permanente Experience with Psycho-

therapy and Medical Utilization. Health Policy Quarterly 1: 159–175.

Demers, R., R. Altamore, H. Mustin, A. Kleinman, and D. Leonardi
1980   An Exploration of the Depth and Dimensions of Illness Behavior. Journal of Family Practice 11:1085–1092.

Ebigbo, P. O.
1982   Somatization among Nigerian Normals and Mentally Ill. Culture, Medicine, and Psychiatry 6:29–43.

Eckman, P.
1980   Biological and Cultural Contributions to Body and Facial Movement in the Expression of Emotions. *In* Explaining Emotions. A. O. Rorty, ed. Berkeley, Los Angeles, London: University of California Press. Pp. 73–201.

Estroff, S.
1981   Making It Crazy: An Ethnography of Psychiatric Clients in an American Community. Berkeley, Los Angeles, London: University of California Press.

Figlio, K.
1982   How Does Illness Mediate Social Relations? *In* The Problem of Medical Knowledge. P. Wright and A. Treacher, eds. Edinburgh: University of Edinburgh Press.

Follette, W. T., and N. A. Cummings
1967   Psychiatric Services and Medical Utilization in a Prepaid Health Plan Setting. Medical Care 5:25–35.

Fordyce, W.
1976   Behavior Methods for Chronic Pain and Illness. St. Louis: Mosby.

Frank, J.
1974   Persuasion and Healing. New York: Schocken.

Frolic, B. M.
1980   Mao's People. Cambridge: Harvard University Press.

Goldberg, D.
1979   Detection and Assessment of Emotional Disorders in a Primary Care Setting. International Journal of Mental Health 8:30–48.

Good, B.
1977   The Heart of What's the Matter. The Semantics of Illness in Iran. Culture, Medicine, and Psychiatry 1:25–58.

Good, B., and M. J. Good
1981   The Meaning of Symptoms: A Cultural Hermeneutic Model for Clinical Practice. *In* The Relevance of Social Science for Medicine. L. Eisenberg and A. Kleinman, eds. Dordrecht: D. Reidel.

Good, B., and A. Kleinman
n.d.   Culture and Anxiety: Cross-Cultural Evidence for the Pattern-

ing of Anxiety Disorders. *In* Anxiety and the Anxiety Disorders. A. H. Tuma and J. D. Maser, eds. Hillside, N.J.: Lawrence Erlbaum Associates.

Hahn, R., and A. Kleinman
1983   Belief as Pathogen, Belief as Medicine: "Voodoo Death" and the "Placebo Phenomenon" in Anthropological Perspective. Medical Anthropology Quarterly 14(4):3, 16−19.

Hankin, J., and J. S. Oktay
1979   Mental Disorder and Primary Care. *In* NIMH Series D, no. 7. DHEW Publication No. ADM 78−661. Washington, D.C.: U.S. Government Printing Office.

Harwood, A., ed.
1981   Ethnicity and Medical Care. Cambridge: Harvard University Press.

Helman, C.
1985   Disease and Pseudo-Disease: A Case History of Pseudo-Angina. *In* Physicians of Western Medicine. R. Hahn and A. Gaines, eds. Dordrecht: D. Reidel.

Hochschild, A.
1983   The Managed Heart. Berkeley, Los Angeles, London: University of California Press.

Hoeper, E., G. Nyczi, P. Cleary, D. Regier, and I. D. Goldberg
1979   Estimated Prevalence of RDC Mental Disorder in Primary Care. International Journal of Mental Health 8:6−15.

Hofer, M.
1984   Relations as Regulators: A Psychobiological Perspective on Bereavement. Psychosomatic Medicine. In press.

Katon, W., A. Kleinman, and G. Rosen
1982   Depression and Somatization. American Journal of Medicine 72(1):127−135, 241−247.

Katon, W., R. Ries, and A. Kleinman
1984   The Prevalence of Somatization in Primary Care. Comprehensive Psychiatry 25(2):208−215.

Keefe, F. J.
1982   Behavioral Assessment and Treatment of Chronic Pain. Journal of Counseling and Clinical Psychology 50(6):896−911.

Keefe, F. J., C. Brown, D. S. Scott, and H. Ziesat
1982   Behavioral Assessment of Chronic Pain. *In* Assessment Strategies in Behavioral Medicine. F. J. Keefe and J. A. Blumenthal, eds. New York: Grune and Stratton.

Kleinman, A.
1977   Depression, Somatization and the New Cross-Cultural Psychiatry. Social Science and Medicine 11:3−10.
1980   Patients and Healers in the Context of Culture. Berkeley, Los Angeles, London: University of California Press.

1982   Neurasthenia and Depression: A Study of Somatization and
            Culture in China. Culture, Medicine, and Psychiatry 6(2):
            117−189.
1984   Somatization. Referential Journal of Psychiatry [Guowai Yixue
            Qingshenbingxue Fence] (in Chinese) 2:65−68.
Kleinman, A., and W. Katon
1983   Somatization and Bereavement. Working Papers of Institute
            of Medicine's Panel on Health Consequences of the Stress
            of Bereavement. Washington, D.C.: National Academy of
            Sciences.
Kleinman, A., and D. Mechanic
1979   Some Observations of Mental Illness and Its Treatment in
            China. The Journal of Nervous and Mental Disease 167:
            267−274.
1981   Psychosocial Aspects of Primary Care and Psychiatry in China.
            In Normal and Abnormal Behavior in Chinese Culture.
            A. Kleinman and T. Y. Lin, eds. Dordrecht: D. Reidel.
Lasch, C.
1979   The Culture of Narcissism. New York: Norton.
Lewis, I.
1971   Ecstatic Religion: An Anthropological Study of Spirit Posses-
            sion and Shamanism. Harmondsworth, England: Penguin.
Liang, H., and J. Shapiro
1983   Son of the Revolution. New York: Knopf.
Lin, K. M., A. Kleinman, T. Y. Lin
1981   Overview of Mental Disorders in Chinese Cultures. *In* Normal
            and Abnormal Behavior in Chinese Culture. A. Kleinman and
            T. Y. Lin, eds. Dordrecht: D. Reidel. Pp. 237−272.
Lin, K. M., and A. Kleinman
1981   Recent Development of Psychiatric Epidemiology in China.
            Culture, Medicine, and Psychiatry 5:135−143.
Lindsay, P. G., and M. Wykoff
1981   The Depression-Pain Syndrome and Its Response to Anti-
            depressants. Psychosomatics 22:571−577.
Lock, M.
1982   Models and Practice in Medicine: Menopause as Syndrome
            or Life Transition? Culture, Medicine, and Psychiatry 6:
            261−280.
Lowy, J. H.
1975   Management of the Persistent Somatizer. International Journal
            of Psychiatry in Medicine 6:227−239.
McIntyre, A.
1981   After Virtue. Notre Dame: University of Notre Dame Press.

Marsella, A.
1979   Depressive Experience and Disorder Across Cultures. *In* Hand-
             book of Cross-Cultural Psychology. Vol. 8. H. Triandis and
             J. Draguns, eds. Boston: Allyn and Bacon.
Mechanic, D.
1972   Social Psychological Factors Affecting the Presentation of
             Bodily Complaints. New England Journal of Medicine 286:
             1132–1139.
1980   The Experience and Reporting of Common Physical Com-
             plaints. Journal of Health and Social Behavior 21:146–155.
Mechanic, D., and A. Kleinman
1980   Ambulatory Medical Care in China. American Journal of Public
             Health 70(1):62–66.
Metzger, T.
1981   Selfhood and Authority in Neo-Confucian China. *In* Normal
             and Abnormal Behavior in Chinese Culture. A. Kleinman and
             T. Y. Lin, eds. Dordrecht: D. Reidel. Pp. 7–28.
Mezzich, J., and E. Raab
1980   Depressive Symptomatology across the Americas. Archives of
             General Psychiatry 37:818–823.
Minuchin, S., B. L. Rosman, and L. Baker
1978   Psychosomatic Families. Cambridge: Harvard University
             Press.
Moore, B.
1970   Reflections on the Causes of Human Misery. Boston: Beacon
             Press.
1978   Injustice: The Social Basis of Obedience and Revolt. New
             York: Sharpe.
Mosher, S. W.
1983   Broken Earth: The Rural Chinese. New York: The Free Press.
Muecke, M. A.
1983   In Search of Healers: Southeast Asian Refugees in the American
             Health Care System. Western Journal of Medicine 139(6):
             835–841.
Myers, F.
1979   Emotions and the Self. Ethos 7:343–370.
Nathanson, C. A.
1977   Self, Illness and Medical Care. Social Science and Medicine
             11:13–25.
Nichter, M.
1981   Idioms of Distress. Culture, Medicine, and Psychiatry 5:
             379–408.

Obeyesekere, G.
1976   The Impact of Ayurvedic Ideas on the Culture and the Individual
             in Sri Lanka. *In* Asian Medical Systems. C. Leslie, ed. Berke-
             ley, Los Angeles, London: University of California Press. Pp.
             201–226.
Orley, J. H., and J. K. Wing
1979   Psychiatric Disorders in Two African Villages. Archives of
             General Psychiatry 36:513–520.
Pennebacker, J., and J. Skelton
1978   Psychological Parameters of Physical Symptoms. Personality
             and Social Psychology Bulletin 4:524–530.
Pickering, G.
1974   Creative Malady. London: Allen and Unwin.
Plough, A.
1981   Medical Technology and the Crisis of Experience. Social
             Science and Medicine 15F:89–101.
Potter, S. H.
1983   The Position of Peasants in Modern China's Social Order.
             Modern China 9(4):465–499.
Racy, J.
1980   Somatization in Saudi Women. British Journal of Psychiatry
             137:212–216.
Regier, D., I. D. Goldberg, and C. H. Taube
1978   The De Facto U.S. Mental Health Service System. Archives of
             General Psychiatry 35:685–693.
Rin, H.
1982   *Linchuang Jingshen Yixue* (Clinical Psychiatric Medicine).
             Taipei, Taiwan: Maochang.
Roberts, A., and L. Reinhardt
1980   The Behavioral Management of Chronic Pain. Pain 8:151–
             162.
Roberts, B., and N. Morton
1952   Prevalence of Psychiatric Illness in a Medical Outpatient Clinic.
             New England Journal of Medicine 245:82.
Romanyshyn, R.
1982   Psychological Life: From Science to Metaphor. Austin: Uni-
             versity of Texas Press.
Rosaldo, M.
1980   Knowledge and Passion. Cambridge: Cambridge University
             Press.
Rosen, G., A. Kleinman, and W. Katon
1982   Somatization in Family Practice. The Journal of Family Practice
             14(3):493–502.

Sethi, B. B., S. C. Gupta, R. Kumar, and P. Kumari
1973   Depression in India: The Journal of Social Psychology 91: 3–13.
Sicherman, B.
1977   The Uses of a Diagnosis: Doctors, Patients, and Neurasthenia. Journal of the History of Medicine and Allied Sciences 32(1): 33–54.
Stein, H.
1982   The Annual Cycle and the Cultural Nexus of Health Behavior among Oklahoma Wheat Farming Families. Culture, Medicine, and Psychiatry 6(1):81–100.
Sternbach, R. A.
1974   Pain Patients, Traits and Treatment. New York: Academic Press.
Stewart, D., and T. Sullivan
1982   Illness Behavior and the Sick Role in Chronic Disease. Social Science and Medicine 16:1397–1404.
Stoeckle, J., I. K. Zola, and G. E. Davidson
1964   The Quality and Significance of Psychological Distress in Medical Patients. Journal of Chronic Disease 17:959.
Stone, D. A.
1979a   Diagnosis and the Dole: The Function of Illness in American Distributive Politics. Journal of Health Politics, Policy and Law 4:507–521.
1979b   Physicians as Gatekeepers: Illness Certification as a Rationing Device. Public Policy 27(2):227–254.
Taussig, M.
1980   The Devil and Commodity Fetishism in South America. Chapel Hill: University of North Carolina Press.
Teja, J. S., R. L. Narang, and A. K. Aggarwal
1971   Depression across Cultures. British Journal of Psychiatry 119: 253–260.
Tessler, R., and D. Mechanic
1978   Psychological Distress and Perceived Health Status. Journal of Health and Social Behavior 19:254–262.
Thurston, A.
n.d.   China's Great Proletarian Cultural Revolution: The Human Cost. Pacific Affairs. In press.
Townsend, J. M.
1978   Cultural Conceptions of Mental Illness. Chicago: University of Chicago Press.
Tseng, W. S.
1974   The Development of Psychiatric Concepts in Chinese Medicine. Archives of General Psychiatry 29:569–575.

Tseng, W. S., and J. Hsu
1975   The Nature of Somatic Complaints among Psychiatric Patients:
              The Chinese Case. Comprehensive Psychiatry 16:237−245.
Turner, J., and C. R. Chapman
1982   Psychological Interventions for Chronic Pain. Pain 12:1−21,
              23−46.
Turner, V.
1967   The Forest of Symbols. Ithaca: Cornell University Press.
Ward, N., V. L. Bloom, and R. O. Friedel
1979   The Effectiveness of Tricyclic Antidepressants in Treatment of
              Coexisting Pain and Depression. Pain 7:331−341.
Weber, M.
1978   Economy and Society. Vol. 2. Berkeley, Los Angeles, London:
              University of California Press.
Wen, J. K., and C. L. Wang
1981   *Shen-K'uei* Syndrome. *In* Normal and Abnormal Behavior in
              Chinese Culture. A. Kleinman and T. Y. Lin, eds. Dordrecht:
              D. Reidel. Pp. 357−370.
Widmer, R. B., and R. J. Cadoret
1978   Depression in Primary Care. Journal of Family Practice 7:
              272−302.
1979   Depression in Family Practice: Changes in Pattern of Patient
              Visits. Journal of Family Practice 9:1017−1021.
Widmer, R. B., R. J. Cadoret, and C. S. Worth
1980   Depression in Family Practice: Some Effects on Spouses and
              Children. Journal of Family Practice 10:45−81.
Wrong, D. H.
1976   Skeptical Sociology. New York: Columbia University Press.
Xu Yun
1983   *Shilun shehui binglixue* (Exploring social pathology). *Yixue yu
              Zhexue* (Medicine and Philosophy) 11:30−33.
Yelin, E., M. Nevitt, and W. Epstein
1980   Toward an Epidemiology of Work Disability. Milbank Memo-
              rial Fund Quarterly 58(3):386−415.
Young, A.
1980   The Discourse on Stress and the Reproduction of Conventional
              Knowledge. Social Science and Medicine 14B:133−147.
Zborowski, M.
1969   People in Pain. San Francisco: Jossey-Bass.
Zheng, Y. P., and D. Yang
1983   The Relationship of Life Event Changes and Stress to Neurosis
              in China. Chinese Journal of Neurology and Psychiatry, Guang-
              dong. (In Chinese.)

Epilogue:
Culture and Depression

Byron Good and Arthur Kleinman

We began the introduction to this volume with the question, Why study depression from a cross-cultural perspective? At the end we return to this question. What can we expect to learn about depression that justifies the effort of cross-national and anthropologically informed studies? Can major questions about social precursors or appropriate treatment be answered solely by expanding our research in these directions? Can such a program of research overcome the serious methodological difficulties that challenge the validity of findings? What kinds of research are likely to yield greatest dividends?

These questions are not merely rhetorical. The claim to priority for *cross-cultural* studies of depression faces skepticism from two opposing perspectives. On the one hand, to many mainstream psychiatric researchers cross-cultural studies seem of little more than esoteric interest. After years of wide-ranging speculation about the nature and causes of depressive illness, researchers and clinicians can now identify a discrete set of depressive disorders and are well on their way to determining their psychophysiological concomitants, epidemiological characteristics, and differential clinical features. Since these characteristics, it is widely assumed, are unlikely to vary substantially in other societies, why should resources be devoted to the study of depression cross-culturally? Many anthropologists, on the other hand, are equally skeptical, but for quite different reasons. Current psychiatric theorizing and research, they argue, are reductionistic, treat symptoms as decontextualized traits, and reify a Western cultural and psychological form, according it the status of universal disease. Why then should such a culture-specific category serve as the basis for cross-cultural research? Does such research not begin with and perpetuate a fundamental category fallacy?

We hope the contributions to this volume will provoke questions in both camps. Given the data reported here, it is simply not tenable, we believe, to argue that dysphoric emotion and depressive illness are invariant across cultures. When culture is treated as a constant (as is common when studies are conducted in our own society), it is relatively easy to view depression as a biological disorder, triggered by social stressors in the presence of ineffective support, and reflected in a set of symptoms or complaints that map back onto the biological substrate of the disorder. Because the analytic categories of professional psychiatry and psychology so fundamentally share assumptions with popular Western cultures, the "order of words" appears to reflect the "order of things," and the complaints of patients are viewed as reflecting an underlying pathological phenomenon, whether that be psychophysiological or cognitive. From this perspective, culture appears epiphenomenal; cultural differences may exist, but they are not considered essential to the phenomenon itself. However, when culture is treated as a significant variable, for example, when the researcher seriously confronts the world of meaning and experience of members of non-Western societies, many of our assumptions about the nature of emotions and illness are cast in sharp relief. Dramatic differences are found across cultures in the social organization, personal experience, and consequences of such emotions as sadness, grief, and anger, of behaviors such as withdrawal or aggression, and of psychological characteristics such as passivity and helplessness or the resort to altered states of consciousness. They are organized differently as psychological realities, communicated in a wide range of idioms, related to quite varied local contexts of power relations, and are interpreted, evaluated, and responded to as fundamentally different meaningful realities. Dysphoria, even the pervasive loss of pleasure in normally valued aspects of the self, objects in the world, or social relationships, is associated with quite different symptoms of distress and has widely varied consequences for the sufferer. Depressive illness and dysphoria are thus not only interpreted differently in non-Western societies and across cultures; they are *constituted* as fundamentally different forms of social reality. It is precisely this conviction that leads anthropologists to argue for the centrality of careful description of local frames of meaning and social relations and for the theoretical and methodological priority of cross-cultural interpretation.

Just as the position that depression is culturally invariant cannot be sustained in the face of cross-cultural studies, so also a purely cultural perspective cannot be maintained in the face of clinical and psychophysiological evidence. Forms of behavior clearly recognizable as depression—syndromes involving loss of pleasure and normal interests, sadness or despair, withdrawal from usual activities and relationships, loss of energy, particular somatic complaints, and in some cases regular swings of mood from sustained dysphoria to sustained euphoria—can be recognized by experienced clinicians in widely varying societies, often associated with important losses or difficult life experiences. In addition, some aspects of depressive illness have now been directly related to psychophysiological abnormalities. This seems particularly true of the vegetative signs and symptoms, shown to be produced by disordered neuroendocrine responses; the specific effects of neurotransmitters, also implicated, are less clear. Such neurophysiological processes seem not only to constrain behavior and experience but also to construct that experience and strongly influence its course through time. We do not interpret these findings as evidence that a disease model is culture-free, as some would argue, or that our current diagnostic criteria should serve as the primary perspective from which to examine cross-cultural data. Such findings do, however, provide a powerful argument for the development of a theoretical perspective that is thoroughly interactionist. Such a perspective challenges us to develop theories that conceive psychophysiology as *human* biology and therefore inseparable from language, meaning, and social relationships, while exploring the cultural meanings of depression both as the interpretation of disordered experience (loss of pleasure, energy, etc.) and as disordered interpretive processes.

The very complexity of dysphoric emotion and depressive illness, particularly when seen in cross-cultural perspective, provides the theoretical mandate. A comprehensive theory of dysphoria and depression must relate wide-ranging human phenomena, from socialization to social dynamics and power relations, from cultural meanings to complaints in clinical settings, from unresolved grief over losses of the most cherished human relationships to mood changes evoked by pharmacology. In our own papers and in the introduction to this collection, we have argued that neither reflectivist theories, which see culture as opaque to a more fundamental level of reality, nor constitutive theories, which conceive culture as constituting reality independent of and autonomous from biology, meet this theoretical challenge. We have argued instead for interpretive theories, which conceive depression as socially produced and culturally constructed through the interpretation of personal distress and social realities in the context of local knowledge and local systems of power. This perspective has provided the framework for our efforts to integrate and respond to the chapters of this volume.

We come away from this project with a sense both of great opportunity and great urgency. The past decade has seen enormous growth in our understanding of depressive illness. New research methods have been developed by teams of clinicians and epidemiologists, social psychologists, psychopharmacologists, and cognitive psychotherapists, producing not only changes in our basic understanding of human behavior but also hope for more beneficial treatments for persons suffering from one of the most persistent and debilitating human ills. Such progress, however, poses a serious threat to understanding. Few of the most basic findings of this research have been subjected to cross-cultural scrutiny, and few of the new research methods have faced the critical challenge of adaptation and translation for transcultural studies. Our very lack of cross-cultural data therefore tempts us to assume that we know more than we actually do, that our knowledge is universal rather than parochial and limited. Belief that science produces universal knowledge combined with our desire to share therapeutic benefits with the non-Western world breeds methodological arrogance. Quick translation of research instruments and approaches, based on the *assumption* of cross-cultural validity rather than skeptical inquiry, threatens to produce data that are artifactual and will obscure understanding in the coming years. *We do not know to what extent our categories of depressive illness are cross-culturally valid*. What evidence we have raises serious questions about the universality of symptom criteria and more fundamentally about our conceptualization of the relation of depression, anxiety, and chronic somatization. However, unless such evidence is greatly expanded and given serious attention, the hypothesis of universalism will become dogma. It is this that lends urgency to the challenge of cross-cultural research.

The sense of opportunity is not for cross-cultural psychiatry alone; current understandings of dysphoria and depression offer a particular challenge to anthropology. During the 1930s and 1940s, the study of emotion was central to American anthropology. However, empirical research failed to sustain many of the speculations of culture and personality theorists, and psychological anthropology turned from systematic study of the emotional life to an almost exclusive focus on cognition. Today there is a renewed interest in cross-cultural studies of emotion, the organization of psychological experience, and "the per-

son,'' but many of the unresolved theoretical confusions and methodological difficulties remain. Some, with little awareness of the problems
involved, treat emotions such as grief, anger, or sadness as privileged
categories. They have little question that some "sentiments" (e.g.,
loyalty, filial feelings, honor and shame) are social, both in form and
function, but these are seen as quite independent of a set of universal
emotions. Others see no difficulty in arguing for complete cultural
relativity of the emotions and even emotional illnesses. In our opinion,
neither position is ultimately tenable. The enormous literature on depression provides an extraordinarily different context for anthropological
investigation from the dominant psychoanalytic context in which culture
and personality theorists worked. There is a clear opportunity for a new
anthropology of the emotions to emerge from this work.

The chapters in this volume offer encouragement. Current anthropological focus on discourse, interpretation, cognition, and linguistic
interaction, combined with a new sophistication in the study of medical
and psychiatric phenomena, suggests that a serious and beneficial
exchange with cross-cultural psychiatrists and psychologists is possible.
The examples in this book of multidisciplinary research efforts, which
combine ethnographic, clinical, and epidemiological approaches, provide new directions for cross-cultural research and raise a host of
hypotheses for exploration. But anthropologists, psychologists, and
psychiatrists must all take up the challenge of working through disciplinary conflicts, engaging not only each other but social scientists and
clinicians from non-Western societies as well, in order to meet the
challenge.

In the final pages of this book, we would like to draw readers' attention
to several issues we believe hold particular promise—and special
urgency—for cross-cultural research. While many additional research
issues have been raised by authors of this book, we suggest seven
priorities that seem especially important.

1. *We need clinical/descriptive research to serve as the basis for
evaluating the cross-cultural validity of our current diagnostic cate
gories of depressive illness.*

The discovery during the 1960s of effective psychopharmaceuticals for
depression led to a concentrated effort to establish clear research diagnostic criteria for depressive disorders. Following the integrative, life
course tradition of the American psychiatrist Adolf Meyer and the

German phenomenological psychiatric tradition of Jaspers and Schneider, researchers turned to careful clinical description. New standards for both the validity of diagnostic categories and the reliability of their application were established, resulting in more than a decade of intensive research, the findings of which are embodied in the American Psychiatric Association's current Diagnostic and Statistical Manual (DSM-III). Unfortunately, similar intensive efforts at clinical description have not been undertaken in non-Western societies. Western diagnostic manuals and epidemiological instruments are being translated for use in a wide variety of societies. Diagnostic criteria—specific symptoms, symptom duration, forms of disability and care seeking—are being carried wholesale into non-Western clinical practice and cross-national research, with little attention being given to the arduous standards for inductive research and clinical description that provide the grounds for claims of validity of these categories in Western patient populations. Cross-national efforts that parallel clinical descriptive research in Western psychiatry could go a long way toward determining the validity of current diagnostic formulations in a variety of cultures and therefore help establish what aspects of such formulations are universal or cross-culturally valid.

Clinical descriptive research, focusing on the "phenomenology" of depressive disorders, provides an ideal context for interdisciplinary cooperation among anthropologists, clinicians, and survey researchers. For such description to achieve its full potential, however, a significantly broadened view of the meaning of "phenomenology" should be accepted. In clinical research, phenomenology has come increasingly to signify a very narrow identification of symptoms expressed by patients. With growth of interest in phenomenological research in the social sciences, the limitations of this psychiatric perspective become particularly noticeable. Phenomenology in the social sciences is associated with a variety of technical methods for describing and analyzing the life world of members of a society—their culturally organized patterns of perceiving time, space, body and person, the symbolic organization of experience, the nature of "realities" in the social world and psychological life, and the forms of discourse and social interaction through which such realities are constructed. Descriptions of clinical phenomenology in psychiatry, however, tend to begin with accepted professional categories of symptoms, then translate the complaints of patients into these categories. Clinical descriptive research that brings together anthropologists, clinicians from the societies involved, and cross-cultural psychiatrists should be a first step in examining questions of validity of psychiatric conceptualizations of depression and our research diagnostic criteria. Such research should precede and accompany any translation of epidemiological instruments for cross-cultural research. Furthermore, phenomenological descriptions and comparisons are needed as much for normal emotional states as for pathological ones. For example, we know hardly anything about the normal experience of grief among members of non-Western societies and Western ethnic minorities. Yet such knowledge is crucial in determining normality and abnormality, the relation of grief to depression, and whether the health consequences of bereavement are the same or different worldwide.

2. *We need to establish new standards for cross-cultural epidemiological studies of depressive disorders.*

Years of research have gone into the development of epidemiological instruments—both psychiatric symptom checklists and formal diagnostic interviews—in the United States and Europe. Coordinated efforts of clinical description, instrument design, factor analysis and scale development, longitudinal studies, and psychophysiological research have been incorporated in such instruments as the Hopkins Symptom Checklist-90 (HSCL-90), the Schedule of Affective Disorders and Schizophrenia (SADS), the Diagnostic Interview Schedule (DIS), and the Present State Examination (PSE). Nothing less would meet current standards for psychiatric epidemiological research. With a few important exceptions, however, this entire process is bypassed in cross-cultural research. The simple translation of instruments developed in this country into other languages seems to meet most standards for cross-cultural research, as long as care is taken in the process of translation.

Why are such standards inadequate? A wide range of research, some reported in this book, indicates great variation in symptom expression and evaluation across cultures, as well as across ethnic groups and communicative contexts in a given society. While differences in somatic complaints and expressions of self-abnegation and guilt have most commonly been noted in cross-cultural research on depression, the more fundamental methodological and epistemological problems raised by such findings are often ignored. Great care has been taken to ensure that domains of psychophysiological importance have been represented in instruments for the study of depressive illness, and this is as it should be. However, few comparable efforts have been made to identify the full range of *semantic domains* represented in the discourse on depression in a non-Western culture and to develop instruments that sample from these semantic domains. In cross-cultural research, the identification and description of the range of symptoms associated with depression in a particular society, analysis of their organization into semantic domains, determination of their frequency for populations of that society, and analysis of the effects of social context on their expression should be required if new or translated epidemiological instruments are to be considered valid for that society. Research based on lesser standards will reproduce current conventional knowledge about the universality of our disease categories rather than seriously confront the problems posed by translations across significantly different life worlds.

3. *Cross-cultural research offers an important opportunity for the investigation of the relation of emotion to depressive illness.*

As we described in the introduction to this volume, research is bedeviled by the alternative conceptualizations of depression as emotion, symptom, and illness. Unfortunately, these difficulties are not merely ones of clear terminology; they represent major substantive problems. Where psychoanalytic theories had difficulty in explaining the relation of depressions associated with significant losses ("reactive depression") to those that seemingly appear without such losses ("endogenous depressions"), current psychophysiological formulations present difficulties for coherent understanding of the relation of affective disorders to emotion in general. Depressive illness, as formulated by biological psychiatry, seems little connected to the profound emotional responses to loss or disappointment, and affective disorders bear little necessary relation to affect in many current conceptual schemes. Renewed theoretical and empirical research is necessary if we are once again to come to a coherent understanding of the relation of normal dysphoria to depressive illness, to conceptualize and investigate the relation between subtypes of depressive disorders (for example, between major depressive disorder and dysthymia), the role of loss and attachment to the development of depression, and differences in illness course and response to treatment for those suffering from depression.

Cross-cultural research provides an important natural experiment for studying the relation of emotion to depressive illness. There appear to be great variations across cultures in the meaning and form of expression of sadness, grief, anger, and aggression. Are these variations directly related to depressive disease? Are they also responsible for different illness experiences of depression? We simply do not know at this time. Coordinated studies of depressive illness and dysphoric emotion in particular societies, focusing on questions such as those raised by Shweder in this volume, provide a significant opportunity to advance our knowledge in a manner that continued studies in American and European populations cannot. Such studies provide an opportunity not merely to advance psychiatric knowledge but to address classic anthropological questions about the cultural relativity of emotions (e.g., does the experience of grief differ across societies?) and whether disordered experience is more usefully conceived as pathology or as deviance or abnormality (e.g., how is abnormal or pathological grief determined in different societies, and is abnormal grieving a universal form of psychopathology?).

4. *The study of depressive illness in relation to local contexts of power has an important potential for advancing our understanding of the social production and maintenance of depression.*

The themes of self-worth, efficacy, and powerlessness run through current theorizing about the social and psychological origins of depression. Several of the chapters in this book point toward important new directions for research into these issues. Beeman's work suggests that sociolinguistic approaches may help us move beyond the study of depression as a characteristic of individuals to analysis of the influence of patterns of communications and social interactions on depressive illness. His approach seems particularly useful for analyzing how gender, class, and work status influence the onset and perpetuation of the depressive experience. Such research would provide a natural link to studies of societal power relations, such as those described here by Kleinman and Kleinman, or studies of the influence of family and social relations on depression, and might lend explanatory force to current theories about the relation of life stresses and depression. These studies currently show that life situations and life events are associated with depression, but they offer little to explain how such situations produce, maintain, or modulate depressive symptoms or depressive illness. The intensive ethnographic study of characteristics of the discourse and interaction patterns of the depressed, in relation to particular localized power contexts, might well provide clues of diagnostic and therapeutic relevance. Such studies could also facilitate a reconceptualization of stress and social support.

Current epidemiological studies reify stressors, supports, and coping mechanisms as atomized, asocial "things" that "impact on" or "buffer" individuals. Systematic reformulation of these concepts as culturally based transactional processes that interrelate individuals, social groups, and power structures might help break the current impasse in efforts to relate stress and depression and provide new avenues for research.

In this context, it should be noted that cross-cultural studies offer a particularly important and unfulfilled opportunity to study gender differences in prevalence of depressive symptoms and episodes. The fact that depression in most societies appears to be more prevalent among women, individuals occupying social statuses of relative powerlessness, and the economically marginal provides an important hypothesis linking social and psychological theories. Detailed studies of the lives of depressed women in America and Great Britain have begun to provide complex models of the vulnerability factors and characteristic provoking incidents that lead to depression. However, there is an increasingly rich ethnographic literature on women in the context of extraordinarily diverse forms of kinship relations, ecological conditions, and social and power relations. Until now, however, these research interests have not been brought together to focus on gender as one of the core social determinants of the distribution of depressive illness and, similarly, on depression as one of the central forms of distress affecting the relatively powerless. Even quite basic questions have hardly been addressed. For example, we do not know whether marriage is a protective factor for men and a risk factor for women with respect to depressive disorders in the non-Western world as it appears to be in the West. Studies of such issues, especially were they to employ ethnographic, clinical, and state-of-the-art epidemiological methods, offer a critical opportunity to expand our parochial theories and stand at an important research frontier.

5. *Cross-cultural studies provide an important opportunity to investigate the hypothesis that depression is a cognitive disorder.*

Several chapters in this volume have noted that the work of Aaron Beck and his colleagues offers an unfulfilled cultural analysis of depression. The cognitive psychotherapists have argued that cognition and discourse are central to any understanding of depression, and that the depressed make mistaken or abnormal judgments about characteristics of their environment and themselves. To the anthropologist, such "logical" patterns appear as cultural logics. It is surprising that a generation of cognitive anthropologists have failed to investigate whether these characteristics are specific to Americans or are more generally typical of those suffering depressive illness in other societies. Given the extent of the cultural patterning of cognition, we would expect disorders of interpretation would take distinctive forms in various cultures. Here is a question for which lack of research leads to inattention to a major aspect of the interaction between culture and cognition. This problem provides a significant opportunity for joint research by cognitive psychotherapists and cognitive anthropologists, research that promises to expand our understanding of both depressive illness and the cultural organization of cognitive processes.

6. *The cross-cultural study of the relation of chronic somatization to depressive disorders offers the opportunity to investigate a problem of great practical significance as well as to advance our understanding of a phenomenon poorly addressed by current psychiatric theory and diagnostic criteria.*

The body is the chief source of idiom and metaphor for the expression of distress. Not surprisingly, therefore, somatic complaints come to express personal demoralization and social oppression. In chronic somatization, depression may result from the social sources of human misery (e.g., a bad marriage, a terrible work relationship, the experience of political oppression and alienation) or from the persistent experience of organic distress (e.g., chronic pain). In the former instance, somatization mediates the sociosomatic dynamic conducing to depressive onset; in the latter, depression in the course of a chronic medical illness mediates the psychosomatic dynamic conducing to symptom amplification.

These are not the only ways depression, somatic complaints, and social problems interact. Both depression and somatization can be configured as problems in the interpretive processes through which persons come to regard the self and the body. These cognitive processes link personal experience (how I monitor my feelings and thoughts) and cultural domain (how we learn to value and interpret certain kinds of experiences). Feelings of pain as much as hopelessness, and egocentric values as much as sociocentric ones, are taken up in this psychocultural dialectic. How disability and despair have meaning in a local cultural system, then, tells us as much about the sociology of depression as about

its physiology. The two are inseparable, even though depression may not
always be part of the causal chain of somatization and somatization may
not always participate in the causation of depression. Chronic somatization forces us to see depressive affect as a component of social structure,
and social structure as an element of affective disorder. The cross-
cultural appraisal of this relationship affords an opportunity to examine
processes that cross-cut the boundaries of academic disciplines and
explore the interaction of culture, social structure, and biology.

Chronic somatization, moreover, configures a major social problem
worldwide, one that greatly affects the health care system and that is
ineffectively managed by standard medical and psychiatric treatment
interventions. In drawing attention to this problem, it is our hope to
encourage interdisciplinary study and thereby to affect the way anthropological and clinical/public health research is conducted. Our present
discipline-based approaches to chronic somatization are not only
methodologically inadequate; they illustrate the failure of our disciplines
to model accurately the core processes of human experience in which
meaning becomes an aspect of biology, and physiology an aspect of
values. We see the interdisciplinary cross-cultural study of chronic
somatization as an opportunity to construct new problematics and paradigms in the human sciences.

7. *We believe serious consideration should be given to adding a
cultural axis to the psychiatric diagnostic process.*

The axial structure of DSM-III represents a compromise among competing and complementary views of psychiatric disorders. It construes
depression, for example, as a heterogeneous psychiatric disease entity
(Axis I), as a pathology embedded in a particular personality (Axis II), as
the consequence of some medical condition (Axis III), as a response to
stressful social precursors (Axis IV), and as a level of social dysfunction
(Axis V). These represent current ways in which clinicians evaluate the
nature and extent of psychopathology.

Why do we suggest a cultural axis? Even though culture may influence
the expression of a psychiatric disorder, what would be meant by an
evaluation along a cultural dimension? There is strong evidence to
suggest that the cultural meaning of a disorder and the social evaluation
of the disorder by members of the sufferer's primary social network have
an important influence on the structure of the illness as a social reality
and thereby on the course of the disorder and its effect on the life of the

sufferer. The social response to the disorder, mediated by cultural explanations and interpretations, has an influence on the disorder which is independent of disease characteristics and etiological processes. An evaluation of the illness, in contrast to diagnosis of the disease, represents a characterization of the disorder *from the perspective of the patient's primary social group* (an "emic" evaluation). In clinical settings in which the professional and popular categories and explanatory frameworks configure psychopathology in quite similar fashion, the importance of the society's evaluation of the sufferer is hidden from view. When the popular meanings and social evaluation of the disorder are radically disjunct from the professional psychiatric evaluation, as is often the case in non-Western societies and at times true when the patient is a member of a distinctive ethnic group or subculture in the West, the difference between the disease reality attended to by the clinician and the illness reality experienced by patient and family have great significance for evaluation, prognosis, and treatment.

We propose that a cultural axis be developed as a research axis for cross-cultural studies, and that social and cross-cultural psychiatrists, anthropologists, and other social science researchers be challenged to demonstrate the utility of such an approach in their research. Researchers should specify the sources of data (an operational definition of "primary social group"), the categories of data to be gathered (e.g., culture-specific illness category, explanatory model, illness idiom, nature of perceived disabilities), and the means of recording data (categorical, descriptive, and linear). For example, an Axis VI assessment might record that a juvenile Puerto Rican patient's family interprets the disorder as an "*ataque de nervios*," that they believe it began with the patient's learning of the death of a friend, that they believe the disorder seriously affects the patient's ability to function in public and work settings, but that they believe the disorder is acute and likely to pass as the patient resolves his grief and matures as an adult. Such information would add significantly to a diagnostic assessment that recorded generalized anxiety disorder, dysthymic disorder, and undiagnosed epileptiform seizures. Perhaps more to the point, an Axis VI assessment that a major depression is interpreted by one patient and his family in somatic terms (as neurasthenia, as undiagnosed medical illness) and by another in a religious idiom (as punishment of God for sins) *may* turn out to have more implications for prognosis and treatment than the diagnosis major depression alone. Establishment of a cultural axis would promote systematic investigation of the nature of culture-specific evaluations of psychiatric disorders and research into the effects of such evaluations on phenomenology, prognosis, and appropriate treatment. We urge psychiatrists and anthropologists to join in consideration of this proposal.

These seven cardinal research themes by no means exhaust our subject, though they finally exhaust what the editors have to offer in this volume. Our simultaneous emphases on interactionism and cultural constructionism have led us along this pathway and away from others. Questions hardly pursued include those concerning the biological bases of cross-cultural differences in depressive disease, the role of religious institutions and cosmologies in the expression and "treatment" of depressive experience, the relationship of depressive disorder to migration and modernization, the cultural transformation of grief into depression, differential lay and professional assessments of treatment outcome, public health policy to foster primary and secondary prevention, and a host of other topics that have spun off from the chapters of this book. We have followed our own interests, placed our own bets. We have tried to avoid, although perhaps we have not always succeeded in doing so, the simplistic solution frameworks that so often bring a halt to the most interesting and productive lines of research and that have plagued the cross-cultural study of depression from its inception. We have urged authors in this volume to systematically relate esoteric historical and native categories to a common, taken-for-granted one of our own, a form of translation we take to be a chief value of anthropological analysis. We have forced disciplinary frameworks into contact and collision, sometimes in spite of the isolationist logic that motivates them. We have taken our readers seriously enough to want them to enter into the debates and controversies, to feel open space and dead ends, to reject or follow new leads.

We have no final answer, no single timeless model of culture and depression to ask as a multiple choice question on the national board exams in medical school, to have quoted in *Time* magazine as an advance in social science. Much like intellectual problems generally, which emerge from dominant concerns and frustrations of an epoch, we have dissolved some of the simpler and cruder issues and provoked new vexations. But we do not see this movement as circular, an emblem of the supposedly "noncumulative" nature of the human sciences. It is apt that theoretical and methodological questions have dominated this book. The relationship of culture and depression confronts us with some of the most difficult questions in science and the humanities. The appropriate conclusion to this volume is a set of questions, some of which motivated our inquiry from its inception, others quite different from our initial ways of configuring issues. But in moving from one set of questions to another, we have progressed methodologically and, not least, in the way we think about cross-cultural work on emotion and mental illness. Our conclusion is a conviction that only an anthropologically informed psychiatry and a clinically sophisticated anthropology are adequate to this line of inquiry, and that this hybridization is not at all a bad model for each of the disciplines themselves. In this sense the difficulties of our subject matter bring fresh themes and approaches to anthropology, psychiatry, and psychology.

CONTRIBUTORS

Beeman, William O., Ph.D.
An anthropological linguist whose field research has been in Iran and Japan, he is Associate Professor, Department of Anthropology, Brown University, Providence, Rhode Island.

Beiser, Morton, M.D.
A psychiatric epidemiologist and cross-cultural psychiatrist whose field research has been in Senegal, in urban North America, and among Southeast Asian refugees and Native Americans, Beiser, who also is Canada Health and Welfare National Health Research Scholar, is Professor and Head, Division of Social and Cultural Psychiatry, University of British Columbia, Vancouver, B.C., Canada.

Bloom, Joseph D., M.D.
A clinical psychiatrist who has conducted cross-cultural research in Alaska and with Native Americans, Bloom is Professor, Department of Psychiatry, Oregon Health Sciences University, Portland, Oregon.

Carr, John E., Ph.D.
A clinical psychologist who has conducted cross-cultural research in Malaysia and in the United States, Carr is Professor and Acting Chairman, Department of Psychiatry and Behavioral Sciences, and Adjunct Professor, Department of Psychology, University of Washington, Seattle, Washington.

Fenton, Fred R., M.D.
A psychiatrist who has worked with the Mental Health Unit, WHO, on cross-cultural studies, he is Professor, Department of Psychiatry, McGill University, Montreal, Quebec, Canada.

Good, Byron, Ph.D.
An anthropologist who has conducted research in Iran, among Iranian refugees in the United States, and in rural and small-town northern

California, Good is Assistant Professor of Medical Anthropology, Department of Social Medicine, Harvard Medical School, Boston, Massachusetts, and Lecturer, Department of Anthropology, Harvard University, Cambridge, Massachusetts.

Good, Mary-Jo DelVecchio, Ph.D.
A sociologist with field research experience in Iran and in northern California, she is Assistant Professor of Medical Sociology, Department of Social Medicine, Harvard Medical School, Boston, Massachusetts, Faculty Member, Center for Middle Eastern Studies, and Lecturer, Department of Sociology, Harvard University, Cambridge, Massachusetts.

Jablensky, Assen, M.D., D.M.Sc.
A Bulgarian psychiatrist attached to the WHO, he has participated in WHO's International Pilot Study of Schizophrenia and in a major cross-cultural study of depression along with numerous other cross-cultural studies. He is a member of the Mental Health Unit, WHO, Geneva, Switzerland.

Jackson, Stanley W., M.D.
A psychiatrist and historian who has investigated the history of depression in the West, Jackson is Professor, Department of Psychiatry, Yale Medical School, New Haven, Connecticut.

Keyes, Charles F., Ph.D.
An anthropologist who has conducted field research in Thailand and cross-cultural studies of Buddhism and ethnicity, Keyes is Professor and Chairman, Department of Anthropology, University of Washington, Seattle, Washington.

Kleinman, Arthur, M.D., M.A.
An anthropologist and psychiatrist who has conducted field research in the People's Republic of China, Taiwan, and North America, he is Professor of Medical Anthropology, Department of Anthropology, Harvard University, Cambridge, Massachusetts, and Department of Social Medicine, Harvard Medical School, and Professor of Psychiatry at Harvard Medical School, Boston, Massachusetts.

Kleinman, Joan, M.A.

A sinologist with field research experience in China and Taiwan, she is a doctoral student in Chinese Language and Literature, University of Washington, Seattle, Washington, and an independent scholar, Cambridge, Massachusetts.

Lutz, Catherine, Ph.D.

An anthropologist who has conducted ethnopsychological studies among the Ifaluk in the South Pacific, Lutz is Professor, Department of Anthropology, State University of New York at Binghampton, Binghampton, New York.

Manson, Spero M., Ph.D.

An anthropologist who has conducted research among American Indian groups and who himself is an American Indian, Manson is Associate Professor, Department of Psychiatry, Oregon Health Sciences University, Portland, Oregon.

Marsella, Anthony J., Ph.D.

A cross-cultural psychologist who has conducted research among ethnic groups in Hawaii, Marsella is Director, WHO Psychiatric Field Research Center, The Queen's Medical Center, Honolulu, Hawaii, and Professor, Department of Psychology, University of Hawaii, Honolulu, Hawaii.

Moradi, Robert, M.D.

A child psychiatrist, originally from Iran, who has investigated the impact of culture change on Iranian immigrants in California, Moradi is on the clinical staff of the Department of Psychiatry, Cedars-Sinai Medical Center, Los Angeles, California.

Obeyesekere, Gananath, Ph.D.

An anthropologist who has conducted field studies in Sri Lanka and who himself is Sinhalese, he is Professor, Department of Anthropology, Princeton University, Princeton, New Jersey.

Sartorius, Norman, M.D., Ph.D.

A psychiatrist with a doctorate in psychology, Sartorius, who has organized and conducted numerous large-scale cross-cultural studies of mental illness for the WHO, is Director, Mental Health Unit, WHO, Geneva, Switzerland.

Schieffelin, Edward L., Ph.D.
An anthropologist who has studied the Kaluli of New Guinea, he is a member of the Institute for the Study of Human Issues, Philadelphia, Pennsylvania.

Shore, James H., M.D.
A cross-cultural psychiatrist and psychiatric epidemiologist who has carried out field research among various American Indian groups, he is Professor and Chairman, Department of Psychiatry, University of Colorado, Denver, Colorado.

Shweder, Richard A., Ph.D.
A psychological anthropologist who has conducted field research on cognitive and moral development in Mexico and India, he is Professor, Committee on Human Development, University of Chicago, Chicago, Illinois.

Vitaliano, Peter P., Ph.D.
A psychologist and epidemiologist whose research has been in North America, Vitaliano is Associate Professor, Department of Psychiatry and Behavioral Sciences, University of Washington, Seattle, Washington.

Index

Author Index

Subject Index

Arthur J. Rubel, Carl W. O'Nell, and Rolando Collado-Ardón, *Susto, a Folk Illness*

Paul U. Unschuld, *Medicine in China: A History of Ideas*

Paul U. Unschuld, *Medicine in China: A History of Pharmaceutics*

Glenn Gritzer and Arnold Arluke, *The Making of Rehabilitation: A Political Economy of Medical Specialization, 1890–1980*

Arthur Kleinman and Byron Good, editors, *Culture and Depression: Studies in the Anthropology and Cross-Cultural Psychiatry of Affect and Disorder*

Designer: U.C. Press Staff
Compositor: Trend Western
Text: 11/13 Times Roman
Display: Times Roman
Printer: Maple-Vail Book Mfg. Group
Binder: Maple-Vail Book Mfg. Group